The Jung Reader

Carl Gustav Jung was the pioneering founder of analytical psychology, a form of analysis that has revolutionised the approach to mental illness and the study of the mind. In this anthology, David Tacey brings together a selection of Jung's essays from his famous *Collected Works*.

Divided into four parts, each with a brand new introduction, this book considers 17 of Jung's most important papers covering:

- the nature of the psyche
- archetypes
- religion and culture
- therapy and healing.

This accessible collection is essential reading for undergraduates on analytical psychology courses, those on psychotherapy training courses, and students studying symbolism and dreams, or archetypal approaches to literature, cinema, religious studies, sociology or philosophy. The text is an informative introduction for general readers as well as analysts and academics who want to learn more about C. G. Jung's contribution to psychoanalysis, and how his ideas are still extremely relevant in the world today.

David Tacey is an Associate Professor in the School of Communication, Arts and Critical Enquiry at La Trobe University, Melbourne, Australia.

The Jung Reader

Edited by David Tacey

Routledge
Taylor & Francis Group
LONDON AND NEW YORK

First published 2012
by Routledge
27 Church Road, Hove, East Sussex, BN3 2FA

Simultaneously published in the USA and Canada
by Routledge
711 Third Avenue, New York NY 10017

Routledge is an imprint of the Taylor & Francis Group, an informa business

© 2012 selection and editorial matter, David Tacey, individual chapters, the copyright holders.

The right of David Tacey to be identified as editor of this work has been asserted by him in accordance with sections 77 and 78 of the Copyright, Designs and Patents Act 1988.

All rights reserved. No part of this book may be reprinted or reproduced or utilised in any form or by any electronic, mechanical, or other means, now known or hereafter invented, including photocopying and recording, or in any information storage or retrieval system, without permission in writing from the publishers.

Trademark notice: Product or corporate names may be trademarks or registered trademarks, and are used only for identification and explanation without intent to infringe.

British Library Cataloguing in Publication Data
A catalogue record for this book is available from the British Library

Library of Congress Cataloging in Publication Data
The Jung reader/edited by David Tacey.
    p. cm.
  Includes bibliographical references and index.
  ISBN 978-0-415-58983-3 (hardback) – ISBN 978-0-415-58984-0 (pbk)
  1. Jung, C. G. (Carl Gustav), 1875-1961. 2. Jungian psychology. 3. Psychoanalysis and art. I. Tacey, David.
  BF109.J8J868 2012
  150.19' 54092–dc23

                                              2011035371

ISBN: 978-0-415-58983-3 (hbk)
ISBN: 978-0-415-58984-0 (pbk)
ISBN: 978-0-203-00000-0 (ebk)

Typeset in Times by RefineCatch Limited, Bungay, Suffolk
Paperback cover design by Andrew Ward

Printed and bound in Great Britain by
TJ International Ltd, Padstow, Cornwall

Contents

Biographical note	vii
General introduction: Jung's analytical psychology	1
Chronology of Jung's life and work	25

PART 1
The nature of the psyche — 29

	Introduction	31
1	Basic postulates of analytical psychology	47
2	The role of the unconscious	61
3	The stages of life	80
4	The relations between the ego and the unconscious	93

PART 2
Archetypes — 135

	Introduction	137
5	On the concept of the archetype	151
6	Phenomenology of the self: The ego; The shadow; The syzygy: anima and animus; The self	155
7	The psychology of the child archetype	179

PART 3
Religion and culture — 201

Introduction — 203

8 The spiritual problem of modern man — 217

9 Psychology and religion: The autonomy of the unconscious — 232

10 Preface to *Answer to Job*: Lectori benevolo — 253

11 Psychology and literature — 257

12 The difference between Eastern and Western thinking — 273

PART 4
Therapy and healing — 287

Introduction — 289

13 The aims of psychotherapy — 303

14 On synchronicity — 315

15 A psychological theory of types — 324

16 The transcendent function — 337

17 Healing the split — 356

Index — 365

Bibliographical note

All references to the works of Jung in the *Collected Works* are to paragraph numbers (indicated by the symbol §), not to page numbers. References to the *Collected Works* will be indicated by the essay title, original date of publication, followed by *CW*, and the volume number. Such references are to *The Collected Works of C. G. Jung*, translated from the German by R. F. C. Hull, edited by Herbert Read, Michael Fordham, Gerhard Adler and William McGuire, and published by Routledge in London and in America by Princeton University Press, 1953–1992.

All references to the works of Sigmund Freud in the *Standard Edition* are to page numbers. References to the *Standard Edition* will be indicated by the essay title, original date of publication, followed by *SE* and the volume number. Such references are to *The Standard Edition of the Complete Psychological Works of Sigmund Freud*, translated from the German and edited by James Strachey, in collaboration with Anna Freud and assisted by Alix Strachey and Alan Tyson, and published in London by The Hogarth Press, 1953–1975.

In the following chapters by C. G. Jung, textual notes which are signed 'EDITORS' refer to comments and information inserted by the editors of *The Collected Works*. Textual notes signed 'Editor' refer to comments added by the editor of the present volume.

General introduction
Jung's analytical psychology

> The intellect, and along with it science, is now placed at the service of a creative power and purpose. Yet this is still 'psychology' although no longer science; it is psychology in the wider meaning of the word.
>
> C. G. Jung[1]

Jung's reputation in its historical context

Carl Gustav Jung was the pioneering founder of analytical psychology, a form of analysis that revolutionised the approach to mental illness and the study of the mind. From its earliest beginnings, as a fledgling science growing up alongside Freudian analysis, Jung's psychology broadened its field of application to include the study of human behaviour and cultural systems. He began with a specific focus, the treatment of the neuroses, and applied his analytic method to the arts, religions, mythologies, philosophies and civilizations. His intellectual movement was intuitive, outward moving and centrifugal, from the clinical to the macrocosmic, from the interiority of the mind to the workings of the universe. Jung became interested in everything that had a 'symbolic' content, from the dreams and fantasies of patients to the rituals and myths of religions, the visionary poems and novels of writers, and the utopian aspirations of political systems. If anything expressed the strivings and ideals of the psyche, Jung found himself interested in it and had something of interest to say about it.

Because of the broad reach of his psychology and the wide application of his method, Jung has become many things to many people. For some clinicians and counsellors, he is a psychiatrist who rejected Freud's method and developed an alternative theory which has given rise to a more profound form of psychotherapy. For those who study their dreams and practise self-analysis, Jung is a mentor and guide. For those interested in gender, Jung was the first modern thinker to postulate the existence of a contrasexual aspect in the psychology of men and women. For those involved in environmentalism, Jung provided a psychological basis for the emerging discipline of eco-psychology. For those who work in the creative arts, art therapy and expressive modalities, Jung is an inspirational thinker. For those who work in, or have benefited from, drug and alcohol recovery programmes, especially those with a spiritual component such as the Alcoholics Anonymous movement, Jung is a father figure. For those who practise personality type indicator tests, as either employers, consultants or workers, Jung is a major influence.

For large numbers of modern people who have lost touch with established religions and yet are interested in spirituality, Jung has shown how the psyche can be encountered in a way that awakens the symbolic life of the soul. For students and readers in the arts and humanities, Jung is an interpreter of symbolic forms that might otherwise remain baffling and impenetrable. For all who take him seriously, he gives a sense of hope if we are prepared to connect with the unconscious and draw from it the directives it can offer to consciousness. His psychology is sometimes called 'depth psychology' because it begins with the unconscious and draws from its deeper regions. Jung referred to his own work as both 'analytical' and 'complex' psychology,[2] but James Hillman provides a case as to why it should be termed 'archetypal' psychology.[3] To add further complication, Jungian analysts often refer to their field today as 'psychoanalysis', going back to the original term that was preferred by Freud.[4]

Archetypes as transpersonal factors

Jung had an intuitive mind and sought the inside story behind appearances. He was not satisfied with the obvious, with what presented itself to our external senses, and was convinced there was something deeper present that we had not yet noticed. He discerned the dark side of the human personality, the shadow behind the light, and saw the feminine element hidden inside men and the masculine in women. Everything hidden interested him, and he saw it as his duty to bring it into consciousness. He was a thinker in search of 'soul' and 'spirit', terms that have become obscure and remote in modern times – most scholars and intellectuals find them embarrassingly archaic. But Jung sought to bring them back to life, regarding them as dynamic and life-giving factors of the psyche. He almost prided himself on championing what the rational mind shied away from.

As a therapist, he penetrated into the psychic structure of our lives, and found there, in addition to complexes, neuroses and knots of libido, universal forces which he called *archetypes*. Hillman writes: 'The archetype is the most ontologically fundamental of all Jung's psychological concepts, with the advantage of precision and yet by definition partly indefinable and open.'[5] For readers interested in the controversial status of archetypal theory, I have provided a critical essay on the topic in the Introduction to Part II of this volume.

When Jung developed his theory of archetypes, he felt he had found a key to unlocking many doors, especially those of religion and mythology, which had become rusty and closed in the modern era. The scientific period had relegated myths and religions to the edges of respectability, finding them to be nothing more than remnants of a less enlightened age or the 'childhood' of humanity. Jung found they were psychotherapeutic systems with far-reaching personal and social consequences. He felt that subtle but powerful forces were enshrined in religions and mythologies, and that we had lost touch with them at our peril.[6] He believed that modernity itself was imperilled if it did not attempt to understand the archetypal forces, once personified as gods and demons. His writings continually emphasise the importance of regaining conscious contact with the archetypal powers of the psyche:

> The archetype ... throws a bridge between present-day consciousness, always in danger of losing its roots, and the natural, unconscious, instinctive wholeness of primeval times. Through this mediation the uniqueness, peculiarity, and one-sidedness of our present individual consciousness are linked up again with its natural roots.[7]

Archetypes are the organs of psychic life, and it is the cultural and spiritual responsibility of every age to 'translate' the archetypes (or gods) into terms that are acceptable to the contemporary mind. In Jewish cultural practice, the art of updating ancient texts so they become relevant to contemporary times is called *midrash*, and arguably Jung practised a version of this in his writings. If we lose the connection between ancient and modern, the mind withers and dies, because it cannot be sundered from its roots without dire consequences. Before it dies, however, it fragments and goes mad, and Jung felt there was ample evidence that the modern world was subject to ever increasing dissociation.[8]

By 1912 Jung had placed analysis within an archetypal context, which meant that clinical problems could no longer be solved within a purely personal frame. By definition, individual complexes and neuroses were linked to archetypal or 'transpersonal' problems found in culture and society. The individual was a representative of a larger, collective and ancestral psychic situation, and Jung attempted 'to solve psychological problems at a step beyond scientific models and therapy in the usual sense.'[9] His psychology is a therapy of culture, and not simply a clinical treatment of patients. The foundational concept of the archetype had made it impossible for Jung to separate the individual from the collective, because in the world he discovered everything was connected to everything else. This led to the theory of synchronicity, an 'acausal connecting principle', which argued for the connectedness of psyche and world and the relativity of time and space in the psychological field.[10] Indeed for Jung, the psyche was no longer 'inside' us, as it was for Freud and his circle. Jung reversed this assumption, and argued that we are inside the psyche, which he saw as a world of cosmological proportions.[11]

Explorations in and beyond science and religion

Modern knowledge has privileged logic and deductive method above intuition and that is why Jung seems to stand out as a special case in the history of modern thought. The strong intuition he possessed is often found in the visionary arts rather than in the sciences. But we are fortunate that Jung remained in the human sciences – medicine, psychiatry, psychology – even if these disciplines were less than hospitable toward him and treated him as an outsider. It was not that he was doing non- or anti-scientific research – in fact some of his work remained empirical to the end – but it was so new, bold, different that scientists tended not to recognise themselves in his work. Instead of dismissing his work as 'unscientific', those who are sympathetic to his project argue that his work is best classified as a branch of hermeneutics, that is, 'the art of interpretation in the service of meaning'.[12] Jung interpreted everything he saw in terms of his vision and that is why his scientific status is questioned. Jung was seeing the world through a lens that the sciences did not understand.

Science in Jung's day operated under the influence of the Enlightenment, a movement from the eighteenth century in which reason was advocated as the primary source of authority. By the early twentieth century, some of this activity had degenerated into *scientism* – a view which denies the validity of any phenomenon not susceptible to scientific investigation. Religion was constructed as the 'enemy' of science, a view which Jung found impossible to condone and which has since been undermined by postmodern investigations.[13] Jung wrote: 'Science comes to a stop at the frontiers of logic, but nature does not.'[14] He was intent on exploring the depths of nature as well as human nature. It is not so much that he was unscientific, as that he was moving further than science would allow. The Australian biologist Grant Watson got it right when he wrote: 'Dr C. G. Jung worked partly as an empiricist and partly as an intuitive.'[15]

Jung made friendly gestures toward religion throughout his career, but religion did not recognise itself in his work. Religious leaders saw Jung as a scientist who was trying to reduce theology and metaphysics to psychological factors. Religion believed Jung was saying that everything religious could be brought down to the level of human subjectivity and fantasy. The charge of 'psychologism' was levelled against him, but it was a misrepresentation of his work. He was interested in building a bridge to the metaphysical, not in collapsing metaphysics into rational explanations. Shamdasani writes: 'Intent on reconciling science and religion through psychology, his work has met with endless controversy at every turn.'[16] Jung was misinterpreted by science and religion; neither saw him as belonging to its world. The truth is that he was trying to develop a position midway between both perspectives. As Jung explains in his memoirs: 'In science I missed the factor of meaning; and in religion, that of empiricism.'[17]

In his personal journal, *The Red Book*, Jung confided that he had been taken over by a different spirit of enquiry: 'The spirit of the depths ... took away my belief in science, he robbed me of the joy of explaining and ordering things, and he let devotion to the ideals of this time die out in me.'[18] Jung experienced an upheaval that reversed some of his original values and directions. A force greater than himself urged him to attend to the realm of ultimate meaning and this encouraged him into philosophical enquiry and religious speculation. He tried to reconcile the 'spirit of the depths' with his scientific career, but he met with opposition and antagonism. He developed a spiritual attitude toward the psyche and took leave of mainstream psychiatry to focus on his exploration of the depths. He gave in to his inner *daimon* or creative genius, but it came at a great price.

The clash with authorities

Jung looked to authorities around him for confirmation but found little solace. Sigmund Freud, his mentor and collaborator from 1906 to 1913, had ruled spirituality a taboo area for scientific enquiry. Freud was 20 years senior to Jung, and Jung looked to him as a father-figure. Freud tolerated Jung while he was a 'follower' but Jung's own interests were derided by Freud as 'mysticism' or 'occultism'. The academic view that Jung was a charlatan is largely a product of Freud and his circle. In his youth, Jung had clashed with his own father, a clergyman. He was interested in his father's profession, and expected good things to come from it, but as he approached adolescence Jung was disappointed by what he saw as the emptiness of his father's religion. He felt his father had little faith and no *experience* to base it on. All he seemed to possess was a set of beliefs. To Jung, his father's sermons were displays of religiosity without spirituality.[19]

Thus Jung felt equally unsupported by his intellectual father, Freud, and his biological father, Paul Jung. In the language of psychoanalysis, he suffered from a father-complex, and in his life and career he had to struggle to discover a fatherly source of authenticating strength within himself. However, even in this context we cannot speak of his complex as purely personal. One might say that in the modern period, there is a spirituality 'complex' in civilization. Science has refused to support spirit, since it has, until recently, been obsessed with demonstrable fact and material causation. Religion has also dispensed with the experiential life of spirit, preferring to focus on the historical sources of revelation and the worship of charismatic leaders. In archetypal terms, spirit is 'unfathered' by either tradition, and Jung's life is a testimony to this problem.

Jung's mother outwardly conformed to her husband's religion, but in her personal life she seemed to be an advocate of popular or 'folk' religion. She was interested in ghosts, spirits of the dead and poltergeists. This interest seemed to be passed on to her son, and for his doctorate Jung wrote a thesis on the psychology of mediumistic or occult phenomena.[20] His mother seemed to exert more influence on him than his father, giving him a lifelong interest in what he called 'night religion'.[21] But Jung's interest in the occult was quickly outgrown, as is often the case in the intellectual development of enquiring minds. Instead of focusing on his mother's 'spirits', Jung developed an interest in, and passion for, *spirit* as an archetypal force. Whereas spirits are conceived as literal and local metaphysical agencies, spirit is a universal force found in all things. Spirit is not just a spooky element in occult events, but an enlivening principle that imbues culture, religion and society.[22] One could argue that Jung's interest in the invisible world progressed from naïve spiritualism to mature spirituality.[23]

Freud, mysticism, libido, incest

Jung was effectively dismissed in 1913 from the Freudian psychoanalytic movement, which was dogmatically atheist. It was also primarily Jewish, and, according to Freud, Jung's 'mysticism' was due to his Germanic Aryan descent, which had left its mark on Jung's character and inclined him to a spiritual disposition. Freud had suppressed his own spiritual instinct and tended to pathologise it in others, as well as to stigmatise it as a racial trace. The highly secular Freud was suspicious of what he called the 'fairytale forest feeling'[24] in Jung's work, and boasted to Karl Abraham: 'We Jews have an easier time, having no mystical element.'[25] This was an error on Freud's part. There are long-standing, highly respected and ongoing traditions of mystical thought in Jewish culture, about which Freud was ignorant.[26] Freud was talking about himself and projecting his disposition upon the Jewish people as a whole. Moreover, it is wrong to ascribe a 'mystical element' to a particular racial group. History shows that this element is found in all peoples at all times. The mystical element, however, can be suppressed or ignored in the service of a triumphant rationalism.

The intellectual argument broke out between these two giants of modern thought when Jung attempted to expand the Freudian theory of libido.[27] Jung felt cramped by the Freudian model, which defined the libido as purely sexual and saw the problems of neurosis as caused by sexual difficulties. Jung wanted to broaden the concept of libido to refer to 'psychic energy' in a more comprehensive sense.[28] To him, the libido was a life-force which could include spiritual, symbolic, and archetypal as well as sexual dynamisms. Jung believed that sex was the most apparent energy-laden aspect on the spectrum of libido, and in its more subtle and elevated aspect, which he called the 'psychic ultra-violet', it was synonymous with spirit.[29] Jung wrote:

> Eros [the personification of libido in Greek mythology] is a questionable fellow [who] belongs on one side to man's primordial animal nature . . . [and] on the other side he is related to the highest forms of the spirit. But he thrives only when spirit and instinct are in right harmony. Too much of the animal distorts the civilized man, too much civilization makes sick animals.[30]

Jung thought Freudian theory was rubbing our noses into our animal nature at the cost of our spiritual lives, which would end up atrophied. Just as the Victorian repression of sexuality made us sick, so Freud's remedy, in which everything lofty and noble is reduced to a construct of sexual repression, is a different kind of distortion.

Jung conceded: 'Freud's sexual theory of neurosis is grounded on a true and factual principle. But it makes the mistake of being one-sided and exclusive; also it commits the imprudence of trying to lay hold of unconfinable Eros with the crude terminology of sex.'[31] Jung called for a holistic emphasis, which was able to balance our biological drives with our transcendental impulses. The religion of his father was too far up in the clouds and had lost the animal instinct to the moralism of Christianity. To that extent, he agreed with Freud, and protested the notion that he was against him: 'It is a widespread error to imagine that I do not see the value of sexuality.'[32] He could see the importance of sexuality but did not consider it to be the only dynamic factor in the psyche. His adopted father, Freud, was concentrating too much on the biological drives and losing the elevated life of the spirit: this was the opposite of his father's position. Jung's task was to hold the tension between these points of view, and not to succumb to an elevated or reductive view of human nature.

Another, related, dispute between them was about the idea of incest. According to Freud, the incest motif in dreams and fantasies was to be interpreted literally, as the desire of the neurotic patient for sexual cohabitation with the parent. Freud staked his theory on the Oedipus complex, the pattern of libido in which the individual seeks sexual union with the parent. Jung, thinking symbolically rather than literally, saw incest as the psyche's way of expressing its desire to return to the source from which the ego had emerged. For Jung, the incest motif signalled the longing of the ego for the embrace and succour of the unconscious. It was the psyche's potent way of calling for a symbolic reconnection with origins and background. Jung published his 'alternative' theory of incest in *Symbols of Transformation* in 1912, and this brought about the final break between him and Freud.

Freud dismissed Jung's theory of incest as mumbo jumbo and as evidence of Jung's 'mysticism'. He thought Jung was finding the sexual theory too hot to handle, and his Swiss prudishness was preventing him from accepting the strictly sexual interpretation. For Freud, Jung's spiritual reading of incest was nothing more than a defence against the realities of the infantile longings that plague the lives of neurotic adults. He charged Jung: 'You hide behind your religious-libidinal cloud.'[33] Jung believed that Freud's interpretation was a defence against the psyche's capacity to use sexual symbols to describe spiritual rebirth.

Freud's habit of reducing everything to the lowest common denominator was a stumbling block not only in his response to incest but in his relations with Jung. If Jung disagreed with his emphasis on sexuality, this was attributed to sexual inhibitions in Jung – an odd accusation, given the biographical evidence which supports the notion that Jung had a full and uninhibited sexual life.[34] Intellectual disagreements were attributed to an Oedipal complex that Freud believed Jung harboured against him. This reductive and circular strategy of Freud's drove Jung to distraction. As he commented to the London psychoanalyst Ernest Jones:

> Freud is convinced that I am thinking under the domination of a father complex against him and then all is complex-nonsense . . . against this insinuation I am completely helpless . . . if Freud understands each attempt to think in a new way about the problems of psychoanalysis as a personal resistance, things become impossible.[35]

Jung wrote to Jones: 'It is an extremely difficult and even unfair standpoint to reduce a different view to personal complexes. This is the psychology of the "nothing but". It removes all seriousness and human consideration and replaces it with personal gossip and suspicion.'[36] Jung felt he was caught up in a dehumanising situation, with an opponent who played dirty tricks and could not be reasoned with.

The remarkable thing was not that Freud and Jung split but that they got together in the first place. They were so different from the outset: Freud was the cheerful pessimist, explaining everything in terms of mechanistic causes and personal impulses, while Jung was the idealistic and romantic explorer of the mind, always looking for traces of the sacred. Yet during the early years of their relationship, each displayed a deep respect and a profound love for the other. It was these affectionate bonds that carried them through the seven years of their association (1906–1913). Freud was originally drawn to Jung because of his intellectual vitality, personal enthusiasm and leadership capacity. Freud was looking for a successor to lead the psychoanalytic movement, and Jung seemed a likely candidate, much to the jealousy of Freud's Viennese circle.

Alleged racism and intellectual hostility

The race issue had played a role in Freud's choice. His Viennese associates were all Jewish, and the strategist in Freud wanted to bequeath his movement to a prominent non-Jew, so that his science could be carried beyond Jewry throughout Europe and America. He wrote to Abraham:

> Jung, being a Christian and the son of a pastor, can only find his way to me against great inner resistances. His adherence is therefore all the more valuable. I was almost going to say it was only his emergence on the scene that has removed from psycho-analysis the danger of becoming a Jewish national affair.[37]

Freud announced that Jung was his 'successor and crown prince',[38] a hasty decision in view of the differences between them. He tried to bury these differences for a greater cause: 'After all, our Aryan comrades are quite indispensable to us; otherwise psycho-analysis would fall a victim to anti-Semitism.'[39] Freud chose Jung to give the signal to the world that psychoanalysis was not an exclusively Jewish science. By this strategy, he hoped psychoanalysis would not fall prey to anti-Semitic attacks. But as soon as their intellectual differences began to surface, and to interfere with his plans for an empire of influence, he changed his mind and decided that Jung must be suffering from 'repressed anti-Semitism'.[40] From the outset, one might say, Freud set up Jung to be a psychological scapegoat and a carrier of anti-Semitism.

Freud played the race card with opportunism: so long as Jung agreed with him, he was constructed as a good leader who would secure a future for psychoanalysis, but when Jung's spirituality interfered with their relations he was branded a racist. This view was shared with the Viennese psychoanalytic circle, who were anxious to find further reason to hate Jung, since his influence on Freud had put them in the shade. When a 'secret committee' of five psychoanalytic pioneers was formed in 1913 to protect the movement from the rupture caused by Jung's defection, as well as to deal with its growing number of dissidents (Adler, Rank, Ferenczi, Reich), a part of its brief was to disestablish Jung and discredit his work. It seems that he was branded a mystic and a racist, slurs which were carried far and wide into the scientific and educated worlds.[41]

Freud wrote to his associate Sabina Spielrein in 1913: 'I am, as you know, cured of the last shred of my predilection for the Aryan cause ... I shall not present my compliments to Jung in Munich, as you know perfectly well ... We are and remain Jews. The others will only exploit us and will never understand or appreciate us.'[42] Not only were personal comments made to this effect, but in his 'History of the Psycho-Analytic Movement' of 1914, Freud made public his racist accusations, describing Jung as one who had tried but failed to give up 'certain racial prejudices which he had previously permitted himself.'[43] Stephen Martin understands the seriousness of this public accusation and its lasting effects:

> Coming from the pen of the master himself in a seemingly official document, this damning, retributive, and, for Freud, clearly face-saving statement began a historical controversy that has simmered and frequently boiled over, with disastrous results, since that time.[44]

Jung was aware of Freud's allegations. In 'The State of Psychotherapy Today', Jung admits that his work had been 'suspected of anti-Semitism' and he states unequivocally: 'This suspicion emanated from Freud.'[45] Even Ernest Jones, a loyal supporter of Freud, wrote: 'I became, of course, aware, somewhat to my astonishment, of how ... many remarks or actions could be interpreted in that sense [as signs of anti-Semitism]. Freud himself was pretty sensitive in this respect.'[46] Jones cites letters of Freud to Abraham, in which instances of intellectual resistance to his work are attributed to anti-Semitism.[47] Jones was never going to be too critical of his leader, but in his three-volume biography of Freud he says enough to alert us to the potential for foul play.

The German Medical Society of Psychotherapy and the Nazi yoke

The other 'evidence' cited in relation to Jung's alleged racism is his involvement with the German Medical Society of Psychotherapy. In early 1933 Jung was Vice President of the Society, and later that year the President, Ernst Kretschmer, vacated the chair and Jung assumed the presidency. Some have viewed this as a sign of his sympathy with the Nazi regime, because by late 1933 all professional societies in Germany were 'conformed' to Nazi ideology. The word used at this time was *Gleichgeschaltung*, which literally means 'bringing into step' with the policies of National Socialism. In his defence, Jung claimed that he accepted the presidency of the German Society to offer support for Jewish medical doctors in the Society. This was a strategy he discussed with his Jewish colleagues in Zurich, who agreed in principle with his optimistic and subversive plan.

In 1934 Jung thought he saw a way for Jewish doctors to become 'extraordinary members' within the umbrella of the Society, beyond the veto power of the Nazi-conformed members.[48] He transformed it into the International General Medical Society of Psychotherapy, and one of his first acts as President was to stipulate that all German Jewish doctors who had been excluded from their national society were entitled to become individual members of the International Society, thus preserving their rights. At the same time, he set up national sections, including Dutch, Danish, Swedish and Swiss – as well as German – ones. In the non-German Societies, the rights and privileges of Jewish members would be preserved in accordance with the laws of those nations.

Meanwhile, as he ascended to the International Presidency, the German Society was officially aligned with Nazi policy under the leadership of Professor Matthias Heinrich Göring, the cousin of the infamous Hermann Göring, the Reich Marshall and Commander in Chief of the German Air Force. As part of his duties as President, Jung was the editor of the Society's journal, the *Zentralblatt für Psychotherapie*. In the autumn of 1933, Professor Göring announced his intention to publish a special supplement for members of the German Society, obliging them to abide by the ideology of the Nazis. Jung was opposed to this idea, but could do little about it since he was no longer president of the German section. However, when the December issue of the *Zentralblatt* appeared, Jung was horrified to discover that the publisher had included Göring's statement in the edition intended for international circulation, which bore Jung's name as editor. Jung claimed this was done without his knowledge or approval, but his critics, always eager to see the worst, have not to believed him.

Although his involvement in the Society had been motivated by noble, even heroic, desires to secure justice for Jewish medical doctors, the Nazi machine had overwhelmed Jung's intentions. Critics claim that Jung should have resigned immediately, sensing his impotence in the face of the might of the Nazis. Instead, Jung stubbornly remained President of the International Society until 1939, clinging to the hope that he might be able to do some good. Scholars have asked: what was he thinking when he tried to 'take on' the Medical Society of Psychotherapy? The notion of moving contrary to the Nazification of German societies seemed foolhardy, or extremely naïve. Was this a sign of Jung's poor judgement in social and political matters? Was he trying to play a messianic role in an impossible situation? His accusers claim he was a 'collaborator' with the Nazi war machine, but Jung's actions and intentions suggest otherwise. At the end of the Society's 1934 congress in Bad Nauheim, Jung issued a circular to all members, stating the principle that 'The International Society is neutral as to politics and creed'.

But those who were not close to Jung felt he was a puppet in the hands of the Nazi regime. The fact that he did not resign when Göring's manifesto was published in Jung's journal was enough to convince his accusers that his work was anti-Jewish. What made matters worse was the bad timing of Jung's attempt to develop a 'national typology' of racial characteristics when tensions were at their peak. In 1918 and again in 1934 he attempted to apply his typological interests to Christians and Jews, suggesting a psychological structural difference between these peoples in terms of origin, history and relationship to place.[49] Jung displayed insensitivity in raising this issue in the social climate of his time, and even though his typology is not derogatory or prejudiced, the fact that it raised the question of differences was itself highly contentious. His statements about 'Jewish psychology' offended some people, even though offence was not intended. Andrew Samuels has argued that the taboo ought to be lifted from Jung's national typology, since we can now view these insights in a different social context.[50]

But the acrimonious break with Freud, untimely theories of national typology, and involvement with the German Society in the Nazi period, have created a momentum of their own, and in some minds an image has built up of Jung as anti-Semitic. This image or slur was a surprise to his personal secretary, Aniela Jaffé, who was a Jew, and who wrote with insight and sensitivity of Jung's conduct during the Nazi time.[51] In turn, several of his close associates, including Erich Neumann, Gerhard Adler, James and Hilda Kirsch, Jolande Jacobi, Rivkah Kluger and Sigmund Hurwitz – all Jewish – have spoken up in his defence.[52] Ernest Harms published an article in 1946 called 'Carl Gustav Jung: Defender of Freud and the Jews', with the subtitle: 'A Chapter of European Psychiatric History under the Nazi Yoke'.[53] Harms addressed the allegations against Jung in a historical manner. He builds a strong case for his claim that the allegations of anti-Semitism and pro-Nazi sympathy are the result of distortions, misinformation and error. He claims that Jung's enemies used this misinformation against him.

In spite of this moral support, slurs have persisted. As the saying has it, 'mud sticks' – especially, as we shall see, when it is the 'black mud' of Freud's invention. It is difficult to get rid of these allegations because they have been reinforced from the Freudian side, which has been smarting for a century over the defection of its 'crown prince'. Since the Freudians have overshadowed Jungians in cultural scale and political influence, the Jungian statements of defence have done little to dislodge the views spread by the secret committee and others.

Pneumaphobia and dread of the spirit

My reading is that it is not so much race as spirituality which is the sticking point. The racial taunt is the outward guise for some other rancour. The anger toward Jung occurs because he stands for 'spirit' and this disturbs those who are rigidly rational. Freud showed phobic signs toward spirit, and in their professional association Jung remembers this exchange:

> I can still recall how Freud said to me, 'My dear Jung, promise me never to abandon the sexual theory. That is the most essential thing of all. You see, we must make a dogma of it, an unshakable bulwark.' He said that to me with great emotion, in the tone of a father saying, 'And promise me this one thing, my dear son: that you will go to church every Sunday.' In some astonishment I asked him, 'A bulwark – against what?' To which he replied, 'Against the black tide of mud' – and here he hesitated for a moment, then added – 'of occultism.'[54]

Freud could not bear to think that his heir was falling victim to the 'black mud' of occultism. Freud referred to everything of a spiritual nature as 'occultism', although this was an undifferentiated judgement. Jung's 'occult' tendencies, as I have said, were overcome as he moved toward a sophisticated understanding of spirituality. But to Freud, spirituality and occultism were both 'black', that is, enemies of reason. 'What Freud seemed to mean by "occultism" was virtually everything that philosophy and religion, including the rising contemporary science of parapsychology, had learned about the psyche.'[55]

In an important letter to Jung, Freud claims the high moral ground, saying he is 'eager for knowledge and not at all superstitious.'[56] Ironically, while treating Jung like an idiot for his interest in the paranormal, Freud profusely demonstrates his own occult beliefs. He describes his long-standing number superstition (numerology), his obsessive fear that he will die at the age of 61, and his interest in thought-transference or telepathy in analysis. He describes these with an air of superiority, having 'seen through' these superstitions by the aid of self-analysis. Yet Freud was still gripped enough by the subject to write a paper on 'Psychoanalysis and Telepathy' in 1921, although it was held over for posthumous publication in 1953.[57] One of his famous papers, 'The Uncanny', demonstrates the profound attraction that the mystical and occult had for him.[58] In this essay Freud 'pleads guilty' to a special interest in the subject, and describes his 'uncanny' personal experiences of déjà vu and superstition. As Jung is writing *Symbols of Transformation* and exploring myth and the configurations of the spirit, Freud is inspired to write *Totem and Taboo*, which is on a similar subject.

One can surmise from this that Freud had a deep interest in spirit, but because he had suppressed it, it never developed beyond an ambivalent and awkward spiritualism. If spirit is thwarted, it can take on inferior appearances. As Jung wrote in another context: 'What is suppressed comes up again in another place in altered form, but this time loaded with resentment that makes the otherwise natural impulse our enemy.'[59] Freud seemed to project his deformed spirit upon Jung, whom he 'treated like a fool riddled with complexes.'[60] Freud taunts Jung for his so called 'spook complex' and says it is 'a charming delusion in which one does not oneself participate.'[61] Yet all indications suggest that it was Freud who was obsessed with 'das Unheimliche', the uncanny.[62]

In *Tabooed Jung*, a study of Jung's exclusion from academic discourses, Christine Gallant writes: 'Jung has always been a tabooed object for the psychoanalytic movement.'[63] In *Totem and Taboo* Freud describes the taboo in this way: 'It has about it a sense of something unapproachable ... principally expressed in prohibitions and restrictions. Our collocation "holy dread" would often coincide in meaning with taboo.'[64] This could describe Jung in 1913: he was 'unapproachable', regarded with 'holy dread', and the secret committee had exercised 'prohibitions' and 'restrictions' to halt his investigations. When an investigator of the mind touches on the numinous, he or she becomes a representative of it, almost by way of contagion. One becomes a carrier of the sacred, and it is a blessing and a curse, because it singles one out as being under the influence of a god, no longer a free agent. The numinous can be infuriating to those who insist on the necessity of human freedom, since the presence of the sacred limits our will. Those who allow themselves to be touched by the sacred become figures of ridicule for those who are afraid of these depths.

Freud had hauled in a fish that was bigger than his theoretical constructs would allow. If we search for the roots of sexuality, Jung believed, we have to be prepared to accept spirit as well, as these are the two faces of the same life-force.[65] Sexuality he said is 'the other face of God, the dark side of the God-image'.[66] This sacred force demands to be known in its totality, and will not be content at being seen as a biological function. What is left out of the picture becomes a source of trouble and discontent. Jung felt he had 'observed in Freud the eruption of unconscious religious factors'.[67] Since Freud had considered 'only half of the whole', the missing element produces 'a counter-effect [which] arises out of the unconscious'.[68] Jung saw this manifesting as a general bitterness toward life and a hardening of heart:

> He gave the impression that at bottom he was working against his own goal and against himself; and there is, after all, no harsher bitterness than that of a person who is his own worst enemy. In his own words, he felt himself menaced by a 'black tide of mud' – he who more than anyone else had tried to let down his buckets into those black depths.[69]

Something came up in the 'buckets' that Freud could not integrate into his system. For Jung, the 'monotony of interpretation' which was characteristic of Freud's reductive method 'expressed a flight from himself, or from that other side of him which might perhaps be called mystical'.[70] 'Freud wanted to teach – or so at least it seemed to me – that, regarded from within, sexuality included spirituality and had an intrinsic meaning. But his concretistic terminology was too narrow to express this idea.'[71] His ambivalent interest in spirit was dealt with by way of projection: Jung was turned into the scorned 'prophet' who was identified with the black mud and sent packing. Freud felt exonerated by having got rid of Jung, whose name and reputation was burdened by projections.

Relevant in this context is John Carroll's work on what he has termed *pneumaphobia*, or fear of the spirit.[72] Carroll argues that pneumaphobia is found in secular and rational contexts which try to eschew or bury the spirit. He finds it expressed in a rancorous and defensive attack on spiritual ideas, since such ideas make some people feel inadequate. The secular consciousness carries a 'wound' about pneuma, and realises it has failed to make an adjustment to it. 'The wound festers and turns to rancour – the compulsion to defame pneuma and those who carry it.'[73] Resentment, hostility and anger – these were diagnosed by Nietzsche as symptoms of those who had lost their transcendent aspiration.[74] The early analysts claimed to be champions of the repressed, and while they dredged up the sexual aspect of libido – often against 'civilised' opposition – they were unable to act as liberators of spiritual energy. 'The assimilation of the fundamental insight that psychic life has two poles', Jung writes, 'still remains a task for the future.'[75]

Jung's psychology and the future

Although Freud used 'mysticism' as a term of abuse, this would not be tolerated today. Public and scholarly attitudes to mysticism changed in the 1940s and 1950s, when the writings of Thomas Merton and Teilhard de Chardin appeared.[76] So, too, the works of Evelyn Underhill, St John of the Cross, Teresa of Avila and Meister Eckhart have been rediscovered by a contemporary culture keen to be informed by mystical vision. The phenomenal interest in the writings of the Islamic poet Rumi has confirmed that the world's hunger for mysticism is at a high level and sustained. In this sense Freud is out of step with contemporary life and speaking from a late-nineteenth-century worldview.

Even in Freudian analysis the idea of mysticism has received renewed support. In *Realms of the Human Unconscious*, Stanislov Grof, a member of the Prague psychoanalytic group, presented his experimental research on altered states of consciousness and indicated that in almost every case his subjects 'transcended the narrow psychodynamic framework and moved into transpersonal realms'.[77] Grof began as a convinced Freudian who shared the typical critiques of Jung, but found his work becoming more 'Jungian' insofar as it affirmed an archetypal basis of mind. In recent years, we witness a number of endorsements of the spiritual life from Freudian quarters, such as *The Psychoanalytic Mystic, Psychoanalysis and Religious Experience*, and *Emotion and Spirit*.[78] Freudians have ignored their founder's jaundiced attitudes toward spirituality and religion.

This shift might have been expected. As a science of the mind, psychoanalysis could not remain faithful to Freud's iron-clad rationality. He drew the boundaries too narrowly and his followers, including Bion, Eigen and Grotstein, have pushed them back, and perhaps destroyed them. The spiritual pole of the libido, as theorised by Jung, has surfaced in the work of post-Freudians, giving the lie to the mechanistic view they inherited.[79] The gap between things Jungian and Freudian is closing, and in 1975 Paul Roazen wrote: 'Few responsible figures in psychoanalysis would be disturbed today if an analyst were to present views identical to Jung's in 1913.'[80]

However, although Freudian theory is becoming more 'Jungian', few if any of these analysts are prepared to acknowledge that a 'reconciliation' with Jung has taken place. In *Jung and the Post-Jungians*, Andrew Samuels discusses 15 ways in which contemporary Freudian theory has come into alignment with Jungian thought, showing that Jung was pointing the way to the future. Samuels concludes: 'Jung is revealed as a surprisingly modern thinker and psychotherapist, who anticipated in a most striking manner many of the ways in which psychoanalytic thinking has developed.'[81] Ironically, Jung is still seen by these writers and analysts as a figure of the past. Christine Gallant observes: 'The theories and findings of the mature Jung and later Jungians are congenial with contemporary psychoanalytic work. Yet little of this goes recognized by today's critics – many of whom would probably bristle at the suggestion that there is less difference between Jung and themselves than they think.'[82] The work of Freud's secret committee is still effective to this day, even though there is no longer any need for the cultural war to continue.

It is clear that the Freudian traditions are more interested in arriving in their own way at a soulful point of view. They do not want to go back to the painful saga of Jung versus Freud, or engage in the personality politics of a hundred years ago. They are more interested in confidently going beyond their founder and moving on. While this is cold comfort for Jungians, in the sense that they remain marginalised, it vindicates the theoretical directions upon which the Jungian project is founded. It also validates the bipolar theory of libido, that whenever the sexual aspect of libido is explored, the spiritual aspect will come up. As Jung wrote: 'all energy can proceed only from the tension of opposites.'[83]

The emergence of holistic science

Writing of the new turn in the direction of knowledge and science in recent decades, Diarmuid O'Murchu said:

> The twenty-first century will, in all probability, experience a momentum towards another view of life, namely, the *holistic* or *systems* view, which seeks to interpret all life-forms, including the universe as a whole, as a process of mutual interdependence, whereby individual parts do not act independently but in relationship with each other for the good of the whole. Already this new orientation, predicted by Teilhard de Chardin almost forty years ago, is beginning to take shape, interestingly and perhaps, ironically, the momentum is arising not from within Christianity but from the combined insights of biology, physics, anthropology, psychology and mysticism.[84]

It is true that Teilhard predicted the turn to holistic science in the 1950s, but Jung predicted it earlier, in the 1920s and 1930s. Writing in 1929, in his commentary on Richard Wilhelm's translation of Chinese alchemical texts, Jung compliments the Eastern systems of knowledge for not losing the vital balance between spirit and matter. The West, he says, has gone over to matter, suppressing spirit and confusing it with intellect. We in the West have become inflated by reason, but:

> The Chinese ... never strayed so far from the central psychic facts as to lose themselves in a one-sided over-development and over-valuation of a single psychic function. They never failed to acknowledge the paradoxicality and polarity of all life. The opposites always balanced one another – a sign of high culture. One-sidedness, though it lends momentum, is a mark of barbarism.[85]

The one-sidedness of the West is 'barbaric' because the spirit withers and dies, and culture drops to a lower level. People become consumed by materialism and high culture absorbs this trend and stops asking the ultimate questions. Eventually culture falls into disorder and violence, as we have seen in the twentieth century, because the psychic energies are askew, or, as the Chinese would say, we have 'lost the Tao', the Way. Jung continues:

> The reaction that is now beginning in the West against the intellect, in favour of feeling, or in favour of intuition, seems to me a sign of cultural advance, a widening of consciousness beyond the narrow confines of a tyrannical intellect.[86]

I am not sure what Jung had in mind here, but there is every indication that knowledge is broadening beyond its previously narrow confines. Many cultural forces have helped to open up the fields of knowledge: feminist scholarship has sought to expose 'objective' knowledge as a construct of a patriarchal worldview; postmodernism has sought to expose the notion of objectivity itself as a cultural fiction;[87] the philosophy of science and paradigm theory has shown that what often passed for science was 'scientism', an ideology posing as science.[88] We are fortunate that, as O'Murchu said, the sciences are in a different mood, thanks to the postmodern turn.

The sciences have taken a leap into intuitive understandings of the world, partly because physics has realised it is impossible to observe matter without at the same time implicating the observer. Contemporary physics,[89] biology,[90] mathematics, neuroscience, economics, ecology and the natural sciences have moved toward an interconnected view of the world, away from the causal model that formed the basis of mechanistic science. Some of these sciences have opened up to the possibility that spirit is the connecting force in the universe.[91] Theology has moved closer to an integrative understanding of reality,[92] and philosophy is recovering its interest in questions of ultimate meaning.[93] Even psychology and psychiatry are moving in the same direction.[94] The world that Jung imagined, where religion, science, philosophy and psychology could work together and bring matter and spirit into a new relationship, is emerging, but it has taken place well after his death.

In *Synchronicity: Nature and Psyche in an Interconnected Universe*, Joseph Cambray writes:

> Jung was radically transgressive; he cared little for the confines or boundaries of different disciplines but sought the most profound patterns in mind, culture,

and nature. Science and religion were not inherently opposed, and he discovered a science of the sacred, especially in his clinical work.[95]

The way in which knowledge is divided into separate compartments in our universities is not conducive to Jung's investigations of the *unus mundus*, or one world. Our university system is only able to reproduce itself, namely, a divided world of specialisations where the 'spiritual' links are ignored. Jung had difficulty with the universities because he was a generalist in a time of specialisation. In his time a generalist was frowned upon as a dilettante who could not be taken seriously. However, Jung was no mere dabbler; he was in search of the unitive threads of existence, which forced him to enter many terrains of knowledge. When he established a Psychology Fund at the Swiss Federal Institute of Technology in Zurich, Jung said of the goal and reach of psychology:

> The treatment of psychology should in general be characterized by the principle of universality. No special theory or special subject should be propounded, but psychology should be taught in its biological, ethnological, medical, philosophical, cultural-historical and religious aspects.[96]

This is a visionary statement about the future role of psychology in the development of knowledge, but ironically the course of mainstream psychology has been in the opposite direction, toward increasing specialisation. In 'Psychology and Literature' Jung suggested that the psychologist has an obligation to go beyond conventional boundaries:

> Since it is a characteristic of the psyche not only to be the source of all productivity but, more especially, to express itself in all the activities and achievements of the human mind, we can nowhere grasp the nature of the psyche *per se* but can meet it only in its various manifestations. The psychologist is therefore obliged to make himself familiar with a wide range of subjects, not out of presumption and inquisitiveness but rather from love of knowledge, and for this purpose he must abandon his thickly walled specialist fortress and set out on the quest for truth.[97]

Jung was urged to familiarise himself with anthropology, sociology, physics, biology, comparative religion, ancient civilisations, theology, classical studies, medieval alchemy, literature, art and at least nine language systems. He was not an expert in these fields, but he was an attentive thinker in search of traces of spirit. When it came to his studies on synchronicity, he teamed up with the Nobel Prize winning physicist Wolfgang Pauli.[98] He had discussions with Einstein so he could be informed about the new scientific investigations in energy and matter.[99] He formed connections with the sinologist Richard Wilhelm, the indologist Heinrich Zimmer, the classicist Karl Kerényi, and the theologian Victor White.

Jung risked being 'undisciplined' in the technical sense and he risked falling out of view, into the gaps between the disciplines he traversed. But in the context of our present quest for knowledge, Jung's efforts make more sense. One expression of the new concern for interconnectedness is the interest in interdisciplinary studies. The impetus for interdisciplinary studies has arisen in the United States, as scholars struggle to piece together the jigsaw puzzle of knowledge. European countries have often remained resistant to this development, sensing that knowledge is best served in a specialist mode. But many in the US and elsewhere are dissatisfied with the specialist knowledges we have inherited, and are looking for broader theories of society and personality. Many realise that scholars often end up knowing 'more and more' about 'less and less', and there is ignorance about, and lack of interest in, the larger questions.

The ecology of the soul

There is another issue that we have to deal with today: the environmental crisis and its 'inconvenient truths'. An ecological emergency is upon us and this has placed the function of knowledge in a different light. Knowledge which continues to fragment the world, to separate humanity from nature, to split spirit from earth and mind from body, is being viewed with a new kind of suspicion, the like of which we have not seen before. The dualistic model of knowledge, which was unrivalled until recently, is being attacked from many quarters, and Jung is coming into favour at this point in time. Today we are in need of large theories that can comprehend the relationships between humanity and nature, and the connections between matter, physics, psyche, mind and behaviour.

The ecological emergency has prompted us to value the whole rather than the part, and Jung offers a vision that is large enough to make sense of the connections between a host of elements that are not usually connected. It could be that these elements have always been connected, but our scientific specialisations have held them apart. Jung's insights into the interconnectedness of the world,[100] together with the revisions of his work by Hillman,[101] have made significant contributions to the rising discipline of *ecopsychology*.[102] One might say that at last Jungian thought has found acknowledgement and respect in a scholarly field. Ecopsychology has brought together natural scientists, philosophers, poets, environmental activists, sociologists and education theorists. This important new discourse is searching for a spiritual orientation and a philosophical foundation for the environmental movement, and it is finding Jung attractive. Before James Lovelock developed his Gaia hypothesis,[103] Jung was proposing unifying principles of the world which are now seen to have ecological consequences. There is a great deal of intellectual excitement about ecopsychology, because it seems to suggest a way out of our dualism, toward a holistic approach which can heal the earth as well as the mind.

Jung's clinical practice was itself an exercise in holistic medicine or ecological healing. He refused to see the body and its diseases as separate from the mind. In turn, the mind was affected by the life of the spirit. A wrong attitude to life, an inadequate moral outlook or prejudice, could have consequences for the health of the body and its organs. One could describe Jung's clinical practice as an application of an 'ecology of soul', where all parts of the human being affect each other. Jung was one of the first of the modern medical practitioners to criticise the medical model and to argue that its limitations were ideological and had to be overcome:

> In the course of the nineteenth century medicine had become, in its methods and theory, one of the disciplines of natural science, and it cherished the same basically philosophical assumption of *material causation*. For medicine, the psyche as a mental 'substance' did not exist, and experimental psychology also did its best to constitute itself a psychology without a psyche.[104]

Jung introduced into medicine the idea that the doctor has a responsibility to bring meaning or spirit into a patient's life. 'A psychoneurosis must be understood, ultimately, as the suffering of a soul which has not discovered its meaning.'[105] 'Not to recognize the spiritual source of such [neuroses] means faulty treatment and failure.'[106] At the time, this was the last thing medicine wanted to hear. It saw itself as a child of natural science and shared its assumption of material causation. To science, meaning seemed insubstantial, ambiguous and elusive. How could such a thing influence the healing of neurosis, much less the organic diseases of the body? The old paradigm assumed that the body was a machine and we could understand its workings in chemical and physical terms. Jung saw this was a flawed argument and that it would eventually be replaced with a more holistic view. For his trouble, Jung was treated as a 'witch doctor' who possessed primitive views on medicine. But it was medicine that was out of date, and in the 90 years or so since Jung made these pronouncements his criticisms have been vindicated.

In our time medicine is becoming more holistic. The general practitioner is not only knowledgeable in Western medicine, but often he or she has an interest in Chinese, Indian or Japanese medicine. A great many doctors practise acupuncture, herbal medicine, naturopathy, osteopathy, and other so-called 'complementary' modalities. In mental health, there is increased suspicion among professionals and patients that medication can treat complex mental illnesses. The mental health industry is moving toward a more holistic paradigm, in which Jung's theories and methods, including his interpretation of dreams, fantasies and visions, and his amplification of images in light of myths and cosmological systems, no longer seem out of place. In this open environment, discourse about soul or spirit no longer grates on the nerves of the medical practitioner. On the contrary, all accounts suggest that such practitioners are eager to be re-educated in a larger model in which soul and spirit are no longer seen as obsolete.[107]

Jung felt that wholeness was the key to healing the personality that had fallen into conflict with itself. To make the conscious listen to the unconscious and to build a bridge between the two was the only way to recover sanity. He felt our mental health had been adversely affected by too much separation from nature. When the human is divorced from the cosmos we are more likely to experience neurosis:

> The psyche is not a hormone but a world of almost cosmic proportions ... Only the individual consciousness that has lost its connection with the psychic totality remains caught in the illusion that the soul is a small circumscribed area, a fit subject for 'scientific' theorizing. The loss of this great relationship is the prime evil of neurosis.[108]

We are not designed to live small, shrunken lives inside our personal shells, but are meant to recognise our at-one-ment with creation. We come from a larger totality and seem to be specks of light from a divine source. If we shut the cosmos out, and experience ourselves as egotistical, we injure our humanity. Hence, for Jung, the way modern people live can be self-destructive. Reconnection with what we have lost, in ways suitable to modern understanding, is what he seeks in his therapy. Speaking of our lost relation to primordial symbols, Jung said: 'It is only possible to live the fullest life when we are in harmony with these symbols; wisdom is a return to them.'[109]

Notes

1 C. G. Jung, *Psychological Types* (1921), *CW 6*, § 84.
2 Jung, 'Problems of Modern Psychotherapy' (1929), *CW 16*, § 115.
3 James Hillman, 'Why "Archetypal" Psychology?', in *Loose Ends: Primary Papers in Archetypal Psychology* (Dallas: Spring Publications, 1978), pp. 138–145.
4 See Murray Stein, ed., *Jungian Psychoanalysis* (Chicago: Open Court, 2010).
5 Hillman, 'Why "Archetypal" Psychology?', p. 142.
6 For a study of the relation between unconscious forces and psychological illness see David Tacey, *Gods and Diseases* (Sydney: HarperCollins, 2011).
7 Jung, 'The Psychology of the Child Archetype' (1940), *CW 9*, Part 2, § 293. See Chapter 7 of this volume.
8 Jung, 'Healing the Split' (1961), *CW 18*. See Chapter 17 of this volume.
9 Hillman, 'Why "Archetypal" Psychology?', p. 142.
10 Jung, 'On Synchronicity' (1951), *CW 8*. See Chapter 14 of this volume.
11 See Jung, 'The Difference Between Eastern and Western Thinking' (1939/1954), *CW 11*. See Chapter 12 of this volume.
12 Anthony Stevens, *Jung: A Very Short Introduction* (Oxford: Oxford University Press, 2001), p. 157.
13 See Graham Ward, ed., *The Postmodern God* (Oxford: Basil Blackwell, 1997).
14 Jung, 'The Psychology of the Transference' (1946), *CW 16*, § 524.
15 Grant Watson, 'The Mystery of Instinct' (1964), reprinted in Dorothy Green, ed., *Descent of Spirit: Writings of E. L. Grant Watson* (Sydney: Primavera Press, 1990), p. 108.

16 Sonu Shamdasani, *Jung and the Making of Modern Psychology: The Dream of a Science* (Cambridge: Cambridge University Press, 2003), p. 2.
17 Jung, *Memories, Dreams, Reflections* (1963) (London: HarperCollins, 1995), p. 91.
18 Jung, *The Red Book: Liber Novus*, Sonu Shamdasani, ed. (New York: W. W. Norton, 2009), p. 229.
19 For more on Jung's relationship with his father, see Chapters 2 and 3 of *Memories, Dreams, Reflections*.
20 Jung, 'On the Psychology and Pathology of So-Called Occult Phenomena' (1902), *CW* 1.
21 Jung, 'Mind and Earth' (1927/1931), *CW* 10, § 59.
22 The notion of spirit is found in almost everything Jung wrote, but a major essay on this subject is 'The Phenomenology of the Spirit in Fairytales' (1945/1948), *CW* 9, Part 1.
23 See my distinction between spiritualism and spirituality in *The Spirituality Revolution: The Emergence of Contemporary Spirituality* (London and New York: Routledge, 2004), pp. 199–214.
24 Freud, letter to Jung, April 22, 1910, in William McGuire, ed., *The Freud/Jung Letters* (Princeton: Princeton University Press, 1974), p. 310.
25 Freud, letter to Karl Abraham, July 31, 1908, in Sigmund Freud and Karl Abraham, *A Psycho-Analytic Dialogue: The Letters of Sigmund Freud and Karl Abraham, 1907–1926* (New York: Basic Books, 1965), p. 52.
26 Cf. Gershom Scholem, *Major Trends in Jewish Mysticism* (1954) (New York: Schocken Books, 1961).
27 Jung's revisioning of the theory of libido was published in German in 1912 in *Wandlungen und Symbole der Libido* [*Transformations and Symbols of the Libido*]. This was published in English in 1916 as *Psychology of the Unconscious*. Jung revised the book in 1952 and it now appears as *Symbols of Transformation, CW* 5.
28 Jung signalled to (warned?) Freud that his concept of libido was about to depart from the 'Freudian' model in a letter to Freud, June 2, 1909, in *The Freud/Jung Letters*, pp. 225–226.
29 Jung, 'On the Nature of the Psyche', *CW* 8, § 420.
30 Jung, 'The Eros Theory', *CW* 7, § 32.
31 Jung, ibid., § 33.
32 Jung, *Memories*, p. 192.
33 Freud, letter to Jung, February 18, 1912, in *The Freud/Jung Letters*, p. 485.
34 Deirdre Bair, *Jung: A Biography* (London: Little, Brown, 2004).
35 Jung to Ernest Jones, November 15, 1912, in the Sigmund Freud Copyrights, Wivenhoe, cited by Sonu Shamdasani, *Jung and the Making of Modern Psychology*, p. 50.
36 Jung to Jones, November 25, 1913, in the Sigmund Freud Copyrights, ibid., cited by Shamdasani, p. 52.
37 Freud, letter to Abraham, May 1, 1908, in Freud and Abraham, *A Psycho-Analytic Dialogue*, p. 34.
38 Freud, letter to Jung, April 16, 1909, in *The Freud/Jung Letters*, p. 218.
39 Freud, letter to Abraham, December 26, 1908, in Freud and Abraham, *A Psycho-Analytic Dialogue*, p. 83.
40 Freud, cited in Ernest Jones, *Sigmund Freud, Life and Work* (1953–57), in *Years of Maturity 1901–1919*, Vol. 2. (London: Hogarth Press, 1967), p. 55.
41 For further discussion of this problem, see Anthony Stevens, 'Jung's Alleged Anti-Semitism', in *Jung: A Very Short Introduction* (Oxford: Oxford University Press, 2001), pp. 140–151.
42 Freud to Sabina Spielrein, quoted in Stevens, 'Jung's Alleged Anti-Semitism', p. 147.
43 Freud, 'On the History of the Psycho-Analytic Movement' (1914), *SE* 14, p. 43.

44 Stephen A. Martin, 'Introduction', in Aryeh Maidenbaum and Stephen A. Martin, eds, *Lingering Shadows: Jungians, Freudians and Anti-Semitism* (Boston: Shambhala, 1991), p. 5.
45 Jung, 'The State of Psychotherapy Today' (1934), *CW* 10, § 354.
46 Ernest Jones, *Sigmund Freud, Life and Work*, Vol. 2., p. 184.
47 Freud to Abraham, July 23, 1908, quoted in Jones, op. cit., p. 56.
48 Geoffrey Cocks, *Psychotherapy in the Third Reich: The Göring Institute* (Oxford: Oxford University Press, 1985), pp. 110, 127–128.
49 Jung, 'The Role of the Unconscious' (1918), *CW* 10; and 'The State of Psychotherapy Today' (1934), *CW* 10.
50 Andrew Samuels, 'Nations, Leaders and a Psychology of Difference', *The Political Psyche* (London and New York: Routledge, 1993).
51 Aniela Jaffé, 'C. G. Jung and National Socialism', in *From the Life and Work of C. G. Jung* (New York: Harper & Row, 1971).
52 See for instance, James Kirsch, 'Carl Gustav Jung and the Jews: The Real Story' (1982), in *Lingering Shadows: Jungians, Freudians and Anti-Semitism*, pp. 51–88.
53 Ernest Harms, 'Carl Gustav Jung: Defender of Freud and the Jews: A Chapter of European Psychiatric History under the Nazi Yoke', *Psychiatric Quarterly* (New York) April 1946, pp. 1–32; reprinted in *Lingering Shadows: Jungians, Freudians and Anti-Semitism*, op. cit., pp. 17–49.
54 Jung, *Memories*, p. 173.
55 Jung, *Memories*, p. 174.
56 Freud, letter to Jung, April 16, 1909, in *The Freud/Jung Letters*, p. 219.
57 Freud, 'Psychoanalysis and Telepathy' (1921), first published in G. Devereux, *Psychoanalysis and the Occult* (New York: International Universities Press, 1953), pp. 56–68. Now in *SE* 18.
58 Freud, 'The Uncanny' (1919), [Das Unheimliche], *SE* 17.
59 Jung, *Aion* (1951), *CW* 9, Part 2, § 51.
60 Jung, letter to Freud, November 11, 1912, in *The Freud/Jung Letters*, p. 516.
61 Freud, letter to Jung, April 16, 1909, in *The Freud/Jung Letters*, p. 220.
62 Cf. G. Devereux, *Psychoanalysis and the Occult* (1953, London: Souvenir Press, 1974); and Nick Totton, 'Funny you should say that: Paranormality, at the margins and the centre of psychotherapy', in *European Journal of Psychotherapy and Counselling* 9(4), 2007, pp. 389–401.
63 Christine Gallant, *Tabooed Jung: Marginality as Power* (New York: New York University Press, 1996), p. 3.
64 Freud, *Totem and Taboo* (1913), *SE* 13, p. 18.
65 Jung's reflections on the spiritual dimension of sexuality are found in 'The Psychology of the Transference' (1946) *CW* 16, and *Mysterium Coniunctionis* (1955–56), *CW* 14.
66 Jung, *Memories*, p. 192.
67 Ibid., p. 174.
68 Ibid., p. 176.
69 Ibid., p. 175.
70 Ibid., p. 175.
71 Ibid., p. 175.
72 John Carroll, *The Western Dreaming* (Sydney: HarperCollins, 2001), p. 53.
73 John Carroll, *The Existential Jesus* (Melbourne: Scribe Publications, 2007), p. 35.
74 Friedrich Nietzsche, *The Birth of Tragedy*, trans. Shaun Whiteside (1872, London: Penguin, 1993).
75 Jung, *Memories*, p. 193.
76 Thomas Merton, *The Seven Storey Mountain* (1948) (New York: Harcourt, Brace and Co., 1998); Teilhard de Chardin, *The Phenomenon of Man* (1959) (New York: Harper Perennial, 1976).

77 Stanislov Grof, *Realms of the Human Unconscious* (New York: Viking, 1975), p. 212.
78 Michael Eigen, *The Psychoanalytic Mystic* (New York: Free Association Books, 1998); William Meissner, *Psychoanalysis and Religious Experience* (New Haven: Yale University Press, 1984); and Neville Symington, *Emotion and Spirit: Questioning the Claims of Psychoanalysis and Religion* (1994) (London: Karnac, 1998).
79 See David Tacey, 'The Gift of the Unknown: Jung(ians) and Freud(ians) at the End of Modernity', in *European Journal of Psychotherapy and Counselling* 9(4), 2007, pp. 423–434.
80 Paul Roazen, *Freud and his Followers* (New York: Knopf, 1975), p. 272.
81 Andrew Samuels, *Jung and the Post-Jungians* (London: Routledge, 1985), p. 9.
82 Christine Gallant, *Tabooed Jung*, p. 4.
83 Jung, 'The Eros Theory', *CW* 7, § 34.
84 Diarmuid O'Murchu, *The God Who Becomes Redundant* (Dublin and London: The Mercier Press/Fowler Wright Books, 1986), p. 9.
85 Jung, 'Commentary on "The Secret of the Golden Flower" ' (1929), *CW* 13, § 7.
86 Ibid., § 7.
87 Jean-Francois Lyotard, *The Postmodern Condition: A Report on Knowledge* (Minneapolis: University of Minnesota Press, 1984).
88 Karl Popper, *Conjectures and Refutations* (London: Routledge and Kegan Paul, 1963), and Thomas Kuhn, *The Structure of Scientific Revolutions* (1962) (Chicago: University of Chicago Press, 1996).
89 David Bohm, *Wholeness and the Implicate Order* (London: Routledge & Kegan Paul, 1980).
90 Rupert Sheldrake, *The Rebirth of Nature: The Greening of Science and God* (New York: Bantam, 1991).
91 Charlene Spretnak, *States of Grace: The Recovery of Meaning in the Postmodern Age* (San Francisco: HarperSanFrancisco, 1991); and Fritjof Capra, *The Tao of Physics* (1975) (Boston: Shambhala, 1991).
92 Thomas Berry, *The Dream of the Earth* (San Francisco: Sierra Club Books, 1988); and Diarmuid O'Murchu, *Quantum Theology* (New York: Crossroad, 1996).
93 Jacques Derrida and Gianni Vattimo, eds, *Religion* (Stanford: Stanford University Press, 1998).
94 Robert A. Emmons, *The Psychology of Ultimate Concerns: Motivation and Spirituality in Personality* (New York and London: The Guilford Press, 1999), and Gregg Jacobs, *The Ancestral Mind* (New York: Viking, 2003).
95 Joseph Cambray, *Synchronicity: Nature and Psyche in an Interconnected Universe* (College Station, TX: Texas A&M University Press, 2009).
96 Jung, cited in C. A. Meier, *The Psychology of Jung. Volume 1: The Unconscious in its Empirical Manifestations* (Boston: Sigo Press, 1984), p. x.
97 Jung, 'Psychology and Literature' (1930/1950), *CW* 15, § 133.
98 C. G. Jung and Wolfgang Pauli, *The Interpretation of Nature and the Psyche* (London and New York: Routledge & Kegan Paul, 1955).
99 On Jung's relationship with Einstein, see Cambray, *Synchronicity*.
100 See in particular, Meredith Sabini, ed., *The Earth Has a Soul: The Nature Writings of C. G. Jung* (Berkeley, California: North Atlantic Books, 2002).
101 James Hillman, 'Anima Mundi: The Return of the Soul to the World' (1982), in Hillman, *The Thought of the Heart and the Soul of the World* (Dallas: Spring Publications, 1992); and James Hillman and Michael Ventura, *We've Had a Hundred Years of Psychotherapy and the World's Getting Worse* (San Francisco: HarperSanFrancisco, 1992).
102 Theodore Roszak, Mary E. Gomes and Allen K. Kanner, eds, *Ecopsychology: Restoring the Earth, Healing the Mind* (San Francisco: Sierra Club Books, 1995).

103 James Lovelock, *Gaia: A New Look at Life on Earth* (New York: Oxford University Press, 1979).
104 Jung, 'Psychotherapists or the Clergy' (1932), *CW* 11, § 490.
105 Jung, ibid., § 497.
106 Jung, 'Basic Postulates of Analytical Psychology' (1931), *CW* 8, § 686; see Chapter 1 of this volume.
107 John Swinton, *Spirituality and Mental Health Care: Rediscovering a 'Forgotten' Dimension* (London: Kingsley, 2001).
108 Jung, 'The State of Psychotherapy Today', op. cit., § 367.
109 Jung, 'The Stages of Life', op. cit., § 794.

Chronology of Jung's life and work

(Adapted and modified from *C. G. Jung: Word and Image*, Aniela Jaffé, ed., Princeton University Press, 1979)

1875	Born on 26 July in Kesswil, Switzerland, to Paul Jung (1842–1896), parson in the Swiss Reformed Church, and Emilie Jung, née Preiswerk (1848–1923).
1879	Family moves to Klein-Hüningen, near Basel.
1895–1900	Medical training and qualification at Basel University.
1896	Death of father.
1900–1909	Works under Eugen Bleuler at the Burghölzli, the insane asylum of Canton Zurich and psychiatric clinic of Zurich University.
1902	Senior Assistant Staff Physician at the Burghölzli; MD dissertation at Zurich University, 'On the Psychology and Pathology of So-Called Occult Phenomena'.
1902–1903	Winter semester with Pierre Janet at the Saltpêtrière, Paris, for study of psychopathology.
1903	Marriage to Emma Rauschenbach (1882–1955); one son and four daughters.
1903–1905	Experimental researches on word association.
1905–1909	Senior Staff Physician at the Burghölzli; conducts courses on hypnotic therapy; research on schizophrenia.
1905–1913	Appointed *Privatdozent* (lecturer) on the medical faculty of Zurich University; lectures on psychoneuroses and psychology.
1906	April: correspondence with Freud begins.
1907	Publishes *Über die Psychologie der Dementia Praecox* (*The Psychology of Dementia Praecox*, 1909); March: first meeting with Freud in Vienna.
1909	Withdraws from the clinic to devote himself to private practice; first visit to the USA, with Freud and Ferenczi; moves to own house in Küsnacht/Zurich.
1910–1914	First president of the International Psychoanalytic Association.

1912	Another visit to the USA; publishes 'The Theory of Psychoanalysis', 'New Paths in Psychology' and *Wandlungen und Symbole der Libido* (*Psychology of the Unconscious*, 1916; for revision, see 1952), leading to:
1913	Break with Freud; designates his psychology as 'Analytical Psychology' (and also 'Complex Psychology'); resigns lectureship at Zurich University.
1913–1919	Period of great psychic disorientation, his 'confrontation with the unconscious'.
1914	Resigns as president of the International Psychoanalytic Association.
1916	Publishes 'Septem Sermones ad Mortuos'; first mandala painting; first description of active imagination in 'The Transcendent Function' (not published until 1957); first use of terms 'collective unconscious', 'individuation', 'anima/animus', 'persona'; begins study of Gnostic writings.
1918	Publishes 'The Role of the Unconscious'.
1918–1919	Commandant of camp for interned British soldiers at Château d'Oex; first use of term 'archetype' in 'Instinct and the Unconscious'.
1920	Journey to Algeria and Tunisia.
1921	Publishes *Psychologische Typen* (*Psychological Types*, 1923); first use of term 'self'.
1923	Builds tower in Bollingen; death of mother; association begins with Richard Wilhelm.
1924–1925	Trip to the USA; visits Pueblo Indians in New Mexico.
1925	First English seminar at the Psychological Club, Zurich.
1925-1926	Expedition to Kenya, Uganda, and the Nile; visit with the Elgonyi on Mount Elgon.
1928	Begins study of alchemy; publishes *Two Essays on Analytical Psychology*.
1928–1930	English seminars on 'Dream Analysis' at the Psychological Club, Zurich.
1929	Publication, with Richard Wilhelm, of *The Secret of the Golden Flower*; publishes *Contributions to Analytical Psychology*.
1930	Vice President of General Medical Society for Psychotherapy, under Ernst Kretschmer as President.
1930–1934	English seminars on 'Interpretation of Visions' at the Psychological Club, Zurich.
1932	Awarded Literature Prize of the City of Zurich.
1933	First lectures at the Eidgenössische Technische Hochschule (ETH), Zurich (Swiss Federal Polytechnic) on modern psychology; publishes *Modern Man in Search of a Soul*; first Eranos lecture, on 'A Study in the Process of Individuation'; cruise to Egypt and Palestine.

1934	Founds International General Medical Society for Psychotherapy and becomes its first president; Eranos lecture on 'Archetypes of the Collective Unconscious'.
1934–1939	English seminars on 'Psychological Aspects of Nietzsche's *Zarathustra*' at the Psychological Club, Zurich.
1934–1939	Editor of *Zentralblatt für Psychotherapie und ihre Grenzgebiete* (Leipzig).
1935	Appointed titular professor at the ETH, Zurich; Eranos lecture on 'Dream Symbols of the Individuation Process'; lectures at the Tavistock, London (*Analytical Psychology: Its Theory and Practice*, published 1968).
1936	Receives honorary doctoral degree from Harvard University; Eranos lecture on 'Ideas of Redemption in Alchemy'; publishes essay 'Wotan'.
1937	Terry Lectures on 'Psychology and Religion' at Yale University; Eranos lecture on 'The Visions of Zosimos'.
1938	Invitation to India for the Indian Science Congress, Calcutta; International Congress for Psychotherapy at Oxford with Jung as president; receives honorary doctorate from Oxford University; appointed Honorary Fellow of the Royal Society of Medicine, London; Eranos lecture on 'Psychological Aspects of the Mother Archetype'.
1939	Eranos lecture on 'Concerning Rebirth'.
1940	Eranos lecture on 'A Psychological Approach to the Dogma of the Trinity'.
1941	Publishes, together with Karl Kerényi, *Essays on a Science of Mythology*; Eranos lecture on 'Transformation Symbolism in the Mass'.
1942	Resigns appointment as professor at the ETH; Eranos lecture on 'The Spirit Mercurius'.
1943	Appointed to the chair of Medical Psychology at Basel University; becomes honorary member of the Swiss Academy of Sciences.
1944	Resigns Basel chair on account of critical illness; publishes *Psychology and Alchemy*.
1945	Eranos lecture on 'The Psychology of the Spirit; receives honorary doctorate from Geneva University.
1946	Eranos lecture on 'The Spirit of Psychology; publishes 'The Psychology of the Transference' and *Essays on Contemporary Events*.
1948	Inauguration of the C. G. Jung Institute, Zurich; Eranos lecture 'On the Self'.
1951	Publishes *Aion*; Eranos lecture 'On Synchronicity'.
1952	Publishes *Symbols of Transformation* (greatly revised edition of *Psychology of the Unconscious*), 'Answer to Job' and, together with

	Wolfgang Pauli, *The Interpretation of Nature and Psyche*, with Jung's contribution 'Synchronicity: An Acausal Connecting Principle'; serious illness.
1953	Publication of the first volume of the American/British edition of the *Collected Works* (translated by R. F. C. Hull), *Psychology and Alchemy*.
1955	Death of his wife (27 November); awarded honorary doctorate of the ETH, on the occasion of his 80th birthday.
1955–1956	Publishes *Mysterium Coniunctionis*, the final work on the psychological significance of alchemy.
1957	Starts work on *Memories, Dreams, Reflections*, with the collaboration of Aniela Jaffé; BBC *Face to Face* interview with John Freeman; publishes 'The Undiscovered Self (Present and Future)'.
1958	Publishes 'Flying Saucers: A Modern Myth'.
1961	Finishes his last work ten days before his death: 'Symbols and the Interpretation of Dreams' in *Man and His Symbols*; dies after short illness on 6 June in Küsnacht/Zurich.

Part I

The nature of the psyche

The nature of the psyche
Introduction

Chapter 1: 'Basic postulates of analytical psychology' (1931)

(From *The Structure and Dynamics of the Psyche*, *The Collected Works* Vol. 8, § 649–688)

'Basic postulates of analytical psychology' is a useful overview of Jung's psychology and a frank self-assessment of its unusual or radical aspects. Jung discusses his soul-centred psychology against a historical background of scientific materialism. Jung's psychology is a reaction to the bleak psychology of his day, which he calls 'psychology without the soul'. But Jung refused to adopt a romantic or idealistic conception of the soul. For him it is a subject of scientific scrutiny and only a sober attitude can do justice to its complexities, functions and pathologies. Soul for Jung is not a theological abstraction, such as we find in Western religion, but an empirical reality. He derives the term soul from the Greek word *psyche*, and thus 'psycho-logy' literally means 'the logos or study of the soul'. Jung wants the discipline of psychology to return to this original foundation. He sees no real reason, apart from modern prejudice and assumptions, as to why psychology has taken a turn to reductive materialism. The study of psyche ought be given back its mystery and philosophical depth. Since soul is primarily unconscious for us today, Jung's psychology begins with the idea of the unconscious, and this marks it off from mainstream psychologies which are psychologies of consciousness.

Jung admits that in some ways his psychology is not 'modern', for to derive a psychology from spiritual principles is to move counter to the reductive bias that is found in everything modern. His psychology represents, in part, a return to 'the teachings of our forefathers' (§ 661). Jung distrusts materialism, since for him it purports to be based on scientific principles, yet is 'a religion or, better, a creed which has absolutely no connection with reason' (§ 651). He despises the fact that materialism has become fused with scientific enquiry, thus generating scientism. Decades before the philosophy of science and the work of Karl Popper and Thomas Kuhn, Jung was arguing that scientific materialism is an ideology and not a science. Materialism is destroying the thinking of our era, and hardly anyone dares to contradict it because:

> To think otherwise than our contemporaries think is somehow illegitimate and disturbing; it is even indecent, morbid or blasphemous, and therefore socially dangerous for the individual. He is stupidly swimming against the social current.
>
> (§ 633)

Jung was aware of the dangers of swimming against the tide, and he practised it on a daily basis. We have to appreciate the personal resolve and professional difficulty that this involved. As we might say today, he must have had enormous resilience and self-belief to withstand the barrage of criticisms that he constantly received.

Jung is not content to assert an opposite position to mainstream psychology; he also turns the tables on this science, arguing that it is inherently irrational in its obsession with material causation. We do not even know what 'matter' is, so how can we pretend to be so certain about it? Matter remains, to this day, mysterious to physicists, chemists and biologists, but the popular worldview asserts a 'materialism' which pure science cannot support. According to Jung, we have merely supplanted the 'metaphysics of mind' that ruled up until the Gothic age with a new 'metaphysics of matter'. It is a creed without substance, except that it serves the ego in its blindness to the invisible dimensions of being.

In reality we are flying blind into the future, with a recklessness that Jung finds alarming. We have left unattended the invisibles and imponderables of the psyche, and Jung's intuition is that this is landing us in social chaos and personal despair. The invisibles require study and attention, and their needs have to be taken seriously, otherwise we face a continued downward course into violence and destruction. After the experience of the First World War, Jung adopts a social dimension in everything he writes, and he does not write as if there is no world crisis outside the clinic. He thinks it is our unsubstantiated worldview that is responsible for the rise of social, political and psychological disorder.

Jung is aware that scientific enquirers will demand proof for his assertions, and he struggles with this demand, claiming that an intuitive understanding leads to the conclusion that all is not well with the world. Jung is no more able to provide 'evidence' for his position than materialism can supply for its view. This is to frustrate him throughout his career, because he feels the rightness of his intuitions, and yet is helpless to make them plain to others. He often resorts to philosophical rather than scientific methods of argument, while arguing that he is not a philosopher but a scientist. He protests that he has empirical facts, but they are not the facts that his colleagues would find convincing. Jung's 'facts' are often *interpretations* of symbolic phenomena such as dreams, visions, fantasies, religions and works of art. He is more of a hermeneut than a scientist, a scholar who interprets the world through a particular kind of vision.

Throughout his career Jung is more interested in 'the West' as the subject of his analysis than he is in the individual sufferer. Western culture is his 'patient', and it is time to analyse this strange specimen and figure out why things are going wrong. His analysis is a psychosocial analysis, or a study of the human condition rather than of any specific group of suffering neurotics. Individuals are suffering because the cultural system is imbalanced, and that is what Jung seeks to address. Our system is wrong because it condones a 'one-sidedness' that does not take the whole psyche and its contents into account. Jung's self-appointed task is to speak on behalf of what has been left out of the Western cultural frame.

Chapter 2: 'The role of the unconscious' (1918)

(From *Civilization in Transition, The Collected Works Vol.* 10, § 1–48)

In 'The role of the unconscious' Jung moves between two points of view. First there is the psychological analysis of the personality, with an emphasis on the dynamics of the unconscious. 'The role of the unconscious,' he says, 'is to act compensatorily to the conscious contents of the moment' (§ 21). The psyche is for him an energic system that is striving to achieve equilibrium and a balanced relationship between its parts. It is only in a state of wholeness, he maintains, that the psyche works effectively and achieves health. Second, there is the psychosocial and often prophetic analysis of civilisation, with a focus on cataclysmic events in recent history. This is for Jung a logical extension of the first theme, because he finds civilisation to be diseased and out of balance. The West is in need of psychological, cultural and religious correction.

The editors of the *Collected Works* have placed this essay in Volume 10, *Civilization in Transition*. Jung is positioning himself as a therapist of culture and not only of individual neurosis. He is a psychologist who refuses to remain within the confines of the clinic. He gives himself freedom to roam across the spectrum of society, politics and culture, making pronouncements about what is wrong with civilisation, and how things might be made better. Jung was not alone in this movement between clinic and civilisation. His mentor and colleague, Freud, did the same thing. In one instant Freud considered a case study, in the next, he reflected on civilisation as a whole, and wrote books with such titles as *Civilization and its Discontents* and *Moses and Monotheism*. In the early days of psychoanalysis, it was not uncommon for pioneers to explore every corner of life and to make some comment. Today, professionals in these fields are more guarded, keeping to their 'specialisations' in a way which would have appalled Freud and Jung, who would have seen this as unadventurous.

This essay was written at the close of the 1914–1918 war. Jung set himself the task of understanding war from a psychological point of view. He was not interested in condemning Germany, but his purpose was to ask the psychological question: where has this eruption of evil come from? What can a psychology of the unconscious contribute to understanding the catastrophe? Jung risks criticism in his attempt at interpretation. Political scientists would argue that a psychology of the unconscious has little to offer to the solution of wars. They would claim that war and social catastrophe can better be understood by exploring known factors such as wealth, class, economics, political relations and social inequality. Why bring in the unknown, when the known is complex enough?

Jung understands this critique, but moves on regardless. The collective crisis is derived from his analysis of the individual. Jung believes that in the early stages of development, a typical pattern emerges whereby we identify ourselves with the good side of our personalities, and disidentify from our dark or evil aspects. This leads to the suppression of aspects that do not fit our idealised self-image. Suppression, or pushing away this unwanted aspect, is followed by repression, a more serious forgetting of the negative aspect, and dissociation from it. This serves us for a time, and helps us to consolidate our lives and gain moral stability and orientation. However, if we do not put an end to repression and begin to retrieve the psychological aspects that belong to our personality, we fall victim to projection, hatred of others and social conflict.

Jung defines projection as a process whereby 'an unconscious content of the subject . . . is transferred to the object, and there magnifies one of its peculiarities to such proportions that it seems a sufficient cause of the disturbance' (§ 41). We find the evil aspects of ourselves in others and despise them for the realities we fail to see in ourselves. This is hardly a new idea, it is found at the heart of religious and cosmological systems. For instance, we read in the *New Testament*: 'Why do you observe the splinter in your brother's eye and never notice the plank in your own? How dare you say to your brother, "Let me take the splinter out of your eye," when all the time there is a plank in your own?'[1] Jung is providing a modern approach to this age-old insight. He argues that we project our negative contents onto those who are 'more or less suitable objects' (§ 41), and the task of withdrawing projections is all the more difficult because we think we have just cause for our criticism of others.

Wars develop when nations claiming to be 'good' attack those deemed to be 'bad'. The state of the world is a reflection of the dissociation within the individual. The upwelling of evil and violence comes from within all of us. We all stand responsible, in his view, for the eruption of evil. Paradoxically, we can only get out of the grip of evil if we befriend it. The cure, Jung felt, is homeopathic: take in and imbibe some of the poison. If we move toward it with awareness, it might not overtake us in such devastating ways. Evil has accumulated in the West because we have been identified with the good for too long. This is why there is a sense of urgency about evil, and why the 'problem of evil' can no longer be relegated to philosophy seminar rooms. It is a problem that each of us has to encounter.

The discovery of the unconscious has forced this awareness upon us. Prior to this discovery, we might have set our minds on the good and repressed the dark side, or projected it upon our neighbour. But now that we are made aware of the totality of the psyche, we have to take responsibility for the darkness that piles up in the inner world. We have to face the darkness within, or 'encounter our own shadow', as Jung was later to put it, as a part of our developmental task. This is a responsibility that confronts individuals, societies and nations. At the time of writing this essay, Jung had not developed his theory of the *shadow* as archetype, although the essay is moving in that direction.

At the heart of Jung's psychology is a moral philosophy. He sometimes denies this in the attempt to present himself as an empirical scientist, but there is a definite philosophy in his psychology. His philosophy appears to be a Western version of the Taoist philosophy of China, which calls for a balance between opposite forces. There is a secret symmetry between conflicting or rival energies, the yin and the yang, and if we bring them into relationship the rivalry can shift to complementarity and vital force. One takes what initially looks like an enemy agent and transforms it into a source of energy. By facing the shadow, we may find our lives are given a new moral integrity, and things move in a more coherent and creative way. In Taoism, the 'Way' is discovered when one discovers the key to a balanced wholeness. Then the psyche can be expected to recover its direction and sense of flow.

Jung did not literally import this philosophy from China, but one could say he had a natural predisposition to think in this way. The West does not have to go to China to discover this approach: it can also be found, to some extent, in the gods of ancient Greece. Apollo, god of the sun, and Dionysus, god of passion and ecstasy, seem to represent a pair of opposites, in which Greece recognised the need for acknowledgement of the light and dark sides of existence. It is sometimes important to respect the light, but at other times it is equally important to recognise the 'dark' side, which was symbolised in the festivals of Dionysus. Only Christianity, Jung argues, fails to provide a cosmology in which humanity can regulate its experience of the opposites. Christian civilisation lost this balance by worshiping a God of light and turning the historical Jesus into a spotless and perfect figure of myth. There is little room in the Christian story for evil or darkness, except as features to be demonised as Satan or Devil.

Jung thought this was its downfall, and it is bringing the West down with it, due to the accumulation of vast amounts of evil. The reason evil is running amok is because we have no symbolic container to hold it. His essay focuses on Germany as a nation in which evil has accumulated without any myth or religion to transform it. Christianity, he argues, 'domesticated the brighter half' of the German psyche, 'but the lower, darker half still awaits redemption and a second spell of domestication'. He adds a prophetic warning:

> Until then, it will remain associated with vestiges of the prehistoric age, with the collective unconscious, which is subject to ever-increasing activation. As the Christian view of the world loses its authority, the more menacingly will the 'blond beast' be heard prowling about in its underground prison, ready at any moment to burst out with devastating consequences.
>
> (§ 17)

It has been remarked that this statement is an accurate anticipation of the spectre of National Socialism and the Nazi uprising of the 1930s and 1940s. The 'blond beast' did awaken from its 'underground prison' with 'devastating consequences', as Jung suggested. This shows that his psychology, by reaching into the deeper levels of experience, can not only analyse the present but predict the future as well.

Every time we walk in the light, or reach for the light, we cast a shadow which we almost never surmise. Often it is others who point out the shadow to us, since although we do not see our failings, others have the knack of spotting them right away! The shadow is projected onto others and plays a role in determining how we experience other people and the outside world. However, it is by no means the case that the shadow is entirely evil or negative. Jung writes:

> The existence within us of something that can turn against us, that can become a serious matter for us, I regard not merely as a dangerous peculiarity, but as a valuable and congenial asset as well. It is a still untouched fortune, an uncorrupted treasure, a sign of youthfulness, an earnest of rebirth.
>
> (§ 20)

He continues:

> The unconscious contains the dark springs of instinct and intuition [and] all those forces which mere reasonableness, propriety, and the orderly course of bourgeois existence could never call awake. [It contains] all those creative forces which lead man onwards to new developments, new forms, and new goals.
>
> (§ 25)

The shadow is a paradoxical reality, containing not only undesirable elements but all the darker, primal, secret impulses that are responsible for creativity, originality and spontaneous expression. A person who places too much emphasis on the light ends up pallid, empty, bloodless, and devoid of adventure – and unprepared for the onslaughts of evil. The shadow is a 'dangerous peculiarity' and a 'valuable and congenial asset as well'. Some Jungians have written about the 'gold' in the shadow, believing that what consciousness rejects is often the stuff of life that gives it its highest value.[2] However, this is to idealise the shadow and put a halo around it. While he points to the paradoxical nature of the shadow, Jung warns against an overvaluation of its positive aspect:

> Nevertheless, to value the unconscious exclusively for the sake of its positive qualities and to regard it as a source of revelation would be fundamentally wrong.
>
> (§ 20)

It would be a mistake to sentimentally distort the unconscious and make of it a personal boon rather than a difficult moral challenge.

Chapter 3: 'The stages of life' (1930/1931)

(From *The Structure and Dynamics of the Psyche, The Collected Works Vol. 8*, § 749–795)

In 'The stages of life' the personality is perceived as a battleground of opposing forces. To the extent that we seek to become more conscious, we rally behind the forces that seek civilisation. But to the extent that we seek to lose ourselves in the unconscious, we support the forces of inertia:

> Everything in us that still belongs to nature shrinks away from a problem, for its name is doubt, and wherever doubt holds sway there is uncertainty and the possibility of divergent ways. And where several ways seem possible, there we have turned away from the certain guidance of instinct and are handed over to fear.
>
> (§ 750)

We fear that civilisation might not prove as reliable a guide as instinct. 'We are beset by an all-too-human fear that consciousness – our Promethean conquest – may in the end not be able to serve us as well as nature' (§ 750). We have departed from the ways of instinct, but wonder if this has been a wise choice. We fear that the light of consciousness will be snuffed out by the problems that beset us. Are we interlopers in the grand scheme of things? In some moments, we are proud of our Promethean theft of fire from the gods. But in darker moments, when we are enshrouded with uncertainty and fear, the child within us cries out for the surer path of nature, the certainty of instinct, the strength of nature. In dark times, we feel as helpless as an orphan, flung out in an unforgiving universe. Indeed, as I will explore, the conquest of consciousness may be styled as a masculine protest against mother nature.

Rage as we might against our isolation in the world, Jung claims we have no alternative but to tread the path we are on. There is no going back, only a movement forward:

> Every problem brings the possibility of a widening of consciousness, but also the necessity of saying goodbye to childlike unconsciousness and trust in nature. This necessity is a psychic fact of such importance that it constitutes one of the most essential symbolic teachings of the Christian religion. It is the sacrifice of the merely natural man, of the unconscious, ingenuous being whose tragic career began with the eating of the apple in Paradise. The biblical fall of man presents the dawn of consciousness as a curse.
>
> (§ 751)

Although innocent unconsciousness is idealised as paradise, we are not free to experiment with ourselves. Our disobedience to the will of God is seen by Jung as necessary. The will of God is synonymous with the will of nature, an eternal, immutable law that we contradict at our peril. Moving away from unconsciousness would be experienced by our early consciousness as a transgression of the natural order. On the other hand, every time we turn away from a problem because it demands too much effort, we are activating the nostalgia for Eden, the sense that we can return to innocence and childhood.

Jung argues that we recapitulate our mythology in our daily lives. His thought is a psychological reworking of the myths of Western culture, in which religious truths becomes psychological. He turns the nouns of religion into the verbs of psychology: metaphysical figures are converted into existential acts or processes of awareness. The key to this shift from mythology to psychology is symbolic awareness: by viewing our lives symbolically, Jung locates the metaphors that are buried in our experience. He is expert at the subtle art of being able to detect mythic currents running through our ordinary lives, in such a way that our lives appear extraordinary. In highlighting the mythic elements, Jung turns the most banal fact into something interesting and exciting. He uses myth to reveal the deeper meaning of our lives, and the awareness of myth enables us to turn events into experiences.

However, one of the unexamined myths in this essay is that of nature-versus-culture. Jung appears to espouse a traditional dualism between earth and spirit, nature and consciousness. His dualism is expressed in emotive language:

> It is just man's turning away from instinct – his opposing himself to instinct – that creates consciousness. Instinct is nature and seeks to perpetuate nature, whereas consciousness can only seek culture or its denial.
>
> (§ 750)

This dualism is tied to a patriarchal view in which spirit is masculine and 'mother earth' is feminine. As such, Jung tends to perpetuate the belief that the masculine is greater than the feminine, and of higher value. The feminine would pull us down to earth and keep us unconscious if it were not for the heroic struggle of spirit, which has to battle against the earth for deliverance. For Jung, the task of consciousness is an *opus contra naturam*, a work against nature. Such views are dismissed today as fantasies of a patriarchal-supremacist system. But in Jung's late career, there are signs that he grew beyond the dualism that is evident in 'The stages of life'. The notion that consciousness and nature are opposed is dropped in his later work. Instead he opts for a more organic approach, in which consciousness is seen as nature striving to become conscious of itself.

If spirit is nature itself struggling to achieve awareness, there is no conflict between these forces. Instead one would construct a different worldview, in which a part of nature seeks to become conscious, and another part seeks to remain unconscious. Nature is an extremely complex field, but the notion that nature is antagonistic to consciousness and seeks to undermine spirit is a view which suits established masculine prejudices. In his essays on alchemy and synchronicity, Jung appears to abandon this masculinist model and adopts a view which is post-heroic and ecological. There is little comfort for ecological thinkers in Jung's 'Stages of life', which sees humanity working against hostile nature in an ongoing struggle for survival.

What has endured from this essay is Jung's popular notion of the midlife crisis. Although the term 'midlife crisis' was coined by the Canadian analyst Elliott Jaques,[3] it was Jung who focused attention on what he called the 'midlife transition', which was the turning point between the first and second 'halves' of life. The midlife transition, he felt, took place roughly between 35 and 40 years of age (§ 758). According to this theory, the ego plays the dominant role in the first half of life, and the unconscious plays an increasingly important role in the second half. This unconscious personality is called the 'second ego' (§ 757), although elsewhere Jung replaces this term with the notion of the *Self*. For Jung, the Self is the archetype of wholeness and governs both conscious and unconscious dynamics of the psyche. The Self comes into play at the midlife transition, where an authority is revealed which is greater than the ego.

The first half of life, according to Jung, is about the development and fulfilment of the ego. Its task is to plant itself in the soil of the world and draw nourishment for its growth. Its aim is to find a place for itself in family, friendship, society and employment and come to terms with the norms of its historical period. We are forced to make these adaptations due to the physical demands of life. The aim of the first half of life is to stabilise the ego, so it can become a container and controller of the human journey. At least, the ego *believes* it is in control, and this attitude is important for developing its confidence. But when the material obligations of life have been discharged, the non-material and spiritual impulses come to the fore and demand attention.

Then the ego is ousted from its central position and becomes aware of a different source of authority. The 'second ego' is not concerned about the ego's goals and ambitions, but may actually thwart those ambitions to make the personality live a larger life, open to the archetypes and the forces of the cosmos. At midlife the ego is cut across by a greater will, and the individual is made to realise that life is about larger forces that course through the personality and demand expression. Typically, the second half of life is about giving rather than receiving, sacrificing rather than gaining, losing rather than winning. But it is a loss by which the spirit gains. It is the paradoxical loss that is found at the heart of religious and spiritual cosmologies.

In our ego-driven and secular society, however, the desire of the personality to push for a 'wider and higher consciousness' (§ 767) is thwarted. There are few social indications that the individual must move from the ego to a higher authority, because those indications are labelled as 'religious' and rejected. Hence the midlife transition can be marked by confusion, anguish and turmoil. Instead of transcending ego, a person at midlife may decide to indulge the ego all the more, and it has become a cliché to suggest that the older person who tries to recover youth is suffering from a midlife crisis. If development is thwarted, and the ego clings to power, we often dig in our heels, refuse to change, and 'somewhere around the age of fifty a period of intolerance and fanaticism is reached' (§ 773). It is clear from Jung's theory that 'religion', or what we today call 'spirituality', is an integral ingredient of a mature personality, and without it we are likely to fall prey to narcissism and stunted development.

Chapter 4: 'The relations between the ego and the unconscious' (1928)

(From *Two Essays on Analytical Psychology, The Collected Works Vol. 7*, § 202–295)

Section One of Part I of this essay discusses the effects of the unconscious upon consciousness. Jung is interested in exploring the effects of the collective unconscious, and how these differ from those of the personal unconscious. To illustrate his argument, he presents a case study of a patient suffering from a mild hysterical neurosis. He does not present a full description of this case, but sketches in a number of features hastily from memory. Jung seems impatient with case material, and wants to move quickly to core issues and not lose sight of them amidst a morass of clinical details.

This essay is written to contrast his approach to that of Freud. Jung argues that the treatment of neurosis is not complete without taking the values and directions of the collective unconscious into account. People can get sick not only from repressed personal materials that have been excluded from consciousness, but from contents that have never entered consciousness. Therapy consists not simply of trawling through the personal life to discern what has been repressed; it is also forced to become spiritual, or at least philosophical, when this is indicated by dreams and fantasies of an archetypal nature. If the psyche seeks a cosmic goal or higher meaning, therapy has to be prepared to venture into these mysterious waters. Jung argues that the lack of a symbolic or spiritual life can make a person mentally and physically ill. A year after writing this essay, he was to make his famous statement, 'the gods have become diseases'.[4]

The patient is an unnamed woman whose neurosis, he surmises, had 'its principal cause in a father-complex' (§ 206). However, in Jung's hands, a father-complex is not the same thing as it is in Freud's. This woman did not seek an incestuous relationship with the father; rather, she sought an archetypal, spiritual relationship with a symbolic father. Jung has a difficult time arguing this case, because the patient is a modern person who had imbibed the 'Freudian' theory from her society, and Jung's theory strikes her as arcane and unacceptable. It is difficult to argue a case for the religious interpretation of a neurosis if the patient is not of that persuasion. Jung has a double task to perform as an analyst. He must interpret his patient's psychological situation as well as present a metapsychological critique of society and the failings of rational thought. He performs a dual role as a psychologist of neurosis and a philosopher of religion.

The patient is unable to make an adjustment to life because her energy seems to 'flow off in every conceivable direction, apparently quite uselessly' (§ 206). She is unable to develop herself professionally, or to form a bond with a partner or engage in sexual relations. These are beyond her reach because she is caught up in what presents initially as a fatal romance with her deceased father. The essay concerns itself with the role of the transference in her recovery. She develops a highly charged, idealised and romantic transference to the analyst, and this seems to replicate the bond with the father. It is not that the transference provides the solution, but it gives visibility to the problem:

> In the course of treatment the patient transferred the father-imago to the doctor, thus making him, in a sense, the father, and in the sense that he is not the father, also making him a substitute for the man she cannot reach. The doctor therefore becomes both a father and a kind of lover. In him the opposites are united, and for this reason he stands for a quasi-ideal solution to the conflict. Without in the least wishing it, he draws upon himself an overvaluation that is almost incredible to the outsider, for to the patient he seems like a saviour or a god.
>
> (§ 206)

Jung admits that this interpretation sounds bizarre to modern ears. But he says that 'this way of speaking is not altogether so laughable as it sounds'. He argues that in our love relations and sexual fantasies we are transferring contents to the beloved that are of a symbolic order. We are loading human relationships with divine projections, and we wonder why our relationships are unable to bear these burdens.

Jung emphasises that the transference to the doctor is a provisional response, and not a solution. Recent research has argued that Jung was not good at holding the romantic transferences of female patients, since he was sometimes tempted to take advantage of them.[5] Such transferences made him feel uncomfortable and he was keen to 'overcome' them. This may account for his impatience with this transference, and why he emphasised that, in contrast to Freudian therapy, the transference to the analyst is 'far from being the cure itself' (§ 206). In his view, healing cannot be achieved if therapy remains within a personalistic frame. Freud saw Jung's eagerness to introduce a cosmic dimension as an expression of Jung's own neurosis: it revealed his desire to place religion above therapy and his incapacity to safely hold the sexuality of his clients.

However, Jung argued in reverse: keeping to the personalistic dimension was a sign of neurosis; introducing a transpersonal perspective was an opportunity for health. The libido, he believed, seeks an archetypal source of a transpersonal nature. He turns to the patient's dreams to discover the symbolic images that point to her attachment. She dreams of herself as a child who is held in the arms of a gigantic father figure. As he lifts her up from the ground, the wind sweeps over the hillside and wheat fields, and she feels nurtured as he rocks her in his arms (§ 211). In this and other dreams, it becomes apparent that her unconscious is seeking to connect with a god, and for lack of a symbolic container, her energies are attaching themselves to the father and analyst. Jung poses a series of questions:

> Was the urge of the unconscious perhaps only apparently reaching out towards the person, but in a deeper sense towards a god? Could the longing for a god be a passion welling up from our darkest, instinctual nature, a passion unswayed by any outside influences, deeper and stronger perhaps than the love for a human person?
>
> (§ 214)

This seemed nonsensical to the patient, who preferred the view that she was attached to the father and the unattainable analyst. Like the majority of modern persons, she was not religiously inclined, and found it difficult to accept that she sought an ecstatic union with a god. The patient 'had a critical and agnostic attitude, and her idea of a possible deity had long since passed into the realm of the inconceivable' (§ 217). Jung avoided futile argument with her point of view. His thesis was not that 'she' was religious but that *something inside her* was religious. The mystery of the soul was not understood by her rational mind.

Her unconscious had fashioned an image of God that 'corresponded to the archaic conception of a nature-daemon, something like Wotan' (§ 217).[6] This 'archaic god-image [was] infinitely far from her conscious idea of God' (§ 217). Jung tried to stay focused on the dreams, and not to worry about the meddlesome intellect. This method seemed to work, as the series of dreams 'produced a living effect – an effect which might well give the psychologist of religion food for reflection' (§ 219). She does not become a convert to any religion or gospel but there is an 'implicit' spirituality at the end of the analysis.[7] She became more sure of herself, less dependent on the analyst, and Jung noted 'a subterranean undermining of the transference' (§ 216). Her romantic relations with a male friend deepened and she found herself in a sustaining love relationship. Jung believes that what he calls a 'transpersonal control-point' was reached in her development. That is, a moment occurred wherein she became aware of her transpersonal life and allowed herself to experience 'a vision of God' (§ 217).

The dreams expressed symbols that were significant and provided a channel, so her spirit could rest in the 'everlasting arms' of her creator.[8] Having made this connection to a transpersonal source, her libido was released from its prison. Energy could flow in two directions: to its transpersonal goal and to sexual relationships. The paradox of the spiritual life is that when we make a connection to spirit, energies are allowed to enter the human realm with renewed vigour. The transpersonal connection does not sap energy from life, but allows vitality to flow into the fleshly, human world. In Jung's psychology, spirit and sex are not opposed but complementary. If we introduce the transpersonal dimension, our personal lives will improve and our sexual relationships will be more rewarding.

Section Two is concerned with 'Phenomena resulting from the assimilation of the unconscious'. This section shows Jung in a critical mode, as he is keen to point out that the assimilation of the unconscious can produce unpleasant effects and dangerous mental states. To the new reader, this emphasis on the negative effects of the unconscious may seem contradictory. Isn't Jung trying to argue that we must, at all costs, learn to assimilate the unconscious? The answer is yes and no. Jung argues that we must attempt to integrate the contents of the unconscious. This is the way we achieve integration of the personality: 'We urge our patients to hold fast to repressed contents that have been re-associated with consciousness, and to assimilate them into their plan of life' (§ 205). However, if the contents of the unconscious are assimilated into the ordinary ego, the results can be disastrous. The ego is not large enough to contain the contents of the unconscious. The function of the ego is to act as the focus of conscious contents and negotiate our relations with the world. It plays an important role in this regard, and that is why Jung grants it the status of an 'archetype'.

However, if the ego is asked to assimilate the unconscious into itself, we are expecting too much of it. It bursts its boundaries and becomes inflated or deflated. If the ego extends itself beyond its boundaries, it becomes arrogant and 'godlike'. The ancient Greeks called a person with such an ego 'hubristic' but we tend to refer to him or her as inflated. In such persons, writes Jung, we notice 'an unmistakable and often unpleasant increase in self-confidence and conceit: they are full of themselves, they know everything, they imagine themselves to be fully informed of everything concerning their unconscious, and are persuaded that they understand perfectly everything that comes out of it' (§ 221). On the other hand, there are others who 'feel themselves more and more crushed under the contents of the unconscious, they lose their self-confidence and abandon themselves with dull resignation to all the extraordinary things that the unconscious produces' (§ 221). If the first response leads to inflation, the second can lead to the equally unbearable state of depression. In the first, the ego has expanded beyond its bounds to include a world that does not belong to it; in the second, the ego has been crushed by alien contents.

We might think of this in terms of the metaphor of water. In the first case, the ego is a small container that attempts to hold a large body of water; it inflates beyond its limits, pretending to hold the ocean of the unconscious. In the second, the ego is blown to pieces by an incoming tsunami that overwhelms it. These inflated and depressive responses reflect the devastating impact that the unconscious can have on the ego. Jung acknowledges that these modes represent 'crude extremes', and that a 'finer shading would have been truer to reality'. He indicates that both these conditions can be found in the one person, so that he or she experiences alternating bouts of mania and depression. Today this condition would be called manic depression or bipolar disorder. Jung detects an underlying parallel between the two conditions:

> The arrogance of the one and the despondency of the other share a common uncertainty as to their boundaries. The one is excessively expanded, the other excessively contracted. Their individual boundaries are in some way obliterated.
>
> (§ 225)

Inflation and deflation are opposite conditions but the cause is the same: the ego is unsure of its extent and capacity. Hence they are mirror images of each other:

> If we analyse these two modes of reaction more deeply, we find that the optimistic self-confidence of the first conceals a profound sense of impotence, for which their conscious optimism acts as an unsuccessful compensation; while the pessimistic resignation of the others masks a defiant will to power, far surpassing in cocksureness the conscious optimism of the first type.
>
> (§ 222)

The states can alternate because each conceals the opposite within itself.

Section Three is concerned with the persona as the mask worn by the personality. This self-explanatory section is a prelude to Section Four, in which Jung introduces another negative response to the unconscious, namely, the 'regressive restoration of the persona'. In this case, the encounter with the unconscious is forgotten or forcibly repressed, and the individual attempts to return to his or her life prior to the encounter. The person scurries toward 'normality' and identification with the social order because the unconscious is so disturbing that the fear of madness causes him or her to regress to an earlier stage of development. This is a study in moral cowardice and yet it is a temptation that many of us face as we strive to restore our balance after a confrontation with the unconscious.

In Section Four Jung also includes a discussion on 'Identification with the collective psyche'. This is an extension of his earlier analysis of the problem of inflation. But he is now concerned with those who not only accept inflation as their destiny, but also 'exalt [inflation] into a system' (§ 260). He argues that this condition produces 'false prophets', which he sees as a problem of the modern age. Indeed, false prophecy is not just a problem in those who seek followings, cults and sects, but also in many patients, who go through this inflated phase in their dealings with the unconscious: 'every analysand starts by unconsciously misusing his newly won knowledge in the interests of his abnormal, neurotic attitude' (§ 223). Jung points out that it is 'weak-minded persons' (§ 260) who succumb to the grandiose illusions of the unconscious. The person who is strong in mind is not tempted to flatter himself by assuming he is identical with the contents of myths and legends. The modern 'prophet' is as likely to be a madman as a prophet, because we are vulnerable to eruptions of the unconscious and what arises may be pathological rather than prophetic. Here Jung is thinking about social and political leaders, founders of new sects, and 'new age' gurus. Jung offers this helpful clarification:

> I would not deny in general the existence of genuine prophets, but in the name of caution I would begin by doubting each individual case; for it is far too serious a matter for us lightly to accept a man as a genuine prophet. Every respectable prophet strives manfully against the unconscious pretensions of his role.
>
> (§ 262)

He believes there is genuine prophecy, but he is not confident about our ability to discern it. Genuine prophecy is rare and we must not assume that it will spring forth because we are in need of it. 'When a prophet appears at a moment's notice, we would be better advised to contemplate a possible psychic disequilibrium' (§ 262).

The last section is concerned with 'individuation' (note: this section of the essay as reproduced here is a shortened version). Having explored the negative responses of inflation and deflation, and the ego's rejection of the unconscious, Jung turns to what he considers to be 'the ideal reaction, namely critical understanding' (§ 254). The point of individuation is to develop and maintain a dialogue between the ego and the unconscious, so that a critical understanding of the psyche's contents can take place. Jung's argument is that bigness and smallness of the ego are illusory, although they are real to the persons who are suffering from these conditions. They need to be scrapped in favour of a measured understanding of our individuality, its shape, proportion, boundaries, capabilities and limitations. 'To find out what is truly individual in ourselves, profound reflection is needed; and suddenly we realize how uncommonly difficult the discovery of individuality is' (§ 242). Jung's insistence on the infrequent occurrence of individuation might seem elitist to some, but Jung is stating a fact as he sees it: individuation is rare.

He refers to individuation as a 'way', and suggests alternative expressions: 'becoming one's own self', 'coming to selfhood' or 'self-realization' (§ 266). Sensing the abuse of his term to support selfish patterns of living, Jung claims that individuation is not to be confused with individualism. The individuated person 'does not become "selfish" in the ordinary sense of the word, but is merely fulfilling the peculiarity of his nature, and this is vastly different from egotism or individualism' (§ 267). The key to individuation, as Jung understands it, is the discovery of the Self. The Self is 'supraordinate to the conscious ego' and 'embraces not only the conscious but also the unconscious psyche, and is therefore, so to speak, a personality which we *also* are' (§ 274). The Self is the centrepiece of individuation because it is large enough to integrate the contents of the unconscious without being overwhelmed or disintegrated. The Self is described as the archetype of wholeness, and it can help to bring the contents of the unconscious into alignment with the conscious attitude.

So long as the ego relates to psychic contents with detachment and critical awareness, the Self emerges to support the ego in its quest for integration:

In this way there arises a consciousness which is no longer imprisoned in the petty, oversensitive, personal world of the ego, but participates freely in the wider world of objective interests. This widened consciousness is no longer that touchy, egotistical bundle of personal wishes, fears, hopes, and ambitions which always has to be compensated or corrected by unconscious counter-tendencies.

(§ 275)

It is clear that in earlier times the Self would have been designated as a religious figure, such as Christ, Moses, Buddha, Mohammed, or similar kinds of prophetic or messianic persons. According to Jung, we have to bring the Self closer to home and no longer experience it in projection upon historical figures. He wants us to imagine a messianic and wondrous figure at the centre of our psychic lives, capable of bringing conflicting forces into a new kind of holistic alignment. This idea creates outrage among some religious commentators, who insist that the saving revelation must come to us from outside. Jung's response is that he is not writing for those who belong to traditional faiths; he is writing for those for whom such faiths are no longer possible.

The Self and its unifying function in the psyche is only touched on in this essay, which is concerned with the self-regulating function of the unconscious in normal and abnormal cases. For a fuller discussion of the dynamics of the Self, see Chapter 6.

Notes

1 Matthew 7: 3–5.
2 Robert Johnson, *Owning Your Own Shadow: Understanding the Dark Side of the Psyche* (HarperSanFrancisco, 1993).
3 Elliott Jaques, 'Death and the Midlife Crisis', *International Journal of Psychoanalysis* 46, 1965, 502–514.
4 C. G. Jung, 'Commentary on "The Secret of the Golden Flower" ' (1929), *CW* Vol. 13, § 54.
5 Jan Wiener, *The Therapeutic Relationship: Transference, Countertransference, and the Making of Meaning* (College Station, TX: Texas A&M University Press, 2009).
6 See Jung's essay, 'Wotan' (1936), *CW* 10, 1964/1970.
7 On the topic of 'implicit spirituality' see David Hay, *Why Spirituality is Difficult for Westerners* (Exeter: Imprint Academic, 2007).
8 Deuteronomy 33: 27: 'The eternal God is your refuge, and underneath are the everlasting arms.'

Chapter I

Basic postulates of analytical psychology[1]

649 It was universally believed in the Middle Ages as well as in the Greco-Roman world that the soul is a substance. Indeed mankind as a whole has held this belief from its earliest beginnings, and it was left for the second half of the nineteenth century to develop a 'psychology without the soul.' Under the influence of scientific materialism, everything that could not be seen with the eyes or touched with the hands was held in doubt; such things were even laughed at because of their supposed affinity with metaphysics. Nothing was considered 'scientific' or admitted to be true unless it could be perceived by the senses or traced back to physical causes. This radical change of view did not begin with philosophical materialism, for the way was being prepared long before. When the spiritual catastrophe of the Reformation put an end to the Gothic Age, with its impetuous yearning for the heights, its geographical confinement, and its restricted view of the world, the vertical outlook of the European mind was henceforth cut across by the horizontal outlook of modern times. Consciousness ceased to grow upward, and grew instead in breadth of view, geographically as well as philosophically. This was the age of the great voyages, of the widening of man's mental horizon by empirical discoveries. Belief in the substantiality of things spiritual yielded more and more to the obtrusive conviction that material things alone have substance, till at last, after nearly four hundred years, the leading European thinkers and investigators came to regard the mind as wholly dependent on matter and material causation.

650 We are certainly not justified in saying that philosophy or natural science has brought about this complete *volte-face*. There were always a fair number of intelligent philosophers and scientists who had enough insight and depth of thought to accept this irrational reversal of standpoint only under protest; a few even resisted it, but they had no following and were powerless against the wave of unreasoning, not to say excitable, surrender to the all-importance of the physical world. Let no one suppose that so radical a change in man's outlook could be brought about by reasoned reflection, for no chain of reasoning can prove or disprove the existence of either mind or matter. Both these concepts, as every intelligent person today can ascertain for himself, are mere symbols that stand for something unknown and unexplored, and this something is postulated or denied according to the temperament of the individual or as the spirit of the age dictates. There is nothing

to prevent the speculative intellect from treating the mind as a complicated biochemical phenomenon and at bottom a mere play of electrons, or on the other hand from regarding the unpredictable behaviour of electrons as the sign of mental life even in them.

651 The fact that a metaphysics of the mind was supplanted in the nineteenth century by a metaphysics of matter is, intellectually considered, a mere trick, but from the psychological point of view it is an unexampled revolution in man's outlook. Other-worldliness is converted into matter-of-factness; empirical boundaries are set to every discussion of man's motivations, to his aims and purposes, and even to the assignment of 'meaning.' The whole invisible inner world seems to have become the visible outer world, and no value exists unless founded on a so-called fact. At least, this is how it appears to the simple mind.

652 It is futile, indeed, to treat this irrational change of opinion as a question of philosophy. We had better not try to do so, for if we maintain that mental and psychic phenomena arise from the activity of the glands we can be sure of the respect and applause of our contemporaries, whereas if we attempted to explain the break up of atoms in the sun as an emanation of the creative *Weltgeist* we should be looked upon as intellectual cranks. And yet both views are equally logical, equally metaphysical, equally arbitrary and equally symbolic. From the standpoint of epistemology it is just as admissible to derive animals from the human species as man from the animal species. But we know how ill Dacqué[2] fared in his academic career because of his sin against the spirit of the age, which will not let itself be trifled with. It is a religion or, better, a creed which has absolutely no connection with reason, but whose significance lies in the unpleasant fact that it is taken as the absolute measure of all truth and is supposed always to have common sense on its side.

653 The spirit of the age cannot be fitted into the categories of human reason. It is more a bias, an emotional tendency that works upon weaker minds, through the unconscious, with an overwhelming force of suggestion that carries them along with it. To think otherwise than as our contemporaries think is somehow illegitimate and disturbing; it is even indecent, morbid or blasphemous, and therefore socially dangerous for the individual. He is stupidly swimming against the social current. Just as formerly the assumption was unquestionable that everything that exists originates in the creative will of a God who is a spirit, so the nineteenth century discovered the equally unquestionable truth that everything arises from material causes. Today the psyche does not build itself a body, but on the contrary matter, by chemical action, produces the psyche. This reversal of outlook would be ludicrous if it were not one of the unquestioned verities of the spirit of the age. It is the popular way of thinking, and therefore it is decent, reasonable, scientific, and normal. Mind must be thought of as an epiphenomenon of matter. The same conclusion is reached even if we say not 'mind' but 'psyche,' and instead of 'matter' speak of 'brain,' 'hormones,' 'instincts,' and 'drives.' To allow the soul or psyche a substantiality of its own is repugnant to the spirit of the age, for that would be heresy.

654   We have now discovered that it was an intellectually unjustified presumption on our forefathers' part to assume that man has a soul; that that soul has substance, is of divine nature and therefore immortal; that there is a power inherent within it which builds up the body, sustains its life, heals its ills and enables the soul to live independently of the body; that there are incorporeal spirits with which the soul associates; and that beyond our empirical present there is a spiritual world from which the soul receives knowledge of spiritual things whose origins cannot be discovered in this visible world. But people who are not above the general level of consciousness have not yet discovered that it is just as presumptuous and fantastic to assume that matter produces mind, that apes give rise to human beings, that from the harmonious interplay of the drives of hunger, love, and power Kant's *Critique of Pure Reason* should have emerged, and that all this could not possibly be other than it is.

655   What or who, indeed, is this all-powerful matter? It is the old Creator God over again, stripped this time of his anthropomorphic features and taking the form of a universal concept whose meaning everyone presumes to understand. Consciousness today has grown enormously in breadth and extent, but unfortunately only in the spatial dimension and not in the temporal, otherwise we should have a much more living sense of history. If our consciousness were not of today only, but had historical continuity, we should be reminded of similar transformations of the gods in Greek philosophy, and this might dispose us to be more critical of our present philosophical assumptions. We are, however, effectively prevented from indulging in such reflections by the spirit of the age. History, for it, is a mere arsenal of convenient arguments that enables us, on occasion, to say: 'Why, even old Aristotle knew that.' This being so, we must ask ourselves how the spirit of the age attains such uncanny power. It is without doubt a psychic phenomenon of the greatest importance – at all events, a prejudice so deeply rooted that until we give it proper consideration we cannot even approach the problem of the psyche.

656   As I have said, the irresistible tendency to explain everything on physical grounds corresponds to the horizontal development of consciousness in the last four centuries, and this horizontal perspective is a reaction against the exclusively vertical perspective of the Gothic Age. It is an ethnopsychological phenomenon, and as such cannot be treated in terms of individual consciousness. Like primitives, we are at first wholly unconscious of our actions, and only discover long afterwards why it was that we acted in a certain way. In the meantime, we content ourselves with all sorts of rationalizations of our behaviour, all of them equally inadequate.

657   If we were conscious of the spirit of the age, we should know why we are so inclined to account for everything on physical grounds; we should know that it is because, up till now, too much was accounted for in terms of spirit. This realization would at once make us critical of our bias. We would say: most likely we are now making exactly the same mistake on the other side. We delude ourselves with the thought that we know much more about matter than about a 'metaphysical' mind or spirit, and so we overestimate material causation and believe that it alone

affords us a true explanation of life. But matter is just as inscrutable as mind. As to the ultimate things we can know nothing, and only when we admit this do we return to a state of equilibrium. This is in no sense to deny the close connection of psychic happenings with the physiological structure of the brain, with the glands and the body in general. We still remain deeply convinced of the fact that the contents of consciousness are to a large extent determined by our sense-perceptions. We cannot fail to recognize that unalterable characteristics of a physical as well as a psychic nature are unconsciously ingrained in us by heredity, and we are profoundly impressed by the power of the instincts which can inhibit or reinforce or otherwise modify even the most spiritual contents. Indeed, we must admit that as to cause, purpose, and meaning the human psyche, wherever we touch it, is first and foremost a faithful reflection of everything we call material, empirical, and mundane. And finally, in face of all these admissions, we must ask ourselves if the psyche is not after all a secondary manifestation – an epiphenomenon – and completely dependent on the physical substrate. Our practical reasonableness and worldly-mindedness prompt us to say yes to this question, and it is only our doubts as to the omnipotence of matter that might lead us to examine in a critical way this verdict of science upon the human psyche.

658　　The objection has already been raised that this view reduces psychic happenings to a kind of activity of the glands; thoughts are regarded as secretions of the brain, and thus we achieve a psychology without the psyche. From this standpoint, it must be confessed, the psyche does not exist in its own right; it is nothing in itself, but is the mere expression of processes in the physical substrate. That these processes have the quality of consciousness is just an irreducible fact – were it otherwise, so the argument runs, we could not speak of psyche at all; there would be no consciousness, and so we should have nothing to say about anything. Consciousness, therefore, is taken as the *sine qua non* of psychic life, that is to say, as the psyche itself. And so it comes about that all modern 'psychologies without the psyche' are psychologies of consciousness, for which an unconscious psychic life simply does not exist.

659　　For there is not *one* modern psychology – there are dozens of them. This is curious enough when we remember that there is only one science of mathematics, of geology, zoology, botany, and so forth. But there are so many psychologies that an American university was able to publish a thick volume under the title *Psychologies of 1930*.[3] I believe there are as many psychologies as philosophies, for there is also no single philosophy, but many. I mention this for the reason that philosophy and psychology are linked by indissoluble bonds which are kept in being by the interrelation of their subject-matters. Psychology takes the psyche for its subject, and philosophy – to put it briefly – takes the world. Until recently psychology was a special branch of philosophy, but now we are coming to something which Nietzsche foresaw – the rise of psychology in its own right, so much so that it is even threatening to swallow philosophy. The inner resemblance between the two disciplines consists in this, that both are systems of opinion about objects which cannot be fully experienced and therefore cannot be adequately comprehended by a purely empirical approach. Both fields of study thus encourage speculation, with the result that opinions are formed in such variety and profusion that many heavy volumes are needed to contain them all. Neither discipline can do without the other, and the one invariably furnishes the unspoken – and generally unconscious – assumptions of the other.

660　　The modern belief in the primacy of physical explanations has led, as already remarked, to a 'psychology without the psyche,' that is, to the view that the psyche is nothing but a product of biochemical processes. As for a modern, scientific psychology which starts from the spirit as such, there simply is none. No one today would venture to found a scientific psychology on the postulate of a psyche independent of the body. The idea of spirit in and for itself, of a self-contained spiritual world-system, which would be the necessary postulate for the existence of autonomous individual souls, is extremely unpopular with us, to say the least. But here I must remark that, in 1914, I attended at Bedford College, London, a joint session of the Aristotelian Society, the Mind Association, and the British Psychological Society, at which a symposium was held on the question, 'Are individual minds contained in God or not?' Should anyone in England dispute the scientific standing of these societies he would not receive a very cordial hearing, for their members include the cream of the British intelligentsia. And perhaps I was the only person in the audience who listened with astonishment to arguments that had the ring of the thirteenth century. This instance may serve to show that the idea of an autonomous spirit whose existence is taken for granted has not died out everywhere in Europe or become a mere fossil left over from the Middle Ages.

661　　If we keep this in mind, we can perhaps summon up courage to consider the possibility of a 'psychology *with* the psyche' – that is, a theory of the psyche ultimately based on the postulate of an autonomous, spiritual principle. We need not be alarmed at the unpopularity of such an undertaking, for to postulate 'spirit' is no more fantastic than to postulate 'matter.' Since we have literally no idea how the psychic can arise out of the physical, and yet cannot deny the reality of psychic events, we are free to frame our assumptions the other way about for once, and to suppose that the psyche arises from a spiritual principle which is as inaccessible to our understanding as matter. It will certainly not be a modern psychology, for to be modern is to deny such a possibility. For better or worse, therefore, we must turn back to the teachings of our forefathers, for it was they who made such assumptions.

662　　The ancient view held that the soul was essentially the life of the body, the life-breath, or a kind of life force which assumed spatial and corporeal form at the moment of conception, or during pregnancy, or at birth, and left the dying body again after the final breath. The soul in itself was a being without extension, and because it existed before taking corporeal form and afterwards as well, it was considered timeless and hence immortal. From the standpoint of modern, scientific psychology, this conception is of course pure illusion. But as it is not our intention to indulge in 'metaphysics,' even of a modern variety, we will examine this time-honoured notion for once in an unprejudiced way and test its empirical justification.

663 The names people give to their experiences are often very revealing. What is the origin of the word *Seele*? Like the English word *soul*, it comes from the Gothic *saiwala* and the old German *saiwalô*, and these can be connected etymologically with the Greek *aiolos*, 'quick-moving, twinkling, iridescent'. The Greek word *psyche* also means 'butterfly'. *Saiwalô* is related on the other side to the Old Slavonic *sila*, 'strength'. These connections throw light on the original meaning of the word *soul*: it is moving force, that is, life-force.

664 The Latin words *animus*, 'spirit', and *anima*, 'soul', are the same as the Greek *anemos*, 'wind'. The other Greek word for 'wind', *pneuma*, also means 'spirit'. In Gothic we find the same word in *us-anan*, 'to breathe out', and in Latin it is *anhelare*, 'to pant'. In Old High German, *spiritus sanctus* was rendered by *atum*, 'breath'. In Arabic, 'wind' is *rīh*, and *rūh* is 'soul, spirit'. The Greek word *psyche* has similar connections; it is related to *psychein*, 'to breathe', *psychos*, 'cool', *psychros*, 'cold, chill', and *physa*, 'bellows'. These connections show clearly how in Latin, Greek, and Arabic the names given to the soul are related to the notion of moving air, the 'cold breath of the spirits.' And this is probably the reason why the primitive view also endows the soul with an invisible breath-body.

665 It is quite understandable that, since breath is the sign of life, it should be taken for life, as are also movement and moving force. According to another primitive view the soul is a fire or flame, because warmth is likewise a sign of life. A very curious, but by no means rare, primitive conception identifies the soul with the name. The name of an individual is his soul, and hence arises the custom of using the ancestor's name to reincarnate the ancestral soul in the new-born child. This means nothing less than that ego-consciousness is recognized as being an expression of the soul. Very often the soul is also identified with the shadow, hence it is a deadly insult to tread on a person's shadow. For the same reason noonday, the ghost-hour of southern latitudes, is considered threatening; one's shadow then grows small, and this means that life is endangered. This conception of the shadow contains an idea which was indicated by the Greeks in the word *synopados*, 'he who follows behind'. They expressed in this way the feeling of an intangible, living presence – the same feeling which led to the belief that the souls of the departed were 'shades.'

666 These indications may serve to show how primitive man experienced the psyche. To him the psyche appears as the source of life, the prime mover, a ghost-like presence which has objective reality. Therefore the primitive knows how to converse with his soul; it becomes vocal within him because it is not simply he himself and his consciousness. To primitive man the psyche is not, as it is to us, the epitome of all that is subjective and subject to the will; on the contrary, it is something objective, self-subsistent, and living its own life.

667 This way of looking at the matter is empirically justified, for not only on the primitive level, but with civilized man as well, psychic happenings have an objective side. In large measure they are withdrawn from our conscious control. We are

unable, for example, to suppress many of our emotions; we cannot change a bad mood into a good one, and we cannot command our dreams to come or go. The most intelligent man may be obsessed at times with thoughts which he cannot drive away even with the greatest effort of will. The mad tricks that memory plays sometimes leave us in helpless amazement, and at any time unexpected fantasies may run through our heads. We believe that we are masters in our own house only because we like to flatter ourselves. In reality we are dependent to a startling degree on the proper functioning of the unconscious psyche, and must trust that it does not fail us. If we study the psychic processes of neurotic persons, it seems perfectly ludicrous that any psychologist could take the psyche as the equivalent of consciousness. And it is well known that the psychic processes of neurotics differ hardly at all from those of so-called normal persons – for what man today is quite sure that he is not neurotic?

668   This being so, we shall do well to admit that there is some justification for the old view of the soul as an objective reality – as something independent, and therefore capricious and dangerous. The further assumption that this being, so mysterious and frightening, is at the same time the source of life is also understandable in the light of psychology. Experience shows us that the sense of the 'I' – the ego-consciousness – grows out of unconscious life. The small child has psychic life without any demonstrable ego-consciousness, for which reason the earliest years leave hardly any traces in the memory. Where do all our good and helpful flashes of intelligence come from? What is the source of our enthusiasms, inspirations, and of our heightened feeling of vitality? The primitive senses in the depths of his soul the springs of life; he is deeply impressed by the life-giving activity of his soul, and he therefore believes in everything that affects it – in magical practices of every kind. That is why, for him, the soul is life itself. He does not imagine that he directs it, but feels himself dependent on it in every respect.

669   However preposterous the idea of the immortality of the soul may seem to us, it is nothing extraordinary to the primitive. The soul is, after all, something out of the common. While everything else that exists takes up a certain amount of room, the soul cannot be located in space. We suppose, of course, that our thoughts are in our heads, but when it comes to our feelings we begin to be uncertain; they appear to dwell more in the region of the heart. Our sensations are distributed over the whole body. Our theory is that the seat of consciousness is in the head, but the Pueblo Indians told me that the Americans were mad because they believed their thoughts were in their heads, whereas any sensible man knows that he thinks with his heart. Certain Negro tribes locate their psychic functioning neither in the head nor in the heart, but in the belly.

670   To this uncertainty about the localization of psychic functions another difficulty is added. Psychic contents in general are nonspatial except in the particular realm of sensation. What bulk can we ascribe to thoughts? Are they small, large, long, thin, heavy, fluid, straight, circular, or what? If we wished to form a living picture of a non-spatial, fourth-dimensional being, we could not do better than to take thought for our model.

671 It would all be so much simpler if only we could deny the existence of the psyche. But here we are with our immediate experiences of something that *is* – something that has taken root in the midst of our measurable, ponderable, three-dimensional reality, that differs mysteriously from this in every respect and in all its parts, and yet reflects it. The psyche could be regarded as a mathematical point and at the same time as a universe of fixed stars. It is small wonder, then, if, to the unsophisticated mind, such a paradoxical being borders on the divine. If it occupies no space, it has no body. Bodies die, but can something invisible and incorporeal disappear? What is more, life and psyche existed for me before I could say 'I,' and when this 'I' disappears, as in sleep or unconsciousness, life and psyche still go on, as our observation of other people and our own dreams inform us. Why should the simple mind deny, in the face of such experiences, that the 'soul' lives in a realm beyond the body? I must admit that I can see as little nonsense in this so-called superstition as in the findings of research regarding heredity or the instincts.

672 We can easily understand why higher and even divine knowledge was formerly attributed to the soul if we remember that in ancient cultures, beginning with primitive times, man always resorted to dreams and visions as a source of information. It is a fact that the unconscious contains subliminal perceptions whose scope is nothing less than astounding. In recognition of this fact, primitive societies used dreams and visions as important sources of information. Great and enduring civilizations like those of India and China were built upon this psychological foundation and developed from it a discipline of self-knowledge which they brought to a high pitch of refinement both in philosophy and in practice.

673 A high regard for the unconscious psyche as a source of knowledge is not nearly such a delusion as our Western rationalism likes to suppose. We are inclined to assume that in the last resort all knowledge comes from without. Yet today we know for certain that the unconscious has contents which would bring an immeasurable increase of knowledge if they could only be made conscious. Modern investigation of animal instinct, for instance in insects, has brought together a rich fund of empirical material which shows that if man sometimes acted as certain insects do he would possess a higher intelligence than at present. It cannot, of course, be proved that insects possess conscious knowledge, but common sense cannot doubt that their unconscious patterns of behaviour are psychic functions. Man's unconscious likewise contains all the patterns of life and behaviour inherited from his ancestors, so that every human child is possessed of a ready-made system of adapted psychic functioning prior to all consciousness. In the conscious life of the adult as well this unconscious, instinctive functioning is continually present and active. In this activity all the functions of the conscious psyche are prefigured. The unconscious perceives, has purposes and intuitions, feels and thinks as does the conscious mind. We find sufficient evidence for this in the field of psychopathology and the investigation of dream-processes. Only in one respect is there an essential difference between the conscious and the unconscious functioning of the psyche. Though consciousness is intensive and

concentrated, it is transitory and is trained upon the immediate present and the immediate field of attention; moreover, it has access only to material that represents one individual's experience stretching over a few decades. A wider range of 'memory' is an artificial acquisition consisting mostly of printed paper. But matters stand very differently with the unconscious. It is not concentrated and intensive, but shades off into obscurity; it is highly extensive and can juxtapose the most heterogeneous elements in the most paradoxical way. More than this, it contains, besides an indeterminable number of subliminal perceptions, the accumulated deposits from the lives of our ancestors, who by their very existence have contributed to the differentiation of the species. If it were possible to personify the unconscious, we might think of it as a collective human being combining the characteristics of both sexes, transcending youth and age, birth and death, and, from having at its command a human experience of one or two million years, practically immortal. If such a being existed, it would be exalted above all temporal change; the present would mean neither more nor less to it than any year in the hundredth millennium before Christ; it would be a dreamer of age-old dreams and, owing to its limitless experience, an incomparable prognosticator. It would have lived countless times over again the life of the individual, the family, the tribe, and the nation, and it would possess a living sense of the rhythm of growth, flowering, and decay.

674 Unfortunately – or rather let us say, fortunately – this being dreams. At least it seems to us as if the collective unconscious, which appears to us in dreams, had no consciousness of its own contents, though of course we cannot be sure of this, any more than we can in the case of insects. The collective unconscious, moreover, seems to be not a person, but something like an unceasing stream or perhaps ocean of images and figures which drift into consciousness in our dreams or in abnormal states of mind.

675 It would be positively grotesque to call this immense system of experience in the unconscious psyche an illusion, for our visible and tangible body is itself just such a system. It still carries within it evolutionary traces from primeval times, and it is certainly a whole that functions purposively – for otherwise we could not live. It would never occur to anyone to look upon comparative anatomy or physiology as nonsense, and neither can we dismiss the investigation of the collective unconscious as illusion or refuse to recognize it as a valuable source of knowledge.

676 Looked at from the outside, the psyche appears to be essentially a reflection of external happenings – to be not only occasioned by them, but to have its origin in them. And it also seems to us, at first, that the unconscious can be explained only from the outside and from the side of consciousness. It is well known that Freud has attempted to do this – an undertaking which could succeed only if the unconscious were actually something that came into being with the existence and consciousness of the individual. But the truth is that the unconscious is always there beforehand as a system of inherited psychic functioning handed down from primeval times. Consciousness is a late-born descendant of the unconscious

psyche. It would certainly show perversity if we tried to explain the lives of our ancestors in terms of their late descendants, and it is just as wrong, in my opinion, to regard the unconscious as a derivative of consciousness. We are probably nearer the truth if we put it the other way round.

677 This was the standpoint of past ages, which, knowing the untold treasures of experience lying hidden beneath the threshold of the ephemeral individual consciousness, always held the individual soul to be dependent on a spiritual world-system. Not only did they make this hypothesis, they assumed without question that this system was a being with a will and consciousness – was even a person – and they called this being God, the quintessence of reality. He was for them the most real of beings, the first cause, through whom alone the soul could be explained. There is some psychological justification for such an hypothesis, for it is only appropriate that an almost immortal being whose experience is almost eternal should be called, in comparison with man, 'divine.'

678 In the foregoing I have shown where the problems lie for a psychology that does not appeal to the physical world as a ground of explanation, but rather to a spiritual system whose active principle is neither matter and its qualities nor any state of energy, but God. At this juncture, we might be tempted by the modern brand of nature philosophy to call energy or the *élan vital* God, and thus to blend into one spirit and nature. So long as such an undertaking is restricted to the misty heights of speculative philosophy, no great harm is done. But if we should operate with this idea in the lower realm of practical psychology, where only practical explanations bear any fruit, we should soon find ourselves involved in the most hopeless difficulties. We do not profess a psychology with merely academic pretensions, or seek explanations that have no bearing on life. What we want is a practical psychology which yields approvable results – one which explains things in a way that must be justified by the outcome for the patient. In practical psychotherapy we strive to fit people for life, and we are not free to set up theories which do not concern our patients and may even injure them. Here we come to a question that is sometimes a matter of life and death – the question whether we base our explanations on 'physis' or spirit. We must never forget that everything spiritual is illusion from the naturalistic standpoint, and that often the spirit has to deny and overcome an insistent physical fact in order to exist at all. If I recognize only naturalistic values, and explain everything in physical terms, I shall depreciate, hinder, or even destroy the spiritual development of my patients. And if I hold exclusively to a spiritual interpretation, then I shall misunderstand and do violence to the natural man in his right to exist as a physical being. More than a few suicides in the course of psychotherapeutic treatment are to be laid at the door of such mistakes. Whether energy is God or God is energy concerns me very little, for how, in any case, can I know such things? But to give appropriate psychological explanations – this I must be able to do.

679 The modern psychologist occupies neither the one position nor the other, but finds himself between the two, dangerously committed to 'this as well as that' – a situation which seductively opens the way to a shallow opportunism. This is

undoubtedly the great danger of the *coincidentia oppositorum* – of intellectual freedom from the opposites. How should anything but a formless and aimless uncertainty result from giving equal value to two contradictory hypotheses? In contrast to this we can readily appreciate the advantage of an explanatory principle that is unequivocal: it allows of a standpoint that can serve as a point of reference. Undoubtedly we are confronted here with a very difficult problem. We must be able to appeal to an explanatory principle founded on reality, and yet it is no longer possible for the modern psychologist to take his stand exclusively on the physical aspect of reality once he has given the spiritual aspect its due. Nor will he be able to put weight on the latter alone, for he cannot ignore the relative validity of the physical aspect. To what, then, can he appeal?

680 The following reflections are my way of attempting to solve this problem. The conflict between nature and spirit is itself a reflection of the paradox of psychic life. This reveals a physical and a spiritual aspect which appear a contradiction because, ultimately, we do not understand the nature of psychic life itself. Whenever, with our human understanding, we want to make a statement about something which in the last analysis we have not grasped and cannot grasp, then we must, if we are honest, be willing to contradict ourselves, we must pull this something into its antithetical parts in order to be able to deal with it at all. The conflict between the physical and the spiritual aspects only shows that psychic life is in the last analysis an incomprehensible 'something.' Without a doubt it is our only immediate experience. All that I experience is psychic. Even physical pain is a psychic image which I experience; my sense-impressions – for all that they force upon me a world of impenetrable objects occupying space – are psychic images, and these alone constitute my immediate experience, for they alone are the immediate objects of my consciousness. My own psyche even transforms and falsifies reality, and it does this to such a degree that I must resort to artificial means to determine what things are like apart from myself. Then I discover that a sound is a vibration of air of such and such a frequency, or that a colour is a wave of light of such and such a length. We are in truth so wrapped about by psychic images that we cannot penetrate at all to the essence of things external to ourselves. All our knowledge consists of the stuff of the psyche which, because it alone is immediate, is superlatively real. Here, then, is a reality to which the psychologist can appeal – namely, psychic reality.

681 If we try to penetrate more deeply into the meaning of this concept, it seems to us that certain psychic contents or images are derived from a 'material' environment to which our bodies belong, while others, which are in no way less real, seem to come from a 'spiritual' source which appears to be very different from the physical environment. Whether I picture to myself the car I wish to buy or try to imagine the state in which the soul of my dead father now is – whether it is an external fact or a thought that concerns me – both happenings are psychic reality. The only difference is that one psychic happening refers to the physical world, and the other to the spiritual world. If I shift my concept of reality on to the plane of the psyche – where alone it is valid – this puts an end to the conflict between

mind and matter, spirit and nature, as contradictory explanatory principles. Each becomes a mere designation for the particular source of the psychic contents that crowd into my field of consciousness. If a fire burns me I do not question the reality of the fire, whereas if I am beset by the fear that a ghost will appear, I take refuge behind the thought that it is only an illusion. But just as the fire is the psychic image of a physical process whose nature is ultimately unknown, so my fear of the ghost is a psychic image from a spiritual source; it is just as real as the fire, for my fear is as real as the pain caused by the fire. As for the spiritual process that underlies my fear of the ghost, it is as unknown to me as the ultimate nature of matter. And just as it never occurs to me to account for the nature of fire except by the concepts of chemistry and physics, so I would never think of trying to explain my fear of ghosts except in terms of spiritual processes.

682   The fact that all immediate experience is psychic and that immediate reality can only be psychic explains why it is that primitive man puts spirits and magical influences on the same plane as physical events. He has not yet torn his original experience into antithetical parts. In his world, spirit and matter still interpenetrate each other, and his gods still wander through forest and field. He is like a child, only half born, still enclosed in his own psyche as in a dream, in a world not yet distorted by the difficulties of understanding that beset a dawning intelligence. When this aboriginal world fell apart into spirit and nature, the West rescued nature for itself. It was prone by temperament to a belief in nature, and only became the more entangled in it with every painful effort to make itself spiritual. The East, on the other hand, took spirit for its own, and by explaining away matter as mere illusion – Maya – continued to dream in Asiatic filth and misery. But since there is only *one* earth and *one* mankind, East and West cannot rend humanity into two different halves. Psychic reality still exists in its original oneness, and awaits man's advance to a level of consciousness where he no longer believes in the one part and denies the other, but recognizes both as constituent elements of one psyche.

683   We could well point to the idea of psychic reality as the most important achievement of modern psychology if it were recognized as such. It seems to me only a question of time for this idea to be generally accepted. It must be accepted in the end, for it alone enables us to understand the manifestations of the psyche in all their variety and uniqueness. Without this idea it is unavoidable that we should explain our psychic experiences in a way that does violence to a good half of them, while with it we can give its due to that side of psychic life which expresses itself in superstition and mythology, religion and philosophy. And this aspect of the psyche is not to be undervalued. Truth that appeals to the testimony of the senses may satisfy reason, but it offers nothing that stirs our feelings and expresses them by giving a meaning to human life. Yet it is most often feeling that is decisive in matters of good and evil, and if feeling does not come to the aid of reason, the latter is usually powerless. Did reason and good intentions save us from the World War, or have they ever saved us from any other catastrophic stupidity? Have any of the great spiritual and social revolutions sprung from reason – for

instance, the transformation of the Greco-Roman world into the age of feudalism, or the explosive spread of Islam?

684   As a physician I am of course not directly concerned with these epochal questions; my duties lie with people who are ill. Medicine has until recently gone on the supposition that illness should be treated and cured by itself; yet voices are now heard which declare this view to be wrong, and demand the treatment of the sick person and not of the sickness. The same demand is forced upon us in the treatment of psychic suffering. More and more we turn our attention from the visible illness and direct it upon the man as a whole. We have come to understand that psychic suffering is not a definitely localized, sharply delimited phenomenon, but rather the symptom of a wrong attitude assumed by the total personality. We can therefore never hope for a thorough cure from a treatment restricted to the illness itself, but only from a treatment of the personality as a whole.

685   I am reminded of a case which is very instructive in this respect. It concerns a highly intelligent young man who had worked out a detailed analysis of his own neurosis after a thorough study of the medical literature. He brought me his findings in the form of a precise and admirably written monograph, fit for publication, and asked me to read the manuscript and to tell him why he was still not cured, although he ought to have been, according to his scientific judgment. After reading his monograph I was forced to admit that, if it were only a question of insight into the causal structure of a neurosis, he should in all truth have been cured. Since he was not, I supposed this must be due to the fact that his attitude to life was somehow fundamentally wrong, though certainly his symptoms did not betray it. During his anamnesis I had been struck by his remark that he often spent his winters at St. Moritz or Nice. I therefore asked him who actually paid for these holidays, and it thereupon came out that a poor school-teacher who loved him almost starved herself to indulge this young man in his visits to pleasure-resorts. His want of conscience was the cause of his neurosis, and this also explains why all his scientific insight availed him nothing. His fundamental error lay in his moral attitude. He found my way of looking at it shockingly unscientific, for morals have nothing to do with science. He thought that he could scientifically unthink the immorality which he himself, at bottom, could not stomach. He would not even admit that any conflict existed, because his mistress gave him the money of her own free will.

686   We can think what we like about this scientifically, but the fact remains that the great majority of civilized persons simply cannot tolerate such behaviour. The moral attitude is a real factor with which the psychologist must reckon if he is not to commit the gravest errors. He must also remember that certain religious convictions not founded on reason are a vital necessity for many people. Again, there are psychic realities which can cause or cure diseases. How often have I heard a patient exclaim: 'If only I knew that my life had some meaning and purpose, there would be no need of all this trouble with my nerves!' Whether the patient is rich or poor, has family and social position or not, alters nothing, for outer circumstances are far from giving his life a meaning. It is much more a question of his

quite irrational need for what we call a spiritual life, and this he cannot obtain from universities, libraries, or even from churches. He cannot accept what these have to offer because it touches only his head but does not stir his heart. In such cases the physician's recognition of the spiritual factors in their true light is vitally important, and the patient's unconscious comes to the aid of this vital need by producing dreams whose content is essentially religious. Not to recognize the spiritual source of such contents means faulty treatment and failure.

687 General conceptions of a spiritual nature are indispensable constituents of psychic life. We can point them out among all peoples who possess some measure of articulated consciousness. Their relative absence or their denial by a civilized people is therefore to be regarded as a sign of degeneration. Whereas, in its development up to the present, psychology has considered psychic processes mainly in the light of their physical causation, the future task of psychology will be the investigation of their spiritual determinants. But the natural history of the mind is no further advanced today than was natural science in the thirteenth century. We are only just beginning to take scientific note of our spiritual experiences.

688 If modern psychology can boast of having removed any of the veils which hid the psyche from us, it is only that one which had concealed from the investigator the psyche's biological aspect. We may compare the present situation to the state of medicine in the sixteenth century, when people began to study anatomy but had not as yet the faintest idea of physiology. So, too, the spiritual aspect of the psyche is known to us only in a very fragmentary way. We have learnt that there are spiritual processes of transformation in the psyche which underlie, for example, the well-known initiation rites of primitive peoples and the states induced by the practice of yoga. But we have not yet succeeded in determining their particular laws. We only know that many of the neuroses arise from a disturbance of these processes. Psychological research has not drawn aside all the many veils from the human psyche; it remains as unapproachable and obscure as all the deep secrets of life. We can only speak of what we have tried to do, and what we hope to do in the future, in the way of attempting a solution of the great riddle.

Notes

1 [First published as 'Die Entschleierung der Seele,' *Europäische Revue* (Berlin), VII: 2/7 (July 1931), which version was translated by W. S. Dell and Cary F. Baynes as 'The Basic Postulates of Analytical Psychology,' *Modern Man in Search of a Soul* (London and New York, 1933). The original version was republished, with slight revisions and the title 'Das Grundproblem der gegenwärtigen Psychologie,' in *Wirklichkeit der Seele* (Psychologische Abhandlungen, IV; Zurich, 1934). The present version is a slight revision of the Dell/Baynes trans.–EDITORS.]
2 [Edgar Dacqué (1878–1945) was a geologist who risked (and lost) his reputation by reversing the Darwinian theory of origin of species.–EDITORS.]
3 [See Bibliography s.v. 'Murchison.' – EDITORS.] [C. Murchison (ed.) *Psychologies of 1930*, International University Series in Psychology (Worcester, Mass: Clark University Press, 1930).]

Chapter 2

The role of the unconscious[1]

1 To the layman's ears, the word 'unconscious' has an undertone of something metaphysical and rather mysterious. This peculiarity, attaching to the whole concept of the unconscious, is primarily due to the fact that the term found its way into ordinary speech as a designation for a metaphysical entity. Eduard von Hartmann, for instance, called the unconscious the 'Universal Ground.' Again, the word was taken up by occultism, because people with these leanings are extremely fond of borrowing scientific terms in order to dress their speculations in a 'scientific' guise. In contradiction to this, the experimental psychologists, who for a long time regarded themselves – not unjustly – as the representatives of the only truly scientific psychology, adopted a negative attitude towards the concept of the unconscious, on the ground that everything psychic is conscious and that consciousness alone deserves the name 'psyche.' They admitted that conscious psychic contents showed varying degrees of clarity, some being 'brighter' or 'darker' than others, but the existence of unconscious contents was denied as being a contradiction in terms.

2 This view stemmed very largely from the circumstance that work in the laboratory was confined exclusively to 'normal' subjects, and also from the nature of the experiments themselves. These were concerned so far as possible with the most elementary psychic processes, while the investigation of the more complex psychic functions, which by their very nature do not lend themselves to experimental procedures based on exact measurement, was almost entirely absent. But a factor far transcending both these reasons in importance was the segregation of experimental psychology from psychopathology. In France, ever since the time of Ribot, psychologists had kept an alert eye on abnormal psychic phenomena, and one of their most eminent representatives, Binet, even made the pronouncement that the pathological psyche exaggerated certain deviations from the normal which were difficult to understand, and, by throwing them into relief, made them more comprehensible. Another French psychologist, Pierre Janet, working at the Salpêtrière, devoted himself almost exclusively and with great success to the study of psychopathological processes. But it is just the abnormal psychic processes which demonstrate most clearly the existence of an unconscious. For this reason it was the medical men, and above all the specialists in the field of psychic

illnesses, who supported the hypothesis of the unconscious and defended it most vigorously. But whereas in France psychology was considerably enriched by the findings of psychopathology and was led to accept the notion of 'unconscious' processes, in Germany it was psychology that enriched psychopathology, supplying it with a number of valuable experimental methods – without, however, taking over from psychopathology its interest in pathological phenomena. This explains in large part why psychopathological research underwent a different development in German science from that followed in France. It became – except for the interest it aroused in academic circles – a task for the medical practitioner, who by his professional work was compelled to understand the complex psychic phenomena exhibited by his patients. In this way there came into being that complex of theoretical views and practical techniques which is known as 'psychoanalysis.' The concept of the unconscious underwent a broad development in the psychoanalytic movement, far more so than in the French school, which was more concerned with the various forms in which unconscious processes manifested themselves than with their causation and their specific content. Fifteen years ago, independently of the Freudian school and on the basis of my own experimental researches, I satisfied myself as to the existence and significance of unconscious processes, indicating at the same time the methods by which these processes might be demonstrated. Later, in collaboration with a number of my pupils, I also demonstrated the significance of unconscious processes in the mentally insane.

3   As a result of this – at first – purely medical development the concept of the unconscious took on a coloration derived from the natural sciences. It has remained a purely medical concept in the Freudian school. According to the views of this school, man, as a civilized being, is unable to act out a large number of instinctive impulses and wishes, for the simple reason that they are incompatible with law and morality. In so far, therefore, as he wants to adapt himself to society, he is obliged to suppress these wishes. The assumption that man has such wishes is altogether plausible, and the truth of it can be seen at any time by every individual with a little application of honesty. But this insight amounts as a rule only to the general statement that socially incompatible and inadmissible wishes exist. Experience shows, however, that the facts are quite different when we come down to individual cases. It then proves, remarkably enough, that very often, as a result of the suppression of an inadmissible wish, the thin wall between wishing and being conscious of the wish is broken, so that the wish becomes unconscious. It is forgotten, and its place is taken by a more or less rational justification – if, indeed, any motivation is sought at all. This process, whereby an inadmissible wish becomes unconscious, is called *repression,* as distinct from *suppression,* which presupposes that the wish remained conscious. Although repressed and forgotten, the incompatible content – whether it consist of wishes or of painful memories – nevertheless exists, and its unperceived presence influences the conscious processes. This influence expresses itself in the form of peculiar disturbances of the conscious, normal functions; we call these disturbances nervous or *psychogenic* disturbances. The remarkable thing is that they do not confine themselves to

purely psychological processes but extend also to physiological ones. In the latter case, as Janet emphasizes, it is never the elementary components of the function that are disturbed, but only the voluntary application of the function under various complex conditions. For instance, an elementary component of the nutritive function consists in the act of swallowing. If choking were regularly to occur whenever food in solid or liquid form was taken, then it would be an anatomical or organic disturbance. But if the choking occurred only in the case of certain foods or at certain meals, or only in the presence of certain persons, or only in certain moods, then it would be a nervous or psychogenic disturbance. The psychogenic disturbance therefore affects merely the act of eating under certain psychological and not physical conditions.

4   Such disturbances of physiological functions are particularly frequent in hysteria. In another, equally large group of illnesses which French doctors call psychasthenia, their place is taken by purely psychological disturbances. These can assume a great variety of forms, such as obsessional ideas, anxiety states, depressions, moods, fantasies, pathological affects and impulses, and so on. At the root of all these disturbances we find repressed psychic contents, i.e., contents that have become unconscious. On the basis of these purely empirical findings, the concept of the unconscious as the sum-total of all incompatible and repressed wishes, including all painful and repressed memories, gradually took form.

5   Now it is an easily demonstrated fact that the overwhelming majority of these incompatible contents have to do with the phenomenon of sexuality. Sexuality is a fundamental instinct which, as everyone knows, is the most hedged about with secrecy and with feelings of delicacy. In the form of love, it is the cause of the stormiest emotions, the wildest longings, the profoundest despairs, the most secret sorrows, and, altogether, of the most painful experiences. Sexuality is an important physical and widely ramified psychic function on which the whole future of humanity depends. It is thus at least as important as the function of nutrition, even though it is an instinct of another kind. But whereas we can allow the nutritive function, from the devouring of a simple piece of bread to a guild banquet, to be seen by all eyes in all its variations, and at most must hold it in check because of an attack of intestinal catarrh or a general food shortage, sexuality comes under a moral taboo and has to submit to a large number of legal regulations and restrictions. It is not, like the nutritive function, at the free disposal of the individual. It is therefore understandable that a great many pressing interests and powerful emotions congregate round this question, for as a rule affects are found at places where adaptation is least complete. Furthermore, sexuality, as I have said, is a fundamental instinct in every human being, and this is reason enough for the well-known Freudian theory which reduces everything to sexuality, and sketches a picture of the unconscious which makes it appear as a kind of lumber-room where all the repressed and inadmissible infantile wishes and all the later, inadmissible sexual wishes are stored. Distasteful as such a view is, we must give it its due if we want to discover all the things that Freud has smuggled into the concept of sexuality. We shall then see that he has widened its boundaries far beyond the

permitted limits, so that a better word for what he actually means would be 'Eros' in the old, philosophical sense of a Pan-Eros who permeates all nature as a creative and procreative force. 'Sexuality' is a most unhappy expression for this. But, such as it is, the concept of sexuality has now been coined and appears to have such definite limits that one even hesitates to use the word 'love' as a synonym. And yet Freud, as can easily be shown from numerous passages in his writings, very often means 'love' when he speaks merely of sexuality.

6   The whole Freudian movement has settled firmly for the sexual theory. There is certainly no unprejudiced thinker or investigator who would not instantly acknowledge the extraordinary importance of sexual or erotic experiences and conflicts. But it will never be proved that sexuality is *the* fundamental instinct and *the* activating principle of the human psyche. Any unprejudiced scientist will, on the contrary, admit that the psyche is an extremely complex structure. Though we can approach it from the biological standpoint and seek to explain it in terms of biological factors, it presents us with a great many other puzzles whose solution makes demands which no isolated science, such as biology, is in a position to satisfy. No matter what instincts, drives or dynamisms biologists may postulate or assume both now and in the future, it will assuredly be quite impossible to set up a sharply defined instinct like sexuality as a fundamental principle of explanation. Biology, indeed science in general, has got beyond this stage: we no longer reduce everything to a single manifest force, as the earlier scientists did with phlogiston and electricity. We have learned to employ a modest abstraction, named energy, as an explanatory principle for all quantitative changes.

7   I am convinced that a truly scientific attitude in psychology must likewise lead to the conclusion that the dynamic processes of the psyche cannot be reduced to this or that concrete instinct – we should merely find ourselves back at the stage of the phlogiston theory. We shall be obliged to take the instincts as constituent parts of the psyche, and then abstract our principle of explanation from their mutual relationship. I have therefore pointed out that we would do well to posit a hypothetical quantity, an 'energy,' as a psychological explanatory principle, and to call it 'libido' in the classical sense of the word, without harbouring any prejudice with regard to its substantiality. With the help of such a quantity, the psychodynamic processes could be explained in an unobjectionable manner, without that unavoidable distortion which a concrete ground of explanation necessarily entails. Thus, when the Freudian school explains that religious feelings or any other sentiments that pertain to the spiritual sphere are 'nothing but' inadmissible sexual wishes which have been repressed and subsequently 'sublimated,' this procedure would be equivalent to a physicist's explanation that electricity is 'nothing but' a waterfall which someone had bought up and piped into a turbine. In other words, electricity is nothing but a 'culturally deformed' waterfall – an argument which might conceivably be raised by the Society for the Preservation of Wild Nature but is hardly a piece of scientific ratiocination. In psychology such an explanation would be appropriate only if it could be proved that the dynamic ground of our being is nothing but sexuality, which amounts to saying, in physics,

that falling water alone can produce electricity. In that case it could rightly be maintained that electricity is nothing but a waterfall conducted along wires.

8   So if we reject the exclusively sexual theory of the unconscious and put in its place an energic view of the psyche, we must say that the unconscious contains everything psychic that has not reached the threshold of consciousness, or whose energy-charge is not sufficient to maintain it in consciousness, or that will reach consciousness only in the future. We can then picture to ourselves how the unconscious must be constituted. We have already taken cognizance of repressions as contents of the unconscious, and to these we must add *everything that we have forgotten*. When a thing is forgotten, it does not mean that it is extinguished; it simply means that the memory has become subliminal. Its energy-charge has sunk so low that it can no longer appear in consciousness; but, though lost to consciousness, it is not lost to the unconscious. It will naturally be objected that this is no more than a *façon de parler*. I would like to make what I mean clear by a hypothetical example. Suppose there are two people, one of whom has never read a book and the other has read a thousand. From the minds of both of them we expunge all memory of the ten years in which the first was merely living and the second was reading his thousand books. Each now knows as little as the other, and yet anyone will be able to find out which of them has read the books and, be it noted, understood them. The experience of reading, though long forgotten, leaves traces behind it, and from these traces the previous experience can be recognized. This long-lasting, indirect influence is due to a fixing of impressions, which are still preserved even when they are no longer capable of reaching consciousness.

9   Besides things that have been forgotten, subliminal perceptions form part of the contents of the unconscious. These may be sense perceptions occurring below the stimulus-threshold of conscious hearing, or in the peripheral field of vision; or they may be apperceptions, by which are meant perceptions of endopsychic or external processes.

10   All this material constitutes the *personal unconscious*. We call it personal because it consists entirely of acquisitions deriving from personal life. Therefore, when anything falls into the unconscious it is taken up in the network of associations formed by this unconscious material. Associative connections of high intensity may then be produced, which cross over or rise up into consciousness in the form of inspirations, intuitions, 'lucky ideas,' and so on.

11   The concept of a personal unconscious does not, however, enable us fully to grasp the nature of the unconscious. If the unconscious were only personal, it would in theory be possible to trace all the fantasies of an insane person back to individual experiences and impressions. No doubt a large proportion of the fantasy-material could be reduced to his personal history, but there are certain fantasies whose roots in the individual's previous history one would seek for in vain. What sort of fantasies are these? They are, in a word, *mythological fantasies*. They are elements which do not correspond to any events or experiences of personal life, but only to myths.

12 Where do these mythological fantasies come from, if they do not spring from the personal unconscious and hence from the experiences of personal life? Indubitably they come from the brain – indeed, precisely from the brain and not from personal memory-traces, but from the inherited brain-structure itself. Such fantasies always have a highly original and 'creative' character. They are like new creations; obviously they derive from the creative activity of the brain and not simply from its mnemonic activity. We receive along with our body a highly differentiated brain which brings with it its entire history, and when it becomes creative it creates out of this history – out of the history of mankind. By 'history' we usually mean the history which we 'make,' and we call this 'objective history.' The truly creative fantasy activity of the brain has nothing to do with this kind of history, but solely with that age-old natural history which has been transmitted in living form since the remotest times, namely, the history of the brain-structure. And this structure tells its own story, which is the story of mankind: the unending myth of death and rebirth, and of the multitudinous figures who weave in and out of this mystery.

13 This unconscious, buried in the structure of the brain and disclosing its living presence only through the medium of creative fantasy, is the *suprapersonal unconscious*. It comes alive in the creative man, it reveals itself in the vision of the artist, in the inspiration of the thinker, in the inner experience of the mystic. The suprapersonal unconscious, being distributed throughout the brain-structure, is like an all-pervading, omnipresent, omniscient spirit. It knows man as he always was, and not as he is at this moment; it knows him as myth. For this reason, also, the connection with the suprapersonal or *collective* unconscious means an extension of man beyond himself; it means death for his personal being and a rebirth in a new dimension, as was literally enacted in certain of the ancient mysteries. It is certainly true that without the sacrifice of man as he is, man as he was – and always will be – cannot be attained. And it is the artist who can tell us most about this sacrifice of the personal man, if we are not satisfied with the message of the Gospels.

14 It should on no account be imagined that there are such things as *inherited ideas*. Of that there can be no question. There are, however, innate possibilities of ideas, *a priori* conditions for fantasy-production, which are somewhat similar to the Kantian categories. Though these innate conditions do not produce any contents of themselves, they give definite form to contents that have already been acquired. Being a part of the inherited structure of the brain, they are the reason for the identity of symbols and myth-motifs in all parts of the earth. The collective unconscious forms the dark background against which the adaptive function of consciousness stands out in sharp relief. One is almost tempted to say that everything of value in the psyche is taken up into the adaptive function, and that everything useless goes to form that inchoate background from which, to the terror of primitive man, menacing shadows and nocturnal spectres detach themselves, demanding sacrifices and ceremonies which to our biologically oriented minds seem futile and meaningless. We laugh at primitive superstitions, thinking

ourselves superior, but we completely forget that we are influenced in just as uncanny a fashion as the primitive by this background, which we are wont to scoff at as a museum of stupidities. Primitive man simply has a different theory – the theory of witchcraft and spirits. I find this theory very interesting and very sensible – actually more sensible than the academic views of modern science. Whereas the highly educated modern man tries to figure out what diet best suits his nervous intestinal catarrh and to what dietetic mistakes the new attack may be due, the primitive, quite correctly, looks for psychological reasons and seeks a psychically effective method of cure. The processes in the unconscious influence us just as much as they do primitives; we are possessed by the demons of sickness no less than they, our psyche is just as much in danger of being struck by some hostile influence, we are just as much the prey of malevolent spirits of the dead, or the victims of a magic spell cast by a strange personality. Only, we call all these things by different names, and that is the only advantage we have over primitive man. It is, as we know, a little thing, yet it makes all the difference. For mankind it was always like a deliverance from a nightmare when the new name was found.

15 This mysterious background, which from time immemorial peopled the nocturnal shadows of the primeval forest with the same yet ever-changing figures, seems like a distorted reflection of life during the day, repeating itself in the dreams and terrors of the night. Shadowily they crowd round, the revenants, the spirits of the dead, fleeting memory-images risen from the prison of the past whence no living thing returns, or feelings left behind by some impressive experience and now personified in spectral form. All this seems but the bitter aftertaste from the emptied beaker of the day, the unwelcome lees, the useless sediment of experience. But if we look closer, we discover that this apparently hostile background sends out powerful emissaries which influence the behaviour of primitives in the highest degree. Sometimes these agencies take on a magical, sometimes a religious form, and sometimes the two forms appear inextricably mixed. Both of them are the most important factors in the primitive mentality after the struggle for existence. In them the spiritual element manifests itself autonomously to the primitive psyche – whose reflexes are purely animal – in projected, sensuous form, and we Europeans must sometimes be struck with wonder at the tremendous influence the experience of the spirit can have on primitive man. For him, the sensuous immediacy of the object attaches to spiritual phenomena as well. A thought *appears to him,* he does not think it; it appears to him in the form of a projected sensuous perception, almost like an hallucination, or at least like an extremely vivid dream. For this reason a thought, for the primitive, can superimpose itself on sensuous reality to such an extent that if a European were to behave in the same way we should say he was mad.

16 These peculiarities of primitive psychology, which I can only touch lightly on here, are of great importance for an understanding of the collective unconscious. A simple reflection will bear this out. As civilized human beings, we in Western Europe have a history reaching back perhaps 2,500 years. Before that there is a prehistoric period of considerably greater duration, during which man reached the

cultural level of, say, the Sioux Indians. Then come the hundreds of thousands of years of neolithic culture, and before that an unimaginably vast stretch of time during which man evolved from the animal. A mere fifty generations ago many of us in Europe were no better than primitives. The layer of culture, this pleasing patina, must therefore be quite extraordinarily thin in comparison with the powerfully developed layers of the primitive psyche. But it is these layers that form the collective unconscious, together with the vestiges of animality that lose themselves in the nebulous abyss of time.

17   Christianity split the Germanic barbarian into an upper and a lower half, and enabled him, by repressing the dark side, to domesticate the brighter half and fit it for civilization. But the lower, darker half still awaits redemption and a second spell of domestication. Until then, it will remain associated with the vestiges of the prehistoric age, with the collective unconscious, which is subject to a peculiar and ever-increasing activation. As the Christian view of the world loses its authority, the more menacingly will the 'blond beast' be heard prowling about in its underground prison, ready at any moment to burst out with devastating consequences. When this happens in the individual it brings about a psychological revolution, but it can also take a social form.

18   In my opinion this problem does not exist for the Jews. The Jew already had the culture of the ancient world and on top of that has taken over the culture of the nations amongst whom he dwells. He has two cultures, paradoxical as that may sound. He is domesticated to a higher degree than we are, but he is badly at a loss for that quality in man which roots him to the earth and draws new strength from below. This chthonic quality is found in dangerous concentration in the Germanic peoples. Naturally the Aryan European has not noticed any signs of this for a very long time, but perhaps he is beginning to notice it in the present war; and again, perhaps not. The Jew has too little of this quality – where has he his own earth underfoot? The mystery of earth is no joke and no paradox. One only needs to see how, in America, the skull and pelvis measurements of all the European races begin to indianize themselves in the second generation of immigrants. That is the mystery of the American earth.

19   The soil of every country holds some such mystery. We have an unconscious reflection of this in the psyche: just as there is a relationship of mind to body, so there is a relationship of body to earth. I hope the reader will pardon my figurative way of speaking, and will try to grasp what I mean. It is not easy to describe, definite though it is. There are people – quite a number of them – who live outside and above their bodies, who float like bodiless shadows above their earth, their earthy component, which is their body. Others live wholly in their bodies. As a rule, the Jew lives in amicable relationship with the earth, but without feeling the power of the chthonic. His receptivity to this seems to have weakened with time. This may explain the specific need of the Jew to reduce everything to its material beginnings; he needs these beginnings in order to counterbalance the dangerous ascendency of his two cultures. A little bit of primitivity does not hurt him; on the contrary, I can understand very well that Freud's and Adler's reduction of

everything psychic to primitive sexual wishes and power-drives has something about it that is beneficial and satisfying to the Jew, because it is a form of simplification. For this reason, Freud is perhaps right to close his eyes to my objections. But these specifically Jewish doctrines are thoroughly unsatisfying to the Germanic mentality; we still have a genuine barbarian in us who is not to be trifled with, and whose manifestation is no comfort for us and not a pleasant way of passing the time. Would that people could learn the lesson of this war! The fact is, our unconscious is not to be got at with over-ingenious and grotesque interpretations. The psychotherapist with a Jewish background awakens in the Germanic psyche not those wistful and whimsical residues from the time of David, but the barbarian of yesterday, a being for whom matters suddenly become *serious* in the most unpleasant way. This annoying peculiarity of the barbarian was apparent also to Nietzsche – no doubt from personal experience – which is why he thought highly of the Jewish mentality and preached about dancing and flying and not taking things seriously. But he overlooked the fact that it is not the barbarian in us who takes things seriously – they become serious for him. He is gripped by the daemon. And who took things more seriously than Nietzsche himself?

20 It seems to me that we should take the problem of the unconscious very seriously indeed. The tremendous compulsion towards goodness and the immense moral force of Christianity are not merely an argument in the latter's favour, they are also a proof of the strength of its suppressed and repressed counterpart – the antichristian, barbarian element. The existence within us of something that can turn against us, that can become a serious matter for us, I regard not merely as a dangerous peculiarity, but as a valuable and congenial asset as well. It is a still untouched fortune, an uncorrupted treasure, a sign of youthfulness, an earnest of rebirth. Nevertheless, to value the unconscious exclusively for the sake of its positive qualities and to regard it as a source of revelation would be fundamentally wrong. The unconscious is, first and foremost, the world of the past, which is activated by the one-sidedness of the conscious attitude. Whenever life proceeds one-sidedly in any given direction, the self-regulation of the organism produces in the unconscious an accumulation of all those factors which play too small a part in the individual's conscious existence. For this reason I have put forward the compensation theory of the unconscious as a complement to the repression theory.

21 The role of the unconscious is to act compensatorily to the conscious contents of the moment. By this I do not mean that it sets up an opposition, for there are times when the tendency of the unconscious coincides with that of consciousness, namely, when the conscious attitude is approaching the optimum. The nearer it approaches the optimum, the more the autonomous activity of the unconscious is diminished, and the more its value sinks until, at the moment when the optimum is reached, it falls to zero. We can say, then, that so long as all goes well, so long as a person travels the road that is, for him, the individual as well as the social optimum, there is no talk of the unconscious. The very fact that we in our age come to speak of the unconscious at all is proof that everything is not in order. This talk of the unconscious cannot be laid entirely at the door of analytical

psychology; its beginnings can be traced back to the time of the French Revolution, and the first signs of it can be found in Mesmer. It is true that in those days they did not speak of the unconscious but of 'animal magnetism.' This is nothing but a rediscovery of the primitive concept of soul-force or soul-stuff, awakened out of the unconscious by a reactivation of archaic forms of thought. At the time when animal magnetism was spreading throughout the Western world as a regular epidemic of table-turning, amounting in the end to a recrudescence of the belief in fetishes (animation of an inanimate object), Robert Mayer elevated the primitive dynamic idea of energy, which rose up from the unconscious and forced itself on him like an inspiration – as he himself describes – to the level of a scientific concept. Meanwhile, the table-turning epidemic burst its bounds altogether and proliferated into spiritualism, which is a modern belief in spirits and a rebirth of the shamanistic form of religion practised by our remote forefathers. This development of reactivated contents from the unconscious is still going on today, and during the last few decades has led to a popularizing of the next higher stage of differentiation – the eclectic or Gnostic systems of Theosophy and Anthroposophy. At the same time, it laid the foundations of French psychopathology, and in particular of the French school of hypnotism. These, in turn, became the main sources of analytical psychology, which now seeks to investigate scientifically the phenomena of the unconscious – the same phenomena which the theosophical and Gnostic sects made accessible to the simple-minded in the form of portentous mysteries.

22 It is evident from this development that analytical psychology does not stand in isolation but finds itself in a definite historical setting. The fact that this whole disturbance or reactivation of the unconscious took place around the year 1800 is, in my view, connected with the French Revolution. This was less a political revolution than a revolution of minds. It was a colossal explosion of all the inflammable matter that had been piling up ever since the Age of Enlightenment. The official deposition of Christianity by the Revolution must have made a tremendous impression on the unconscious pagan in us, for from then on he found no rest. In the greatest German of the age, Goethe, he could really live and breathe, and in Hölderlin he could at least cry loudly for the glory that was Greece. After that, the dechristianization of man's view of the world made rapid progress despite occasional reactionaries. Hand in hand with this went the importation of strange gods. Besides the fetishism and shamanism already mentioned, the prime import was Buddhism, retailed by Schopenhauer. Mystery religions spread apace, including that higher form of shamanism, Christian Science. This picture reminds us vividly of the first centuries of our era, when Rome began to find the old gods ridiculous and felt the need to import new ones on a large scale. As today, they imported pretty well everything that existed, from the lowest, most squalid superstition to the noblest flowerings of the human spirit. Our time is fatally reminiscent of that epoch, when again everything was not in order, and again the unconscious burst forth and brought back things immemorially buried. If anything, the chaos of minds was perhaps less pronounced then than it is today.

23   As the reader will have remarked, I have omitted to speak here of the medical aspect of the unconscious, for instance the question of how the unconscious produces nervous symptoms. But I have touched on this question in the earlier pages and can now leave it alone. At all events, I am not getting away from my subject, because psychotherapy is concerned not only with family quarrels, unhappy love-affairs, and the like, but with the question of psychological adaptation in general, and the attitude we are to take towards people and things, and also towards ourselves. A doctor who treats the body must know the body, and a doctor who treats the psyche must know the psyche. If he knows the psyche only under the aspect of sexuality or of the personal lust for power, he knows it only in part. This part has to be known, of course, but the other parts are equally important, and particularly the question I have touched on here concerning the relation between conscious and unconscious. A biologically trained eye is not sufficient to grasp this problem, for in practice it is more than a matter of eugenics, and the observation of human life in the light of self-preservation and propagation is too one-sided. Certainly the unconscious presents us with very different aspects; but so far we have fixed our attention too much on certain outward peculiarities, for instance the archaic language of the unconscious, and have taken it all quite literally. The language of the unconscious is particularly rich in images, as our dreams prove. But it is a primitive language, a faithful reflection of the colourful, ever-changing world. The unconscious is of like nature: it is a compensatory image of the world. In my view it cannot be maintained either that the unconscious has a merely sexual nature or that it is a metaphysical reality, nor can it be exalted into a 'universal ground.' It is to be understood as a psychic phenomenon, like consciousness. We no more know what the psyche is than we know what life is. They are interpenetrating mysteries, giving us every reason for uncertainty as to how much 'I' am the world, and how much 'world' is 'I'. The unconscious at any rate is real, because it *works*. I like to visualize the unconscious as a world seen in a mirror: our consciousness presents to us a picture of the outer world, but also of the world within, this being a compensatory mirror-image of the outer world. We could also say that the outer world is a compensatory mirror-image of the inner world. At all events we stand between two worlds, or between two totally different psychological systems of perception; between perception of external sensory stimuli and perception of the unconscious. The picture we have of the outer world makes us understand everything as the effect of physical and physiological forces; the picture of the inner world shows everything as the effect of spiritual agencies. Then, it is no longer the force of gravity that welds the stars together, but the creative hand of a demiurge; love is no longer the effect of a sexual stimulus, but of psychic predestination, and so forth.

24   The right way may perhaps be found in the approximation of the two worlds. Schiller thought he had found this way in art, in what he called the 'symbol' of art. The artist, therefore, should know the secret of the middle path. My own experiences led me to doubt this. I am of the opinion that the union of rational and irrational truth is to be found not so much in art as in the symbol

per se; for it is the essence of the symbol to contain both the rational and the irrational. It always expresses the one through the other; it comprises both without being either.

25   How does a symbol originate? This question brings us to the most important function of the unconscious: the *symbol-creating function*. There is something very remarkable about this function, because it has only a relative existence. The compensatory function, on the other hand, is the natural, automatic function of the unconscious and is constantly present. It owes its existence to the simple fact that all the impulses, thoughts, wishes, and tendencies which run counter to the rational orientation of daily life are denied expression, thrust into the background, and finally fall into the unconscious. There all the things which we have repressed and suppressed, which we have deliberately ignored and devalued, gradually accumulate and, in time, acquire such force that they begin to influence consciousness. This influence would be in direct opposition to our conscious orientation if the unconscious consisted only of repressed and suppressed material. But this, as we have seen, is not the case. The unconscious also contains the dark springs of instinct and intuition, it contains all those forces which mere reasonableness, propriety, and the orderly course of bourgeois existence could never call awake, all those creative forces which lead man onwards to new developments, new forms, and new goals. I therefore call the influence of the unconscious not merely complementary but compensatory, because it adds to consciousness everything that has been excluded by the drying up of the springs of intuition and by the fixed pursuit of a single goal.

26   This function, as I say, works automatically, but, owing to the notorious atrophy of instinct in civilized man, it is often too weak to swing his one-sided orientation of consciousness in a new direction against the pressures of society. Therefore, artificial aids have always been needed to bring the healing forces of the unconscious into play. It was chiefly the religions that performed this task. By taking the manifestations of the unconscious as divine or daemonic signs, revelations, or warnings, they offered it some idea or view that served as a favourable gradient. In this way they directed particular attention to all phenomena of unconscious origin, whether they were dreams, visions, feelings, fantasies, or projections of the same in strange or unusual personalities, or in any striking processes of organic and inorganic nature. This concentration of attention enabled the unconscious contents and forces to overflow into conscious life, thereby influencing it and altering it. From this standpoint, religious ideas are an artificial aid that benefits the unconscious by endowing its compensatory function – which, if disregarded, would remain ineffective – with a higher value for consciousness. Faith, superstition, or any strongly feeling-toned idea gives the unconscious content a value which ordinarily it does not possess, but which it might in time attain, though in a very unpleasant form. When, therefore, unconscious contents accumulate as a result of being consistently ignored, they are bound to exert an influence that is pathological. There are just as many neurotics among primitives as among civilized Europeans. Hysterical Africans are by no means rare in Africa. These

disagreeable manifestations of the unconscious account in large measure for the primitive fear of demons and the resultant rites of propitiation.

27   The compensatory function of the unconscious naturally does not contain in itself the conscious valuation, although it is wholly dependent on the conscious way of thinking. The unconscious can supply, at most, the germs of conscious convictions or of symbol-formation. We can say, therefore, that the symbol-creating function of the unconscious exists and does not exist, depending on the conditions. It shares this paradoxical quality with symbols in general. One is reminded of the story of the young rabbi who was a pupil of Kant's. One day an old rabbi came to guide him back to the faith of his fathers, but all arguments were in vain. At last the old rabbi drew forth the ominous *shofar*, the horn that is blown at the cursing of heretics (as happened to Spinoza), and asked the young man if he knew what it was. 'Of course I know,' answered the young man coolly, 'it is the horn of a ram.' At that the old rabbi reeled back and fell to the ground in horror.

28   What is the *shofar*? It is *also* only the horn of a ram. Sometimes a symbol can be no more than that, but only when it is dead. The symbol is killed when we succeed in reducing the *shofar* to a ram's horn. But again, through symbolization a ram's horn can become the *shofar*.

29   The compensatory function expresses itself in quite definite arrangements of psychic material, for instance in dreams, in which nothing 'symbolic' is to be found any more than in a ram's horn. In order to discover their symbolic quality a quite definite conscious attitude is needed, namely, the willingness to understand the dream-content symbolically, first of all as a mere hypothesis, and then leave experience to decide whether it is necessary or desirable to understand the dream in this way. I will give a brief example which may help to elucidate this difficult question. An elderly woman-patient, who, like many others, was upset by the problem of the war, once told me the following dream which she had shortly before she visited me:

30   *She was singing hymns that put particular emphasis on her belief in Christ, among others the hymn that goes:*

> Christ's blood and righteousness shall be
> My festal dress and jewellery;
> So shall I stand before the Lord
> When heaven shall grant me my reward.
> They shall be saved at Judgment Day
> Who put their trust in Christ alway.

While she was singing it, she saw a bull tearing around madly in front of the window. Suddenly it gave a jump and broke one of its legs. She saw that the bull was in agony, and thought, turning her eyes away, that somebody ought to kill it. Then she awoke.

31   The bull's agony reminded her of the torturings of animals whose unwilling witness she had been. She abominated such things and was extraordinarily upset

by them because of her unconscious identification with the tortured animal. There was something in her that could be expressed by the image of an animal being tortured. This image was evidently evoked by the special emphasis on the belief in Christ in the hymns she was singing, for it was while she was singing that the bull got excited and broke its leg. This odd combination of ideas immediately led to an association concerning the profound religious disquiet she had felt during the war, which shook her belief in the goodness of God and in the adequacy of the Christian view of the world. This shock should have been assuaged by the emphasis on Christian faith in the hymn, but instead it aroused that animal element in the unconscious which was personified by the bull. This is just the element that is represented by the Christian symbol as having been conquered and offered up in sacrifice. In the Christian mystery it is the sacrificed Lamb, or more correctly, the 'little ram.' In its sister-religion, Mithraism, which was also Christianity's most successful rival, the central symbol of the cult was the sacrifice not of a ram but of a bull. The usual altarpiece showed the overcoming of the bull by the divine saviour Mithras. We have, therefore, a very close historical connection between Christianity and the bull sacrifice. Christianity suppressed this animal element, but the moment the absolute validity of the Christian faith is shaken, that element is thrust into the foreground again. The animal instinct seeks to break out, but in so doing breaks a leg – in other words, instinct cripples itself. From the purely animal drives there also come all those factors which limit the sway of instinct. From the same root that produces wild, untamed, blind instinct there grow up the natural laws and cultural forms that tame and break its pristine power. But when the animal in us is split off from consciousness by being repressed, it may easily burst out in full force, quite unregulated and uncontrolled. An outburst of this sort always ends in catastrophe – the animal destroys itself. What was originally something dangerous now becomes something to be pitied, something that really needs our compassion. The tremendous forces unleashed by the war bring about their own destruction because there is no human hand to preserve and guide them. Our view of the world has proved too narrow to channel these forces into a cultural form.

32   Had I tried to explain to my elderly woman-patient that the bull was a sexual symbol, she would have got nothing out of it; on the contrary, she would merely have lost her religious point of view and been none the better off. In such cases it is not a question of an either/or explanation. If we are willing to adopt a symbolical standpoint, even if only as an hypothesis, we shall see that the dream is an attempt on the part of the unconscious to bring the Christian principle into harmony with its apparently irreconcilable opposite – animal instinct – by means of understanding and compassion. It is no accident that official Christianity has no relation to the animal. This omission, particularly striking in comparison with Buddhism, is often felt by sensitive people and has moved one modern poet to sing of a Christ who sacrifices his life for the sufferings of dumb animals. The Christian love of your neighbour can extend to the animal too, the *animal in us,* and can surround with love all that a rigidly anthropomorphic view of the world

has cruelly repressed. By being repressed into the unconscious, the source from which it originated, the animal in us only becomes more beastlike, and that is no doubt the reason why no religion is so defiled with the spilling of innocent blood as Christianity, and why the world has never seen a bloodier war than the war of the Christian nations. The repressed animal bursts forth in its most savage form when it comes to the surface, and in the process of destroying itself leads to international suicide. If every individual had a better relation to the animal within him, he would also set a higher value on life. Life would be the absolute, the supreme moral principle, and he would react instinctively against any institution or organization that had the power to destroy life on a large scale.

33   This dream, then, simply shows the dreamer the value of Christianity and contrasts it with an untamed force of nature, which, left to its raging, hurts itself and demands pity. A purely analytical reduction that traced the religious emotion back to the repression of animal instinct would, in this particular case, be sterile and uselessly destructive. If, on the other hand, we assert that the dream is to be understood symbolically and is trying to give the dreamer an opportunity to become reconciled with herself, we have taken the first step in an interpretation which will bring the contradictory values into harmony and open up a new path of inner development. Subsequent dreams would then, in keeping with this hypothesis, provide the means for understanding the wider implications of the union of the animal component with the highest moral and intellectual achievements of the human spirit. In my experience this is what actually happens, for the unconscious is continuously compensatory in its action upon the conscious situation of the moment. It is therefore not a matter of indifference *what* our conscious attitude is towards the unconscious. The more negative, critical, hostile, or disparaging we are, the more it will assume these aspects, and the more the true value of the unconscious will escape us.

34   Thus the unconscious has a symbol-creating function only when we are willing to recognize in it a symbolic element. The products of the unconscious are pure nature. *Naturam si sequemur ducem, nunquam aberrabimus*,[2] said the ancients. But nature is not, in herself, a guide, for she is not there for man's sake. Ships are not guided by the phenomenon of magnetism. We have to make the compass a guide and, in addition, allow for a specific correction, for the needle does not even point exactly to the north. So it is with the guiding function of the unconscious. It can be used as a source of symbols, but with the necessary conscious correction that has to be applied to every natural phenomenon in order to make it serve our purpose.

35   Many people will find this view extremely unscientific, for nowhere do they see any reduction to fundamental causes, so that they could declare with certainty that such-and-such a thing is 'nothing but' this or that. For all those who seek to explain things in this way, sexuality as a causative factor is very convenient. Indeed, in the case I have described a sexual explanation could be offered without much difficulty. But – what would the patient get out of it? What use is it to a woman on the threshold of old age if her problem is answered in this way? Or should psychotherapy be reserved for patients under forty?

36   Naturally we can ask in return: What does the patient get out of an answer that takes religious problems seriously? What is a religious problem anyway? And what has a scientific method to do with religion?

37   It seems to me that the patient is the proper authority to deal with questions of this sort. What does he get out of them however they are answered? Why should he bother his head about science? If he is a religious person, his relationship to God will mean infinitely more to him than any scientifically satisfactory explanation, just as it is a matter of indifference to a sick man *how* he gets well so long as he does get well. Our patient, indeed any patient, is treated correctly only when he is treated as an individual. This means entering into his particular problem and not giving him an explanation based on 'scientific' principles that goes clean over his head although it may be quite correct biologically.

38   In my view the first duty of a scientific psychologist is to keep close to the living facts of the psyche, to observe these facts carefully, and thus open himself to those deeper experiences of which at present he has absolutely no knowledge. When, therefore, this or that individual psyche has a sexual conflict, and another one has a religious problem, the true scientist will first of all acknowledge the patent difference between them. He will devote himself as much to the religious problem as to the sexual problem, regardless of whether the biologist's credo allows room for the gods or not. The really unprejudiced investigator will not let his subjective credo influence or in any way distort the material lying before him, and pathological material is no exception to this. Nowadays it is a piece of unwarranted naïveté to regard a neurotic conflict as exclusively a sexual or as exclusively a power problem. This procedure is just as arbitrary as the assertion that there is no such thing as the unconscious and no neurotic conflicts. When we see all round us how powerful ideas can be, we must admit that they must be equally powerful in the psyche of the individual, whether or not he is aware of it. No one doubts that sexuality is a psychologically effective factor, and it cannot be doubted that ideas are psychologically effective factors too. Between the world of ideas and the world of instinct there is, however, a polar difference, so that as a rule only one pole is conscious. The other pole then dominates the unconscious. Thus, when anyone in his conscious life is wholly under the sway of instinct, his unconscious will place just as one-sided an emphasis on the value of ideas. And since the influence of the unconscious does in the end reach consciousness indirectly, and secretly determines its attitude, it gives rise to a compromise formation: instinct surreptitiously becomes a fixed idea, it loses its reality and is blown up by the unconscious into a one-sided, universal principle. We see the contrary often happening too, when a person consciously takes his stand on the world of ideas and is gradually forced to experience how his instinct secretly makes his ideas the instrument of unconscious wishes.

39   As the contemporary world and its newspapers present the spectacle of a gigantic psychiatric clinic, every attentive observer has ample opportunity to see these formulations being enacted before his eyes. A principle of cardinal importance in studying these phenomena is the one already stressed by analytical

psychology: that the unconscious of one person is projected upon another person, so that the first accuses the second of what he overlooks in himself. This principle is of such alarming general validity that everyone would do well, before railing at others, to sit down and consider very carefully whether the brick should not be thrown at his own head.

40   This seemingly irrelevant aside brings us to one of the most remarkable features of the unconscious: it is, as it were, present before our eyes in all its parts, and is accessible to observation at any time.

41   The reason for this paradoxical quality is that the unconscious, in so far as it is activated in any way by small amounts of energy, is projected upon certain more or less suitable objects. The reader will ask how anyone can know this. The existence of projections was gradually recognized when it was found that the process of psychological adaptation was marked by disturbances and defects whose cause appeared to lie in the object. Closer investigation revealed that the 'cause' was an unconscious content of the subject, which, because not recognized by him, apparently transferred itself to the object, and there magnified one of its peculiarities to such proportions that it seemed a sufficient cause of the disturbance.

42   The fact of projection was first recognized from disturbances of psychological adaptation. Later, it was recognized also from what *promoted* adaptation, that is to say from the apparently positive qualities of the object. Here it was the valuable qualities of the subject's own personality which he had overlooked that appeared in the object and made it especially desirable.

43   But the full extent of these projections from the unconscious became known through analysis of those obscure and inexplicable feelings and emotions which give some intangible, magical quality to certain places, certain moods of nature, certain works of art, and also to certain ideas and certain people. This magic likewise comes from projection, but a projection of the collective unconscious. If it is inanimate objects that have the 'magical' quality, often their mere statistical incidence is sufficient to prove that their significance is due to the projection of a mythological content from the collective unconscious. Mostly these contents are motifs already known to us from myths and fairytales. I would mention as an example the mysterious house where a witch or magician dwells, where some monstrous crime is being committed or has been committed, where there is a ghost, where a hidden treasure lies buried, and so on. The projection of this primordial image can be recognized when, one day, a person somehow comes upon this mysterious house – when, in other words, a real but quite ordinary house makes a magical impression upon him. Generally, too, the whole atmosphere of the place seems symbolic and is, therefore, the projection of a coherent unconscious system.

44   We find this phenomenon beautifully developed in primitive man. The country he inhabits is at the same time the topography of his unconscious. In that stately tree dwells the thunder-god; this spring is haunted by the Old Woman; in that wood the legendary king is buried; near that rock no one may light a fire because it is the abode of a demon; in yonder pile of stones dwell the ancestral spirits, and

when any woman passes it she must quickly utter an apotropaic formula lest she become pregnant, for one of the spirits could easily enter her body. All kinds of objects and signs mark these places, and pious awe surrounds the marked spot. Thus does primitive man dwell in his land and at the same time in the land of his unconscious. Everywhere his unconscious jumps out at him, alive and real. How different is our relationship to the land we dwell in! Feelings totally strange to us accompany the primitive at every step. Who knows what the cry of a bird means to him, or the sight of that old tree! A whole world of feeling is closed to us and is replaced by a pale aestheticism. Nevertheless, the world of primitive feeling is not entirely lost to us; it lives on in the unconscious. The further we remove ourselves from it with our enlightenment and our rational superiority, the more it fades into the distance, but is made all the more potent by everything that falls into it, thrust out by our one-sided rationalism. This lost bit of nature seeks revenge and returns in faked, distorted form, for instance as a tango epidemic, as Futurism, Dadaism, and all the other crazes and crudities in which our age abounds.

45   Even the primitive's distrust of the neighbouring tribe, which we thought we had long ago outgrown thanks to our global organizations, has come back again in this war, swollen to gigantic proportions. It is no longer a matter of burning down the neighbouring village, or of making a few heads roll: whole countries are devastated, millions are slaughtered. The enemy nation is stripped of every shred of decency, and our own faults appear in others, fantastically magnified. Where are the superior minds, capable of reflection, today? If they exist at all, nobody heeds them: instead there is a general running amok, a universal fatality against whose compelling sway the individual is powerless to defend himself. And yet this collective phenomenon is the fault of the individual as well, for nations are made up of individuals. Therefore the individual must consider by what means he can counteract the evil. Our rationalistic attitude leads us to believe that we can work wonders with international organizations, legislation, and other well-meant devices. But in reality only a change in the attitude of the individual can bring about a renewal in the spirit of the nations. Everything begins with the individual.

46   There are well-meaning theologians and humanitarians who want to break the power principle – in others. We must begin by breaking it in ourselves. Then the thing becomes credible. We should listen to the voice of nature that speaks to us from the unconscious. Then everyone will be so preoccupied with himself that he will give up trying to put the world to rights.

47   The layman may feel somewhat astonished that I have included these general problems in my discussion of a psychological concept. They are not a digression from my theme, as might appear, but are an essential part of it. The question of the relations between conscious and unconscious is not a special question, but one which is bound up in the most intimate way with our history, with the present time, and with our view of the world. Very many things are unconscious for us only because our view of the world allows them no room; because by education and training we have never come to grips with them, and, whenever they came to consciousness as occasional fantasies, have instantly suppressed them. The

borderline between conscious and unconscious is in large measure determined by our view of the world. That is why we must talk about general problems if we wish to deal adequately with the concept of the unconscious. And if we are to grasp its nature, we must concern ourselves not only with contemporary problems, but also with the history of the human mind.

48   This preoccupation with the unconscious is a problem of practical as well as theoretical importance. For just as our view of the world up till now has been a decisive factor in the shaping of the unconscious and its contents, so the remoulding of our views in accordance with the active forces of the unconscious is laid upon us as a practical necessity. It is impossible to cure a neurosis permanently with individual nostrums, for man cannot exist merely as an isolated individual outside the human community. The principle on which he builds his life must be one that is generally acceptable, otherwise it will lack that natural morality which is indispensable to man as a member of the herd. But such a principle, if it is not left in the darkness of the unconscious, becomes a formulated view of the world which is felt as a necessity by all who are in the habit of consciously scrutinizing their thoughts and actions. This may explain why I have touched on questions each one of which would need for its full presentation more than one head and more than one lifetime.

Notes

1 [Originally published as 'Ueber das Unbewusste,' *Schweizerland: Monatshefte für Schweizer Art und Arbeit* (Zurich), IV (1918), no. 9, 464–72, and no. 11–12, 548–58. – EDITORS.]
2 'If we take Nature for our guide, we shall never go astray.'

Chapter 3

The stages of life[1]

749 To discuss the problems connected with the stages of human development is an exacting task, for it means nothing less than unfolding a picture of psychic life in its entirety from the cradle to the grave. Within the framework of a lecture such a task can be carried out only on the broadest lines, and it must be well understood that no attempt will be made to describe the normal psychic occurrences within the various stages. We shall restrict ourselves, rather, to certain 'problems,' that is, to things that are difficult, questionable, or ambiguous; in a word, to questions which allow of more than one answer – and, moreover, answers that are always open to doubt. For this reason there will be much to which we must add a question-mark in our thoughts. Worse still, there will be some things we must accept on faith, while now and then we must even indulge in speculations.

750 If psychic life consisted only of self-evident matters of fact – which on a primitive level is still the case – we could content ourselves with a sturdy empiricism. The psychic life of civilized man, however, is full of problems; we cannot even think of it except in terms of problems. Our psychic processes are made up to a large extent of reflections, doubts, experiments, all of which are almost completely foreign to the unconscious, instinctive mind of primitive man. It is the growth of consciousness which we must thank for the existence of problems; they are the Danaän gift of civilization. It is just man's turning away from instinct – his opposing himself to instinct – that creates consciousness. Instinct is nature and seeks to perpetuate nature, whereas consciousness can only seek culture or its denial. Even when we turn back to nature, inspired by a Rousseauesque longing, we 'cultivate' nature. As long as we are still submerged in nature we are unconscious, and we live in the security of instinct which knows no problems. Everything in us that still belongs to nature shrinks away from a problem, for its name is doubt, and wherever doubt holds sway there is uncertainty and the possibility of divergent ways. And where several ways seem possible, there we have turned away from the certain guidance of instinct and are handed over to fear. For consciousness is now called upon to do that which nature has always done for her children – namely, to give a certain, unquestionable, and unequivocal decision. And here we are beset by an all-too-human fear that consciousness – our Promethean conquest – may in the end not be able to serve us as well as nature.

751   Problems thus draw us into an orphaned and isolated state where we are abandoned by nature and are driven to consciousness. There is no other way open to us; we are forced to resort to conscious decisions and solutions where formerly we trusted ourselves to natural happenings. Every problem, therefore, brings the possibility of a widening of consciousness, but also the necessity of saying goodbye to childlike unconsciousness and trust in nature. This necessity is a psychic fact of such importance that it constitutes one of the most essential symbolic teachings of the Christian religion. It is the sacrifice of the merely natural man, of the unconscious, ingenuous being whose tragic career began with the eating of the apple in Paradise. The biblical fall of man presents the dawn of consciousness as a curse. And as a matter of fact it is in this light that we first look upon every problem that forces us to greater consciousness and separates us even further from the paradise of unconscious childhood. Every one of us gladly turns away from his problems; if possible, they must not be mentioned, or, better still, their existence is denied. We wish to make our lives simple, certain, and smooth, and for that reason problems are taboo. We want to have certainties and no doubts – results and no experiments – without even seeing that certainties can arise only through doubt and results only through experiment. The artful denial of a problem will not produce conviction; on the contrary, a wider and higher consciousness is required to give us the certainty and clarity we need.

752   This introduction, long as it is, seemed to me necessary in order to make clear the nature of our subject. When we must deal with problems, we instinctively resist trying the way that leads through obscurity and darkness. We wish to hear only of unequivocal results, and completely forget that these results can only be brought about when we have ventured into and emerged again from the darkness. But to penetrate the darkness we must summon all the powers of enlightenment that consciousness can offer; as I have already said, we must even indulge in speculations. For in treating the problems of psychic life we perpetually stumble upon questions of principle belonging to the private domains of the most heterogeneous branches of knowledge. We disturb and anger the theologian no less than the philosopher, the physician no less than the educator; we even grope about in the field of the biologist and of the historian. This extravagant behaviour is due not to arrogance but to the circumstance that man's psyche is a unique combination of factors which are at the same time the special subjects of far-reaching lines of research. For it is out of himself and out of his peculiar constitution that man has produced his sciences. They are *symptoms* of his psyche.

753   If, therefore, we ask ourselves the unavoidable question, 'Why does man, in obvious contrast to the animal world, have problems at all?' we run into that inextricable tangle of thoughts which many thousands of incisive minds have woven in the course of the centuries. I shall not perform the labours of a Sisyphus upon this masterpiece of confusion, but will try to present quite simply my contribution toward man's attempt to answer this basic question.

754   There are no problems without consciousness. We must therefore put the question in another way and ask, 'How does consciousness arise in the first place?'

Nobody can say with certainty; but we can observe small children in the process of becoming conscious. Every parent can see it if he pays attention. And what we see is this: when the child recognizes someone or something – when he 'knows' a person or a thing – then we feel that the child has consciousness. That, no doubt, is also why in Paradise it was the tree of knowledge which bore such fateful fruit.

755   But what is recognition or 'knowledge' in this sense? We speak of 'knowing' something when we succeed in linking a new perception to an already existing context, in such a way that we hold in consciousness not only the perception but parts of this context as well. 'Knowing' is based, therefore, upon the perceived connection between psychic contents. We can have no knowledge of a content that is not connected with anything, and we cannot even be conscious of it should our consciousness still be on this low initial level. Accordingly the first stage of consciousness which we can observe consists in the mere connection between two or more psychic contents. At this level, consciousness is merely sporadic, being limited to the perception of a few connections, and the content is not remembered later on. It is a fact that in the early years of life there is no continuous memory; at most there are islands of consciousness which are like single lamps or lighted objects in the far-flung darkness. But these islands of memory are not the same as those earliest connections which are merely perceived; they contain a new, very important series of contents belonging to the perceiving subject himself, the so-called ego. This series, like the initial series of contents, is at first merely perceived, and for this reason the child logically begins by speaking of itself objectively, in the third person. Only later, when the ego-contents – the so-called ego-complex – have acquired an energy of their own (very likely as a result of training and practice) does the feeling of subjectivity or 'I-ness' arise. This may well be the moment when the child begins to speak of itself in the first person. The continuity of memory probably begins at this stage. Essentially, therefore, it would be a continuity of ego-memories.

756   In the childish stage of consciousness there are as yet no problems; nothing depends upon the subject, for the child itself is still wholly dependent on its parents. It is as though it were not yet completely born, but were still enclosed in the psychic atmosphere of its parents. Psychic birth, and with it the conscious differentiation from the parents, normally takes place only at puberty, with the eruption of sexuality. The physiological change is attended by a psychic revolution. For the various bodily manifestations give such an emphasis to the ego that it often asserts itself without stint or moderation. This is sometimes called 'the unbearable age'.

757   Until this period is reached the psychic life of the individual is governed largely by instinct, and few or no problems arise. Even when external limitations oppose his subjective impulses, these restraints do not put the individual at variance with himself. He submits to them or circumvents them, remaining quite at one with himself. He does not yet know the state of inner tension induced by a problem. This state only arises when what was an external limitation becomes an inner one;

when one impulse is opposed by another. In psychological language we would say: the problematical state, the inner division with oneself, arises when, side by side with the series of ego-contents, a second series of equal intensity comes into being. This second series, because of its energy value, has a functional significance equal to that of the ego-complex; we might call it another, second ego which can on occasion even wrest the leadership from the first. This produces the division with oneself, the state that betokens a problem.

758   To recapitulate what we have said: the first stage of consciousness, consisting in merely recognizing or 'knowing,' is an anarchic or chaotic state. The second, that of the developed ego-complex, is monarchic or monistic. The third brings another step forward in consciousness, and consists in an awareness of the divided, or dualistic, state.

759   And here we come to our real theme – the problem of the stages of life. First of all we must deal with the period of youth. It extends roughly from the years just after puberty to middle life, which itself begins between the thirty-fifth and fortieth year.

760   I might well be asked why I begin with the second stage, as though there were no problems connected with childhood. The complex psychic life of the child is, of course, a problem of the first magnitude to parents, educators, and doctors, but when normal the child has no real problems of its own. It is only the adult human being who can have doubts about himself and be at variance with himself.

761   We are all familiar with the sources of the problems that arise in the period of youth. For most people it is the demands of life which harshly put an end to the dream of childhood. If the individual is sufficiently well prepared, the transition to a profession or career can take place smoothly. But if he clings to illusions that are contrary to reality, then problems will surely arise. No one can take the step into life without making certain assumptions, and occasionally these assumptions are false – that is, they do not fit the conditions into which one is thrown. Often it is a question of exaggerated expectations, underestimation of difficulties, unjustified optimism, or a negative attitude. One could compile quite a list of the false assumptions that give rise to the first conscious problems.

762   But it is not always the contradiction between subjective assumptions and external facts that gives rise to problems; it may just as often be inner, psychic difficulties. They may exist even when things run smoothly in the outside world. Very often it is the disturbance of psychic equilibrium caused by the sexual instinct; equally often it is the feeling of inferiority which springs from an unbearable sensitivity. These inner conflicts may exist even when adaptation to the outer world has been achieved without apparent effort. It even seems as if young people who have had a hard struggle for existence are spared inner problems, while those who for some reason or other have no difficulty with adaptation run into problems of sex or conflicts arising from a sense of inferiority.

763   People whose own temperaments offer problems are often neurotic, but it would be a serious misunderstanding to confuse the existence of problems with

neurosis. There is a marked difference between the two in that the neurotic is ill because he is unconscious of his problems, while the person with a difficult temperament suffers from his conscious problems without being ill.

764 If we try to extract the common and essential factors from the almost inexhaustible variety of individual problems found in the period of youth, we meet in all cases with one particular feature; a more or less patent clinging to the childhood level of consciousness, a resistance to the fateful forces in and around us which would involve us in the world. Something in us wishes to remain a child, to be unconscious or, at most, conscious only of the ego; to reject everything strange, or else subject it to our will; to do nothing, or else indulge our own craving for pleasure or power. In all this there is something of the inertia of matter; it is a persistence in the previous state whose range of consciousness is smaller, narrower, and more egoistic than that of the dualistic phase. For here the individual is faced with the necessity of recognizing and accepting what is different and strange as a part of his own life, as a kind of 'also I.'

765 The essential feature of the dualistic phase is the widening of the horizon of life, and it is this that is so vigorously resisted. To be sure, this expansion – or diastole, as Goethe called it – had started long before this. It begins at birth, when the child abandons the narrow confinement of the mother's body; and from then on it steadily increases until it reaches a climax in the problematical state, when the individual begins to struggle against it.

766 What would happen to him if he simply changed himself into that foreign-seeming 'also-I' and allowed the earlier ego to vanish into the past? We might suppose this to be a quite practical course. The very aim of religious education, from the exhortation to put off the old Adam right back to the rebirth rituals of primitive races, is to transform the human being into the new, future man, and to allow the old to die away.

767 Psychology teaches us that, in a certain sense, there is nothing in the psyche that is old; nothing that can really, finally die away. Even Paul was left with a thorn in the flesh. Whoever protects himself against what is new and strange and regresses to the past falls into the same neurotic condition as the man who identifies himself with the new and runs away from the past. The only difference is that the one has estranged himself from the past and the other from the future. In principle both are doing the same thing: they are reinforcing their narrow range of consciousness instead of shattering it in the tension of opposites and building up a state of wider and higher consciousness.

768 This outcome would be ideal if it could be brought about in the second stage of life – but there's the rub. For one thing, nature cares nothing whatsoever about a higher level of consciousness; quite the contrary. And then society does not value these feats of the psyche very highly; its prizes are always given for achievement and not for personality, the latter being rewarded for the most part posthumously. These facts compel us towards a particular solution: we are forced to limit ourselves to the attainable, and to differentiate particular aptitudes in which the socially effective individual discovers his true self.

769 Achievement, usefulness and so forth are the ideals that seem to point the way out of the confusions of the problematical state. They are the lodestars that guide us in the adventure of broadening and consolidating our physical existence; they help us to strike our roots in the world, but they cannot guide us in the development of that wider consciousness to which we give the name of culture. In the period of youth, however, this course is the normal one and in all circumstances preferable to merely tossing about in a welter of problems.

770 The dilemma is often solved, therefore, in this way: whatever is given to us by the past is adapted to the possibilities and demands of the future. We limit ourselves to the attainable, and this means renouncing all our other psychic potentialities. One man loses a valuable piece of his past, another a valuable piece of his future. Everyone can call to mind friends or schoolmates who were promising and idealistic youngsters, but who, when we meet them again years later, seem to have grown dry and cramped in a narrow mould. These are examples of the solution mentioned above.

771 The serious problems in life, however, are never fully solved. If ever they should appear to be so it is a sure sign that something has been lost. The meaning and purpose of a problem seem to lie not in its solution but in our working at it incessantly. This alone preserves us from stultification and petrifaction. So also the solution of the problems of youth by restricting ourselves to the attainable is only temporarily valid and not lasting in a deeper sense. Of course, to win for oneself a place in society and to transform one's nature so that it is more or less fitted to this kind of existence is in all cases a considerable achievement. It is a fight waged within oneself as well as outside, comparable to the struggle of the child for an ego. That struggle is for the most part unobserved because it happens in the dark; but when we see how stubbornly childish illusions and assumptions and egoistic habits are still clung to in later years we can gain some idea of the energies that were needed to form them. And so it is with the ideals, convictions, guiding ideas and attitudes which in the period of youth lead us out into life, for which we struggle, suffer, and win victories: they grow together with our own being, we apparently change into them, we seek to perpetuate them indefinitely and as a matter of course, just as the young person asserts his ego in spite of the world and often in spite of himself.

772 The nearer we approach to the middle of life, and the better we have succeeded in entrenching ourselves in our personal attitudes and social positions, the more it appears as if we had discovered the right course and the right ideals and principles of behaviour. For this reason we suppose them to be eternally valid, and make a virtue of unchangeably clinging to them. We overlook the essential fact that the social goal is attained only at the cost of a diminution of personality. Many – far too many – aspects of life which should also have been experienced lie in the lumber-room among dusty memories; but sometimes, too, they are glowing coals under grey ashes.

773 Statistics show a rise in the frequency of mental depressions in men about forty. In women the neurotic difficulties generally begin somewhat earlier. We see that

in this phase of life – between thirty-five and forty – an important change in the human psyche is in preparation. At first it is not a conscious and striking change; it is rather a matter of indirect signs of a change which seems to take its rise in the unconscious. Often it is something like a slow change in a person's character; in another case certain traits may come to light which had disappeared since childhood; or again, one's previous inclinations and interests begin to weaken and others take their place. Conversely – and this happens very frequently – one's cherished convictions and principles, especially the moral ones, begin to harden and to grow increasingly rigid until, somewhere around the age of fifty, a period of intolerance and fanaticism is reached. It is as if the existence of these principles were endangered and it were therefore necessary to emphasize them all the more.

774 The wine of youth does not always clear with advancing years; sometimes it grows turbid. All the phenomena mentioned above can best be seen in rather one-sided people, turning up sometimes sooner and sometimes later. Their appearance, it seems to me, is often delayed by the fact that the parents of the person in question are still alive. It is then as if the period of youth were being unduly drawn out. I have seen this especially in the case of men whose fathers were long-lived. The death of the father then has the effect of a precipitate and almost catastrophic ripening.

775 I know of a pious man who was a churchwarden and who, from the age of forty onward, showed a growing and finally unbearable intolerance in matters of morality and religion. At the same time his moods grew visibly worse. At last he was nothing more than a darkly lowering pillar of the Church. In this way he got along until the age of fifty-five, when suddenly, sitting up in bed in the middle of the night, he said to his wife: 'Now at last I've got it! I'm just a plain rascal.' Nor did this realization remain without results. He spent his declining years in riotous living and squandered a goodly part of his fortune. Obviously quite a likable fellow, capable of both extremes!

776 The very frequent neurotic disturbances of adult years all have one thing in common: they want to carry the psychology of the youthful phase over the threshold of the so-called years of discretion. Who does not know those touching old gentlemen who must always warm up the dish of their student days, who can fan the flame of life only by reminiscences of their heroic youth, but who, for the rest, are stuck in a hopelessly wooden Philistinism? As a rule, to be sure, they have this one merit which it would be wrong to undervalue: they are not neurotic, but only boring and stereotyped. The neurotic is rather a person who can never have things as he would like them in the present, and who can therefore never enjoy the past either.

777 As formerly the neurotic could not escape from childhood, so now he cannot part with his youth. He shrinks from the grey thoughts of approaching age, and, feeling the prospect before him unbearable, is always straining to look behind him. Just as the childish person shrinks back from the unknown in the world and in human existence, so the grown man shrinks back from the second half of life.

It is as if unknown and dangerous tasks awaited him, or as if he were threatened with sacrifices and losses which he does not wish to accept, or as if his life up to now seemed to him so fair and precious that he could not relinquish it.

778   Is it perhaps at bottom the fear of death? That does not seem to me very probable, because as a rule death is still far in the distance and therefore somewhat abstract. Experience shows us, rather, that the basic cause of all the difficulties of this transition is to be found in a deep-seated and peculiar change within the psyche. In order to characterize it I must take for comparison the daily course of the sun – but a sun that is endowed with human feeling and man's limited consciousness. In the morning it rises from the nocturnal sea of unconsciousness and looks upon the wide, bright world which lies before it in an expanse that steadily widens the higher it climbs in the firmament. In this extension of its field of action caused by its own rising, the sun will discover its significance; it will see the attainment of the greatest possible height, and the widest possible dissemination of its blessings, as its goal. In this conviction the sun pursues its course to the unforeseen zenith – unforeseen, because its career is unique and individual, and the culminating point could not be calculated in advance. At the stroke of noon the descent begins. And the descent means the reversal of all the ideals and values that were cherished in the morning. The sun falls into contradiction with itself. It is as though it should draw in its rays instead of emitting them. Light and warmth decline and are at last extinguished.

779   All comparisons are lame, but this simile is at least not lamer than others. A French aphorism sums it up with cynical resignation: *Si jeunesse savait, si vieillesse pouvait.*

780   Fortunately we are not rising and setting suns, for then it would fare badly with our cultural values. But there is something sunlike within us, and to speak of the morning and spring, of the evening and autumn of life is not mere sentimental jargon. We thus give expression to psychological truths and, even more, to physiological facts, for the reversal of the sun at noon changes even bodily characteristics. Especially among southern races one can observe that older women develop deep, rough voices, incipient moustaches, rather hard features and other masculine traits. On the other hand the masculine physique is toned down by feminine features, such as adiposity and softer facial expressions.

781   There is an interesting report in the ethnological literature about an Indian warrior chief to whom in middle life the Great Spirit appeared in a dream. The spirit announced to him that from then on he must sit among the women and children, wear women's clothes, and eat the food of women. He obeyed the dream without suffering a loss of prestige. This vision is a true expression of the psychic revolution of life's noon, of the beginning of life's decline. Man's values, and even his body, do tend to change into their opposites.

782   We might compare masculinity and femininity and their psychic components to a definite store of substances of which, in the first half of life, unequal use is made. A man consumes his large supply of masculine substance and has left over only the smaller amount of feminine substance, which must now be put to use.

Conversely, the woman allows her hitherto unused supply of masculinity to become active.

783 This change is even more noticeable in the psychic realm than in the physical. How often it happens that a man of forty-five or fifty winds up his business, and the wife then dons the trousers and opens a little shop where he perhaps performs the duties of a handyman. There are many women who only awaken to social responsibility and to social consciousness after their fortieth year. In modern business life, especially in America, nervous breakdowns in the forties are a very common occurrence. If one examines the victims one finds that what has broken down is the masculine style of life which held the field up to now, and that what is left over is an effeminate man. Contrariwise, one can observe women in these self-same business spheres who have developed in the second half of life an uncommonly masculine tough-mindedness which thrusts the feelings and the heart aside. Very often these changes are accompanied by all sorts of catastrophes in marriage, for it is not hard to imagine what will happen when the husband discovers his tender feelings and the wife her sharpness of mind.

784 The worst of it all is that intelligent and cultivated people live their lives without even knowing of the possibility of such transformations. Wholly unprepared, they embark upon the second half of life. Or are there perhaps colleges for forty-year-olds which prepare them for their coming life and its demands as the ordinary colleges introduce our young people to a knowledge of the world? No, thoroughly unprepared we take the step into the afternoon of life; worse still, we take this step with the false assumption that our truths and ideals will serve us as hitherto. But we cannot live the afternoon of life according to the programme of life's morning; for what was great in the morning will be little at evening, and what in the morning was true will at evening have become a lie. I have given psychological treatment to too many people of advancing years, and have looked too often into the secret chambers of their souls, not to be moved by this fundamental truth.

785 Ageing people should know that their lives are not mounting and expanding, but that an inexorable inner process enforces the contraction of life. For a young person it is almost a sin, or at least a danger, to be too preoccupied with himself; but for the ageing person it is a duty and a necessity to devote serious attention to himself. After having lavished its light upon the world, the sun withdraws its rays in order to illuminate itself. Instead of doing likewise, many old people prefer to be hypochondriacs, niggards, pedants, applauders of the past or else eternal adolescents – all lamentable substitutes for the illumination of the self, but inevitable consequences of the delusion that the second half of life must be governed by the principles of the first.

786 I said just now that we have no schools for forty-year-olds. That is not quite true. Our religions were always such schools in the past, but how many people regard them like that today? How many of us older ones have been brought up in such a school and really prepared for the second half of life, for old age, death and eternity?

787 A human being would certainly not grow to be seventy or eighty years old if this longevity had no meaning for the species. The afternoon of human life must also have a significance of its own and cannot be merely a pitiful appendage to life's morning. The significance of the morning undoubtedly lies in the development of the individual, our entrenchment in the outer world, the propagation of our kind, and the care of our children. This is the obvious purpose of nature. But when this purpose has been attained – and more than attained – shall the earning of money, the extension of conquests, and the expansion of life go steadily on beyond the bounds of all reason and sense? Whoever carries over into the afternoon the law of the morning, or the natural aim, must pay for it with damage to his soul, just as surely as a growing youth who tries to carry over his childish egoism into adult life must pay for this mistake with social failure. Money-making, social achievement, family and posterity are nothing but plain nature, not culture. Culture lies outside the purpose of nature. Could by any chance culture be the meaning and purpose of the second half of life?

788 In primitive tribes we observe that the old people are almost always the guardians of the mysteries and the laws, and it is in these that the cultural heritage of the tribe is expressed. How does the matter stand with us? Where is the wisdom of our old people, where are their precious secrets and their visions? For the most part our old people try to compete with the young. In the United States it is almost an ideal for a father to be the brother of his sons, and for the mother to be if possible the younger sister of her daughter.

789 I do not know how much of this confusion is a reaction against an earlier exaggeration of the dignity of age, and how much is to be charged to false ideals. These undoubtedly exist, and the goal of those who hold them lies behind, and not ahead. Therefore they are always striving to turn back. We have to grant these people that it is hard to see what other goal the second half of life can offer than the well-known aims of the first. Expansion of life, usefulness, efficiency, the cutting of a figure in society, the shrewd steering of offspring into suitable marriages and good positions – are not these purposes enough? Unfortunately not enough meaning and purpose for those who see in the approach of old age a mere diminution of life and can feel their earlier ideals only as something faded and worn out. Of course, if these persons had filled up the beaker of life earlier and emptied it to the lees, they would feel quite differently about everything now; they would have kept nothing back, everything that wanted to catch fire would have been consumed, and the quiet of old age would be very welcome to them. But we must not forget that only a very few people are artists in life; that the art of life is the most distinguished and rarest of all the arts. Who ever succeeded in draining the whole cup with grace? So for many people all too much unlived life remains over – sometimes potentialities which they could never have lived with the best of wills, so that they approach the threshold of old age with unsatisfied demands which inevitably turn their glances backward.

790 It is particularly fatal for such people to look back. For them a prospect and a goal in the future are absolutely necessary. That is why all great religions hold out

the promise of a life beyond, of a supramundane goal which makes it possible for mortal man to live the second half of life with as much purpose and aim as the first. For the man of today the expansion of life and its culmination are plausible goals, but the idea of life after death seems to him questionable or beyond belief. Life's cessation, that is, death, can only be accepted as a reasonable goal either when existence is so wretched that we are only too glad for it to end, or when we are convinced that the sun strives to its setting 'to illuminate distant races' with the same logical consistency it showed in rising to the zenith. But to believe has become such a difficult art today that it is beyond the capacity of most people, particularly the educated part of humanity. They have become too accustomed to the thought that, with regard to immortality and such questions, there are innumerable contradictory opinions and no convincing proofs. And since 'science' is the catchword that seems to carry the weight of absolute conviction in the temporary world, we ask for 'scientific' proofs. But educated people who can think know very well that proof of this kind is a philosophical impossibility. We simply cannot know anything whatever about such things.

791   May I remark that for the same reasons we cannot know, either, whether something *does* happen to a person after death? No answer of any kind is permissible, either for or against. We simply have no definite scientific knowledge about it one way or the other, and are therefore in the same position as when we ask whether the planet Mars is inhabited or not. And the inhabitants of Mars, if there are any, are certainly not concerned whether we affirm or deny their existence. They may exist or they may not. And that is how it stands with so-called immortality – with which we may shelve the problem.

792   But here my medical conscience awakens and urges me to say a word which has an important bearing on this question. I have observed that a life directed to an aim is in general better, richer, and healthier than an aimless one, and that it is better to go forwards with the stream of time than backwards against it. To the psychotherapist an old man who cannot bid farewell to life appears as feeble and sickly as a young man who is unable to embrace it. And as a matter of fact, it is in many cases a question of the selfsame childish greediness, the same fear, the same defiance and wilfulness, in the one as in the other. As a doctor I am convinced that it is hygienic – if I may use the word – to discover in death a goal towards which one can strive, and that shrinking away from it is something unhealthy and abnormal, which robs the second half of life of its purpose. I therefore consider that all religions with a supramundane goal are eminently reasonable from the point of view of psychic hygiene. When I live in a house which I know will fall about my head within the next two weeks, all my vital functions will be impaired by this thought; but if on the contrary I feel myself to be safe, I can dwell there in a normal and comfortable way. From the standpoint of psychotherapy it would therefore be desirable to think of death as only a transition, as part of a life process whose extent and duration are beyond our knowledge.

793   In spite of the fact that the majority of people do not know why the body needs salt, everyone demands it nonetheless because of an instinctive need. It is the

same with the things of the psyche. By far the greater portion of mankind have from time immemorial felt the need of believing in a continuance of life. The demands of therapy, therefore, do not lead us into any bypaths but down the middle of the highway trodden by humanity. For this reason we are thinking correctly, and in harmony with life, even though we do not understand what we think.

794   Do we ever understand what we think? We only understand that kind of thinking which is a mere equation, from which nothing comes out but what we have put in. That is the working of the intellect. But besides that there is a thinking in primordial images, in symbols which are older than the historical man, which are inborn in him from the earliest times, and, eternally living, outlasting all generations, still make up the groundwork of the human psyche. It is only possible to live the fullest life when we are in harmony with these symbols; wisdom is a return to them. It is a question neither of belief nor of knowledge, but of the agreement of our thinking with the primordial images of the unconscious. They are the unthinkable matrices of all our thoughts, no matter what our conscious mind may cogitate. One of these primordial thoughts is the idea of life after death. Science and these primordial images are incommensurables. They are irrational data, *a priori* conditions of the imagination which are simply there, and whose purpose and justification science can only investigate *a posteriori*, much as it investigates a function like that of the thyroid gland. Before the nineteenth century the thyroid was regarded as a meaningless organ merely because it was not understood. It would be equally shortsighted of us today to call the primordial images senseless. For me these images are something like psychic organs, and I treat them with the very greatest respect. It happens sometimes that I must say to an older patient: 'Your picture of God or your idea of immortality is atrophied, consequently your psychic metabolism is out of gear.' The ancient *athanasias pharmakon,* the medicine of immortality, is more profound and meaningful than we supposed.

795   In conclusion I would like to come back for a moment to the comparison with the sun. The one hundred and eighty degrees of the arc of life are divisible into four parts. The first quarter, lying to the east, is childhood, that state in which we are a problem for others but are not yet conscious of any problems of our own. Conscious problems fill out the second and third quarters; while in the last, in extreme old age, we descend again into that condition where, regardless of our state of consciousness, we once more become something of a problem for others. Childhood and extreme old age are, of course, utterly different, and yet they have one thing in common: submersion in unconscious psychic happenings. Since the mind of a child grows out of the unconscious its psychic processes, though not easily accessible, are not as difficult to discern as those of a very old person who is sinking again into the unconscious, and who progressively vanishes within it. Childhood and old age are the stages of life without any conscious problems, for which reason I have not taken them into consideration here.

Note

1 [Originally published as 'Die seelischen Probleme der menschlichen Altersstufen,' *Neue Zürcher Zeitung*, March 14 and 16, 1930. Revised and largely rewritten, it was republished as 'Die Lebenswende,' *Seelenprobleme der Gegenwart* (Psychologische Abhandlungen, III; Zurich, 1931), which version was translated by W. S. Dell and Cary F. Baynes as 'The Stages of Life,' *Modern Man in Search of a Soul* (London and New York, 1933). The present translation is based on this. – EDITORS.]

Chapter 4

The relations between the ego and the unconscious[1]

PART I: THE EFFECTS OF THE UNCONSCIOUS UPON CONSCIOUSNESS

1 The personal and the collective unconscious

202 In Freud's view, as most people know, the contents of the unconscious are reducible to infantile tendencies which are repressed because of their incompatible character. Repression is a process that begins in early childhood under the moral influence of the environment and continues throughout life. By means of analysis the repressions are removed and the repressed wishes made conscious.

203 According to this theory, the unconscious contains only those parts of the personality which could just as well be conscious, and have been suppressed only through the process of education. Although from one point of view the infantile tendencies of the unconscious are the most conspicuous, it would nonetheless be a mistake to define or evaluate the unconscious entirely in these terms. The unconscious has still another side to it: it includes not only repressed contents, but all psychic material that lies below the threshold of consciousness. It is impossible to explain the subliminal nature of all this material on the principle of repression, for in that case the removal of repression ought to endow a person with a prodigious memory which would thenceforth forget nothing.

204 We therefore emphatically affirm that in addition to the repressed material the unconscious contains all those psychic components that have fallen below the threshold, as well as subliminal sense-perceptions. Moreover we know, from abundant experience as well as for theoretical reasons, that the unconscious also contains all the material that has *not yet* reached the threshold of consciousness. These are the seeds of future conscious contents. Equally we have reason to suppose that the unconscious is never quiescent in the sense of being inactive, but is ceaselessly engaged in grouping and regrouping its contents. This activity should be thought of as completely autonomous only in pathological cases; normally it is co-ordinated with the conscious mind in a compensatory relationship.

205 It is to be assumed that all these contents are of a personal nature in so far as they are acquired during the individual's life. Since this life is limited, the number

of acquired contents in the unconscious must also be limited. This being so, it might be thought possible to empty the unconscious either by analysis or by making a complete inventory of the unconscious contents, on the ground that the unconscious cannot produce anything more than what is already known and assimilated into consciousness. We should also have to suppose, as already said, that if one could arrest the descent of conscious contents into the unconscious by doing away with repression, unconscious productivity would be paralysed. This is possible only to a very limited extent, as we know from experience. We urge our patients to hold fast to repressed contents that have been re-associated with consciousness, and to assimilate them into their plan of life. But this procedure, as we may daily convince ourselves, makes no impression on the unconscious, since it calmly goes on producing dreams and fantasies which, according to Freud's original theory, must arise from personal repressions. If in such cases we pursue our observations systematically and without prejudice, we shall find material which, although similar in form to the previous personal contents, yet seems to contain allusions that go far beyond the personal sphere.

206   Casting about in my mind for an example to illustrate what I have just said, I have a particularly vivid memory of a woman patient with a mild hysterical neurosis which, as we expressed it in those days [about 1910], had its principal cause in a 'father-complex.' By this we wanted to denote the fact that the patient's peculiar relationship to her father stood in her way. She had been on very good terms with her father, who had since died. It was a relationship chiefly of feeling. In such cases it is usually the intellectual function that is developed, and this later becomes the bridge to the world. Accordingly our patient became a student of philosophy. Her energetic pursuit of knowledge was motivated by her need to extricate herself from the emotional entanglement with her father. This operation may succeed if her feelings can find an outlet on the new intellectual level, perhaps in the formation of an emotional tie with a suitable man, equivalent to the former tie. In this particular case, however, the transition refused to take place, because the patient's feelings remained suspended, oscillating between her father and a man who was not altogether suitable. The progress of her life was thus held up, and that inner disunity so characteristic of a neurosis promptly made its appearance. The so-called normal person would probably be able to break the emotional bond in one or the other direction by a powerful act of will, or else – and this is perhaps the more usual thing – he would come through the difficulty unconsciously, on the smooth path of instinct, without ever being aware of the sort of conflict that lay behind his headaches or other physical discomforts. But any weakness of instinct (which may have many causes) is enough to hinder a smooth unconscious transition. Then all progress is delayed by conflict, and the resulting stasis of life is equivalent to a neurosis. In consequence of the standstill, psychic energy flows off in every conceivable direction, apparently quite uselessly. For instance, there are excessive innervations of the sympathetic system, which lead to nervous disorders of the stomach and intestines; or the vagus (and consequently the heart) is stimulated; or fantasies and memories, uninteresting enough in

themselves, become overvalued and prey on the conscious mind (mountains out of molehills). In this state a new motive is needed to put an end to the morbid suspension. Nature herself paves the way for this, unconsciously and indirectly, through the phenomenon of the transference (Freud). In the course of treatment the patient transfers the father-imago to the doctor, thus making him, in a sense, the father, and in the sense that he is *not* the father, also making him a substitute for the man she cannot reach. The doctor therefore becomes both a father and a kind of lover – in other words, an object of conflict. In him the opposites are united, and for this reason he stands for a quasi-ideal solution of the conflict. Without in the least wishing it, he draws upon himself an over-valuation that is almost incredible to the outsider, for to the patient he seems like a saviour or a god. This way of speaking is not altogether so laughable as it sounds. It is indeed a bit much to be a father and lover at once. Nobody could possibly stand up to it in the long run, precisely because it is too much of a good thing. One would have to be a demigod at least to sustain such a role without a break, for all the time one would have to be the giver. To the patient in the state of transference, this provisional solution naturally seems ideal, but only at first; in the end she comes to a standstill that is just as bad as the neurotic conflict was. Fundamentally, nothing has yet happened that might lead to a real solution. The conflict has merely been transferred. Nevertheless a successful transference can – at least temporarily – cause the whole neurosis to disappear, and for this reason it has been very rightly recognized by Freud as a healing factor of first-rate importance, but, at the same time, as a provisional state only, for although it holds out the possibility of a cure, it is far from being the cure itself.

207   This somewhat lengthy discussion seemed to me essential if my example was to be understood, for my patient had arrived at the state of transference and had already reached the upper limit where the standstill begins to make itself disagreeable. The question now arose: what next? I had of course become the complete saviour, and the thought of having to give me up was not only exceedingly distasteful to the patient, but positively terrifying. In such a situation 'sound common sense' generally comes out with a whole repertory of admonitions: 'you simply must,' 'you really ought,' 'you just cannot,' etc. So far as sound common sense is, happily, not too rare and not entirely without effect (pessimists, I know, exist), a rational motive can, in the exuberant feeling of buoyancy you get from the transference, release so much enthusiasm that a painful sacrifice can be risked with a mighty effort of will. If successful – and these things sometimes are – the sacrifice bears blessed fruit, and the erstwhile patient leaps at one bound into the state of being practically cured. The doctor is generally so delighted that he fails to tackle the theoretical difficulties connected with this little miracle.

208   If the leap does not succeed – and it did not succeed with my patient – one is then faced with the problem of resolving the transference. Here 'psychoanalytic' theory shrouds itself in a thick darkness. Apparently we are to fall back on some nebulous trust in fate: somehow or other the matter will settle itself. 'The transference stops automatically when the patient runs out of money,' as a slightly cynical

colleague once remarked to me. Or the ineluctable demands of life make it impossible for the patient to linger on in the transference – demands which compel the involuntary sacrifice, sometimes with a more or less complete relapse as a result. (One may look in vain for accounts of such cases in the books that sing the praises of psychoanalysis!)

209 To be sure, there are hopeless cases where nothing helps; but there are also cases that do not get stuck and do not inevitably leave the transference situation with bitter hearts and sore heads. I told myself, at this juncture with my patient, that there must be a clear and respectable way out of the impasse. My patient had long since run out of money – if indeed she ever possessed any – but I was curious to know what means nature would devise for a satisfactory way out of the transference deadlock. Since I never imagined that I was blessed with that 'sound common sense' which always knows exactly what to do in every quandary, and since my patient knew as little as I, I suggested to her that we could at least keep an eye open for any movements coming from a sphere of the psyche uncontaminated by our superior wisdom and our conscious plannings. That meant first and foremost her dreams.

210 Dreams contain images and thought-associations which we do not create with conscious intent. They arise spontaneously without our assistance and are representatives of a psychic activity withdrawn from our arbitrary will. Therefore the dream is, properly speaking, a highly objective, natural product of the psyche, from which we might expect indications, or at least hints, about certain basic trends in the psychic process. Now, since the psychic process, like any other life-process, is not just a causal sequence, but is also a process with a teleological orientation, we might expect dreams to give us certain *indicia* about the objective causality as well as about the objective tendencies, precisely because dreams are nothing less than self-representations of the psychic life-process.

211 On the basis of these reflections, then, we subjected the dreams to a careful examination. It would lead too far to quote word for word all the dreams that now followed. Let it suffice to sketch their main character: the majority referred to the person of the doctor, that is to say, the actors were unmistakably the dreamer herself and her doctor. The latter, however, seldom appeared in his natural shape, but was generally distorted in a remarkable way. Sometimes his figure was of supernatural size, sometimes he seemed to be extremely aged, then again he resembled her father, but was at the same time curiously woven into nature, as in the following dream: *Her father (who in reality was of small stature) was standing with her on a hill that was covered with wheat-fields. She was quite tiny beside him, and he seemed to her like a giant. He lifted her up from the ground and held her in his arms like a little child. The wind swept over the wheat-fields, and as the wheat swayed in the wind, he rocked her in his arms.*

212 From this dream and from others like it I could discern various things. Above all I got the impression that her unconscious was holding unshakably to the idea of my being the father-lover, so that the fatal tie we were trying to undo appeared

to be doubly strengthened. Moreover one could hardly avoid seeing that the unconscious placed a special emphasis on the supernatural, almost 'divine' nature of the father-lover, thus accentuating still further the over-valuation occasioned by the transference. I therefore asked myself whether the patient had still not understood the wholly fantastic character of her transference, or whether perhaps the unconscious could never be reached by understanding at all, but must blindly and idiotically pursue some nonsensical chimera. Freud's idea that the unconscious can 'do nothing but wish,' Schopenhauer's blind and aimless Will, the gnostic demiurge who in his vanity deems himself perfect and then in the blindness of his limitation creates something lamentably imperfect – all these pessimistic suspicions of an essentially negative background to the world and the soul came threateningly near. And there would indeed be nothing to set against this except a well-meaning 'you ought,' reinforced by a stroke of the axe that would cut down the whole phantasmagoria for good and all.

213   But, as I turned the dreams over and over in my mind, there dawned on me another possibility. I said to myself: it cannot be denied that the dreams continue to speak in the same old metaphors with which our conversations have made the patient as well as myself sickeningly familiar. But the patient has an undoubted understanding of her transference fantasy. She knows that I appear to her as a semi-divine father-lover, and she can, at least intellectually, distinguish this from my factual reality. Therefore the dreams are obviously reiterating the conscious standpoint minus the conscious criticism, which they completely ignore. They reiterate the conscious contents, not *in toto*, but insist on the fantastic standpoint as opposed to 'sound common sense.'

214   I naturally asked myself what was the source of this obstinacy and what was its purpose? That it must have some purposive meaning I was convinced, for there is no truly living thing that does not have a final meaning, that can in other words be explained as a mere left-over from antecedent facts. But the energy of the transference is so strong that it gives one the impression of a vital instinct. That being so, what is the purpose of such fantasies? A careful examination and analysis of the dreams, especially of the one just quoted, revealed a very marked tendency – in contrast to conscious criticism, which always seeks to reduce things to human proportions – to endow the person of the doctor with superhuman attributes. He had to be gigantic, primordial, huger than the father, like the wind that sweeps over the earth – was he then to be made into a god? Or, I said to myself, was it rather the case that the unconscious was trying to *create* a god out of the person of the doctor, as it were to free a vision of God from the veils of the personal, so that the transference to the person of the doctor was no more than a misunderstanding on the part of the conscious mind, a stupid trick played by 'sound common sense'? Was the urge of the unconscious perhaps only apparently reaching out towards the person, but in a deeper sense towards a god? Could the longing for a god be a *passion* welling up from our darkest, instinctual nature, a passion unswayed by any outside influences, deeper and stronger perhaps than the love for a human person? Or was it perhaps the highest and truest meaning of that inappropriate

love we call 'transference,' a little bit of real *Gottesminne*, that has been lost to consciousness ever since the fifteenth century?

215 No one will doubt the reality of a passionate longing for a human person; but that a fragment of religious psychology, an historical anachronism, indeed something of a medieval curiosity – we are reminded of Mechtild of Magdeburg – should come to light as an immediate living reality in the middle of the consulting-room, and be expressed in the prosaic figure of the doctor, seems almost too fantastic to be taken seriously.

216 A genuinely scientific attitude must be unprejudiced. The sole criterion for the validity of an hypothesis is whether or not it possesses an heuristic – i.e., explanatory – value. The question now is, can we regard the possibilities set forth above as a valid hypothesis? There is no *a priori* reason why it should not be just as possible that the unconscious tendencies have a goal beyond the human person, as that the unconscious can 'do nothing but wish.' Experience alone can decide which is the more suitable hypothesis. This new hypothesis was not entirely plausible to my very critical patient. The earlier view that I was the father-lover, and as such presented an ideal solution of the conflict, was incomparably more attractive to her way of feeling. Nevertheless her intellect was sufficiently keen to appreciate the theoretical possibility of the new hypothesis. Meanwhile the dreams continued to disintegrate the person of the doctor and swell him to ever vaster proportions. Concurrently with this there now occurred something which at first I alone perceived, and with the utmost astonishment, namely a kind of subterranean undermining of the transference. Her relations with a certain friend deepened perceptibly, notwithstanding the fact that consciously she still clung to the transference. So that when the time came for leaving me, it was no catastrophe, but a perfectly reasonable parting. I had the privilege of being the only witness during the process of severance. I saw how the transpersonal control-point developed – I cannot call it anything else – a *guiding function* and step by step gathered to itself all the former personal over-valuations; how, with this afflux of energy, it gained influence over the resisting conscious mind without the patient's consciously noticing what was happening. From this I realized that the dreams were not just fantasies, but self-representations of unconscious developments which allowed the psyche of the patient gradually to grow out of the pointless personal tie.[2]

217 This change took place, as I showed, through the unconscious development of a transpersonal control-point; a virtual goal, as it were, that expressed itself symbolically in a form which can only be described as a vision of God. The dreams swelled the human person of the doctor to superhuman proportions, making him a gigantic primordial father who is at the same time the wind, and in whose protecting arms the dreamer rests like an infant. If we try to make the patient's conscious, and traditionally Christian, idea of God responsible for the divine image in the dreams, we would still have to lay stress on the distortion. In religious matters the patient had a critical and agnostic attitude, and her idea of a possible deity had long since passed into the realm of the inconceivable, i.e., had dwindled into a complete abstraction. In contrast to this, the god-image of the

dreams corresponded to the archaic conception of a nature-daemon, something like Wotan. θεὸς τὸ πνεῦμα, 'God is spirit,' is here translated back into its original form where πνεῦμα means 'wind': God is the wind, stronger and mightier than man, an invisible breath-spirit. As in Hebrew *ruah*, so in Arabic *ruh* means breath and spirit.[3] Out of the purely personal form the dreams develop an archaic god-image that is infinitely far from the conscious idea of God. It might be objected that this is simply an infantile image, a childhood memory. I would have no quarrel with this assumption if we were dealing with an old man sitting on a golden throne in heaven. But there is no trace of any sentimentality of that kind; instead, we have a primordial idea that can correspond only to an archaic mentality.

218 These primordial ideas, of which I have given a great many examples in my *Symbols of Transformation*, oblige one to make, in regard to unconscious material, a distinction of quite a different character from that between 'preconscious' and 'unconscious' or 'subconscious' and 'unconscious.' The justification for these distinctions need not be discussed here. They have their specific value and are worth elaborating further as points of view. The fundamental distinction which experience has forced upon me claims to be no more than that. It should be evident from the foregoing that we have to distinguish in the unconscious a layer which we may call the *personal unconscious*. The materials contained in this layer are of a personal nature in so far as they have the character partly of acquisitions derived from the individual's life and partly of psychological factors which could just as well be conscious. It can readily be understood that incompatible psychological elements are liable to repression and therefore become unconscious. But on the other hand this implies the possibility of making and keeping the repressed contents conscious once they have been recognized. We recognize them as personal contents because their effects, or their partial manifestation, or their source can be discovered in our personal past. They are the integral components of the personality, they belong to its inventory, and their loss to consciousness produces an inferiority in one respect or another – an inferiority, moreover, that has the psychological character not so much of an organic lesion or an inborn defect as of a lack which gives rise to a feeling of moral resentment. The sense of moral inferiority always indicates that the missing element is something which, to judge by this feeling about it, really ought not be missing, or which could be made conscious if only one took sufficient trouble. The moral inferiority does not come from a collision with the generally accepted and, in a sense, arbitrary moral law, but from the conflict with one's own self which, for reasons of psychic equilibrium, demands that the deficit be redressed. Whenever a sense of moral inferiority appears, it indicates not only a need to assimilate an unconscious component, but also the possibility of such assimilation. In the last resort it is a man's moral qualities which force him, either through direct recognition of the need or indirectly through a painful neurosis, to assimilate his unconscious self and to keep himself fully conscious. Whoever progresses along this road of self-realization must inevitably bring into consciousness the contents of the personal unconscious, thus enlarging the scope of his personality. I should add at once that this enlargement

has to do primarily with one's moral consciousness, one's knowledge of oneself, for the unconscious contents that are released and brought into consciousness by analysis are usually unpleasant – which is precisely why these wishes, memories, tendencies, plans, etc. were repressed. These are the contents that are brought to light in much the same way by a thorough confession, though to a much more limited extent. The rest comes out as a rule in dream analysis. It is often very interesting to watch how the dreams fetch up the essential points, bit by bit and with the nicest choice. The total material that is added to consciousness causes a considerable widening of the horizon, a deepened self-knowledge which, more than anything else, one would think, is calculated to humanize a man and make him modest. But even self-knowledge, assumed by all wise men to be the best and most efficacious, has different effects on different characters. We make very remarkable discoveries in this respect in practical analysis, but I shall deal with this question in the next chapter.

219   As my example of the archaic idea of God shows, the unconscious seems to contain other things besides personal acquisitions and belongings. My patient was quite unconscious of the derivation of 'spirit' from 'wind,' or of the parallelism between the two. This content was not the product of her thinking, nor had she ever been taught it. The critical passage in the New Testament was inaccessible to her – τὸ πνεῦμα, πνεῖ ὅπου θέλει – since she knew no Greek. If we must take it as a wholly personal acquisition, it might be a case of so-called cryptomnesia,[4] the unconscious recollection of a thought which the dreamer had once read somewhere. I have nothing against such a possibility in this particular case; but I have seen a sufficient number of other cases – many of them are to be found in the book mentioned above – where cryptomnesia can be excluded with certainty. Even if it were a case of cryptomnesia, which seems to me very improbable, we should still have to explain what the predisposition was that caused just this image to be retained and later, as Semon puts it, 'ecphorated' (ἐψορεῖν, Latin *efferre*, 'to produce'). In any case, cryptomnesia or no cryptomnesia, we are dealing with a genuine and thoroughly primitive god-image that grew up in the unconscious of a civilized person and produced a living effect – an effect which might well give the psychologist of religion food for reflection. There is nothing about this image that could be called personal: it is a wholly collective image, the ethnic origin of which has long been known to us. Here is an historical image of world-wide distribution that has come into existence again through a natural psychic function. This is not so very surprising, since my patient was born into the world with a human brain which presumably still functions today much as it did of old. We are dealing with a reactivated *archetype*, as I have elsewhere called these primordial images.[5] These ancient images are restored to life by the primitive, analogical mode of thinking peculiar to dreams. It is not a question of inherited ideas, but of inherited thought-patterns.[6]

220   In view of these facts we must assume that the unconscious contains not only personal, but also impersonal collective components in the form of inherited categories[7] or archetypes. I have therefore advanced the hypothesis that at its deeper

levels the unconscious possesses collective contents in a relatively active state. That is why I speak of a collective unconscious.

II Phenomena resulting from the assimilation of the unconscious

221 The process of assimilating the unconscious leads to some very remarkable phenomena. It produces in some patients an unmistakable and often unpleasant increase of self-confidence and conceit: they are full of themselves, they know everything, they imagine themselves to be fully informed of everything concerning their unconscious, and are persuaded that they understand perfectly everything that comes out of it. At every interview with the doctor they get more and more above themselves. Others on the contrary feel themselves more and more crushed under the contents of the unconscious, they lose their self-confidence and abandon themselves with dull resignation to all the extraordinary things that the unconscious produces. The former, overflowing with feelings of their own importance, assume a responsibility for the unconscious that goes much too far, beyond all reasonable bounds; the others finally give up all sense of responsibility, overcome by a sense of the powerlessness of the ego against the fate working through the unconscious.

222 If we analyse these two modes of reaction more deeply, we find that the optimistic self-confidence of the first conceals a profound sense of impotence, for which their conscious optimism acts as an unsuccessful compensation; while the pessimistic resignation of the others masks a defiant will to power, far surpassing in cocksureness the conscious optimism of the first type.

223 With these two modes of reaction I have sketched only two crude extremes. A finer shading would have been truer to reality. As I have said elsewhere, every analysand starts by unconsciously misusing his newly won knowledge in the interests of his abnormal, neurotic attitude, unless he is sufficiently freed from his symptoms in the early stages to be able to dispense with further treatment altogether. A very important contributory factor is that in the early stages everything is still understood on the objective level, i.e., without distinction between imago and object, so that everything is referred directly to the object. Hence the man for whom 'other people' are the objects of prime importance will conclude from any self-knowledge he may have imbibed at this stage of the analysis: 'Aha! so that is what other people are like!' He will therefore feel it his duty, according to his nature, tolerant or otherwise, to enlighten the world. But the other man, who feels himself to be more the object of his fellows than their subject, will be weighed down by this self-knowledge and become correspondingly depressed. (I am naturally leaving out of account those numerous and more superficial natures who experience these problems only by the way.) In both cases the relation to the object is reinforced – in the first case in an active, in the second case in a reactive sense. The collective element is markedly accentuated. The one extends the sphere of his action, the other the sphere of his suffering.

224 Adler has employed the term 'godlikeness' to characterize certain basic features

of neurotic power psychology. If I likewise borrow the same term from *Faust*, I use it here more in the sense of that well-known passage where Mephisto writes 'Eritis sicut Deus, scientes bonum et malum' in the student's album, and makes the following aside:

> Just follow the old advice
> And my cousin the snake.
> There'll come a time when your godlikeness
> Will make you quiver and quake.[8]

The godlikeness evidently refers to knowledge, the knowledge of good and evil. The analysis and conscious realization of unconscious contents engender a certain superior tolerance, thanks to which even relatively indigestible portions of one's unconscious characterology can be accepted. This tolerance may look very wise and superior, but often it is no more than a grand gesture that brings all sorts of consequences in its train. Two spheres have been brought together which before were kept anxiously apart. After considerable resistances have been overcome, the union of opposites is successfully achieved, at least to all appearances. The deeper understanding thus gained, the juxtaposition of what was before separated, and hence the apparent overcoming of the moral conflict, give rise to a feeling of superiority that may well be expressed by the term 'godlikeness.' But this same juxtaposition of good and evil can have a very different effect on a different kind of temperament. Not everyone will feel himself a superman, holding in his hands the scales of good and evil. It may also seem as though he were a helpless object caught between hammer and anvil; not in the least a Hercules at the parting of the ways, but rather a rudderless ship buffeted between Scylla and Charybdis. For without knowing it, he is caught up in perhaps the greatest and most ancient of human conflicts, experiencing the throes of eternal principles in collision. Well might he feel himself like a Prometheus chained to the Caucasus, or as one crucified. This would be a 'godlikeness' in suffering. Godlikeness is certainly not a scientific concept, although it aptly characterizes the psychological state in question. Nor do I imagine that every reader will immediately grasp the peculiar state of mind implied by 'godlikeness.' The term belongs too exclusively to the sphere of *belles-lettres*. So I should probably be better advised to give a more circumspect description of this state. The insight and understanding, then, gained by the analysand usually reveal much to him that was before unconscious. He naturally applies this knowledge to his environment; in consequence he sees, or thinks he sees, many things that before were invisible. Since his knowledge was helpful to him, he readily assumes that it would be useful also to others. In this way he is liable to become arrogant; it may be well meant, but it is nonetheless annoying to other people. He feels as though he possesses a key that opens many, perhaps even all, doors. Psychoanalysis itself has this same bland unconsciousness of its limitations, as can clearly be seen from the way it meddles with works of art.

225   Since human nature is not compounded wholly of light, but also abounds in

shadows, the insight gained in practical analysis is often somewhat painful, the more so if, as is generally the case, one has previously neglected the other side. Hence there are people who take their newly won insight very much to heart, far too much in fact, quite forgetting that they are not unique in having a shadow-side. They allow themselves to get unduly depressed and are then inclined to doubt everything, finding nothing right anywhere. That is why many excellent analysts with very good ideas can never bring themselves to publish them, because the psychic problem, as they see it, is so overwhelmingly vast that it seems to them almost impossible to tackle it scientifically. One man's optimism makes him overweening, while another's pessimism makes him over-anxious and despondent. Such are the forms which the great conflict takes when reduced to a smaller scale. But even in these lesser proportions the essence of the conflict is easily recognized: the arrogance of the one and the despondency of the other share a common uncertainty as to their boundaries. The one is excessively expanded, the other excessively contracted. Their individual boundaries are in some way obliterated. If we now consider the fact that, as a result of psychic compensation, great humility stands very close to pride, and that 'pride goeth before a fall,' we can easily discover behind the haughtiness certain traits of an anxious sense of inferiority. In fact we shall see clearly how his uncertainty forces the enthusiast to puff up his truths, of which he feels none too sure, and to win proselytes to his side in order that his followers may prove to himself the value and trustworthiness of his own convictions. Nor is he altogether so happy in his fund of knowledge as to be able to hold out alone; at bottom he feels isolated by it, and the secret fear of being left alone with it induces him to trot out his opinions and interpretations in and out of season, because only when convincing someone else does he feel safe from gnawing doubts.

226   It is just the reverse with our despondent friend. The more he withdraws and hides himself, the greater becomes his secret need to be understood and recognized. Although he speaks of his inferiority he does not really believe it. There arises within him a defiant conviction of his unrecognized merits, and in consequence he is sensitive to the slightest disapprobation, always wearing the stricken air of one who is misunderstood and deprived of his rightful due. In this way he nurses a morbid pride and an insolent discontent – which is the very last thing he wants and for which his environment has to pay all the more dearly.

227   Both are at once too small and too big; their individual mean, never very secure, now becomes shakier than ever. It sounds almost grotesque to describe such a state as 'godlike.' But since each in his way steps beyond his human proportions, both of them are a little 'superhuman' and therefore, figuratively speaking, godlike. If we wish to avoid the use of this metaphor, I would suggest that we speak instead of 'psychic inflation.' The term seems to me appropriate in so far as the state we are discussing involves an extension of the personality beyond individual limits, in other words, a state of being puffed up. In such a state a man fills a space which normally he cannot fill. He can only fill it by appropriating to himself contents and qualities which properly exist for themselves alone and

should therefore remain outside our bounds. What lies outside ourselves belongs either to someone else, or to everyone, or to no one. Since psychic inflation is by no means a phenomenon induced exclusively by analysis, but occurs just as often in ordinary life, we can investigate it equally well in other cases. A very common instance is the humourless way in which many men identify themselves with their business or their titles. The office I hold is certainly my special activity; but it is also a collective factor that has come into existence historically through the cooperation of many people and whose dignity rests solely on collective approval. When, therefore, I identify myself with my office or title, I behave as though I myself were the whole complex of social factors of which that office consists, or as though I were not only the bearer of the office, but also and at the same time the approval of society. I have made an extraordinary extension of myself and have usurped qualities which are not in me but outside me. *L'état c'est moi* is the motto for such people.

228 In the case of inflation through knowledge we are dealing with something similar in principle, though psychologically more subtle. Here it is not the dignity of an office that causes the inflation, but very significant fantasies. I will explain what I mean by a practical example, choosing a mental case whom I happened to know personally and who is also mentioned in a publication by Maeder.[9] The case is characterized by a high degree of inflation. (In mental cases we can observe all the phenomena that are present only fleetingly in normal people, in a cruder and enlarged form.)[10] The patient suffered from paranoid dementia with megalomania. He was in telephonic communication with the Mother of God and other great ones. In human reality he was a wretched locksmith's apprentice who at the age of nineteen had become incurably insane. He had never been blessed with intelligence, but he had, among other things, hit upon the magnificent idea that the world was his picture-book, the pages of which he could turn at will. The proof was quite simple: he had only to turn round, and there was a new page for him to see.

229 This is Schopenhauer's 'world as will and idea' in unadorned, primitive concreteness of vision. A shattering idea indeed, born of extreme alienation and seclusion from the world, but so naïvely and simply expressed that at first one can only smile at the grotesqueness of it. And yet this primitive way of looking lies at the very heart of Schopenhauer's brilliant vision of the world. Only a genius or a madman could so disentangle himself from the bonds of reality as to see the world as his picture-book. Did the patient actually work out or build up such a vision, or did it just befall him? Or did he perhaps fall into it? His pathological disintegration and inflation point rather to the latter. It is no longer *he* that thinks and speaks, but *it* thinks and speaks within him: he hears voices. So the difference between him and Schopenhauer is that, in him, the vision remained at the stage of a mere spontaneous growth, while Schopenhauer abstracted it and expressed it in language of universal validity. In so doing he raised it out of its subterranean beginnings into the clear light of collective consciousness. But it would be quite wrong to suppose that the patient's vision had a purely personal character or

Relations between ego and unconscious | 105

value, as though it were something that belonged to him. If that were so, he would be a philosopher. A man is a philosopher of genius only when he succeeds in transmuting the primitive and merely natural vision into an abstract idea belonging to the common stock of consciousness. This achievement, and this alone, constitutes his personal value, for which he may take credit without necessarily succumbing to inflation. But the sick man's vision is an impersonal value, a natural growth against which he is powerless to defend himself, by which he is actually swallowed up and 'wafted' clean out of the world. Far from *his* mastering the idea and expanding *it* into a philosophical view of the world, it is truer to say that the undoubted grandeur of his vision blew *him* up to pathological proportions. The personal value lies entirely in the philosophical achievement, not in the primary vision. To the philosopher as well this vision comes as so much increment, and is simply a part of the common property of mankind, in which, in principle, everyone has a share. The golden apples drop from the same tree, whether they be gathered by an imbecile locksmith's apprentice or by a Schopenhauer.

230   There is, however, yet another thing to be learnt from this example, namely that these transpersonal contents are not just inert or dead matter that can be annexed at will. Rather they are living entities which exert an attractive force upon the conscious mind. Identification with one's office or one's title is very attractive indeed, which is precisely why so many men are nothing more than the decorum accorded to them by society. In vain would one look for a personality behind the husk. Underneath all the padding one would find a very pitiable little creature. That is why the office – or whatever this outer husk may be – is so attractive: it offers easy compensation for personal deficiencies.

231   Outer attractions, such as offices, titles, and other social regalia are not the only things that cause inflation. These are simply impersonal quantities that lie outside in society, in the collective consciousness. But just as there is a society outside the individual, so there is a collective psyche outside the personal psyche, namely the collective unconscious, concealing, as the above example shows, elements that are no whit less attractive. And just as a man may suddenly step into the world on his professional dignity ('Messieurs, à présent je suis Roy'), so another may disappear out of it equally suddenly when it is his lot to behold one of those mighty images that put a new face upon the world. These are the magical *représentations collectives* which underlie the slogan, the catchword, and, on a higher level, the language of the poet and mystic. I am reminded of another mental case who was neither a poet nor anything very outstanding, just a naturally quiet and rather sentimental youth. He had fallen in love with a girl and, as so often happens, had failed to ascertain whether his love was requited. His primitive *participation mystique* took it for granted that his agitations were plainly the agitations of the other, which on the lower levels of human psychology is naturally very often the case. Thus he built up a sentimental love-fantasy which precipitately collapsed when he discovered that the girl would have none of him. He was so desperate that he went straight to the river to drown himself. It was late at night, and the stars gleamed up at him from the dark water. It seemed to him that the stars were

swimming two by two down the river, and a wonderful feeling came over him. He forgot his suicidal intentions and gazed fascinated at the strange, sweet drama. And gradually he became aware that every star was a face, and that all these pairs were lovers, who were carried along locked in a dreaming embrace. An entirely new understanding came to him: all had changed – his fate, his disappointment, even his love, receded and fell away. The memory of the girl grew distant, blurred; but instead, he felt with complete certainty that untold riches were promised him. He knew that an immense treasure lay hidden for him in the neighbouring observatory. The result was that he was arrested by the police at four o'clock in the morning, attempting to break into the observatory.

232   What had happened? His poor head had glimpsed a Dantesque vision, whose loveliness he could never have grasped had he read it in a poem. But he saw it, and it transformed him. What had hurt him most was now far away; a new and undreamed of world of stars, tracing their silent courses far beyond this grievous earth, had opened out to him the moment he crossed 'Proserpine's threshold.' The intuition of untold wealth – and could any fail to be touched by this thought? – came to him like a revelation. For his poor turnip-head it was too much. He did not drown in the river, but in an eternal image, and its beauty perished with him.

233   Just as one man may disappear in his social role, so another may be engulfed in an inner vision and be lost to his surroundings. Many fathomless transformations of personality, like sudden conversions and other far-reaching changes of mind, originate in the attractive power of a collective image,[11] which, as the present example shows, can cause such a high degree of inflation that the entire personality is disintegrated. This disintegration is a mental disease, of a transitory or a permanent nature, a 'splitting of the mind' or 'schizophrenia,' in Bleuler's term.[12] The pathological inflation naturally depends on some innate weakness of the personality against the autonomy of collective unconscious contents.

234   We shall probably get nearest to the truth if we think of the conscious and personal psyche as resting upon the broad basis of an inherited and universal psychic disposition which is as such unconscious, and that our personal psyche bears the same relation to the collective psyche as the individual to society.

235   But equally, just as the individual is not merely a unique and separate being, but is also a social being, so the human psyche is not a self-contained and wholly individual phenomenon, but also a collective one. And just as certain social functions or instincts are opposed to the interests of single individuals, so the human psyche exhibits certain functions or tendencies which, on account of their collective nature, are opposed to individual needs. The reason for this is that every man is born with a highly differentiated brain and is thus assured of a wide range of mental functioning which is neither developed ontogenetically nor acquired. But, to the degree that human brains are uniformly differentiated, the mental functioning thereby made possible is also collective and universal. This explains, for example, the interesting fact that the unconscious processes of the most widely separated peoples and races show a quite remarkable correspondence, which displays itself, among other things, in the extraordinary but well-authenticated

analogies between the forms and motifs of autochthonous myths. The universal similarity of human brains leads to the universal possibility of a uniform mental functioning. This functioning is the *collective psyche.* Inasmuch as there are differentiations corresponding to race, tribe, and even family, there is also a collective psyche limited to race, tribe, and family over and above the 'universal' collective psyche. To borrow an expression from Pierre Janet,[13] the collective psyche comprises the *parties inférieures* of the psychic functions, that is to say those deep-rooted, well-nigh automatic portions of the individual psyche which are inherited and are to be found everywhere, and are thus impersonal or suprapersonal. Consciousness plus the personal unconscious constitutes the *parties supérieures* of the psychic functions, those portions, therefore, that are developed ontogenetically and acquired. Consequently, the individual who annexes the unconscious heritage of the collective psyche to what has accrued to him in the course of his ontogenetic development, as though it were part of the latter, enlarges the scope of his personality in an illegitimate way and suffers the consequences. In so far as the collective psyche comprises the *parties inférieures* of the psychic functions and thus forms the basis of every personality, it has the effect of crushing and devaluing the personality. This shows itself either in the aforementioned stifling of self-confidence or else in an unconscious heightening of the ego's importance to the point of a pathological will to power.

236   By raising the personal unconscious to consciousness, the analysis makes the subject aware of things which he is generally aware of in others, but never in himself. This discovery makes him therefore less individually unique, and more collective. His collectivization is not always a step to the bad; it may sometimes be a step to the good. There are people who repress their good qualities and consciously give free rein to their infantile desires. The lifting of personal repressions at first brings purely personal contents into consciousness; but attached to them are the collective elements of the unconscious, the ever-present instincts, qualities, and ideas (images) as well as all those 'statistical' quotas of average virtue and average vice which we recognize when we say, 'Everyone has in him something of the criminal, the genius, and the saint.' Thus a living picture emerges, containing pretty well everything that moves upon the checkerboard of the world, the good and the bad, the fair and the foul. A sense of solidarity with the world is gradually built up, which is felt by many natures as something very positive and in certain cases actually is the deciding factor in the treatment of neurosis. I have myself seen cases who, in this condition, managed for the first time in their lives to arouse love, and even to experience it themselves; or, by daring to leap into the unknown, they get involved in the very fate for which they were suited. I have seen not a few who, taking this condition as final, remained for years in a state of enterprising euphoria. I have often heard such cases referred to as shining examples of analytical therapy. But I must point out that cases of this euphoric and enterprising type are so utterly lacking in differentiation from the world that nobody could pass them as fundamentally cured. To my way of thinking they are as much cured as not cured. I have had occasion to follow up the lives of such

patients, and it must be owned that many of them showed symptoms of maladjustment, which, if persisted in, gradually leads to the sterility and monotony so characteristic of those who have divested themselves of their egos. Here too I am speaking of the borderline cases, and not of the less valuable, normal, average folk for whom the question of adaptation is more technical than problematical. If I were more of a therapist than an investigator, I would naturally be unable to check a certain optimism of judgment, because my eyes would then be glued to the number of cures. But my conscience as an investigator is concerned not with quantity but with quality. Nature is aristocratic, and one person of value outweighs ten lesser ones. My eye followed the valuable people, and from them I learned the dubiousness of the results of a purely personal analysis, and also to understand the reasons for this dubiousness.

237   If, through assimilation of the unconscious, we make the mistake of including the collective psyche in the inventory of personal psychic functions, a dissolution of the personality into its paired opposites inevitably follows. Besides the pair of opposites already discussed, megalomania and the sense of inferiority, which are so painfully evident in neurosis, there are many others, from which I will single out only the specifically moral pair of opposites, namely good and evil. The specific virtues and vices of humanity are contained in the collective psyche like everything else. One man arrogates collective virtue to himself as his personal merit, another takes collective vice as his personal guilt. Both are as illusory as the megalomania and the inferiority, because the imaginary virtues and the imaginary wickednesses are simply the moral pair of opposites contained in the collective psyche, which have become perceptible or have been rendered conscious artificially. How much these paired opposites are contained in the collective psyche is exemplified by primitives: one observer will extol the greatest virtues in them, while another will record the very worst impressions of the selfsame tribe. For the primitive, whose personal differentiation is, as we know, only just beginning, both judgments are true, because his psyche is essentially collective and therefore for the most part unconscious. He is still more or less identical with the collective psyche, and for that reason shares equally in the collective virtues and vices, without any personal attribution and without inner contradiction. The contradiction arises only when the personal development of the psyche begins, and when reason discovers the irreconcilable nature of the opposites. The consequence of this discovery is the conflict of repression. We want to be good, and therefore must repress evil; and with that the paradise of the collective psyche comes to an end. Repression of the collective psyche was absolutely necessary for the development of personality. In primitives, development of personality, or more accurately, development of the person, is a question of magical prestige. The figure of the medicine-man or chief leads the way: both make themselves conspicuous by the singularity of their ornaments and their mode of life, expressive of their social roles. The singularity of his outward tokens marks the individual off from the rest, and the segregation is still further enhanced by the possession of special ritual secrets. By these and similar means the primitive creates around him a shell,

which might be called a persona (mask). Masks, as we know, are actually used among primitives in totem ceremonies – for instance, as a means of enhancing or changing the personality. In this way the outstanding individual is apparently removed from the sphere of the collective psyche, and to the degree that he succeeds in identifying himself with his persona, he actually is removed. This removal means magical prestige. One could easily assert that the impelling motive in this development is the will to power. But that would be to forget that the building up of prestige is always a product of collective compromise: not only must there be one who wants prestige, there must also be a public seeking somebody on whom to confer prestige. That being so, it would be incorrect to say that a man creates prestige for himself out of his individual will to power; it is on the contrary an entirely collective affair. Since society as a whole needs the magically effective figure, it uses this need of the will to power in the individual, and the will to submit in the mass, as a vehicle, and thus brings about the creation of personal prestige. The latter is a phenomenon which, as the history of political institutions shows, is of the utmost importance for the comity of nations.

238   The importance of personal prestige can hardly be overestimated, because the possibility of regressive dissolution in the collective psyche is a very real danger, not only for the outstanding individual but also for his followers. This possibility is most likely to occur when the goal of prestige – universal recognition – has been reached. The person then becomes a collective truth, and that is always the beginning of the end. To gain prestige is a positive achievement not only for the outstanding individual but also for the clan. The individual distinguishes himself by his deeds, the many by their renunciation of power. So long as this attitude needs to be fought for and defended against hostile influences, the achievement remains positive; but as soon as there are no more obstacles and universal recognition has been attained, prestige loses its positive value and usually becomes a dead letter. A schismatic movement then sets in, and the whole process begins again from the beginning.

239   Because personality is of such paramount importance for the life of the community, everything likely to disturb its development is sensed as a danger. But the greatest danger of all is the premature dissolution of prestige by an invasion of the collective psyche. Absolute secrecy is one of the best known primitive means of exorcising this danger. Collective thinking and feeling and collective effort are far less of a strain than individual functioning and effort; hence there is always a great temptation to allow collective functioning to take the place of individual differentiation of the personality. Once the personality has been differentiated and safeguarded by magical prestige, its levelling down and eventual dissolution in the collective psyche (e.g., Peter's denial) occasion a 'loss of soul' in the individual, because an important personal achievement has been either neglected or allowed to slip into regression. For this reason taboo infringements are followed by Draconian punishments altogether in keeping with the seriousness of the situation. So long as we regard these things from the causal point of view, as mere historical survivals and metastases of the incest taboo,[14] it is impossible to

understand what all these measures are for. If, however, we approach the problem from the teleological point of view, much that was quite inexplicable becomes clear.

240   For the development of personality, then, strict differentiation from the collective psyche is absolutely necessary, since partial or blurred differentiation leads to an immediate melting away of the individual in the collective. There is now a danger that in the analysis of the unconscious the collective and the personal psyche may be fused together, with, as I have intimated, highly unfortunate results. These results are injurious both to the patient's life-feeling and to his fellow men, if he has any influence at all on his environment. Through his identification with the collective psyche he will infallibly try to force the demands of his unconscious upon others, for identity with the collective psyche always brings with it a feeling of universal validity – 'godlikeness' – which completely ignores all differences in the personal psyche of his fellows. (The feeling of universal validity comes, of course, from the universality of the collective psyche.) A collective attitude naturally presupposes this same collective psyche in others. But that means a ruthless disregard not only of individual differences but also of differences of a more general kind within the collective psyche itself, as for example differences of race.[15] This disregard for individuality obviously means the suffocation of the single individual, as a consequence of which the element of differentiation is obliterated from the community. The element of differentiation is the individual. All the highest achievements of virtue, as well as the blackest villainies, are individual. The larger a community is, and the more the sum total of collective factors peculiar to every large community rests on conservative prejudices detrimental to individuality, the more will the individual be morally and spiritually crushed, and, as a result, the one source of moral and spiritual progress for society is choked up. Naturally the only thing that can thrive in such an atmosphere is sociality and whatever is collective in the individual. Everything individual in him goes under, i.e., is doomed to repression. The individual elements lapse into the unconscious, where, by the law of necessity, they are transformed into something essentially baleful, destructive, and anarchical. Socially, this evil principle shows itself in the spectacular crimes – regicide and the like – perpetrated by certain prophetically-inclined individuals; but in the great mass of the community it remains in the background, and only manifests itself indirectly in the inexorable moral degeneration of society. It is a notorious fact that the morality of society as a whole is in inverse ratio to its size; for the greater the aggregation of individuals, the more the individual factors are blotted out, and with them morality, which rests entirely on the moral sense of the individual and the freedom necessary for this. Hence every man is, in a certain sense, unconsciously a worse man when he is in society than when acting alone; for he is carried by society and to that extent relieved of his individual responsibility. Any large company composed of wholly admirable persons has the morality and intelligence of an unwieldy, stupid, and violent animal. The bigger the organization, the more unavoidable is its immorality and blind stupidity (*Senatus bestia,*

senatores boni viri). Society, by automatically stressing all the collective qualities in its individual representatives, puts a premium on mediocrity, on everything that settles down to vegetate in an easy, irresponsible way. Individuality will inevitably be driven to the wall. This process begins in school, continues at the university, and rules all departments in which the State has a hand. In a small social body, the individuality of its members is better safeguarded, and the greater is their relative freedom and the possibility of conscious responsibility. Without freedom there can be no morality. Our admiration for great organizations dwindles when once we become aware of the other side of the wonder: the tremendous piling up and accentuation of all that is primitive in man, and the unavoidable destruction of his individuality in the interests of the monstrosity that every great organization in fact is. The man of today, who resembles more or less the collective ideal, has made his heart into a den of murderers, as can easily be proved by the analysis of his unconscious, even though he himself is not in the least disturbed by it. And in so far as he is normally 'adapted'[16] to his environment, it is true that the greatest infamy on the part of his group will not disturb him, so long as the majority of his fellows steadfastly believe in the exalted morality of their social organization. Now, all that I have said here about the influence of society upon the individual is identically true of the influence of the collective unconscious upon the individual psyche. But, as is apparent from my examples, the latter influence is as invisible as the former is visible. Hence it is not surprising that its inner effects are not understood, and that those to whom such things happen are called pathological freaks and treated as crazy. If one of them happened to be a real genius, the fact would not be noted until the next generation or the one after. So obvious does it seem to us that a man should drown in his own dignity, so utterly incomprehensible that he should seek anything other than what the mob wants, and that he should vanish permanently from view in this other. One could wish both of them a sense of humour, that – according to Schopenhauer – truly 'divine' attribute of man which alone befits him to maintain his soul in freedom.

241   The collective instincts and fundamental forms of thinking and feeling whose activity is revealed by the analysis of the unconscious constitute, for the conscious personality, an acquisition which it cannot assimilate without considerable disturbance. It is therefore of the utmost importance in practical treatment to keep the integrity of the personality constantly in mind. For, if the collective psyche is taken to be the personal possession of the individual, it will result in a distortion or an overloading of the personality which is very difficult to deal with. Hence it is imperative to make a clear distinction between personal contents and those of the collective psyche. This distinction is far from easy, because the personal grows out of the collective psyche and is intimately bound up with it. So it is difficult to say exactly what contents are to be called personal and what collective. There is no doubt, for instance, that archaic symbolisms such as we frequently find in fantasies and dreams are collective factors. All basic instincts and basic forms of thinking and feeling are collective. Everything that all men agree in regarding as universal is collective, likewise everything that is universally

understood, universally found, universally said and done. On closer examination one is always astonished to see how much of our so-called individual psychology is really collective. So much, indeed, that the individual traits are completely overshadowed by it. Since, however, individuation[17] is an ineluctable psychological necessity, we can see from the ascendancy of the collective what very special attention must be paid to this delicate plant 'individuality' if it is not to be completely smothered.

242   Human beings have one faculty which, though it is of the greatest utility for collective purposes, is most pernicious for individuation, and that is the faculty of imitation. Collective psychology cannot dispense with imitation, for without it all mass organizations, the State and the social order, are impossible. Society is organized, indeed, less by law than by the propensity to imitation, implying equally suggestibility, suggestion, and mental contagion. But we see every day how people use, or rather abuse, the mechanism of imitation for the purpose of personal differentiation: they are content to ape some eminent personality, some striking characteristic or mode of behaviour, thereby achieving an outward distinction from the circle in which they move. We could almost say that as a punishment for this the uniformity of their minds with those of their neighbours, already real enough, is intensified into an unconscious, compulsive bondage to the environment. As a rule these specious attempts at individual differentiation stiffen into a pose, and the imitator remains at the same level as he always was, only several degrees more sterile than before. To find out what is truly individual in ourselves, profound reflection is needed; and suddenly we realize how uncommonly difficult the discovery of individuality is.

III The persona as a segment of the collective psyche

243   In this chapter we come to a problem which, if overlooked, is liable to cause the greatest confusion. It will be remembered that in the analysis of the personal unconscious the first things to be added to consciousness are the personal contents, and I suggested that these contents, which have been repressed but are capable of becoming conscious, should be called the *personal unconscious.* I also showed that to annex the deeper layers of the unconscious, which I have called the *collective unconscious,* produces an enlargement of the personality leading to the state of inflation. This state is reached by simply continuing the analytical work, as in the case of the young woman discussed above. By continuing the analysis we add to the personal consciousness certain fundamental, general, and impersonal characteristics of humanity, thereby bringing about the inflation[18] I have just described, which might be regarded as one of the unpleasant consequences of becoming fully conscious.

244   From this point of view the conscious personality is a more or less arbitrary segment of the collective psyche. It consists in a sum of psychic facts that are felt to be personal. The attribute 'personal' means: pertaining exclusively to this

particular person. A consciousness that is purely personal stresses its proprietary and original right to its contents with a certain anxiety, and in this way seeks to create a whole. But all those contents that refuse to fit into this whole are either overlooked and forgotten or repressed and denied. This is one way of educating oneself, but it is too arbitrary and too much of a violation. Far too much of our common humanity has to be sacrificed in the interests of an ideal image into which one tries to mould oneself. Hence these purely 'personal' people are always very sensitive, for something may easily happen that will bring into consciousness an unwelcome portion of their real ('individual') character.

245   This arbitrary segment of collective psyche – often fashioned with considerable pains – I have called the *persona*. The term *persona* is really a very appropriate expression for this, for originally it meant the mask once worn by actors to indicate the role they played. If we endeavour to draw a precise distinction between what psychic material should be considered personal, and what impersonal, we soon find ourselves in the greatest dilemma, for by definition we have to say of the persona's contents what we have said of the impersonal unconscious, namely, that it is collective. It is only because the persona represents a more or less arbitrary and fortuitous segment of the collective psyche that we can make the mistake of regarding it *in toto* as something individual. It is, as its name implies, only a mask of the collective psyche, a mask that *feigns individuality,* making others and oneself believe that one is individual, whereas one is simply acting a role through which the collective psyche speaks.

246   When we analyse the persona we strip off the mask, and discover that what seemed to be individual is at bottom collective; in other words, that the persona was only a mask of the collective psyche. Fundamentally the persona is nothing real: it is a compromise between individual and society as to what a man should appear to be. He takes a name, earns a title, exercises a function, he is this or that. In a certain sense all this is real, yet in relation to the essential individuality of the person concerned it is only a secondary reality, a compromise formation, in making which others often have a greater share than he. The persona is a semblance, a two-dimensional reality, to give it a nickname.

247   It would be wrong to leave the matter as it stands without at the same time recognizing that there is, after all, something individual in the peculiar choice and delineation of the persona, and that despite the exclusive identity of the ego-consciousness with the persona the unconscious self, one's real individuality, is always present and makes itself felt indirectly if not directly. Although the ego-consciousness is at first identical with the persona – that compromise role in which we parade before the community – yet the unconscious self can never be repressed to the point of extinction. Its influence is chiefly manifest in the special nature of the contrasting and compensating contents of the unconscious. The purely personal attitude of the conscious mind evokes reactions on the part of the unconscious, and these, together with personal repressions, contain the seeds of individual development in the guise of collective fantasies. Through the analysis of the personal unconscious, the conscious mind becomes suffused with

collective material which brings with it the elements of individuality. I am well aware that this conclusion must be almost unintelligible to anyone not familiar with my views and technique, and particularly so to those who habitually regard the unconscious from the standpoint of Freudian theory. But if the reader will recall my example of the philosophy student, he can form a rough idea of what I mean. At the beginning of the treatment the patient was quite unconscious of the fact that her relation to her father was a fixation, and that she was therefore seeking a man like her father, whom she could then meet with her intellect. This in itself would not have been a mistake if her intellect had not had that peculiarly protesting character such as is unfortunately often encountered in intellectual women. Such an intellect is always trying to point out mistakes in others; it is pre-eminently critical, with a disagreeably personal undertone, yet it always wants to be considered objective. This invariably makes a man bad-tempered, particularly if, as so often happens, the criticism touches on some weak spot which, in the interests of fruitful discussion, were better avoided. But far from wishing the discussion to be fruitful, it is the unfortunate peculiarity of this feminine intellect to seek out a man's weak spots, fasten on them, and exasperate him. This is not usually a conscious aim, but rather has the unconscious purpose of forcing a man into a superior position and thus making him an object of admiration. The man does not as a rule notice that he is having the role of the hero thrust upon him; he merely finds her taunts so odious that in future he will go a long way to avoid meeting the lady. In the end the only man who can stand her is the one who gives in at the start, and therefore has nothing wonderful about him.

248 My patient naturally found much to reflect upon in all this, for she had no notion of the game she was playing. Moreover she still had to gain insight into the regular romance that had been enacted between her and her father ever since childhood. It would lead us too far to describe in detail how, from her earliest years, with unconscious sympathy, she had played upon the shadow-side of her father which her mother never saw, and how, far in advance of her years, she became her mother's rival. All this came to light in the analysis of the personal unconscious. Since, if only for professional reasons, I could not allow myself to be irritated, I inevitably became the hero and father-lover. The transference too consisted at first of contents from the personal unconscious. My role as a hero was just a sham, and so, as it turned me into the merest phantom, she was able to play her traditional role of the supremely wise, very grown-up, all-understanding mother-daughter-beloved – an empty role, a persona behind which her real and authentic being, her individual self, lay hidden. Indeed, to the extent that she at first completely identified herself with her role, she was altogether unconscious of her real self. She was still in her nebulous infantile world and had not yet discovered the real world at all. But as, through progressive analysis, she became conscious of the nature of her transference, the dreams I spoke of in Chapter I began to materialize. They brought up bits of the collective unconscious, and that was the end of her infantile world and of all the heroics. She came to herself and to her own real potentialities. This is roughly the way things go in most cases, if

the analysis is carried far enough. That the consciousness of her individuality should coincide exactly with the reactivation of an archaic god-image is not just an isolated coincidence, but a very frequent occurrence which, in my view, corresponds to an unconscious law.

249 After this digression, let us turn back to our earlier reflections.

250 Once the personal repressions are lifted, the individuality and the collective psyche begin to emerge in a coalescent state, thus releasing the hitherto repressed personal fantasies. The fantasies and dreams which now appear assume a somewhat different aspect. An infallible sign of collective images seems to be the appearance of the 'cosmic' element, i.e., the images in the dream or fantasy are connected with cosmic qualities, such as temporal and spatial infinity, enormous speed and extension of movement, 'astrological' associations, telluric, lunar, and solar analogies, changes in the proportions of the body, etc. The obvious occurrence of mythological and religious motifs in a dream also points to the activity of the collective unconscious. The collective element is very often announced by peculiar symptoms,[19] as for example by dreams where the dreamer is flying through space like a comet, or feels that he is the earth, or the sun, or a star; or else is of immense size, or dwarfishly small; or that he is dead, is in a strange place, is a stranger to himself, confused, mad, etc. Similarly, feelings of disorientation, of dizziness and the like, may appear along with symptoms of inflation.

251 The forces that burst out of the collective psyche have a confusing and blinding effect. One result of the dissolution of the persona is a release of involuntary fantasy, which is apparently nothing else than the specific activity of the collective psyche. This activity throws up contents whose existence one had never suspected before. But as the influence of the collective unconscious increases, so the conscious mind loses its power of leadership. Imperceptibly it becomes the led, while an unconscious and impersonal process gradually takes control. Thus, without noticing it, the conscious personality is pushed about like a figure on a chess-board by an invisible player. It is this player who decides the game of fate, not the conscious mind and its plans. This is how the resolution of the transference, apparently so impossible to the conscious mind, was brought about in my earlier example.

252 The plunge into this process becomes unavoidable whenever the necessity arises of overcoming an apparently insuperable difficulty. It goes without saying that this necessity does not occur in every case of neurosis, since perhaps in the majority the prime consideration is only the removal of temporary difficulties of adaptation. Certainly severe cases cannot be cured without a far-reaching change of character or of attitude. In by far the greater number, adaptation to external reality demands so much work that inner adaptation to the collective unconscious cannot be considered for a very long time. But when this inner adaptation becomes a problem, a strange, irresistible attraction proceeds from the unconscious and exerts a powerful influence on the conscious direction of life. The predominance of unconscious influences, together with the associated disintegration of the persona and the deposition of the conscious mind from power, constitute a state of

psychic disequilibrium which, in analytical treatment, is artificially induced for the therapeutic purpose of resolving a difficulty that might block further development. There are of course innumerable obstacles that can be overcome with good advice and a little moral support, aided by goodwill and understanding on the part of the patient. Excellent curative results can be obtained in this way. Cases are not uncommon where there is no need to breathe a word about the unconscious. But again, there are difficulties for which one can foresee no satisfactory solution. If in these cases the psychic equilibrium is not already disturbed before treatment begins, it will certainly be upset during the analysis, and sometimes without any interference by the doctor. It often seems as though these patients had only been waiting to find a trustworthy person in order to give up and collapse. Such a loss of balance is similar in principle to a psychotic disturbance; that is, it differs from the initial stages of mental illness only by the fact that it leads in the end to greater health, while the latter leads to yet greater destruction. It is a condition of panic, a letting go in face of apparently hopeless complications. Mostly it was preceded by desperate efforts to master the difficulty by force of will; then came the collapse, and the once guiding will crumbles completely. The energy thus freed disappears from consciousness and falls into the unconscious. As a matter of fact, it is at these moments that the first signs of unconscious activity appear. (I am thinking of the example of that young man who was weak in the head.) Obviously the energy that fell away from consciousness has activated the unconscious. The immediate result is a change of attitude. One can easily imagine that a stronger head would have taken that vision of the stars as a healing apparition, and would have looked upon human suffering *sub specie aeternitatis*, in which case his senses would have been restored.[20]

253 Had this happened, an apparently insurmountable obstacle would have been removed. Hence I regard the loss of balance as purposive, since it replaces a defective consciousness by the automatic and instinctive activity of the unconscious, which is aiming all the time at the creation of a new balance and will moreover achieve this aim, provided that the conscious mind is capable of assimilating the contents produced by the unconscious, i.e., of understanding and digesting them. If the unconscious simply rides roughshod over the conscious mind, a psychotic condition develops. If it can neither completely prevail nor yet be understood, the result is a conflict that cripples all further advance. But with this question, namely the understanding of the collective unconscious, we come to a formidable difficulty which I have made the theme of my next chapter.

IV Negative attempts to free the individuality from the collective psyche

Regressive restoration of the persona

254 A collapse of the conscious attitude is no small matter. It always feels like the end of the world, as though everything had tumbled back into original chaos. One

feels delivered up, disoriented, like a rudderless ship that is abandoned to the moods of the elements. So at least it seems. In reality, however, one has fallen back upon the collective unconscious, which now takes over the leadership. We could multiply examples of cases where, at the critical moment, a 'saving' thought, a vision, an 'inner voice,' came with an irresistible power of conviction and gave life a new direction. Probably we could mention just as many cases where the collapse meant a catastrophe that destroyed life, for at such moments morbid ideas are also liable to take root, or ideals wither away, which is no less disastrous. In the one case some psychic oddity develops, or a psychosis; in the other, a state of disorientation and demoralization. But once the unconscious contents break through into consciousness, filling it with their uncanny power of conviction, the question arises of how the individual will react. Will he be overpowered by these contents? Will he credulously accept them? Or will he reject them? (I am disregarding the ideal reaction, namely critical understanding.) The first case signifies paranoia or schizophrenia; the second may either become an eccentric with a taste for prophecy, or he may revert to an infantile attitude and be cut off from human society; the third signifies the *regressive restoration of the persona*. This formulation sounds very technical, and the reader may justifiably suppose that it has something to do with a complicated psychic reaction such as can be observed in the course of analytical treatment. It would, however, be a mistake to think that cases of this kind make their appearance only in analytical treatment. The process can be observed just as well, and often better, in other situations of life, namely in all those careers where there has been some violent and destructive intervention of fate. Every one, presumably, has suffered adverse turns of fortune, but mostly they are wounds that heal and leave no crippling mark. But here we are concerned with experiences that are destructive, that can smash a man completely or at least cripple him for good. Let us take as an example a businessman who takes too great a risk and consequently becomes bankrupt. If he does not allow himself to be discouraged by this depressing experience, but, undismayed, keeps his former daring, perhaps with a little salutary caution added, his wound will be healed without permanent injury. But if, on the other hand, he goes to pieces, abjures all further risks, and laboriously tries to patch up his social reputation within the confines of a much more limited personality, doing inferior work with the mentality of a scared child, in a post far below him, then, technically speaking, he will have restored his persona in a regressive way. He will as a result of his fright have slipped back to an earlier phase of his personality; he will have demeaned himself, pretending that he is as he was *before* the crucial experience, though utterly unable even to think of repeating such a risk. Formerly perhaps he wanted more than he could accomplish; now he does not even dare to attempt what he has it in him to do.

255 Such experiences occur in every walk of life and in every possible form, hence in psychological treatment also. Here again it is a question of widening the personality, of taking a risk on one's circumstances or on one's nature. What the critical experience is in actual treatment can be seen from the case of our philosophy

student: it is the transference. As I have already indicated, it is possible for the patient to slip over the reef of the transference unconsciously, in which case it does not become an experience and nothing fundamental happens. The doctor, for the sake of mere convenience, might well wish for such patients. But if they are intelligent, the patients soon discover the existence of this problem for themselves. If then the doctor, as in the above case, is exalted into the father-lover and consequently has a flood of demands let loose against him, he must perforce think out ways and means of parrying the onslaught, without himself getting drawn into the maelstrom and without injury to the patient. A violent rupture of the transference may bring on a complete relapse, or worse; so the problem must be handled with great tact and foresight. Another possibility is the pious hope that 'in time' the 'nonsense' will stop of its own accord. Certainly everything stops in time, but it may be an unconscionably long time, and the difficulties may be so unbearable for both sides that one might as well give up the idea of time as a healing factor at once.

256 A far better instrument for 'combatting' the transference would seem to be offered by the Freudian theory of neurosis. The dependence of the patient is explained as an infantile sexual demand that takes the place of a rational application of sexuality. Similar advantages are offered by the Adlerian theory,[21] which explains the transference as an infantile power-aim, and as a 'security measure.' Both theories fit the neurotic mentality so neatly that every case of neurosis can be explained by both theories at once.[22] This highly remarkable fact, which any unprejudiced observer is bound to corroborate, can only rest on the circumstance that Freud's 'infantile eroticism' and Adler's 'power drive' are one and the same thing, regardless of the clash of opinions between the two schools. It is simply a fragment of uncontrolled, and at first uncontrollable, primordial instinct that comes to light in the phenomenon of transference. The archaic fantasy-forms that gradually reach the surface of consciousness are only a further proof of this.

257 We can try both theories to make the patient see how infantile, impossible, and absurd his demands are, and perhaps in the end he will actually come to his senses again. My patient, however, was not the only one who did not do this. True enough, the doctor can always save his face with these theories and extricate himself from a painful situation more or less humanely. There are indeed patients with whom it is, or seems to be, unrewarding to go to greater lengths; but there are also cases where these procedures cause senseless psychic injury. In the case of my student I dimly felt something of the sort, and I therefore abandoned my rationalistic attempts in order – with ill-concealed mistrust – to give nature a chance to correct what seemed to me to be her own foolishness. As already mentioned, this taught me something extraordinarily important, namely the existence of an unconscious self-regulation. Not only can the unconscious 'wish,' it can also cancel its own wishes. This realization, of such immense importance for the integrity of the personality, must remain sealed to anyone who cannot get over the idea that it is simply a question of infantilism. He will turn round on the

threshold of this realization and tell himself: 'It was all nonsense of course. I am a crazy visionary! The best thing to do would be to bury the unconscious or throw it overboard with all its works.' The meaning and purpose he so eagerly desired he will see only as infantile maunderings. He will understand that his longing was absurd; he learns to be tolerant with himself, resigned. What can he do? Rather than face the conflict he will turn back and, as best he can, regressively restore his shattered persona, discounting all those hopes and expectations that had blossomed under the transference. He will become smaller, more limited, more rationalistic than he was before. One could not say that this result would be an unqualified misfortune in all cases, for there are all too many who, on account of their notorious ineptitude, thrive better in a rationalistic system than in freedom. Freedom is one of the more difficult things. Those who can stomach this way out can say with Faust:

> This earthly circle I know well enough.
> Towards the Beyond the view has been cut off;
> Fool – who directs that way his dazzled eye,
> Contrives himself a double in the sky!
> Let him look round him here, not stray beyond;
> To a sound man this world must needs respond.
> To roam into eternity is vain!
> What he perceives, he can attain.
> Thus let him walk along his earthlong day;
> Though phantoms haunt him, let him go his way.[23]

258   Such a solution would be perfect if a man were really able to shake off the unconscious, drain it of its energy and render it inactive. But experience shows that the unconscious can be deprived of its energy only in part: it remains continually active, for it not only contains but is itself the source of the libido from which the psychic elements flow. It is therefore a delusion to think that by some kind of magical theory or method the unconscious can be finally emptied of libido and thus, as it were, eliminated. One may for a while play with this delusion, but the day comes when one is forced to say with Faust:

> But now such spectredom so throngs the air
> That none knows how to dodge it, none knows where.
> Though one day greet us with a rational gleam,
> The night entangles us in webs of dream.
> We come back happy from the fields of spring –
> And a bird croaks. Croaks what? Some evil thing.
> Enmeshed in superstition night and morn,
> It forms and shows itself and comes to warn.
> And we, so scared, stand without friend or kin,
> And the door creaks – and nobody comes in.[24]

120　The nature of the psyche

Nobody, of his own free will, can strip the unconscious of its effective power. At best, one can merely deceive oneself on this point. For, as Goethe says:

> Unheard by the outward ear
> In the heart I whisper fear;
> Changing shape from hour to hour
> I employ my savage power.[25]

Only one thing is effective against the unconscious, and that is hard outer necessity. (Those with rather more knowledge of the unconscious will see behind the outer necessity the same face which once gazed at them from within.) An inner necessity can change into an outer one, and so long as the outer necessity is real, and not just faked, psychic problems remain more or less ineffective. This is why Mephisto offers Faust, who is sick of the 'madness of magic,' the following advice:

> Right. There is one way that needs
> No money, no physician, and no witch.
> Pack up your things and get back to the land
> And there begin to dig and ditch;
> Keep to the narrow round, confine your mind,
> And live on fodder of the simplest kind,
> A beast among the beasts; and don't forget
> To use your own dung on the crops you set![26]

It is a well-known fact that the 'simple life' cannot be faked, and therefore the unproblematical existence of a poor man, who really is delivered over to fate, cannot be bought by such cheap imitations. Only the man who lives such a life not as a mere possibility, but is actually driven to it by the necessity of his own nature, will blindly pass over the problem of his soul, since he lacks the capacity to grasp it. But once he has seen the Faustian problem, the escape into the 'simple life' is closed for ever. There is of course nothing to stop him from taking a two-room cottage in the country, or from pottering about in a garden and eating raw turnips. But his soul laughs at the deception. Only what is really oneself has the power to heal.

259　The regressive restoration of the persona is a possible course only for the man who owes the critical failure of his life to his own inflatedness. With diminished personality, he turns back to the measure he can fill. But in every other case resignation and self-belittlement are an evasion, which in the long run can be kept up only at the cost of neurotic sickliness. From the conscious point of view of the person concerned, his condition does not look like an evasion at all, but seems to be due to the impossibility of coping with the problem. Usually he is a lonely figure, with little or nothing to help him in our present-day culture. Even psychology has only purely reductive interpretations to offer, since it inevitably underlines the archaic and infantile character of these transitional states and makes them unacceptable to him. The fact that a medical theory may also serve the purpose of enabling the doctor to pull his own head more or less elegantly out of the noose does not occur to him. That is precisely why these reductive theories fit the essence of neurosis so beautifully – because they are of such great service to the doctor.

Identification with the collective psyche

260 The second way leads to identification with the collective psyche. This would amount to an acceptance of inflation, but now exalted into a system. That is to say, one would be the fortunate possessor of *the* great truth which was only waiting to be discovered, of the eschatological knowledge which spells the healing of the nations. This attitude is not necessarily megalomania in direct form, but in the milder and more familiar form of prophetic inspiration and desire for martyrdom. For weak-minded persons, who as often as not possess more than their fair share of ambition, vanity, and misplaced naïveté, the danger of yielding to this temptation is very great. Access to the collective psyche means a renewal of life for the individual, no matter whether this renewal is felt as pleasant or unpleasant. Everybody would like to hold fast to this renewal: one man because it enhances his life-feeling, another because it promises a rich harvest of knowledge, a third because he discovered the key that will transform his whole life. Therefore all those who do not wish to deprive themselves of the great treasures that lie buried in the collective psyche will strive by every means possible to maintain their newly won connection with the primal source of life.[27] Identification would seem to be the shortest road to this, for the dissolution of the persona in the collective psyche positively invites one to wed oneself with the abyss and blot out all memory in its embrace. This piece of mysticism is innate in all better men as the 'longing for the mother,' the nostalgia for the source from which we came.

261 As I have shown in my book on libido, there lie at the root of the regressive longing, which Freud conceives as 'infantile fixation' or the 'incest wish,' a specific value and a specific need which are made explicit in myths. It is precisely the strongest and best among men, the heroes, who give way to their regressive longing and purposely expose themselves to the danger of being devoured by the monster of the maternal abyss. But if a man is a hero, he is a hero because, in the final reckoning, he did not let the monster devour him, but subdued it, not once but many times. Victory over the collective psyche alone yields the true value – the capture of the hoard, the invincible weapon, the magic talisman, or whatever it be that the myth deems most desirable. Anyone who identifies with the collective psyche – or, in mythological terms, lets himself be devoured by the monster – and vanishes in it, attains the treasure that the dragon guards, but he does so in spite of himself and to his own greatest harm.

262 Probably no one who was conscious of the absurdity of this identification would have the courage to make a principle of it. But the danger is that very many people lack the necessary humour, or else it fails them at this particular juncture;

they are seized by a sort of pathos, everything seems pregnant with meaning, and all effective self-criticism is checked. I would not deny in general the existence of genuine prophets, but in the name of caution I would begin by doubting each individual case; for it is far too serious a matter for us lightly to accept a man as a genuine prophet. Every respectable prophet strives manfully against the unconscious pretensions of his role. When therefore a prophet appears at a moment's notice, we would be better advised to contemplate a possible psychic disequilibrium.

263 But besides the possibility of becoming a prophet, there is another alluring joy, subtler and apparently more legitimate: the joy of becoming a prophet's disciple. This, for the vast majority of people, is an altogether ideal technique. Its advantages are: the *odium dignitatis*, the superhuman responsibility of the prophet, turns into the so much sweeter *otium indignitatis*. The disciple is unworthy; modestly he sits at the Master's feet and guards against having ideas of his own. Mental laziness becomes a virtue; one can at least bask in the sun of a semidivine being. He can enjoy the archaism and infantilism of his unconscious fantasies without loss to himself, for all responsibility is laid at the Master's door. Through his deification of the Master, the disciple, apparently without noticing it, waxes in stature; moreover, does he not possess the great truth – not his own discovery, of course, but received straight from the Master's hands? Naturally the disciples always stick together, not out of love, but for the very understandable purpose of effortlessly confirming their own convictions by engendering an air of collective agreement.

264 Now this is an identification with the collective psyche that seems altogether more commendable: somebody else has the honour of being a prophet, but also the dangerous responsibility. For one's own part, one is a mere disciple, but nonetheless a joint guardian of the great treasure which the Master has found. One feels the full dignity and burden of such a position, deeming it a solemn duty and a moral necessity to revile others not of a like mind, to enrol proselytes and to hold up a light to the Gentiles, exactly as though one were the prophet oneself. And these people, who creep about behind an apparently modest persona, are the very ones who, when inflated by identification with the collective psyche, suddenly burst upon the world scene. For, just as the prophet is a primordial image from the collective psyche, so also is the disciple of the prophet.

265 In both cases inflation is brought about by the collective unconscious, and the independence of the individuality suffers injury. But since by no means all individualities have the strength to be independent, the disciple-fantasy is perhaps the best they can accomplish. The gratifications of the accompanying inflation at least do something to make up for the loss of spiritual freedom. Nor should we underestimate the fact that the life of a real or imagined prophet is full of sorrows, disappointments, and privations, so that the hosanna-shouting band of disciples has the value of a compensation. All this is so humanly understandable that it would be a matter for astonishment if it led to any further destination whatever.

PART II: INDIVIDUATION

I The function of the unconscious

266 There is a destination, a possible goal, beyond the alternative stages dealt with in our last chapter. That is the way of individuation. Individuation means becoming an 'in-dividual,' and, in so far as 'individuality' embraces our innermost, last, and incomparable uniqueness, it also implies becoming one's own self. We could therefore translate individuation as 'coming to selfhood' or 'self-realization.'

267 The possibilities of development discussed in the preceding chapters were, at bottom, alienations of the self, ways of divesting the self of its reality in favour of an external role or in favour of an imagined meaning. In the former case the self retires into the background and gives place to social recognition; in the latter, to the auto-suggestive meaning of a primordial image. In both cases the collective has the upper hand. Self-alienation in favour of the collective corresponds to a social ideal; it even passes for social duty and virtue, although it can also be misused for egotistical purposes. Egoists are called 'selfish,' but this, naturally, has nothing to do with the concept of 'self' as I am using it here. On the other hand, self-realization seems to stand in opposition to self-alienation. This misunderstanding is quite general, because we do not sufficiently distinguish between individualism and individuation. Individualism means deliberately stressing and giving prominence to some supposed peculiarity rather than to collective considerations and obligations. But individuation means precisely the better and more complete fulfilment of the collective qualities of the human being, since adequate consideration of the peculiarity of the individual is more conducive to a better social performance than when the peculiarity is neglected or suppressed. The idiosyncrasy of an individual is not to be understood as any strangeness in his substance or in his components, but rather as a unique combination, or gradual differentiation, of functions and faculties which in themselves are universal. Every human face has a nose, two eyes, etc., but these universal factors are variable, and it is this variability which makes individual peculiarities possible. Individuation, therefore, can only mean a process of psychological development that fulfils the individual qualities given; in other words, it is a process by which a man becomes the definite, unique being he in fact is. In so doing he does not become 'selfish' in the ordinary sense of the word, but is merely fulfilling the peculiarity of his nature, and this, as we have said, is vastly different from egotism or individualism.

268 Now in so far as the human individual, as a living unit, is composed of purely universal factors, he is wholly collective and therefore in no sense opposed to collectivity. Hence the individualistic emphasis on one's own peculiarity is a contradiction of this basic fact of the living being. Individuation, on the other hand, aims at a living co-operation of all factors. But since the universal factors always appear only in individual form, a full consideration of them will also produce an individual effect, and one which cannot be surpassed by anything else, least of all by individualism.

269	The aim of individuation is nothing less than to divest the self of the false wrappings of the persona on the one hand, and of the suggestive power of primordial images on the other. From what has been said in the previous chapters it should be sufficiently clear what the persona means psychologically. But when we turn to the other side, namely to the influence of the collective unconscious, we find we are moving in a dark interior world that is vastly more difficult to understand than the psychology of the persona, which is accessible to everyone. Everyone knows what is meant by 'putting on official airs' or 'playing a social role.' Through the persona a man tries to appear as this or that, or he hides behind a mask, or he may even build up a definite persona as a barricade. So the problem of the persona should present no great intellectual difficulties.

270	It is, however, another thing to describe, in a way that can be generally understood, those subtle inner processes which invade the conscious mind with such suggestive force. Perhaps we can best portray these influences with the help of examples of mental illness, creative inspiration, and religious conversion. A most excellent account – taken from life, so to speak – of such an inner transformation is to be found in H. G. Wells' *Christina Alberta's Father*.[28] Changes of a similar kind are described in Léon Daudet's eminently readable *L'Hérédo*. A wide range of material is contained in William James' *Varieties of Religious Experience*. Although in many cases of this kind there are certain external factors which either directly condition the change, or at least provide the occasion for it, yet it is not always the case that the external factor offers a sufficient explanation of these changes of personality. We must recognize the fact that they can also arise from subjective inner causes, opinions, convictions, where external stimuli play no part at all, or a very insignificant one. In pathological changes of personality this can even be said to be the rule. The cases of psychosis that present a clear and simple reaction to some overwhelming outside event belong to the exceptions. Hence, for psychiatry, the essential aetiological factor is the inherited or acquired pathological disposition. The same is probably true of most creative intuitions, for we are hardly likely to suppose a purely causal connection between the falling apple and Newton's theory of gravitation. Similarly all religious conversions that cannot be traced back directly to suggestion and contagious example rest upon independent interior processes culminating in a change of personality. As a rule these processes have the peculiarity of being subliminal, i.e., unconscious, in the first place and of reaching consciousness only gradually. The moment of irruption can, however, be very sudden, so that consciousness is instantaneously flooded with extremely strange and apparently quite unsuspected contents. That is how it looks to the layman and even to the person concerned, but the experienced observer knows that psychological events are never sudden. In reality the irruption has been preparing for many years, often for half a lifetime, and already in childhood all sorts of remarkable signs could have been detected which, in more or less symbolic fashion, hinted at abnormal future developments. I am reminded, for instance, of a mental case who refused all nourishment and created quite extraordinary difficulties in connection with nasal feeding. In fact an anaesthetic was necessary before the tube could be inserted. The patient was able in some remarkable way to swallow his tongue by pressing it back into the throat, a fact that was quite new and unknown to me at the time. In a lucid interval I obtained the following history from the man. As a boy he had often revolved in his mind the idea of how he could take his life, even if every conceivable measure were employed to prevent him. He first tried to do it by holding his breath, until he found that by the time he was in a semi-conscious state he had already begun to breathe again. So he gave up these attempts and thought: perhaps it would work if he refused food. This fantasy satisfied him until he discovered that food could be poured into him through the nasal cavity. He therefore considered how this entrance might be closed, and thus it was that he hit upon the idea of pressing his tongue backwards. At first he was unsuccessful, and so he began a regular training, until at last he succeeded in swallowing his tongue in much the same way as sometimes happens accidentally during anaesthesia, evidently in his case by artificially relaxing the muscles at the root of the tongue.

271   In this strange manner the boy paved the way for his future psychosis. After the second attack he became incurably insane. This is only one example among many others, but it suffices to show how the subsequent, apparently sudden irruption of alien contents is really not sudden at all, but is rather the result of an unconscious development that has been going on for years.

272   The great question now is: in what do these unconscious processes consist? And how are they constituted? Naturally, so long as they are unconscious, nothing can be said about them. But sometimes they manifest themselves, partly through symptoms, partly through actions, opinions, affects, fantasies, and dreams. Aided by such observational material we can draw indirect conclusions as to the momentary state and constitution of the unconscious processes and their development. We should not, however, labour under the illusion that we have now discovered the real nature of the unconscious processes. We never succeed in getting further than the hypothetical 'as if.'

273   'No mortal mind can plumb the depths of nature' – nor even the depths of the unconscious. We do know, however, that the unconscious never rests. It seems to be always at work, for even when asleep we dream. There are many people who declare that they never dream, but the probability is that they simply do not remember their dreams. It is significant that people who talk in their sleep mostly have no recollection either of the dream which started them talking, or even of the fact that they dreamed at all. Not a day passes but we make some slip of the tongue, or something slips our memory which at other times we know perfectly well, or we are seized by a mood whose cause we cannot trace, etc. These things are all symptoms of some consistent unconscious activity which becomes directly visible at night in dreams, but only occasionally breaks through the inhibitions imposed by our daytime consciousness.

274   So far as our present experience goes, we can lay it down that the unconscious processes stand in a compensatory relation to the conscious mind. I expressly use the word 'compensatory' and not the word 'contrary' because conscious and

unconscious are not necessarily in opposition to one another, but complement one another to form a totality, which is the *self*. According to this definition the self is a quantity that is supraordinate to the conscious ego. It embraces not only the conscious but also the unconscious psyche, and is therefore, so to speak, a personality which we *also* are. It is easy enough to think of ourselves as possessing part-souls. Thus we can, for instance, see ourselves as a persona without too much difficulty. But it transcends our powers of imagination to form a clear picture of what we are as a self, for in this operation the part would have to comprehend the whole. There is little hope of our ever being able to reach even approximate consciousness of the self, since however much we may make conscious there will always exist an indeterminate and indeterminable amount of unconscious material which belongs to the totality of the self. Hence the self will always remain a supraordinate quantity.

275   The unconscious processes that compensate the conscious ego contain all those elements that are necessary for the self-regulation of the psyche as a whole. On the personal level, these are the not consciously recognized personal motives which appear in dreams, or the meanings of daily situations which we have overlooked, or conclusions we have failed to draw, or affects we have not permitted, or criticisms we have spared ourselves. But the more we become conscious of ourselves through self-knowledge, and act accordingly, the more the layer of the personal unconscious that is superimposed on the collective unconscious will be diminished. In this way there arises a consciousness which is no longer imprisoned in the petty, oversensitive, personal world of the ego, but participates freely in the wider world of objective interests. This widened consciousness is no longer that touchy, egotistical bundle, of personal wishes, fears, hopes, and ambitions which always has to be compensated or corrected by unconscious counter-tendencies; instead, it is a function of relationship to the world of objects, bringing the individual into absolute, binding, and indissoluble communion with the world at large. The complications arising at this stage are no longer egotistic wish-conflicts, but difficulties that concern others as much as oneself. At this stage it is fundamentally a question of collective problems, which have activated the collective unconscious because they require collective rather than personal compensation. We can now see that the unconscious produces contents which are valid not only for the person concerned, but for others as well, in fact for a great many people and possibly for all.

276   The Elgonyi, natives of the Elgon forests, of central Africa, explained to me that there are two kinds of dreams: the ordinary dream of the little man, and the 'big vision' that only the great man has, e.g., the medicine-man or chief. Little dreams are of no account, but if a man has a 'big dream' he summons the whole tribe in order to tell it to everybody.

277   How is a man to know whether his dream is a 'big' or a 'little' one? He knows it by an instinctive feeling of significance. He feels so overwhelmed by the impression it makes that he would never think of keeping the dream to himself. He *has* to tell it, on the psychologically correct assumption that it is of general

significance. Even with us the collective dream has a feeling of importance about it that impels communication. It springs from a conflict of relationship and must therefore be built into our conscious relations, because it compensates these and not just some inner personal quirk.

278   The processes of the collective unconscious are concerned not only with the more or less personal relations of an individual to his family or to a wider social group, but with his relations to society and to the human community in general. The more general and impersonal the condition that releases the unconscious reaction, the more significant, bizarre, and overwhelming will be the compensatory manifestation. It impels not just private communication, but drives people to revelations and confessions, and even to a dramatic representation of their fantasies.

279   I will explain by an example how the unconscious manages to compensate relationships. A somewhat arrogant gentleman once came to me for treatment. He ran a business in partnership with his younger brother. Relations between the two brothers were very strained, and this was one of the essential causes of my patient's neurosis. From the information he gave me, the real reason for the tension was not altogether clear. He had all kinds of criticisms to make of his brother, whose gifts he certainly did not show in a very favourable light. The brother frequently came into his dreams, always in the role of a Bismarck, Napoleon, or Julius Caesar. His house looked like the Vatican or Yildiz Kiosk. My patient's unconscious evidently had the need to exalt the rank of the younger brother. From this I concluded that he was setting himself too high and his brother too low. The further course of analysis entirely justified this inference.

280   Another patient, a young woman who clung to her mother in an extremely sentimental way, always had very sinister dreams about her. She appeared in the dreams as a witch, as a ghost, as a pursuing demon. The mother had spoilt her beyond all reason and had so blinded her by tenderness that the daughter had no conscious idea of her mother's harmful influence. Hence the compensatory criticism exercised by the unconscious.

281   I myself once happened to put too low a value on a patient, both intellectually and morally. In a dream I saw a castle perched on a high cliff, and on the topmost tower was a balcony, and there sat my patient. I did not hesitate to tell her this dream at once, naturally with the best results.

282   We all know how apt we are to make fools of ourselves in front of the very people we have unjustly underrated. Naturally the case can also be reversed, as once happened to a friend of mine. While still a callow student he had written to Virchow, the pathologist, craving an audience with 'His Excellency.' When, quaking with fear, he presented himself and tried to give his name, he blurted out, 'My name is Virchow.' Whereupon His Excellency, smiling mischievously, said, 'Ah! So your name is Virchow too?' The feeling of his own nullity was evidently too much for the unconscious of my friend, and in consequence it instantly prompted him to present himself as equal to Virchow in grandeur.

283   In these more personal relations there is of course no need for any very collective compensations. On the other hand, the figures employed by the unconscious

in our first case are of a definitely collective nature: they are universally recognized heroes. Here there are two possible interpretations: either my patient's younger brother is a man of acknowledged and far-reaching collective importance, or my patient is overestimating his own importance not merely in relation to his brother but in relation to everybody else as well. For the first assumption there was no support at all, while for the second there was the evidence of one's own eyes. Since the man's extreme arrogance affected not only himself, but a far wider social group, the compensation availed itself of a collective image.

284   The same is true of the second case. The 'witch' is a collective image; hence we must conclude that the blind dependence of the young woman applied as much to the wider social group as it did to her mother personally. This was indeed the case, in so far as she was still living in an exclusively infantile world, where the world was identical with her parents. These examples deal with relations within the personal orbit. There are, however, impersonal relations which occasionally need unconscious compensation. In such cases collective images appear with a more or less mythological character. Moral, philosophical, and religious problems are, on account of their universal validity, the most likely to call for mythological compensation. In the aforementioned novel by H. G. Wells we find a classical type of compensation: Mr. Preemby, a midget personality, discovers that he is really a reincarnation of Sargon, King of Kings. Happily, the genius of the author rescues poor old Sargon from pathological absurdity, and even gives the reader a chance to appreciate the tragic and eternal meaning in this lamentable affray. Mr. Preemby, a complete nonentity, recognizes himself as the point of intersection of all ages past and future. This knowledge is not too dearly bought at the cost of a little madness, provided that Preemby is not in the end devoured by that monster of a primordial image – which is in fact what nearly happens to him.

285   The universal problem of evil and sin is another aspect of our impersonal relations to the world. Almost more than any other, therefore, this problem produces collective compensations. One of my patients, aged sixteen, had as the initial symptom of a severe compulsion neurosis the following dream: *He is walking along an unfamiliar street. It is dark, and he hears steps coming behind him. With a feeling of fear he quickens his pace. The footsteps come nearer, and his fear increases. He begins to run. But the footsteps seem to be overtaking him. Finally he turns round, and there he sees the devil. In deathly terror he leaps into the air and hangs there suspended.* This dream was repeated twice, a sign of its special urgency.

286   It is a notorious fact that the compulsion neuroses, by reason of their meticulousness and ceremonial punctilio, not only have the surface appearance of a moral problem but are indeed brimfull of inhuman beastliness and ruthless evil, against the integration of which the very delicately organized personality puts up a desperate struggle. This explains why so many things have to be performed in ceremonially 'correct' style, as though to counteract the evil hovering in the background. After this dream the neurosis started, and its essential feature was that the patient had, as he put it, to keep himself in a 'provisional' or 'uncontaminated'

state of purity. For this purpose he either severed or made 'invalid' all contact with the world and with everything that reminded him of the transitoriness of human existence, by means of lunatic formalities, scrupulous cleansing ceremonies, and the anxious observance of innumerable rules and regulations of an unbelievable complexity. Even before the patient had any suspicion of the hellish existence that lay before him, the dream showed him that if he wanted to come down to earth again there would have to be a pact with evil.

287 Elsewhere I have described a dream that illustrates the compensation of a religious problem in a young theological student.[29] He was involved in all sorts of difficulties of belief, a not uncommon occurrence in the man of today. In his dream he was the pupil of the 'white magician,' who, however, was dressed in black. After having instructed him up to a certain point, the white magician told him that they now needed the 'black magician.' The black magician appeared, but clad in a white robe. He declared that he had found the keys of paradise, but needed the wisdom of the white magician in order to understand how to use them. This dream obviously contains the problem of opposites which, as we know, has found in Taoist philosophy a solution very different from the views prevailing in the West. The figures employed by the dream are impersonal collective images corresponding to the nature of the impersonal religious problem. In contrast to the Christian view, the dream stresses the relativity of good and evil in a way that immediately calls to mind the Taoist symbol of Yin and Yang.

288 We should certainly not conclude from these compensations that, as the conscious mind becomes more deeply engrossed in universal problems, the unconscious will bring forth correspondingly far-reaching compensations. There is what one might call a legitimate and an illegitimate interest in impersonal problems. Excursions of this kind are legitimate only when they arise from the deepest and truest needs of the individual; illegitimate when they are either mere intellectual curiosity or a flight from unpleasant reality. In the latter case the unconscious produces all too human and purely personal compensations, whose manifest aim is to bring the conscious mind back to ordinary reality. People who go illegitimately mooning after the infinite often have absurdly banal dreams which endeavour to damp down their ebullience. Thus, from the nature of the compensation, we can at once draw conclusions as to the seriousness and rightness of the conscious strivings.

289 There are certainly not a few people who are afraid to admit that the unconscious could ever have 'big' ideas. They will object, 'But do you really believe that the unconscious is capable of offering anything like a constructive criticism of our Western mentality?' Of course, if we take the problem intellectually and impute rational intentions to the unconscious, the thing becomes absurd. But it would never do to foist our conscious psychology upon the unconscious. Its mentality is an instinctive one; it has no differentiated functions, and it does not 'think' as we understand 'thinking.' It simply creates an image that answers to the conscious situation. This image contains as much thought as feeling, and is anything rather than a product of rationalistic reflection. Such an image would be

better described as an artist's vision. We tend to forget that a problem like the one which underlies the dream last mentioned cannot, even to the conscious mind of the dreamer, be an intellectual problem, but is profoundly emotional. For a moral man the ethical problem is a passionate question which has its roots in the deepest instinctual processes as well as in his most idealistic aspirations. The problem for him is devastatingly real. It is not surprising, therefore, that the answer likewise springs from the depths of his nature. The fact that everyone thinks his psychology is the measure of all things, and, if he also happens to be a fool, will inevitably think that such a problem is beneath his notice, should not trouble the psychologist in the least, for he has to take things objectively, as he finds them, without twisting them to fit his subjective suppositions. The richer and more capacious natures may legitimately be gripped by an impersonal problem, and to the extent that this is so, their unconscious can answer in the same style. And just as the conscious mind can put the question, 'Why is there this frightful conflict between good and evil?,' so the unconscious can reply, 'Look closer! Each needs the other. The best, just because it is the best, holds the seed of evil, and there is nothing so bad but good can come of it.'

290   It might then dawn on the dreamer that the apparently insoluble conflict is, perhaps, a prejudice, a frame of mind conditioned by time and place. The seemingly complex dream-image might easily reveal itself as plain, instinctive common sense, as the tiny germ of a rational idea, which a maturer mind could just as well have thought consciously. At all events Chinese philosophy thought of it ages ago. The singularly apt, plastic configuration of thought is the prerogative of that primitive, natural spirit which is alive in all of us and is only obscured by a one-sided conscious development. If we consider the unconscious compensations from this angle, we might justifiably be accused of judging the unconscious too much from the conscious standpoint. And indeed, in pursuing these reflections, I have always started from the view that the unconscious simply reacts to the conscious contents, albeit in a very significant way, but that it lacks initiative. It is, however, far from my intention to give the impression that the unconscious is merely reactive in all cases. On the contrary, there is a host of experiences which seem to prove that the unconscious is not only spontaneous but can actually take the lead. There are innumerable cases of people who lingered on in a pettifogging unconsciousness, only to become neurotic in the end. Thanks to the neurosis contrived by the unconscious, they are shaken out of their apathy, and this in spite of their own laziness and often desperate resistance.

291   Yet it would, in my view, be wrong to suppose that in such cases the unconscious is working to a deliberate and concerted plan and is striving to realize certain definite ends. I have found nothing to support this assumption. The driving force, so far as it is possible for us to grasp it, seems to be in essence only an urge towards self-realization. If it were a matter of some general teleological plan, then all individuals who enjoy a surplus of unconsciousness would necessarily be driven towards higher consciousness by an irresistible urge. That is plainly not the case. There are vast masses of the population who, despite their notorious

unconsciousness, never get anywhere near a neurosis. The few who are smitten by such a fate are really persons of the 'higher' type who, for one reason or another, have remained too long on a primitive level. Their nature does not in the long run tolerate persistence in what is for them an unnatural torpor. As a result of their narrow conscious outlook and their cramped existence they save energy; bit by bit it accumulates in the unconscious and finally explodes in the form of a more or less acute neurosis. This simple mechanism does not necessarily conceal a 'plan.' A perfectly understandable urge towards self-realization would provide a quite satisfactory explanation. We could also speak of a retarded maturation of the personality.

292   Since it is highly probable that we are still a long way from the summit of absolute consciousness, presumably everyone is capable of wider consciousness, and we may assume accordingly that the unconscious processes are constantly supplying us with contents which, if consciously recognized, would extend the range of consciousness. Looked at in this way, the unconscious appears as a field of experience of unlimited extent. If it were merely reactive to the conscious mind, we might aptly call it a psychic mirror-world. In that case, the real source of all contents and activities would lie in the conscious mind, and there would be absolutely nothing in the unconscious except the distorted reflections of conscious contents. The creative process would be shut up in the conscious mind, and anything new would be nothing but conscious invention or cleverness. The empirical facts give the lie to this. Every creative man knows that spontaneity is the very essence of creative thought. Because the unconscious is not just a reactive mirror-reflection, but an independent, productive activity, its realm of experience is a self-contained world, having its own reality, of which we can only say that it affects us as we affect it – precisely what we say about our experience of the outer world. And just as material objects are the constituent elements of this world, so psychic factors constitute the objects of that other world.

293   The idea of psychic objectivity is by no means a new discovery. It is in fact one of the earliest and most universal acquisitions of humanity: it is nothing less than the conviction as to the concrete existence of a spirit-world. The spirit-world was certainly never an invention in the sense that fire-boring was an invention; it was far rather the experience, the conscious acceptance of a reality in no way inferior to that of the material world. I doubt whether primitives exist anywhere who are not acquainted with magical influence or a magical substance. ('Magical' is simply another word for 'psychic'.) It would also appear that practically all primitives are aware of the existence of spirits.[30] 'Spirit' is a psychic fact. Just as we distinguish our own bodiliness from bodies that are strange to us, so primitives – if they have any notion of 'souls' at all – distinguish between their own souls and the spirits, which are felt as strange and as 'not belonging.' They are objects of outward perception, whereas their own soul (or one of several souls where a plurality is assumed), though believed to be essentially akin to the spirits, is not usually an object of so-called sensible perception. After death the soul (or one of the plurality of souls) becomes a spirit which survives the dead man, and often it

shows a marked deterioration of character that partly contradicts the notion of personal immortality. The Bataks,[31] of Sumatra, go so far as to assert that the people who were good in this life turn into malign and dangerous spirits. Nearly everything that the primitives say about the tricks which the spirits play on the living, and the general picture they give of the *revenants*, corresponds down to the last detail with the phenomena established by spiritualistic experience. And just as the communications from the 'Beyond' can be seen to be the activities of broken-off bits of the psyche, so these primitive spirits are manifestations of unconscious complexes.[32] The importance that modern psychology attaches to the 'parental complex' is a direct continuation of primitive man's experience of the dangerous power of the ancestral spirits. Even the error of judgment which leads him unthinkingly to assume that the spirits are realities of the external world is carried on in our assumption (which is only partially correct) that the real parents are responsible for the parental complex. In the old trauma theory of Freudian psychoanalysis, and in other quarters as well, this assumption even passed for a scientific explanation. (It was in order to avoid this confusion that I advocated the term 'parental imago.'[33])

294   The simple soul is of course quite unaware of the fact that his nearest relations, who exercise immediate influence over him, create in him an image which is only partly a replica of themselves, while its other part is compounded of elements derived from himself. The imago is built up of parental influences plus the specific reactions of the child; it is therefore an image that reflects the object with very considerable qualifications. Naturally, the simple soul believes that his parents are as he sees them. The image is unconsciously projected, and when the parents die, the projected image goes on working as though it were a spirit existing on its own. The primitive then speaks of parental spirits who return by night (*revenants*), while the modern man calls it a father or mother complex.

295   The more limited a man's field of consciousness is, the more numerous the psychic contents (imagos) which meet him as quasi-external apparitions, either in the form of spirits, or as magical potencies projected upon living people (magicians, witches, etc.). At a rather higher stage of development, where the idea of the soul already exists, not all the imagos continue to be projected (where this happens, even trees and stones talk), but one or the other complex has come near enough to consciousness to be felt as no longer strange, but as somehow 'belonging.' Nevertheless, the feeling that it 'belongs' is not at first sufficiently strong for the complex to be sensed as a subjective content of consciousness. It remains in a sort of no man's land between conscious and unconscious, in the half-shadow, in part belonging or akin to the conscious subject, in part an autonomous being, and meeting consciousness as such. At all events it is not necessarily obedient to the subject's intentions, it may even be of a higher order, more often than not a source of inspiration or warning, or of 'supernatural' information. Psychologically such a content could be explained as a partly autonomous complex that is not yet fully integrated. The archaic souls, the *ba* and *ka* of the Egyptians, are complexes of this kind. At a still higher level, and particularly among the civilized peoples of

the West, this complex is invariably of the feminine gender – anima and ψυχή – a fact for which deeper and cogent reasons are not lacking.

Notes

1. [Originally published as *Die Beziehungen zwischen dem Ich und dem Unbewessten* (Zurich, Rascher Verlag,1928), which version was translated by H. G. and C. F. Baynes as 'The Relations Between the Ego and the Unconscious,' in *Two Essays on Analytical Psychology* (London and New York, 1928). The present translation by R. F. C. Hull is based on this. – Editor.]
2. Cf. the 'transcendent function' in *Psychological Types*, Def. 51, 'Symbol.'
3. For a fuller elaboration of this theme see *Symbols of Transformation*, index, s.v. 'wind.'
4. Cf. Flournoy, *Des Indes à la planète Mars: Étude sur un cas de somnambulisme avec glossolalie* (trans, by D. B. Vermilye as *From India to the Planet Mars*), and Jung, 'Psychology and Pathology of So-called Occult Phenomena,' pars. 138ff.
5. Cf. *Psychological Types*, Def. 26.
6. Consequently, the accusation of 'fanciful mysticism' levelled at my ideas is lacking in foundation.
7. Hubert and Mauss, *Mélanges d'histoire des religions*, p. xxix.
8. *Faust*, Part I, 3rd scene in Faust's study.
9. Maeder, 'Psychologische Untersuchungen an Dementia-Praecox-Kranken' (1910), pp. 209ff.
10. When I was still a doctor at the psychiatric clinic in Zurich, I once took an intelligent layman through the sick-wards. He had never seen a lunatic asylum from the inside before. When we had finished our round, he exclaimed, 'I tell you, it's just like Zurich in miniature! A quintessence of the population. It is as though all the types one meets every day on the streets had been assembled here in their classical purity. Nothing but oddities and picked specimens from top to bottom of society!' I had never looked at it from this angle before, but my friend was not far wrong.
11. Cf. *Psychological Types*, Def. 26, 'Image.' Léon Daudet, in *L'Hérédo*, calls this process 'autofécondation intérieure,' by which he means the reawakening of an ancestral soul.
12. Bleuler, *Dementia Praecox or the Group of Schizophrenias* (orig. 1911).
13. *Les Névroses* (1898).
14. Freud, *Totem and Taboo*.
15. Thus it is a quite unpardonable mistake to accept the conclusions of a Jewish psychology as generally valid. Nobody would dream of taking Chinese or Indian psychology as binding upon ourselves. The cheap accusation of anti-Semitism that has been levelled at me on the ground of this criticism is about as intelligent as accusing me of an anti-Chinese prejudice. No doubt, on an earlier and deeper level of psychic development, where it is still impossible to distinguish between an Aryan, Semitic, Hamitic, or Mongolian mentality, all human races have a common collective psyche. But with the beginning of racial differentiation essential differences are developed in the collective psyche as well. For this reason we cannot transplant the spirit of a foreign race *in globo* into our own mentality without sensible injury to the latter, a fact which does not, however, deter sundry natures of feeble instinct from affecting Indian philosophy and the like.
16. Cf. 'adjustment' and 'adaptation' in *Psychological Types* (1923 edn., p. 419).
17. Ibid., Def. 29: 'Individuation is a process of differentiation, having for its goal the development of the individual personality.' – 'Since the individual is not only a single entity, but also, by his very existence, presupposes a collective relationship, the process of individuation does not lead to isolation, but to an intenser and more universal collective solidarity.'

18 This phenomenon, which results from the extension of consciousness, is in no sense specific to analytical treatment. It occurs whenever people are overpowered by knowledge or by some new realization. 'Knowledge puffeth up,' Paul writes to the Corinthians, for the new knowledge had turned the heads of many, as indeed constantly happens. The inflation has nothing to do with the *kind* of knowledge, but simply and solely with the fact that any new knowledge can so seize hold of a weak head that he no longer sees and hears anything else. He is hypnotized by it, and instantly believes he has solved the riddle of the universe. But that is equivalent to almighty self-conceit. This process is such a general reaction that, in Genesis 2:17, eating of the tree of knowledge is represented as a deadly sin. It may not be immediately apparent why greater consciousness followed by self-conceit should be such a dangerous thing. Genesis represents the act of becoming conscious as a taboo infringement, as though knowledge meant that a sacrosanct barrier had been impiously overstepped. I think that Genesis is right in so far as every step towards greater consciousness is a kind of Promethean guilt: through knowledge, the gods are as it were robbed of their fire, that is, something that was the property of the unconscious powers is torn out of its natural context and subordinated to the whims of the conscious mind. The man who has usurped the new knowledge suffers, however, a transformation or enlargement of consciousness, which no longer resembles that of his fellow men. He has raised himself above the human level of his age ('ye shall become like unto God'), but in so doing has alienated himself from humanity. The pain of this loneliness is the vengeance of the gods, for never again can he return to mankind. He is, as the myth says, chained to the lonely cliffs of the Caucasus, forsaken of God and man.

19 It may not be superfluous to note that collective elements in dreams are not restricted to this stage of the analytical treatment. There are many psychological situations in which the activity of the collective unconscious can come to the surface. But this is not the place to enlarge upon these conditions.

20 Cf. Flournoy, 'Automatisme téléologique antisuicide: un cas de suicide empêché par une hallucination' (1907), 113–37; and Jung, 'The Psychology of Dementia Praecox,' pars. 304ff.

21 Adler, *The Neurotic Constitution* (orig. 1912).

22 Cf. supra, pars. 44ff., for an example of such a case.

23 *Faust*, trans. by Louis MacNeice, p. 283 (Part II, Act V).

24 Ibid., p. 281 (Part II, Act V).

25 Ibid., p. 282 (Part II, Act V), modified.

26 Ibid., p. 67 (Part I, Witch's Kitchen scene), modified.

27 I would like to call attention here to an interesting remark of Kant's. In his lectures on psychology (*Vorlesungen über Psychologie*, Leipzig, 1889) he speaks of the 'treasure lying within the field of dim representations, that deep abyss of human knowledge forever beyond our reach.' This treasure, as I have demonstrated in my *Symbols of Transformation*, is the aggregate of all those primordial images in which the libido is invested, or rather, which are self-representations of the libido.

28 [Concerning the origin of this novel in a conversation between Wells and Jung, cf. Bennet, *What Jung Really Said*, p. 93. – EDITORS.]

29 'Archetypes of the Collective Unconscious,' par. 71.

30 In cases of reports to the contrary, it must always be borne in mind that the fear of spirits is sometimes so great that people will actually deny that there are any spirits to fear. I have come across this myself among the dwellers on Mount Elgon.

31 Warnecke, *Die Religion der Batak* (1909).

32 Cf. 'The Psychological Foundations of Belief in Spirits.'

33 [This term was taken up by psychoanalysis, but in analytical psychology it has been largely replaced by 'primordial image of the parent' or 'parental archetype.' – EDITORS.]

Part II

Archetypes

Archetypes
Introduction

Chapter 5: 'On the concept of the archetype' (1938/1954)

(From 'Psychological aspects of the mother archetype', *The Archetypes and the Collective Unconscious, The Collected Works Vol.* 9, Part I, § 148–155)

Archetypal theory

To help the reader gain an overview of the theory of archetypes, an essay is needed which ranges beyond the selections published in this anthology. Jung's writings on archetypal theory are diverse and complicated, and yet not all have to be consulted to gain a critical perspective on the subject. What follows is my attempt to provide a fair and balanced assessment of a hotly contested topic.

With Jung's theory of archetypes we come to the structural core of his psychology. Many artists, literary scholars, anthropologists and others have found his theory to be persuasive and illuminating. It appears to explain a great deal about the study of cultures, religions and the history of ideas. However, scientists have almost universally refuted Jung's theory of archetypes.[1] I am not sure if the theory has always been fairly dismissed, or even if it has been understood before being refuted. James Hillman, making light of the controversy, said the theory should be reframed as myth rather than science. But it seems that the theory of archetypes stands midway between myth and science, and has a foot in both camps. I would like to believe that the scientific reputation of archetypes can be recovered, as scientists come to terms with its complexity and explanatory power.

Archetypes are 'identical psychic structures common to all',[2] which constitute 'the archaic heritage of humanity'.[3] Jung claims a distinguished lineage for his archetypes; he resists the notion that he is responsible for inventing them, and argues that he has rediscovered them from historical sources. In this context, he claims as precedents Plato's 'ideas' (§ 149), Kant's 'categories' (§ 150) and Schopenhauer's 'prototypes'.[4] The precise terminology is apparently not important, although the term 'archetype' can be found in a range of ancient texts.[5] What is important is our awareness that universal forces exist and have been noted throughout history. In 'Instinct and the unconscious', Jung views archetypes as the psychological equivalents of instincts. He says the archetype is 'the instinct's perception of itself, or the self-portrait of the instinct'.[6] He argues that the theory of archetypes ought not to come as a shock to scientific investigators; just as 'instincts' are integral to biology, so 'archetypes' are the foundation categories of psychology.

In 'On the nature of the psyche' Jung compares the structure of the psyche to a light spectrum, arguing that instinct represents the 'psychic infra-red, the biological instinctual psyche', and the archetype represents 'the psychic ultraviolet', which 'describes a field which exhibits none of the peculiarities of the physiological'.[7] He says 'there is probably no alternative now but to describe [archetypes], in accordance with their chiefest effect, as "spirit" ... If so, the position of the archetype would be located beyond the psychic sphere.'[8] There is a note of reluctance in these pronouncements, because Jung knows he is going outside the bounds of science, and science will dismiss him as soon as he begins to speak of *spirit* as a determining influence.

In an attempt to bolster his theory, Jung makes use of the philosopher Kant, who is not widely read today but is still influential in the philosophical tradition. Kant distinguished between *phenomena*, the things that can be presented to the senses, and *noumena*, things that remain outside our perception. Jung used this terminology to distinguish between the *archetype in itself*, which is beyond the scrutiny of reason and hence noumenal, and the *archetypal image*, which is a cultural or personal representation of an archetype in time and space and hence phenomenal. Jung referred to himself as a 'phenomenologist' of the archetype,[9] an explorer of the aspects of archetypal reality that can be studied. As a scientist, his intention is to focus on the archetypal images and leave the noumenal archetype to philosophers. The archetype *in itself* thus remains beyond the range of science. As Jung put it: 'The finite will never be able to grasp the infinite.'[10] At times, Jung seems to posit his theory and then disown it insofar as it shades into metaphysics and abstraction: 'I believe only what I know. Everything else is hypothesis and beyond that I can leave a lot of things to the Unknown.'[11]

In formulating his theory of archetypes, Jung knew enough biology to appreciate that images or representations could not be inherited genetically. According to the principles of biological science, no 'content' can be inherited; only a content-free ordering structure could be inherited. The archetype in itself is thus for Jung an empty or imageless inherited form, and can only be 'filled out', as he put it, by experience of the world around us. He was claiming a biological explanation for the archetype which was similar to the biological hypothesis of the instincts: 'The representations are not inherited, only the forms, and in that respect they correspond in every way to the instincts, which are also determined in form only' (§ 155). Nevertheless, even in making these clarifications in the interests of science, Jung's theory was misunderstood and rejected by the sciences. Anthony Stevens goes so far as to say that the theory of archetypes was met with 'universal derision'.[12] Jung seemed to write the epitaph to his own theory when he said: 'Anyone who continues to think as Plato did must pay for his anachronism by seeing the . . . metaphysical essence of the Idea relegated to the unverifiable realm of faith and superstition' (§ 149).

To be fair to Jung's critics, there is some confusion in the theory which can give rise to a hostile reception. In his early writings he used the term 'primordial image' to refer to the most basic and inherited structure of the psyche. He did this, for instance, in *Transformations and Symbols of the Libido* (1912), the book which marked the parting of the ways with Freud. He used 'primordial image' because he had not yet arrived at the term 'archetype', which was not employed until 1919.[13] He was aware that an 'image' could not be inherited or genetically reproduced, and so 'primordial image' was an unfortunate term. It almost defies belief that Jung would continue to use this term in his late work, thus undermining his own distinctions. For instance, as late as 1938/1954 Jung is still writing that 'a primordial image is determined as to its content only when it has become conscious and is therefore filled out with the material of conscious experience' (§ 155). But how can an 'image' be without 'content'? Surely he means an imprint or image-former, not an image.

Even when he revised the retitled *Symbols of Transformation* in 1952 he did not take the opportunity to correct this scientific error because he uses 'primordial image' and 'archetype' interchangeably.[14] Jaffé, Samuels and Hobson have said that such carelessness in his language did nothing to help his cause or to pacify his critics.[15] Hobson argues that Jung uses terms loosely and 'seems to forget his own stringent criteria'.[16] Hobson says Jung uses the word 'form' in confusing ways, sometimes referring to the archetype as a 'form without content', and sometimes referring to the content itself as 'form'. Jung seemed to write hastily and without the necessary attention to detail. He was his own worst enemy, since his readers – especially those studying him to find fault – could easily gain the impression that he was running counter to science and opting for a 'mysticism' of inherited images or genetically acquired representations.

Natural and social scientists did not listen to Jung's clarifications and modifications; it seemed the die was cast by 1912. Scientists assumed he was saying that images, ideas and symbolisms were inherited, and they knew this to be impossible. To give a few examples: the influential folklorist Weston La Barre denounced Jung's theories, claiming that his 'archetypal folk-symbolisms are inherited phylogenetically'.[17] Not only was this not possible, but such views, according to La Barre, underestimate the influence of culture in generating folk symbolisms. Perhaps La Barre had only read early Jung, before the distinction between archetype and image was made. In his later work Jung is in defensive mode and points out that culture and society are decisive factors in the construction of archetypal images. The archetypes, once activated, can only be fleshed out by cultural experience. Based on the same assumption, the ethnologist William Bascom writes: 'It has been necessary to reject Jung's archetypes . . . because they disregard the influence of culture on both symbolism and folklore.'[18] Alan Dundes works from the same premise when he writes: 'Since they are pre-cultural, [archetypes] are essentially beyond the influence of cultural conditioning, and therefore Jung's theory eliminates the need for the study of cultural conditioning to understand archetypes.'[19]

Continuing the tradition of critique, the French anthropologist Claude Lévi-Strauss dismisses Jung as a muddle-headed thinker. In his work *Structural Anthropology*, he distances himself from Jung, even though he arrives at the same theory about pre-existing unconscious structures.[20] In *The Savage Mind*, Lévi-Strauss accuses Jung of biological naïveté by identifying the archetype with images and not with the forms underlying them.[21] This was to accuse Jung of proposing a form of outmoded Lamarckism. Whether this was a critique based on the early Jung that did not consider the late work, or whether it was a deliberate attempt to destroy his reputation, is a fact still to be decided. There is some reason to assume that these scholars had been influenced by the Freudian campaign, and were unable to think clearly about the value of Jung's work. Freud's dismissal of Jung was the only 'text' they had in mind.

A recent dismissal of Jung's theory shows how automatic the stance has become: ' "Archetypes," ' writes psychologist Noel Smith, 'are the mystical concepts invented by psychoanalyst Karl [*sic*] Jung. There is no objective evidence for them nor is any possible.'[22] Commenting on this passage, John Haule writes: 'It is not unusual for such repudiations to include a misspelling of Jung's name or more serious errors of fact. They reveal that the scholar in question is dealing with Jung's rumored reputation and not with any ascertainable facts.'[23] A systematic misreading of his ideas has taken place for nearly a hundred years, resulting in violations of his work and reputation.

This was enough to drive Jung out of his wits and his exasperation is evident in numerous places:

> Again and again I encounter the mistaken notion that an archetype is determined in regard to its content, in other words that it is a kind of unconscious idea (if such an expression be permissible). It is necessary to point out once more that archetypes are not determined as to their content, but only as regards their form, and then only to a very limited degree. A primordial image is determined as to its content only when it has become conscious and is therefore filled out with the material of conscious experience ... The archetype in itself is empty and purely formal, nothing but a possibility of representation which is given *a priori*.
>
> (§ 155)

But by this stage the scientific world had stopped listening. Anthony Stevens argues that '[i]t was in vain for Jung to protest that he was not arguing for innate ideas',[24] since scholars such as Lévi-Strauss had already switched off. The damage was done, and science moved on. Every now and then we find someone who is startled by Jung's misfortune. In 'Jung and His Critics', Carlos Drake says a 'misunderstanding of the nature of the archetype is pervasive in folklore and anthropology'.[25] Indeed it is, but such comments are found in specialist journals while in the wider world of scholarship, negative views continue as before. Jungian scholars often try to clarify the mistakes and point to the errors, but it is hard to change a prejudice once it has become confirmed by decades of agreement. Scientists won't read Jungian defences of the theory because 'Jung' has already been discredited.

The result was that Jung was either forgotten and ignored, or shunted off to the literature department, and to religious studies and cinema studies, where the explanatory powers of his theories were obvious. Archetypal symbolism, and its relationship with myth, dream and fantasy, is so apparent in the arts that his theory of archetypes cannot disappear while artists continue to dredge up mythic patterns from the unconscious. The critic Northrop Frye referred to Jung's writings as 'primarily studies in literary criticism',[26] and it is hard not to see this as a backhanded remark. Jung's relegation to the arts is not an outcome that anyone should be proud of, and I hope the sciences can reopen the case against Jung and evaluate the evidence in a new light.

Anthony Stevens has noted a great deal of recent scientific research which seems to confirm, or to run parallel with, Jung's theory:

> A number of evolutionary psychologists and psychiatrists both in Britain and the United States have detected and announced the presence of neuropsychic propensities virtually indistinguishable from archetypes. Paul Gilbert refers to them as 'psychobiological response patterns', Russell Gardner as 'master programmes' or 'propensity states', while Brant Wenegrat borrows the sociobiological term 'genetically transmitted response strategies'. David Buss refers to 'evolved psychological mechanisms' and Randolph Nesse to 'prepared tendencies'.[27]

It seems that evolutionary psychology, which takes into account the biological sciences and the impact of nature on the mind, is moving into areas that are similar to the theories of Jung. The conventional nature/nurture dichotomy is breaking down, and scientists are discovering that nature and nurture are interdependent. Evolutionary psychologists claim: 'There is nothing in the logic of development to justify the idea that traits can be divided into genetically versus environmentally controlled sets or arranged along a spectrum that reflects the influence of genes versus environment.'[28] Not Jung, but sociobiologist Robin Fox, said: 'What we are equipped with is innate *propensities* that require environmental input for their realization.'[29]

It seems that some scientific researchers are 'rediscovering' the theory of archetypes, though most avoid the term 'archetype' since it has become tainted and scientists do not wish to be relegated to the eccentric fringe. I have noted this in the work of the Harvard neuroscientist Gregg Jacobs, whose work *The Ancestral Mind* posits an unconscious storehouse of propensities which are indistinguishable from Jung's archetypes.[30] But he does not make the connection with Jung because, I presume, he dares not associate himself with a discredited source.

Reputations are fragile, easily tainted, and hard to repair once they have been degraded. Apart from Stevens, there are several scientific researchers who are prepared to try to rehabilitate Jung's standing in the scientific world. Among these writers I would include Rupert Sheldrake,[31] Joseph Cambray,[32] and Jean Knox.[33] Jung has lost the first bout with science, but the signs are that the future might arrive at a different assessment.

Chapter 6: 'Phenomenology of the Self: The ego; The shadow; The syzygy: Anima and animus; The Self' (1951)

(From *Aion, The Collected Works Vol.* 9, Part II, §1–67)

I: The ego

The ego is to be distinguished from what Jung terms 'the Self' or 'whole person', insofar as the ego is 'the centre of the field of consciousness' (§ 1) and the Self is the centre of the totality of consciousness and the unconscious. 'The ego is, by definition, subordinate to the self and is related to it like a part to the whole' (§ 9). The ego has some freedom 'inside the field of consciousness' (§ 9), but this is radically curtailed by the influence of complexes and archetypes. 'The most decisive qualities in a person are often unconscious and can be perceived only by others, or have to be laboriously discovered with outside help' (§ 7). The ego is an archetype and we might refer to it as the archetype of conscious life, 'to which all conscious contents are related' (§ 1). By 'ego' Jung is referring to something more than the popular meaning of 'ego', which is used in colloquial language as a synonym for ambition, pride or personal striving.

Our culture tends to be obsessed by the ego, since we pursue a cult of consciousness to the exclusion of all else. The unconscious and its archetypes are often dismissed as illusory, and as a result we overvalue the ego and see it as the sole player in the psychic economy. As if to compensate for the overvaluation, some get into the habit of putting the ego down and undervaluing its role. Those who are inclined to a spiritual standpoint often view the ego with disdain and attempt to obliterate it in a quest for a spiritual Self. However, as Jung writes, 'it must be reckoned a psychic catastrophe when the ego is assimilated by the self' (§ 45). The ego's task is to orient our lives in consciousness and facilitate our relations with others and the world. The popular notion that spiritual awareness must seek to eradicate the ego is a dangerous misconception, and may arise from the equation of ego with pride. But if the ego in Jung's sense is lost, the personality 'finds itself in the psychically relative space-time continuum that is characteristic of the unconscious as such' (§ 45). This is a polite way of saying that the individual has fallen into a condition of madness.

Jung emphasises that the ego must not be lost to the unconscious because it 'exists in an absolute space and an absolute time', and 'it is a vital necessity that this should be so' (§ 45). The personality cannot be comprised only of watery depths, but must have some dry land upon which to build its dwelling. For Jung, a spirituality that does not include a stable foothold in the world is highly suspect and to be dismissed as a form of psychopathology. Behind this view, it seems to me, is a theology of incarnation: Jung believes that eternity cannot enter time and space if the human instrument, in turn, cannot secure itself in reality. Eternity needs time, or God needs humanity, so that it can pour itself into time and space and realise its nature. If the human being is too 'cosmic', the quest of incarnation is aborted.

II: The shadow

I have commented extensively on the formation and problem of the shadow in the introduction to Chapter 2. However, Chapter 2 was mostly concerned with the collective aspect of the shadow, whereas in Chapter 6 the shadow is considered from an individual and clinical point of view. The contents of this chapter are taken from a lecture delivered to the Swiss Society for Practical Psychology in 1948, and are admirable for their practical suggestions. Jung argues that the shadow is the most accessible of the archetypes, and a rudimentary amount of self-reflection, as well as the critical comments of one's friends and foes, serve to remind the individual of his or her shadow side. However, 'although with insight and good will the shadow can to some extent be assimilated into the conscious personality, experience shows that there are certain features which offer the most obstinate resistance to moral control and prove almost impossible to influence' (§ 16).

The main obstacle to integrating the shadow is projection, which is stubborn and difficult to overcome. The ego is convinced that the traits peculiar to the shadow are to be found in others, and the extent to which it is bound to this belief is the extent to which it remains unconscious. Jung is careful not to punish the ego for this failing, because 'it is not the conscious subject but the unconscious which does the projecting. Hence one meets with projections, one does not make them' (§ 17). Jung shows sensitivity in this discussion and distinguishes between guilt and responsibility. The ego is not *blamed* for the projections, but it is the *responsibility* of the ego to become conscious of them and to withdraw them from the environment. Such withdrawal is felt to be of the utmost moral and social significance. 'The effect of projection is to isolate the subject from the environment, since instead of a real relation to it there is now only an illusory one' (§ 17). Jung's psychology is deeply concerned with the relation to the social and political environment, and how to improve this relation for the benefit of humanity.

III: The syzygy: Anima and animus

'Whereas the shadow can be seen through and recognised fairly easily, the anima and animus are much further away from consciousness and in normal circumstances are seldom if ever realized' (§ 19). If the integration of the shadow is apprenticeship work, the integration of the anima or animus is a masterful achievement. We all have masculine and feminine aspects in our personalities, and Jung was the first of the psychologists to postulate a bisexual complexity at the heart of every individual. Some found his theory radical and challenging; the notion of an interior contrasexual component was destabilising to established gender norms. Today Jung's insights have become generally accepted and one might even say they are now mainstream. It has almost become a cliché to speak of men 'getting in touch with their feminine sides'. It is curious that this theme is often mocked or parodied in movies, as if society is uncomfortable about this psychological complexity and has to make fun of it. Somehow it is the feminine in men that causes discomfort, while the masculine in women seems to be more acceptable.

It is a fact that men and women have both male and female hormones, and it is a matter of which hormone predominates as to whether the person is male or female. Jung argues that men typically develop the masculine side of their nature, and their feminine side falls into the unconscious. In these depths it tends to form a semi-autonomous personality that Jung calls the anima. He uses the same reasoning for women, who typically develop the more feminine aspect of their nature, and their masculine side falls into the unconscious and becomes a part-personality that he calls the animus. The aim of psychological development is to dissolve the anima and animus sub-personalities, and integrate them into the conscious personality. The more feminine a woman is or tries to be, or the more masculine a man is or tries to be, the more the unconscious will produce a counter-personality of the contrasexual type, and this will emerge in dreams, visions, fantasies, projections and everything that comes up from the unconscious.

Once integrated, these sub-personalities become what Jung calls 'functions of relationship to the unconscious', that is, bridges that connect the conscious to the unconscious. While the anima and animus remain autonomous and split off, the person is not an integrated whole, but a site of conflicted and plural selves, each of which struggles for leadership and control. Wholeness is the ideal psychological state, but it is rarely achieved. For the most part, we oscillate between one attitude and another, in a back and forth movement, much like the swing of a pendulum.

Jung believes that the typical way we encounter the anima and animus is through projections upon the opposite sex. Archetypes form the basis of most intimate relationships, according to his theory. In the first half of life, it is biologically important that we project these archetypes. It is to the benefit of the species, if not to the individual, that the anima and animus are projected onto others and form the basis of relationships. The anima of a man is often formed around the early experiences of key women in his life, such as the mother, sisters, aunts, friends, and nannies. Similarly, in women, the animus is shaped on the experience of father, brothers, cousins, uncles and significant male others. Projections take place because the ego is ignorant of its deeper nature, and because instinct ensures that the sexes are brought together for procreation.

When men and women meet and become involved, the man projects his anima onto the woman and experiences the other part of himself through her, and vice versa for the woman. In many cases, this leads to happy relationships and stable marriages, at least until such time as the psyche decides that one or both partners must develop the contrasexual elements in their personalities. Then the trouble starts. The projection begins to slip, and the beloved no longer seems like the ideal mate. This is a sign that the ego's relation to the anima or animus has to change. This creates havoc in relationships, and many do not survive this process of differentiating the archetypal image from the real person.

While Jung's theory of the contrasexual component of the personality seems radical in certain respects, there are other parts of it which are conservative. His notion that a woman's consciousness is governed by Eros, the 'function of relationship', and a man's by Logos, the function of 'discrimination and cognition' (§ 29), strikes us today as cramped and sexist. He seems to suggest that women are designed to feel and men are designed to think, and this is, after all, a description of a patriarchal social order that our time has been working hard to undermine. Jung wants women to be 'feminine' and men to be 'masculine', but this begs many questions about social conditioning and gender construction. We live in a different world to the one envisaged by Jung – so much so that it seems he has confused archetype with stereotype.

Today the notion that men and women should be uniformly masculine or feminine seems outrageous, due to decades of social reform, feminism, and gender experimentation. Jung's theory has little to say to gays and lesbians, who do not fit the categories in which he is thinking. A 'feminine' man or a 'masculine' woman is for Jung a sign that each is identified with the contrasexual component, and he rules against this kind of character. Having discovered the contrasexual element in the psyche, Jung was concerned to limit and contain this potentially disruptive element. It was as if he experienced a backlash in himself against his own radical ideas. A conventional gender identity has to be preserved, he argued, even though elements of the contrasexual polarity were to be allowed. If men showed too much femininity, especially in the choice of a homosexual partner, Jung would express disapproval and suspect such men of suffering from a mother-complex, and of being 'anima possessed'. If women became too masculine, Jung would refer to them as 'opinionated', 'irritating' and 'animus ridden'.

Jung has a way of talking about women's 'problems' that are irritating for many of us today. He speaks of Logos (or thinking) in women as a 'regrettable accident' (§ 29), and says: 'No matter how friendly and obliging a woman's Eros may be, no logic on earth can shake her if she is ridden by the animus' (§ 29). Jung is trying to be descriptive and candid, but to us these pronouncements are offensive and they turn potential readers away. As a student of mine put it, Jung is at his most cringe-making when talking about gender. All I can say in his defence is that we should not throw it all out because some of it is unpalatable. We have to strip back the sexist remarks and boorish comments and focus on the core concepts. Jung's theory of our contrasexual nature remains invaluable to our understanding of development, and our task is to retrieve the theory from its sexism, so that we can do justice to the gender diversity that is valued today. As Andrew Samuels put it, with regard to gender and sexuality followers of this tradition are forced to be post-Jungian rather than Jungian.[34]

IV: The Self

In some ways, the Self seems more abstract and hypothetical than the anima, animus and shadow. While they are identifiable in dreams and projections, the Self seems almost an act of faith on Jung's part, especially because nothing equivalent to the Self has been postulated before in psychology. Nevertheless Jung asserts that the Self 'exists and can be experienced' and it 'confronts the subject independently of him, like anima or animus' (§ 59). It is to religion and cosmology that we must turn to find an equivalent to the Self, and here we run into difficulty. In the West, the equivalents to the Self – Christ, Moses, Mohammed – have been external, historical figures, not elements of the psyche. That which 'saves', which gathers the fragmented person into a whole, which 'subdues the lawless powers belonging to the world of darkness and depicts or creates an order that transforms the chaos into a cosmos' (§ 60), has been experienced in the past as an outside messianic figure.

One would have to turn to esoteric traditions in the West to find a redemptive factor which is located within the personality. In the East it is a different story, because concepts of the Atman, the Tao and the God Within are mainstream and not tucked away in esoteric fields. The East has no problem in imagining a redemptive agency inside the human person. Jung wants to bring into Western psychology an idea which is alien to Western thinking. Indeed Jung had to go back to the ancient and discredited fields of medieval alchemy and hermetic studies to find ideas similar to what he proposed in the concept of the Self. His notion of the Self would draw some people to him in attitudes of appreciation and acknowledgement, but it would alienate a great many more. The Self, we might say, is the point at which his psychology transforms into a kind of religious experience. It is the point at which science gives way to metaphysics, although Jung still claims that the Self is 'empirical' (§ 59).

Although some of us might be tempted to rail against the West for its externalising attitude and extraverted bias, the West could have a good reason for its traditional focus. As soon as the ego gets a hint of the proximity of the divine to its immediate reality, this goes to its head and it becomes inflated. I have discussed this in my notes on Chapter 4. The proximity of the divine figure to the ego puts the ego in danger of hubris, and it is a danger to which the ego usually succumbs. Once the 'self . . . becomes assimilated to the ego' (§ 47), the divine vision is shattered, the incarnational process is corrupted, and the individuation of the personality terminated. Since inflation is such a typical response of the ego, the West may have protected us from this peril, as in the Christian prayer, 'lead us not into temptation, but deliver us from evil'. The proximity of the divine is a blessing and a curse, and to the extent that the ego is not prepared for this revelation, it is primarily a curse.

So why has Jung made it his task to make the proximity of the divine known to us? He seems to think that we are ready for this news, and for the integration of the metaphorical East (interior, introverted spirituality) into the West. It is hard to know what evidence Jung has for supposing that this revelation would not be catastrophic – that the West is capable of handling this event without going crazy. It is significant that Western religions, apart from a few dissenting voices, attack Jung for what they perceive as his attempt to pass off narcissism and self-absorption as religious experience. A statement from the Vatican makes it clear that the Catholic Church sees Jung as an evil-doer and false prophet.[35] But the Church appears not to understand that Jung is advocating the Self, not the ego, as the seat of spirituality and healing. Because the Self is such an alien idea, many do not know how to comprehend it: when Jung points to the interior realm, they assume he is championing the ego. The official voices of Western religion are not ready for his message, but see it as egotism dressed up as 'new age' religion.[36] Since the inner redemptive figure is not seen, all pathways of interiority are dismissed as vain and delusory.

The inner redemptive figure has not yet risen above the horizon of awareness and Jung would argue that this is because we have for too long projected this figure upon external objects. He believes that the historical process has brought us to a place where we can no longer look outward for salvation. The traditional forms of religions have collapsed for the educated West, and the time seems right to turn to the saving forces of the psyche. The turn to the East in educated Westerners is a part of this process of accessing the interior divine. Jung is right to insist that none of this spiritual transformation can work unless Westerners discover the vital meaning of humility. Without humility, and a genuine desire to *serve* the archetypal forces, we would not be able to attend to the birth of the Self in a sound way. The West has to overcome its hubris so that the ego can be an instrument of this transformation. Jung saw Nietzsche as the personification of what could go wrong in the West: after the death of God, the ego develops the idea that the 'Superman' could replace him. But for Jung, the death of God can only be replaced by a rebirth of God. It is the relocation of the divine that concerns Jung in his reflections on the Self.

Chapter 7: 'The psychology of the child archetype' (1940)

(From *The Archetypes and the Collective Unconscious, The Collected Works Vol. 9, Part I, § 259–305)

This is a fine example of Jung's archetypal analysis. The motif of the child in mythology, folklore and dream is dealt with in an insightful and erudite manner, and one can see the advantages of the multi-disciplinary approach. Before the archetypal method, scholars of mythology would have to approach this subject from specialist positions, thus missing the insights afforded by a global view. 'The customary treatment of mythological motifs so far in separate departments of science, such as philology, ethnology, the history of civilization, and comparative religion, was not exactly a help to us in recognizing their universality' (§ 259). The benefit of viewing the child motif as an archetype is that all of these disciplinary angles can be considered, and one can view it as a 'structural element of the psyche' and 'a living function actually present' in modern persons (§ 259). It is no longer 'out there' in myth, the past, and scholarship, but also 'in here' in the psyche of the living human subject. The archetype affords a universal perspective that was not possible before, although critics of this approach accuse it of broad generalisation and dilettantism.

Jung explores the psychology of what he calls 'primitive mentality', although today we would refer to indigenous mentality. He argues that archetypes are present in the myths and rituals of indigenous peoples, but he counters the suggestion that they are present through 'migration' or cross-cultural transmission. Instead he claims they have arisen directly from the collective unconscious. Jung opposes the theory, often found in the social sciences, that myths are pre-scientific attempts to describe the seasons and physical processes. They are not allegories of the outside world, but revelations of an inside world:

> The primitive mentality does not *invent* myths, it *experiences* them. Myths are original revelations of the preconscious psyche, involuntary statements about unconscious psychic happenings, and anything but allegories of physical processes. Such allegories would be an idle amusement for an unscientific intellect. Myths, on the contrary, have a vital meaning.
>
> (§ 261)

That 'vital meaning' is psychic and spiritual – both at the same time – and Jung argues against any so-called 'scientific' reduction of archetype and myth to external factors. Science appears to him to be 'unscientific' in its systematic avoidance of psychic reality and its attempts to explain away archetypal materials as 'primitive' descriptions of the physical world. Myths and archetypal fantasies are 'self-portraits of what is going on in the unconscious, or statements of the unconscious psyche about itself' (§ 262).

When it comes to myths and symbols, writes Jung, we are in the presence of mystery. We have to accept that full knowledge of these materials is denied us:

> In the last analysis . . . it is impossible to say what they refer to. Every interpretation necessarily remains an 'as if'. The ultimate core of meaning may be circumscribed, but not described.
>
> (§ 265)

Jung insists that we have to stay with a large element of uncertainty and resist the temptation to state absolutely what archetypal images 'mean'. The archetype of

Introduction to Part II   149

the child, as this essay reveals, is complex, profound, mystical and multi-layered. It can be understood to mean a great many things. Jung's preference for mystery is what frustrates scientists and those who want straight answers. But I have found Jung's insistence on the unknowability of archetypes to be genuine. There is a secret to creation, a 'hidden cause' (§ 266) in the psyche, and Jung wants to honour this as best he can. It is better, finally, not to presume to know reality, than to lay claim to a false image of reality and prevent the truth from disclosing itself. He adopts a wait-and-see approach which is full of reverence for life.

Jung insists that when we interpret archetypal reality we can never escape the realm of metaphor and arrive at a more literal level. We are caught up in poetic discourse whether we like it or not, because archetypes are not reducible to concepts or logic:

> Even the best attempts at explanation are only more or less successful translations into another metaphorical language. Indeed, language itself is only an image. The most we can do is to *dream the myth onwards* and give it a modern dress.
>
> (§ 271)

He sounds like a Buddhist monk who invites us to appreciate the mystery of creation and not to explain it away. Closer to the West, Jung reminds us of the poet John Keats, who wrote that the poet should aspire to a state of 'negative capability'; 'that is when a man is capable of being in uncertainties, mysteries, doubts without any irritable reaching after fact and reason.'[37] The best we can do is keep the mystery alive by 'dreaming it onwards' and giving it a 'modern dress'. The task of interpretation, and of art and science, is to relate these unknowable mysteries to consciousness, thus maintaining a vital link between the present and the past.

Notes

1. The foremost study of the science of archetypes remains Anthony Stevens' *Archetypes Revisited: An Updated Natural History of the Self* (London: Routledge, 2002).
2. Jung, *Symbols of Transformation* (1912/1952), *CW* 5, § 224.
3. Ibid., § 259.
4. Jung, 'Instinct and the Unconscious' (1919), *CW* 8, § 276.
5. Jung cites ancient writers who used the term, including Philo Judaeus, Irenaeus and Dionysius the Areopagite, in 'Archetypes of the Collective Unconscious' (1934/1954), *CW* 9, Part 1, § 5.
6. Ibid., § 277.
7. Jung, 'On the Nature of the Psyche' (1947/1954), *CW* 8, § 420.
8. Ibid.
9. Jung, 'Psychology and Religion' (1938/1940), *CW* 11, § 2.
10. Jung, 'The Structure of the Psyche' (1927/1931), *CW* 8, § 283.
11. Jung, 'Psychology and Religion', § 79.
12. Anthony Stevens, *The Two-Million-Year-Old Self* (College Station, TX: Texas A&M Press, 1993), p. 21.

13 Jung first used the term 'archetype' in 'Instinct and the Unconscious' (1919), § 270.
14 Jung, *Symbols*, § 450.
15 Aniela Jaffé, *The Myth of Meaning* (1967) (New York: Penguin Books, 1975), p. 17; Andrew Samuels, *Jung and the Post-Jungians* (London and New York: Routledge, 1985), p. 33; R. F. Hobson, 'The archetypes of the collective unconscious' (1961), in Michael Fordham, Rosemary Gordon, Judith Hubback, Kenneth Lambert and Mary Williams, eds, *Analytical Psychology: A Modern Science* (London: Academic Press, 1980), pp. 66–75.
16 R. F. Hobson, op. cit., p. 73.
17 Weston La Barre, 'Folklore and Psychology', in *The Journal of American Folklore*, Vol. LXI, Oct–Dec 1948, 382–390, p. 383.
18 William R. Bascom, 'Four Functions of Folklore', in *The Journal of American Folklore*, Vol. LXVII, Feb 1954, p. 343.
19 Alan Dundes, *The Study of Folklore* (Englewood Cliffs, NJ: Prentice-Hall, 1965), p. 291.
20 Claude Lévi-Strauss, *Structural Anthropology* (Garden City, NY: Anchor, 1967), p. 18.
21 Claude Lévi-Strauss, *The Savage Mind* (Chicago: University of Chicago Press, 1968), p. 65.
22 Noel W. Smith, *An Analysis of Ice Age Art: Its Psychology and Belief System* (New York: Peter Lang, 1992), p. 13.
23 John Ryan Haule, *Jung in the 21st Century*, Volume 1, *Evolution and Archetype* (London and New York: Routledge, 2011), p. 9.
24 Anthony Stevens, *The Two-Million-Year-Old Self*, p. 13.
25 Carlos Drake, 'Jung and His Critics', *The Journal of American Folklore*, Vol. 80, No. 318, Oct–Dec 1967, 321–333, p. 329.
26 Northrop Frye, *Fables of Identity: Studies in Poetic Mythology* (New York: Harcourt, Brace & World, 1963), p. 17.
27 Anthony Stevens, *On Jung*, 2nd edn. (Princeton, NJ: Princeton University Press, 1999), p. 285.
28 J. Tooby and L. Cosmides, 'The Psychological Foundations of Culture', in J. Barkow, J. Tooby and L. Cosmides, eds, *The Adapted Mind: Evolutionary Psychology and the Generation of Culture* (New York: Oxford University Press, 1992), p. 83.
29 Robin Fox, *The Search for Society: Quest for a Biosocial Science and Morality* (New Brunswick, NJ: Rutgers University Press, 1989), p. 45.
30 Gregg Jacobs, *The Ancestral Mind* (New York: Viking, 2003).
31 Rupert Sheldrake, *The Presence of the Past* (London: Collins, 1988) and *The Rebirth of Nature: The Greening of Science and God* (New York: Bantam, 1991).
32 Joseph Cambray, *Synchronicity: Nature and Psyche in an Interconnected Universe* (College Station, TX: Texas A&M University Press, 2009).
33 Jean Knox, *Archetype, Attachment, Analysis: Jungian Psychology and the Emergent Mind* (New York: Routledge, 2003).
34 Andrew Samuels, *Jung and the Post-Jungians* (London and New York: Routledge, 1985).
35 Pontifical Council for Culture and Pontifical Council for Interreligious Dialogue 2003: Jesus Christ: The Bearer of the Water of Life: A Christian Reflection on the 'New Age'. Vatican, Rome. Retrieved from http://www.vatican.va/roman_curia/pontifical_councils/interelg/documents/rc_pc_interelg_doc_20030203_new-age_en.html
36 See David Tacey, *Jung and the New Age* (London and New York: Routledge, 2001).
37 John Keats, Letter to George and Tom Keats, 22 December 1818, in Jane Campion, ed., *Bright Star: The Complete Poems and Selected Letters of John Keats* (London: Vintage Books, 2009), p. 492.

Chapter 5

On the concept of the archetype[1]

148   The concept of the Great Mother belongs to the field of comparative religion and embraces widely varying types of mother-goddess. The concept itself is of no immediate concern to psychology, because the image of a Great Mother in this form is rarely encountered in practice, and then only under very special conditions. The symbol is obviously a derivative of the *mother archetype*. If we venture to investigate the background of the Great Mother image from the standpoint of psychology, then the mother archetype, as the more inclusive of the two, must form the basis of our discussion. Though lengthy discussion of the *concept* of an archetype is hardly necessary at this stage, some preliminary remarks of a general nature may not be out of place.

149   In former times, despite some dissenting opinion and the influence of Aristotle, it was not too difficult to understand Plato's conception of the Idea as supraordinate and pre-existent to all phenomena. 'Archetype,' far from being a modern term, was already in use before the time of St. Augustine, and was synonymous with 'Idea' in the Platonic usage. When the *Corpus Hermeticum*, which probably dates from the third century, describes God as τὸ ἀρχέτυπον φῶς, the 'archetypal light,' it expresses the idea that he is the prototype of all light; that is to say, pre-existent and supraordinate to the phenomenon 'light.' Were I a philosopher, I should continue in this Platonic strain and say: Somewhere, in 'a place beyond the skies,' there is a prototype or primordial image of the mother that is pre-existent and supraordinate to all phenomena in which the 'maternal,' in the broadest sense of the term, is manifest. But I am an empiricist, not a philosopher; I cannot let myself presuppose that my peculiar temperament, my own attitude to intellectual problems, is universally valid. Apparently this is an assumption in which only the philosopher may indulge, who always takes it for granted that his own disposition and attitude are universal, and will not recognize the fact, if he can avoid it, that his 'personal equation' conditions his philosophy. As an empiricist, I must point out that there is a temperament which regards ideas as real entities and not merely as *nomina*. It so happens – by the merest accident, one might say – that for the past two hundred years we have been living in an age in which it has become unpopular or even unintelligible to suppose that ideas could be anything but *nomina*. Anyone who continues to think as Plato did must pay for his anachronism by

seeing the 'supracelestial,' i.e., metaphysical, essence of the Idea relegated to the unverifiable realm of faith and superstition, or charitably left to the poet. Once again, in the age-old controversy over universals, the nominalistic standpoint has triumphed over the realistic, and the Idea has evaporated into a mere *flatus vocis*. This change was accompanied – and, indeed, to a considerable degree caused – by the marked rise of empiricism, the advantages of which were only too obvious to the intellect. Since that time the Idea is no longer something *a priori*, but is secondary and derived. Naturally, the new nominalism promptly claimed universal validity for itself in spite of the fact that it, too, is based on a definite and limited thesis coloured by temperament. This thesis runs as follows: we accept as valid anything that comes from outside and can be verified. The ideal instance is verification by experiment. The antithesis is: we accept as valid anything that comes from inside and cannot be verified. The hopelessness of this position is obvious. Greek natural philosophy with its interest in matter, together with Aristotelian reasoning, has achieved a belated but overwhelming victory over Plato.

150   Yet every victory contains the germ of future defeat. In our own day signs foreshadowing a change of attitude are rapidly increasing. Significantly enough, it is Kant's doctrine of categories, more than anything else, that destroys in embryo every attempt to revive metaphysics in the old sense of the word, but at the same time paves the way for a rebirth of the Platonic spirit. If it be true that there can be no metaphysics transcending human reason, it is no less true that there can be no empirical knowledge that is not already caught and limited by the *a priori* structure of cognition. During the century and a half that have elapsed since the appearance of the *Critique of Pure Reason*, the conviction has gradually gained ground that thinking, understanding, and reasoning cannot be regarded as independent processes subject only to the eternal laws of logic, but that they are *psychic functions* co-ordinated with the personality and subordinate to it. We no longer ask, 'Has this or that been seen, heard, handled, weighed, counted, thought, and found to be logical?' We ask instead, '*Who* saw, heard, or thought?' Beginning with 'the personal equation' in the observation and measurement of minimal processes, this critical attitude has gone on to the creation of an empirical psychology such as no time before ours has known. Today we are convinced that in all fields of knowledge psychological premises exist which exert a decisive influence upon the choice of material, the method of investigation, the nature of the conclusions, and the formulation of hypotheses and theories. We have even come to believe that Kant's personality was a decisive conditioning factor of his *Critique of Pure Reason*. Not only our philosophers, but our own predilections in philosophy, and even what we are fond of calling our 'best' truths are affected, if not dangerously undermined, by this recognition of a personal premise. All creative freedom, we cry out, is taken away from us! What? Can it be possible that a man only thinks or says or does what he himself *is*?

151   Provided that we do not again exaggerate and so fall a victim to unrestrained 'psychologizing,' it seems to me that the critical standpoint here defined is inescapable. It constitutes the essence, origin, and method of modern psychology. There *is*

an *a priori* factor in all human activities, namely the inborn, preconscious and unconscious individual structure of the psyche. The preconscious psyche – for example, that of a new-born infant – is not an empty vessel into which, under favourable conditions, practically anything can be poured. On the contrary, it is a tremendously complicated, sharply defined individual entity which appears indeterminate to us only because we cannot see it directly. But the moment the first visible manifestations of psychic life begin to appear, one would have to be blind not to recognize their individual character, that is, the unique personality behind them. It is hardly possible to suppose that all these details come into being only at the moment in which they appear. When it is a case of morbid predispositions already present in the parents, we infer hereditary transmission through the germ-plasm; it would not occur to us to regard epilepsy in the child of an epileptic mother as an unaccountable mutation. Again, we explain by heredity the gifts and talents which can be traced back through whole generations. We explain in the same way the reappearance of complicated instinctive actions in animals that have never set eyes on their parents and therefore could not possibly have been 'taught' by them.

152 Nowadays we have to start with the hypothesis that, so far as predisposition is concerned, there is no essential difference between man and all other creatures. Like every animal, he possesses a preformed psyche which breeds true to his species and which, on closer examination, reveals distinct features traceable to family antecedents. We have not the slightest reason to suppose that there are certain human activities or functions that could be exempted from this rule. We are unable to form any idea of what those dispositions or aptitudes are which make instinctive actions in animals possible. And it is just as impossible for us to know the nature of the preconscious psychic disposition that enables a child to react in a human manner. We can only suppose that his behaviour results from patterns of functioning, which I have described as *images*. The term 'image' is intended to express not only the form of the activity taking place, but the typical situation in which the activity is released.[2] These images are 'primordial' images in so far as they are peculiar to whole species, and if they ever 'originated' their origin must have coincided at least with the beginning of the species. They are the 'human quality' of the human being, the specifically human form his activities take. This specific form is hereditary and is already present in the germ-plasm. The idea that it is not inherited but comes into being in every child anew would be just as preposterous as the primitive belief that the sun which rises in the morning is a different sun from that which set the evening before.

153 Since everything psychic is preformed, this must also be true of the individual functions, especially those which derive directly from the unconscious predisposition. The most important of these is creative fantasy. In the products of fantasy the primordial images are made visible, and it is here that the concept of the archetype finds its specific application. I do not claim to have been the first to point out this fact. The honour belongs to Plato. The first investigator in the field of ethnology to draw attention to the widespread occurrence of certain 'elementary ideas' was Adolf Bastian. Two later investigators, Hubert and Mauss,[3] followers

of Dürkheim, speak of 'categories' of the imagination. And it was no less an authority than Hermann Usener[4] who first recognized unconscious preformation under the guise of 'unconscious thinking.' If I have any share in these discoveries, it consists in my having shown that archetypes are not disseminated only by tradition, language, and migration, but that they can rearise spontaneously, at any time, at any place, and without any outside influence.

154 The far-reaching implications of this statement must not be overlooked. For it means that there are present in every psyche forms which are unconscious but nonetheless active – living dispositions, ideas in the Platonic sense, that preform and continually influence our thoughts and feelings and actions.

155 Again and again I encounter the mistaken notion that an archetype is determined in regard to its content, in other words that it is a kind of unconscious idea (if such an expression be admissible). It is necessary to point out once more that archetypes are not determined as regards their content, but only as regards their form and then only to a very limited degree. A primordial image is determined as to its content only when it has become conscious and is therefore filled out with the material of conscious experience. Its form, however, as I have explained elsewhere, might perhaps be compared to the axial system of a crystal, which, as it were, preforms the crystalline structure in the mother liquid, although it has no material existence of its own. This first appears according to the specific way in which the ions and molecules aggregate. The archetype in itself is empty and purely formal, nothing but a *facultas praeformandi*, a possibility of representation which is given *a priori*. The representations themselves are not inherited, only the forms, and in that respect they correspond in every way to the instincts, which are also determined in form only. The existence of the instincts can no more be proved than the existence of the archetypes, so long as they do not manifest themselves concretely. With regard to the definiteness of the form, our comparison with the crystal is illuminating inasmuch as the axial system determines only the stereometric structure but not the concrete form of the individual crystal. This may be either large or small, and it may vary endlessly by reason of the different size of its planes or by the growing together of two crystals. The only thing that remains constant is the axial system, or rather, the invariable geometric proportions underlying it. The same is true of the archetype. In principle, it can be named and has an invariable nucleus of meaning – but always only in principle, never as regards its concrete manifestation. In the same way, the specific appearance of the mother-image at any given time cannot be deduced from the mother archetype alone, but depends on innumerable other factors.

Notes

1 [Originally published as the first part of a lecture, 'Die psychologischen Aspekte des Mutterarchetypus,' in *Eranos-Jahrbuch 1938*. Later revised and published in *Von den Wurzeln des Bewusstseins* (Zurich, 1954). The present translation by R. F. C. Hull is based on the latter. – Editor.]
2 Cf. my 'Instinct and the Unconscious,' par. 277.
3 [Cf. the previous paper, 'Concerning the Archetypes,' par. 137, n. 25.–EDITORS.]
4 Usener, *Das Weihnachtsfest*, p. 3.

Chapter 6

Phenomenology of the self[1]

The ego; The shadow; The syzygy:
anima and animus; The self

I: The ego

1 Investigation of the psychology of the unconscious confronted me with facts which required the formulation of new concepts. One of these concepts is the *self.* The entity so denoted is not meant to take the place of the one that has always been known as the *ego,* but includes it in a supraordinate concept. We understand the ego as the complex factor to which all conscious contents are related. It forms, as it were, the centre of the field of consciousness; and, in so far as this comprises the empirical personality, the ego is the subject of all personal acts of consciousness. The relation of a psychic content to the ego forms the criterion of its consciousness, for no content can be conscious unless it is represented to a subject.

2 With this definition we have described and delimited the *scope* of the subject. Theoretically, no limits can be set to the field of consciousness, since it is capable of indefinite extension. Empirically, however, it always finds its limit when it comes up against the *unknown*. This consists of everything we do not know, which, therefore, is not related to the ego as the centre of the field of consciousness. The unknown falls into two groups of objects: those which are outside and can be experienced by the senses, and those which are inside and are experienced immediately. The first group comprises the unknown in the outer world; the second the unknown in the inner world. We call this latter territory the *unconscious*.

3 The ego, as a specific content of consciousness, is not a simple or elementary factor but a complex one which, as such, cannot be described exhaustively. Experience shows that it rests on two seemingly different bases: the *somatic* and the *psychic*. The somatic basis is inferred from the totality of endosomatic perceptions, which for their part are already of a psychic nature and are associated with the ego, and are therefore conscious. They are produced by endosomatic stimuli, only some of which cross the threshold of consciousness. A considerable proportion of these stimuli occur unconsciously, that is, subliminally. The fact that they are subliminal does not necessarily mean that their status is merely physiological, any more than this would be true of a psychic content. Sometimes they are capable of crossing the threshold, that is, of becoming perceptions. But there is no doubt

that a large proportion of these endosomatic stimuli are simply incapable of consciousness and are so elementary that there is no reason to assign them a psychic nature – unless of course one favours the philosophical view that all life-processes are psychic anyway. The chief objection to this hardly demonstrable hypothesis is that it enlarges the concept of the psyche beyond all bounds and interprets the life-process in a way not absolutely warranted by the facts. Concepts that are too broad usually prove to be unsuitable instruments because they are too vague and nebulous. I have therefore suggested that the term 'psychic' be used only where there is evidence of a will capable of modifying reflex or instinctual processes. Here I must refer the reader to my paper 'On the Nature of the Psyche,'[2] where I have discussed this definition of the 'psychic' at somewhat greater length.

4   The somatic basis of the ego consists, then, of conscious and unconscious factors. The same is true of the psychic basis: on the one hand the ego rests on the *total field of consciousness,* and on the other, on the *sum total of unconscious contents*. These fall into three groups: first, temporarily subliminal contents that can be reproduced voluntarily (memory); second, unconscious contents that cannot be reproduced voluntarily; third, contents that are not capable of becoming conscious at all. Group two can be inferred from the spontaneous irruption of subliminal contents into consciousness. Group three is hypothetical; it is a logical inference from the facts underlying group two. It contains contents which have *not yet* irrupted into consciousness, or which never will.

5   When I said that the ego 'rests' on the total field of consciousness I do not mean that it *consists* of this. Were that so, it would be indistinguishable from the field of consciousness as a whole. The ego is only the latter's point of reference, grounded on and limited by the somatic factor described above.

6   Although its bases are in themselves relatively unknown and unconscious, the ego is a conscious factor par excellence. It is even acquired, empirically speaking, during the individual's lifetime. It seems to arise in the first place from the collision between the somatic factor and the environment, and, once established as a subject, it goes on developing from further collisions with the outer world and the inner.

7   Despite the unlimited extent of its bases, the ego is never more and never less than consciousness as a whole. As a conscious factor the ego could, theoretically at least, be described completely. But this would never amount to more than a picture of the *conscious personality*; all those features which are unknown or unconscious to the subject would be missing. A total picture would have to include these. But a total description of the personality is, even in theory, absolutely impossible, because the unconscious portion of it cannot be grasped cognitively. This unconscious portion, as experience has abundantly shown, is by no means unimportant. On the contrary, the most decisive qualities in a person are often unconscious and can be perceived only by others, or have to be laboriously discovered with outside help.

8   Clearly, then, the *personality as a total phenomenon* does not coincide with the ego, that is, with the conscious personality, but forms an entity that has to be

distinguished from the ego. Naturally the need to do this is incumbent only on a psychology that reckons with the fact of the unconscious, but for such a psychology the distinction is of paramount importance. Even for jurisprudence it should be of some importance whether certain psychic facts are conscious or not – for instance, in adjudging the question of responsibility.

9   I have suggested calling the total personality which, though present, cannot be fully known, the *self*. The ego is, by definition, subordinate to the self and is related to it like a part to the whole. Inside the field of consciousness it has, as we say, free will. By this I do not mean anything philosophical, only the well-known psychological fact of 'free choice,' or rather the subjective feeling of freedom. But, just as our free will clashes with necessity in the outside world, so also it finds its limits outside the field of consciousness in the subjective inner world, where it comes into conflict with the facts of the self. And just as circumstances or outside events 'happen' to us and limit our freedom, so the self acts upon the ego like an *objective occurrence* which free will can do very little to alter. It is, indeed, well known that the ego not only can do nothing against the self, but is sometimes actually assimilated by unconscious components of the personality that are in the process of development and is greatly altered by them.

10   It is, in the nature of the case, impossible to give any general description of the ego except a formal one. Any other mode of observation would have to take account of the *individuality* which attaches to the ego as one of its main characteristics. Although the numerous elements composing this complex factor are, in themselves, everywhere the same, they are infinitely varied as regards clarity, emotional colouring, and scope. The result of their combination – the ego – is therefore, so far as one can judge, individual and unique, and retains its identity up to a certain point. Its stability is relative, because far-reaching changes of personality can sometimes occur. Alterations of this kind need not always be pathological; they can also be developmental and hence fall within the scope of the normal.

11   Since it is the point of reference for the field of consciousness, the ego is the subject of all successful attempts at adaptation so far as these are achieved by the will. The ego therefore has a significant part to play in the psychic economy. Its position there is so important that there are good grounds for the prejudice that the ego is the centre of the personality, and that the field of consciousness is the psyche *per se*. If we discount certain suggestive ideas in Leibniz, Kant, Schelling, and Schopenhauer, and the philosophical excursions of Carus and von Hartmann, it is only since the end of the nineteenth century that modern psychology, with its inductive methods, has discovered the foundations of consciousness and proved empirically the existence of a psyche outside consciousness. With this discovery the position of the ego, till then absolute, became relativized; that is to say, though it retains its quality as the centre of the field of consciousness, it is questionable whether it is the centre of the personality. It is part of the personality but not the whole of it. As I have said, it is simply impossible to estimate how large or how small its share is; how free or how dependent it is on the qualities of this

'extra-conscious' psyche. We can only say that its freedom is limited and its dependence proved in ways that are often decisive. In my experience one would do well not to underestimate its dependence on the unconscious. Naturally there is no need to say this to persons who already overestimate the latter's importance. Some criterion for the right measure is afforded by the psychic consequences of a wrong estimate, a point to which we shall return later on.

12   We have seen that, from the standpoint of the psychology of consciousness, the unconscious can be divided into three groups of contents. But from the standpoint of the psychology of the personality a twofold division ensues: an 'extra-conscious' psyche whose contents are *personal,* and an 'extra-conscious' psyche whose contents are *impersonal* and *collective*. The first group comprises contents which are integral components of the individual personality and could therefore just as well be conscious; the second group forms, as it were, an omnipresent, unchanging, and everywhere identical *quality or substrate of the psyche per se*. This is, of course, no more than a hypothesis. But we are driven to it by the peculiar nature of the empirical material, not to mention the high probability that the general similarity of psychic processes in all individuals must be based on an equally general and impersonal principle that conforms to law, just as the instinct manifesting itself in the individual is only the partial manifestation of an instinctual substrate common to all men.

II: The shadow

13   Whereas the contents of the personal unconscious are acquired during the individual's lifetime, the contents of the collective unconscious are invariably archetypes that were present from the beginning. Their relation to the instincts has been discussed elsewhere.[3] The archetypes most clearly characterized from the empirical point of view are those which have the most frequent and the most disturbing influence on the ego. These are the *shadow,* the *anima,* and the *animus*.[4] The most accessible of these, and the easiest to experience, is the shadow, for its nature can in large measure be inferred from the contents of the personal unconscious. The only exceptions to this rule are those rather rare cases where the positive qualities of the personality are repressed, and the ego in consequence plays an essentially negative or unfavourable role.

14   The shadow is a moral problem that challenges the whole ego-personality, for no one can become conscious of the shadow without considerable moral effort. To become conscious of it involves recognizing the dark aspects of the personality as present and real. This act is the essential condition for any kind of self-knowledge, and it therefore, as a rule, meets with considerable resistance. Indeed, self-knowledge as a psychotherapeutic measure frequently requires much painstaking work extending over a long period.

15   Closer examination of the dark characteristics – that is, the inferiorities constituting the shadow – reveals that they have an *emotional* nature, a kind of autonomy, and accordingly an obsessive or, better, possessive quality. Emotion, incidentally,

is not an activity of the individual but something that happens to him. Affects occur usually where adaptation is weakest, and at the same time they reveal the reason for its weakness, namely a certain degree of inferiority and the existence of a lower level of personality. On this lower level with its uncontrolled or scarcely controlled emotions one behaves more or less like a primitive, who is not only the passive victim of his affects but also singularly incapable of moral judgment.

16   Although, with insight and good will, the shadow can to some extent be assimilated into the conscious personality, experience shows that there are certain features which offer the most obstinate resistance to moral control and prove almost impossible to influence. These resistances are usually bound up with *projections,* which are not recognized as such, and their recognition is a moral achievement beyond the ordinary. While some traits peculiar to the shadow can be recognized without too much difficulty as one's own personal qualities, in this case both insight and good will are unavailing because the cause of the emotion appears to lie, beyond all possibility of doubt, in the *other person*. No matter how obvious it may be to the neutral observer that it is a matter of projections, there is little hope that the subject will perceive this himself. He must be convinced that he throws a very long shadow before he is willing to withdraw his emotionally-toned projections from their object.

17   Let us suppose that a certain individual shows no inclination whatever to recognize his projections. The projection-making factor then has a free hand and can realize its object – if it has one – or bring about some other situation characteristic of its power. As we know, it is not the conscious subject but the unconscious which does the projecting. Hence one meets with projections, one does not make them. The effect of projection is to isolate the subject from his environment, since instead of a real relation to it there is now only an illusory one. Projections change the world into the replica of one's own unknown face. In the last analysis, therefore, they lead to an autoerotic or autistic condition in which one dreams a world whose reality remains forever unattainable. The resultant *sentiment d'incomplétude* and the still worse feeling of sterility are in their turn explained by projection as the malevolence of the environment, and by means of this vicious circle the isolation is intensified. The more projections are thrust in between the subject and the environment, the harder it is for the ego to see through its illusions. A forty-five-year-old patient who had suffered from a compulsion neurosis since he was twenty and had become completely cut off from the world once said to me: 'But I can never admit to myself that I've wasted the best twenty-five years of my life!'

18   It is often tragic to see how blatantly a man bungles his own life and the lives of others yet remains totally incapable of seeing how much the whole tragedy originates in himself, and how he continually feeds it and keeps it going. Not *consciously,* of course – for consciously he is engaged in bewailing and cursing a faithless world that recedes further and further into the distance. Rather, it is an unconscious factor which spins the illusions that veil his world. And what is being spun is a cocoon, which in the end will completely envelop him.

19   One might assume that projections like these, which are so very difficult if not impossible to dissolve, would belong to the realm of the shadow – that is, to the negative side of the personality. This assumption becomes untenable after a certain point, because the symbols that then appear no longer refer to the same but to the opposite sex, in a man's case to a woman and vice versa. The source of projections is no longer the shadow – which is always of the same sex as the subject – but a contrasexual figure. Here we meet the animus of a woman and the anima of a man, two corresponding archetypes whose autonomy and unconsciousness explain the stubbornness of their projections. Though the shadow is a motif as well known to mythology as anima and animus, it represents first and foremost the personal unconscious, and its content can therefore be made conscious without too much difficulty. In this it differs from anima and animus, for whereas the shadow can be seen through and recognized fairly easily, the anima and animus are much further away from consciousness and in normal circumstances are seldom if ever realized. With a little self-criticism one can see through the shadow – so far as its nature is personal. But when it appears as an archetype, one encounters the same difficulties as with anima and animus. In other words, it is quite within the bounds of possibility for a man to recognize the relative evil of his nature, but it is a rare and shattering experience for him to gaze into the face of absolute evil.

III: The syzygy: anima and animus

20 What, then, is this projection-making factor? The East calls it the 'Spinning Woman'[5] – Maya, who creates illusion by her dancing. Had we not long since known it from the symbolism of dreams, this hint from the Orient would put us on the right track: the enveloping, embracing, and devouring element points unmistakably to the mother,[6] that is, to the son's relation to the real mother, to her imago, and to the woman who is to become a mother for him. His Eros is passive like a child's; he hopes to be caught, sucked in, enveloped, and devoured. He seeks, as it were, the protecting, nourishing, charmed circle of the mother, the condition of the infant released from every care, in which the outside world bends over him and even forces happiness upon him. No wonder the real world vanishes from sight!

21   If this situation is dramatized, as the unconscious usually dramatizes it, then there appears before you on the psychological stage a man living regressively, seeking his childhood and his mother; fleeing from a cold cruel world which denies him understanding. Often a mother appears beside him who apparently shows not the slightest concern that her little son should become a man, but who, with tireless and self-immolating effort, neglects nothing that might hinder him from growing up and marrying. You behold the secret conspiracy between mother and son, and how each helps the other to betray life.

22   Where does the guilt lie? With the mother, or with the son? Probably with both. The unsatisfied longing of the son for life and the world ought to be taken

seriously. There is in him a desire to touch reality, to embrace the earth and fructify the field of the world. But he makes no more than a series of fitful starts, for his initiative as well as his staying power are crippled by the secret memory that the world and happiness may be had as a gift – from the mother. The fragment of world which he, like every man, must encounter again and again is never quite the right one, since it does not fall into his lap, does not meet him half way, but remains resistant, has to be conquered, and submits only to force. It makes demands on the masculinity of a man, on his ardour, above all on his courage and resolution when it comes to throwing his whole being into the scales. For this he would need a faithless Eros, one capable of forgetting his mother and undergoing the pain of relinquishing the first love of his life. The mother, foreseeing this danger, has carefully inculcated into him the virtues of faithfulness, devotion, loyalty, so as to protect him from the moral disruption which is the risk of every life adventure. He has learnt these lessons only too well, and remains true to his mother. This naturally causes her the deepest anxiety (when, to her greater glory, he turns out to be a homosexual, for example) and at the same time affords her an unconscious satisfaction that is positively mythological. For, in the relationship now reigning between them, there is consummated the immemorial and most sacred archetype of the marriage of mother and son. What, after all, has commonplace reality to offer, with its registry offices, pay envelopes, and monthly rent, that could outweigh the mystic awe of the *hieros gamos*? Or the star-crowned woman whom the dragon pursues, or the pious obscurities veiling the marriage of the Lamb?

23   This myth, better than any other, illustrates the nature of the collective unconscious. At this level the mother is both old and young, Demeter and Persephone, and the son is spouse and sleeping suckling rolled into one. The imperfections of real life, with its laborious adaptations and manifold disappointments, naturally cannot compete with such a state of indescribable fulfilment.

24   In the case of the son, the projection-making factor is identical with the mother-imago, and this is consequently taken to be the real mother. The projection can only be dissolved when the son sees that in the realm of his psyche there is an imago not only of the mother but of the daughter, the sister, the beloved, the heavenly goddess, and the chthonic Baubo. Every mother and every beloved is forced to become the carrier and embodiment of this omnipresent and ageless image, which corresponds to the deepest reality in a man. It belongs to him, this perilous image of Woman; she stands for the loyalty which in the interests of life he must sometimes forgo; she is the much needed compensation for the risks, struggles, sacrifices that all end in disappointment; she is the solace for all the bitterness of life. And, at the same time, she is the great illusionist, the seductress, who draws him into life with her Maya – and not only into life's reasonable and useful aspects, but into its frightful paradoxes and ambivalences where good and evil, success and ruin, hope and despair, counterbalance one another. Because she is his greatest danger she demands from a man his greatest, and if he has it in him she will receive it.

25   This image is 'My Lady Soul,' as Spitteler called her. I have suggested instead the term 'anima,' as indicating something specific, for which the expression 'soul' is too general and too vague. The empirical reality summed up under the concept of the anima forms an extremely dramatic content of the unconscious. It is possible to describe this content in rational, scientific language, but in this way one entirely fails to express its living character. Therefore, in describing the living processes of the psyche, I deliberately and consciously give preference to a dramatic, mythological way of thinking and speaking, because this is not only more expressive but also more exact than an abstract scientific terminology, which is wont to toy with the notion that its theoretic formulations may one fine day be resolved into algebraic equations.

26   The projection-making factor is the anima, or rather the unconscious as represented by the anima. Whenever she appears, in dreams, visions, and fantasies, she takes on personified form, thus demonstrating that the factor she embodies possesses all the outstanding characteristics of a feminine being.[7] She is not an invention of the conscious, but a spontaneous product of the unconscious. Nor is she a substitute figure for the mother. On the contrary, there is every likelihood that the numinous qualities which make the mother-imago so dangerously powerful derive from the collective archetype of the anima, which is incarnated anew in every male child.

27   Since the anima is an archetype that is found in men, it is reasonable to suppose that an equivalent archetype must be present in women; for just as the man is compensated by a feminine element, so woman is compensated by a masculine one. I do not, however, wish this argument to give the impression that these compensatory relationships were arrived at by deduction. On the contrary, long and varied experience was needed in order to grasp the nature of anima and animus empirically. Whatever we have to say about these archetypes, therefore, is either directly verifiable or at least rendered probable by the facts. At the same time, I am fully aware that we are discussing pioneer work which by its very nature can only be provisional.

28   Just as the mother seems to be the first carrier of the projection-making factor for the son, so is the father for the daughter. Practical experience of these relationships is made up of many individual cases presenting all kinds of variations on the same basic theme. A concise description of them can, therefore, be no more than schematic.

29   Woman is compensated by a masculine element and therefore her unconscious has, so to speak, a masculine imprint. This results in a considerable psychological difference between men and women, and accordingly I have called the projection-making factor in women the animus, which means mind or spirit. The animus corresponds to the paternal Logos just as the anima corresponds to the maternal Eros. But I do not wish or intend to give these two intuitive concepts too specific a definition. I use Eros and Logos merely as conceptual aids to describe the fact that woman's consciousness is characterized more by the connective quality of Eros than by the discrimination and cognition associated with Logos. In men,

Eros, the function of relationship, is usually less developed than Logos. In women, on the other hand, Eros is an expression of their true nature, while their Logos is often only a regrettable accident. It gives rise to misunderstandings and annoying interpretations in the family circle and among friends. This is because it consists of *opinions* instead of reflections, and by opinions I mean *a priori* assumptions that lay claim to absolute truth. Such assumptions, as everyone knows, can be extremely irritating. As the animus is partial to argument, he can best be seen at work in disputes where both parties know they are right. Men can argue in a very womanish way, too, when they are anima-possessed and have thus been transformed into the animus of their own anima. With them the question becomes one of personal vanity and touchiness (as if they were females); with women it is a question of *power,* whether of truth or justice or some other 'ism' – for the dressmaker and hairdresser have already taken care of their vanity. The 'Father' (i.e., the sum of conventional opinions) always plays a great role in female argumentation. No matter how friendly and obliging a woman's Eros may be, no logic on earth can shake her if she is ridden by the animus. Often the man has the feeling – and he is not altogether wrong – that only seduction or a beating or rape would have the necessary power of persuasion. He is unaware that this highly dramatic situation would instantly come to a banal and unexciting end if he were to quit the field and let a second woman carry on the battle (his wife, for instance, if she herself is not the fiery war horse). This sound idea seldom or never occurs to him, because no man can converse with an animus for five minutes without becoming the victim of his own anima. Anyone who still had enough sense of humour to listen objectively to the ensuing dialogue would be staggered by the vast number of commonplaces, misapplied truisms, clichés from newspapers and novels, shop-soiled platitudes of every description interspersed with vulgar abuse and brain-splitting lack of logic. It is a dialogue which, irrespective of its participants, is repeated millions and millions of times in all the languages of the world and always remains essentially the same.

30 This singular fact is due to the following circumstance: when animus and anima meet, the animus draws his sword of power and the anima ejects her poison of illusion and seduction. The outcome need not always be negative, since the two are equally likely to fall in love (a special instance of love at first sight). The language of love is of astonishing uniformity, using the well-worn formulas with the utmost devotion and fidelity, so that once again the two partners find themselves in a banal collective situation. Yet they live in the illusion that they are related to one another in a most individual way.

31 In both its positive and its negative aspects the anima/animus relationship is always full of 'animosity,' i.e., it is emotional, and hence collective. Affects lower the level of the relationship and bring it closer to the common instinctual basis, which no longer has anything individual about it. Very often the relationship runs its course heedless of its human performers, who afterwards do not know what happened to them.

32 Whereas the cloud of 'animosity' surrounding the man is composed chiefly of sentimentality and resentment, in woman it expresses itself in the form of opinionated views, interpretations, insinuations, and misconstructions, which all have the purpose (sometimes attained) of severing the relation between two human beings. The woman, like the man, becomes wrapped in a veil of illusions by her demon-familiar, and, as the daughter who alone understands her father (that is, is eternally right in everything), she is translated to the land of sheep, where she is put to graze by the shepherd of her soul, the animus.

33 Like the anima, the animus too has a positive aspect. Through the figure of the father he expresses not only conventional opinion but – equally – what we call 'spirit,' philosophical or religious ideas in particular, or rather the attitude resulting from them. Thus the animus is a psychopomp, a mediator between the conscious and the unconscious and a personification of the latter. Just as the anima becomes, through integration, the Eros of consciousness, so the animus becomes a Logos; and in the same way that the anima gives relationship and relatedness to a man's consciousness, the animus gives to woman's consciousness a capacity for reflection, deliberation, and self-knowledge.

34 The effect of anima and animus on the ego is in principle the same. This effect is extremely difficult to eliminate because, in the first place, it is uncommonly strong and immediately fills the ego-personality with an unshakable feeling of rightness and righteousness. In the second place, the cause of the effect is projected and appears to lie in objects and objective situations. Both these characteristics can, I believe, be traced back to the peculiarities of the archetype. For the archetype, of course, exists *a priori*. This may possibly explain the often totally irrational yet undisputed and indisputable existence of certain moods and opinions. Perhaps these are so notoriously difficult to influence because of the powerfully suggestive effect emanating from the archetype. Consciousness is fascinated by it, held captive, as if hypnotized. Very often the ego experiences a vague feeling of moral defeat and then behaves all the more defensively, defiantly, and self-righteously, thus setting up a vicious circle which only increases its feeling of inferiority. The bottom is then knocked out of the human relationship, for, like megalomania, a feeling of inferiority makes mutual recognition impossible, and without this there is no relationship.

35 As I said, it is easier to gain insight into the shadow than into the anima or animus. With the shadow, we have the advantage of being prepared in some sort by our education, which has always endeavoured to convince people that they are not one-hundred-per-cent pure gold. So everyone immediately understands what is meant by 'shadow,' 'inferior personality,' etc. And if he has forgotten, his memory can easily be refreshed by a Sunday sermon, his wife, or the tax collector. With the anima and animus, however, things are by no means so simple. Firstly, there is no moral education in this respect, and secondly, most people are content to be self-righteous and prefer mutual vilification (if nothing worse!) to the recognition of their projections. Indeed, it seems a very natural state of affairs for men to have irrational moods and women irrational opinions. Presumably this situation

is grounded on instinct and must remain as it is to ensure that the Empedoclean game of the hate and love of the elements shall continue for all eternity. Nature is conservative and does not easily allow her courses to be altered; she defends in the most stubborn way the inviolability of the preserves where anima and animus roam. Hence it is much more difficult to become conscious of one's anima/animus projections than to acknowledge one's shadow side. One has, of course, to overcome certain moral obstacles, such as vanity, ambition, conceit, resentment, etc., but in the case of projections all sorts of purely intellectual difficulties are added, quite apart from the contents of the projection which one simply doesn't know how to cope with. And on top of all this there arises a profound doubt as to whether one is not meddling too much with nature's business by prodding into consciousness things which it would have been better to leave asleep.

36   Although there are, in my experience, a fair number of people who can understand without special intellectual or moral difficulties what is meant by anima and animus, one finds very many more who have the greatest trouble in visualizing these empirical concepts as anything concrete. This shows that they fall a little outside the usual range of experience. They are unpopular precisely because they seem unfamiliar. The consequence is that they mobilize prejudice and become taboo like everything else that is unexpected.

37   So if we set it up as a kind of requirement that projections should be dissolved, because it is wholesomer that way and in every respect more advantageous, we are entering upon new ground. Up till now everybody has been convinced that the idea 'my father,' 'my mother,' etc., is nothing but a faithful reflection of the real parent, corresponding in every detail to the original, so that when someone says 'my father' he means no more and no less than what his father is in reality. This is actually what he supposes he does mean, but a supposition of identity by no means brings that identity about. This is where the fallacy of the *enkekalymmenos* ('the veiled one') comes in.[8] If one includes in the psychological equation X's picture of his father, which he takes for the real father, the equation will not work out, because the unknown quantity he has introduced does not tally with reality. X has overlooked the fact that his idea of a person consists, in the first place, of the possibly very incomplete picture he has received of the real person and, in the second place, of the subjective modifications he has imposed upon this picture. X's idea of his father is a complex quantity for which the real father is only in part responsible, an indefinitely larger share falling to the son. So true is this that every time he criticizes or praises his father he is unconsciously hitting back at himself, thereby bringing about those psychic consequences that overtake people who habitually disparage or overpraise themselves. If, however, X carefully compares his reactions with reality, he stands a chance of noticing that he has miscalculated somewhere by not realizing long ago from his father's behaviour that the picture he has of him is a false one. But as a rule X is convinced that he is right, and if anybody is wrong it must be the other fellow. Should X have a poorly developed Eros, he will be either indifferent to the inadequate relationship he has with his father or else annoyed by the inconsistency and general incomprehensibility of a

father whose behaviour never really corresponds to the picture X has of him. Therefore X thinks he has every right to feel hurt, misunderstood, and even betrayed.

38   One can imagine how desirable it would be in such cases to dissolve the projection. And there are always optimists who believe that the golden age can be ushered in simply by telling people the right way to go. But just let them try to explain to these people that they are acting like a dog chasing its own tail. To make a person see the shortcomings of his attitude considerably more than mere 'telling' is needed, for more is involved than ordinary common sense can allow. What one is up against here is the kind of fateful misunderstanding which, under ordinary conditions, remains forever inaccessible to insight. It is rather like expecting the average respectable citizen to recognize himself as a criminal.

39   I mention all this just to illustrate the order of magnitude to which the anima/animus projections belong, and the moral and intellectual exertions that are needed to dissolve them. Not all the contents of the anima and animus are projected, however. Many of them appear spontaneously in dreams and so on, and many more can be made conscious through active imagination. In this way we find that thoughts, feelings, and affects are alive in us which we would never have believed possible. Naturally, possibilities of this sort seem utterly fantastic to anyone who has not experienced them himself, for a normal person 'knows what he thinks.' Such a childish attitude on the part of the 'normal person' is simply the rule, so that no one without experience in this field can be expected to understand the real nature of anima and animus. With these reflections one gets into an entirely new world of psychological experience, provided of course that one succeeds in realizing it in practice. Those who do succeed can hardly fail to be impressed by all that the ego does not know and never has known. This increase in self-knowledge is still very rare nowadays and is usually paid for in advance with a neurosis, if not with something worse.

40   The autonomy of the collective unconscious expresses itself in the figures of anima and animus. They personify those of its contents which, when withdrawn from projection, can be integrated into consciousness. To this extent, both figures represent *functions* which filter the contents of the collective unconscious through to the conscious mind. They appear or behave as such, however, only so long as the tendencies of the conscious and unconscious do not diverge too greatly. Should any tension arise, these functions, harmless till then, confront the conscious mind in personified form and behave rather like systems split off from the personality, or like part souls. This comparison is inadequate in so far as nothing previously belonging to the ego-personality has split off from it; on the contrary, the two figures represent a disturbing accretion. The reason for their behaving in this way is that though the *contents* of anima and animus can be integrated they themselves cannot, since they are archetypes. As such they are the foundation stones of the psychic structure, which in its totality exceeds the limits of consciousness and therefore can never become the object of direct cognition. Though the effects of anima and animus can be made conscious, they themselves are factors

transcending consciousness and beyond the reach of perception and volition. Hence they remain autonomous despite the integration of their contents, and for this reason they should be borne constantly in mind. This is extremely important from the therapeutic standpoint, because constant observation pays the unconscious a tribute that more or less guarantees its co-operation. The unconscious as we know can never be 'done with' once and for all. It is, in fact, one of the most important tasks of psychic hygiene to pay continual attention to the symptomatology of unconscious contents and processes, for the good reason that the conscious mind is always in danger of becoming one-sided, of keeping to well-worn paths and getting stuck in blind alleys. The complementary and compensating function of the unconscious ensures that these dangers, which are especially great in neurosis, can in some measure be avoided. It is only under ideal conditions, when life is still simple and unconscious enough to follow the serpentine path of instinct without hesitation or misgiving, that the compensation works with entire success. The more civilized, the more unconscious and complicated a man is, the less he is able to follow his instincts. His complicated living conditions and the influence of his environment are so strong that they drown the quiet voice of nature. Opinions, beliefs, theories, and collective tendencies appear in its stead and back up all the aberrations of the conscious mind. Deliberate attention should then be given to the unconscious so that the compensation can set to work. Hence it is especially important to picture the archetypes of the unconscious not as a rushing phantasmagoria of fugitive images but as constant, autonomous factors, which indeed they are.

41   Both these archetypes, as practical experience shows, possess a fatality that can on occasion produce tragic results. They are quite literally the father and mother of all the disastrous entanglements of fate and have long been recognized as such by the whole world. Together they form a divine pair,[9] one of whom, in accordance with his Logos nature, is characterized by *pneuma* and *nous,* rather like Hermes with his ever-shifting hues, while the other, in accordance with her Eros nature, wears the features of Aphrodite, Helen (Selene), Persephone, and Hecate. Both of them are unconscious powers, 'gods' in fact, as the ancient world quite rightly conceived them to be. To call them by this name is to give them that central position in the scale of psychological values which has always been theirs whether consciously acknowledged or not; for their power grows in proportion to the degree that they remain unconscious. Those who do not see them are in their hands, just as a typhus epidemic flourishes best when its source is undiscovered. Even in Christianity the divine syzygy has not become obsolete, but occupies the highest place as Christ and his bride the Church.[10] Parallels like these prove extremely helpful in our attempts to find the right criterion for gauging the significance of these two archetypes. What we can discover about them from the conscious side is so slight as to be almost imperceptible. It is only when we throw light into the dark depths of the psyche and explore the strange and tortuous paths of human fate that it gradually becomes clear to us how immense is the influence wielded by these two factors that complement our conscious life.

168 Archetypes

42   Recapitulating, I should like to emphasize that the integration of the shadow, or the realization of the personal unconscious, marks the first stage in the analytic process, and that without it a recognition of anima and animus is impossible. The shadow can be realized only through a relation to a partner, and anima and animus only through a relation to a partner of the opposite sex, because only in such a relation do their projections become operative. The recognition of the anima gives rise, in a man, to a triad, one third of which is transcendent: the masculine subject, the opposing feminine subject, and the transcendent anima. With a woman the situation is reversed. The missing fourth element that would make the triad a quaternity is, in a man, the archetype of the Wise Old Man, which I have not discussed here, and in a woman the Chthonic Mother. These four constitute a half immanent and half transcendent quaternity, an archetype which I have called the *marriage quaternio*.[11] The marriage quaternio provides a schema not only for the self but also for the structure of primitive society with its cross-cousin marriage, marriage classes, and division of settlements into quarters. The self, on the other hand, is a God-image, or at least cannot be distinguished from one. Of this the early Christian spirit was not ignorant, otherwise Clement of Alexandria could never have said that he who knows himself knows God.[12]

IV: The Self[13]

43 We shall now turn to the question of whether the increase in self-knowledge resulting from the withdrawal of impersonal projections – in other words, the integration of the contents of the collective unconscious – exerts a specific influence on the ego-personality. To the extent that the integrated contents are *parts of the self*, we can expect this influence to be considerable. Their assimilation augments not only the area of the field of consciousness but also the importance of the ego, especially when, as usually happens, the ego lacks any critical approach to the unconscious. In that case it is easily overpowered and becomes identical with the contents that have been assimilated. In this way, for instance, a masculine consciousness comes under the influence of the anima and can even be possessed by her.

44   I have discussed the wider effects of the integration of unconscious contents elsewhere[14] and can therefore omit going into details here. I should only like to mention that the more numerous and the more significant the unconscious contents which are assimilated to the ego, the closer the approximation of the ego to the self, even though this approximation must be a never-ending process. This inevitably produces an inflation of the ego,[15] unless a critical line of demarcation is drawn between it and the unconscious figures. But this act of discrimination yields practical results only if it succeeds in fixing reasonable boundaries to the ego and in granting the figures of the unconscious – the self, anima, animus, and shadow – relative autonomy and reality (of a psychic nature). To psychologize this reality out of existence either is ineffectual, or else merely increases the inflation of the ego. One cannot dispose of facts by declaring them unreal. The projection-making

factor, for instance, has undeniable reality. Anyone who insists on denying it becomes identical with it, which is not only dubious in itself but a positive danger to the well-being of the individual. Everyone who has dealings with such cases knows how perilous an inflation can be. No more than a flight of steps or a smooth floor is needed to precipitate a fatal fall. Besides the 'pride goeth before a fall' motif there are other factors of a no less disagreeable psychosomatic and psychic nature which serve to reduce 'puffed-up-ness.' This condition should not be interpreted as one of conscious self-aggrandizement. Such is far from being the rule. In general we are not directly conscious of this condition at all, but can at best infer its existence indirectly from the symptoms. These include the reactions of our immediate environment. Inflation magnifies the blind spot in the eye, and the more we are assimilated by the projection-making factor, the greater becomes the tendency to identify with it. A clear symptom of this is our growing disinclination to take note of the reactions of the environment and pay heed to them.

45 It must be reckoned a psychic catastrophe when the *ego is assimilated by the self*. The image of wholeness then remains in the unconscious, so that on the one hand it shares the archaic nature of the unconscious and on the other finds itself in the psychically relative space-time continuum that is characteristic of the unconscious as such.[16] Both these qualities are numinous and hence have an unlimited determining effect on ego-consciousness, which is differentiated, i.e., separated, from the unconscious and moreover exists in an absolute space and an absolute time. It is a vital necessity that this should be so. If, therefore, the ego falls for any length of time under the control of an unconscious factor, its adaptation is disturbed and the way opened for all sorts of possible accidents.

46 Hence it is of the greatest importance that the ego should be anchored in the world of consciousness and that consciousness should be reinforced by a very precise adaptation. For this, certain virtues like attention, conscientiousness, patience, etc., are of great value on the moral side, just as accurate observation of the symptomatology of the unconscious and objective self-criticism are valuable on the intellectual side.

47 However, accentuation of the ego personality and the world of consciousness may easily assume such proportions that the figures of the unconscious are psychologized and the *self consequently becomes assimilated to the ego*. Although this is the exact opposite of the process we have just described it is followed by the same result: inflation. The world of consciousness must now be levelled down in favour of the reality of the unconscious. In the first case, reality had to be protected against an archaic, 'eternal' and 'ubiquitous' dream-state; in the second, room must be made for the dream at the expense of the world of consciousness. In the first case, mobilization of all the virtues is indicated; in the second, the presumption of the ego can only be damped down by moral defeat. This is necessary, because otherwise one will never attain that median degree of modesty which is essential for the maintenance of a balanced state. It is not a question, as one might think, of relaxing morality itself but of making a moral effort in a different direction. For instance, a man who is not conscientious enough has to

make a moral effort in order to come up to the mark; while for one who is sufficiently rooted in the world through his own efforts it is no small moral achievement to inflict defeat on his virtues by loosening his ties with the world and reducing his adaptive performance. (One thinks in this connection of Brother Klaus, now canonized, who for the salvation of his soul left his wife to her own devices, along with numerous progeny.)

48 Since real moral problems all begin where the penal code leaves off, their solution can seldom or never depend on precedent, much less on precepts and commandments. The real moral problems spring from *conflicts of duty*. Anyone who is sufficiently humble, or easy-going, can always reach a decision with the help of some outside authority. But one who trusts others as little as himself can never reach a decision at all, unless it is brought about in the manner which Common Law calls an 'Act of God.' The Oxford Dictionary defines this concept as the 'action of uncontrollable natural forces.' In all such cases there is an unconscious authority which puts an end to doubt by creating a *fait accompli*. (In the last analysis this is true also of those who get their decision from a higher authority, only in more veiled form.) One can describe this authority either as the 'will of God' or as an 'action of uncontrollable natural forces,' though psychologically it makes a good deal of difference how one thinks of it. The rationalistic interpretation of this inner authority as 'natural forces' or the instincts satisfies the modern intellect but has the great disadvantage that the apparent victory of instinct offends our moral self-esteem; hence we like to persuade ourselves that the matter has been decided solely by the rational motions of the will. Civilized man has such a fear of the 'crimen laesae maiestatis humanae' that whenever possible he indulges in a retrospective coloration of the facts in order to cover up the feeling of having suffered a moral defeat. He prides himself on what he believes to be his self-control and the omnipotence of his will, and despises the man who lets himself be outwitted by mere nature.

49 If, on the other hand, the inner authority is conceived as the 'will of God' (which implies that 'natural forces' are divine forces), our self-esteem is benefited because the decision then appears to be an act of obedience and the result a divine intention. This way of looking at it can, with some show of justice, be accused not only of being very convenient but of cloaking moral laxity in the mantle of virtue. The accusation, however, is justified only when one is in fact knowingly hiding one's own egoistic opinion behind a hypocritical façade of words. But this is by no means the rule, for in most cases instinctive tendencies assert themselves for or against one's subjective interests no matter whether an outside authority approves or not. The inner authority does not need to be consulted first, as it is present at the outset in the intensity of the tendencies struggling for decision. In this struggle the individual is never a spectator only; he takes part in it more or less 'voluntarily' and tries to throw the weight of his feeling of moral freedom into the scales of decision. Nevertheless, it remains a matter of doubt how much his seemingly free decision has a causal, and possibly unconscious, motivation. This may be quite as much an 'act of God' as any natural cataclysm. The problem seems to me

unanswerable, because we do not know where the roots of the feeling of moral freedom lie; and yet they exist no less surely than the instincts, which are felt as compelling forces.

50   All in all, it is not only more beneficial but more 'correct' psychologically to explain as the 'will of God' the natural forces that appear in us as instincts. In this way we find ourselves living in harmony with the *habitus* of our ancestral psychic life; that is, we function as man has functioned at all times and in all places. The existence of this habitus is proof of its viability, for, if it were not viable, all those who obeyed it would long since have perished of maladaptation. On the other hand, by conforming to it one has a reasonable life expectancy. When an habitual way of thinking guarantees as much as this there is not only no ground for declaring it incorrect but, on the contrary, every reason to take it as 'true' or 'correct' in the psychological sense. Psychological truths are not metaphysical insights; they are habitual modes of thinking, feeling, and behaving which experience has proved appropriate and useful.

51   So when I say that the impulses which we find in ourselves should be understood as the 'will of God,' I wish to emphasize that they ought not to be regarded as an arbitrary wishing and willing, but as absolutes which one must learn how to handle correctly. The will can control them only in part. It may be able to suppress them, but it cannot alter their nature, and what is suppressed comes up again in another place in altered form, but this time loaded with a resentment that makes the otherwise harmless natural impulse our enemy. I should also like the term 'God' in the phrase 'the will of God' to be understood not so much in the Christian sense as in the sense intended by Diotima, when she said: 'Eros, dear Socrates, is a mighty daemon.' The Greek words *daimon* and *daimonion* express a determining power which comes upon man from outside, like providence or fate, though the ethical decision is left to man. He must know, however, what he is deciding about and what he is doing. Then, if he obeys he is following not just his own opinion, and if he rejects he is destroying not just his own invention.

52   The purely biological or scientific standpoint falls short in psychology because it is, in the main, intellectual only. That this should be so is not a disadvantage, since the methods of natural science have proved of great heuristic value in psychological research. But the psychic phenomenon cannot be grasped in its totality by the intellect, for it consists not only of *meaning* but also of *value*, and this depends on the intensity of the accompanying feeling-tones. Hence at least the two 'rational' functions[17] are needed in order to map out anything like a complete diagram of a given psychic content.

53   If, therefore, in dealing with psychic contents one makes allowance not only for intellectual judgments but for value judgments as well, not only is the result a more complete picture of the content in question, but one also gets a better idea of the particular position it holds in the hierarchy of psychic contents in general. The feeling-value is a very important criterion which psychology cannot do without, because it determines in large measure the role which the content will play in the psychic economy. That is to say, the affective value gives the measure of the

intensity of an idea, and the intensity in its turn expresses that idea's energic tension, its effective potential. The shadow, for instance, usually has a decidedly negative feeling-value, while the anima, like the animus, has more of a positive one. Whereas the shadow is accompanied by more or less definite and describable feeling-tones, the anima and animus exhibit feeling qualities that are harder to define. Mostly they are felt to be fascinating or numinous. Often they are surrounded by an atmosphere of sensitivity, touchy reserve, secretiveness, painful intimacy, and even absoluteness. The relative autonomy of the anima- and animus-figures expresses itself in these qualities. In order of affective rank they stand to the shadow very much as the shadow stands in relation to ego-consciousness. The main affective emphasis seems to lie on the latter; at any rate it is able, by means of a considerable expenditure of energy, to repress the shadow, at least temporarily. But if for any reason the unconscious gains the upper hand, then the valency of the shadow and of the other figures increases proportionately, so that the scale of values is reversed. What lay furthest away from waking consciousness and seemed unconscious assumes, as it were, a threatening shape, and the affective value increases the higher up the scale you go: ego-consciousness, shadow, anima, self. This reversal of the conscious waking state occurs regularly during the transition from waking to sleeping, and what then emerge most vividly are the very things that were unconscious by day. Every *abaissement du niveau mental* brings about a relative reversal of values.

54 I am speaking here of the *subjective* feeling-value, which is subject to the more or less periodic changes described above. But there are also *objective* values which are founded on a *consensus omnium* – moral, aesthetic, and religious values, for instance, and these are universally recognized ideals or feeling-toned collective ideas (Lévy-Bruhl's 'représentations collectives').[18] The subjective feeling-tones or 'value quanta' are easily recognized by the kind and number of constellations, or symptoms of disturbance,[19] they produce. Collective ideals often have no subjective feeling-tone, but nevertheless retain their feeling-value. This value, therefore, cannot be demonstrated by subjective symptoms, though it may be by the attributes attaching to these collective ideas and by their characteristic symbolism, quite apart from their suggestive effect.

55 The problem has a practical aspect, since it may easily happen that a collective idea, though significant in itself, is – because of its lack of subjective feeling-tone – represented in a dream only by a subsidiary attribute, as when a god is represented by his theriomorphic attribute, etc. Conversely, the idea may appear in consciousness lacking the affective emphasis that properly belongs to it, and must then be transposed back into its archetypal context – a task that is usually discharged by poets and prophets. Thus Hölderlin, in his 'Hymn to Liberty,' lets this concept, worn stale by frequent use and misuse, rise up again in its pristine splendour:

>   Since her arm out of the dust has raised me,
>   Beats my heart so boldly and serene;

And my cheek still tingles with her kisses,
Flushed and glowing where her lips have been.
Every word she utters, by her magic
Rises new-created, without flaw;
Hearken to the tidings of my goddess,
Hearken to the Sovereign, and adore![20]

56 It is not difficult to see here that the idea of liberty has been changed back to its original dramatic state – into the shining figure of the anima, freed from the weight of the earth and the tyranny of the senses, the psychopomp who leads the way to the Elysian fields.

57 The first case we mentioned, where the collective idea is represented in a dream by a lowly aspect of itself, is certainly the more frequent: the 'goddess' appears as a black cat, and the Deity as the *lapis exilis* (stone of no worth). Interpretation then demands a knowledge of certain things which have less to do with zoology and mineralogy than with the existence of an historical *consensus omnium* in regard to the object in question. These 'mythological' aspects are always present, even though in a given case they may be unconscious. If for instance one doesn't happen to recall, when considering whether to paint the garden gate green or white, that green is the colour of life and hope, the symbolic aspect of 'green' is nevertheless present as an unconscious *sous-entendu*. So we find something which has the highest significance for the life of the unconscious standing lowest on the scale of conscious values, and vice versa. The figure of the shadow already belongs to the realm of bodiless phantoms – not to speak of anima and animus, which do not seem to appear at all except as projections upon our fellow human beings. As for the self, it is completely outside the personal sphere, and appears, if at all, only as a religious mythologem, and its symbols range from the highest to the lowest. Anyone who identifies with the daylight half of his psychic life will therefore declare the dreams of the night to be null and void, notwithstanding that the night is as long as the day and that all consciousness is manifestly founded on unconsciousness, is rooted in it and every night is extinguished in it. What is more, psychopathology knows with tolerable certainty what the unconscious can do to the conscious, and for this reason devotes to the unconscious an attention that often seems incomprehensible to the layman. We know, for instance, that what is small by day is big at night, and the other way round; thus we also know that besides the small by day there always looms the big by night, even when it is invisible.

58 This knowledge is an essential prerequisite for any integration – that is to say a content can only be integrated when its double aspect has become conscious and when it is grasped not merely intellectually but understood according to its feeling-value. Intellect and feeling, however, are difficult to put into one harness – they conflict with one another by definition. Whoever identifies with an intellectual standpoint will occasionally find his feeling confronting him like an enemy in the guise of the anima; conversely, an intellectual animus will make

violent attacks on the feeling standpoint. Therefore, anyone who wants to achieve the difficult feat of realizing something not only intellectually, but also according to its feeling-value, must for better or worse come to grips with the anima/animus problem in order to open the way for a higher union, a *coniunctio oppositorum*. This is an indispensable prerequisite for wholeness.

59   Although 'wholeness' seems at first sight to be nothing but an abstract idea (like anima and animus), it is nevertheless empirical in so far as it is anticipated by the psyche in the form of spontaneous or autonomous symbols. These are the quaternity or mandala symbols, which occur not only in the dreams of modern people who have never heard of them, but are widely disseminated in the historical records of many peoples and many epochs. Their significance as *symbols of unity and totality* is amply confirmed by history as well as by empirical psychology. What at first looks like an abstract idea stands in reality for something that exists and can be experienced, that demonstrates its *a priori* presence spontaneously. Wholeness is thus an objective factor that confronts the subject independently of him, like anima or animus; and just as the latter have a higher position in the hierarchy than the shadow, so wholeness lays claim to a position and a value superior to those of the syzygy. The syzygy seems to represent at least a substantial portion of it, if not actually two halves of the totality formed by the royal brother-sister pair, and hence the tension of opposites from which the divine child[21] is born as the symbol of unity.

60   Unity and totality stand at the highest point on the scale of objective values because their symbols can no longer be distinguished from the *imago Dei*. Hence all statements about the God-image apply also to the empirical symbols of totality. Experience shows that individual mandalas are symbols of *order*, and that they occur in patients principally during times of psychic disorientation or re-orientation. As magic circles they bind and subdue the lawless powers belonging to the world of darkness, and depict or create an order that transforms the chaos into a cosmos.[22] The mandala at first comes into the conscious mind as an unimpressive point or dot,[23] and a great deal of hard and painstaking work as well as the integration of many projections are generally required before the full range of the symbol can be anything like completely understood. If this insight were purely intellectual it could be achieved without much difficulty, for the world-wide pronouncements about the God within us and above us, about Christ and the *corpus mysticum*, the personal, and suprapersonal atman, etc., are all formulations that can easily be mastered by the philosophic intellect. This is the common source of the illusion that one is then in possession of the thing itself. But actually one has acquired nothing more than its name, despite the age-old prejudice that the name magically represents the thing, and that it is sufficient to pronounce the name in order to posit the thing's existence. In the course of the millennia the reasoning mind has been given every opportunity to see through the futility of this conceit, though that has done nothing to prevent the intellectual mastery of a thing from being accepted at its face value. It is precisely our experiences in psychology which demonstrate as plainly as could be wished that the

intellectual 'grasp' of a psychological fact produces no more than a concept of it, and that a concept is no more than a name, a *flatus vocis*. These intellectual counters can be bandied about easily enough. They pass lightly from hand to hand, for they have no weight or substance. They sound full but are hollow; and though purporting to designate a heavy task and obligation, they commit us to nothing. The intellect is undeniably useful in its own field, but is a great cheat and illusionist outside of it whenever it tries to manipulate values.

61 It would seem that one can pursue any science with the intellect alone except psychology, whose subject – the psyche – has more than the two aspects mediated by sense-perception and thinking. The function of value – feeling – is an integral part of our conscious orientation and ought not to be missing in a psychological judgment of any scope, otherwise the model we are trying to build of the real process will be incomplete. Every psychic process has a value quality attached to it, namely its feeling-tone. This indicates the degree to which the subject is *affected* by the process or how much it means to him (in so far as the process reaches consciousness at all). It is through the 'affect' that the subject becomes involved and so comes to feel the whole weight of reality. The difference amounts roughly to that between a severe illness which one reads about in a textbook and the real illness which one has. In psychology one possesses nothing unless one has experienced it in reality. Hence a purely intellectual insight is not enough, because one knows only the words and not the substance of the thing from inside.

62 There are far more people who are afraid of the unconscious than one would expect. They are even afraid of their own shadow. And when it comes to the anima and animus, this fear turns to panic. For the syzygy does indeed represent the psychic contents that irrupt into consciousness in a psychosis (most clearly of all in the paranoid forms of schizophrenia).[24] The overcoming of this fear is often a moral achievement of unusual magnitude, and yet it is not the only condition that must be fulfilled on the way to a real experience of the self.

63 The shadow, the syzygy, and the self are psychic factors of which an adequate picture can be formed only on the basis of a fairly thorough experience of them. Just as these concepts arose out of an experience of reality, so they can be elucidated only by further experience. Philosophical criticism will find everything to object to in them unless it begins by recognizing that they are concerned with *facts*, and that the 'concept' is simply an abbreviated description or definition of these facts. Such criticism has as little effect on the object as zoological criticism on a duck-billed platypus. It is not the concept that matters; the concept is only a word, a counter, and it has meaning and use only because it stands for a certain sum of experience. Unfortunately I cannot pass on this experience to my public. I have tried in a number of publications, with the help of case material, to present the nature of these experiences and also the method of obtaining them. Wherever my methods were really applied the facts I give have been confirmed. One could see the moons of Jupiter even in Galileo's day if one took the trouble to use his telescope.

64 Outside the narrower field of professional psychology these figures meet with understanding from all who have any knowledge of comparative mythology.

They have no difficulty in recognizing the shadow as the adverse representative of the dark chthonic world, a figure whose characteristics are universal. The syzygy is immediately comprehensible as the psychic prototype of all divine couples. Finally the self, on account of its empirical peculiarities, proves to be the *eidos* behind the supreme ideas of unity and totality that are inherent in all monotheistic and monistic systems.

65 I regard these parallels as important because it is possible, through them, to relate so-called *metaphysical* concepts, which have lost their root connection with natural experience, to living, universal psychic processes, so that they can recover their true and original meaning. In this way the connection is reestablished between the ego and projected contents now formulated as 'metaphysical' ideas. Unfortunately, as already said, the fact that metaphysical ideas exist and are believed in does nothing to prove the actual existence of their content or of the object they refer to, although the coincidence of idea and reality in the form of a special psychic state, a state of grace, should not be deemed impossible, even if the subject cannot bring it about by an act of will. Once metaphysical ideas have lost their capacity to recall and evoke the original experience they have not only become useless but prove to be actual impediments on the road to wider development. One clings to possessions that have once meant wealth; and the more ineffective, incomprehensible, and lifeless they become the more obstinately people cling to them. (Naturally it is only sterile ideas that they cling to; living ideas have content and riches enough, so there is no need to cling to them.) Thus in the course of time the meaningful turns into the meaningless. This is unfortunately the fate of metaphysical ideas.

66 Today it is a real problem what on earth such ideas can mean. The world – so far as it has not completely turned its back on tradition – has long ago stopped wanting to hear a 'message'; it would rather be told what the message means. The words that resound from the pulpit are incomprehensible and cry for an explanation. How has the death of Christ brought us redemption when no one feels redeemed? In what way is Jesus a God-man and what is such a being? What is the Trinity about, and the parthenogenesis, the eating of the body and the drinking of the blood, and all the rest of it? What connection can there be between the world of such concepts and the everyday world, whose material reality is the concern of natural science on the widest possible scale? At least sixteen hours out of twenty-four we live exclusively in this everyday world, and the remaining eight we spend preferably in an unconscious condition. Where and when does anything take place to remind us even remotely of phenomena like angels, miraculous feedings, beatitudes, the resurrection of the dead, etc.? It was therefore something of a discovery to find that during the unconscious state of sleep intervals occur, called 'dreams,' which occasionally contain scenes having a not inconsiderable resemblance to the motifs of mythology. For myths are miracle tales and treat of all those things which, very often, are also objects of belief.

67 In the everyday world of consciousness such things hardly exist; that is to say, until 1933 only lunatics would have been found in possession of living fragments

of mythology. After this date the world of heroes and monsters spread like a devastating fire over whole nations, proving that the strange world of myth had suffered no loss of vitality during the centuries of reason and enlightenment. If metaphysical ideas no longer have such a fascinating effect as before, this is certainly not due to any lack of primitivity in the European psyche, but simply and solely to the fact that the erstwhile symbols no longer express what is now welling up from the unconscious as the end-result of the development of Christian consciousness through the centuries. This end-result is a true *antimimon pneuma*, a false spirit of arrogance, hysteria, woolly-mindedness, criminal amorality, and doctrinaire fanaticism, a purveyor of shoddy spiritual goods, spurious art, philosophical stutterings, and Utopian humbug, fit only to be fed wholesale to the mass man of today. That is what the post-Christian spirit looks like.

Notes

1 [Originally published as the first four chapters of *Aion: Untersuchungen zur Symbolgeschichte* (Zurich, Rascher Verlag, 1951), which version was translated by R. F. C. Hull. – Editor.]
2 Pars. 371ff.
3 'Instinct and the Unconscious' and 'On the Nature of the Psyche,' pars. 397ff.
4 The contents of this and the following chapter are taken from a lecture delivered to the Swiss Society for Practical Psychology, in Zurich, 1948. The material was first published in the *Wiener Zeitschrift für Nervenheilkunde und deren Grenzgebiete*, I (1948): 4.
5 Erwin Rousselle, 'Seelische Führung im lebenden Taoismus,' Pl. I, pp. 150, 170. Rousselle calls the spinning woman the 'animal soul.' There is a saying that runs, 'The spinner sets in motion.' I have defined the anima as a personification of the unconscious.
6 Here and in what follows, the word 'mother' is not meant in the literal sense but as a symbol of everything that functions as a mother.
7 Naturally, she is a typical figure in *belles-lettres*. Recent publications on the subject of the anima include Linda Fierz-David, *The Dream of Poliphilo,* and my 'Psychology of the Transference.' The anima as a psychological idea first appears in the 16th-cent. humanist Richardus Vitus. Cf. my *Mysterium Coniunctionis,* pars. 91ff.
8 The fallacy, which stems from Eubulides the Megarian, runs: 'Can you recognize your father?' Yes. 'Can you recognize this veiled one?' No. 'This veiled one is your father. Hence you can recognize your father and not recognize him.'
9 Naturally this is not meant as a psychological definition, let alone a metaphysical one. As I pointed out in 'The Relations between the Ego and the Unconscious' (pars. 296ff.), the syzygy consists of three elements: the femininity pertaining to the man and the masculinity pertaining to the woman; the experience which man has of woman and vice versa; and, finally, the masculine and feminine archetypal image. The first element can be integrated into the personality by the process of conscious realization, but the last one cannot.
10 'For the Scripture says, God made man male and female; the male is Christ, the female is the Church.' – Second Epistle of Clement to the Corinthians, xiv, 2 (trans. by Lake, I, p. 151). In pictorial representations, Mary often takes the place of the Church.
11 'The Psychology of the Transference,' pars. 425ff. Cf. infra, pars. 358ff., the Naassene *quaternio*.
12 Cf. infra, par. 347.

13 The material for this chapter is drawn from a paper, 'Über das Selbst,' published in the *Eranos-Jahrbuch 1948.*
14 'The Relations between the Ego and the Unconscious.'
15 In the sense of the words used in I Cor. 5: 2: 'Inflati estis [πεφνστώμενοτ] et non magis luctum habuistis' (And you are puffed up, and have not rather mourned) – with reference to a case of tolerated incest with the mother ('that a man should have his father's wife').
16 Cf. 'On the Nature of the Psyche,' pars. 414ff., 439ff.
17 Cf. *Psychological Types*, Defs., 'Rational' and 'Irrational.'
18 *Les Fonctions mentales dans les sociétés inférieures.*
19 'On Psychic Energy,' pars. 14ff., 20ff.
20 *Sämtliche Werke*, I, p. 126.
21 Cf. my 'Psychology of the Child Archetype'; also *Psychology and Alchemy*, index, s.v. 'filius Philosophorum,' 'child,' 'hermaphrodite.'
22 Cf. *Psychology and Alchemy*, Part II, ch. 3.
23 [Cf. infra, par. 340.]
24 A classic case is the one published by Nelken: 'Analytische Beobachtungen über Phantasien eines Schizophrenen.' Another is Schreber's *Memoirs of My Nervous Illness.*

Chapter 7

The psychology of the child archetype[1]

I Introduction

259 The author of the companion essay[2] on the mythology of the 'child' or the child god has asked me for a psychological commentary on the subject of his investigations. I am glad to accede to his request, although the undertaking seems to me no small venture in view of the great significance of the child motif in mythology. Kerényi himself has enlarged upon the occurrence of this motif in Greece and Rome, with parallels drawn from Indian, Finnish, and other sources, thus indicating that the presentation of the theme would allow of yet further extensions. Though a comprehensive description would contribute nothing decisive in principle, it would nevertheless produce an overwhelming impression of the world-wide incidence and frequency of the motif. The customary treatment of mythological motifs so far in separate departments of science, such as philology, ethnology, the history of civilization, and comparative religion, was not exactly a help to us in recognizing their universality; and the psychological problems raised by this universality could easily be shelved by hypotheses of migration. Consequently Adolf Bastian's[3] ideas met with little success in their day. Even then there was sufficient empirical material available to permit far-reaching psychological conclusions, but the necessary premises were lacking. Although the psychological knowledge of that time included myth-formation in its province – witness Wundt's *Völkerpsychologie* – it was not in a position to demonstrate this same process as a living function actually present in the psyche of civilized man, any more than it could understand mythological motifs as structural elements of the psyche. True to its history, when psychology was metaphysics first of all, then the study of the senses and their functions, and then of the conscious mind and *its* functions, psychology identified its proper subject with the conscious psyche and its contents and thus completely overlooked the existence of a nonconscious psyche. Although various philosophers, among them Leibniz, Kant, and Schelling, had already pointed very clearly to the problem of the dark side of the psyche, it was a physician who felt impelled, from his scientific and medical experience, to point to the *unconscious* as the essential basis of the psyche. This was C. G. Carus,[4] the authority whom Eduard von Hartmann followed. In recent times

it was, once again, medical psychology that approached the problem of the unconscious without philosophical preconceptions. It became clear from many separate investigations that the psychopathology of the neuroses and of many psychoses cannot dispense with the hypothesis of a dark side of the psyche, i.e., the unconscious. It is the same with the psychology of dreams, which is really the *terra intermedia* between normal and pathological psychology. In the dream, as in the products of psychoses, there are numberless interconnections to which one can find parallels only in mythological associations of ideas (or perhaps in certain poetic creations which are often characterized by a borrowing, not always conscious, from myths). Had thorough investigation shown that in the majority of such cases it was simply a matter of forgotten knowledge, the physician would not have gone to the trouble of making extensive researches into individual and collective parallels. But, in point of fact, typical mythologems were observed among individuals to whom all knowledge of this kind was absolutely out of the question, and where indirect derivation from religious ideas that might have been known to them, or from popular figures of speech, was impossible.[5] Such conclusions forced us to assume that we must be dealing with 'autochthonous' revivals independent of all tradition, and, consequently, that 'myth-forming' structural elements must be present in the unconscious psyche.[6]

260   These products are never (or at least very seldom) myths with a definite form, but rather mythological components which, because of their typical nature, we can call 'motifs,' 'primordial images,' types or – as I have named them – *archetypes*. The child archetype is an excellent example. Today we can hazard the formula that the archetypes appear in myths and fairytales just as they do in dreams and in the products of psychotic fantasy. The medium in which they are embedded is, in the former case, an ordered and for the most part immediately understandable context, but in the latter case a generally unintelligible, irrational, not to say delirious sequence of images which nonetheless does not lack a certain hidden coherence. In the individual, the archetypes appear as involuntary manifestations of unconscious processes whose existence and meaning can only be inferred, whereas the myth deals with traditional forms of incalculable age. They hark back to a prehistoric world whose spiritual preconceptions and general conditions we can still observe today among existing primitives. Myths on this level are as a rule tribal history handed down from generation to generation by word of mouth. Primitive mentality differs from the civilized chiefly in that the conscious mind is far less developed in scope and intensity. Functions such as thinking, willing, etc. are not yet differentiated; they are pre-conscious, and in the case of thinking, for instance, this shows itself in the circumstance that the primitive does not think *consciously*, but that thoughts *appear*. The primitive cannot assert that he thinks; it is rather that 'something thinks in him.' The spontaneity of the act of thinking does not lie, causally, in his conscious mind, but in his unconscious. Moreover, he is incapable of any conscious effort of will; he must put himself beforehand into the 'mood of willing,' or let himself be put – hence his *rites d'entrée et de sortie*. His consciousness is menaced by an almighty

unconscious: hence his fear of magical influences which may cross his path at any moment; and for this reason, too, he is surrounded by unknown forces and must adjust himself to them as best he can. Owing to the chronic twilight state of his consciousness, it is often next to impossible to find out whether he merely dreamed something or whether he really experienced it. The spontaneous manifestation of the unconscious and its archetypes intrudes everywhere into his conscious mind, and the mythical world of his ancestors – for instance, the *alchera* or *bugari* of the Australian aborigines – is a reality equal if not superior to the material world.[7] It is not the world as we know it that speaks out of his unconscious, but the unknown world of the psyche, of which we know that it mirrors our empirical world only in part, and that, for the other part, it moulds this empirical world in accordance with its own psychic assumptions. The archetype does not proceed from physical facts, but describes how the psyche experiences the physical fact, and in so doing the psyche often behaves so autocratically that it denies tangible reality or makes statements that fly in the face of it.

261   The primitive mentality does not *invent* myths, it *experiences* them. Myths are original revelations of the preconscious psyche, involuntary statements about unconscious psychic happenings, and anything but allegories of physical processes.[8] Such allegories would be an idle amusement for an unscientific intellect. Myths, on the contrary, have a vital meaning. Not merely do they represent, they *are* the psychic life of the primitive tribe, which immediately falls to pieces and decays when it loses its mythological heritage, like a man who has lost his soul. A tribe's mythology is its living religion, whose loss is always and everywhere, even among the civilized, a moral catastrophe. But religion is a vital link with psychic processes independent of and beyond consciousness, in the dark hinterland of the psyche. Many of these unconscious processes may be indirectly occasioned by consciousness, but never by conscious choice. Others appear to arise spontaneously, that is to say, from no discernible or demonstrable conscious cause.

262   Modern psychology treats the products of unconscious fantasy-activity as self-portraits of what is going on in the unconscious, or as statements of the unconscious psyche about itself. They fall into two categories. First, fantasies (including dreams) of a personal character, which go back unquestionably to personal experiences, things forgotten or repressed, and can thus be completely explained by individual anamnesis. Second, fantasies (including dreams) of an impersonal character, which cannot be reduced to experiences in the individual's past, and thus cannot be explained as something individually acquired. These fantasy-images undoubtedly have their closest analogues in mythological types. We must therefore assume that they correspond to certain *collective* (and not personal) structural elements of the human psyche in general, and, like the morphological elements of the human body, are *inherited*. Although tradition and transmission by migration certainly play a part, there are, as we have said, very many cases that cannot be accounted for in this way and drive us to the hypothesis of 'autochthonous revival.' These cases are so numerous that we are obliged to assume the

existence of a collective psychic substratum. I have called this the *collective unconscious.*

263 The products of this second category resemble the types of structures to be met with in myth and fairytale so much that we must regard them as related. It is therefore wholly within the realm of possibility that both, the mythological types as well as the individual types, arise under quite similar conditions. As already mentioned, the fantasy-products of the second category (as also those of the first) arise in a state of reduced intensity of consciousness (in dreams, delirium, reveries, visions, etc.). In all these states the check put upon unconscious contents by the concentration of the conscious mind ceases, so that the hitherto unconscious material streams, as though from opened side-sluices, into the field of consciousness. This mode of origination is the general rule.[9]

264 Reduced intensity of consciousness and absence of concentration and attention, Janet's *abaissement du niveau mental*, correspond pretty exactly to the primitive state of consciousness in which, we must suppose, myths were originally formed. It is therefore exceedingly probable that the mythological archetypes, too, made their appearance in much the same manner as the manifestations of archetypal structures among individuals today.

265 The methodological principle in accordance with which psychology treats the products of the unconscious is this: Contents of an archetypal character are manifestations of processes in the collective unconscious. Hence they do not refer to anything that is or has been conscious, but to something essentially unconscious. In the last analysis, therefore, it is impossible to say what they refer to. Every interpretation necessarily remains an 'as-if.' The ultimate core of meaning may be circumscribed, but not described. Even so, the bare circumscription denotes an essential step forward in our knowledge of the pre-conscious structure of the psyche, which was already in existence when there was as yet no unity of personality (even today the primitive is not securely possessed of it) and no consciousness at all. We can also observe this pre-conscious state in early childhood, and as a matter of fact it is the dreams of this early period that not infrequently bring extremely remarkable archetypal contents to light.[10]

266 If, then, we proceed in accordance with the above principle, there is no longer any question whether a myth refers to the sun or the moon, the father or the mother, sexuality or fire or water; all it does is to circumscribe and give an approximate description of an *unconscious core of meaning*. The ultimate meaning of this nucleus was never conscious and never will be. It was, and still is, only interpreted, and every interpretation that comes anywhere near the hidden sense (or, from the point of view of scientific intellect, nonsense, which comes to the same thing) has always, right from the beginning, laid claim not only to absolute truth and validity but to instant reverence and religious devotion. Archetypes were, and still are, living psychic forces that demand to be taken seriously, and they have a strange way of making sure of their effect. Always they were the bringers of protection and salvation, and their violation has as its consequence the 'perils of the soul' known to us from the psychology of primitives. Moreover,

267   they are the unfailing causes of neurotic and even psychotic disorders, behaving exactly like neglected or maltreated physical organs or organic functional systems. An archetypal content expresses itself, first and foremost, in metaphors. If such a content should speak of the sun and identify with it the lion, the king, the hoard of gold guarded by the dragon, or the power that makes for the life and health of man, it is neither the one thing nor the other, but the unknown third thing that finds more or less adequate expression in all these similes, yet – to the perpetual vexation of the intellect – remains unknown and not to be fitted into a formula. For this reason the scientific intellect is always inclined to put on airs of enlightenment in the hope of banishing the spectre once and for all. Whether its endeavours were called euhemerism, or Christian apologetics, or Enlightenment in the narrow sense, or Positivism, there was always a myth hiding behind it, in new and disconcerting garb, which then, following the ancient and venerable pattern, gave itself out as ultimate truth. In reality we can never legitimately cut loose from our archetypal foundations unless we are prepared to pay the price of a neurosis, any more than we can rid ourselves of our body and its organs without committing suicide. If we cannot deny the archetypes or otherwise neutralize them, we are confronted, at every new stage in the differentiation of consciousness to which civilization attains, with the task of finding a new *interpretation* appropriate to this stage, in order to connect the life of the past that still exists in us with the life of the present, which threatens to slip away from it. If this link-up does not take place, a kind of rootless consciousness comes into being no longer oriented to the past, a consciousness which succumbs helplessly to all manner of suggestions and, in practice, is susceptible to psychic epidemics. With the loss of the past, now become 'insignificant,' devalued, and incapable of revaluation, the saviour is lost too, for the saviour is either the insignificant thing itself or else arises out of it. Over and over again in the 'metamorphosis of the gods' he rises up as the prophet or first-born of a new generation and appears unexpectedly in the unlikeliest places (sprung from a stone, tree, furrow, water, etc.) and in ambiguous form (Tom Thumb, dwarf, child, animal, and so on).

268   This archetype of the 'child god' is extremely widespread and intimately bound up with all the other mythological aspects of the child motif. It is hardly necessary to allude to the still living 'Christ-child,' who, in the legend of Saint Christopher, also has the typical feature of being 'smaller than small and bigger than big.' In folklore the child motif appears in the guise of the *dwarf* or the *elf* as personifications of the hidden forces of nature. To this sphere also belongs the little metal man of late antiquity, the ἀνθρωπάριον,[11] who, till far into the Middle Ages, on the one hand inhabited the mine-shafts,[12] and on the other represented the alchemical metals,[13] above all Mercurius reborn in perfect form (as the hermaphrodite, *filius sapientiae*, or *infans noster*).[14] Thanks to the religious interpretation of the 'child,' a fair amount of evidence has come down to us from the Middle Ages showing that the 'child' was not merely a traditional figure, but a vision spontaneously experienced (as a so-called 'irruption of the unconscious'). I would mention Meister Eckhart's vision of the 'naked boy' and the dream of Brother Eustachius.[15]

Interesting accounts of these spontaneous experiences are also to be found in English ghost-stories, where we read of the vision of a 'Radiant Boy' said to have been seen in a place where there are Roman remains.[16] This apparition was supposed to be of evil omen. It almost looks as though we were dealing with the figure of a *puer aeternus* who had become inauspicious through 'metamorphosis,' or in other words had shared the fate of the classical and the Germanic gods, who have all become bugbears. The mystical character of the experience is also confirmed in Part II of Goethe's *Faust*, where Faust himself is transformed into a boy and admitted into the 'choir of blessed youths,' this being the 'larval stage' of Doctor Marianus.[17]

269   In the strange tale called *Das Reich ohne Raum*, by Bruno Goetz, a *puer aeternus* named Fo (= Buddha) appears with whole troops of 'unholy' boys of evil significance. (Contemporary parallels are better let alone.) I mention this instance only to demonstrate the enduring vitality of the child archetype.

270   The child motif not infrequently occurs in the field of psychopathology. The 'imaginary' child is common among women with mental disorders and is usually interpreted in a Christian sense. Homunculi also appear, as in the famous Schreber case,[18] where they come in swarms and plague the sufferer. But the clearest and most significant manifestation of the child motif in the therapy of neuroses is in the maturation process of personality induced by the analysis of the unconscious, which I have termed the process of *individuation*.[19] Here we are confronted with preconscious processes which, in the form of more or less well-formed fantasies, gradually pass over into the conscious mind, or become conscious as dreams, or, lastly, are made conscious through the method of active imagination.[20] This material is rich in archetypal motifs, among them frequently that of the child. Often the child is formed after the Christian model; more often, though, it develops from earlier, altogether non-Christian levels – that is to say, out of chthonic animals such as crocodiles, dragons, serpents, or monkeys. Sometimes the child appears in the cup of a flower, or out of a golden egg, or as the centre of a mandala. In dreams it often appears as the dreamer's son or daughter or as a boy, youth, or young girl; occasionally it seems to be of exotic origin, Indian or Chinese, with a dusky skin, or, appearing more cosmically, surrounded by stars or with a starry coronet; or as the king's son or the witch's child with daemonic attributes. Seen as a special instance of 'the treasure hard to attain' motif,[21] the child motif is extremely variable and assumes all manner of shapes, such as the jewel, the pearl, the flower, the chalice, the golden egg, the quaternity, the golden ball, and so on. It can be interchanged with these and similar images almost without limit.

II The psychology of the child archetype

The archetype as a link with the past

271 As to the *psychology* of our theme I must point out that every statement going beyond the purely phenomenal aspects of an archetype lays itself open to the

criticism we have expressed above. Not for a moment dare we succumb to the illusion that an archetype can be finally explained and disposed of. Even the best attempts at explanation are only more or less successful translations into another metaphorical language. (Indeed, language itself is only an image.) The most we can do is to *dream the myth onwards* and give it a modern dress. And whatever explanation or interpretation does to it, we do to our own souls as well, with corresponding results for our own well-being. The archetype – let us never forget this – is a psychic organ present in all of us. A bad explanation means a correspondingly bad attitude to this organ, which may thus be injured. But the ultimate sufferer is the bad interpreter himself. Hence the 'explanation' should always be such that the functional significance of the archetype remains unimpaired, so that an adequate and meaningful connection between the conscious mind and the archetypes is assured. For the archetype is an element of our psychic structure and thus a vital and necessary component in our psychic economy. It represents or personifies certain instinctive data of the dark, primitive psyche, the real but invisible roots of consciousness. Of what elementary importance the connection with these roots is, we see from the preoccupation of the primitive mentality with certain 'magic' factors, which are nothing less than what we would call archetypes. This original form of *religio* ('linking back') is the essence, the working basis of all religious life even today, and always will be, whatever future form this life may take.

272   There is no 'rational' substitute for the archetype any more than there is for the cerebellum or the kidneys. We can examine the physical organs anatomically, histologically, and embryologically. This would correspond to an outline of archetypal phenomenology and its presentation in terms of comparative history. But we only arrive at the *meaning* of a physical organ when we begin to ask teleological questions. Hence the query arises: What is the biological purpose of the archetype? Just as physiology answers such a question for the body, so it is the business of psychology to answer it for the archetype.

273   Statements like 'The child motif is a vestigial memory of one's own childhood' and similar explanations merely beg the question. But if, giving this proposition a slight twist, we were to say, 'The child motif is a picture of certain *forgotten* things in our childhood,' we are getting closer to the truth. Since, however, the archetype is always an image belonging to the whole human race and not merely to the individual, we might put it better this way: 'The child motif represents the pre-conscious, childhood aspect of the collective psyche.'[22]

274   We shall not go wrong if we take this statement for the time being *historically*, on the analogy of certain psychological experiences which show that certain phases in an individual's life can become autonomous, can personify themselves to the extent that they result in a *vision of oneself* – for instance, one sees oneself as a child. Visionary experiences of this kind, whether they occur in dreams or in the waking state, are, as we know, conditional on a dissociation having previously taken place between past and present. Such dissociations come about because of various incompatibilities; for instance, a man's present state may have come into

conflict with his childhood state, or he may have violently sundered himself from his original character in the interests of some arbitrary persona[23] more in keeping with his ambitions. He has thus become unchildlike and artificial, and has lost his roots. All this presents a favourable opportunity for an equally vehement confrontation with the primary truth.

275   In view of the fact that men have not yet ceased to make statements about the child god, we may perhaps extend the individual analogy to the life of mankind and say in conclusion that humanity, too, probably always comes into conflict with its childhood conditions, that is, with its original, unconscious, and instinctive state, and that the danger of the kind of conflict which induces the vision of the 'child' actually exists. Religious observances, i.e., the retelling and ritual repetition of the mythical event, consequently serve the purpose of bringing the image of childhood, and everything connected with it, again and again before the eyes of the conscious mind so that the link with the original condition may not be broken.

The function of the archetype

276   The child motif represents not only something that existed in the distant past but also something that exists *now;* that is to say, it is not just a vestige but a system functioning in the present whose purpose is to compensate or correct, in a meaningful manner, the inevitable one-sidednesses and extravagances of the conscious mind. It is in the nature of the conscious mind to concentrate on relatively few contents and to raise them to the highest pitch of clarity. A necessary result and precondition is the exclusion of other potential contents of consciousness. The exclusion is bound to bring about a certain one-sidedness of the conscious contents. Since the differentiated consciousness of civilized man has been granted an effective instrument for the practical realization of its contents through the dynamics of his will, there is all the more danger, the more he trains his will, of his getting lost in one-sidedness and deviating further and further from the laws and roots of his being. This means, on the one hand, the possibility of human freedom, but on the other it is a source of endless transgressions against one's instincts. Accordingly, primitive man, being closer to his instincts, like the animal, is characterized by fear of novelty and adherence to tradition. To our way of thinking he is painfully backward, whereas we exalt progress. But our progressiveness, though it may result in a great many delightful wish-fulfilments, piles up an equally gigantic Promethean debt which has to be paid off from time to time in the form of hideous catastrophes. For ages man has dreamed of flying, and all we have got for it is saturation bombing! We smile today at the Christian hope of a life beyond the grave, and yet we often fall into chiliasms a hundred times more ridiculous than the notion of a happy Hereafter. Our differentiated consciousness is in continual danger of being uprooted; hence it needs compensation through the still existing state of childhood.

277   The symptoms of compensation are described, from the progressive point of view, in scarcely flattering terms. Since, to the superficial eye, it looks like a

retarding operation, people speak of inertia, backwardness, scepticism, fault-finding, conservatism, timidity, pettiness, and so on. But inasmuch as man has, in high degree, the capacity for cutting himself off from his own roots, he may also be swept uncritically to catastrophe by his dangerous one-sidedness. The retarding ideal is always more primitive, more natural (in the good sense as in the bad), and more 'moral' in that it keeps faith with law and tradition. The progressive ideal is always more abstract, more unnatural, and less 'moral' in that it demands disloyalty to tradition. Progress enforced by will is always *convulsive*. Backwardness may be closer to naturalness, but in its turn it is always menaced by painful awakenings. The older view of things realized that progress is only possible *Deo concedente*, thus proving itself conscious of the opposites and repeating the age-old *rites d'entrée et de sortie* on a higher plane. The more differentiated consciousness becomes, the greater the danger of severance from the root-condition. Complete severance comes when the *Deo concedente* is forgotten. Now it is an axiom of psychology that when a part of the psyche is split off from consciousness it is only *apparently* inactivated; in actual fact it brings about a possession of the personality, with the result that the individual's aims are falsified in the interests of the split-off part. If, then, the childhood state of the collective psyche is repressed to the point of total exclusion, the unconscious content overwhelms the conscious aim and inhibits, falsifies, even destroys its realization. Viable progress only comes from the co-operation of both.

The futurity of the archetype

278   One of the essential features of the child motif is its futurity. The child is potential future. Hence the occurrence of the child motif in the psychology of the individual signifies as a rule an anticipation of future developments, even though at first sight it may seem like a retrospective configuration. Life is a flux, a flowing into the future, and not a stoppage or a backwash. It is therefore not surprising that so many of the mythological saviours are child gods. This agrees exactly with our experience of the psychology of the individual, which shows that the 'child' paves the way for a future change of personality. In the individuation process, it anticipates the figure that comes from the synthesis of conscious and unconscious elements in the personality. It is therefore a symbol which unites the opposites;[24] a mediator, bringer of healing, that is, one who makes whole. Because it has this meaning, the child motif is capable of the numerous transformations mentioned above: it can be expressed by roundness, the circle or sphere, or else by the quaternity as another form of wholeness.[25] I have called this wholeness that transcends consciousness the 'self.'[26] The goal of the individuation process is the synthesis of the self. From another point of view the term 'entelechy' might be preferable to 'synthesis.' There is an empirical reason why 'entelechy' is, in certain conditions, more fitting: the symbols of wholeness frequently occur at the beginning of the individuation process, indeed they can often be observed in the first dreams of early infancy. This observation says much for the *a priori* existence of potential

wholeness,[27] and on this account the idea of *entelechy* instantly recommends itself. But in so far as the individuation process occurs, empirically speaking, as a synthesis, it looks, paradoxically enough, as if something already existent were being put together. From this point of view, the term 'synthesis' is also applicable.

Unity and plurality of the child motif

279 In the manifold phenomenology of the 'child' we have to distinguish between the *unity* and *plurality* of its respective manifestations. Where, for instance, numerous homunculi, dwarfs, boys, etc., appear, having no individual characteristics at all, there is the probability of a *dissociation*. Such forms are therefore found especially in schizophrenia, which is essentially a fragmentation of personality. The many children then represent the products of its dissolution. But if the plurality occurs in normal people, then it is the representation of an as yet incomplete synthesis of personality. The personality (viz., the 'self') is still in the *plural stage*, i.e., an ego may be present, but it cannot experience its wholeness within the framework of its own personality, only within the community of the family, tribe, or nation; it is still in the stage of unconscious identification with the plurality of the group. The Church takes due account of this widespread condition in her doctrine of the *corpus mysticum*, of which the individual is by nature a member.

280 If, however, the child motif appears in the form of a unity, we are dealing with an unconscious and provisionally complete synthesis of the personality, which in practice, like everything unconscious, signifies no more than a possibility.

Child god and child hero

281 Sometimes the 'child' looks more like a *child god*, sometimes more like a young *hero*. Common to both types is the miraculous birth and the adversities of early childhood – abandonment and danger through persecution. The god is by nature wholly supernatural; the hero's nature is human but raised to the limit of the supernatural – he is 'semi-divine.' While the god, especially in his close affinity with the symbolic animal, personifies the collective unconscious which is not yet integrated into a human being, the hero's supernaturalness includes human nature and thus represents a synthesis of the ('divine,' i.e., not yet humanized) unconscious and human consciousness. Consequently he signifies the potential anticipation of an individuation process which is approaching wholeness.

282 For this reason the various 'child'-fates may be regarded as illustrating the kind of psychic events that occur in the entelechy or genesis of the 'self.' The 'miraculous birth' tries to depict the way in which this genesis is experienced. Since it is a psychic genesis, everything must happen non-empirically, e.g., by means of a virgin birth, or by miraculous conception, or by birth from unnatural organs. The motifs of 'insignificance,' exposure, abandonment, danger, etc. try to show how precarious is the psychic possibility of wholeness, that is, the enormous difficulties to be met with in attaining this 'highest good.' They also signify the

powerlessness and helplessness of the life-urge which subjects every growing thing to the law of maximum self-fulfilment, while at the same time the environmental influences place all sorts of insuperable obstacles in the way of individuation. More especially the threat to one's inmost self from dragons and serpents points to the danger of the newly acquired consciousness being swallowed up again by the instinctive psyche, the unconscious. The lower vertebrates have from earliest times been favourite symbols of the collective psychic substratum,[28] which is localized anatomically in the subcortical centres, the cerebellum and the spinal cord. These organs constitute the snake.[29] Snake-dreams usually occur, therefore, when the conscious mind is deviating from its instinctual basis.

283 The motif of 'smaller than small yet bigger than big' complements the impotence of the child by means of its equally miraculous deeds. This paradox is the essence of the hero and runs through his whole destiny like a red thread. He can cope with the greatest perils, yet, in the end, something quite insignificant is his undoing: Baldur perishes because of the mistletoe, Maui because of the laughter of a little bird, Siegfried because of his one vulnerable spot, Heracles because of his wife's gift, others because of common treachery, and so on.

284 The hero's main feat is to overcome the monster of darkness: it is the long-hoped-for and expected triumph of consciousness over the unconscious. Day and light are synonyms for consciousness, night and dark for the unconscious. The coming of consciousness was probably the most tremendous experience of primeval times, for with it a world came into being whose existence no one had suspected before. 'And God said: "Let there be light!"' is the projection of that immemorial experience of the separation of the conscious from the unconscious. Even among primitives today the possession of a soul is a precarious thing, and the 'loss of soul' a typical psychic malady which drives primitive medicine to all sorts of psychotherapeutic measures. Hence the 'child' distinguishes itself by deeds which point to the conquest of the dark.

III The special phenomenology of the child archetype

The abandonment of the child

285 Abandonment, exposure, danger, etc. are all elaborations of the 'child's' insignificant beginnings and of its mysterious and miraculous birth. This statement describes a certain psychic experience of a creative nature, whose object is the emergence of a new and as yet unknown content. In the psychology of the individual there is always, at such moments, an agonizing situation of conflict from which there seems to be no way out – at least for the conscious mind, since as far as this is concerned, *tertium non datur*. But out of this collision of opposites the unconscious psyche always creates a third thing of an irrational nature,[30] which the conscious mind neither expects nor understands. It presents itself in a form that is neither a straight 'yes' nor a straight 'no,' and is consequently rejected by

both. For the conscious mind knows nothing beyond the opposites and, as a result, has no knowledge of the thing that unites them. Since, however, the solution of the conflict through the union of opposites is of vital importance, and is moreover the very thing that the conscious mind is longing for, some inkling of the creative act, and of the significance of it, nevertheless gets through. From this comes the numinous character of the 'child.' A meaningful but unknown content always has a secret fascination for the conscious mind. The new configuration is a nascent whole; it is on the way to wholeness, at least in so far as it excels in 'wholeness' the conscious mind when torn by opposites and surpasses it in completeness. For this reason all uniting symbols have a redemptive significance.

286   Out of this situation the 'child' emerges as a symbolic content, manifestly separated or even isolated from its background (the mother), but sometimes including the mother in its perilous situation, threatened on the one hand by the negative attitude of the conscious mind and on the other by the *horror vacui* of the unconscious, which is quite ready to swallow up all its progeny, since it produces them only in play, and destruction is an inescapable part of its play. Nothing in all the world welcomes this new birth, although it is the most precious fruit of Mother Nature herself, the most pregnant with the future, signifying a higher stage of self-realization. That is why Nature, the world of the instincts, takes the 'child' under its wing: it is nourished or protected by animals.

287   'Child' means something evolving towards independence. This it cannot do without detaching itself from its origins: abandonment is therefore a necessary condition, not just a concomitant symptom. The conflict is not to be overcome by the conscious mind remaining caught between the opposites, and for this very reason it needs a symbol to point out the necessity of detaching itself from its origins. Because the symbol of the 'child' fascinates and grips the conscious mind, its redemptive effect passes over into consciousness and brings about that separation from the conflict-situation which the conscious mind by itself was unable to achieve. The symbol anticipates a nascent state of consciousness. So long as this is not actually in being, the 'child' remains a mythological projection which requires religious repetition and renewal by ritual. The Christ Child, for instance, is a religious necessity only so long as the majority of men are incapable of giving psychological reality to the saying: 'Except ye become as little children. . . .' Since all such developments and transitions are extraordinarily difficult and dangerous, it is no wonder that figures of this kind persist for hundreds or even thousands of years. Everything that man should, and yet cannot, be or do – be it in a positive or negative sense – lives on as a mythological figure and anticipation alongside his consciousness, either as a religious projection or – what is still more dangerous – as unconscious contents which then project themselves spontaneously into incongruous objects, e.g., hygienic and other 'salvationist' doctrines or practices. All these are so many rationalized substitutes for mythology, and their unnaturalness does more harm than good.

288   The conflict-situation that offers no way out, the sort of situation that produces the 'child' as the irrational third, is of course a formula appropriate only to a

psychological, that is, modern stage of development. It is not strictly applicable to the psychic life of primitives, if only because primitive man's childlike range of consciousness still excludes a whole world of possible psychic experiences. Seen on the nature-level of the primitive, our modern *moral* conflict is still an *objective* calamity that threatens life itself. Hence not a few child-figures are culture-heroes and thus identified with things that promote culture, e.g., fire,[31] metal, corn, maize, etc. As bringers of light, that is, enlargers of consciousness, they overcome darkness, which is to say that they overcome the earlier unconscious state. Higher consciousness, or knowledge going beyond our present-day consciousness, is equivalent to being *all alone in the world*. This loneliness expresses the conflict between the bearer or symbol of higher consciousness and his surroundings. The conquerors of darkness go far back into primeval times, and, together with many other legends, prove that there once existed a state of *original psychic distress*, namely *unconsciousness*. Hence in all probability the 'irrational' fear which primitive man has of the dark even today. I found a form of religion among a tribe living on Mount Elgon that corresponded to pantheistic optimism. Their optimistic mood was, however, always in abeyance between six o'clock in the evening and six o'clock in the morning, during which time it was replaced by fear, for in the night the dark being Ayik has his dominion – the 'Maker of Fear.' During the daytime there were no monster snakes anywhere in the vicinity, but at night they were lurking on every path. At night the whole of mythology was let loose.

The invincibility of the child

289 It is a striking paradox in all child myths that the 'child' is on the one hand delivered helpless into the power of terrible enemies and in continual danger of extinction, while on the other he possesses powers far exceeding those of ordinary humanity. This is closely related to the psychological fact that though the child may be 'insignificant,' unknown, 'a mere child,' he is also divine. From the conscious standpoint we seem to be dealing with an insignificant content that has no releasing, let alone redeeming, character. The conscious mind is caught in its conflict-situation, and the combatant forces seem so overwhelming that the 'child' as an isolated content bears no relation to the conscious factors. It is therefore easily overlooked and falls back into the unconscious. At least, this is what we should have to fear if things turned out according to our conscious expectations. Myth, however, emphasizes that it is not so, but that the 'child' is endowed with superior powers and, despite all dangers, will unexpectedly pull through. The 'child' is born out of the womb of the unconscious, begotten out of the depths of human nature, or rather out of living Nature herself. It is a personification of vital forces quite outside the limited range of our conscious mind; of ways and possibilities of which our one-sided conscious mind knows nothing; a wholeness which embraces the very depths of Nature. It represents the strongest, the most ineluctable urge in every being, namely the urge to realize itself. It is, as it were, an incarnation of *the inability to do otherwise*, equipped with all the powers of nature

and instinct, whereas the conscious mind is always getting caught up in its supposed ability to do otherwise. The urge and compulsion to self-realization is a law of nature and thus of invincible power, even though its effect, at the start, is insignificant and improbable. Its power is revealed in the miraculous deeds of the child hero, and later in the *athla* ('works') of the bondsman or thrall (of the Heracles type), where, although the hero has outgrown the impotence of the 'child,' he is still in a menial position. The figure of the thrall generally leads up to the real epiphany of the semi-divine hero. Oddly enough, we have a similar modulation of themes in alchemy – in the synonyms for the *lapis*. As the *materia prima*, it is the *lapis exilis et vilis*. As a substance in process of transmutation, it is *servus rubeus* or *fugitivus;* and finally, in its true apotheosis, it attains the dignity of a *filius sapientiae* or *deus terrenus*, a 'light above all lights,' a power that contains in itself all the powers of the upper and nether regions. It becomes a *corpus glorificatum* which enjoys everlasting incorruptibility and is therefore a panacea ('bringer of healing').[32] The size and invincibility of the 'child' are bound up in Hindu speculation with the nature of the atman, which corresponds to the 'smaller than small yet bigger than big' motif. As an individual phenomenon, the self is 'smaller than small'; as the equivalent of the cosmos, it is 'bigger than big.' The self, regarded as the counter-pole of the world, its 'absolutely other,' is the *sine qua non* of all empirical knowledge and consciousness of subject and object. Only because of this psychic 'otherness' is consciousness possible at all. Identity does not make consciousness possible; it is only separation, detachment, and agonizing confrontation through opposition that produce consciousness and insight. Hindu introspection recognized this psychological fact very early and consequently equated the subject of cognition with the subject of ontology in general. In accordance with the predominantly introverted attitude of Indian thinking, the object lost the attribute of absolute reality and, in some systems, became a mere illusion. The Greek-Occidental type of mind could not free itself from the conviction of the world's absolute existence – at the cost, however, of the cosmic significance of the self. Even today Western man finds it hard to see the psychological necessity for a transcendental subject of cognition as the counter-pole of the empirical universe, although the postulate of a world-confronting self, at least as a *point of reflection*, is a logical necessity. Regardless of philosophy's perpetual attitude of dissent or only half-hearted assent, there is always a compensating tendency in our unconscious psyche to produce a symbol of the self in its cosmic significance. These efforts take on the archetypal forms of the hero myth such as can be observed in almost any individuation process.

290   The phenomenology of the 'child's' birth always points back to an original psychological state of non-recognition, i.e., of darkness or twilight, of non-differentiation between subject and object, of unconscious identity of man and the universe. This phase of non-differentiation produces the *golden egg*, which is both man and universe and yet neither, but an irrational third. To the twilight consciousness of primitive man it seems as if the egg came out of the womb of the wide world and were, accordingly, a cosmic, objective, external occurrence. To a

differentiated consciousness, on the other hand, it seems evident that this egg is nothing but a symbol thrown up by the psyche or – what is even worse – a fanciful speculation and therefore 'nothing but' a primitive phantasm to which no 'reality' of any kind attaches. Present-day medical psychology, however, thinks somewhat differently about these 'phantasms.' It knows only too well what dire disturbances of the bodily functions and what devastating psychic consequences can flow from 'mere' fantasies. 'Fantasies' are the natural expressions of the life of the unconscious. But since the unconscious is the psyche of all the body's autonomous functional complexes, its 'fantasies' have an aetiological significance that is not to be despised. From the psychopathology of the individuation process we know that the formation of symbols is frequently associated with physical disorders of a psychic origin, which in some cases are felt as decidedly 'real.' In medicine, fantasies are *real things* with which the psychotherapist has to reckon very seriously indeed. He cannot therefore deprive of all justification those primitive phantasms whose content is so real that it is projected upon the external world. In the last analysis the human body, too, is built of the stuff of the world, the very stuff wherein fantasies become visible; indeed, without it they could not be experienced at all. Without this stuff they would be like a sort of abstract crystalline lattice in a solution where the crystallization process had not yet started.

291   The symbols of the self arise in the depths of the body and they express its materiality every bit as much as the structure of the perceiving consciousness. The symbol is thus a living body, *corpus et anima;* hence the 'child' is such an apt formula for the symbol. The uniqueness of the psyche can never enter wholly into reality, it can only be realized approximately, though it still remains the absolute basis of all consciousness. The deeper 'layers' of the psyche lose their individual uniqueness as they retreat farther and farther into darkness. 'Lower down,' that is to say as they approach the autonomous functional systems, they become increasingly collective until they are universalized and extinguished in the body's materiality, i.e., in chemical substances. The body's carbon is simply carbon. Hence 'at bottom' the psyche is simply 'world.' In this sense I hold Kerényi to be absolutely right when he says that in the symbol the *world itself* is speaking. The more archaic and 'deeper,' that is the more *physiological,* the symbol is, the more collective and universal, the more 'material' it is. The more abstract, differentiated, and specific it is, and the more its nature approximates to conscious uniqueness and individuality, the more it sloughs off its universal character. Having finally attained full consciousness, it runs the risk of becoming a mere allegory which nowhere oversteps the bounds of conscious comprehension, and is then exposed to all sorts of attempts at rationalistic and therefore inadequate explanation.

The hermaphroditism of the child

292   It is a remarkable fact that perhaps the majority of cosmogonic gods are of a bisexual nature. The hermaphrodite means nothing less than a union of the

strongest and most striking opposites. In the first place this union refers back to a primitive state of mind, a twilight where differences and contrasts were either barely separated or completely merged. With increasing clarity of consciousness, however, the opposites draw more and more distinctly and irreconcilably apart. If, therefore, the hermaphrodite were only a product of primitive non-differentiation, we would have to expect that it would soon be eliminated with increasing civilization. This is by no means the case; on the contrary, man's imagination has been preoccupied with this idea over and over again on the high and even the highest levels of culture, as we can see from the late Greek and syncretic philosophy of Gnosticism. The hermaphroditic *rebis* has an important part to play in the natural philosophy of the Middle Ages. And in our own day we hear of Christ's androgyny in Catholic mysticism.[33]

293   We can no longer be dealing, then, with the continued existence of a primitive phantasm, or with an original contamination of opposites. Rather, as we can see from medieval writings,[34] the primordial idea has become a *symbol of the creative union of opposites*, a 'uniting symbol' in the literal sense. In its functional significance the symbol no longer points back, but forward to a goal not yet reached. Notwithstanding its monstrosity, the hermaphrodite has gradually turned into a subduer of conflicts and a bringer of healing, and it acquired this meaning in relatively early phases of civilization. This vital meaning explains why the image of the hermaphrodite did not fade out in primeval times but, on the contrary, was able to assert itself with increasing profundity of symbolic content for thousands of years. The fact that an idea so utterly archaic could rise to such exalted heights of meaning not only points to the vitality of archetypal ideas, it also demonstrates the rightness of the principle that the archetype, because of its power to unite opposites, mediates between the unconscious substratum and the conscious mind. It throws a bridge between present-day consciousness, always in danger of losing its roots, and the natural, unconscious, instinctive wholeness of primeval times. Through this mediation the uniqueness, peculiarity, and one-sidedness of our present individual consciousness are linked up again with its natural, racial roots. Progress and development are ideals not lightly to be rejected, but they lose all meaning if man only arrives at his new state as a fragment of himself, having left his essential hinterland behind him in the shadow of the unconscious, in a state of primitivity or, indeed, barbarism. The conscious mind, split off from its origins, incapable of realizing the meaning of the new state, then relapses all too easily into a situation far worse than the one from which the innovation was intended to free it – *exempla sunt odiosa!* It was Friedrich Schiller who first had an inkling of this problem; but neither his contemporaries nor his successors were capable of drawing any conclusions. Instead, people incline more than ever to educate *children* and nothing more. I therefore suspect that the *furor paedogogicus* is a god-sent method of by-passing the central problem touched on by Schiller, namely the *education of the educator*. Children are educated by what the grown-up *is* and not by what he *says*. The popular faith in words is a veritable disease of the mind, for a superstition of this sort always leads farther and farther away from man's

foundations and seduces people into a disastrous identification of the personality with whatever slogan may be in vogue. Meanwhile everything that has been overcome and left behind by so-called 'progress' sinks deeper and deeper into the unconscious, from which there re-emerges in the end the primitive condition of *identity with the mass*. Instead of the expected progress, this condition now becomes reality.

294   As civilization develops, the bisexual primordial being turns into a symbol of the unity of personality, a symbol of the self, where the war of opposites finds peace. In this way the primordial being becomes the distant goal of man's self-development, having been from the very beginning a projection of his unconscious wholeness. Wholeness consists in the union of the conscious and the unconscious personality. Just as every individual derives from masculine and feminine genes, and the sex is determined by the predominance of the corresponding genes, so in the psyche it is only the conscious mind, in a man, that has the masculine sign, while the unconscious is by nature feminine. The reverse is true in the case of a woman. All I have done in my anima theory is to rediscover and reformulate this fact.[35] It had long been known.

295   The idea of the *coniunctio* of male and female, which became almost a technical term in Hermetic philosophy, appears in Gnosticism as the *mysterium iniquitatis*, probably not uninfluenced by the Old Testament 'divine marriage' as performed, for instance, by Hosea.[36] Such things are hinted at not only by certain traditional customs,[37] but by the quotation from the Gospel according to the Egyptians in the second epistle of Clement: 'When the two shall be one, the outside as the inside, and the male with the female neither male nor female.'[38] Clement of Alexandria introduces this logion with the words: 'When ye have trampled on the garment of shame (with thy feet) . . .,'[39] which probably refers to the body; for Clement as well as Cassian (from whom the quotation was taken over), and the pseudo-Clement, too, interpreted the words in a spiritual sense, in contrast to the Gnostics, who would seem to have taken the *coniunctio* all too literally. They took care, however, through the practice of abortion and other restrictions, that the biological meaning of their acts did not swamp the religious significance of the rite. While, in Church mysticism, the primordial image of the *hieros gamos* was sublimated on a lofty plane and only occasionally – as for instance with Mechthild of Magdeburg[40] – approached the physical sphere in emotional intensity, for the rest of the world it remained very much alive and continued to be the object of especial psychic preoccupation. In this respect the symbolical drawings of Opicinus de Canistris[41] afford us an interesting glimpse of the way in which this primordial image was instrumental in uniting opposites, even in a pathological state. On the other hand, in the Hermetic philosophy that throve in the Middle Ages the *coniunctio* was performed wholly in the physical realm in the admittedly abstract theory of the *coniugium solis et lunae*, which despite this drawback gave the creative imagination much occasion for anthropomorphic flights.

296   Such being the state of affairs, it is readily understandable that the primordial image of the hermaphrodite should reappear in modern psychology in the guise of

the male-female antithesis, in other words as *male* consciousness and personified *female* unconscious. But the psychological process of bringing things to consciousness has complicated the picture considerably. Whereas the old science was almost exclusively a field in which only the man's unconscious could project itself, the new psychology had to acknowledge the existence of an autonomous female psyche as well. Here the case is reversed, and a feminine consciousness confronts a masculine personification of the unconscious, which can no longer be called *anima* but *animus*. This discovery also complicates the problem of the *coniunctio*.

297   Originally this archetype played its part entirely in the field of fertility magic and thus remained for a very long time a purely biological phenomenon with no other purpose than that of fecundation. But even in early antiquity the symbolical meaning of the act seems to have increased. Thus, for example, the physical performance of the *hieros gamos* as a sacred rite not only became a mystery – it faded to a mere conjecture.⁴² As we have seen, Gnosticism, too, endeavoured in all seriousness to subordinate the physiological to the metaphysical. Finally, the Church severed the *coniunctio* from the physical realm altogether, and natural philosophy turned it into an abstract *theoria*. These developments meant the gradual transformation of the archetype into a psychological process which, in theory, we can call a combination of conscious and unconscious processes. In practice, however, it is not so simple, because as a rule the feminine unconscious of a man is projected upon a feminine partner, and the masculine unconscious of a woman is projected upon a man. The elucidation of these problems is a special branch of psychology and has no part in a discussion of the mythological hermaphrodite.

The child as beginning and end

298   Faust, after his death, is received as a boy into the 'choir of blessed youths.' I do not know whether Goethe was referring, with this peculiar idea, to the *cupids* on antique grave-stones. It is not unthinkable. The figure of the *cucullatus* points to the hooded, that is, the *invisible* one, the genius of the departed, who reappears in the child-like frolics of a new life, surrounded by the sea-forms of dolphins and tritons. The sea is the favourite symbol for the unconscious, the mother of all that lives. Just as the 'child' is, in certain circumstances (e.g., in the case of Hermes and the Dactyls), closely related to the phallus, symbol of the begetter, so it comes up again in the sepulchral phallus, symbol of a renewed begetting.

299   The 'child' is therefore *renatus in novam infantiam*. It is thus both beginning and end, an initial and a terminal creature. The initial creature existed before man was, and the terminal creature will be when man is not. Psychologically speaking, this means that the 'child' symbolizes the pre-conscious and the post-conscious essence of man. His pre-conscious essence is the unconscious state of earliest childhood; his post-conscious essence is an anticipation by analogy of life after death. In this idea the all-embracing nature of psychic wholeness is expressed.

Wholeness is never comprised within the compass of the conscious mind – it includes the indefinite and indefinable extent of the unconscious as well. Wholeness, empirically speaking, is therefore of immeasurable extent, older and younger than consciousness and enfolding it in time and space. This is no speculation, but an immediate psychic experience. Not only is the conscious process continually accompanied, it is often guided, helped, or interrupted, by unconscious happenings. The child had a psychic life before it had consciousness. Even the adult still says and does things whose significance he realizes only later, if ever. And yet he said them and did them as if he knew what they meant. Our dreams are continually saying things beyond our conscious comprehension (which is why they are so useful in the therapy of neuroses). We have intimations and intuitions from unknown sources. Fears, moods, plans, and hopes come to us with no visible causation. These concrete experiences are at the bottom of our feeling that we know ourselves very little; at the bottom, too, of the painful conjecture that we might have surprises in store for ourselves.

300 Primitive man is no puzzle to himself. The question 'What is man?' is the question that man has always kept until last. Primitive man has so much psyche outside his conscious mind that the experience of something psychic outside him is far more familiar to him than to us. Consciousness hedged about by psychic powers, sustained or threatened or deluded by them, is the age-old experience of mankind. This experience has projected itself into the archetype of the child, which expresses man's wholeness. The 'child' is all that is abandoned and exposed and at the same time divinely powerful; the insignificant, dubious beginning, and the triumphal end. The 'eternal child' in man is an indescribable experience, an incongruity, a handicap, and a divine prerogative; an imponderable that determines the ultimate worth or worthlessness of a personality.

IV Conclusion

301 I am aware that a psychological commentary on the child archetype without detailed documentation must remain a mere sketch. But since this is virgin territory for the psychologist, my main endeavour has been to stake out the possible extent of the problems raised by our archetype and to describe, at least cursorily, its different aspects. Clear-cut distinctions and strict formulations are quite impossible in this field, seeing that a kind of fluid interpenetration belongs to the very nature of all archetypes. They can only be roughly circumscribed at best. Their living meaning comes out more from their presentation as a whole than from a single formulation. Every attempt to focus them more sharply is immediately punished by the intangible core of meaning losing its luminosity. No archetype can be reduced to a simple formula. It is a vessel which we can never empty, and never fill. It has a potential existence only, and when it takes shape in matter it is no longer what it was. It persists throughout the ages and requires interpreting ever anew. The archetypes are the imperishable elements of the unconscious, but they change their shape continually.

302 It is a well-nigh hopeless undertaking to tear a single archetype out of the living tissue of the psyche; but despite their interwovenness they do form units of meaning that can be apprehended intuitively. Psychology, as one of the many expressions of psychic life, operates with ideas which in their turn are derived from archetypal structures and thus generate a somewhat more abstract kind of myth. Psychology therefore translates the archaic speech of myth into a modern mythologem – not yet, of course, recognized as such – which constitutes one element of the myth 'science.' This seemingly hopeless undertaking is a *living and lived myth*, satisfying to persons of a corresponding temperament, indeed beneficial in so far as they have been cut off from their psychic origins by neurotic dissociation.

303 As a matter of experience, we meet the child archetype in spontaneous and in therapeutically induced individuation processes. The first manifestation of the 'child' is as a rule a totally unconscious phenomenon. Here the patient identifies himself with his personal infantilism. Then, under the influence of therapy, we get a more or less gradual separation from and objectification of the 'child,' that is, the identity breaks down and is accompanied by an intensification (sometimes technically induced) of fantasy, with the result that archaic or mythological features become increasingly apparent. Further transformations run true to the hero myth. The theme of 'mighty feats' is generally absent, but on the other hand the mythical dangers play all the greater part. At this stage there is usually another identification, this time with the hero, whose role is attractive for a variety of reasons. The identification is often extremely stubborn and dangerous to the psychic equilibrium. If it can be broken down and if consciousness can be reduced to human proportions, the figure of the hero can gradually be differentiated into a symbol of the self.

304 In practical reality, however, it is of course not enough for the patient merely to *know about* such developments; what counts is his experience of the various transformations. The initial stage of personal infantilism presents the picture of an 'abandoned' or 'misunderstood' and unjustly treated child with overweening pretensions. The epiphany of the hero (the second identification) shows itself in a corresponding inflation: the colossal pretension grows into a conviction that one is something extraordinary, or else the impossibility of the pretension ever being fulfilled only proves one's own inferiority, which is favourable to the role of the heroic sufferer (a negative inflation). In spite of their contradictoriness, both forms are identical, because conscious megalomania is balanced by unconscious compensatory inferiority and conscious inferiority by unconscious megalomania (you never get one without the other). Once the reef of the second identification has been successfully circumnavigated, conscious processes can be cleanly separated from the unconscious, and the latter observed objectively. This leads to the possibility of an accommodation with the unconscious, and thus to a possible synthesis of the conscious and unconscious elements of knowledge and action. This in turn leads to a shifting of the centre of personality from the ego to the self.[43]

305   In this psychological framework the motifs of abandonment, invincibility, hermaphroditism, and beginning and end take their place as distinct categories of experience and understanding.

Notes

1 [Originally published as 'Zur Psychologie des Kind-Archetypus,' in *Das göttliche Kind* (Amsterdam and Leipzig, 1940). The volume contained a companion essay by Karl Kerényi and was included as part of a larger volume translated by R. F. C. Hull as *Essays on a Science of Mythology* (New York, Bollingen Series, 1949). The text of the present essay is a revision of the 1949 version. – Editor.]
2 Kerényi, 'The Primordial Child in Primordial Times.'
3 *Der Mensch in der Geschichte* (1860).
4 *Psyche* (1846).
5 A working example in 'The Concept of the Collective Unconscious,' pars. 105ff., above.
6 Freud, in his *Interpretation of Dreams* (p. 261), paralleled certain aspects of infantile psychology with the Oedipus legend and observed that its 'universal validity' was to be explained in terms of the same infantile premise. The real working out of mythological material was then taken up by my pupils (A. Maeder, 'Essai d'interprétation de quelques rêves,' 1907, and 'Die Symbolik in den Legenden, Märchen, Gebräuchen, und Träumen,' 1908; F. Riklin, 'Über Gefängnispsychosen,' 1907, and *Wishfulfilment and Symbolism in Fairy Tales*, orig. 1908); and by K. Abraham, *Dreams and Myths*, orig. 1909. They were succeeded by Otto Rank of the Viennese school (*The Myth of the Birth of the Hero*, orig. 1922). In the *Psychology of the Unconscious* (orig. 1911; revised and expanded as *Symbols of Transformation*), I presented a somewhat more comprehensive examination of psychic and mythological parallels. Cf. also my essay in this volume, 'Concerning the Archetypes, with Special Reference to the Anima Concept.'
7 This fact is well known, and the relevant ethnological literature is too extensive to be mentioned here.
8 Cf. 'The Structure of the Psyche,' pars. 330ff.
9 Except for certain cases of spontaneous vision, *automatismes téléologiques* (Flournoy), and the processes in the method of 'active imagination' which I have described [e.g., in 'The Transcendent Function' and *Mysterium Coniunctionis*, pars. 706, 753f.– EDITORS].
10 The relevant material can be found in the unpublished reports of the seminars I gave at the Federal Polytechnic Institute (ETH) in Zurich in 1936–39, and in Michael Fordham's book *The Life of Childhood*.
11 Berthelot, *Alchimistes grecs*, III, xxv.
12 Agricola, *De animantibus subterraneis* (1549); Kircher, *Mundus subterraneus* (1678), VIII, 4.
13 Mylius, *Philosophia reformata* (1622).
14 'Allegoria super librum Turbae' in *Artis auriferae*, I (1572), p. 161.
15 *Texte aus der deutschen Mystik des 14. und 15. Jahrhunderts*, ed. Spamer, pp. 143, 150.
16 Ingram, *The Haunted Homes and Family Traditions of Great Britain*, pp. 43ff.
17 An old alchemical authority variously named Morienes, Morienus, Marianus ('De compositione alchemiae,' Manget, *Bibliotheca chemica curiosa*, I, pp. 509ff.). In view of the explicitly alchemical character of *Faust*, Part II, such a connection would not be surprising.
18 Schreber, *Memoirs of My Nervous Illness*.

19 For a general presentation see infra, 'Conscious, Unconscious, and Individuation.' Special phenomena in the following text, also in *Psychology and Alchemy*, Part II.
20 'The Relations between the Ego and the Unconscious,' Part II, ch. 3 [also 'The Transcendent Function' – EDITORS].
21 *Symbols of Transformation*, index, s.v.
22 It may not be superfluous to point out that lay prejudice is always inclined to identify the child motif with the concrete experience 'child,' as though the real child were the cause and pre-condition of the existence of the child motif. In psychological reality, however, the empirical idea 'child' is only the means (and not the only one) by which to express a psychic fact that cannot be formulated more exactly. Hence by the same token the mythological idea of the child is emphatically not a copy of the empirical child but a *symbol* clearly recognizable as such: it is a wonder-child, a divine child, begotten, born, and brought up in quite extraordinary circumstances, and not – this is the point – a human child. Its deeds are as miraculous or monstrous as its nature and physical constitution. Only on account of these highly unempirical properties is it necessary to speak of a 'child motif' at all. Moreover, the mythological 'child' has various forms: now a god, giant, Tom Thumb, animal, etc., and this points to a causality that is anything but rational or concretely human. The same is true of the 'father' and 'mother' archetypes which, mythologically speaking, are equally irrational symbols.
23 *Psychological Types*, Def. 48; and *Two Essays on Analytical Psychology*, index, s.v. 'persona.'
24 *Psychological Types*, ch. V, 3: 'The Significance of the Uniting Symbol.'
25 *Psychology and Alchemy*, pars. 327ff.; 'Psychology and Religion,' pars.108ff.
26 *Two Essays on Analytical Psychology*, pars. 399ff. [Cf. also *Aion* (Part II of this volume), ch. 4.–EDITORS.]
27 *Psychology and Alchemy*, pars. 328ff.
28 Higher vertebrates symbolize mainly affects.
29 This interpretation of the snake is found as early as Hippolytus, *Elenchos*, IV, 49–51 (Legge trans., I, p. 117). Cf. also Leisegang, *Die Gnosis*, p. 146.
30 *Psychological Types*, Def. 51.
31 Even Christ is of a fiery nature ('he that is near to me is near to the fire' – Origen, *In Jeremiam Homiliae*, XX, 3); likewise the Holy Ghost.
32 The material is collected in *Psychology and Alchemy*, Parts II and III. For Mercurius as a servant, see the parable of Eirenaeus Philalethes, *Ripley Reviv'd: or, An Exposition upon Sir George Ripley's Hermetico-Poetical Works* (1678).
33 Koepgen, *Die Gnosis des Christentums*, pp. 315ff.
34 For the *lapis* as mediator and medium, cf. *Tractatus aureus*, in Manget, *Bibliotheca chemica curiosa*, I, p. 408b, and *Artis auriferae* (1572), p. 641.
35 *Psychological Types*, Def. 48; and 'Relations between the Ego and the Unconscious,' pars. 296ff.
36 Hosea 1: 2ff.
37 Cf. Fendt, *Gnostische Mysterien*.
38 James, *The Apocryphal New Testament*, p. 11.
39 Clement, *Stromata*, III, 13, 92, 2.
40 *The Flowing Light of the Godhead*.
41 Salomon, *Opicinus de Canistris*.
42 Cf. the diatribe by Bishop Asterius (Foucart, *Les Mystères d'Eleusis*, pp. 477ff.). According to Hippolytus' account the hierophant actually made himself impotent by a draught of hemlock. The self-castration of priests in the worship of the Mother Goddess is of similar import.
43 A more detailed account of these developments is to be found in 'The Relations between the Ego and the Unconscious.'

Part III

Religion and culture

Religion and culture

Introduction

Chapter 8: 'The spiritual problem of modern man' (1928/1931)

(From *Civilization in Transition, The Collected Works Vol.* 10, § 148–196)

The spiritual 'problem' of Western humanity consists, for Jung, of a cluster of problems. First, the modern person has been educated to believe in reason and the evidence of the senses. This means that the truly modern person has become alienated from religion and from all forms of non-rational activity. He or she engages in what Jung calls 'directed' or logical thinking,[1] thus preventing the psyche from expressing itself. This has created a divided personality, with the conscious part identified with society and its values, and the unconscious part unattended, unsupported and lacking in direction. The unconscious is liable to become unruly, dangerous or monstrous in this split-off condition, thus creating the social climate for conflict, war, and a general discontent that is liable to lead to addictions, compulsions, fanaticisms and revolutionary movements. When spirit is neglected it becomes the source of many pathologies.

Second, the non-rational life of the soul has changed; it is no longer adequately expressed by the values of Christianity, nor by any other religion that is concerned primarily with the good, the light and the holy. There has been such a piling-up of evil and darkness in the psyche that the soul can no longer identify itself with images of goodness. The soul requires a different kind of expression, one which can acknowledge – and transform – the dark forces that have gathered in the inner world. This means there can be no going back to the religious forms of the past, and the spiritual 'problem' is not solved by returning to religious life in the old way. Religions now appear somewhat alien to the soul: 'For modern man . . . the various forms of religion no longer appear to come from within, from the psyche; they seem more like items from the inventory of the outside world' (§ 168).

Third, the new religious expressions, which have yet to be realised, will need to emerge from within the conditions of the modern soul and need to be experiential. The new religious life of humanity cannot be based on external belief, received tradition or moral instruction. Jung suggests that the imitation of Christ or any other messianic figure is no longer possible; instead, we have to allow the spirit within to guide and direct us (§ 171). This points to a religion based on the indwelling of the Holy Spirit – although the modern spirit is anything but 'holy' when it is first encountered. Jung seems to follow the thinking of the twelfth-century Calabrian abbot Joachim of the Flowers, who advocated a tripartite view of history: an Old Testament world governed by God the Father, a Christian world governed by God the Son, and a future, third world governed by the Spirit. Jung's work points to a new era that does not so much represent the destruction of Father and Son, as their completion in a higher spiritual order. The Holy Spirit – the least known member of the Trinity – is on Jung's mind as a clue to the landscape of the future.

'We are only at the threshold of a new spiritual epoch', writes Jung (§ 190), and as such, we do not have the cultural forms to direct this new spiritual life. We cannot expect religious tradition, society or governments to do the work for us: these are 'old world' expressions which are opposed to radical change. Society wants to remain humanist and secular, religion wants to remain true to the past, and education wants to remain true to reason. Consequently, humanity is left stranded and without resources. If change is to come it is going to be from our own efforts: 'Great innovations never come from above; they come invariably from below, just as trees never grow from the sky downward, but upward from the earth' (§ 177). Jung places emphasis on personal initiative and industry. We have to motivate ourselves to meet the spiritual challenges of our time: 'The modern man . . . must be proficient in the highest degree, for unless he can atone by creative ability for his break with tradition, he is merely disloyal to the past' (§ 153). Jung is scathing toward the 'pseudo-moderns' who do not meet the challenges of the age, but who merely enjoy their freedom from the past. He sees them as hedonistic and as giving the 'truly modern' person a bad name. If the spiritual life is not attended to, or we do not contribute to rebuilding it in some way, our lives are empty and we drag civilisation to the edge of ruin.

Rebuilding is essential, but Jung admits that at first we do not know how to rebuild or where to start. He criticises the new spiritual movements of his time, especially Madame Blavatsky's Theosophy and Rudolph Steiner's Anthroposophy. It is hard to know why Jung is so scathing toward these movements; after all, they are new responses to the life of the spirit and they seem to fulfil his requirements about facing our spiritual challenges in an experiential manner. Perhaps these movements are too close to Jung's psychology for comfort, and he feels impelled to attack them. Perhaps he sees in them the awkward, gauche, imprecise qualities that are found in all new movements of the spirit, including his own. He claims that Theosophy is 'an amateurish, indeed barbarous imitation of the East' (§ 188), but the same could be said by Buddhist monks of Jung's psychology, especially its appropriation of the Atman, the Tao and the mandala in the concept of the Self. His use of Eastern ideas is amateurish and imprecise, even if it is well intended.

Jung seems touchy about the East, and is only too aware of how much he has borrowed from it. Jung wants the West to arrive at its own 'East', by finding an equivalent introverted and experiential attitude in itself:

It seems to be quite true that the East is at the bottom of the spiritual change we are passing through today. Only, this East is not a Tibetan monastery full of Mahatmas, but lies essentially within us. It is our own psyche, constantly at work creating new spiritual forms and spiritual forces which may help us to subdue the boundless lust for prey of Aryan man.

(§ 190)

For Jung the East is a symbol of the unexplored potential of the Western psyche, and he wants us to make contact with that psychic reality – and not project our interiority upon the Oriental world. The turn to the East seems to follow much of Jung's logic: the Western world is empty, burnt out, needs renewal, but he steps in with moral criticism if such a turn means that the interiority of the West is neglected as we journey to the East.

Chapter 9: 'Psychology and religion: The autonomy of the unconscious' (1938/1940)

(From *Psychology and Religion: West and East, The Collected Works Vol.* 11, § 1–55)

It is a shock to Western thought to imagine that the 'unconscious' is capable of a higher form of intelligence than our reason. Psychic forces not only possess insight and wisdom, but 'the unconscious is capable at times of manifesting an intelligence and purposiveness superior to the actual conscious insight' (§ 63). Not only are psychic forces invisible, but they possess an intelligence that points to some higher purpose. Science, however, claims that such purpose has been 'added' to the data by Jung. Jung argues that life is given splendour and hope once we see the meaningfulness which is observable in the psychic depths. This is not a distortion of reality, but life as it is meant to be lived. Science is the distortion, in that it avoids viewing life through the lens of the deeper intelligence which underpins existence.

At this point we begin to wonder about the appropriateness of the term 'the unconscious'. If the unconscious possesses direction, purpose, wisdom, and if it is 'superior to conscious insight', in what sense is it unconscious? Jung admits that 'the concept of the unconscious is an assumption for the sake of convenience' (§ 64). In another essay he refers to the unconscious as 'a multiple consciousness'.[2] In his view, it is we who are unconscious and the psyche which is conscious, in the sense of being intelligent and aware of its goal. We are unaware of our goal, and only catch glimpses of it during a lifetime. But because we start with the ego or the socially conditioned self, the rest of the psyche is unknown to us, and we call it 'the unconscious' even though we demean it by using that term.

This is one example of the terminological tangles in which Jung found himself. He followed Freud at first, and for Freud the ego is the seat of human identity. But because Jung went into 'wisdom' that went beyond Freud, the psychoanalytic legacy became a burden as he tried to explore his intuitions. In the East, for instance, there is no such thing as the 'unconscious', and the cosmic forces or archetypes are regarded as supremely intelligent and conscious. I have often reflected that the East gets this right, and we in the West are slow to learn that the ego is the seat of unconsciousness, whereas the archetypal forces are intelligent. Coming out of Freud, but moving closer to mysticism and the East, Jung is caught between them, and uses language that can confuse the early reader of his work.

Jung announces that the unconscious 'has religious tendencies' (§ 39) and that the psyche is a 'religious phenomenon' (§ 63). He defines his work as 'the psychology of the *homo religiosus*' (§ 11). He sees forces in the psyche that seek *religio* or 'binding back' to the sacred. These forces, apparently subjective, are actually objective in that they participate in ultimate reality. Jung discerns something going on in the psychic background which is of monumental significance, but humanity, as yet, continues to avoid it.

What does Jung mean by religious? He does not mean 'religion' in the conventional sense. Jung was not keen on organisational religion, and rebelled against his father's dedication to what he saw as a 'dead' or moribund tradition. Jung's main interest was in religious experience, namely, the fact of having been encountered by, or brought into contact with, the *numinosum*. This term refers to a god or spirit as a power that can impact on our experience and turn lives around. 'The *numinosum*,' he writes, 'is an experience of the subject independent of his will' (§ 6). This is the hallmark of Jung's work. He is not interested in our personal intention, our independent actions or choices. He is riveted by something that comes to greet us which is outside our will and contrary to our intentions. There is something outside consciousness which eclipses us on all sides. In a time governed by humanism and ideals of independence, Jung's ideas strike many as archaic, medieval, and counter-modern. But those with an interest in the sources of mystery from which our lives emerge will be intrigued by what Jung calls his 'unusual argument' (§ 4).

'The *numinosum*,' he says, 'is the influence of an invisible presence that causes a peculiar alteration of consciousness' (§ 6). This sounds strange to modern ears and many would prefer to run from this perspective. Fear of the numinous or *pneumaphobia* is what drives many of us away from Jung's insights. There is a natural, perhaps an innate, resistance to 'prophets' who tell us that God is near. This is not only an intellectual shock but an emotional rebuke to our self and its autonomy. We live in a period of history in which notions of liberty are held in high esteem. Jung's work is not about freedom, but about the bonds that tie us to invisible presences. 'Freedom,' wrote Camille Paglia, 'is the most overrated modern idea',[3] and those who live by the idea of freedom will not like what they encounter in Jung's work.

Jung tells us how we are bound, but just as importantly, he tells us how we can achieve a degree of freedom. Although urging us to become aware of the invisible presences in our lives, Jung has a humanistic side, and is concerned that we find our relation to these presences, so that we discover an element of freedom and maintain dignity in the face of an archetypal destiny. The first task is to become aware of the archetypes, to respect them. Having brought them to awareness, we might be able to achieve some autonomy. In his view, our freedom is limited by complexes and archetypes, and curtailed by a fate that works through the unconscious. But some liberation is possible even if the cards are stacked against an entirely free life because of our embeddedness in a matrix we can barely discern.

There is a positive side, however, to such embeddedness. It not only limits our freedom, but connects us to forces beyond the ego. The ego might feel alone, even alienated from the world, history and cosmos, but this alienation is an illusion of its making. It is a 'myth' that many of us live by, and it is a myth that Jung's work challenges. In certain respects, Jung's work is similar to that of Karl Marx: both saw alienation as the modern condition, and both sought to overcome alienation and achieve an authentic existence. But whereas for Marx the work of transformation was to be achieved by social rebellion against capitalism, for Jung, the transformation was psychological and achieved by rebellion against the hegemony of the ego. For him, we need to change the *locus* of our identity from the ego and its typical isolation, to the soul and connectedness. By returning to the soul, humanity can recover its roots and kinship with nature and the historical process. Marx's revolution has been tried and found wanting; Jung's revolution has not been tried and is a task for the future.

Chapter 10: Preface to *Answer to Job*: Lectori benevolo (1952)

(From *Psychology and Religion: West and East, The Collected Works* Vol. 11, § 553–559)

Jung's short preface to his book *Answer to Job* is probably his clearest and most concise statement about the problem of literalism in Western religions. *Answer to Job* (not reproduced here) is concerned with the problem of evil and the role of the feminine in religion, but in addition he develops an argument about the right interpretation of sacred images. Jung believes that the churches have been involved in a self-deceiving falsehood. They have tended to read their images, miracles and wonders as literal events or physical facts, whereas it is obvious that such important moments in the Christian story as the virgin birth, the physical resurrection and the second coming are not events on the stage of history but images of myth. They are *myths* which have been woven around the bare 'facts' of the historical figure of Jesus, his ministry of love and forgiveness and his crucifixion on Calvary. Jung does not doubt that Jesus existed, but feels that this figure released so many archetypal patterns that his life was appropriated by myths before anyone had a chance to know him. Jung would include Jesus' followers in this category; no one knew Jesus as a real figure, because his life was shot through with mythic currents.

Today we tend to dismiss myths as 'false' but Jung would insist that they are 'true'. He did not mean that they are literally true, but that they are spiritually true, that is, they express age-old truths of the spirit and timeless patterns of the soul. Christ became a universal symbol of the spirit, and it can be said that spirit does not have a 'normal' birth, that is, it is not dependent on sexual processes or biological facts for its existence. It precedes sexuality, biology and the body, and it can be said to be 'virginal' in a metaphorical sense. The spirit cannot be destroyed by death or the annihilation of the body, and thus it can be said to be immortal, to 'rise again' after death and lead a life of its own in the mind of God. Jung's theory of the metaphorical nature of the Christian mysteries does not please Christian readers, who insist on the 'truth' of such mysteries. Jung is saying that simple-minded believers lack imagination and do not understand the nature of truth. Truth is not something that one can see or touch, or an event which can be beheld by eyewitnesses. The resurrection cannot be captured by photography. The outward body dies and the spirit lives on. Truth is internal, hidden from the common eye, and revealed only to the poet, the prophet or the philosopher.

Christians tend not to believe in a hidden level of truth in the Bible and think of God's word as matter of fact or non-metaphorical. That is why Jung's reading of these mysteries is considered heretical. Jung's hope, however, is not to humiliate religious tradition but to make it see the deeper meaning of its miracles. He thinks literalism is killing the church and destroying an otherwise good religion. If religion could understand its miracles as symbols and scriptures as poetry, it would not be rejected by thinking people who cannot 'believe' in the supernatural, and it would build a bridge between dogmas and the psyche. So long as these events are literalised, they remain 'out there', lost in the past and caught in projections. If they are transformed into symbols of spirit, we can reclaim this heritage even in a technological age. They can come alive again in the soul.

Jung made it clear from the beginning that he was not a believer in miracles or wonders. He felt a mixture of poor judgement and bad taste on the part of the churches had conspired to read them literally.

> Religious statements are of this type [metaphorical in nature]. They refer without exception to things that cannot be established as physical facts. If they did not do this, they would inevitably fall into the category of the natural sciences. Taken as referring to anything physical, they make no sense whatever, and science would dismiss them as non-experienceable. They would be mere miracles, which are sufficiently exposed to doubt as it is, and yet they could not demonstrate the reality of the spirit or the meaning that underlies them.
>
> (§ 554)

Religious statements are not literally true, but nor are they lies, as atheists contend. The rational person protests that if they are not true as facts, they cannot be true in any way. Such thinking lands us in the spiritual wasteland in which many of us flounder. The mysteries of religions are truths of the spirit, but this is not self-evident to most of us today. Not even those who are professionally involved in religious life understand this. Too often, those who devote their lives to religion do not perceive that religion is a call to personal transformation. We need to be inducted into the language of myth and symbol, initiated into it, either by training, education, or an analysis of the unconscious. The unconscious still speaks in the language of myth, the same language that is found in religious systems.

The traditions demand that people return to belief in miracles, but Jung points out that this is impossible for the modern intellect; nor does it connect us to the meaning of miracles:

> Miracles appeal only to the understanding of those who cannot perceive the meaning. They are mere substitutes for the not understood reality of the spirit.
> (§ 554)

Literalism satisfies the religious institutions and their requirements, but not the soul or spirit, which hungers for the meaning in and behind miracles. We can no longer be fed miracles and wonders, because we are no longer satisfied by superstitious tales and need to know the meaning of the transformations of spirit. Miracles are for those without faith or imagination. One does not need miracles if there is true faith. To confuse the sacred narrative of the mystical body with facts about the physical body is not a work of divine inspiration but of cultural manipulation. It is interesting to note how close Jung's critique of religion is at this point to that of Marx and Freud.

Jung felt that unless Western religion could overcome its obsession with literalism there was little hope for its revival. He wanted to bring the myths of religion to life by bringing them into contact with the soul, so they could be experienced as truths within the individual. The historical emphasis in religion was killing it off, because everything was being kept outside the subjective arena. Myths had to be pried apart from their historical associations and linked to the human heart. In the current dogmatic climate, myths were dying for want of being understood as living organs of the soul.

Chapter 11: 'Psychology and literature' (1930/1950)

(From *The Spirit in Man, Art, and Literature, The Collected Works Vol.* 15, § 133–162)

One of the first things Jung does in this essay is offer an apology for trespassing on the field of literature. He feels some kind of explanation is in order and says:

> Since it is a characteristic of the psyche not only to be the source of all productivity but, more especially, to express itself in all the activities and achievements of the human mind, we can nowhere grasp the nature of the psyche *per se* but can meet it only in its various manifestations. The

psychologist is therefore obliged to make himself familiar with a wide range of subjects, not out of presumption and inquisitiveness but rather from love of knowledge, and for this purpose he must abandon his thickly walled specialist fortress and set out on the quest for truth.[4]

He adds: '[although] the poetic imagination . . . constitutes the proper province of literary science and aesthetics . . . it is also a psychic phenomenon, and as such it probably must be taken into account by the psychologist.' This 'probably' does not seem too convincing, but at this stage in the history of psychoanalysis researchers were not confident about how much trespassing they could do.

Jung says he cannot confine himself to psychology or psychiatry, and his interest has 'burst the framework' of the study of medicine. The complex nature of the psyche has made him a generalist, not because he wants to be but because he has to be. The pursuit of psyche urged him into areas of knowledge that he would not have explored unless he had been prompted. Jung risked being 'undisciplined' in the technical sense and he risked falling out of view, into the gaps between the disciplines. He went outside boundaries because he was motivated by the desire to think his way to a new place beyond conventional specialisations. He was in search of meaning, and meaning is not confined to any discipline.

One of Jung's major themes is that the personality of the artist does not, and cannot, explain the art: 'The personal psychology of the artist may explain many aspects of his work, but not the work itself' (§ 134). He is making a deliberate move against Freudian reductionism. In Freudian interpretations, the work of art is often reduced to the psychological problems of the artist. Jung protests that in this kind of analysis 'the artist's creativity is reduced to a mere symptom' (§ 134). Such interpretations find in the work of art, for instance, the mother complex or Oedipal conflicts of the artist. In Jung's view this brings the psychoanalytic interpretation of art into deserved ridicule and ill-repute. Many have become wary of psychoanalytic interpretations of poetry, painting and narrative because they are narrow and dogmatic, rarely focused on the work, or what it might mean to society or culture, but intent only on reducing it to personal problems.

Jung is also making a case against humanism in literary criticism. Contrary to Freudian readings, in which the artist becomes a neurotic sufferer, humanism tends to exalt the artist and celebrate him or her as a hero, saint or visionary. Humanism falls prey to what is called the 'intentional fallacy', that is, the notion that an artist knows exactly what he or she is doing in their work. This assumes that the conscious intentions of the artist exhaust the meanings of the work, and if we want to discover the meaning of any work, we need only contact the artist and ask him or her about it. This is the opposite of the Freudian reading, in which it is assumed that art works contain unconscious impulses. Jung agrees with Freud that art contains unconscious materials, but disagrees with the view that these can be reduced to personal problems.

Jung's approach conforms in a fascinating way to the ideas of post-structuralism and postmodernism. These theories tend to emphasise the objectivity of the work of art, and do not collapse it into the psychology of the artist. French theorists such as Roland Barthes wrote about the 'death of the author', by which he meant that the artist's intentions ought not to be viewed as the explanatory principles of the art. According to Barthes we are to look beyond the artist's intentions to explore the work in its own right, regardless of what was in the artist's mind at the time of conception. This comes close to Jung's approach – meaning that he anticipated the ideas of postmodernism and post-structuralism by several decades.[5]

Jung distinguishes between what he calls 'psychological' and 'visionary' modes of expression. These are unhappy terms, and even the editors of his essay begin to argue with Jung in a footnote to paragraph 139. The editors suggest that Jung meant to distinguish between personalistic and archetypal modes of expression. This seems a happier choice of terms. What Jung calls the 'psychological' and his editors call the 'personalistic' mode is not of interest to Jung. He argues that 'psychological' writings are conscious and deliberate, and as such, there is nothing for the psychologist to interpret: 'The so-called "psychological novel" is by no means as rewarding for the psychologist as the literary minded suppose' (§ 136). 'There is nothing the psychologist can add to it that has not already been said in better words by the poet' (§ 138). This mode of creativity, he argues, is so carefully controlled that there are no deeper structures to discern. As a literary scholar, I have to disagree with him. Often a text gives the impression of being deliberately crafted, but underneath there remain strange elements to be excavated. In other words, the unconscious insinuates itself, even when the conscious appears to be in control.[6]

Jung was mainly concerned with what he called the 'visionary' mode. He claims that works in this mode tend to seize hold of the artist and make of him or her an often unwilling instrument. Jung waxes lyrical about this mode and betrays a romantic fascination for its apparent lack of control:

> The visionary mode of artistic creation . . . is something strange that derives its existence from the hinterland of man's mind, as if it had emerged from the abyss of prehuman ages. . . . It is a primordial experience which surpasses man's understanding and to which in his weakness he may easily succumb. The very enormity of the experience gives it its value and its shattering impact. Sublime, pregnant with meaning, yet chilling the blood with its strangeness, it arises from timeless depths. . . . This disturbing spectacle of some tremendous process that in every way transcends our human feeling and understanding makes quite other demands upon the powers of the artist than do the experiences of the foreground of life.
>
> (§ 141)

Jung gives several examples of this mode, mainly from German culture, which is what he knew best. He cites Goethe's *Faust, Part Two*, Wagner's *The Ring of the Nibelungen*, Nietzsche's *Thus Spake Zarathustra*; and he also mentions, from Italian literature, Dante's *The Divine Comedy*, and from English literature,

William Blake's poetry. These are works in which there has been an eruption of the unconscious, and the artist is seized by something beyond his control, acting as an instrument for archetypal processes. Jung says we normally feel ambivalent about such works, because they are so foreign to normal life and everyday experience: 'We are astonished, confused, bewildered, put on guard or even repelled; we demand commentaries and explanations' (§ 143).

As an example of being *repelled* by a visionary work, Jung gives the example of James Joyce's *Ulysses*. He wrote a separate, long essay on this modernist novel, but it was not one of his best papers, and Jung seems not to have understood the work.[7] He refers to it as having the design and content of a psychotic mental state. Jung likes some visionary works but not others; he prefers them to be coherent in style, not fragmented and confused. Ironically, they are meant to portray explosions of the unconscious, but they must not *be* explosive in their style, like Joyce. Jung's taste in art is curiously restricted: he likes a work to have romantic content, which can be passionate and turbulent, but he expects the form or shape to be classical and restrained.

Jung argues that some works of art become 'great' because they express not only the unconscious impulses of the artist but the unconscious life of the time. He ascribes to such works not only aesthetic and moral significance, but prophetic meaning. They anticipate contents of the collective psyche that have not yet reached the threshold of awareness. Such works tell us what is happening on the inside of our culture, and he sees visionary works of art, like religions and myths, as having a therapeutic value: 'What is of particular importance for the study of literature, however, is that the manifestations of the collective unconscious are compensatory to the conscious attitude, so that they have the effect of bringing a one-sided, unadapted, or dangerous state of consciousness back into equilibrium' (§ 152). Works of art which are able to bring archetypal currents to the surface serve to compensate the one-sidedness of society, and, to the extent that they bring unruly contents into alignment with consciousness, help to prevent future outbreaks of disorder. Art is a form of collective therapy; it supplies what is missing from awareness, relates it to consciousness, and thereby helps a society to reach wholeness.

Jung's theory of the collective unconscious enables him to emphasise the social significance of works which have archetypal content. He summarises his theory of art as follows:

> The creative process . . . consists in the unconscious activation of an archetypal image, and in elaborating and shaping this image into the finished work. By giving it shape, the artist translates it into the language of the present, and so makes it possible for us to find our way back to the deepest springs of life. Therein lies the social significance of art; it is constantly at work educating the spirit of the age, conjuring up the forms in which the age is most lacking.[8]

Visionary art is to society what the dream is to the individual: the means whereby suppressed contents are brought to the surface so that a transformation can occur.

As with dreams, visionary works need to be interpreted and call for hermeneutical responses. Aesthetic works have begun the work of interpretation for us by 'translating' an archetypal content into 'the language of the present'. Such works 'give shape' to contents which must still be understood by the mind and society, because visionary works, like dreams, speak in symbols which the intellect does not comprehend. Jung's theory of art had been anticipated by Shakespeare, who wrote in *A Midsummer Night's Dream*:

> And as imagination bodies forth
> The forms of things unknown, the poet's pen
> Turns them to shapes, and gives to airy nothing
> A local habitation and a name.[9]

Shakespeare's 'airy nothing' is similar to Jung's 'unconscious', and the work of art gives archetypal contents 'a local habitation and a name'. The artist is a magus who 'bodies forth / the forms of things unknown', and allows those forms to resonate in the imagination of an age. If the works are great, they may reverberate throughout the ages to come.

Chapter 12: 'The difference between Eastern and Western thinking' (1939/1954)

(From 'Psychological commentary on *The Tibetan Book of the Great Liberation*', in *Psychology and Religion: West and East, The Collected Works Vol. 11*, § 759–787)

This paper, written in English, is the first section of Jung's commentary on *The Tibetan Book of the Great Liberation*. Jung thinks that the East has a better grasp of psychology than the West, but is reluctant to admit it because he is a Westerner through and through. He admires the East, but cannot become an advocate of the East, although he is tempted in this direction. Whenever Jung discusses the East, his writing is full of admiration and longing, undercut by resistances. The question he raises is: how did East and West arrive at such different concepts of mind? 'It is safe to assume that what the East calls "mind" has more to do with our "unconscious" than with mind as we understand it, which is more or less identical with consciousness' (§ 774). 'The Eastern mind, however, has no difficulty in conceiving of a consciousness without an ego. Consciousness is deemed capable of transcending its ego condition; indeed, in its "higher" forms, the ego disappears' (§ 774). 'To us, consciousness is inconceivable without an ego; it is equated with the relation of contents to an ego. If there is no ego there is nobody to be conscious of anything' (§ 774).

The difference between East and West is that the West sees mind originating in the human being, and the East sees mind as a quality or dimension of the cosmos. The East can conceive of mind without a human presence. Its concept of mind is universal whereas the West's is anthropocentric. The West asserts that there is no evidence for the existence of a universal mind, and science does not regard this as a sensible hypothesis. Jung is not including his psychology in this generalisation, as his vision allows for a universal mind, a thesis which he develops in his theory of synchronicity. Jung is in the West but not *of* the West. He is alarmed at what a shrunken thing mind has become:

> The development of Western philosophy during the last two centuries has succeeded in isolating the mind in its own sphere and in severing it from its primordial oneness with the universe. Man himself has ceased to be the microcosm and eidolon [image, double] of the cosmos, and his 'anima' is no longer the consubstantial *scintilla*, or spark of the *Anima Mundi*, the World Soul.
>
> (§ 759)

We have cut off mind from the cosmos, and Jung is alarmed at this development because he sees it as the seal of our alienation.

But we have to read Jung closely; he is not being as categorical as it might appear. He says the West has lost the universal mind, but he does not think we have lost it forever. In fact, the discovery of the unconscious might have given us the capacity to recover it again. What we call 'our' mind, 'our' psyche may be nothing more than a manner of speaking. Our anthropocentricism may be an illusion, a failure to see beyond certain facts. The truth may be more shocking than anything Western science has imagined. Our human mind and psyche may be part of a continuum of mind that we do not see. We have habitually and systematically blocked out the universal dimension, failing to realise that our souls are 'sparks' or *scintilla* of the soul of the world. 'It is just possible that our mind is nothing but a perceptible manifestation of a Universal Mind' (§ 760). The lost or forgotten 'universal mind', he supposes, is to be found in an inchoate condition in our unconscious. It is the psychology of the unconscious that opens a potential bridge between Eastern and Western conceptions of mind.

While Jung says that 'it is useless to build false and treacherous bridges over yawning gaps' (§ 773), he is nevertheless cautiously excited about the prospect of finding the Eastern mind in the Western unconscious. He assumes that the East has become attractive to the West, and the West is desirous of what the East possesses. He is worried about this desirous attitude because he thinks we have a consumerist hunger, which may blind us to the possibilities of our own transformation. It is easier for us to see universal mind as a treasure of the East, and to go in search of that treasure in a literal way. But if we do this, the Western psyche is still locked in its personalism and confinement: it has merely 'added' universal mind as an exotic possession. The original dualism between personal and universal remains, and has merely been submerged by our acquisitive hunger. Jung is urging us to find universal mind as a buried treasure in the field.

Jung discusses a number of different, contrary points of view between East and West. 'Introversion is the style of the East, an habitual and collective attitude, just as extraversion is the style of the West' (§ 770). 'The East bases itself upon psychic reality, that is, upon the psyche as the main and unique condition of existence' (§ 770); whereas 'we in the West believe that a truth is satisfactory only if it can be verified by external facts' (§ 778). The West has developed its relationship with the world – the study of nature, science, technology, medicine – whereas the East has developed its relationship with the inner world and perfected the art of spirituality, which Jung refers to as 'the self-liberating power of the introverted mind' (§ 773). Each civilisation developed its strengths and neglected its weaknesses and blind spots. Jung emphasises the disproportionate developments of each: 'What we [in the West] have to show in the way of spiritual insight and psychological technique must seem, when compared with yoga, just as backward as Eastern astrology and medicine when compared with Western science' (§ 778).

But despite these vast differences, 'the two contradictory worlds have met' (§ 778). The East is becoming rapidly Westernised and the West is borrowing and adapting from the East. Each world is exploring the other for what it lacks in itself. Jung seems to worry that in its fascination for Western technology and science, the East is losing its spiritual strength and, on the other hand, in its interest in Eastern spirituality the West is avoiding its own soul. He is not sanguine about the possibility of achieving a global civilisation in which both inner and outer worlds are developed and respected. If the West seduces the East with its science and technology, and fails to develop its own interiority, we are not necessarily moving toward psychological integration. Yet he is not pessimistic either, and evinces a sense of excitement about the possibilities of what he calls 'the spiritual adventure of our age' (§ 763).

Notes

1 Jung, 'Two Kinds of Thinking', *Symbols of Transformation* (1912/1952), *CW* 5.
2 Jung, 'On the Nature of the Psyche' (1947/1954), *CW* 8, § 388.
3 Camille Paglia, *Sexual Personae* (London: Penguin, 1990), p. 39.
4 No paragraph numbers can be given, since the Introduction from which this and the following quote are taken was found posthumously and unpublished in Jung's papers, so was not awarded paragraph numbers in the usual way.
5 See Christopher Hauke, *Jung and the Postmodern* (London and Philadelphia: Routledge, 2000).
6 See David Tacey, *Patrick White: Fiction and the Unconscious* (Melbourne: Oxford University Press, 1988).
7 Jung, '"Ulysses": A Monologue' (1932), *CW* 15.
8 Jung, 'On the Relation of Analytical Psychology to Poetry' (1922), *CW* 15, § 130.
9 Shakespeare, *A Midsummer Night's Dream*, Act V, Scene 1, lines 14–17. See also Herbert Read, *The Forms of Things Unknown* (New York: Horizon Press, 1960).

Chapter 8

The spiritual problem of modern man[1]

148 The spiritual problem of modern man is one of those questions which are so much a part of the age we live in that we cannot see them in the proper perspective. Modern man is an entirely new phenomenon; a modern problem is one which has just arisen and whose answer still lies in the future. In speaking of the spiritual problem of modern man we can at most frame a question, and we should perhaps frame it quite differently if we had but the faintest inkling of the answer the future will give. The question, moreover, seems rather vague; but the truth is that it has to do with something so universal that it exceeds the grasp of any single individual. We have reason enough, therefore, to approach such a problem in all modesty and with the greatest caution. This open avowal of our limitations seems to me essential, because it is these problems more than any others which tempt us to the use of high-sounding and empty words, and because I shall myself be forced to say certain things which may sound immoderate and incautious, and could easily lead us astray. Too many of us already have fallen victim to our own grandiloquence.

149 To begin at once with an example of such apparent lack of caution, I must say that the man we call modern, the man who is aware of the immediate present, is by no means the average man. He is rather the man who stands upon a peak, or at the very edge of the world, the abyss of the future before him, above him the heavens, and below him the whole of mankind with a history that disappears in primeval mists. The modern man – or, let us say again, the man of the immediate present – is rarely met with, for he must be conscious to a superlative degree. Since to be wholly of the present means to be fully conscious of one's existence as a man, it requires the most intensive and extensive consciousness, with a minimum of unconsciousness. It must be clearly understood that the mere fact of living in the present does not make a man modern, for in that case everyone at present alive would be so. He alone is modern who is fully conscious of the present.

150 The man who has attained consciousness of the present is solitary. The 'modern' man has at all times been so, for every step towards fuller consciousness removes him further from his original, purely animal *participation mystique* with the herd, from submersion in a common unconsciousness. Every step forward means tearing oneself loose from the maternal womb of unconsciousness in which the

mass of men dwells. Even in a civilized community the people who form, psychologically speaking, the lowest stratum live in a state of unconsciousness little different from that of primitives. Those of the succeeding strata live on a level of consciousness which corresponds to the beginnings of human culture, while those of the highest stratum have a consciousness that reflects the life of the last few centuries. Only the man who is modern in our meaning of the term really lives in the present; he alone has a present-day consciousness, and he alone finds that the ways of life on those earlier levels have begun to pall upon him. The values and strivings of those past worlds no longer interest him save from the historical standpoint. Thus he has become 'unhistorical' in the deepest sense and has estranged himself from the mass of men who live entirely within the bounds of tradition. Indeed, he is completely modern only when he has come to the very edge of the world, leaving behind him all that has been discarded and outgrown, and acknowledging that he stands before the Nothing out of which All may grow.[2]

151   This sounds so grand that it borders suspiciously on bathos, for nothing is easier than to affect a consciousness of the present. A great horde of worthless people do in fact give themselves a deceptive air of modernity by skipping the various stages of development and the tasks of life they represent. Suddenly they appear by the side of the truly modern man – uprooted wraiths, bloodsucking ghosts whose emptiness casts discredit upon him in his unenviable loneliness. Thus it is that the few present-day men are seen by the undiscerning eyes of the masses only through the dismal veil of those spectres, the pseudo-moderns, and are confused with them. It cannot be helped; the 'modern' man is questionable and suspect, and has been so at all times, beginning with Socrates and Jesus.

152   An honest admission of modernity means voluntarily declaring oneself bankrupt, taking the vows of poverty and chastity in a new sense, and – what is still more painful – renouncing the halo of sanctity which history bestows. To be 'unhistorical' is the Promethean sin, and in this sense the modern man is sinful. A higher level of consciousness is like a burden of guilt. But, as I have said, only the man who has outgrown the stages of consciousness belonging to the past, and has amply fulfilled the duties appointed for him by his world, can achieve full consciousness of the present. To do this he must be sound and proficient in the best sense – a man who has achieved as much as other people, and even a little more. It is these qualities which enable him to gain the next highest level of consciousness.

153   I know that the idea of proficiency is especially repugnant to the pseudo-moderns, for it reminds them unpleasantly of their trickery. This, however, should not prevent us from taking it as our criterion of the modern man. We are even forced to do so, for unless he is proficient, the man who claims to be modern is nothing but a trickster. He must be proficient in the highest degree, for unless he can atone by creative ability for his break with tradition; he is merely disloyal to the past. To deny the past for the sake of being conscious only of the present would be sheer futility. Today has meaning only if it stands between yesterday and tomorrow. It is a process of transition that forms the link between past

and future. Only the man who is conscious of the present in this sense may call himself modern.

154   Many people call themselves modern – especially the pseudo-moderns. Therefore the really modern man is often to be found among those who call themselves old-fashioned. They do this firstly in order to make amends for their guilty break with tradition by laying all the more emphasis on the past, and secondly in order to avoid the misfortune of being taken for pseudo-moderns. Every good quality has its bad side, and nothing good can come into the world without at once producing a corresponding evil. This painful fact renders illusory the feeling of elation that so often goes with consciousness of the present – the feeling that we are the culmination of the whole history of mankind, the fulfilment and end-product of countless generations. At best it should be a proud admission of our poverty: we are also the disappointment of the hopes and expectations of the ages. Think of nearly two thousand years of Christian Idealism followed, not by the return of the Messiah and the heavenly millennium, but by the World War among Christian nations with its barbed wire and poison gas. What a catastrophe in heaven and on earth!

155   In the face of such a picture we may well grow humble again. It is true that modern man is a culmination, but tomorrow he will be surpassed. He is indeed the product of an age-old development, but he is at the same time the worst conceivable disappointment of the hopes of mankind. The modern man is conscious of this. He has seen how beneficent are science, technology, and organization, but also how catastrophic they can be. He has likewise seen how all well-meaning governments have so thoroughly paved the way for peace on the principle 'in time of peace prepare for war' that Europe has nearly gone to rack and ruin. And as for ideals, neither the Christian Church, nor the brotherhood of man, nor international social democracy, nor the solidarity of economic interests has stood up to the acid test of reality. Today, ten years after the war,[3] we observe once more the same optimism, the same organizations, the same political aspirations, the same phrases and catchwords at work. How can we but fear that they will inevitably lead to further catastrophes? Agreements to outlaw war leave us sceptical, even while we wish them every possible success. At bottom, behind every such palliative measure there is a gnawing doubt. I believe I am not exaggerating when I say that modern man has suffered an almost fatal shock, psychologically speaking, and as a result has fallen into profound uncertainty.

156   These statements make it clear enough that my views are coloured by a professional bias. A doctor always spies out diseases, and I cannot cease to be a doctor. But it is essential to the physician's art that he should not discover diseases where none exists. I will therefore not make the assertion that Western man, and the white man in particular, is sick, or that the Western world is on the verge of collapse. I am in no way competent to pass such a judgment.

157   Whenever you hear anyone talking about a cultural or even about a human problem, you should never forget to inquire who the speaker really is. The more general the problem, the more he will smuggle his own, most personal psychology

into the account he gives of it. This can, without a doubt, lead to intolerable distortions and false conclusions which may have very serious consequences. On the other hand, the very fact that a general problem has gripped and assimilated the whole of a person is a guarantee that the speaker has really experienced it, and perhaps gained something from his sufferings. He will then reflect the problem for us in his personal life and thereby show us a truth. But if he projects his own psychology into the problem, he falsifies it by his personal bias, and on the pretence of presenting it objectively so distorts it that no truth emerges but merely a deceptive fiction.

158   It is of course only from my own experience with other persons and with myself that I draw my knowledge of the spiritual problem of modern man. I know something of the intimate psychic life of many hundreds of educated persons, both sick and healthy, coming from every quarter of the civilized, white world; and upon this experience I base my statements. No doubt I can draw only a one-sided picture, for everything I have observed lies in the psyche – it is all *inside*. I must add at once that this is a remarkable fact in itself, for the psyche is not always and everywhere to be found on the inside. There are peoples and epochs where it is found *outside*, because they were wholly unpsychological. As examples we may choose any of the ancient civilizations, but especially that of Egypt with its monumental objectivity and its naïve confession of sins that have not been committed. We can no more feel psychic problems lurking behind the Apis tombs of Saqqara and the Pyramids than we can behind the music of Bach.

159   Whenever there exists some external form, be it an ideal or a ritual, by which all the yearnings and hopes of the soul are adequately expressed – as for instance in a living religion – then we may say that the psyche is outside and that there is no psychic problem, just as there is then no unconscious in our sense of the word. In consonance with this truth, the discovery of psychology falls entirely within the last decades, although long before that man was introspective and intelligent enough to recognize the facts that are the subject-matter of psychology. It was the same with technical knowledge. The Romans were familiar with all the mechanical principles and physical facts which would have enabled them to construct a steam engine, but all that came of it was the toy made by Hero of Alexandria. The reason for this is that there was no compelling necessity to go further. This need arose only with the enormous division of labour and the growth of specialization in the nineteenth century. So also a spiritual need has produced in our time the 'discovery' of psychology. The psychic facts still existed earlier, of course, but they did not attract attention – no one noticed them. People got along without them. But today we can no longer get along unless we pay attention to the psyche.

160   It was men of the medical profession who were the first to learn this truth. For the priest, the psyche can only be something that needs fitting into a recognized, form or system of belief in order to ensure its undisturbed functioning. So long as this system gives true expression to life, psychology can be nothing but a technical adjuvant to healthy living, and the psyche cannot be regarded as a factor *sui generis*. While man still lives as a herd-animal he has no psyche of his own, nor

The spiritual problem of modern man   221

does he need any, except the usual belief in the immortality of the soul. But as soon as he has outgrown whatever local form of religion he was born to – as soon as this religion can no longer embrace his life in all its fullness – then the psyche becomes a factor in its own right which cannot be dealt with by the customary measures. It is for this reason that we today have a psychology, founded on experience, and not upon articles of faith or the postulates of any philosophical system. The very fact that we have such a psychology is to me symptomatic of a profound convulsion of the collective psyche. For the collective psyche shows the same pattern of change as the psyche of the individual. So long as all goes well and all our psychic energies find an outlet in adequate and well-regulated ways, we are disturbed by nothing from within. No uncertainty or doubt besets us, and we *cannot* be divided against ourselves. But no sooner are one or two channels of psychic activity blocked up than phenomena of obstruction appear. The stream tries to flow back against the current, the inner man wants something different from the outer man, and we are at war with ourselves. Only then, in this situation of distress, do we discover the psyche as something which thwarts our will, which is strange and even hostile to us, and which is incompatible with our conscious standpoint. Freud's psychoanalytic endeavours show this process in the clearest way. The very first thing he discovered was the existence of sexually perverse and criminal fantasies which at their face value are wholly incompatible with the conscious outlook of civilized man. A person who adopted the standpoint of these fantasies would be nothing less than a rebel, a criminal, or a madman.

161   We cannot suppose that the unconscious or hinterland of man's mind has developed this aspect only in recent times. Probably it was always there, in every culture. And although every culture had its destructive opponent, a Herostratus who burned down its temples, no culture before ours was ever forced to take these psychic undercurrents in deadly earnest. The psyche was merely part of a metaphysical system of some sort. But the conscious, modern man can no longer refrain from acknowledging the might of the psyche, despite the most strenuous and dogged efforts at self-defence. This distinguishes our time from all others. We can no longer deny that the dark stirrings of the unconscious are active powers, that psychic forces exist which, for the present at least, cannot be fitted into our rational world order. We have even elevated them into a science – one more proof of how seriously we take them. Previous centuries could throw them aside unnoticed; for us they are a shirt of Nessus which we cannot strip off.

162   The revolution in our conscious outlook, brought about by the catastrophic results of the World War, shows itself in our inner life by the shattering of our faith in ourselves and our own worth. We used to regard foreigners as political and moral reprobates, but the modern man is forced to recognize that he is politically and morally just like anyone else. Whereas formerly I believed it was my bounden duty to call others to order, I must now admit that I need calling to order myself, and that I would do better to set my own house to rights first. I admit this the more readily because I realize only too well that my faith in the rational organization of the world – that old dream of the millennium when peace and harmony

reign – has grown pale. Modern man's scepticism in this respect has chilled his enthusiasm for politics and world-reform; more than that, it is the worst possible basis for a smooth flow of psychic energies into the outer world, just as doubt concerning the morality of a friend is bound to prejudice the relationship and hamper its development. Through his scepticism modern man is thrown back on himself; his energies flow towards their source, and the collision washes to the surface those psychic contents which are at all times there, but lie hidden in the silt so long as the stream flows smoothly in its course. How totally different did the world appear to medieval man! For him the earth was eternally fixed and at rest in the centre of the universe, circled by a sun that solicitously bestowed its warmth. Men were all children of God under the loving care of the Most High, who prepared them for eternal blessedness; and all knew exactly what they should do and how they should conduct themselves in order to rise from a corruptible world to an incorruptible and joyous existence. Such a life no longer seems real to us, even in our dreams. Science has long ago torn this lovely veil to shreds. That age lies as far behind as childhood, when one's own father was unquestionably the handsomest and strongest man on earth.

163 Modern man has lost all the metaphysical certainties of his medieval brother, and set up in their place the ideals of material security, general welfare and humanitarianism. But anyone who has still managed to preserve these ideals unshaken must have been injected with a more than ordinary dose of optimism. Even security has gone by the board, for modern man has begun to see that every step forward in material 'progress' steadily increases the threat of a still more stupendous catastrophe. The imagination shrinks in terror from such a picture. What are we to think when the great cities today are perfecting defence measures against gas attacks, and even practise them in dress rehearsals? It can only mean that these attacks have already been planned and provided for, again on the principle 'in time of peace prepare for war.' Let man but accumulate sufficient engines of destruction and the devil within him will soon be unable to resist putting them to their fated use. It is well known that fire-arms go off of themselves if only enough of them are together.

164 An intimation of the terrible law that governs blind contingency, which Heraclitus called the rule of *enantiodromia* (a running towards the opposite), now steals upon modern man through the by-ways of his mind, chilling him with fear and paralysing his faith in the lasting effectiveness of social and political measures in the face of these monstrous forces. If he turns away from the terrifying prospect of a blind world in which building and destroying successively tip the scales, and then gazes into the recesses of his own mind, he will discover a chaos and a darkness there which everyone would gladly ignore. Science has destroyed even this last refuge; what was once a sheltering haven has become a cesspool.

165 And yet it is almost a relief to come upon so much evil in the depths of our own psyche. Here at least, we think, is the root of all the evil in mankind. Even though we are shocked and disillusioned at first, we still feel, just because these things are part of our psyche, that we have them more or less in hand and can correct them

or at any rate effectively suppress them. We like to assume that, if we succeeded in this, we should at least have rooted out some fraction of the evil in the world. Given a widespread knowledge of the unconscious, everyone could see when a statesman was being led astray by his own bad motives. The very newspapers would pull him up: 'Please have yourself analysed; you are suffering from a repressed father-complex.'

166 I have purposely chosen this grotesque example to show to what absurdities we are led by the illusion that because something is psychic it is under our control. It is, however, true that much of the evil in the world comes from the fact that man in general is hopelessly unconscious, as it is also true that with increasing insight we can combat this evil at its source in ourselves, in the same way that science enables us to deal effectively with injuries inflicted from without.

167 The rapid and worldwide growth of a psychological interest over the last two decades shows unmistakably that modern man is turning his attention from outward material things to his own inner processes. Expressionism in art prophetically anticipated this subjective development, for all art intuitively apprehends coming changes in the collective unconsciousness.

168 The psychological interest of the present time is an indication that modern man expects something from the psyche which the outer world has not given him: doubtless something which our religion ought to contain, but no longer does contain, at least for modern man. For him the various forms of religion no longer appear to come from within, from the psyche; they seem more like items from the inventory of the outside world. No spirit not of this world vouchsafes him inner revelation; instead, he tries on a variety of religions and beliefs as if they were Sunday attire, only to lay them aside again like worn-out clothes.

169 Yet he is somehow fascinated by the almost pathological manifestations from the hinterland of the psyche, difficult though it is to explain how something which all previous ages have rejected should suddenly become interesting. That there is a general interest in these matters cannot be denied, however much it offends against good taste. I am not thinking merely of the interest taken in psychology as a science, or of the still narrower interest in the psychoanalysis of Freud, but of the widespread and ever-growing interest in all sorts of psychic phenomena, including spiritualism, astrology, Theosophy, parapsychology, and so forth. The world has seen nothing like it since the end of the seventeenth century. We can compare it only to the flowering of Gnostic thought in the first and second centuries after Christ. The spiritual currents of our time have, in fact, a deep affinity with Gnosticism. There is even an 'Église gnostique de la France,' and I know of two schools in Germany which openly declare themselves Gnostic. The most impressive movement numerically is undoubtedly Theosophy, together with its continental sister, Anthroposophy; these are pure Gnosticism in Hindu dress. Compared with them the interest in scientific psychology is negligible. What is striking about these Gnostic systems is that they are based exclusively on the manifestations of the unconscious, and that their moral teachings penetrate into the dark side of life, as is clearly shown by the refurbished European version of

Kundalini-yoga. The same is true of parapsychology, as everyone acquainted with this subject will agree.

170 The passionate interest in these movements undoubtedly arises from psychic energy which can no longer be invested in obsolete religious forms. For this reason such movements have a genuinely religious character, even when they pretend to be scientific. It changes nothing when Rudolf Steiner calls his Anthroposophy 'spiritual science,' or when Mrs. Eddy invents a 'Christian Science.' These attempts at concealment merely show that religion has grown suspect – almost as suspect as politics and world-reform.

171 I do not believe that I am going too far when I say that modern man, in contrast to his nineteenth-century brother, turns to the psyche with very great expectations, and does so without reference to any traditional creed but rather with a view to Gnostic experience. The fact that all the movements I have mentioned give themselves a scientific veneer is not just a grotesque caricature or a masquerade, but a positive sign that they are actually pursuing 'science,' i.e., *knowledge,* instead of *faith,* which is the essence of the Western forms of religion. Modern man abhors faith and the religions based upon it. He holds them valid only so far as their knowledge-content seems to accord with his own experience of the psychic background. He wants to *know* – to experience for himself.

172 The age of discovery has only just come to an end in our day, when no part of the earth remains unexplored; it began when men would no longer *believe* that the Hyperboreans were one-footed monsters, or something of that kind, but wanted to find out and see with their own eyes what existed beyond the boundaries of the known world. Our age is apparently setting out to discover what exists in the psyche beyond consciousness. The question asked in every spiritualistic circle is: What happens after the medium has lost consciousness? Every Theosophist asks: What shall I experience at the higher levels of consciousness? The question which every astrologer asks is: What are the operative forces that determine my fate despite my conscious intention? And every psychoanalyst wants to know: What are the unconscious drives behind the neurosis?

173 Our age wants to experience the psyche for itself. It wants original experience and not assumptions, though it is willing to make use of all the existing assumptions as a means to this end, including those of the recognized religions and the authentic sciences. The European of yesterday will feel a slight shudder run down his spine when he gazes more deeply into these delvings. Not only does he consider the subject of this so-called research obscure and shuddersome, but even the methods employed seem to him a shocking misuse of man's finest intellectual attainments. What is the professional astronomer to say when he is told that at least a thousand times more horoscopes are cast today than were cast three hundred years ago? What will the educator and advocate of philosophical enlightenment say about the fact that the world has not grown poorer by a single superstition since the days of antiquity? Freud himself, the founder of psychoanalysis, has taken the greatest pains to throw as glaring a light as possible on the dirt and darkness and evil of the psychic background, and to interpret it in such a way as to

make us lose all desire to look for anything behind it except refuse and smut. He did not succeed, and his attempt at deterrence has even brought about the exact opposite – an admiration for all this filth. Such a perverse phenomenon would normally be inexplicable were it not that even the scatologists are drawn by the secret fascination of the psyche.

174   There can be no doubt that from the beginning of the nineteenth century – ever since the time of the French Revolution – the psyche has moved more and more into the foreground of man's interest, and with a steadily increasing power of attraction. The enthronement of the Goddess of Reason in Notre Dame seems to have been a symbolic gesture of great significance for the Western world – rather like the hewing down of Wotan's oak by Christian missionaries. On both occasions no avenging bolt from heaven struck the blasphemer down.

175   It is certainly more than an amusing freak of history that just at the time of the Revolution a Frenchman, Anquetil du Perron, should be living in India and, at the beginning of the nineteenth century, brought back with him a translation of the *Oupnek'hat,* a collection of fifty Upanishads, which gave the West its first deep insight into the baffling mind of the East. To the historian this is a mere coincidence independent of the historical nexus of cause and effect. My medical bias prevents me from seeing it simply as an accident. Everything happened in accordance with a psychological law which is unfailingly valid in personal affairs. If anything of importance is devalued in our conscious life, and perishes – so runs the law – there arises a compensation in the unconscious. We may see in this an analogy to the conservation of energy in the physical world, for our psychic processes also have a quantitative, energic aspect. No psychic value can disappear without being replaced by another of equivalent intensity. This is a fundamental rule which is repeatedly verified in the daily practice of the psychotherapist and never fails. The doctor in me refuses point blank to consider the life of a people as something that does not conform to psychological law. For him the psyche of a people is only a somewhat more complex structure than the psyche of an individual. Moreover, has not a poet spoken of the 'nations of his soul'? And quite correctly, it seems to me, for in one of its aspects the psyche is not individual, but is derived from the nation, from the collectivity, from humanity even. In some way or other we are part of a single, all-embracing psyche, a single 'greatest man,' the *homo maximus,* to quote Swedenborg.

176   And so we can draw a parallel: just as in me, a single individual, the darkness calls forth a helpful light, so it does in the psychic life of a people. In the crowds that poured into Notre Dame, bent on destruction, dark and nameless forces were at work that swept the individual off his feet; these forces worked also upon Anquetil du Perron and provoked an answer which has come down in history and speaks to us through the mouths of Schopenhauer and Nietzsche. For he brought the Eastern mind to the West, and its influence upon us we cannot as yet measure. Let us beware of underestimating it! So far, indeed, there is little of it to be seen on the intellectual surface: a handful of orientalists, one or two Buddhist enthusiasts, a few sombre celebrities like Madame Blavatsky and Annie Besant with her

Krishnamurti. These manifestations are like tiny scattered islands in the ocean of mankind; in reality they are the peaks of submarine mountain-ranges. The cultural Philistines believed until recently that astrology had been disposed of long since and was something that could safely be laughed at. But today, rising out of the social deeps, it knocks at the doors of the universities from which it was banished some three hundred years ago. The same is true of Eastern ideas; they take root in the lower levels and slowly grow to the surface. Where did the five or six million Swiss francs for the Anthroposophist temple at Dornach come from? Certainly not from one individual. Unfortunately there are no statistics to tell us the exact number of avowed Theosophists today, not to mention the unavowed. But we can be sure there are several millions of them. To this number we must add a few million Spiritualists of Christian or Theosophist leanings.

177   Great innovations never come from above; they come invariably from below, just as trees never grow from the sky downward, but upward from the earth. The upheaval of our world and the upheaval of our consciousness are one and the same. Everything has become relative and therefore doubtful. And while man, hesitant and questioning, contemplates a world that is distracted with treaties of peace and pacts of friendship, with democracy and dictatorship, capitalism and Bolshevism, his spirit yearns for an answer that will allay the turmoil of doubt and uncertainty. And it is just the people from the obscurer levels who follow the unconscious drive of the psyche; it is the much-derided, silent folk of the land, who are less infected with academic prejudices than the shining celebrities are wont to be. Looked at from above, they often present a dreary or laughable spectacle; yet they are as impressively simple as those Galileans who were once called blessed. Is it not touching to see the offscourings of man's psyche gathered together in compendia a foot thick? We find the merest babblings, the most absurd actions, the wildest fantasies recorded with scrupulous care in the volumes of *Anthropophyteia*,[4] while men like Havelock Ellis and Freud have dealt with like matters in serious treatises which have been accorded all scientific honours. Their reading public is scattered over the breadth of the civilized, white world. How are we to explain this zeal, this almost fanatical worship of everything unsavoury? It is because these things are psychological – they are of the substance of the psyche and therefore as precious as fragments of manuscript salvaged from ancient middens. Even the secret and noisome things of the psyche are valuable to modern man because they serve his purpose. But what purpose?

178   Freud prefixed to his *Interpretation of Dreams* the motto: *Flectere si nequeo superos Acheronta movebo* – 'If I cannot bend the gods on high, I will at least set Acheron in uproar.' But to what purpose?

179   The gods whom we are called upon to dethrone are the idolized values of our conscious world. Nothing, as we know, discredited the ancient gods so much as their love-scandals, and now history is repeating itself. People are laying bare the dubious foundations of our belauded virtues and incomparable ideals, and are calling out to us in triumph: 'There are your man-made gods, mere snares and delusions tainted with human baseness – whited sepulchres full of dead men's

The spiritual problem of modern man 227

bones and of all uncleanness.' We recognize a familiar strain, and the Gospel words which we failed to digest at Confirmation come to life again.

180 I am deeply convinced that these are not just vague analogies. There are too many persons to whom Freudian psychology is dearer than the Gospels, and to whom Bolshevism means more than civic virtue. And yet they are all our brothers, and in each of us there is at least one voice which seconds them, for in the end there is one psyche which embraces us all.

181 The unexpected result of this development is that an uglier face is put upon the world. It becomes so ugly that no one can love it any longer; we cannot even love ourselves, and in the end there is nothing in the outer world to draw us away from the reality of the life within. Here, no doubt, we have the true significance of this whole development. After all, what does Theosophy, with its doctrines of *karma* and reincarnation, seek to teach except that this world of appearance is but a temporary health-resort for the morally unperfected? It depreciates the intrinsic value of the present-day world no less radically than does the modern outlook, but with the help of a different technique; it does not vilify our world, but grants it only a relative meaning in that it promises other and higher worlds. The result in either case is the same.

182 I admit that all these ideas are extremely unacademic, the truth being that they touch modern man on the side where he is least conscious. Is it again a mere coincidence that modern thought has had to come to terms with Einstein's relativity theory and with nuclear theories which lead us away from determinism and border on the inconceivable? Even physics is volatilizing our material world. It is no wonder, then, in my opinion, if modern man falls back on the reality of psychic life and expects from it that certainty which the world denies him.

183 Spiritually the Western world is in a precarious situation, and the danger is greater the more we blind ourselves to the merciless truth with illusions about our beauty of soul. Western man lives in a thick cloud of incense which he burns to himself so that his own countenance may be veiled from him in the smoke. But how do we strike men of another colour? What do China and India think of us? What feelings do we arouse in the black man? And what about all those whom we rob of their lands and exterminate with rum and venereal disease?

184 I have an American Indian friend who is a Pueblo chieftain. Once when we were talking confidentially about the white man, he said to me: 'We don't understand the whites. They are always wanting something, always restless, always looking for something. What is it? We don't know. We can't understand them. They have such sharp noses, such thin, cruel lips, such lines in their faces. We think they are all crazy.'

185 My friend had recognized, without being able to name it, the Aryan bird of prey with his insatiable lust to lord it in every land, even those that concern him not at all. And he had also noted that megalomania of ours which leads us to suppose, among other things, that Christianity is the only truth and the white Christ the only redeemer. After setting the whole East in turmoil with our science and technology, and exacting tribute from it, we send our missionaries even to China. The comedy

of Christianity in Africa is really pitiful. There the stamping out of polygamy, no doubt highly pleasing to God, has given rise to prostitution on such a scale that in Uganda alone twenty thousand pounds are spent annually on preventives of venereal infection. And the good European pays his missionaries for these edifying achievements! Need we also mention the story of suffering in Polynesia and the blessings of the opium trade?

186   That is how the European looks when he is extricated from the cloud of his own moral incense. No wonder that unearthing the psyche is like undertaking a full-scale drainage operation. Only a great idealist like Freud could devote a lifetime to such unclean work. It was not he who caused the bad smell, but all of us – we who think ourselves so clean and decent from sheer ignorance and the grossest self-deception. Thus our psychology, the acquaintance with our own souls, begins in every respect from the most repulsive end, that is to say with all those things which we do not wish to see.

187   But if the psyche consisted only of evil and worthless things, no power on earth could induce the normal man to find it attractive. That is why people who see in Theosophy nothing but lamentable intellectual superficiality, and in Freudian psychology nothing but sensationalism, prophesy an early and inglorious end to these movements. They overlook the fact that such movements derive their force from the fascination of the psyche, and that it will express itself in these forms until they are replaced by something better. They are transitional or embryonic stages from which new and riper forms will emerge.

188   We have not yet realized that Western Theosophy is an amateurish, indeed barbarous imitation of the East. We are just beginning to take up astrology again, which to the Oriental is his daily bread. Our studies of sexual life, originating in Vienna and England, are matched or surpassed by Hindu teachings on this subject. Oriental texts ten centuries old introduce us to philosophical relativism, while the idea of indeterminacy, newly broached in the West, is the very basis of Chinese science. As to our discoveries in psychology, Richard Wilhelm has shown me that certain complicated psychic processes are recognizably described in ancient Chinese texts. Psychoanalysis itself and the lines of thought to which it gives rise – a development which we consider specifically Western – are only a beginner's attempt compared with what is an immemorial art in the East. It may not perhaps be known that parallels between psychoanalysis and yoga have already been drawn by Oscar Schmitz.[5]

189   Another thing we have not realized is that while we are turning the material world of the East upside down with our technical proficiency, the East with its superior psychic proficiency is throwing our spiritual world into confusion. We have never yet hit upon the thought that while we are overpowering the Orient from without, it may be fastening its hold on us from within. Such an idea strikes us as almost insane, because we have eyes only for obvious causal connections and fail to see that we must lay the blame for the confusion of our intellectual middle class at the doors of Max Müller, Oldenberg, Deussen, Wilhelm, and others like them. What does the example of the Roman Empire teach us? After the

conquest of Asia Minor, Rome became Asiatic; Europe was infected by Asia and remains so today. Out of Cilicia came the Mithraic cult, the religion of the Roman legions, and it spread from Egypt to fog-bound Britain. Need I point out the Asiatic origin of Christianity?

190   The Theosophists have an amusing idea that certain Mahatmas, seated somewhere in the Himalayas or Tibet, inspire and direct every mind in the world. So strong, in fact, can be the influence of the Eastern belief in magic that Europeans of sound mind have assured me that every good thing I say is unwittingly inspired in me by the Mahatmas, my own inspirations being of no account whatever. This myth of the Mahatmas, widely circulated in the West and firmly believed, far from being nonsense, is – like every myth – an important psychological truth. It seems to be quite true that the East is at the bottom of the spiritual change we are passing through today. Only, this East is not a Tibetan monastery full of Mahatmas, but lies essentially within us. It is our own psyche, constantly at work creating new spiritual forms and spiritual forces which may help us to subdue the boundless lust for prey of Aryan man. We shall perhaps come to know something of that narrowing of horizons which has grown in the East into a dubious quietism, and also something of that stability which human existence acquires when the claims of the spirit become as imperative as the necessities of social life. Yet in this age of Americanization we are still far from anything of the sort; it seems to me that we are only at the threshold of a new spiritual epoch. I do not wish to pass myself off as a prophet, but one can hardly attempt to sketch the spiritual problem of modern man without mentioning the longing for rest in a period of unrest, the longing for security in an age of insecurity. It is from need and distress that new forms of existence arise, and not from idealistic requirements or mere wishes.

191   To me the crux of the spiritual problem today is to be found in the fascination which the psyche holds for modern man. If we are pessimists, we shall call it a sign of decadence; if we are optimistically inclined, we shall see in it the promise of a far-reaching spiritual change in the Western world. At all events, it is a significant phenomenon. It is the more noteworthy because it is rooted in the deeper social strata, and the more important because it touches those irrational and – as history shows – incalculable psychic forces which transform the life of peoples and civilizations in ways that are unforeseen and unforeseeable. These are the forces, still invisible to many persons today, which are at the bottom of the present 'psychological' interest. The fascination of the psyche is not by any means a morbid perversity; it is an attraction so strong that it does not shrink even from what it finds repellent.

192   Along the great highways of the world everything seems desolate and outworn. Instinctively modern man leaves the trodden paths to explore the by-ways and lanes, just as the man of the Greco-Roman world cast off his defunct Olympian gods and turned to the mystery cults of Asia. Our instinct turns outward, and appropriates Eastern theosophy and magic; but it also turns inward, and leads us to contemplate the dark background of the psyche. It does this with the same scepticism and the same ruthlessness which impelled the Buddha to sweep aside

his two million gods that he might attain the original experience which alone is convincing.

193   And now we must ask a final question. Is what I have said of modern man really true, or is it perhaps an illusion? There can be no doubt whatever that to many millions of Westerners the facts I have adduced are wholly irrelevant and fortuitous, and regrettable aberrations to a large number of educated persons. But – did a cultivated Roman think any differently when he saw Christianity spreading among the lower classes? Today the God of the West is still a living person for vast numbers of people, just as Allah is beyond the Mediterranean, and the one believer holds the other an inferior heretic, to be pitied and tolerated failing all else. To make matters worse, the enlightened European is of the opinion that religion and such things are good enough for the masses and for women, but of little consequence compared with immediate economic and political questions.

194   So I am refuted all along the line, like a man who predicts a thunderstorm when there is not a cloud in the sky. Perhaps it is a storm below the horizon, and perhaps it will never reach us. But what is significant in psychic life always lies below the horizon of consciousness, and when we speak of the spiritual problem of modern man we are speaking of things that are barely visible – of the most intimate and fragile things, of flowers that open only in the night. In daylight everything is clear and tangible, but the night lasts as long as the day, and we live in the nighttime also. There are people who have bad dreams which even spoil their days for them. And for many people the day's life is such a bad dream that they long for the night when the spirit awakes. I believe that there are nowadays a great many such people, and this is why I also maintain that the spiritual problem of modern man is much as I have presented it.

195   I must plead guilty, however, to the charge of one-sidedness, for I have passed over in silence the spirit of the times, about which everyone has so much to say because it is so clearly apparent to us all. It shows itself in the ideal of internationalism and supernationalism, embodied in the League of Nations, and the like; we see it also in sport and, significantly, in cinema and jazz. These are characteristic symptoms of our time, which has extended the humanistic ideal even to the body. Sport puts an exceptional valuation on the body, and this tendency is emphasized still further in modern dancing. The cinema, like the detective story, enables us to experience without danger to ourselves all the excitements, passions, and fantasies which have to be repressed in a humanistic age. It is not difficult to see how these symptoms link up with our psychological situation. The fascination of the psyche brings about a new self-appraisal, a reassessment of our fundamental human nature. We can hardly be surprised if this leads to a rediscovery of the body after its long subjection to the spirit – we are even tempted to say that the flesh is getting its own back. When Keyserling sarcastically singles out the chauffeur as the culture-hero of our time, he has struck, as he often does, close to the mark. The body lays claim to equal recognition; it exerts the same fascination as the psyche. If we are still caught in the old idea of an antithesis between mind and matter, this state of affairs must seem like an unbearable contradiction. But if we

can reconcile ourselves to the mysterious truth that the spirit is the life of the body seen from within, and the body the outward manifestation of the life of the spirit – the two being really one – then we can understand why the striving to transcend the present level of consciousness through acceptance of the unconscious must give the body its due, and why recognition of the body cannot tolerate a philosophy that denies it in the name of the spirit. These claims of physical and psychic life, incomparably stronger than they were in the past, may seem a sign of decadence, but they may also signify a rejuvenation, for as Hölderlin says:

> Where danger is,
> Arises salvation also.

And indeed we see, as the Western world strikes up a more rapid tempo – the American tempo – the exact opposite of quietism and world-negating resignation. An unprecedented tension arises between outside and inside, between objective and subjective reality. Perhaps it is a final race between aging Europe and young America; perhaps it is a healthier or a last desperate effort to escape the dark sway of natural law, and to wrest a yet greater and more heroic victory of waking consciousness over the sleep of the nations. This is a question only history can answer.

Notes

1 [First pub. as 'Das Seelenproblem des modernen Menschen,' *Europäische Revue* (Berlin), IV (1928), 700–715. Revised and expanded in *Seelenprobleme der Gegenwart* (Zurich, 1931), pp. 401–35. Trans. by W. S. Dell and Cary F. Baynes in *Modern Man in Search of a Soul* (London and New York, 1933), pp. 226–54. The latter version has been consulted.–EDITORS.]
2 ['In this, your Nothing, I may find my All!' *Faust, Part Two.*–Trans.]
3 [This essay was originally written in 1928.–EDITORS.]
4 [See bibliography.] [Friedrich H. Krauss (ed.) *Anthropophyteia, 10 Volumes* (Leipzig: Ethnologischer Verlag, 1904–1913)].
5 [*Psychoanalyse und Yoga.* See bibliography.] [Oscar A. H. Schmitz, *Psychoanalyse und Yoga* (Darmstadt: Otto Reichl Verlag, 1923).]

Chapter 9

Psychology and religion[1]
The autonomy of the unconscious

1. As it seems to be the intention of the founder of the Terry Lectures to enable representatives of science, as well as of philosophy and other spheres of human knowledge, to contribute to the discussion of the eternal problem of religion, and since Yale University has bestowed upon me the great honour of delivering the Terry Lectures for 1937, I assume that it will be my task to show what psychology, or rather that special branch of medical psychology which I represent, has to do with or to say about religion. Since religion is incontestably one of the earliest and most universal expressions of the human mind, it is obvious that any psychology which touches upon the psychological structure of human personality cannot avoid taking note of the fact that religion is not only a sociological and historical phenomenon, but also something of considerable personal concern to a great number of individuals.

2. Although I have often been called a philosopher, I am an empiricist and adhere as such to the phenomenological standpoint. I trust that it does not conflict with the principles of scientific empiricism if one occasionally makes certain reflections which go beyond a mere accumulation and classification of experience. As a matter of fact I believe that experience is not even possible without reflection, because 'experience' is a process of assimilation without which there could be no understanding. As this statement indicates, I approach psychological matters from a scientific and not from a philosophical standpoint. Inasmuch as religion has a very important psychological aspect, I deal with it from a purely empirical point of view, that is, I restrict myself to the observation of phenomena and I eschew any metaphysical or philosophical considerations. I do not deny the validity of these other considerations, but I cannot claim to be competent to apply them correctly.

3. I am aware that most people believe they know all there is to be known about psychology, because they think that psychology is nothing but what they know of themselves. But I am afraid psychology is a good deal more than that. While having little to do with philosophy, it has much to do with empirical facts, many of which are not easily accessible to the experience of the average man. It is my intention to give you a few glimpses of the way in which practical psychology comes up against the problem of religion. It is self-evident that the vastness of the

problem requires far more than three lectures, as the necessary elaboration of concrete detail takes a great deal of time and explanation. My first lecture will be a sort of introduction to the problem of practical psychology and religion. The second is concerned with facts which demonstrate the existence of an authentic religious function in the unconscious. The third deals with the religious symbolism of unconscious processes.

4   Since I am going to present a rather unusual argument, I cannot assume that my audience will be fully acquainted with the methodological standpoint of the branch of psychology I represent. This standpoint is exclusively phenomenological, that is, it is concerned with occurrences, events, experiences – in a word, with facts. Its truth is a fact and not a judgment. When psychology speaks, for instance, of the motif of the virgin birth, it is only concerned with the fact that there is such an idea, but it is not concerned with the question whether such an idea is true or false in any other sense. The idea is psychologically true inasmuch as it exists. Psychological existence is subjective in so far as an idea occurs in only one individual. But it is objective in so far as that idea is shared by a society – by a *consensus gentium*.

5   This point of view is the same as that of natural science. Psychology deals with ideas and other mental contents as zoology, for instance, deals with the different species of animals. An elephant is 'true' because it exists. The elephant is neither an inference nor a statement nor the subjective judgment of a creator. It is a phenomenon. But we are so used to the idea that psychic events are wilful and arbitrary products, or even the inventions of a human creator, that we can hardly rid ourselves of the prejudiced view that the psyche and its contents are nothing but our own arbitrary invention or the more or less illusory product of supposition and judgment. The fact is that certain ideas exist almost everywhere and at all times and can even spontaneously create themselves quite independently of migration and tradition. They are not made by the individual, they just happen to him – they even force themselves on his consciousness. This is not Platonic philosophy but empirical psychology.

6   In speaking of religion I must make clear from the start what I mean by that term. Religion, as the Latin word denotes, is a careful and scrupulous observation of what Rudolf Otto[2] aptly termed the *numinosum*, that is, a dynamic agency or effect not caused by an arbitrary act of will. On the contrary, it seizes and controls the human subject, who is always rather its victim than its creator. The *numinosum* – whatever its cause may be – is an experience of the subject independent of his will. At all events, religious teaching as well as the *consensus gentium* always and everywhere explain this experience as being due to a cause external to the individual. The *numinosum* is either a quality belonging to a visible object or the influence of an invisible presence that causes a peculiar alteration of consciousness. This is, at any rate, the general rule.

7   There are, however, certain exceptions when it comes to the question of religious practice or ritual. A great many ritualistic performances are carried out for the sole purpose of producing at will the effect of the *numinosum* by means of

certain devices of a magical nature, such as invocation, incantation, sacrifice, meditation and other yoga practices, self-inflicted tortures of various descriptions, and so forth. But a religious belief in an external and objective divine cause is always prior to any such performance. The Catholic Church, for instance, administers the sacraments for the purpose of bestowing their spiritual blessings upon the believer; but since this act would amount to enforcing the presence of divine grace by an indubitably magical procedure, it is logically argued that nobody can compel divine grace to be present in the sacramental act, but that it is nevertheless inevitably present since the sacrament is a divine institution which God would not have caused to be if he had not intended to lend it his support.[3]

8   Religion appears to me to be a peculiar attitude of mind which could be formulated in accordance with the original use of the word *religio*, which means a careful consideration and observation of certain dynamic factors that are conceived as 'powers': spirits, daemons, gods, laws, ideas, ideals, or whatever name man has given to such factors in his world as he has found powerful, dangerous, or helpful enough to be taken into careful consideration, or grand, beautiful, and meaningful enough to be devoutly worshipped and loved. In colloquial speech one often says of somebody who is enthusiastically interested in a certain pursuit that he is almost 'religiously devoted' to his cause; William James, for instance, remarks that a scientist often has no creed, but his 'temper is devout.'[4]

9   I want to make clear that by the term 'religion'[5] I do not mean a creed. It is, however, true that every creed is originally based on the one hand upon the experience of the *numinosum* and on the other hand upon πίστιῳ, that is to say, trust or loyalty, faith and confidence in a certain experience of a numinous nature and in the change of consciousness that ensues. The conversion of Paul is a striking example of this. We might say, then, that the term 'religion' designates the attitude peculiar to a consciousness which has been changed by experience of the *numinosum*.

10   Creeds are codified and dogmatized forms of original religious experience.[6] The contents of the experience have become sanctified and are usually congealed in a rigid, often elaborate, structure of ideas. The practice and repetition of the original experience have become a ritual and an unchangeable institution. This does not necessarily mean lifeless petrifaction. On the contrary, it may prove to be a valid form of religious experience for millions of people for thousands of years, without there arising any vital necessity to alter it. Although the Catholic Church has often been accused of particular rigidity, she nevertheless admits that dogma is a living thing and that its formulation is therefore capable of change and development. Even the number of dogmas is not limited and can be multiplied in the course of time. The same holds true of the ritual. Yet all changes and developments are determined within the framework of the facts as originally experienced, and this sets up a special kind of dogmatic content and emotional value. Even Protestantism, which has abandoned itself apparently to an almost unlimited emancipation from dogmatic tradition and codified ritual and has thus split into more than four hundred denominations – even Protestantism is bound at least to be

Christian and to express itself within the framework of the belief that God revealed himself in Christ, who suffered for mankind. This is a definite framework with definite contents which cannot be combined with or supplemented by Buddhist or Islamic ideas and feelings. Yet it is unquestionably true that not only Buddha and Mohammed, Confucius and Zarathustra, represent religious phenomena, but also Mithras, Attis, Cybele, Mani, Hermes, and the deities of many other exotic cults. The psychologist, if he takes up a scientific attitude, has to disregard the claim of every creed to be the unique and eternal truth. He must keep his eye on the human side of the religious problem, since he is concerned with the original religious experience quite apart from what the creeds have made of it.

11   As I am a doctor and a specialist in nervous and mental diseases, my point of departure is not a creed but the psychology of the *homo religiosus*, that is, of the man who takes into account and carefully observes certain factors which influence him and his general condition. It is easy to designate and define these factors in accordance with historical tradition or ethnological knowledge, but to do the same thing from the standpoint of psychology is an uncommonly difficult task. What I can contribute to the question of religion is derived entirely from my practical experience, both with my patients and with so-called normal persons. As our experience with people depends to a large extent upon what we do with them, I can see no other way of proceeding than to give you at least a general idea of the line I take in my professional work.

12   Since every neurosis is connected with man's most intimate life, there will always be some hesitation when a patient has to give a complete account of all the circumstances and complications which originally led him into a morbid condition. But why shouldn't he be able to talk freely? Why should he be afraid or shy or prudish? The reason is that he is 'carefully observing' certain external factors which together constitute what one calls public opinion or respectability or reputation. And even if he trusts his doctor and is no longer shy of him, he will be reluctant or even afraid to admit certain things to *himself*, as if it were dangerous to become conscious of himself. One is usually afraid of things that seem to be overpowering. But is there anything in man that is stronger than himself? We should not forget that every neurosis entails a corresponding amount of demoralization. If a man is neurotic, he has lost confidence in himself. A neurosis is a humiliating defeat and is felt as such by people who are not entirely unconscious of their own psychology. And one is defeated by something 'unreal.' Doctors may have assured the patient, long ago, that there is nothing the matter with him, that he does not suffer from a real heart-disease or from a real cancer. His symptoms are quite imaginary. The more he believes that he is a *malade imaginaire*, the more a feeling of inferiority permeates his whole personality. 'If my symptoms are imaginary,' he will say, 'where have I picked up this confounded imagination and why should I put up with such a perfect nuisance?' It is indeed pathetic to have an intelligent man almost imploringly assure you that he is suffering from an intestinal cancer and declare at the same time in a despondent voice that of course he knows his cancer is a purely imaginary affair.

13 Our usual materialistic conception of the psyche is, I am afraid, not particularly helpful in cases of neurosis. If only the soul were endowed with a subtle body, then one could at least say that this breath- or vapour-body was suffering from a real though somewhat ethereal cancer, in the same way as the gross material body can succumb to a cancerous disease. That, at least, would be something real. Medicine therefore feels a strong aversion for anything of a psychic nature – either the body is ill or there is nothing the matter. And if you cannot prove that the body is really ill, that is only because our present techniques do not enable the doctor to discover the true nature of the undoubtedly organic trouble.

14 But what, actually, is the psyche? Materialistic prejudice explains it as a mere epiphenomenal by-product of organic processes in the brain. Any psychic disturbance must therefore be an organic or physical disorder which is undiscoverable only because of the inadequacy of our present methods of diagnosis. The undeniable connection between psyche and brain gives this point of view a certain weight, but not enough to make it an unshakable truth. We do not know whether there is a real disturbance of the organic processes in the brain in a case of neurosis, and if there are disorders of an endocrine nature it is impossible to say whether they might not be effects rather than causes.

15 On the other hand, it cannot be doubted that the real causes of neurosis are psychological. Not so long ago it was very difficult to imagine how an organic or physical disorder could be relieved by quite simple psychological means, yet in recent years medical science has recognized a whole class of diseases, the psychosomatic disorders, in which the patient's psychology plays the essential part. Since my readers may not be familiar with these medical facts I may instance a case of hysterical fever, with a temperature of 102°, which was cured in a few minutes through confession of the psychological cause. A patient with psoriasis extending over practically the whole body was told that I did not feel competent to treat his skin trouble, but that I should concentrate on his psychological conflicts, which were numerous. After six weeks of intense analysis and discussion of his purely psychological difficulties, there came about as an unexpected by-product the almost complete disappearance of the skin disease. In another case, the patient had recently undergone an operation for distention of the colon. Forty centimetres of it had been removed, but this was followed by another extraordinary distention. The patient was desperate and refused to permit a second operation, though the surgeon thought it vital. As soon as certain intimate psychological facts were discovered, the colon began to function normally again.

16 Such experiences make it exceedingly difficult to believe that the psyche is nothing, or that an imaginary fact is unreal. Only, it is not there where a near-sighted mind seeks it. It exists, but not in physical form. It is an almost absurd prejudice to suppose that existence can only be physical. As a matter of fact, the only form of existence of which we have immediate knowledge is psychic. We might well say, on the contrary, that physical existence is a mere inference, since we know of matter only in so far as we perceive psychic images mediated by the senses.

17 We are surely making a great mistake when we forget this simple yet fundamental truth. Even if a neurosis had no cause at all other than imagination, it would, none the less, be a very real thing. If a man imagined that I was his archenemy and killed me, I should be dead on account of mere imagination. Imaginary conditions do exist and they may be just as real and just as harmful or dangerous as physical conditions. I even believe that psychic disturbances are far more dangerous than epidemics or earthquakes. Not even the medieval epidemics of bubonic plague or smallpox killed as many people as certain differences of opinion in 1914 or certain political 'ideals' in Russia.

18 Although the mind cannot apprehend its own form of existence, owing to the lack of an Archimedean point outside, it nevertheless exists. Not only does the psyche exist, it is existence itself.

19 What, then, shall we say to our patient with the imaginary cancer? I would tell him: 'Yes, my friend, you are really suffering from a cancer-like thing, you really do harbour in yourself a deadly evil. However, it will not kill your body, because it is imaginary. But it will eventually kill your soul. It has already spoilt and even poisoned your human relations and your personal happiness and it will go on growing until it has swallowed your whole psychic existence. So that in the end you will not be a human being any more, but an evil destructive tumour.'

20 It is obvious to our patient that he is not the author of his morbid imagination, although his theoretical turn of mind will certainly suggest that he is the owner and maker of his own imaginings. If a man is suffering from a real cancer, he never believes himself to be responsible for such an evil, despite the fact that the cancer is in his own body. But when it comes to the psyche we instantly feel a kind of responsibility, as if we were the makers of our psychic conditions. This prejudice is of relatively recent date. Not so very long ago even highly civilized people believed that psychic agencies could influence our minds and feelings. There were ghosts, wizards, and witches, daemons and angels, and even gods, who could produce certain psychological changes in human beings. In former times the man with the idea that he had cancer might have felt quite differently about his idea. He would probably have assumed that somebody had worked witchcraft against him or that he was possessed. He never would have thought of himself as the originator of such a fantasy.

21 As a matter of fact, I take his cancer to be a spontaneous growth, which originated in the part of the psyche that is not identical with consciousness. It appears as an autonomous formation intruding upon consciousness. Of consciousness one might say that it is our own psychic existence, but the cancer has *its* own psychic existence, independent of ourselves. This statement seems to formulate the observable facts completely. If we submit such a case to an association experiment,[7] we soon discover that he is not master in his own house. His reactions will be delayed, altered, suppressed, or replaced by autonomous intruders. There will be a number of stimulus-words which cannot be answered by his conscious intention. They will be answered by certain autonomous contents, which are very often unconscious even to himself. In our case we shall certainly discover answers that

come from the psychic complex at the root of the cancer idea. Whenever a stimulus-word touches something connected with the hidden complex, the reaction of the conscious ego will be disturbed, or even replaced, by an answer coming from the complex. It is just as if the complex were an autonomous being capable of interfering with the intentions of the ego. Complexes do indeed behave like secondary or partial personalities possessing a mental life of their own.

22   Many complexes are split off from consciousness because the latter preferred to get rid of them by repression. But there are others that have never been in consciousness before and therefore could never have been arbitrarily repressed. They grow out of the unconscious and invade the conscious mind with their weird and unassailable convictions and impulses. Our patient belonged to the latter category. Despite his culture and intelligence, he was a helpless victim of something that obsessed and possessed him. He was unable to help himself in any way against the demonic power of his morbid idea. It proliferated in him like a carcinoma. One day the idea appeared and from then on it remained unshakable; there were only short intervals when he was free from it.

23   The existence of such cases does something to explain why people are afraid of becoming conscious of themselves. There might really be something behind the screen – one never knows – and so people prefer 'to consider and observe carefully' the factors external to their consciousness. In most people there is a sort of primitive δεισιδαιμονία with regard to the possible contents of the unconscious. Beneath all natural shyness, shame, and tact, there is a secret fear of the unknown 'perils of the soul.' Of course one is reluctant to admit such a ridiculous fear. But one should realize that this fear is by no means unjustified; on the contrary, it is only too well founded. We can never be sure that a new idea will not seize either upon ourselves or upon our neighbours. We know from modern as well as from ancient history that such ideas are often so strange, indeed so bizarre, that they fly in the face of reason. The fascination which is almost invariably connected with ideas of this sort produces a fanatical obsession, with the result that all dissenters, no matter how well meaning or reasonable they are, get burnt alive or have their heads cut off or are disposed of in masses by the more modern machine-gun. We cannot even console ourselves with the thought that such things belong to the remote past. Unfortunately they seem to belong not only to the present, but, quite particularly, to the future. 'Homo homini lupus' is a sad yet eternal truism. There is indeed reason enough for man to be afraid of the impersonal forces lurking in his unconscious. We are blissfully unconscious of these forces because they never, or almost never, appear in our personal relations or under ordinary circumstances. But if people crowd together and form a mob, then the dynamisms of the collective man are let loose – beasts or demons that lie dormant in every person until he is part of a mob. Man in the mass sinks unconsciously to an inferior moral and intellectual level, to that level which is always there, below the threshold of consciousness, ready to break forth as soon as it is activated by the formation of a mass.

24   It is, to my mind, a fatal mistake to regard the human psyche as a purely personal affair and to explain it exclusively from a personal point of view. Such a mode of

explanation is only applicable to the individual in his ordinary everyday occupations and relationships. If, however, some slight trouble occurs, perhaps in the form of an unforeseen and somewhat unusual event, instantly instinctual forces are called up, forces which appear to be wholly unexpected, new, and strange. They can no longer be explained in terms of personal motives, being comparable rather to certain primitive occurrences like panics at solar eclipses and the like. To explain the murderous outbreak of Bolshevism, for instance, as a personal father-complex appears to me singularly inadequate.

25   The change of character brought about by the uprush of collective forces is amazing. A gentle and reasonable being can be transformed into a maniac or a savage beast. One is always inclined to lay the blame on external circumstances, but nothing could explode in us if it had not been there. As a matter of fact, we are constantly living on the edge of a volcano, and there is, so far as we know, no way of protecting ourselves from a possible outburst that will destroy everybody within reach. It is certainly a good thing to preach reason and common sense, but what if you have a lunatic asylum for an audience or a crowd in a collective frenzy? There is not much difference between them because the madman and the mob are both moved by impersonal, overwhelming forces.

26   As a matter of fact, it only needs a neurosis to conjure up a force that cannot be dealt with by rational means. Our cancer case shows clearly how impotent man's reason and intellect are against the most palpable nonsense. I always advise my patients to take such obvious but invincible nonsense as the manifestation of a power and a meaning they have not yet understood. Experience has taught me that it is much more effective to take these things seriously and then look for a suitable explanation. But an explanation is suitable only when it produces a hypothesis equal to the morbid effect. Our patient is confronted with a power of will and suggestion more than equal to anything his consciousness can put against it. In this precarious situation it would be bad strategy to convince him that in some incomprehensible way he is at the back of his own symptom, secretly inventing and supporting it. Such a suggestion would instantly paralyse his fighting spirit, and he would get demoralized. It is far better for him to understand that his complex is an autonomous power directed against his conscious personality. Moreover, such an explanation fits the actual facts much better than a reduction to personal motives. An apparently personal motivation does exist, but it is not made by his will, it just happens to him.

27   When in the Babylonian epic Gilgamesh's arrogance and hybris defy the gods, they create a man equal in strength to Gilgamesh in order to check the hero's unlawful ambition. The very same thing has happened to our patient: he is a thinker who has settled, or is always going to settle, the world by the power of his intellect and reason. His ambition has at least succeeded in forging his own personal fate. He has forced everything under the inexorable law of his reason, but somewhere nature escaped and came back with a vengeance in the form of an unassailable bit of nonsense, the cancer idea. This was the clever device of the unconscious to keep him on a merciless and cruel leash. It was the worst blow that

could be dealt to all his rational ideals and especially to his belief in the all-powerful human will. Such an obsession can occur only in a person who makes habitual misuse of reason and intellect for egotistical power purposes.

28   Gilgamesh, however, escaped the vengeance of the gods. He had warning dreams to which he paid attention. They showed him how he could overcome his enemy. Our patient, living in an age when the gods have become extinct and have fallen into bad repute, also had such dreams, but he did not listen to them. How could an intelligent man be so superstitious as to take dreams seriously! The very common prejudice against dreams is but one symptom of a far more serious undervaluation of the human psyche in general. The marvellous development of science and technics is counterbalanced by an appalling lack of wisdom and introspection. It is true that our religion speaks of an immortal soul; but it has very few kind words to say for the human psyche as such, which would go straight to eternal damnation were it not for a special act of Divine Grace. These two important factors are largely responsible for the general undervaluation of the psyche, but not entirely so. Older by far than these relatively recent developments are the primitive fear of and aversion to everything that borders on the unconscious.

29   Consciousness must have been a very precarious thing in its beginnings. In relatively primitive societies we can still observe how easily consciousness gets lost. One of the 'perils of the soul,'[8] for instance, is the loss of a soul. This is what happens when part of the psyche becomes unconscious again. Another example is 'running amok,'[9] the equivalent of 'going berserk' in Germanic saga.[10] This is a more or less complete trance-state, often accompanied by devastating social effects. Even a quite ordinary emotion can cause considerable loss of consciousness. Primitives therefore cultivate elaborate forms of politeness, speaking in a hushed voice, laying down their weapons, crawling on all fours, bowing the head, showing the palms. Even our own forms of politeness still exhibit a 'religious' consideration of possible psychic dangers. We propitiate fate by magically wishing one another a good day. It is not good form to keep the left hand in your pocket or behind your back when shaking hands. If you want to be particularly ingratiating you use both hands. Before people of great authority we bow with uncovered head, i.e., we offer our head unprotected in order to propitiate the powerful one, who might quite easily fall sudden prey to a fit of uncontrollable violence. In war-dances primitives can become so excited that they may even shed blood.

30   The life of the primitive is filled with constant regard for the ever-lurking possibility of psychic danger, and the procedures employed to diminish the risks are very numerous. The setting up of tabooed areas is an outward expression of this fact. The innumerable taboos are delimited psychic areas which are meticulously and fearfully observed. I once made a terrific mistake when I was with a tribe on the southern slopes of Mount Elgon, in East Africa. I wanted to inquire about the ghost-houses I frequently found in the woods, and during a palaver I mentioned the word *selelteni*, meaning 'ghost.' Instantly everybody was silent and painfully embarrassed. They all looked away from me because I had spoken aloud a

carefully hushed-up word, and had thus invited most dangerous consequences. I had to change the subject in order to be able to continue the meeting. The same men assured me that they never had dreams; they were the prerogative of the chief and of the medicine man. The medicine man then confessed to me that he no longer had any dreams either, they had the District Commissioner instead. 'Since the English are in the country we have no dreams any more,' he said. 'The District Commissioner knows everything about war and diseases, and about where we have got to live.' This strange statement is based on the fact that dreams were formerly the supreme political guide, the voice of *Mungu*, 'God.' Therefore it would have been unwise for an ordinary man to suggest that he had dreams.

31   Dreams are the voice of the Unknown, ever threatening new schemes, new dangers, sacrifices, warfare, and other troublesome things. An African Negro once dreamt that his enemies had taken him prisoner and burnt him alive. The next day he called his relatives together and implored them to burn him. They consented so far as to bind his feet together and put them in the fire. He was of course badly crippled but had escaped his foes.[11]

32   There are any amount of magical rites that exist for the sole purpose of erecting a defence against the unexpected, dangerous tendencies of the unconscious. The peculiar fact that the dream is a divine voice and messenger and yet an unending source of trouble does not disturb the primitive mind in the least. We find obvious remnants of this primitive thinking in the psychology of the Hebrew prophets.[12] Often enough they hesitate to listen to the voice. And it was, we must admit, rather hard on a pious man like Hosea to marry a harlot in order to obey the Lord's command. Since the dawn of humanity there has been a marked tendency to limit this unruly and arbitrary 'supernatural' influence by means of definite forms and laws. And this process has continued throughout history in the form of a multiplication of rites, institutions, and beliefs. During the last two thousand years we find the institution of the Christian Church taking over a mediating and protective function between these influences and man. It is not denied in medieval ecclesiastical writings that a divine influx may occur in dreams, but this view is not exactly encouraged, and the Church reserves the right to decide whether a revelation is to be considered authentic or not.[13] In spite of the Church's recognition that certain dreams are sent by God, she is disinclined, and even averse, to any serious concern with dreams, while admitting that some might conceivably contain an immediate revelation. Thus the change of mental attitude that has taken place in recent centuries is, from this point of view at least, not wholly unwelcome to the Church, because it effectively discouraged the earlier introspective attitude which favoured a serious consideration of dreams and inner experiences.

33   Protestantism, having pulled down so many walls carefully erected by the Church, immediately began to experience the disintegrating and schismatic effect of individual revelation. As soon as the dogmatic fence was broken down and the ritual lost its authority, man had to face his inner experience without the protection and guidance of dogma and ritual, which are the very quintessence of Christian as well as of pagan religious experience. Protestantism has, in the main,

lost all the finer shades of traditional Christianity: the mass, confession, the greater part of the liturgy, and the vicarious function of priesthood.

34   I must emphasize that this statement is not a value-judgment and is not intended to be one. I merely state the facts. Protestantism has, however, intensified the authority of the Bible as a substitute for the lost authority of the Church. But as history has shown, one can interpret certain biblical texts in many ways. Nor has scientific criticism of the New Testament been very helpful in enhancing belief in the divine character of the holy scriptures. It is also a fact that under the influence of a so-called scientific enlightenment great masses of educated people have either left the Church or become profoundly indifferent to it. If they were all dull rationalists or neurotic intellectuals the loss would not be regrettable. But many of them are religious people, only incapable of agreeing with the existing forms of belief. Otherwise, one could hardly explain the remarkable effect of the Buchman movement on the more-or-less educated Protestant classes. The Catholic who has turned his back on the Church usually develops a secret or manifest leaning towards atheism, whereas the Protestant follows, if possible, a sectarian movement. The absolutism of the Catholic Church seems to demand an equally absolute negation, whereas Protestant relativism permits of variations.

35   It may perhaps be thought that I have gone a bit too far into the history of Christianity, and for no other purpose than to explain the prejudice against dreams and inner experiences. But what I have just said might have been part of my conversation with our cancer patient. I told him that it would be better to take his obsession seriously instead of reviling it as pathological nonsense. But to take it seriously would mean acknowledging it as a sort of diagnostic statement of the fact that, in a psyche which really existed, trouble had arisen in the form of a cancer-like growth. 'But,' he will certainly ask, 'what could that growth be?' And I shall answer: 'I do not know,' as indeed I do not. Although, as I mentioned before, it is surely a compensatory or complementary unconscious formation, nothing is yet known about its specific nature or about its content. It is a spontaneous manifestation of the unconscious, based on contents which are not to be found in consciousness.

36   My patient is now very curious how I shall set about getting at the contents that form the root of the obsession. I then inform him, at the risk of shocking him severely, that his dreams will provide us with all the necessary information. We will take them as if they issued from an intelligent, purposive, and, as it were, personal source. This is of course a bold hypothesis and at the same time an adventure, because we are going to give extraordinary credit to a discredited entity – the psyche – whose very existence is still denied by not a few contemporary psychologists as well as by philosophers. A famous anthropologist, when I showed him my way of proceeding, made the typical remark: 'That's all very interesting indeed, but dangerous.' Yes, I admit it is dangerous, just as dangerous as a neurosis. If you want to cure a neurosis you have to risk something. To do something without taking a risk is merely ineffectual, as we know only too well. A surgical operation for cancer is a risk too, and yet it has to be done. For the sake

of better understanding I have often felt tempted to advise my patients to think of the psyche as a subtle body in which subtle tumours can grow. The prejudiced belief that the psyche is unimaginable and consequently less than air, or that it is a more or less intellectual system of logical concepts, is so great that when people are not conscious of certain contents they assume these do not exist. They have no confidence and no belief in a reliable psychic functioning outside consciousness, and dreams are thought to be only ridiculous. Under such conditions my proposal arouses the worst suspicions. And indeed I have heard every argument under the sun used against the vague spectres of dreams.

37   Yet in dreams we find, without any profound analysis, the same conflicts and complexes whose existence can also be demonstrated by the association test. Moreover, these complexes form an integral part of the existing neurosis. We have, therefore, reason to believe that dreams can give us at least as much information as the association test can about the content of a neurosis. As a matter of fact, they give very much more. The symptom is like the shoot above ground, yet the main plant is an extended rhizome underground. The rhizome represents the content of a neurosis; it is the matrix of complexes, of symptoms, and of dreams. We have every reason to believe that dreams mirror exactly the underground processes of the psyche. And if we get there, we literally get at the 'roots' of the disease.

38   As it is not my intention to go any further into the psychopathology of neuroses, I propose to choose another case as an example of how dreams reveal the unknown inner facts of the psyche and of what these facts consist. The dreamer was another intellectual, of remarkable intelligence and learning. He was neurotic and was seeking my help because he felt that his neurosis had become overpowering and was slowly but surely undermining his morale. Fortunately his intellectual integrity had not yet suffered and he had the free use of his fine intelligence. For this reason I set him the task of observing and recording his dreams himself. The dreams were not analysed or explained to him and it was only very much later that we began their analysis. Thus the dreams I am going to relate have not been tampered with at all. They represent an entirely uninfluenced natural sequence of events. The patient had never read any psychology, much less any analytical psychology.

39   Since the series consists of over four hundred dreams, I could not possibly convey an impression of the whole material; but I have published elsewhere a selection of seventy-four dreams containing motifs of special religious interest.[14] The dreamer, it should be said, was a Catholic by education, but no longer a practising one, nor was he interested in religious problems. He was one of those scientifically minded intellectuals who would be simply amazed if anybody should saddle them with religious views of any kind. If one holds that the unconscious has a psychic existence independent of consciousness, a case such as that of our dreamer might be of particular interest, provided we are not mistaken in our conception of the religious character of certain dreams. And if one lays stress on the conscious mind alone and does not credit the unconscious with an independent

existence, it will be interesting to find out whether or not the dreams really derive their material from conscious contents. Should the facts favour the hypothesis of the unconscious, one could then use dreams as possible sources of information about the religious tendencies of the unconscious.

40   One cannot expect dreams to speak of religion as we know it. There are, however, two dreams among the four hundred that obviously deal with religion. I will now give the text which the dreamer himself had taken down:

All the houses have something theatrical about them, with stage scenery and decorations. The name of Bernard Shaw is mentioned. The play is supposed to take place in the distant future. There is a notice in English and German on one of the sets:

This is the universal Catholic Church.
It is the Church of the Lord.
All those who feel that they are the instruments of the Lord may enter.

Under this is printed in smaller letters: 'The Church was founded by Jesus and Paul' – like a firm advertising its long standing.
I say to my friend, 'Come on, let's have a look at this.' He replies, 'I do not see why a lot of people have to get together when they're feeling religious.' I answer, 'As a Protestant you will never understand.' A woman nods emphatic approval. Then I see a sort of proclamation on the wall of the church. It runs:

Soldiers!
When you feel you are under the power of the Lord, do not address him directly. The Lord cannot be reached by words. We also strongly advise you not to indulge in any discussions among yourselves concerning the attributes of the Lord. It is futile, for everything valuable and important is ineffable.
(Signed) Pope . . . (Name illegible)

Now we go in. The interior resembles a mosque, more particularly the Hagia Sophia: no seats – wonderful effect of space; no images, only framed texts decorating the walls (like the Koran texts in the Hagia Sophia). One of the texts reads 'Do not flatter your benefactor.' The woman who had nodded approval bursts into tears and cries, 'Then there's nothing left!' I reply, 'I find it quite right!' but she vanishes. At first I stand with a pillar in front of me and can see nothing. Then I change my position and see a crowd of people. I do not belong to them and stand alone. But they are quite clear, so that I can see their faces. They all say in unison, 'We confess that we are under the power of the Lord. The Kingdom of Heaven is within us.' They repeat this three times with great solemnity. Then the organ starts to play and they sing a Bach fugue with chorale. But the original text is omitted; sometimes there is only a sort of coloratura singing, then the words are repeated: 'Everything else is paper' (meaning that it does not make a living impression on me). When the chorale has faded away the gemütlich *part of the ceremony begins; it is almost like a students' party. The people are all cheerful and equable. We move about, converse, and greet one another, and wine (from an episcopal seminary) is served with other refreshments. The health of the Church is drunk and, as if to express everybody's pleasure at the increase in membership, a loudspeaker blares a ragtime melody with the refrain, 'Charles is also with us now.' A priest explains to me: 'These somewhat trivial amusements are officially approved and permitted. We must adapt a little to American methods. With a large crowd such as we have here this is inevitable. But we differ in principle from the American churches by our decidedly anti-ascetic tendency.' Thereupon I awake with a feeling of great relief.*

41   There are, as you know, numerous works on the phenomenology of dreams, but very few that deal with their psychology. This for the obvious reason that a psychological interpretation of dreams is an exceedingly ticklish and risky business. Freud has made a courageous attempt to elucidate the intricacies of dream psychology with the help of views which he gathered in the field of psychopathology.[15] Much as I admire the boldness of his attempt, I cannot agree either with his method or with its results. He explains the dream as a mere façade behind which something has been carefully hidden. There is no doubt that neurotics hide disagreeable things, probably just as much as normal people do. But it is a serious question whether this category can be applied to such a normal and world-wide phenomenon as the dream. I doubt whether we can assume that a dream is something other than it appears to be. I am rather inclined to quote another Jewish authority, the Talmud, which says: 'The dream is its own interpretation.' In other words *I take the dream for what it is*. The dream is such a difficult and complicated thing that I do not dare to make any assumptions about its possible cunning or its tendency to deceive. The dream is a natural occurrence, and there is no earthly reason why we should assume that it is a crafty device to lead us astray. It occurs when consciousness and will are to a large extent extinguished. It seems to be a natural product which is also found in people who are not neurotic. Moreover, we know so little about the psychology of the dream process that we must be more than careful when we introduce into its explanation elements that are foreign to the dream itself.

42   For all these reasons I hold that our dream really is speaking of religion and that it intends to do so. Since the dream has a coherent and well-designed structure, it suggests a certain logic and a certain intention, that is, it has a meaningful motivation which finds direct expression in the dream-content.

43   The first part of the dream is a serious statement in favour of the Catholic Church. A certain Protestant point of view – that religion is just an individual experience – is discouraged by the dreamer. The second, more grotesque part is the Church's adaptation to a decidedly worldly standpoint, and the end is a statement in favour of an anti-ascetic tendency which would not and could not be backed up by the real Church. Nevertheless the dreamer's anti-ascetic priest makes it a matter of principle. Spiritualization and sublimation are essentially

Christian principles, and any insistence upon the contrary would amount to blasphemous paganism. Christianity has never been worldly nor has it ever looked with favour on good food and wine, and it is more than doubtful whether the introduction of jazz into the cult would be a particular asset. The 'cheerful and equable' people who peripatetically converse with each other in more or less Epicurean style remind one much more of an ancient philosophical ideal which is rather distasteful to the contemporary Christian. In the first and second part the importance of masses or crowds of people is emphasized.

44   Thus the Catholic Church, though highly recommended, appears coupled with a strange pagan point of view which is irreconcilable with a fundamentally Christian attitude. The actual irreconcilability does not appear in the dream. It is hushed up as it were by a cosy ('gemütlich') atmosphere in which dangerous contrasts are blurred and blended. The Protestant conception of an individual relationship to God is swamped by mass organization and a correspondingly collective religious feeling. The insistence on crowds and the insinuation of a pagan ideal are remarkable parallels to things that are actually happening in Europe today. Everybody was astonished at the pagan tendencies of modern Germany because nobody knew how to interpret Nietzsche's Dionysian experience. Nietzsche was but one of the thousands and millions of Germans yet unborn in whose unconscious the Teutonic cousin of Dionysus – Wotan – came to birth during the Great War.[16] In the dreams of the Germans whom I treated then I could clearly see the Wotanistic revolution coming on, and in 1918 I published an article in which I pointed out the peculiar kind of new development to be expected in Germany.[17] Those Germans were by no means people who had studied *Thus Spake Zarathustra*, and certainly the young people who resurrected the pagan sacrifices of sheep knew nothing of Nietzsche's experience.[18] That is why they called their god Wotan and not Dionysus. In Nietzsche's biography you will find irrefutable proof that the god he originally meant was really Wotan, but, being a philologist and living in the seventies and eighties of the nineteenth century, he called him Dionysus. Looked at from a comparative point of view, the two gods have much in common.

45   There is apparently no opposition to collective feeling, mass religion, and paganism anywhere in the dream of my patient, except for the Protestant friend who is soon reduced to silence. One curious incident merits our attention, and that is the unknown woman who at first backs up the eulogy of Catholicism and then suddenly bursts into tears, saying: 'Then there's nothing left,' and vanishes without returning.

46   Who is this woman? To the dreamer she is a vague and unknown person, but when he had that dream he was already well acquainted with her as the 'unknown woman' who had frequently appeared in previous dreams.

47   As this figure plays a great role in men's dreams, it bears the technical name of the 'anima,'[19] with reference to the fact that, from time immemorial, man in his myths has expressed the idea of a male and female coexisting in the same body. Such psychological intuitions were usually projected in the form of the divine

syzygy, the divine pair, or in the idea of the hermaphroditic nature of the creator.[20] Edward Maitland, the biographer of Anna Kingsford, relates in our own day an inner experience of the bisexual nature of the Deity.[21] Then there is Hermetic philosophy with its hermaphrodite and its androgynous inner man,[22] the *homo Adamicus*, who, 'although he appears in masculine form, always carries about with him Eve, or his wife, hidden in his body,' as a medieval commentator on the *Hermetis Tractatus aureus* says.[23]

48   The anima is presumably a psychic representation of the minority of female genes in a man's body. This is all the more probable since the same figure is not to be found in the imagery of a woman's unconscious. There is a corresponding figure, however, that plays an equivalent role, yet it is not a woman's image but a man's. This masculine figure in a woman's psychology has been termed the 'animus.'[24] One of the most typical manifestations of both figures is what has long been called 'animosity.' The anima causes illogical moods, and the animus produces irritating platitudes and unreasonable opinions. Both are frequent dream-figures. As a rule they personify the unconscious and give it its peculiarly disagreeable or irritating character. The unconscious in itself has no such negative qualities. They appear only when it is personified by these figures and when they begin to influence consciousness. Being only partial personalities, they have the character either of an inferior woman or of an inferior man – hence their irritating effect. A man experiencing this influence will be subject to unaccountable moods, and a woman will be argumentative and produce opinions that are beside the mark.[25]

49   The negative reaction of the anima to the church dream indicates that the dreamer's feminine side, his unconscious, disagrees with his conscious attitude. The disagreement started with the text on the wall: 'Do not flatter your benefactor,' which the dreamer agreed with. The meaning of the text seems sound enough, so that one does not understand why the woman should feel so desperate about it. Without delving further into this mystery, we must content ourselves for the time being with the statement that there is a contradiction in the dream and that a very important minority has left the stage under vivid protest and pays no more attention to the proceedings.

50   We gather, then, from the dream that the unconscious functioning of the dreamer's mind has produced a pretty flat compromise between Catholicism and pagan *joie de vivre*. The product of the unconscious is manifestly not expressing a fixed point of view or a definite opinion, rather it is a dramatic exposition of an act of reflection. It could be formulated perhaps as follows: 'Now what about this religious business? You are a Catholic, are you not? Is that not good enough? But asceticism – well, well, even the church has to adapt a little – movies, radio, spiritual five o'clock tea and all that – why not some ecclesiastical wine and gay acquaintances?' But for some secret reason this awkward mystery woman, well known from many former dreams, seems to be deeply disappointed and quits.

51   I must confess that I find myself in sympathy with the anima. Obviously the compromise is too cheap and too superficial, but it is characteristic of the dreamer as well as of many other people to whom religion does not matter very much.

Religion was of no concern to my patient and he certainly never expected that it would concern him in any way. But he had come to me because of a very alarming experience. Being highly rationalistic and intellectual he had found that his attitude of mind and his philosophy forsook him completely in the face of his neurosis and its demoralizing forces. He found nothing in his whole *Weltanschauung* that would help him to gain sufficient control of himself. He was therefore very much in the situation of a man deserted by his hitherto cherished convictions and ideals. It is by no means extraordinary that under such conditions a man should return to the religion of his childhood in the hope of finding something helpful there. It was, however, not a conscious attempt or decision to revivify his earlier religious beliefs. He merely dreamed it; that is, his unconscious produced a peculiar statement about his religion. It is just as if the spirit and the flesh, the eternal enemies in a Christian consciousness, had made peace with each other in the form of a curious mitigation of their contradictory nature. Spirituality and worldliness come together in unexpected amity. The effect is slightly grotesque and comical. The inexorable severity of the spirit seems to be undermined by an almost antique gaiety perfumed with wine and roses. At all events the dream describes a spiritual and worldly atmosphere that dulls the sharpness of a moral conflict and swallows up in oblivion all mental pain and distress.

52   If this was a wish-fulfilment it was surely a conscious one, for it was precisely what the patient had already done to excess. And he was not unconscious of this either, since wine was one of his most dangerous enemies. The dream, on the other hand, is an impartial statement of the patient's spiritual condition. It gives a picture of a degenerate religion corrupted by worldliness and mob instincts. There is religious sentimentality instead of the *numinosum* of divine experience. This is the well-known characteristic of a religion that has lost its living mystery. It is readily understandable that such a religion is incapable of giving help or of having any other moral effect.

53   The over-all aspect of the dream is definitely unfavourable, although certain other aspects of a more positive nature are dimly visible. It rarely happens that dreams are either exclusively positive or exclusively negative. As a rule one finds both aspects, but usually one is stronger than the other. It is obvious that such a dream provides the psychologist with enough material to raise the problem of a religious attitude. If our dream were the only one we possess we could hardly hope to unlock its innermost meaning, but we have quite a number of dreams in our series which point to a remarkable religious problem. I never, if I can help it, interpret one dream by itself. As a rule a dream belongs in a series. Since there is a continuity of consciousness despite the fact that it is regularly interrupted by sleep, there is probably also a continuity of unconscious processes – perhaps even more than with the events of consciousness. In any case my experience is in favour of the probability that dreams are the visible links in a chain of unconscious events. If we want to shed any light on the deeper reasons for the dream, we must go back to the series and find out where it is located in the long chain of four hundred dreams.

54   We find our dream wedged in between two important dreams of an uncanny quality. The dream before reports that there is a gathering of many people and that a peculiar ceremony is taking place, apparently of magical character, for the purpose of 'reconstructing the gibbon.' The dream after is concerned with a similar theme – the magical transformation of animals into human beings.[26]

55   Both dreams are intensely disagreeable and very alarming to the patient. Whereas the church dream manifestly moves on the surface and expresses opinions which in other circumstances could just as well have been thought consciously, these two dreams are strange and remote in character and their emotional effect is such that the dreamer would avoid them if possible. As a matter of fact, the text of the second dream says: 'If one runs away, all is lost.' Curiously enough, this remark coincides with that of the unknown woman: 'Then there's nothing left.' The inference to be drawn from these remarks is that the church dream was an attempt to escape from other dream ideas of a much deeper significance. These ideas appear in the dreams occurring immediately before and after it.

Notes

1 [Written in English and delivered in 1937, at Yale University, Connecticut, as the fifteenth series of the Dwight Harrington Terry Lectures. What is reproduced here is the first part of the lecture series. The complete lectures were published by Yale University Press (and by Oxford University Press, London) in 1938. The text was augmented by Jung in 1940. – Editor.]
2 *The Idea of the Holy*.
3 *Gratia adiuvans* and *gratia sanctificans* are the effects of the *sacramentum ex opere operato*. The sacrament owes its undoubted efficacy to the fact that it is directly instituted by Christ himself. The Church is powerless to connect the rite with grace in such a way that the sacramental act would produce the presence and effect of grace. Consequently the rite performed by the priest is not a *causa instrumentalis*, but merely a *causa ministerialis*.
4 'But our esteem for facts has not neutralized in us all religiousness. It is itself almost religious. Our scientific temper is devout.' *Pragmatism*, p. 14.
5 'Religion is that which gives reverence and worship to some higher nature [which is called divine].' Cicero, *De inventione rhetorica*, II, 53, 161. For 'testimony given under the sanction of religion on the faith of an oath' cf. Cicero, *Pro Coelio*, 55.
6 Heinrich Scholz (*Die Religionsphilosophie des Als-Ob*) insists on a similar standpoint. Cf. also Pearcy, *A Vindication of Paul*.
7 Cf. my 'Studies in Word Association.'
8 Frazer, *Taboo and the Perils of the Soul*, pp. 30ff.; Crawley, *The Idea of the Soul*, pp. 82ff.; Lévy-Bruhl, *Primitive Mentality*.
9 Fenn, *Running Amok*.
10 Ninck, *Wodan und germanischer Schicksalsglaube*.
11 Lévy-Bruhl, *How Natives Think*, and *Primitive Mentality*, ch. 3, 'Dreams,' pp. 97ff.
12 Haeussermann, *Wortempfang und Symbol in der alttestamentlichen Prophetie*.
13 In his excellent treatise on dreams and their functions, Benedictus Pererius, S.J. (*De Magia; De Observatione Somniorum et de Divinatione Astrologica libri tres*, 1598) says: 'For God is not constrained by such laws of time, nor does he await opportune moments for his operation; for he inspires dreams where he will, when he will, and in whomsoever he will' (p. 147). The following passage throws an interesting light on

the relation of the Church to the problem of dreams: 'For we read in Cassian's 22nd Collation, that the old governors and directors of the monks were well versed in seeking out and testing the causes of certain dreams' (p. 142). Pererius classifies dreams as follows: 'Many [dreams] are natural, some are of human origin, and some are even divine' (p. 145). There are four causes of dreams: (1) An affection of the body. (2) An affect or vehement commotion of the mind caused by love, hope, fear, or hatred (pp. 126ff.). (3) The power and cunning of the demon, i.e. of a heathen god or the Christian devil. ('For the devil is able to know natural effects which will needs come about at some future time from fixed causes; he can know those things which he himself is going to bring about at a later time; he can know things, both present and past, which are hidden from men, and make them known to men in dreams' [p. 129]. Concerning the diagnosis of demonic dreams, the author says: 'It can be surmised that dreams are sent by the devil, firstly if dreams often occur which signify future or hidden events, knowledge whereof is advantageous not to any useful end whether for oneself or for others, but only for the vain display of curious information, or even for the doing of some evil act...' [p. 130].) (4) Dreams sent by God. Concerning the signs indicating the divine nature of a dream, the author says: '... from the importance of the matters made known by the dream, especially if, in the dream, those things are made known to a man of which certain knowledge can come to him only by God's leave and bounty. Of such sort are those things which in the schools of the theologians are called contingent future events; further, the secrets of the heart which are wholly hidden from all men's understanding; and lastly, those highest mysteries of our faith which are known to no man unless he be taught them by God [!] ... That this [is divine] is especially declared by a certain enlightenment and moving of the spirits, whereby God so illumines the mind, so acts upon the will, and so assures the dreamer of the credibility and authority of his dream that he so clearly recognizes and so certainly judges God to be its author that he not only desires to believe it, but must believe it without any doubt whatsoever' (pp. 131ff.). Since the demon, as stated above, is also capable of producing dreams accurately predicting future events, the author adds a quotation from Gregory the Great (*Dialogorum Libri IV*, cap. 48, in Migne, *P.L.*, vol. 77, col. 412): 'Holy men discern between illusions and revelations, the very words and images of visions, by a certain inward sensibility, so that they know what they receive from the good spirit and what they endure from the deceiver. For if a man's mind were not careful in this regard, it would plunge itself into many vanities through the deceiving spirit, who is sometimes wont to foretell many true things, in order that he may entirely prevail to ensnare the soul by some one single falsity' (p. 132). It seemed to be a welcome safeguard against this uncertainty if dreams were concerned with the 'highest mysteries of our faith.' Athanasius, in his biography of St. Anthony, gives us some idea of how clever the devils are in foretelling future events, (Cf. Budge, *The Book of Paradise*, I, pp. 37ff.) The same author says they sometimes appear even in the shape of monks, singing psalms, reading the Bible aloud, and making disturbing remarks about the moral conduct of the brethren (pp. 33ff. and 47). Pererius, however, seems to trust his own criterion, for he continues: 'As therefore the natural light of our minds enables us clearly to discern the truth of first principles, so that they are embraced by our assent immediately and without any argument; so in dreams sent by God the divine light shining upon our minds brings it about that we understand and believe with certainty that those dreams are true and of God.' He does not touch on the delicate question of whether *every* unshakable conviction derived from a dream necessarily proves the divine origin of the dream. He merely takes it for granted that a dream of this sort would naturally exhibit a character consistent with the 'highest mysteries of our faith,' and not perchance with those of another one. The humanist Kaspar Peucer (in his *Commentarius de praecipuis generibus divinationum*, 1560) is far more definite and restrictive in this respect.

He says (p. 270): 'Those dreams are of God which the sacred scriptures affirm to be sent from on high, not to every one promiscuously, nor to those who strive after and expect revelations of their own opinion, but to the Holy Patriarchs and Prophets by the will and judgment of God. [Such dreams are concerned] not with light matters, or with trifles and ephemeral things, but with Christ, the governance of the Church, with empires and their well ordering, and other remarkable events; and to these God always adds sure testimonies, such as the gift of interpretation and other things, by which it is clear that they are not rashly to be objected to, nor are they of natural origin, but are divinely inspired.' His crypto-Calvinism is palpably manifest in his words, particularly when one compares them with the natural theology of his Catholic contemporaries. It is probable that Peucer's hint about 'revelations' refers to certain heretical innovations. At any rate, in the next paragraph, where he deals with dreams of diabolical origin, he says these are the dreams 'which the devil shows nowadays to Anabaptists, and at all times to Enthusiasts and suchlike fanatics.' Pererius with more perspicacity and human understanding devotes one chapter to the question 'Whether it be lawful for a Christian man to observe dreams?' (pp. 142ff.) and another to the question 'To what kind of man does it belong to interpret dreams aright?' (pp. 245ff.). In the first he reaches the conclusion that important dreams should be considered. I quote his words: 'Finally, to consider whether the dreams which ofttimes disturb us and move us to evil courses are put before us by the devil, as likewise on the other hand to ponder whether those by which we are aroused and incited to good, as for example to celibacy, almsgiving, and entering the religious life, are sent us by God, is the part not of a superstitious mind, but of one that is religious, prudent, and careful and solicitous for its salvation.' Only stupid people would observe all the other futile dreams. In the second chapter, he answers that nobody should or could interpret dreams 'unless he be divinely inspired and instructed.' 'Even so,' he adds, 'the things of God knoweth no man, but the Spirit of God' (I Cor. 2:11). This statement, eminently true in itself, reserves the art of interpretation to such persons as are endowed by their office with the gift of the Holy Spirit. It is obvious, however, that a Jesuit author could not envisage a descent of the Holy Spirit outside the Church.

14 'Dream Symbols of the Individuation Process.' [Orig. in *Eranos-Jahrbuch 1935*. A revised and expanded version of this appears in *Psychology and Alchemy*, as Part II.– EDITORS.] Although the dreams cited here are mentioned in the above publication, they are examined there from a different standpoint. Since dreams have many aspects they can be studied from various angles.

15 Freud, *The Interpretation of Dreams*. Silberer (*Der Traum*, 1919) presents a more cautious and more balanced point of view. As to the difference between Freud's and my own views, I would refer the reader to my little essay on this subject, 'Freud and Jung: Contrasts.' Further material in *Two Essays on Analytical Psychology*, pars. 16ff.; Kranefeldt, *Secret Ways of the Mind*; Gerhard Adler, *Entdeckung der Seele*; and Toni Wolff, 'Einführung in die Grundlagen der komplexen Psychologie,' in *Die kulturelle Bedeutung der komplexen Psychologie*.

16 Cf. the relation of Odin as the god of poets, seers, and raving enthusiasts, and of Mimir, the Wise One, to Dionysus and Silenus. The word Odin has a root-connection with Gall. *oὔατεις*, Ir. *fáith*, L. *vates*, similar to μάντις and μαίνομαι. Ninck, *Wodan und germanischer Schicksalsglaube*, pp. 30ff.

17 'The Role of the Unconscious.'

18 Cf. my 'Wotan,' *Neue Schweizer Rundschau*, 1936 [an abbreviated version in the *Saturday Review of Literature*, Oct. 16, 1937; subsequently published in *Essays on Contemporary Events*, 1947, now in *Coll. Works*, vol. 10]. The Wotan parallels in Nietzsche's work are to be found in the poem 'To the Unknown God' (*Werke*, ed. Baeumler, V, p. 457); *Thus Spake Zarathustra*, trans. by Thomas Common, pp. 293ff.,

19 Cf. my *Two Essays*, pars. 296ff.; *Psychological Types*, Defs. 48, 49; 'Archetypes of the Collective Unconscious,' pars. 52ff.; and 'Concerning the Archetypes.'
20 Cf. my 'Concerning the Archetypes,' pars. 120ff.
21 Maitland, *Anna Kingsford*, I, pp. 129ff. [Cf. 'Comm. on *Golden Flower*,' par. 40.]
22 The statement about the hermaphroditic nature of the Deity in *Corpus Hermeticum*, Lib. I (ed. Scott, *Hermetica*, 1, p. 118): 'For the first Mind was bisexual,' is probably taken from Plato, *Symposium*, XIV. It is questionable whether the later medieval representations of the hermaphrodite stem from 'Poimandres' (*Hermetica*, I), since the hermaphrodite figure was practically unknown in the West before the *Poimander* was printed by Marsilio Ficino in 1471. It is possible, however, that one of the few scholars of those days who understood Greek got the idea from one of the Greek codices then extant, as for instance the Codex Laurentianus 71, 33, the Codex Parisinus Graecus 1220, or the Codices Vaticanus Graecus 237 and 951, all from the 14th century. There are no older codices. The first Latin translation by Marsilio Ficino had a sensational effect. But before that date we have the hermaphroditic symbols from the Codex Germanicus Monacensis 598, dated 1417. It seems to me more probable that the hermaphrodite symbol derives from Arabic or Syriac MSS. translated in the 11th or 12th century. In the old Latin 'Tractatulus Avicennae,' which is strongly influenced by Arabic tradition, we find: '[The elixir] is a voluptuous serpent impregnating itself' (*Artis auriferae*, I, 1593, p. 406). Although the author was a Pseudo-Avicenna and not the authentic Ibn Sina (970–1037), he is one of the Arabic-Latin sources for medieval Hermetic literature. We find the same passage in 'Rosinus ad Sarratantam' (*Artis aurif.*, I, p. 303). 'Rosinus' is an Arabic-Latin corruption of 'Zosimos,' a Greek neo-Platonic philosopher of the 3rd century. His treatise 'Ad Sarratantam' belongs to the same class of literature, and since the history of these texts is still shrouded in darkness, nobody can say who copied from whom. The *Turba philosophorum*, Sermo LXV, a Latin text of Arabic origin, makes the same allusion: 'The composite brings itself forth.' (Ruska, *Turba philosophorum*, 1931, p. 165.) So far as I can judge, the first text that definitely mentions the hermaphrodite is the 'Liber de arte chymica' of the 16th century (*Artis aurif.*, I, pp. 575ff.). On p. 610 it says: 'For that Mercurius is all metals, male and female, and an hermaphroditic monster even in the marriage of soul and body.' Of the later literature I mention only Hieronymus Reusner, *Pandora* (1588); 'Splendor Solis' (*Aureum vellus,* 1598); Michael Maier, *Symbola aureae mensae* (1617) and *Atalanta fugiens* (1618); J. D. Mylius, *Philosophia reformata* (1622).
23 The 'Tractatus aureus Hermetis' is of Arabic origin and does not belong to the *Corpus Hermeticum*. Its history is unknown (first printed in *Ars chemica,* 1566). Dominicus Gnosius wrote a commentary on the text in his *Hermetis Trismegisti Tractatus vere Aureus de Lapide philosophici secreto* (1610). On p. 101 he says: 'As a shadow continually follows the body of one who walks in the sun . . . so our Adamic hermaphrodite, though he appears in masculine form, nevertheless always carries about with him Eve, or his feminine part, hidden in his body.' This commentary, together with the text, is reproduced in Manget, *Bibliotheca chemica curiosa,* I (1702), pp. 401ff.
24 There is a description of both these figures in *Two Essays,* Part II, pars. 296ff. See also *Psychological Types,* Def. 48, and Emma Jung, 'On the Nature of the Animus.' [Cf. also *Aion,* ch. III.]
25 Anima and animus do not only occur in negative form. They may sometimes appear as a source of enlightenment, as messengers (ἄγγελοι), and as mystagogues. [Cf. Jung, *Aion (Coll. Works,* Vol. 9, pt. 11), p. 16; 'Psychology of the Transference,' par. 504.–EDITORS.]
26 [Cf. *Psychology and Alchemy,* pars. 164ff., 183ff.–EDITORS.]

Chapter 10

Preface to *Answer to Job*[1]
Lectori benevolo

> *I am distressed for thee, my brother . . .*
> II Samuel 1:26 (AV)

553 On account of its somewhat unusual content, my little book requires a short preface. I beg of you, dear reader, not to overlook it. For, in what follows, I shall speak of the venerable objects of religious belief. Whoever talks of such matters inevitably runs the risk of being torn to pieces by the two parties who are in mortal conflict about those very things. This conflict is due to the strange supposition that a thing is true only if it presents itself as a *physical* fact. Thus some people believe it to be physically true that Christ was born as the son of a virgin, while others deny this as a physical impossibility. Everyone can see that there is no logical solution to this conflict and that one would do better not to get involved in such sterile disputes. Both are right and both are wrong. Yet they could easily reach agreement if only they dropped the word 'physical.' 'Physical' is not the only criterion of truth: there are also *psychic* truths which can neither be explained nor proved nor contested in any physical way. If, for instance, a general belief existed that the river Rhine had at one time flowed backwards from its mouth to its source, then this belief would in itself be a fact even though such an assertion, physically understood, would be deemed utterly incredible. Beliefs of this kind are psychic facts which cannot be contested and need no proof.

554 Religious statements are of this type. They refer without exception to things that cannot be established as physical facts. If they did not do this, they would inevitably fall into the category of the natural sciences. Taken as referring to anything physical, they make no sense whatever, and science would dismiss them as non-experienceable. They would be mere miracles, which are sufficiently exposed to doubt as it is, and yet they could not demonstrate the reality of the spirit or *meaning* that underlies them, because meaning is something that always demonstrates itself and is experienced on its own merits. The spirit and meaning of Christ are present and perceptible to us even without the aid of miracles. Miracles appeal only to the understanding of those who cannot perceive the meaning. They are mere substitutes for the not understood reality of the spirit. This is not to say that the living presence of the spirit is not occasionally

accompanied by marvellous physical happenings. I only wish to emphasize that these happenings can neither replace nor bring about an understanding of the spirit, which is the one essential thing.

555   The fact that religious statements frequently conflict with the observed physical phenomena proves that in contrast to physical perception the spirit is autonomous, and that psychic experience is to a certain extent independent of physical data. The psyche is an autonomous factor, and religious statements are psychic confessions which in the last resort are based on unconscious, i.e., on transcendental, processes. These processes are not accessible to physical perception but demonstrate their existence through the confessions of the psyche. The resultant statements are filtered through the medium of human consciousness: that is to say, they are given visible forms which in their turn are subject to manifold influences from within and without. That is why whenever we speak of religious contents we move in a world of images that point to something ineffable. We do not know how clear or unclear these images, metaphors, and concepts are in respect of their transcendental object. If, for instance, we say 'God,' we give expression to an image or verbal concept which has undergone many changes in the course of time. We are, however, unable to say with any degree of certainty – unless it be by faith – whether these changes affect only the images and concepts, or the Unspeakable itself. After all, we can imagine God as an eternally flowing current of vital energy that endlessly changes shape just as easily as we can imagine him as an eternally unmoved, unchangeable essence. Our reason is sure only of one thing: that it manipulates images and ideas which are dependent on human imagination and its temporal and local conditions, and which have therefore changed innumerable times in the course of their long history. There is no doubt that there is something behind these images that transcends consciousness and operates in such a way that the statements do not vary limitlessly and chaotically, but clearly all relate to a few basic principles or archetypes. These, like the psyche itself, or like matter, are unknowable as such. All we can do is to construct models of them which we know to be inadequate, a fact which is confirmed again and again by religious statements.

556   If, therefore, in what follows I concern myself with these 'metaphysical' objects, I am quite conscious that I am moving in a world of images and that none of my reflections touches the essence of the Unknowable. I am also too well aware of how limited are our powers of conception – to say nothing of the feebleness and poverty of language – to imagine that my remarks mean anything more in principle than what a primitive man means when he conceives of his god as a hare or a snake. But, although our whole world of religious ideas consists of anthropomorphic images that could never stand up to rational criticism, we should never forget that they are based on numinous archetypes, i.e., on an emotional foundation which is unassailable by reason. We are dealing with psychic facts which logic can overlook but not eliminate. In this connection Tertullian has already appealed, quite rightly, to the testimony of the soul. In his *De testimonio animae,* he says:

Preface to *Answer to job* 255

These testimonies of the soul are as simple as they are true, as obvious as they are simple, as common as they are obvious, as natural as they are common, as divine as they are natural. I think that they cannot appear to any one to be trifling and ridiculous if he considers the majesty of Nature, whence the authority of the soul is derived. What you allow to the mistress you will assign to the disciple. Nature is the mistress, the soul is the disciple; what the one has taught, or the other has learned, has been delivered to them by God, who is, in truth, the Master even of the mistress herself. What notion the soul is able to conceive of her first teacher is in your power to judge, from that soul which is in you. Feel that which causes you to feel; think upon that which is in forebodings your prophet; in omens, your augur; in the events which befall you, your foreseer. Strange if, being given by God, she knows how to act the diviner for men! Equally strange if she knows Him by whom she has been given![2]

557 I would go a step further and say that the statements made in the Holy Scriptures are also utterances of the soul – even at the risk of being suspected of psychologism. The statements of the conscious mind may easily be snares and delusions, lies, or arbitrary opinions, but this is certainly not true of the statements of the soul: to begin with they always go over our heads because they point to realities that transcend consciousness. These *entia* are the archetypes of the collective unconscious, and they precipitate complexes of ideas in the form of mythological motifs. Ideas of this kind are never invented, but enter the field of inner perception as finished products, for instance in dreams. They are spontaneous phenomena which are not subject to our will, and we are therefore justified in ascribing to them a certain autonomy. They are to be regarded not only as objects but as subjects with laws of their own. From the point of view of consciousness, we can, of course, describe them as objects, and even explain them up to a point, in the same measure as we can describe and explain a living human being. But then we have to disregard their autonomy. If that is considered, we are compelled to treat them as subjects; in other words, we have to admit that they possess spontaneity and purposiveness, or a kind of consciousness and free will. We observe their behaviour and consider their statements. This dual standpoint, which we are forced to adopt towards every relatively independent organism, naturally has a dual result. On the one hand it tells me what I do to the object, and on the other hand what it does (possibly to me). It is obvious that this unavoidable dualism will create a certain amount of confusion in the minds of my readers, particularly as in what follows we shall have to do with the archetype of Deity.

558 Should any of my readers feel tempted to add an apologetic 'only' to the God-images as we perceive them, he would immediately fall foul of experience, which demonstrates beyond any shadow of doubt the extraordinary numinosity of these images. The tremendous effectiveness (mana) of these images is such that they not only give one the feeling of pointing to the *Ens realissimum,* but make one convinced that they actually express it and establish it as a fact. This makes

discussion uncommonly difficult, if not impossible. It is, in fact, impossible to demonstrate God's reality to oneself except by using images which have arisen spontaneously or are sanctified by tradition, and whose psychic nature and effects the naïve-minded person has never separated from their unknowable metaphysical background. He instantly equates the effective image with the transcendental x to which it points. The seeming justification for this procedure appears self-evident and is not considered a problem so long as the statements of religion are not seriously questioned. But if there is occasion for criticism, then it must be remembered that the image and the statement are psychic processes which are different from their transcendental object; they do not posit it, they merely point to it. In the realm of psychic processes criticism and discussion are not only permissible but are unavoidable.

559　In what follows I shall attempt just such a discussion, such a 'coming to terms' with certain religious traditions and ideas. Since I shall be dealing with numinous factors, my feeling is challenged quite as much as my intellect. I cannot, therefore, write in a coolly objective manner, but must allow my emotional subjectivity to speak if I want to describe what I feel when I read certain books of the Bible, or when I remember the impressions I have received from the doctrines of our faith. I do not write as a biblical scholar (which I am not), but as a layman and physician who has been privileged to see deeply into the psychic life of many people. What I am expressing is first of all my own personal view, but I know that I also speak in the name of many who have had similar experiences.

Note

1　[Originally published as the 'Note to the Kind Reader' in the book, *Antwort auf Hiob* (Zurich, 1952). The present translation by R. F. C. Hull was first published, in book form, in London, 1954. In 1956, it was reprinted and published by Pastoral Psychology Book Club, Great Neck, New York. Only minor stylistic alterations have been made in the version here published. – Editor.]
2　Chap V, in Migne, Jaques Paul. (ed.) *Patrologiae cursus completus*, Latin Series, Paris, 1844–64. Vol. 1, columns. 615f. (trans. by C. Dodgson, I, pp. 138f., slightly modified).

Chapter 11

Psychology and literature[1]

Introduction

Psychology, which once eked out a modest existence in a small and highly academic backroom, has, in fulfilment of Nietzsche's prophecy, developed in the last few decades into an object of public interest which has burst the framework assigned to it by the universities. In the form of psychotechnics it makes its voice heard in industry, in the form of psychotherapy it has invaded wide areas of medicine, in the form of philosophy it has carried forward the legacy of Schopenhauer and von Hartmann, it has quite literally rediscovered Bachofen and Carus, through it mythology and the psychology of primitives have acquired a new focus of interest, it will revolutionize the science of comparative religion, and not a few theologians want to apply it even to the cure of souls. Will Nietzsche be proved right in the end with his 'scientia ancilla psychologiae'?

At present, unfortunately, this encroaching advance of psychology is still a welter of chaotic cross-currents, each of the conflicting schools attempting to cover up the confusion by an all the more vociferous dogmatism and a fanatical defence of its own standpoint. Equally onesided are the attempts to open up all these different areas of knowledge and life to psychological research. Onesidedness and rigidity of principle are, however, the childish errors of every young science that has to perform pioneer work with but few intellectual tools. Despite all [my] tolerance and realization of the necessity of doctrinal opinions of various kinds, I have never wearied of emphasizing that onesidedness and dogmatism harbour in themselves the gravest dangers precisely in the domain of psychology. The psychologist should constantly bear in mind that his hypothesis is no more at first than the expression of his own subjective premise and can therefore never lay immediate claim to general validity. What the individual researcher has to contribute in explanation of any one of the countless aspects of the psyche is merely a point of view, and it would be doing the grossest violence to the object of research if he tried to make this one point of view into a generally binding truth. The phenomenology of the psyche is so colourful, so variegated in form and meaning, that we cannot possibly reflect all its riches in *one* mirror. Nor in our description of it can we ever embrace the whole, but must be content to shed light only on single parts of the total phenomenon.

Since it is a characteristic of the psyche not only to be the source of all productivity but, more especially, to express itself in all the activities and achievements of the human mind, we can nowhere grasp the nature of the psyche *per se* but can meet it only in its various manifestations. The psychologist is therefore obliged to make himself familiar with a wide range of subjects, not out of presumption and inquisitiveness but rather from love of knowledge, and for this purpose he must abandon his thickly walled specialist fortress and set out on the quest for truth. He will not succeed in banishing the psyche to the confines of the laboratory or of the consulting room, but must follow it through all those realms where its visible manifestations are to be found, however strange they may be to him.

Thus it comes that I, unperturbed by the fact that I am by profession a doctor, speak to you today as a psychologist about the poetic imagination, although this constitutes the proper province of literary science and of aesthetics. On the other hand, it is also a psychic phenomenon, and as such it probably must be taken into account by the psychologist. In so doing I shall not encroach on the territory either of the literary historian or of the aesthetician, for nothing is further from my intentions than to replace their points of view by psychological ones. Indeed, I would be making myself guilty of that same sin of onesidedness which I have just censured. Nor shall I presume to put before you a complete theory of poetic creativity, as that would be altogether impossible for me. My observations should be taken as nothing more than points of view by which a psychological approach to poetry might be oriented in a general way.

133 It is obvious enough that psychology, being a study of psychic processes, can be brought to bear on the study of literature, for the human psyche is the womb of all the arts and sciences. The investigation of the psyche should therefore be able on the one hand to explain the psychological structure of a work of art, and on the other to reveal the factors that make a person artistically creative. The psychologist is thus faced with two separate and distinct tasks, and must approach them in radically different ways.

134 In the case of a work of art we are confronted with a product of complicated psychic activities – but a product that is apparently intentional and consciously shaped. In the case of the artist we must deal with the psychic apparatus itself. In the first instance the object of analysis and interpretation is a concrete artistic achievement, while in the second it is the creative human being as a unique personality. Although these two objects are intimately related and even interdependent, neither of them can explain the other. It is of course possible to draw inferences about the artist from the work of art, and *vice versa,* but these inferences are never conclusive. At best they are probably surmises or lucky guesses. A knowledge of Goethe's particular relation to his mother throws some light on Faust's exclamation: 'The mothers, the mothers, how eerily it sounds!' But it does not enable us to see how the attachment to his mother could produce the *Faust* drama itself, however deeply we sense the importance of this relationship for Goethe the man from the many telltale traces it has left behind in his

work. Nor are we more successful in reasoning in the reverse direction. There is nothing in *The Ring of the Nibelungs* that would lead us to discern or to infer the fact that Wagner had a tendency towards transvestism, even though a secret connection does exist between the heroics of the Nibelungs and a certain pathological effeminacy in the man Wagner. The personal psychology of the artist may explain many aspects of his work, but not the work itself. And if ever it did explain his work successfully, the artist's creativity would be revealed as a mere symptom. This would be detrimental both to the work of art and to its repute.

135   The present state of psychological knowledge does not allow us to establish those rigorous causal connections in the realm of art which we would expect a science to do. Psychology, after all, is the newest of the sciences. It is only in the realm of the psychophysical instincts and reflexes that we can confidently operate with the concept of causality. From the point where true psychic life begins – that is, at a level of greater complexity – the psychologist must content himself with widely ranging descriptions of psychic processes, and with portraying as vividly as he can the warp and woof of the mind in all its amazing intricacy. At the same time, he should refrain from calling any one of these processes 'necessary' in the sense that it is causally determined. If the psychologist were able to demonstrate definite causalities in a work of art and in the process of artistic creation, he would leave aesthetics no ground to stand on and would reduce it to a special branch of his own science. Although he should never abandon his claim to investigate and establish the causality of complex psychic processes – to do so would be to deny psychology the right to exist – he will never be able to make good this claim in the fullest sense, because the creative urge which finds its clearest expression in art is irrational and will in the end make a mock of all our rationalistic undertakings. All conscious psychic processes may well be causally explicable; but the creative act, being rooted in the immensity of the unconscious, will forever elude our attempts at understanding. It describes itself only in its manifestations; it can be guessed at, but never wholly grasped. Psychology and aesthetics will always have to turn to one another for help, and the one will not invalidate the other. It is an important principle of psychology that any given psychic material can be shown to derive from causal antecedents; it is a principle of aesthetics that a psychic product can be regarded as existing in and for itself. Whether the work of art or the artist himself is in question, both principles are valid in spite of their relativity.

I The work of art

136   There is a fundamental difference of attitude between the psychologist's approach to a literary work and that of a literary critic. What is of decisive importance and value for the latter may be quite irrelevant for the former. Indeed, literary products of highly dubious merit are often of the greatest interest to the psychologist. The so-called 'psychological novel' is by no means as rewarding for the psychologist as the literary-minded suppose. Considered as a self-contained whole, such a

novel explains itself. It has done its own work of psychological interpretation, and the psychologist can at most criticize or enlarge upon this.

137 In general, it is the non-psychological novel that offers the richest opportunities for psychological elucidation. Here the author, having no intentions of this sort, does not show his characters in a psychological light and thus leaves room for analysis and interpretation, or even invites it by his unprejudiced mode of presentation. Good examples of such novels are those of Benoit, or English fiction after the manner of Rider Haggard, as well as that most popular article of literary mass-production, the detective story, first exploited by Conan Doyle. I would also include Melville's *Moby Dick,* which I consider to be the greatest American novel, in this broad class of writings. An exciting narrative that is apparently quite devoid of psychological intentions is just what interests the psychologist most of all. Such a tale is constructed against a background of unspoken psychological assumptions, and the more unconscious the author is of them, the more this background reveals itself in unalloyed purity to the discerning eye. In the psychological novel, on the other hand, the author himself makes the attempt to raise the raw material of his work into the sphere of psychological discussion, but instead of illuminating it he merely succeeds in obscuring the psychic background. It is from novels of this sort that the layman gets his 'psychology'; whereas novels of the first kind require the psychologist to give them a deeper meaning.

138 I have been speaking in terms of the novel, but what I am discussing is a psychological principle which is not restricted to this form of literature. We meet with it also in poetry, and in *Faust* it is so obvious that it divides the first part from the second. The love-tragedy of Gretchen is self-explanatory; there is nothing the psychologist can add to it that has not already been said in better words by the poet. But the second part cries out for interpretation. The prodigious richness of the imaginative material has so overtaxed, or outstripped, the poet's powers of expression that nothing explains itself any more and every line only makes the reader's need of an interpretation more apparent. *Faust* is perhaps the best illustration of these two extremes in the psychology of art.

139 For the sake of clarity I would like to call the one mode of artistic creation *psychological,*[2] and the other *visionary.* The psychological mode works with materials drawn from man's conscious life – with crucial experiences, powerful emotions, suffering, passion, the stuff of human fate in general. All this is assimilated by the psyche of the poet, raised from the commonplace to the level of poetic experience, and expressed with a power of conviction that gives us a greater depth of human insight by making us vividly aware of those everyday happenings which we tend to evade or to overlook because we perceive them only dully or with a feeling of discomfort. The raw material of this kind of creation is derived from the contents of man's consciousness, from his eternally repeated joys and sorrows, but clarified and transfigured by the poet. There is no work left for the psychologist to do – unless perhaps we expect him to explain why Faust fell in love with Gretchen, or why Gretchen was driven to murder her child. Such themes constitute the lot of humankind; they are repeated millions of times and account for the hideous

monotony of the police court and the penal code. No obscurity surrounds them, for they fully explain themselves in their own terms.

140   Countless literary products belong to this class: all the novels dealing with love, the family milieu, crime and society, together with didactic poetry, the greater number of lyrics, and drama both tragic and comic. Whatever artistic form they may take, their contents always derive from the sphere of conscious human experience – from the psychic foreground of life, we might say. That is why I call this mode of creation 'psychological'; it remains within the limits of the psychologically intelligible. Everything it embraces – the experience as well as its artistic expression – belongs to the realm of a clearly understandable psychology. Even the psychic raw material, the experiences themselves, have nothing strange about them; on the contrary, they have been known from the beginning of time – passion and its fated outcome, human destiny and its sufferings, eternal nature with its beauty and horror.

141   The gulf that separates the first from the second part of *Faust* marks the difference between the psychological and the visionary modes of artistic creation. Here everything is reversed. The experience that furnishes the material for artistic expression is no longer familiar. It is something strange that derives its existence from the hinterland of man's mind, as if it had emerged from the abyss of prehuman ages, or from a superhuman world of contrasting light and darkness. It is a primordial experience which surpasses man's understanding and to which in his weakness he may easily succumb. The very enormity of the experience gives it its value and its shattering impact. Sublime, pregnant with meaning, yet chilling the blood with its strangeness, it arises from timeless depths; glamorous, daemonic, and grotesque, it bursts asunder our human standards of value and aesthetic form, a terrifying tangle of eternal chaos, a *crimen laesae majestatis humanae*. On the other hand, it can be a revelation whose heights and depths are beyond our fathoming, or a vision of beauty which we can never put into words. This disturbing spectacle of some tremendous process that in every way transcends our human feeling and understanding makes quite other demands upon the powers of the artist than do the experiences of the foreground of life. These never rend the curtain that veils the cosmos; they do not exceed the bounds of our human capacities, and for this reason they are more readily shaped to the demands of art, however shattering they may be for the individual. But the primordial experiences rend from top to bottom the curtain upon which is painted the picture of an ordered world, and allow a glimpse into the unfathomable abyss of the unborn and of things yet to be. Is it a vision of other worlds, or of the darknesses of the spirit, or of the primal beginnings of the human psyche? We cannot say that it is any or none of these.

> Formation, transformation,
> Eternal Mind's eternal recreation.

142   We find such a vision in the *Shepherd of Hermas,* in Dante, in the second part of *Faust,* in Nietzsche's Dionysian experience,[3] in Wagner's *Ring, Tristan,*

Parsifal, in Spitteler's *Olympian Spring,* in William Blake's paintings and poetry, in the *Hypnerotomachia* of the monk Francesco Colonna,[4] in Jacob Boehme's poetic-philosophic stammerings,[5] and in the magnificent but scurrilous imagery of E. T. A. Hoffmann's tale *The Golden Bowl.*[6] In more restricted and succinct form, this primordial experience is the essential content of Rider Haggard's *She* and *Ayesha,* of Benoît's *L'Atlantide,* of Alfred Kubin's *Die andere Seite,* of Meyrink's *Das grüne Gesicht,* of Goetz's *Das Reich ohne Raum,* and of Barlach's *Der tote Tag.* The list might be greatly extended.

143   In dealing with the psychological mode of creation, we need never ask ourselves what the material consists of or what it means. But this question forces itself upon us when we turn to the visionary mode. We are astonished, confused, bewildered, put on our guard or even repelled;[7] we demand commentaries and explanations. We are reminded of nothing in everyday life, but rather of dreams, night-time fears, and the dark, uncanny recesses of the human mind. The public for the most part repudiates this kind of literature, unless it is crudely sensational, and even the literary critic finds it embarrassing. It is true that Dante and Wagner have made his task somewhat easier for him by disguising the visionary experience in a cloak of historical or mythical events, which are then erroneously taken to be the real subject-matter. In both cases the compelling power and deeper meaning of the work do not lie in the historical or mythical material, but in the visionary experience it serves to express. Rider Haggard, pardonably enough, is generally regarded as a romantic story-teller, but in his case too the tale is only a means – admittedly a rather lush one – for capturing a meaningful content.

144   It is strange that a deep darkness surrounds the sources of the visionary material. This is the exact opposite of what we find in the psychological mode of creation, and we are led to suspect that this obscurity is not unintentional. We are naturally inclined to suppose, under the influence of Freudian psychology, that some highly personal experiences must lie behind all this phantasmagoric darkness, which would help to explain that strange vision of chaos, and why it sometimes seems as if the poet were intentionally concealing the source of his experience. From here it is only a step to the conjecture that this kind of art is pathological and neurotic, but a step that is justified in so far as the visionary material exhibits peculiarities which are observed in the fantasies of the insane. Conversely, psychotic products often contain a wealth of meaning such as is ordinarily found only in the works of a genius. One will naturally feel tempted to regard the whole phenomenon from the standpoint of pathology and to explain the strange images as substitute figures and attempts at concealment. It is easy enough to suppose that an intimate personal experience underlies the 'primordial vision,' an experience that cannot be reconciled with morality. It may, for instance, have been a love affair that seemed morally or aesthetically incompatible with the personality as a whole or with the poet's fictitious view of himself. His ego then sought to repress this experience altogether, or at least its salient features, and make it unrecognizable, i.e., unconscious. For this purpose the whole arsenal of pathological fantasy is called into play, and because this manoeuvre is bound to

be unsatisfactory, it has to be repeated in an almost endless series of fictions. This would account for the proliferation of monstrous, daemonic, grotesque, and perverse figures, which all act as substitutes for the 'unacceptable' reality and at the same time conceal it.

145 Such a view of the poet's psychology has aroused considerable attention and is the only theoretical attempt that has been made so far to give a 'scientific' explanation of the sources of visionary material. If I now put forward my own view, I do so because I assume it is not so well-known, and is less understood, than the one I have just described.

146 The reduction of the vision to a personal experience makes it something unreal and unauthentic – a mere substitute, as we have said. The vision thus loses its primordial quality and becomes nothing but a symptom; the teeming chaos shrinks to the proportions of a psychic disturbance. We feel reassured by this explanation, and turn back to our picture of a well-ordered cosmos. As practical and reasonable human beings, we never expected it to be perfect; we accept these unavoidable imperfections which we call abnormalities and diseases, and take it for granted that human nature is not exempt from them. The frightening revelation of abysses that defy human understanding is dismissed as illusion, and the poet is regarded as the victim and perpetrator of deception. His primordial experience was 'human, all too human,' so much so that he could not face it and had to conceal its meaning from himself.

147 We should do well, I think, to bear clearly in mind the full consequences of this reduction of art to personal factors, and see where it leads. The truth is that it deflects our attention from the psychology of the work of art and focuses it on the psychology of the artist. The latter presents a problem that cannot be denied, but the work of art exists in its own right and cannot be got rid of by changing it into a personal complex. As to what it means to the artist, whether it is just a game, or a mask, or a source of suffering, or a positive achievement, these are questions which we shall discuss in the next section. Our task for the moment is to interpret the work of art psychologically, and to do this we must take its foundation – the primordial experience – as seriously as we do the experiences underlying personalistic art, which no one doubts are real and important. It is certainly much more difficult to believe that a visionary experience can be real, for it has all the appearance of something that does not fall to the ordinary lot of man. It has about it a fatal suggestion of vague metaphysics, so that we feel obliged to intervene in the name of well-intentioned reasonableness. We are driven to the conclusion that such things simply cannot be taken seriously, or else the world would sink back into benighted superstition. Anyone who does not have distinct leanings towards the occult will be inclined to dismiss visionary experiences as 'lively fantasy' or 'poetic licence.' The poets themselves contribute to this by putting a wholesome distance between themselves and their work. Spitteler, for example, maintained that his *Olympian Spring* 'meant' nothing, and that he could just as well have sung: 'May is come, tra-la-la-la-la!' Poets are human too, and what they say about their work is often far from being the best word on the subject. It seems as if we

have to defend the seriousness of the visionary experience against the personal resistance of the poet himself.

148   In the *Shepherd of Hermas,* the *Divine Comedy,* and *Faust,* we catch echoes of a preliminary love-episode which culminates in a visionary experience. There is no ground for the assumption that the normal, human experience in the first part of *Faust* is repudiated or concealed in the second, or that Goethe was normal at the time when he wrote Part I but in a neurotic state of mind when he wrote Part II. These three works cover a period of nearly two thousand years, and in each of them we find the undisguised personal love-episode not only connected with the weightier visionary experience but actually subordinated to it. This testimony is significant, for it shows that in the work of art (irrespective of the personal psychology of the poet) the vision represents a deeper and more impressive experience than human passion. In works of art of this nature – and we must never confuse them with the artist as a person – it cannot be doubted that the vision is a genuine primordial experience, no matter what the rationalists may say. It is not something derived or secondary, it is not symptomatic of something else, it is a true symbol – that is, an expression for something real but unknown. The love-episode is a real experience really suffered, and so is the vision. It is not for us to say whether its content is of a physical, psychic, or metaphysical nature. In itself it had psychic reality, and this is no less real than physical reality. Human passion falls within the sphere of conscious experience, while the object of the vision lies beyond it. Through our senses we experience the known, but our intuitions point to things that are unknown and hidden, that by their very nature are secret. If ever they become conscious, they are intentionally kept secret and concealed, for which reason they have been regarded from earliest times as mysterious, uncanny, and deceptive. They are hidden from man, and he hides himself from them out of religious awe, protecting himself with the shield of science and reason. The ordered cosmos he believes in by day is meant to protect him from the fear of chaos that besets him by night – his enlightenment is born of night-fears! What if there were a living agency beyond our everyday human world – something even more purposeful than electrons? Do we delude ourselves in thinking that we possess and control our own psyches, and is what science calls the 'psyche' not just a question-mark arbitrarily confined within the skull, but rather a door that opens upon the human world from a world beyond, allowing unknown and mysterious powers to act upon man and carry him on the wings of the night to a more than personal destiny? It even seems as if the love-episode had served as a mere release, or had been unconsciously arranged for a definite purpose, and as if the personal experience were only a prelude to the all-important 'divine comedy.'

149   The creator of this kind of art is not the only one who is in touch with the night-side of life; prophets and seers are nourished by it too. St. Augustine says: 'And higher still we soared, thinking in our minds and speaking and marvelling at Your works: and so we came to our own souls, and went beyond them to reach at last that region of richness unending, where You feed Israel forever with the food of truth...'[8] But this same region also has its victims: the great evil-doers and

destroyers who darken the face of the times, and the madmen who approach too near to the fire: 'Who among us shall dwell with the devouring fire? Who among us shall dwell with everlasting burnings?'[9] It is true indeed that those whom the gods wish to destroy they first make mad. However dark and unconscious this night-world may be, it is not wholly unfamiliar. Man has known it from time immemorial, and for primitives it is a self-evident part of their cosmos. It is only we who have repudiated it because of our fear of superstition and metaphysics, building up in its place an apparently safer and more manageable world of consciousness in which natural law operates like human law in a society. The poet now and then catches sight of the figures that people the night-world – spirits, demons, and gods; he feels the secret quickening of human fate by a suprahuman design, and has a presentiment of incomprehensible happenings in the pleroma. In short, he catches a glimpse of the psychic world that terrifies the primitive and is at the same time his greatest hope. It would, incidentally, be an interesting subject for research to investigate how far our recently invented fear of superstition and our materialistic outlook are derived from, and are a further development of, primitive magic and the fear of ghosts. At any rate the fascination exerted by depth psychology and the equally violent resistance it evokes are not without relevance to our theme.

150   From the very beginnings of human society we find traces of man's efforts to banish his dark forebodings by expressing them in a magical or propitiatory form. Even in the Rhodesian rock-drawings of the Stone Age there appears, side by side with amazingly lifelike pictures of animals, an abstract pattern – a double cross contained in a circle. This design has turned up in practically every culture, and we find it today not only in Christian churches but in Tibetan monasteries as well. It is the so-called sun-wheel, and since it dates from a time when the wheel had not yet been invented, it cannot have had its origin in any experience of the external world. It is rather a symbol for some inner experience, and as a representation of this it is probably just as lifelike as the famous rhinoceros with tick-birds on its back. There has never been a primitive culture that did not possess a highly developed system of secret teaching, a body of lore concerning the things that lie beyond man's earthly existence, and of wise rules of conduct.[10] The men's councils and the totem clans preserve this knowledge, and it is handed down to the younger men in the rites of initiation. The mysteries of the Graeco-Roman world performed the same function, which has left behind a rich deposit in the world's mythologies.

151   It is therefore to be expected that the poet will turn to mythological figures in order to give suitable expression to his experience. Nothing would be more mistaken than to suppose that he is working with second-hand material. On the contrary, the primordial experience is the source of his creativeness, but it is so dark and amorphous that it requires the related mythological imagery to give it form. In itself it is wordless and imageless, for it is a vision seen 'as in a glass, darkly.' It is nothing but a tremendous intuition striving for expression. It is like a whirlwind that seizes everything within reach and assumes visible form as it

swirls upward. Since the expression can never match the richness of the vision and can never exhaust its possibilities, the poet must have at his disposal a huge store of material if he is to communicate even a fraction of what he has glimpsed, and must make use of difficult and contradictory images in order to express the strange paradoxes of his vision. Dante decks out his experience in all the imagery of heaven, purgatory, and hell; Goethe brings in the Blocksberg and the Greek underworld; Wagner needs the whole corpus of Nordic myth, including the Parsifal saga; Nietzsche resorts to the hieratic style of the bard and legendary seer; Blake presses into his service the phantasmagoric world of India, the Old Testament, and the Apocalypse; and Spitteler borrows old names for the new figures that pour in alarming profusion from his muse's cornucopia. Nothing is missing in the whole gamut that ranges from the ineffably sublime to the perversely grotesque.

152 The psychologist can do little to elucidate this variegated spectacle except provide comparative material and a terminology for its discussion. Thus, what appears in the vision is the imagery of the collective unconscious. This is the matrix of consciousness and has its own inborn structure. According to phylogenetic law, the psychic structure must, like the anatomical, show traces of the earlier stages of evolution it has passed through. This is in fact so in the case of the unconscious, for in dreams and mental disturbances psychic products come to the surface which show all the traits of primitive levels of development, not only in their form but also in their content and meaning, so that we might easily take them for fragments of esoteric doctrines. Mythological motifs frequently appear, but clothed in modern dress; for instance, instead of the eagle of Zeus, or the great roc, there is an airplane; the fight with the dragon is a railway smash; the dragon-slaying hero is an operatic tenor; the Earth Mother is a stout lady selling vegetables; the Pluto who abducts Persephone is a reckless chauffeur, and so on. What is of particular importance for the study of literature, however, is that the manifestations of the collective unconscious are compensatory to the conscious attitude, so that they have the effect of bringing a one-sided, unadapted, or dangerous state of consciousness back into equilibrium. This function can also be observed in the symptomatology of neurosis and in the delusions of the insane, where the process of compensation is often perfectly obvious – for instance in the case of people who have anxiously shut themselves off from the world and suddenly discover that their most intimate secrets are known and talked about by everybody. The compensation is, of course, not always as crass as this; with neurotics it is much more subtle, and in dreams – particularly, in one's own dreams – it is often a complete mystery at first not only to the layman but even to the specialist, however staggeringly simple it turns out to be once it has been understood. But, as we know, the simplest things are often the most difficult to understand.

153 If we disregard for the moment the possibility that *Faust* was compensatory to Goethe's conscious attitude, the question that arises is this: in what relation does it stand to the conscious outlook of his time, and can this relation also be regarded as compensatory? Great poetry draws its strength from the life of mankind, and

we completely miss its meaning if we try to derive it from personal factors. Whenever the collective unconscious becomes a living experience and is brought to bear upon the conscious outlook of an age, this event is a creative act which is of importance for a whole epoch. A work of art is produced that may truthfully be called a message to generations of men. So *Faust* touches something in the soul of every German, as Jacob Burckhardt has already remarked.[11] So also Dante's fame is immortal, and the *Shepherd of Hermas* was very nearly included in the New Testament canon. Every period has its bias, its particular prejudice, and its psychic malaise. An epoch is like an individual; it has its own limitations of conscious outlook, and therefore requires a compensatory adjustment. This is effected by the collective unconscious when a poet or seer lends expression to the unspoken desire of his times and shows the way, by word or deed, to its fulfilment – regardless whether this blind collective need results in good or evil, in the salvation of an epoch or its destruction.

154   It is always dangerous to speak of one's own times, because what is at stake is too vast to be comprehended.[12] A few hints must therefore suffice. Francesco Colonna's book takes the form of a dream which depicts the apotheosis of love. It does not tell the story of a human passion, but describes a relationship to the anima, man's subjective image of woman, incarnated in the fictitious figure of the lady Polia. The relationship is played out in the pagan setting of classical antiquity, and this is remarkable because the author, so far as we know, was a monk. His book, written in 1453, compensates the medieval Christian outlook by conjuring up a simultaneously older and more youthful world from Hades, which is at the same time the grave and the fruitful mother.[13] The *Hypnerotomachia* of Colonna, says Linda Fierz-David, 'is the symbol of the living process of growth which had been set going, obscurely and incomprehensibly, in the men of his time, and had made of the Renaissance the beginning of a new era.'[14] Already in Colonna's time the Church was being weakened by schisms, and the age of the great voyages and of scientific discovery was dawning. These tensions between the old and the new are symbolized by the paradoxical figure of Polia, the 'modern' soul of the monk Francesco Colonna. After three centuries of religious schism and the scientific discovery of the world, Goethe paints a picture of the megalomania that threatens the Faustian man, and attempts to redeem the inhumanity of this figure by uniting him with the Eternal Feminine, the maternal Sophia. She is the highest manifestation of the anima, stripped of the pagan savagery of the nymph Polia. But this compensation of Faust's inhumanity had no lasting effect, for Nietzsche, after proclaiming the death of God, announces the birth of the Superman, who in turn is doomed to destruction. Nietzsche's contemporary, Spitteler, transforms the waxing and waning of the gods into a myth of the seasons. If we compare his *Prometheus and Epimetheus*[15] with the drama that is being enacted on the world stage today, the prophetic significance of the great work of art will become painfully apparent.[16] Each of these poets speaks with the voice of thousands and tens of thousands, foretelling changes in the conscious outlook of his time.

2 The artist

155 The secret of creativeness, like that of the freedom of the will, is a transcendental problem which the psychologist cannot answer but can only describe. The creative personality, too, is a riddle we may try to answer in various ways, but always in vain. Nevertheless, modern psychologists have not been deterred from investigating the problem of the artist and his art. Freud thought he had found a key to the work of art by deriving it from the personal experience of the artist.[17] This was a possible approach, for it was conceivable that a work of art might, like a neurosis, be traced back to complexes. It was Freud's great discovery that neuroses have a quite definite psychic cause, and that they originate in real or imagined emotional experiences in early childhood. Some of his followers, in particular Rank and Stekel, adopted a similar approach and arrived at similar results. It is undeniable that the artist's personal psychology may occasionally be traced out in the roots and in the furthest ramifications of his work. This view, that personal factors in many ways determine the artist's choice of material and the form he gives it, is not in itself new. Credit, however, is certainly due to the Freudian school for showing how far-reaching this influence is and the curious analogies to which it gives rise.

156 Freud considers a neurosis to be a substitute for a direct means of gratification. For him it is something inauthentic – a mistake, a subterfuge, an excuse, a refusal to face facts; in short, something essentially negative that should never have been. One hardly dares to put in a good word for a neurosis, since it is apparently nothing but a meaningless and therefore irritating disturbance. By treating a work of art as something that can be analysed in terms of the artist's repressions we bring it into questionable proximity with a neurosis, where, in a sense, it finds itself in good company, for the Freudian method treats religion and philosophy in the same way. No legitimate objection can be raised to this if it is admitted to be no more than an unearthing of those personal determinants without which a work of art is unthinkable. But if it is claimed that such an analysis explains the work of art itself, then a categorical denial is called for. The essence of a work of art is not to be found in the personal idiosyncrasies that creep into it – indeed, the more there are of them, the less it is a work of art – but in its rising above the personal and speaking from the mind and heart of the artist to the mind and heart of mankind. The personal aspect of art is a limitation and even a vice. Art that is only personal, or predominantly so, truly deserves to be treated as a neurosis. When the Freudian school advances the opinion that all artists are undeveloped personalities with marked infantile autoerotic traits, this judgment may be true of the artist as a man, but it is not applicable to the man as an artist. In this capacity he is neither autoerotic, nor heteroerotic, nor erotic in any sense. He is in the highest degree objective, impersonal, and even inhuman – or suprahuman – for as an artist he is nothing but his work, and not a human being.

157 Every creative person is a duality or a synthesis of contradictory qualities. On the one side he is a human being with a personal life, while on the other he is an impersonal creative process. As a human being he may be sound or morbid, and

his personal psychology can and should be explained in personal terms. But he can be understood as an artist only in terms of his creative achievement. We should make a great mistake if we reduced the mode of life of an English gentleman, or a Prussian officer, or a cardinal, to personal factors. The gentleman, the officer, and the high ecclesiastic function as impersonal officials, and each role has its own objective psychology. Although the artist is the exact opposite of an official, there is nevertheless a secret analogy between them in so far as a specifically artistic psychology is more collective than personal in character. Art is a kind of innate drive that seizes a human being and makes him its instrument. The artist is not a person endowed with free will who seeks his own ends, but one who allows art to realize its purposes through him. As a human being he may have moods and a will and personal aims, but as an artist he is 'man' in a higher sense – he is 'collective man,' a vehicle and moulder of the unconscious psychic life of mankind. That is his office, and it is sometimes so heavy a burden that he is fated to sacrifice happiness and everything that makes life worth living for the ordinary human being. As K. G. Carus says: 'Strange are the ways by which genius is announced, for what distinguishes so supremely endowed a being is that, for all the freedom of his life and the clarity of his thought, he is everywhere hemmed round and prevailed upon by the Unconscious, the mysterious god within him; so that ideas flow to him – he knows not whence; he is driven to work and to create – he knows not to what end; and is mastered by an impulse for constant growth and development – he knows not whither.'[18]

158   In these circumstances it is not at all surprising that the artist is an especially interesting specimen for the critical analysis of the psychologist. His life cannot be otherwise than full of conflicts, for two forces are at war within him: on the one hand the justified longing of the ordinary man for happiness, satisfaction, and security, and on the other a ruthless passion for creation which may go so far as to override every personal desire. If the lives of artists are as a rule so exceedingly unsatisfactory, not to say tragic, it is not because of some sinister dispensation of fate, but because of some inferiority in their personality or an inability to adapt. A person must pay dearly for the divine gift of creative fire. It is as though each of us was born with a limited store of energy. In the artist, the strongest force in his make-up, that is, his creativeness, will seize and all but monopolize this energy, leaving so little over that nothing of value can come of it. The creative impulse can drain him of his humanity to such a degree that the personal ego can exist only on a primitive or inferior level and is driven to develop all sorts of defects – ruthlessness, selfishness ('autoeroticism'), vanity, and other infantile traits. These inferiorities are the only means by which it can maintain its vitality and prevent itself from being wholly depleted. The autoeroticism of certain artists is like that of illegitimate or neglected children who from their earliest years develop bad qualities to protect themselves from the destructive influence of a loveless environment. Such children easily become ruthless and selfish, and later display an invincible egoism by remaining all their lives infantile and helpless or by actively offending against morality and the law. How can we doubt that it is his art that

explains the artist, and not the insufficiencies and conflicts of his personal life? These are nothing but the regrettable results of his being an artist, a man upon whom a heavier burden is laid than upon ordinary mortals. A special ability demands a greater expenditure of energy, which must necessarily leave a deficit on some other side of life.

159   It makes no difference whether the artist knows that his work is generated, grows and matures within him, or whether he imagines that it is his own invention. In reality it grows out of him as a child its mother. The creative process has a feminine quality, and the creative work arises from unconscious depths – we might truly say from the realm of the Mothers. Whenever the creative force predominates, life is ruled and shaped by the unconscious rather than by the conscious will, and the ego is swept along on an underground current, becoming nothing more than a helpless observer of events. The progress of the work becomes the poet's fate and determines his psychology. It is not Goethe that creates *Faust*, but *Faust* that creates Goethe.[19] And what is *Faust*? *Faust* is essentially a symbol. By this I do not mean that it is an allegory pointing to something all too familiar, but the expression of something profoundly alive in the soul of every German, which Goethe helped to bring to birth. Could we conceive of anyone but a German writing *Faust* or *Thus Spake Zarathustra*? Both of them strike a chord that vibrates in the German psyche, evoking a 'primordial image,' as Burckhardt once called it – the figure of a healer or teacher of mankind, or of a wizard. It is the archetype of the Wise Old Man, the helper and redeemer, but also of the magician, deceiver, corrupter, and tempter. This image has lain buried and dormant in the unconscious since the dawn of history; it is awakened whenever the times are out of joint and a great error deflects society from the right path. For when people go astray they feel the need of a guide or teacher, and even of a physician. The seductive error is like a poison that can also act as a cure, and the shadow of a saviour can turn into a fiendish destroyer. These opposing forces are at work in the mythical healer himself: the physician who heals wounds is himself the bearer of a wound, a classic example being Chiron.[20] In Christianity it is the wound in the side of Christ, the great physician. Faust, characteristically enough, is unwounded, which means that he is untouched by the moral problem. A man can be as high-minded as Faust and as devilish as Mephistopheles if he is able to split his personality into two halves, and only then is he capable of feeling 'six thousand feet beyond good and evil.' Mephistopheles was cheated of his reward, Faust's soul, and for this he presented a bloody reckoning a hundred years later. But who now seriously believes that poets utter truths that apply to all men? And if they do, in what way would we have to regard the work of art?

160   In itself, an archetype is neither good nor evil. It is morally neutral, like the gods of antiquity, and becomes good or evil only by contact with the conscious mind, or else a paradoxical mixture of both. Whether it will be conducive to good or evil is determined, knowingly or unknowingly, by the conscious attitude. There are many such archetypal images, but they do not appear in the dreams of individuals or in works of art unless they are activated by a deviation from the

middle way. Whenever conscious life becomes one-sided or adopts a false attitude, these images 'instinctively' rise to the surface in dreams and in the visions of artists and seers to restore the psychic balance, whether of the individual or of the epoch.

161 In this way the work of the artist meets the psychic needs of the society in which he lives, and therefore means more than his personal fate, whether he is aware of it or not. Being essentially the instrument of his work, he is subordinate to it, and we have no right to expect him to interpret it for us. He has done his utmost by giving it form, and must leave the interpretation to others and to the future. A great work of art is like a dream; for all its apparent obviousness it does not explain itself and is always ambiguous. A dream never says 'you ought' or 'this is the truth.' It presents an image in much the same way as nature allows a plant to grow, and it is up to us to draw conclusions. If a person has a nightmare, it means he is either too much given to fear or too exempt from it; if he dreams of a wise old man, it means he is either too much of a pedant or else in need of a teacher. In a subtle way both meanings come to the same thing, as we realize when we let a work of art act upon us as it acted upon the artist. To grasp its meaning, we must allow it to shape us as it shaped him. Then we also understand the nature of his primordial experience. He has plunged into the healing and redeeming depths of the collective psyche, where man is not lost in the isolation of consciousness and its errors and sufferings, but where all men are caught in a common rhythm which allows the individual to communicate his feelings and strivings to mankind as a whole.

162 This re-immersion in the state of *participation mystique* is the secret of artistic creation and of the effect which great art has upon us, for at that level of experience it is no longer the weal or woe of the individual that counts, but the life of the collective. That is why every great work of art is objective and impersonal, and yet profoundly moving. And that is also why the personal life of the artist is at most a help or a hindrance, but is never essential to his creative task. He may go the way of the Philistine, a good citizen, a fool, or a criminal. His personal career may be interesting and inevitable, but it does not explain his art.

Notes

1 [First published as 'Psychologie und Dichtung' in *Philosophie der Literaturwissenschaft* (Berlin, 1930), ed. by Emil Ermatinger; expanded and revised in *Gestaltungen des Unbewussten* (Zurich, 1950). The original version was translated by Eugene Jolas as 'Psychology and Poetry,' *transition: An International Quarterly for Creative Experiment*, no, 19/20 (June, 1930); also translated by W. S. Dell and Cary F. Baynes, in *Modern Man in Search of a Soul* (London and New York, 1933).

   A typescript of an introduction was found among Jung's posthumous papers; it is first published here, in translation. Evidently Jung used the introduction when he read the essay as a lecture, though nothing certain is known of such an occasion. Cf. p. 132, par. (1).–EDITORS.]

2 [The designation 'psychological' is somewhat confusing in this context because, as the subsequent discussion makes clear, the 'visionary' mode deals equally with

'psychological' material. Moreover, 'psychological' is used in still another sense in pars. 136–37, where the 'psychological novel' is contrasted with the 'non-psychological novel.'

[The term 'personalistic' suggests itself as coming closer to defining the material in question, which derives from 'the sphere of conscious human experience – from the psychic foreground of life' (par. 140). The term 'personalistic' occurs elsewhere in Jung's writings, e.g., in *The Practice of Psychotherapy*, pp. 95 and 185 n. 34. Both times it characterizes a particular kind of psychology. The second instance is the more significant in that 'personalistic' is contrasted with 'archetypal,' and this would appear to be precisely the distinction intended between the two kinds of psychological material and the two modes of artistic creation.–EDITORS.]

3 Cf. my essay 'Wotan,' pars, 375ff.
4 Recently interpreted along the lines of analytical psychology by Linda Fierz-David, in *The Dream of Poliphilo*.
5 Some samples of Boehme may be found in my *Psychology and Alchemy*, pars. 214 ff., and in 'A Study in the Process of Individuation,' pars. 533ff., 578ff.
6 Cf. the detailed study by Aniela Jaffé in *Gestaltungen des Unbewussten*.
7 One has only to think of James Joyce's *Ulysses*, which is a work of the greatest significance in spite or perhaps because of its nihilistic tendencies.
8 *Confessions* (trans. Sheed), p. 158.
9 Isaiah 33:14.
10 Die *Stammeslehren der Dschagga*, edited by Bruno Gutmann, comprises no less than three volumes and runs to 1975 pages!
11 Letter to Albert Brenner. [In 1855. See Dru trans, of Burckhardt's letters, p. 116, and Jung, *Symbols of Transformation*, par. 45, n. 45.–EDITORS.]
12 Written in 1929.
13 *The Dream of Poliphilo*, pp. 234ff.
14 Ibid., p. 27.
15 I am referring to the first version, written in prose.
16 Cf. *Psychological Types*, Pars. 321ff.
17 See his. essays on Jensen's *Gradiva* (Standard Edition, IX), and on Leonardo da Vinci (XI).
18 *Psyche*, ed, Ludwig Klages, p. 158.
19 Eckermann's dream, in which he saw Faust and Mephistopheles falling to earth in the form of a double meteor, recalls the motif of the Dioscuri (cf. the motif of the two friends in my essay 'Concerning Rebirth,' pp. 135ff.), and this sheds light on an essential characteristic of Goethe's psyche. An especially subtle point here is Eckermann's remark that the swift and horned figure of Mephisto reminded him of Mercurius. This observation is in full accord with the alchemical nature of Goethe's masterpiece. (I have to thank my colleague W. Kranefeldt for refreshing my memory of Eckermann's *Conversations*.)
20 Cf. C. Kerényi, *Asklepios*, pp. 78f.

Chapter 12

The difference between Eastern and Western thinking[1]

759 Dr. Evans-Wentz has entrusted me with the task of commenting on a text which contains an important exposition of Eastern 'psychology.' The very fact that I have to use quotation marks shows the dubious applicability of this term. It is perhaps not superfluous to mention that the East has produced nothing equivalent to what we call psychology, but rather philosophy or metaphysics. Critical philosophy, the mother of modern psychology, is as foreign to the East as to medieval Europe. Thus the word 'mind,' as used in the East, has the connotation of something metaphysical. Our Western conception of mind has lost this connotation since the Middle Ages, and the word has now come to signify a 'psychic function.' Despite the fact that we neither know nor pretend to know what 'psyche' is, we can deal with the phenomenon of 'mind.' We do not assume that the mind is a metaphysical entity or that there is any connection between an individual mind and a hypothetical Universal Mind. Our psychology is, therefore, a science of mere phenomena without any metaphysical implications. The development of Western philosophy during the last two centuries has succeeded in isolating the mind in its own sphere and in severing it from its primordial oneness with the universe. Man himself has ceased to be the microcosm and eidolon of the cosmos, and his 'anima' is no longer the consubstantial *scintilla*, or spark of the *Anima Mundi*, the World Soul.

760 Psychology accordingly treats all metaphysical claims and assertions as mental phenomena, and regards them as statements about the mind and its structure that derive ultimately from certain unconscious dispositions. It does not consider them to be absolutely valid or even capable of establishing a metaphysical truth. We have no intellectual means of ascertaining whether this attitude is right or wrong. We only know that there is no evidence for, and no possibility of proving, the validity of a metaphysical postulate such as 'Universal Mind.' If the mind asserts the existence of a Universal Mind, we hold that it is merely making an assertion. We do not assume that by such an assertion the existence of a Universal Mind has been established. There is no argument against this reasoning, but no evidence, either, that our conclusion is ultimately right. In other words, it is just as possible that our mind is nothing but a perceptible manifestation of a Universal Mind. Yet we do not know, and we cannot even see, how it would be possible to recognize

whether this is so or not. Psychology therefore holds that the mind cannot establish or assert anything beyond itself.

761 If, then, we accept the restrictions imposed upon the capacity of our mind, we demonstrate our common sense. I admit it is something of a sacrifice, inasmuch as we bid farewell to that miraculous world in which mind-created things and beings move and live. This is the world of the primitive, where even inanimate objects are endowed with a living, healing, magic power, through which they participate in us and we in them. Sooner or later we had to understand that their potency was really ours, and that their significance was our projection. The theory of knowledge is only the last step out of humanity's childhood, out of a world where mind-created figures populated a metaphysical heaven and hell.

762 Despite this inevitable epistemological criticism, however, we have held fast to the religious belief that the organ of faith enables man to know God. The West thus developed a new disease: the conflict between science and religion. The critical philosophy of science became as it were negatively metaphysical – in other words, materialistic – on the basis of an error in judgment; matter was assumed to be a tangible and recognizable reality. Yet this is a thoroughly metaphysical concept hypostatized by uncritical minds. Matter is an hypothesis. When you say 'matter,' you are really creating a symbol for something unknown, which may just as well be 'spirit' or anything else; it may even be God. Religious faith, on the other hand, refuses to give up its pre-critical *Weltanschauung*. In contradiction to the saying of Christ, the faithful try to *remain* children instead of becoming *as* children. They cling to the world of childhood. A famous modern theologian confesses in his autobiography that Jesus has been his good friend 'from childhood on.' Jesus is the perfect example of a man who preached something different from the religion of his forefathers. But the *imitatio Christi* does not appear to include the mental and spiritual sacrifice which he had to undergo at the beginning of his career and without which he would never have become a saviour.

763 The conflict between science and religion is in reality a misunderstanding of both. Scientific materialism has merely introduced a new hypostasis, and that is an intellectual sin. It has given another name to the supreme principle of reality and has assumed that this created a new thing and destroyed an old thing. Whether you call the principle of existence 'God,' 'matter,' 'energy,' or anything else you like, you have created nothing; you have simply changed a symbol. The materialist is a metaphysician *malgré lui*. Faith, on the other hand, tries to retain a primitive mental condition on merely sentimental grounds. It is unwilling to give up the primitive, childlike relationship to mind-created and hypostatized figures; it wants to go on enjoying the security and confidence of a world still presided over by powerful, responsible, and kindly parents. Faith may include a *sacrificium intellectus* (provided there is an intellect to sacrifice), but certainly not a sacrifice of feeling. In this way the faithful *remain* children instead of becoming *as* children, and they do not gain their life because they have not lost it. Furthermore, faith collides with science and thus gets its deserts, for it refuses to share in the spiritual adventure of our age.

764 Any honest thinker has to admit the insecurity of all metaphysical positions, and in particular of all creeds. He has also to admit the unwarrantable nature of all metaphysical assertions and face the fact that there is no evidence whatever for the ability of the human mind to pull itself up by its own bootstrings, that is, to establish anything transcendental.

765 Materialism is a metaphysical reaction against the sudden realization that cognition is a mental faculty and, if carried beyond the human plane, a projection. The reaction was 'metaphysical' in so far as the man of average philosophical education failed to see through the implied hypostasis, not realizing that 'matter' was just another name for the supreme principle. As against this, the attitude of faith shows how reluctant people were to accept philosophical criticism. It also demonstrates how great is the fear of letting go one's hold on the securities of childhood and of dropping into a strange, unknown world ruled by forces unconcerned with man. Nothing really changes in either case; man and his surroundings remain the same. He has only to realize that he is shut up inside his mind and cannot step beyond it, even in insanity; and that the appearance of his world or of his gods very much depends upon his own mental condition.

766 In the first place, the structure of the mind is responsible for anything we may assert about metaphysical matters, as I have already pointed out. We have also begun to understand that the intellect is not an *ens per se*, or an independent mental faculty, but a psychic function dependent upon the conditions of the psyche as a whole. A philosophical statement is the product of a certain personality living at a certain time in a certain place, and not the outcome of a purely logical and impersonal procedure. To that extent it is chiefly subjective; whether it has an objective validity or not depends on whether there are few or many persons who argue in the same way. The isolation of man within his mind as a result of epistemological criticism has naturally led to psychological criticism. This kind of criticism is not popular with the philosophers, since they like to consider the philosophic intellect as the perfect and unconditioned instrument of philosophy. Yet this intellect of theirs is a function dependent upon an individual psyche and determined on all sides by subjective conditions, quite apart from environmental influences. Indeed, we have already become so accustomed to this point of view that 'mind' has lost its universal character altogether. It has become a more or less individualized affair, with no trace of its former cosmic aspect as the *anima rationalis*. Mind is understood nowadays as a subjective, even an arbitrary, thing. Now that the formerly hypostatized 'universal ideas' have turned out to be mental principles, it is dawning upon us to what an extent our whole experience of so-called reality is psychic; as a matter of fact, everything thought, felt, or perceived is a psychic image, and the world itself exists only so far as we are able to produce an image of it. We are so deeply impressed with the truth of our imprisonment in, and limitation by, the psyche that we are ready to admit the existence in it even of things we do *not* know: we call them 'the unconscious.'

767 The seemingly universal and metaphysical scope of the mind has thus been narrowed down to the small circle of individual consciousness, profoundly aware

of its almost limitless subjectivity and of its infantile-archaic tendency to heedless projection and illusion. Many scientifically minded persons have even sacrificed their religious and philosophical leanings for fear of uncontrolled subjectivism. By way of compensation for the loss of a world that pulsed with our blood and breathed with our breath, we have developed an enthusiasm for *facts* – mountains of facts, far beyond any single individual's power to survey. We have the pious hope that this incidental accumulation of facts will form a meaningful whole, but nobody is quite sure, because no human brain can possibly comprehend the gigantic sum total of this mass-produced knowledge. The facts bury us, but whoever dares to speculate must pay for it with a bad conscience – and rightly so, for he will instantly be tripped up by the facts.

768   Western psychology knows the mind as the mental functioning of a psyche. It is the 'mentality' of an individual. An impersonal Universal Mind is still to be met with in the sphere of philosophy, where it seems to be a relic of the original human 'soul.' This picture of our Western outlook may seem a little drastic, but I do not think it is far from the truth. At all events, something of the kind presents itself as soon as we are confronted with the Eastern mentality. In the East, mind is a cosmic factor, the very essence of existence; while in the West we have just begun to understand that it is the essential condition of cognition, and hence of the cognitive existence of the world. There is no conflict between religion and science in the East, because no science is there based upon the passion for facts, and no religion upon mere faith; there is religious cognition and cognitive religion.[2] With us, man is incommensurably small and the grace of God is everything; but in the East, man is God and he redeems himself. The gods of Tibetan Buddhism belong to the sphere of illusory separateness and mind-created projections, and yet they exist; but so far as we are concerned an illusion remains an illusion, and thus is nothing at all. It is a paradox, yet nevertheless true, that with us a thought has no proper reality; we treat it as if it were a nothingness. Even though the thought be true in itself, we hold that it exists only by virtue of certain facts which it is said to formulate. We can produce a most devastating fact like the atom bomb with the help of this ever-changing phantasmagoria of virtually nonexistent thoughts, but it seems wholly absurd to us that one could ever establish the reality of thought itself.

769   'Psychic reality' is a controversial concept, like 'psyche' or 'mind.' By the latter terms some understand consciousness and its contents, others allow the existence of 'dark' or 'subconscious' representations. Some include instincts in the psychic realm, others exclude them. The vast majority consider the psyche to be a result of biochemical processes in the brain cells. A few conjecture that it is the psyche that makes the cortical cells function. Some identify 'life' with psyche. But only an insignificant minority regards the psychic phenomenon as a category of existence *per se* and draws the necessary conclusions. It is indeed paradoxical that *the* category of existence, the indispensable *sine qua non* of all existence, namely the psyche, should be treated as if it were only semi-existent. Psychic existence is the only category of existence of which we have *immediate*

knowledge, since nothing can be known unless it first appears as a psychic image. Only psychic existence is immediately verifiable. To the extent that the world does not assume the form of a psychic image, it is virtually non-existent. This is a fact which, with few exceptions – as for instance in Schopenhauer's philosophy – the West has not yet fully realized. But Schopenhauer was influenced by Buddhism and by the Upanishads.

770   Even a superficial acquaintance with Eastern thought is sufficient to show that a fundamental difference divides East and West. The East bases itself upon psychic reality, that is, upon the psyche as the main and unique condition of existence. It seems as if this Eastern recognition were a psychological or temperamental fact rather than a result of philosophical reasoning. It is a typically introverted point of view, contrasted with the equally typical extraverted point of view of the West.[3] Introversion and extraversion are known to be temperamental or even constitutional attitudes which are never intentionally adopted in normal circumstances. In exceptional cases they may be produced at will, but only under very special conditions. Introversion is, if one may so express it, the 'style' of the East, an habitual and collective attitude, just as extraversion is the 'style' of the West. Introversion is felt here as something abnormal, morbid, or otherwise objectionable. Freud identifies it with an autoerotic, 'narcissistic' attitude of mind. He shares his negative position with the National Socialist philosophy of modern Germany,[4] which accuses introversion of being an offence against community feeling. In the East, however, our cherished extraversion is depreciated as illusory desirousness, as existence in the *samsāra*, the very essence of the *nidāna*-chain which culminates in the sum of the world's sufferings.[5] Anyone with practical knowledge of the mutual depreciation of values between introvert and extravert will understand the emotional conflict between the Eastern and the Western standpoint. For those who know something of the history of European philosophy the bitter wrangling about 'universals' which began with Plato will provide an instructive example. I do not wish to go into all the ramifications of this conflict between introversion and extraversion, but I must mention the religious aspects of the problem. The Christian West considers man to be wholly dependent upon the grace of God, or at least upon the Church as the exclusive and divinely sanctioned earthly instrument of man's redemption. The East, however, insists that man is the sole cause of his higher development, for it believes in 'self-liberation.'

771   The religious point of view always expresses and formulates the essential psychological attitude and its specific prejudices, even in the case of people who have forgotten, or who have never heard of, their own religion. In spite of everything, the West is thoroughly Christian as far as its psychology is concerned. Tertullian's *anima naturaliter Christiana* holds true throughout the West – not, as he thought, in the religious sense, but in a psychological one. Grace comes from elsewhere; at all events from outside. Every other point of view is sheer heresy. Hence it is quite understandable why the human psyche is suffering from undervaluation. Anyone who dares to establish a connection between the psyche and the idea of God is immediately accused of 'psychologism' or suspected of morbid

'mysticism.' The East, on the other hand, compassionately tolerates those 'lower' spiritual stages where man, in his blind ignorance of karma, still bothers about sin and tortures his imagination with a belief in absolute gods, who, if he only looked deeper, are nothing but the veil of illusion woven by his own unenlightened mind. The psyche is therefore all-important; it is the all-pervading Breath, the Buddha-essence; it is the Buddha-Mind, the One, the *Dharmakāya*. All existence emanates from it, and all separate forms dissolve back into it. This is the basic psychological prejudice that permeates Eastern man in every fibre of his being, seeping into all his thoughts, feelings, and deeds, no matter what creed he professes.

772　In the same way Western man is Christian, no matter to what denomination his Christianity belongs. For him man is small inside, he is next to nothing; moreover, as Kierkegaard says, 'before God man is always wrong.' By fear, repentance, promises, submission, self-abasement, good deeds, and praise he propitiates the great power, which is not himself but *totaliter aliter*, the Wholly Other, altogether perfect and 'outside,' the only reality.[6] If you shift the formula a bit and substitute for God some other power, for instance the world or money, you get a complete picture of Western man – assiduous, fearful, devout, self-abasing, enterprising, greedy, and violent in his pursuit of the goods of this world: possessions, health, knowledge, technical mastery, public welfare, political power, conquest, and so on. What are the great popular movements of our time? Attempts to grab the money or property of others and to protect our own. The mind is chiefly employed in devising suitable 'isms' to hide the real motives or to get more loot. I refrain from describing what would happen to Eastern man should he forget his ideal of Buddhahood, for I do not want to give such an unfair advantage to my Western prejudices. But I cannot help raising the question of whether it is possible, or indeed advisable, for either to imitate the other's standpoint. The difference between them is so vast that one can see no reasonable possibility of this, much less its advisability. You cannot mix fire and water. The Eastern attitude stultifies the Western, and vice versa. You cannot be a good Christian and redeem yourself, nor can you be a Buddha and worship God. It is much better to accept the conflict, for it admits only of an irrational solution, if any.

773　By an inevitable decree of fate the West is becoming acquainted with the peculiar facts of Eastern spirituality. It is useless either to belittle these facts, or to build false and treacherous bridges over yawning gaps. Instead of learning the spiritual techniques of the East by heart and imitating them in a thoroughly Christian way – *imitatio Christi!* – with a correspondingly forced attitude, it would be far more to the point to find out whether there exists in the unconscious an introverted tendency similar to that which has become the guiding spiritual principle of the East. We should then be in a position to build on our own ground with our own methods. If we snatch these things directly from the East, we have merely indulged our Western acquisitiveness, confirming yet again that 'everything good is outside,' whence it has to be fetched and pumped into our barren souls.[7] It seems to me that we have really learned something from the East when we understand that the psyche contains riches enough without having to be primed from outside, and when we feel capable of evolving out of ourselves with or without divine grace. But we cannot embark upon this ambitious enterprise until we have learned how to deal with our spiritual pride and blasphemous self-assertiveness. The Eastern attitude violates the specifically Christian values, and it is no good blinking this fact. If our new attitude is to be genuine, i.e., grounded in our own history, it must be acquired with full consciousness of the Christian values and of the conflict between them and the introverted attitude of the East. We must get at the Eastern values from within and not from without, seeking them in ourselves, in the unconscious. We shall then discover how great is our fear of the unconscious and how formidable are our resistances. Because of these resistances we doubt the very thing that seems so obvious to the East, namely, the *self-liberating power of the introverted mind.*

774 This aspect of the mind is practically unknown to the West, though it forms the most important component of the unconscious. Many people flatly deny the existence of the unconscious, or else they say that it consists merely of instincts, or of repressed or forgotten contents that were once part of the conscious mind. It is safe to assume that what the East calls 'mind' has more to do with our 'unconscious' than with mind as we understand it, which is more or less identical with consciousness. To us, consciousness is inconceivable without an ego; it is equated with the relation of contents to an ego. If there is no ego there is nobody to be conscious of anything. The ego is therefore indispensable to the conscious process. The Eastern mind, however, has no difficulty in conceiving of a consciousness without an ego. Consciousness is deemed capable of transcending its ego condition; indeed, in its 'higher' forms, the ego disappears altogether. Such an ego-less mental condition can only be unconscious to us, for the simple reason that there would be nobody to witness it. I do not doubt the existence of mental states transcending consciousness. But they lose their consciousness to exactly the same degree that they transcend consciousness. I cannot imagine a conscious mental state that does not relate to a subject, that is, to an ego. The ego may be depotentiated – divested, for instance, of its awareness of the body – but so long as there is awareness of something, there must be somebody who is aware. The unconscious, however, is a mental condition of which no ego is aware. It is only by indirect means that we eventually become conscious of the existence of an unconscious. We can observe the manifestation of unconscious fragments of the personality, detached from the patient's consciousness, in insanity. But there is no evidence that the unconscious contents are related to an unconscious centre analogous to the ego; in fact there are good reasons why such a centre is not even probable.

775 The fact that the East can dispose so easily of the ego seems to point to a mind that is not to be identified with our 'mind.' Certainly the ego does not play the same role in Eastern thought as it does with us. It seems as if the Eastern mind were less egocentric, as if its contents were more loosely connected with the subject, and as if greater stress were laid on mental states which include a depotentiated ego. It also seems as if *hatha* yoga were chiefly useful as a means for

extinguishing the ego by fettering its unruly impulses. There is no doubt that the higher forms of yoga, in so far as they strive to reach samādhi, seek a mental condition in which the ego is practically dissolved. Consciousness in our sense of the word is rated a definitely inferior condition, the state of *avidyā* (ignorance), whereas what we call the 'dark background of consciousness' is understood to be a 'higher' consciousness.[8] Thus our concept of the 'collective unconscious' would be the European equivalent of *buddhi*, the enlightened mind.

776 In view of all this, the Eastern form of 'sublimation' amounts to a withdrawal of the centre of psychic gravity from ego-consciousness, which holds a middle position between the body and the ideational processes of the psyche. The lower, semi-physiological strata of the psyche are subdued by *askesis*, i.e., exercises, and kept under control. They are not exactly denied or suppressed by a supreme effort of the will, as is customary in Western sublimation. Rather, the lower psychic strata are adapted and shaped through the patient practice of *hatha* yoga until they no longer interfere with the development of 'higher' consciousness. This peculiar process seems to be aided by the fact that the ego and its desires are checked by the greater importance which the East habitually attaches to the 'subjective factor.'[9] By this I mean the 'dark background' of consciousness, the unconscious. The introverted attitude is characterized in general by an emphasis on the *a priori* data of apperception. As is well known, the act of apperception consists of two phases: first the perception of the object, second the assimilation of the perception to a preexisting pattern or concept by means of which the object is 'comprehended.' The psyche is not a nonentity devoid of all quality; it is a definite system made up of definite conditions and it reacts in a specific way. Every new representation, be it a perception or a spontaneous thought, arouses associations which derive from the storehouse of memory. These leap immediately into consciousness, producing the complex picture of an 'impression,' though this is already a sort of interpretation. The unconscious disposition upon which the quality of the impression depends is what I call the 'subjective factor.' It deserves the qualification 'subjective' because objectivity is hardly ever conferred by a first impression. Usually a rather laborious process of verification, comparison, and analysis is needed to modify and adapt the immediate reactions of the subjective factor.

777 The prominence of the subjective factor does not imply a *personal subjectivism*, despite the readiness of the extraverted attitude to dismiss the subjective factor as 'nothing but' subjective. The psyche and its structure are real enough. They even transform material objects into psychic images, as we have said. They do not perceive waves, but sound; not wave-lengths, but colours. Existence is as we see and understand it. There are innumerable things that can be seen, felt, and understood in a great variety of ways. Quite apart from merely personal prejudices, the psyche assimilates external facts in its own way, which is based ultimately upon the laws or patterns of apperception. These laws do not change, although different ages or different parts of the world call them by different names. On a primitive level people are afraid of witches; on the modern level we are apprehensively aware of microbes. There everybody believes in ghosts, here

everybody believes in vitamins. Once upon a time men were possessed by devils, now they are not less obsessed by ideas, and so on.

778   The subjective factor is made up, in the last resort, of the eternal patterns of psychic functioning. Anyone who relies upon the subjective factor is therefore basing himself on the reality of psychic law. So he can hardly be said to be wrong. If by this means he succeeds in extending his consciousness downwards, to touch the basic laws of psychic life, he is in possession of that truth which the psyche will naturally evolve if not fatally interfered with by the non-psychic, i.e., the external, world. At any rate, his truth could be weighed against the sum of all knowledge acquired through the investigation of externals. We in the West believe that a truth is satisfactory only if it can be verified by external facts. We believe in the most exact observation and exploration of nature; our truth must coincide with the behaviour of the external world, otherwise it is merely 'subjective.' In the same way that the East turns its gaze from the dance of *prakriti* (physis) and from the multitudinous illusory forms of *māyā*, the West shuns the unconscious and its futile fantasies. Despite its introverted attitude, however, the East knows very well how to deal with the external world. And despite its extraversions the West, too, has a way of dealing with the psyche and its demands; it has an institution called the Church, which gives expression to the unknown psyche of man through its rites and dogmas. Nor are natural science and modern techniques by any means the invention of the West. Their Eastern equivalents are somewhat old-fashioned, or even primitive. But what we have to show in the way of spiritual insight and psychological technique must seem, when compared with yoga, just as backward as Eastern astrology and medicine when compared with Western science. I do not deny the efficacy of the Christian Church; but, if you compare the *Exercitia* of Ignatius Loyola with yoga, you will take my meaning. There is a difference, and a big one. To jump straight from that level into Eastern yoga is no more advisable than the sudden transformation of Asian peoples into half-baked Europeans. I have serious doubts as to the blessings of Western civilization, and I have similar misgivings as to the adoption of Eastern spirituality by the West. Yet the two contradictory worlds have met. The East is in full transformation; it is thoroughly and fatally disturbed. Even the most efficient methods of European warfare have been successfully imitated. The trouble with us seems to be far more psychological. Our blight is ideologies – they are the long-expected Antichrist! National Socialism comes as near to being a religious movement as any movement since A.D. 622.[9a] Communism claims to be paradise come to earth again. We are far better protected against failing crops, inundations, epidemics, and invasions from the Turk than we are against our own deplorable spiritual inferiority, which seems to have little resistance to psychic epidemics.

779   In its religious attitude, too, the West is extraverted. Nowadays it is gratuitously offensive to say that Christianity implies hostility, or even indifference, to the world and the flesh. On the contrary, the good Christian is a jovial citizen, an enterprising business man, an excellent soldier, the very best in every profession there is. Worldly goods are often interpreted as special rewards for Christian

behaviour, and in the Lord's Prayer the adjective ἐπιούσιος, *supersubstantialis*,[10] referring to the bread, has long since been omitted, for the real bread obviously makes so very much more sense! It is only logical that extraversion, when carried to such lengths, cannot credit man with a psyche which contains anything not imported into it from outside, either by human teaching or divine grace. From this point of view it is downright blasphemy to assert that man has it in him to accomplish his own redemption. Nothing in our religion encourages the idea of the self-liberating power of the mind. Yet a very modern form of psychology – 'analytical' or 'complex' psychology – envisages the possibility of there being certain processes in the unconscious which, by virtue of their symbolism, compensate the defects and anfractuosities of the conscious attitude. When these unconscious compensations are made conscious through the analytical technique, they produce such a change in the conscious attitude that we are entitled to speak of a new level of consciousness. The method cannot, however, produce the actual process of unconscious compensation; for that we depend upon the unconscious psyche or the 'grace of God' – names make no difference. But the unconscious process itself hardly ever reaches consciousness without technical aid. When brought to the surface, it reveals contents that offer a striking contrast to the general run of conscious thinking and feeling. If that were not so, they would not have a compensatory effect. The first effect, however, is usually a conflict, because the conscious attitude resists the intrusion of apparently incompatible and extraneous tendencies, thoughts, feelings, etc. Schizophrenia yields the most startling examples of such intrusions of utterly foreign and unacceptable contents. In schizophrenia it is, of course, a question of pathological distortions and exaggerations, but anybody with the slightest knowledge of the normal material will easily recognize the sameness of the underlying patterns. It is, as a matter of fact, the same imagery that one finds in mythology and other archaic thought-forms.

780   Under normal conditions, every conflict stimulates the mind to activity for the purpose of creating a satisfactory solution. Usually – i.e., in the West – the conscious standpoint arbitrarily decides against the unconscious, since anything coming from inside suffers from the prejudice of being regarded as inferior or somehow wrong. But in the cases with which we are here concerned it is tacitly agreed that the apparently incompatible contents shall not be suppressed again, and that the conflict shall be accepted and suffered. At first no solution appears possible, and this fact, too, has to be borne with patience. The suspension thus created 'constellates' the unconscious – in other words, the conscious suspense produces a new compensatory reaction in the unconscious. This reaction (usually manifested in dreams) is brought to conscious realization in its turn. The conscious mind is thus confronted with a new aspect of the psyche, which arouses a different problem or modifies an old one in an unexpected way. The procedure is continued until the original conflict is satisfactorily resolved. The whole process is called the 'transcendent function.' It is a process and a method at the same time. The production of unconscious compensations is a spontaneous *process*; the conscious realization is a *method*. The function is called 'transcendent' because it facilitates

the transition from one psychic condition to another by means of the mutual confrontation of opposites.

781 This is a very sketchy description of the transcendent function, and for details I must refer the reader to the relevant literature.[11] But I felt it necessary to call attention to these psychological observations and methods because they indicate the way by which we may find access to the sort of 'mind' referred to in our text. This is the image-creating mind, the matrix of all those patterns that give apperception its peculiar character. These patterns are inherent in the unconscious 'mind'; they are its structural elements, and they alone can explain why certain mythological motifs are more or less ubiquitous, even where migration as a means of transmission is exceedingly improbable. Dreams, fantasies, and psychoses produce images to all appearances identical with mythological motifs of which the individuals concerned had absolutely no knowledge, not even indirect knowledge acquired through popular figures of speech or through the symbolic language of the Bible.[12] The psychopathology of schizophrenia, as well as the psychology of the unconscious, demonstrate the production of archaic material beyond a doubt. Whatever the structure of the unconscious may be, one thing is, certain: it contains an indefinite number of motifs or patterns of an archaic character, in principle identical with the root ideas of mythology and similar thought-forms.

782 Because the unconscious is the matrix mind, the quality of creativeness attaches to it. It is the birthplace of thought-forms such as our text considers the Universal Mind to be. Since we cannot attribute any particular form to the unconscious, the Eastern assertion that the Universal Mind is without form, the *arupaloka*, yet is the source of all forms, seems to be psychologically justified. In so far as the forms or patterns of the unconscious belong to no time in particular, being seemingly eternal, they convey a peculiar feeling of timelessness when consciously realized. We find similar statements in primitive psychology: for instance, the Australian word *aljira*[13] means 'dream' as well as 'ghostland' and the 'time' in which the ancestors lived and still live. It is, as they say, the 'time when there was no time.' This looks like an obvious concretization and projection of the unconscious with all its characteristic qualities – its dream manifestations, its ancestral world of thought-forms, and its timelessness.

783 An introverted attitude, therefore, which withdraws its emphasis from the external world (the world of consciousness) and localizes it in the subjective factor (the background of consciousness) necessarily calls forth the characteristic manifestations of the unconscious, namely, archaic thought-forms imbued with 'ancestral' or 'historic' feeling, and, beyond them, the sense of indefiniteness, timelessness, oneness. The extraordinary feeling of oneness is a common experience in all forms of 'mysticism' and probably derives from the general contamination of contents, which increases as consciousness dims. The almost limitless contamination of images in dreams, and particularly in the products of insanity, testifies to their unconscious origin. In contrast to the clear distinction and differentiation of forms in consciousness, unconscious contents are incredibly vague and for this reason capable of any amount of contamination. If we tried to conceive of a state in which

nothing is distinct, we should certainly feel the whole as one. Hence it is not unlikely that the peculiar experience of oneness derives from the subliminal awareness of all-contamination in the unconscious.

784 By means of the transcendent function we not only gain access to the 'One Mind' but also come to understand why the East believes in the possibility of self-liberation. If, through introspection and the conscious realization of unconscious compensations, it is possible to transform one's mental condition and thus arrive at a solution of painful conflicts, one would seem entitled to speak of 'self-liberation.' But, as I have already hinted, there is a hitch in this proud claim to self-liberation, for a man cannot produce these unconscious compensations at will. He has to rely upon the possibility that they *may* be produced. Nor can he alter the peculiar character of the compensation: *est ut est aut non est* – 'it is as it is or it isn't at all.' It is a curious thing that Eastern philosophy seems to be almost unaware of this highly important fact. And it is precisely this fact that provides the psychological justification for the Western point of view. It seems as if the Western mind had a most penetrating intuition of man's fateful dependence upon some dark power which must co-operate if all is to be well. Indeed, whenever and wherever the unconscious fails to co-operate, man is instantly at a loss, even in his most ordinary activities. There may be a failure of memory, of co-ordinated action, or of interest and concentration; and such failure may well be the cause of serious annoyance, or of a fatal accident, a professional disaster, or a moral collapse. Formerly, men called the gods unfavourable; now we prefer to call it a neurosis, and we seek the cause in lack of vitamins, in endocrine disturbances, overwork, or sex. The co-operation of the unconscious, which is something we never think of and always take for granted, is, when it suddenly fails, a very serious matter indeed.

785 In comparison with other races – the Chinese for instance – the white man's mental equilibrium, or, to put it bluntly, his brain, seems to be his tender spot. We naturally try to get as far away from our weaknesses as possible, a fact which may explain the sort of extraversion that is always seeking security by dominating its surroundings. Extraversion goes hand in hand with mistrust of the inner man, if indeed there is any consciousness of him at all. Moreover, we all tend to under-value the things we are afraid of. There must be some such reason for our absolute conviction that *nihil est in intellectu quod non antea fuerit in sensu*, which is the motto of Western extraversion. But, as we have emphasized, this extraversion is psychologically justified by the vital fact that unconscious compensation lies beyond man's control. I know that yoga prides itself on being able to control even the unconscious processes, so that nothing can happen in the psyche as a whole that is not ruled by a supreme consciousness. I have not the slightest doubt that such a condition is more or less possible. But it is possible only at the price of becoming identical with the unconscious. Such an identity is the Eastern equivalent of our Western fetish of 'complete objectivity,' the machine-like subservience to one goal; to one idea or cause, at the cost of losing every trace of inner life. From the Eastern point of view this complete objectivity is appalling, for it

amounts to complete identity with the samsāra; to the West, on the other hand, samādhi is nothing but a meaningless dream-state. In the East, the inner man has always had such a firm hold on the outer man that the world had no chance of tearing him away from his inner roots; in the West, the outer man gained the ascendancy to such an extent that he was alienated from his innermost being. The One Mind, Oneness, indefiniteness, and eternity remained the prerogative of the One God. Man became small, futile, and essentially in the wrong.

786   I think it is becoming clear from my argument that the two standpoints, however contradictory, each have their psychological justification. Both are one-sided in that they fail to see and take account of those factors which do not fit in with their typical attitude. The one underrates the world of consciousness, the other the world of the One Mind. The result is that, in their extremism, both lose one half of the universe; their life is shut off from total reality, and is apt to become artificial and inhuman. In the West, there is the mania for 'objectivity,' the asceticism of the scientist or of the stockbroker, who throw away the beauty and universality of life for the sake of the ideal, or not so ideal, goal. In the East, there is the wisdom, peace, detachment, and inertia of a psyche that has returned to its dim origins, having left behind all the sorrow and joy of existence as it is and, presumably, ought to be. No wonder that one-sidedness produces very similar forms of monasticism in both cases, guaranteeing to the hermit, the holy man, the monk or the scientist unswerving singleness of purpose. I have nothing against one-sidedness as such. Man, the great experiment of nature, or his own great experiment, is evidently entitled to all such undertakings – if he can endure them. Without one-sidedness the spirit of man could not unfold in all its diversity. But I do not think there is any harm in trying to understand both sides.

787   The extraverted tendency of the West and the introverted tendency of the East have one important purpose in common: both make desperate efforts to conquer the mere naturalness of life. It is the assertion of mind over matter, the *opus contra naturam*, a symptom of the youthfulness of man, still delighting in the use of the most powerful weapon ever devised by nature: the conscious mind. The afternoon of humanity, in a distant future, may yet evolve a different ideal. In time, even conquest will cease to be the dream.

Notes

1 [Written in English in 1939 and first published in *The Tibetan Book of the Great Liberation*, the texts of which were translated from Tibetan by various hands and edited by W. Y. Evans-Wentz (London and New York, 1954), pp. xxix–lxiv. The commentary is republished here with only minor alterations.–EDITORS.]
2 I am purposely leaving out of account the modernized East.
3 *Psychological Types*, Defs. 19 and 34.
4 Written in the year 1939.
5 *Samyutta-nikāya* 12, *Nidāna-samyutta.*
6 [Cf. Otto, *The Idea of the Holy*, pp. 26ff.–EDITORS.]
7 'Whereas who holdeth not God as such an inner possession, but with every means must fetch Him from without . . . verily such a man hath Him not, and easily something

cometh to trouble him.' Meister Eckhart (Büttner, II, p. 185). Cf. *Meister Eckhart*, trans. by Evans, II, p. 8.

8 In so far as 'higher' and 'lower' are categorical judgments of consciousness, Western psychology does not differentiate unconscious contents in this way. It appears that the East recognizes subhuman psychic conditions, a real 'subconsciousness' comprising the instincts and semi-physiological psychisms, but classed as a 'higher consciousness.'

9 *Psychological Types* (1933 edn., pp. 472ff.)

9a [Date of Mohammed's flight (*hegira*) to Medina: beginning of Moslem era.]

10 This is not the unacceptable translation of ἐπιούσιος by Jerome but the ancient spiritual interpretation by Tertullian, Origen, and others.

11 *Psychological Types*, Def. 51. [Cf. also 'The Transcendent Function.']

12 Some people find such statements incredible. But either they have no knowledge of primitive psychology, or they are ignorant of the results of psychopathological research. Specific observations occur in my *Symbols of Transformation* and *Psychology and Alchemy*, Part II; Nelken, 'Analytische Beobachtungen über Phantasien eines Schizophrenen,' pp. 504ff.; Spielrein, 'Über den psychologischen Inhalt eines Falls von Schizophrenie,' pp. 329ff.; and C. A. Meier, 'Spontanmanifestationen des kollektiven Unbewussten.'

13 Lévy-Bruhl, *La Mythologie primitive*, pp. xxiii ff.

Part IV

Therapy and healing

Therapy and healing
Introduction

Chapter 13: 'The aims of psychotherapy' (1931)

(From 'General problems of psychotherapy', in *The Practice of Psychotherapy, The Collected Works Vol.* 16, § 66–113)

Throughout his career Jung claimed not to be a 'Jungian' in the sense of being narrowly confined to his own therapeutic method or outlook. Here he says he has 'always felt the need for a conspectus of many viewpoints' and has 'given divergent opinions their due' (§ 66). Jung is philosophical about the 'plurality of contradictory opinions' (§ 71) and does not see them as a threat to the coherence of the field of psychotherapy. He argues that the psyche is complex and many faceted, and 'such opinions could never arise, much less secure a following, if they did not correspond to some . . . fundamental psychological fact that is more or less universal' (§ 66). 'Were we to exclude one such opinion as simply wrong or worthless, we should be . . . doing violence to our own empirical material' (§ 66). It is odd, therefore, that Jungian psychology has been charged by critics with being highly specialised and esoteric, given Jung's own openness to other views. Andrew Samuels has argued in a number of places, including *The Plural Psyche*, that Jungian therapy is innately diverse and accommodating.[1]

Jung argues that the aim of his therapy differs from that of Freud or Adler, in that they seek to make the patient 'normal' by treating a disordered pleasure principle (Freud) or power impulse (Adler). Jung is less interested in adjusting the patient to society than in helping the patient connect to his or her inner life. Jung's interests are introverted and in his view neurosis arises because the conscious mind is out of relationship with the unconscious. He argues that Freud and Adler are helpful to younger patients, but less helpful to 'persons over forty'. Most of his clients are of a mature age and adapted to society; they are 'often of outstanding ability, to whom normalization means nothing' (§ 84). Their problem is not how to fit in with the social fabric, but how to overcome the 'senselessness of their lives' (§ 83). In such cases, therapy is 'less a question of treatment than of developing the creative possibilities latent in the patient' (§ 82). The aim of this kind of therapy is not normalisation but individuation.

The method in such cases must be receptive to the lost or hidden aspects of the patient, and conducted in a questing spirit. Too much technique can hinder therapy, he asserts, and the therapist must adopt a position of humility or 'not knowing'. The aim of therapy is to *draw out* what is within the patient, not to impose a new set of external requirements. 'Education' derives from the Latin *educare*, meaning to 'draw out', and what Jung proposes for therapy is an education of the heart and the interior life. Jung reveals himself as the original anti-psychiatrist, the doctor who heals because he does not know what the problem is in advance. The key element is not the knowledge of the therapist or a professional system of answers, but the attitude of humility before the inner life. Therapy occurs when the therapist is amazed, even confounded, by the patient's neurosis. The neurosis is the result of a one-sidedness in the patient, and the aim is to find the missing pieces that can restore the psyche to health.

The mature client, Jung writes, must often discover a spiritual outlook, even if he or she has previously rejected spirituality. By 'spirituality' Jung means a receptivity to the mystery of life and the interior realm. It is by a new receptivity that lost parts of the personality can be allowed back into the conscious domain. 'My aim,' he declares, 'is to bring about a psychic state in which my patient begins to experiment with his own nature – a state of fluidity, change and growth' (§ 99). 'Many neuroses are caused primarily by the fact that people blind themselves to their own religious promptings because of a childish passion for rational enlightenment' (§ 99). Jung makes it clear here and elsewhere that he is not advocating adherence to formal religion, but emphasising the need for 'the religious attitude', which is to be distinguished from 'dogmas and creeds' (§ 99).

Jung sees the task of therapy as one of rebuilding the personality according to the promptings and signals that arise from the psyche. Chief among these are dreams and fantasies, which he sees as intelligent messages from the unconscious which guide the person to a better apprehension of the psychic totality. However, these expressions come from a deep source that is hard to fathom. Jung admits he often fails to discern what a dream means and has no comprehensive or systematic theory of symbols. He says the point is not to interpret in a narrow or rational way, but to hold the dream and reflect on it. 'If we carry [a dream] around with us and turn it over and over, something almost always comes of it' (§ 86). We should not expect the dream to lend itself to being translated into purely conceptual language; rather, we have to go to the dream as if to a foreign shore, leaving some of our familiarity behind.

Jung encourages his clients to paint their dreams and fantasies, even if they are not gifted with artistic talent. He invites them to paint, draw, sculpt and write the images that arise from the unconscious, and this chapter offers practical advice about the use of art work in therapeutic contexts. Jung made extensive use of painting and sculpting in his self-guided therapeutic work, and a number of his striking, brightly coloured works can be found in *The Red Book*.[2] However, Jung cautions his clients and readers about the dangers of aestheticism – viewing these works purely in artistic terms and forgetting their therapeutic intent. He thinks we should not get too caught up with aesthetic matters, technique, styles and trends. We should allow the unconscious as much freedom as possible, and this often means that such works are primitive or infantile. For him, the expressive function of art is more important than formal considerations.

For Jung, the aim of dream work is to move toward the soul and feel its non-rational claims on us, not to feed the ego with new insights about how it can continue on its present course. The dream may seek to subvert the ego and cut across its one-sided orientation. Thus dream work is not to be seen as comforting or consoling, but must be regarded as the psyche's attempt to provide constructive criticism to the individual. Jung is convinced that the sources of pathology reside not so much in the unconscious but in the ego and its rigidities. Therapy is to be seen as potentially deeply disturbing, since what one has come to see as given and natural is deconstructed by the therapeutic process. The aim of therapy is to unravel the habitual stance of the ego, and open it to a range of possibilities and meanings. In particular, Jung is at pains to challenge the personalistic perspective of the ego, that is, the notion that the psyche as it perceives it is a personal construction. Healing often involves the acceptance of transpersonal forces in the psyche, and the adoption of a humble attitude toward this otherness. We are healed when we see ourselves in a new light, no longer confined to the ego, but connected to the ancestral, the archetypal and the other.

Chapter 14: 'On synchronicity' (1951)

(From *The Structure and Dynamics of the Psyche, The Collected Works Vol.* 8, § 969–997)

Speaking of connectedness, we move to the concept of synchronicity. Jung coined this term in the 1950s, and by this term he meant 'an acausal connecting principle' that linked psyche and world. Jung's thinking had been moving in this direction for some time, since he had noted what he called 'meaningful correspondences' between psyche and world. The biologist and neo-vitalist Hans Dreisch had already postulated the notion of the *psychoid*, a theoretical point at which mind and matter, or spirit and nature, meet. Jung had suspected that there was a link between inner and outer worlds, but for decades he lacked the science to be able to explore this possibility. It was Jung's conversations with Albert Einstein that sparked his interest in the concept of synchronicity. As he wrote in a letter to Carl Seelig:

> It was Einstein who first started me off thinking about a possible relativity of time as well as space, and their psychic conditionality. More than thirty years later this stimulus led to my relation with the physicist Professor Wolfgang Pauli and to my thesis of psychic synchronicity.[3]

There has been a tendency in recent intellectual history to relegate Jung to the arts and humanities, but in the theory of synchronicity he reveals himself to be at the leading edge of scientific notions about time and relativity. In his book *Synchronicity: Nature and Psyche in an Interconnected Universe*, the scientist and analyst Joseph Cambray attempts to restore Jung to the scientific tradition in the study of time and space.[4] If Einstein explored the relativity of physical time and space, and revolutionised science in this undertaking, Jung explored the relativity of psychic time and space, and yet few took him seriously in this endeavour. Jung's theory of synchronicity was seen as vague, murky, mystical, and yet arguably Einstein's general theory of relativity is no less 'mystical'. Jung's explorations in synchronicity were often dismissed as speculative, and yet the Nobel Prize-winning physicist Wolfgang Pauli took them seriously enough to engage with Jung in a joint adventure into the 'interpretation of nature and the psyche'.[5]

It was in his work with Pauli that Jung published his comprehensive essay, *Synchronicity: An Acausal Connecting Principle*.[6] It is in this essay, published in 1952, that the full theory is expounded, whereas the chapter presented in this anthology is an earlier paper, delivered at the 1951 Eranos conference at Ascona, Switzerland. Gilles Quispel reports that after Jung delivered his Eranos lecture, he told Quispel that 'now the concept of projection should be revised completely'.[7] This seems entirely credible, because up to this time the link between psyche and world had been 'explained away' in terms of the psyche's 'projections' upon the world, a view which had been current in psychoanalysis since the early days. Freud worked within the Cartesian worldview, which assumed that the human mind was animated by psychological forces and the external world was inanimate. Any experience of 'animation' in the world was dismissed by Freud and his followers as an example of mind-created projections. Freud had declared that the early view of the world, in which spirits and gods are believed to reside in the universe, 'is nothing but psychology projected into the external world'.[8] For a number of years Jung agreed, and his work is replete with comments that coincide with Freud's view, such as: 'Sooner or later we had to understand that the potency [of the world of objects] was really ours, and that their significance was our projection.'[9]

But as his research deepened he began to think of the world in different terms. It could be that the 'modern' view of the world is itself primitive, whereas the ancient, animated worldview represents a more sophisticated grasp of reality. Not that Jung believed literally in the ancient gods and spirits of the natural world; he did not. But he began to see that the so-called 'primitive' philosophy may have grasped something that we in the modern world have lost. What we must do is see beyond the literalism of the ancient world and its cosmologies, and appreciate the fact that the world may be constituted by spirit and psyche in ways we cannot conceive, given our scientific orientation. The 'personifications' of spirits and gods may be a poetic form of thinking but that thinking is not fundamentally wrong. Namely, spirit and animation may be inherent in the world, and not 'projected' into it by the human mind. Because this spiritual reality is invisible and unseen, we rely on the mythic imagination to give form to what remains unknown. Reality could be quite other than we currently imagine; it could be far more mysterious than normal perception allows.

Jung believed that synchronicities happen all the time, but 'after the first momentary astonishment they are as a rule quickly forgotten' (§ 972). But if we allow ourselves to be touched by them, they can be transformative. He believed that synchronicity often occurs during therapeutic treatment, because therapy activates the levels of mind at which synchronicities take place. Hence synchronicity is an important therapeutic tool, and just as important as dreams and fantasies in showing patients aspects of reality that they have refused to take into account. They can be profound turning points, if we are receptive to them.

Jung recounts the story of a case which has been much discussed since. A young woman patient, described as 'psychologically inaccessible', seemed to be unable to make meaningful contact with the unconscious and hence was in a stalemate situation. Her neurosis could not be moved because her 'excellent education' proved to be an obstacle and 'she always knew better about everything' (§ 982). Nothing diminishes the possibility of transformation more than a hardened rationality. The patient had an impressive dream in which someone had given her a golden scarab, a costly piece of jewellery. As she told the dream, Jung heard a gentle tapping on the window behind him. He opened the window and into the room flew a scarab beetle, 'whose golden-green colour most nearly resembles that of a golden scarab' (§ 982). He handed the beetle to his patient with the words, 'Here is your scarab', and this experience 'punctured the desired hole in her rationalism and broke the ice of her intellectual resistance'. The treatment, he said, 'could now be continued with satisfactory results' (§ 982).

Synchronicities like this can have a greater impact than the analyst's words or special pleadings. It is as if the world is speaking directly to oneself, and such an experience can achieve a great deal in an instant – that is, once we are caught and held by it, and do not defend against it. The psyche is made real and immediate in such moments, and intellectual resistances collapse. Moreover, it becomes clear to the individual that the psyche is not a personal possession or an abstract conception, but something which has an objective dimension. Psyche bursts its subjective boundaries and becomes cosmological. Psyche is no longer inside us, but we are inside the psyche. When psyche speaks to us through the world, we are more likely to be convinced by its authority and suggestive power. We are awoken to its broader cosmic dimension and become aware that 'either the psyche cannot be localized in space, or that space is relative to the psyche' (§ 996). 'The same applies to the temporal determination of the psyche and the psychic relativity of time' (§ 996).

If healing takes place when we feel connected to forces beyond ourselves, synchronicity is a wonderful, rich and largely unexplored source of healing. Jung is aware that the notion of synchronicity represents a radical challenge to science and calls into question the Cartesian basis of knowledge. 'I do not need to emphasize,' he says, 'that the verification of these findings must have far-reaching consequences' (§ 996).

Chapter 15: 'A psychological theory of types' (1931)

(From 'Four papers on psychological typology', in *Psychological Types, The Collected Works Vol. 6*, § 951–959)

After the acrimonious break with Freud, Jung set himself the task of reflecting on structural differences in human personalities. Did he and Freud quarrel because they were different 'types'? To ask this question in the racially charged atmosphere of his day was controversial, but Jung was thinking along the lines of psychological, not racial typology. Jung and Freud were confronted with the same clinical material, but Jung interpreted it one way, and Freud another. Jung believed there was something structural which lay beneath their differences. Freud looked outside the human subject to family relationships, social interactions, and the early childhood environment. He was most interested in 'object relations', and Jung deemed his orientation to be 'extraverted'. Jung, on the other hand, was 'introverted'; his focus was primarily on the psychological contents of the subject. 'With Freud objects are of the greatest significance and possess almost exclusively the determining power, while the subject remains remarkably insignificant'. For Freud, 'objects either promote or hinder the subject's desire for pleasure'.[10]

Jung's terms introversion and extraversion[11] have entered into the colloquial language of most nations, and are used without people realising their origins in his psychology. Jung writes:

> Introversion or extraversion, as a typical attitude, means an essential bias which conditions the whole psychic process, establishes the habitual mode of reaction, and thus determines not only the style of behaviour but also the quality of subjective experience. Not only that, it determines the kind of compensation the unconscious will produce.
>
> (§ 940)

According to his theory, only the *conscious* attitude of the individual is extraverted or introverted. In the unconscious, a 'compensation' develops, because the psyche strives for wholeness, and this can occur at the cost of the conscious attitude. Hence an introvert will be compensated by an extraverted tendency in the unconscious, but this extraversion is not the same as that of a natural extravert. It is said to be 'inferior', that is, 'less developed [and] more primitive' (§ 953). When it expresses itself it may appear in a dubious or maladapted form, such as we often see when introverts try to be extraverted at parties or social occasions. Similarly the extravert will be compensated by an unlived introversion, which may seek expression at certain times of life, especially at midlife, when the habitual stance no longer suffices. This inferior introversion may make the extravert prey to various kinds of fundamentalist philosophies.

Until recently an introverted attitude was constructed as antisocial, and even viewed as a form of pathology. I once heard it remarked that 'there are no introverts, only wounded extraverts'. This prejudice has a long history, and many continue to think this way. Somehow our culture is so determined to make everyone extraverted, that is, focused on outward things and people, that introversion is seen as some kind of affliction. But Jung discovered that a large percentage of the population of any country is naturally oriented toward an introverted point of view. It is not as if such people are a handicap to society or self-obsessed, but they typically withdraw from the object at first approach, and reflect and take stock when confronted by an external situation.

> There is a whole class of men who, at the moment of reaction to a given situation, at first draw back a little as if with an unvoiced 'No', and only after that are able to react; and there is another class who, in the same situation, come out with an immediate reaction, apparently quite confident that their behaviour is self-evidently right. The former class would therefore be characterized by a negative relation to the object, and the latter by a positive one'
>
> (§ 937).

In therapeutic analysis, patients are encouraged to develop their 'inferior' attitude, but not in an overly confident manner, so that it lands them in a difficult or embarrassing situation. According to Jung, one has to proceed with caution as one explores the undeveloped attitude because, like everything unconscious, it requires deliberation and a critical approach. However, he thought the inferiority could not be overcome, and indeed should not be overcome because it acts as a necessary doorway into the unconscious. We cannot become fully conscious of all our faculties and aptitudes because we remain partial beings who have to learn to live with a certain lack of development in some aspects of our characters.

In addition to the attitude-types, Jung designated four functions of consciousness: thinking, feeling, intuition and sensation. Sensation tells us that a thing exists, thinking tells us what it is, feeling tells us its value, and intuition tells us its possibilities in time. Jung insists that these are not arbitrary designations, but are based on decades of clinical experience and empirical experimentation (§ 958). Nevertheless his critics argue that they remain speculative and hypothetical. They seem to correlate in some ways to the ancient classification of character according to the four elements (air, water, earth and fire). This system was adapted by astrology, and 'the astrological type theory, to the astonishment of the enlightened ... still remains intact today, and is even enjoying a new vogue' (§ 933). A different kind of 'fourfold' typology lasted at least seventeen hundred years, known as the Galenic temperaments or four humours: phlegmatic, sanguine, choleric and melancholic. Jung points out that the four functions are not to be confused with intelligence as such, since 'intelligence ... is not a function but a modality' (§ 949). In particular, thinking is not to be confused with intelligence, as is often the case. Jung says it ought to be clear to most people what 'thinking' means, and in a swipe at pedantic scholars, he says 'it is only the philosopher who does not know what it means; no layman will find it incomprehensible' (§ 949).

Jung refers to thinking and feeling as rational functions, and to sensation and intuition as non-rational. Significantly, he defines intuition as 'perception via the unconscious' (§ 951). It is a unique way of seeing which 'sees through' to the depths, and which is sometimes dubbed *clairvoyance*. As an intuitive, Jung spent a lot of time reflecting on the nature and purpose of intuition, which rationalists denigrate as 'mysticism' but Jung sought to normalise as an innate human capacity. Intuition does not merely look at an object (sensation), or recognise its meaning (thinking), or establish its value (feeling), but 'points to possibilities as to whence it came and whither it is going in a given situation' (§ 958).

In most individuals, there is a 'superior' function through which the personality expresses itself and shows its strengths, and an 'inferior' function which is hidden or only emerges at various times when the normal defences are relaxed. A thinking type typically has inferior feeling, according to this model, although thinking will often be complemented by one of the 'auxiliary' functions, sensation or intuition. Similar patterns occur in all four types: a superior function, aided by an auxiliary function, and compensated in the unconscious by an inferior function. An intuitive type will tend to have inferior sensation, and either feeling or thinking as an auxiliary function. It has almost become a cliché in the Jungian world to refer to one's 'inferior sensation function', since those who are drawn to Jungian psychology are often intuitive by nature, and have a problematical relation with reality. However, this kind of formulation ought not be used as an excuse for failing to adjust to reality.

This typology has become popular and a modified version of it is referred to as the Myers-Briggs Type Indicator or MBTI. In the guise of MBTI tests and programmes, it has been widely used in the public domain, especially in workplace cultures and personnel offices. People often forget that Jung was the originator of the model and the theory behind it. The success of these programmes has been prodigious, but it has come at a cost. In the wider domain, people tend to focus on the superior and auxiliary functions, in terms of what these can do for us in facilitating social adaptation, employment opportunities and career advancement. In Jung's research, however, much emphasis was placed on the so-called inferior function, because this was seen as a vital doorway into the unconscious, and a necessary burden that the individuating person had to face if he or she wished to become integrated.

Jung's research was interested in the encounter with the inferior function as the locus of our engagement with the gods or archetypes of our deeper nature. It is through the pathway of the inferior function that the numinous reveals itself – precisely because this is our least adapted area, where the ego does not dominate. In a sense, his theory of types was a prelude to his theory of archetypes, but these areas of his thought have become separated today. Jung's typology has been appropriated by a modern world concerned with results, productivity and growth, and has lost the spiritual emphasis on humility and our need to live in the presence of our undeveloped aspects. The popular deployment of Jung's model has meant that everything in the psyche is seen as an opportunity for growth. His psychology of the sacred sits oddly against this commercial emphasis on ego development.

Chapter 16: 'The transcendent function' (1916/1957)

(From *The Structure and Dynamics of the Psyche, The Collected Works Vol.* 8, § 131–193)

Jung begins this essay by asserting that 'there is nothing mysterious or metaphysical about the term "transcendent function"' (§ 131). He was always attempting to claim scientific status for his ideas, even though his ideas overspill scientific boundaries and become overtly philosophical. One senses that if Jung were writing today he would not have to protest so much. Psychotherapists today allow themselves to be speculative and 'mysterious' in their research, and this is no longer seen as disastrous to their reputations, as Jung sensed it was for his.

In 'The transcendent function' Jung is in Hegelian territory, even though he never mentions Hegel. But the notion of presenting the conscious attitude as a thesis, compensated and/or contradicted by the unconscious as an antithesis, and resolving these in the expectation of finding a *synthesis* is similar to Hegelian dialectics.[12] Jung disliked Hegel, though it is difficult to determine his reasons. Jung may have seen him as a dangerous critic of Kant, his favourite philosopher. Jung referred to Hegel as 'a psychologist in disguise who projected great truths out of the subjective sphere into a cosmos he himself had created'.[13] But one might equally say that Jung was a philosopher in disguise, who developed 'great truths' in the realm of pure thought and sought to apply them to his clients.

'The confrontation of the two positions generates a tension charged with energy and creates a living, third thing' (§ 189), says Jung. This third thing, or *tertium* as he calls it, is the transcendent function, which 'arises from the union of conscious and unconscious contents' (§ 131). This is an abstract way of talking about the psyche's tendency to create wholeness, unity and homeostasis among its warring parts. The function can hardly be distinguished from the practical experience of individuation. As such, the transcendent function seems to be an operational arm of the archetype of the Self, whose task is to ensure stability and bring about a reconciliation between conscious and unconscious. The transcendent function seems never to come into being without the support of imagination, symbol and image, since these alone are broad enough to accommodate the contents of conscious and unconscious. Cognitive concepts or pure thinking cannot activate the transcendent function, because they favour the conscious standpoint and are not open to non-rational contents or directives.

It is assumed that neurosis occurs because there is a highly charged content of the unconscious which is not connected with the conscious mind. It produces disturbing effects because it has nowhere to go, other than to create havoc in a person's life. What is needed to produce the transcendent function is access to unconscious material. Dreams and fantasies are the primary data which tell us what the unconscious is doing and what it wants. However, Jung points out that dreams are often difficult to work with, and speak such an alien language that clients are unable to understand them. Even a highly skilled therapist is frequently unable to determine what individual dreams mean (§ 141). Dream interpretation remains central, but Jung suggests that dream work may be supplemented by a number of other methods and techniques. The patient's transference to the therapist is seen as a key indicator of the unconscious process.

One way to generate healing is by a method that is called 'active imagination'. In this activity, unconscious materials are encountered in a state of therapeutic receptivity. The patient 'makes himself as conscious as possible of the mood he is in, sinking himself in it without reserve and noting down on paper all the fantasies and other associations that come up' (§ 167). Fantasy must be allowed free reign, but not, Jung advises, to trigger a 'free association' process that leads away from the original 'object' or mood. In this paper Jung is concerned with patients who are depressed, and it is one of his remarkably few papers on this condition, which has become epidemic in our time. Jung distrusts free association because it invites the mind to dissociate from the source of the depression and replace it with all kinds of diversional interests. 'Out of this preoccupation with the object there comes a more or less complete expression of the mood, which reproduces the content of the depression in some way, either concretely or symbolically' (§ 167). The point of this procedure is to enrich and clarify the affect, 'whereby the affect and its contents are brought nearer to consciousness, becoming at the same time more impressive and more understandable' (§ 167). The act of taking the unconscious seriously, he argues, seems to guarantee its cooperation: this is part of Jung's optimism as a psychotherapist.

Jung discusses other ways in which the unconscious can be awoken. Some might work with plastic materials to create models or sculptures, others might express themselves in bodily movements, dance or automatic writing. 'Visual types' might prefer to paint a picture, or 'audio-verbal types' might hear inner words or voices. Obviously, the insane see images and hear voices on a regular basis, but Jung is inviting normal people to explore these expressions for therapeutic reasons. Needless to say, there are inherent dangers in awakening the unconscious, especially if it gains the upper hand and cannot be contained.

Jung cautions that 'the rediscovered unconscious often has a really dangerous effect on the ego' (§ 183). Many of us are likely to overvalue the contents of the unconscious, 'precisely because they were boundlessly undervalued before' (§ 176). If this happens, the ego can be rendered incapable of a moral reaction. If the ego is awestruck by the unconscious and unable to respond, the transcendent function cannot operate. Jung describes a psychological dialectic in which now the unconscious and now the ego must take the lead and bring about a process of reconciliation. This bespeaks a delicate balancing act: the ego has to listen to the unconscious, but it cannot be annulled or rendered inactive. Jung considers two forms of passivity that he thinks must be avoided: aestheticism, in which the archetypal images are enjoyed for artistic reasons but not understood, and intellectualism, in which the rational mind seeks to reduce the products of the unconscious to an intellectual system. In the Jungian world today, aestheticism

Introduction to Part IV 299

and intellectualism are rife, suggesting that a lot of people have not understood Jung's meaning. Jung seeks the transformation of personality, and is wary of those seeking head trips or artistic fascination.

Jung emphasises the role of the transference in the healing process. 'The patient clings by means of the transference to the person who seems to promise him a renewal of attitude' (§ 146). The 'trained analyst mediates the transcendent function for the patient, i.e., helps him to bring conscious and unconscious together and so arrive at a new attitude' (§ 146). This paper, together with Jung's essay 'The psychology of the transference',[14] make it clear that he held the transference in higher regard than is often thought. When Jungian psychology developed its identity, independently of Freudian practice, it tended to emphasise that it was about the study of archetypal imagery and amplification. It argued that the focus of therapy was on the inner life of the patient, not on the role of the analyst, and that 'transference' was a clinical focus of the non-Jungian traditions. It was felt that Jungians, especially those trained in Zurich, could get along without it.[15]

However, these and other essays make it clear that this assumption is false, and the Jungian practitioner is closer to his Freudian cousins than perhaps either would like to imagine. The similarities were masked in the early days to exaggerate the differences, but today it is clear that Jungian and Freudian practitioners are part of the one broad tradition of psychoanalysis. In recognition of this fact, practitioners who have hitherto referred to themselves as 'Jungian analysts' have adopted the convention of referring to themselves as 'psychoanalysts'.[16]

Chapter 17: 'Healing the split' (1961)

(From 'Symbols and the interpretation of dreams', *The Symbolic Life, The Collected Works Vol.* 18, § 578–607)

We move from 'splits' in patients to splits in the collective psyche. Jung thought that the prevalence of neuroses in individuals is directly related to the dissociated condition of modern consciousness. The modern mind has been severed from its psychological and historical roots, and yet we expect it to keep on growing and to serve our desire for continued progress. The past has been forgotten or repressed as we speed toward an uncertain future. The dark background of consciousness, its origins in the non-rational sources of instinct and spirit, its powerful symbolic heritage in religions, myths and cosmologies, has been ditched in favour of being modern and up to date. Jung suspects that what we call 'modern' is a synonym for illness or disease: it is an epidemic of superficiality, denial and groundlessness. 'The modern standpoint is surely onesided and unjust. It does not even accord with the known facts' (§ 607). The modern is what the runaway ego has made of our world, and if we do not arrest this movement we will lose all substance and meaning.

'Healing the split' is the last section of Jung's final work, *Man and His Symbols*, and was completed ten days before his death. It was his attempt, after a lifetime of clinical research and professional engagement, to connect with a wider, popular audience beyond his specialist areas. Jung has a number of 'messages' to deliver to humanity at large, and these are delivered with earnestness. His core message is that things are not what they seem. There is more to reality than meets the eye, and we would do well to concentrate on this 'more' and reconcile ourselves to it. We have left too much out of our picture of the world, and the ego that seeks to describe reality for us is flawed and irresponsible. To follow the ego's directives, with its promises of freedom and independence, is to end in a fool's paradise. Despite such promises, the pursuit of the ego to the exclusion of all else leads to isolation from others, disconnection from the past, and irreality. We are learning what the East has always taught: that to follow surface appearances is to succumb to *maya* or illusion and to bring upon oneself a burden of suffering.

How do we plant our consciousness again in the dark soil of instinct and spirit? First we have to learn to be self-critical, to distrust habitual attitudes, to break with conventions. We need to risk forging a relationship with the age-old wisdom of the psyche, to listen to an ancient source inside us which sees reality through different eyes. We need to learn the language of this different source, which speaks in archetypes, myths and symbols. This is 'the language of nature, which is strange and incomprehensible to us' (§ 586), but we must take the trouble to familiarise ourselves with it. The ego refers to myths as lies and distortion, but it is the ego which is the real distortion. Jung asks us to turn reality on its head and view things from the inside out. If we can find the humility and self-criticism to take the non-ego into account, we might start to live with authenticity. We might begin to heal the split.

Jung insists that we cannot wait for society to recover the symbolic life for us. He has little faith in the official institutions of the modern era: 'Man today is painfully aware of the fact that neither his great religions nor his various philosophies seem to provide him with those powerful ideas that would give him the certainty and security he needs in face of the present condition of the world' (§ 599). We must work at a personal level on a recovery of the symbolic life. 'As any change must begin somewhere, it is the single individual who will undergo it and carry it through. The change must begin with one individual; it might be any one of us' (§ 599). It is by reflecting on our dreams that we can make contact with the archetypal symbols that well up from the depths. These symbols are 'natural attempts to reconcile and reunite often widely separated opposites' (§ 595).

For Jung, dreams are a true and reliable guide in a time of cultural decay and disorientation: 'The symbol-producing function of our dreams is an attempt to bring our original mind back to consciousness' (§ 591). It is an article of faith that the 'original mind' is a reality and can be accessed to our advantage, even now. 'We *have been* that mind,' he says, 'but we have never *known* it. We got rid of it before understanding it' (§ 591). Jung ends with an impassioned plea for bringing back the original mind that can restore sanity, proportion and balance to our lives. He is certain that we cannot return the world to order by our rational devices. He implores us to find the humility to call on a will which is greater than ours. I will close with one of Jung's favourite anecdotes, about why the modern person is out of touch with this greater source:

> Christians often ask why God does not speak to them, as he is believed to have done in former days. When I hear such questions, it always makes me think of the Rabbi who was asked how it could be that God often showed himself to people in the olden days but that nowadays one no longer saw him. The Rabbi replied: 'Nor is there anyone nowadays who could stoop so low.'
>
> (§ 600)

Notes

1. Andrew Samuels, *The Plural Psyche* (London and New York: Routledge, 1989).
2. Jung, *The Red Book: Liber Novus*, Sonu Shamdasani, ed. (New York: W. W. Norton, 2009).
3. Jung, letter to Carl Seelig, 25 February 1953, in Gerhard Adler, ed., *C.G. Jung Letters, Vol. 2, 1951–1961* (Princeton: Princeton University Press, 1971), p. 109.
4. Joseph Cambray, *Synchronicity: Nature and Psyche in an Interconnected Universe* (College Station, TX: Texas A&M University Press, 2009).
5. Wolfgang Pauli and C. G. Jung, *The Interpretation of Nature and the Psyche* (1952) (London: Routledge & Kegan Paul, 1955).
6. The full paper appears as 'Synchronicity: An Acausal Connecting Principle' (1952), in *CW* 8, § 816–968.
7. Gilles Quispel, quoted in Robert Segal, June Singer, and Murray Stein, eds, *The Allure of Gnosticism: The Gnostic Experience in Jungian Psychology and Contemporary Culture* (Chicago: Open Court, 1995), p. 19.
8. Freud, *The Psychopathology of Everyday Life* (1901), *SE* 6, pp. 258–259.
9. Jung, 'Psychological Commentary on *The Tibetan Book of the Great Liberation*' (1939/1954), *CW* 11, § 761.
10. Jung, 'On the Psychology of the Unconscious' (1917/1926/1943), *CW* 7, § 58, § 59.
11. Although some English dictionaries spell the word as 'extroversion', the correct spelling is extraversion.
12. See Frederick G. Weiss, ed., *Hegel: The Essential Writings* (New York: Harper & Row, 1974).
13. Jung, 'On the Nature of the Psyche' (1947/1954), *CW* 8, § 358.
14. Jung, 'The Psychology of the Transference' (1946), *CW* 16.
15. For the best overview of the role of transference in the Jungian tradition, see Jan Wiener, *The Therapeutic Relationship: Transference, Countertransference, and the Making of Meaning* (College Station, TX: Texas A&M University Press, 2009).
16. See Murray Stein, ed., *Jungian Psychoanalysis* (Chicago: Open Court, 2010).

Chapter 13

The aims of psychotherapy[1]

66 It is generally agreed today that neuroses are functional psychic disturbances and are therefore to be cured preferably by psychological treatment. But when we come to the question of the structure of the neuroses and the principles of therapy, all agreement ends, and we have to acknowledge that we have as yet no fully satisfactory conception of the nature of the neuroses or of the principles of treatment. While it is true that two currents or schools of thought have gained a special hearing, they by no means exhaust the number of divergent opinions that actually exist. There are also numerous non-partisans who, amid the general conflict of opinion, have their own special views. If, therefore, we wanted to paint a comprehensive picture of this diversity, we should have to mix upon our palette all the hues and shadings of the rainbow. I would gladly paint such a picture if it lay within my power, for I have always felt the need for a conspectus of the many viewpoints. I have never succeeded in the long run in not giving divergent opinions their due. Such opinions could never arise, much less secure a following, if they did not correspond to some special disposition, some special character, some fundamental psychological fact that is more or less universal. Were we to exclude one such opinion as simply wrong and worthless, we should be rejecting this particular disposition or this particular fact as a misinterpretation – in other words, we should be doing violence to our own empirical material. The wide approval which greeted Freud's explanation of neurosis in terms of sexual causation and his view that the happenings in the psyche turn essentially upon infantile pleasure and its satisfaction should be instructive to the psychologist. It shows him that this manner of thinking and feeling coincides with a fairly widespread trend or spiritual current which, independently of Freud's theory, has made itself felt in other places, in other circumstances, in other minds, and in other forms. I should call it a manifestation of the collective psyche. Let me remind you here of the works of Havelock Ellis and August Forel and the contributors to *Anthropophyteia*;[2] then of the changed attitude to sex in Anglo-Saxon countries during the post-Victorian period, and the broad discussion of sexual matters in literature, which had already started with the French realists. Freud is one of the exponents of a contemporary psychological fact which has a special history of its own; but for obvious reasons we cannot go into that here.

67 The acclaim which Adler, like Freud, has met with on both sides of the Atlantic points similarly to the undeniable fact that, for a great many people, the need for self-assertion arising from a sense of inferiority is a plausible basis of explanation. Nor can it be disputed that this view accounts for psychic actualities which are not given their due in the Freudian system. I need hardly mention in detail the collective psychological forces and social factors that favour the Adlerian view and make it their theoretical exponent. These matters are sufficiently obvious.

68 It would be an unpardonable error to overlook the element of truth in both the Freudian and the Adlerian viewpoints, but it would be no less unpardonable to take either of them as the sole truth. Both truths correspond to psychic realities. There are in fact some cases which by and large can best be described and explained by the one theory, and some by the other.

69 I can accuse neither of these two investigators of any fundamental error; on the contrary, I endeavour to apply both hypotheses as far as possible because I fully recognize their relative rightness. It would certainly never have occurred to me to depart from Freud's path had I not stumbled upon facts which forced me into modifications. And the same is true of my relation to the Adlerian viewpoint.

70 After what has been said it seems hardly necessary to add that I hold the truth of my own deviationist views to be equally relative, and feel myself so very much the mere exponent of another disposition that I could almost say with Coleridge: 'I believe in the one and only saving Church, of which at present I am the only member.'[3]

71 It is in applied psychology, if anywhere, that we must be modest today and bear with an apparent plurality of contradictory opinions; for we are still far from having anything like a thorough knowledge of the human psyche, that most challenging field of scientific inquiry. At present we have merely more or less plausible opinions that cannot be squared with one another.

72 If, therefore, I undertake to say something about my views I hope I shall not be misunderstood. I am not advertising a novel truth, still less am I announcing a final gospel. I can only speak of attempts to throw light on psychic facts that are obscure to me, or of efforts to overcome therapeutic difficulties.

73 And it is just with this last point that I should like to begin, for here lies the most pressing need for modifications. As is well known, one can get along for quite a time with an inadequate theory, but not with inadequate therapeutic methods. In my psychotherapeutic practice of nearly thirty years I have met with a fair number of failures which made a far deeper impression on me than my successes. Anybody can have successes in psychotherapy, starting with the primitive medicine-man and faith-healer. The psychotherapist learns little or nothing from his successes, for they chiefly confirm him in his mistakes. But failures are priceless experiences because they not only open the way to a better truth but force us to modify our views and methods.

74 I certainly recognize how much my work has been furthered first by Freud and then by Adler, and in practice I try to acknowledge this debt by making use of

their views, whenever possible, in the treatment of my patients. Nevertheless I must insist that I have experienced failures which, I felt, might have been avoided had I considered the facts that subsequently forced me to modify their views.

75 To describe all the situations I came up against is almost impossible, so I must content myself with singling out a few typical cases. It was with older patients that I had the greatest difficulties, that is, with persons over forty. In handling younger people I generally get along with the familiar viewpoints of Freud and Adler, for these tend to bring the patient to a certain level of adaptation and normality. Both views are eminently applicable to the young, apparently without leaving any disturbing after-effects. In my experience this is not so often the case with older people. It seems to me that the basic facts of the psyche undergo a very marked alteration in the course of life, so much so that we could almost speak of a psychology of life's morning and a psychology of its afternoon. As a rule, the life of a young person is characterized by a general expansion and a striving towards concrete ends; and his neurosis seems mainly to rest on his hesitation or shrinking back from this necessity. But the life of an older person is characterized by a contraction of forces, by the affirmation of what has been achieved, and by the curtailment of further growth. His neurosis comes mainly from his clinging to a youthful attitude which is now out of season. Just as the young neurotic is afraid of life, so the older one shrinks back from death. What was a normal goal for the young man becomes a neurotic hindrance to the old – just as, through his hesitation to face the world, the young neurotic's originally normal dependence on his parents grows into an incest-relationship that is inimical to life. It is natural that neurosis, resistance, repression, transference, 'guiding fictions,' and so forth should have one meaning in the young person and quite another in the old, despite apparent similarities. The aims of therapy should undoubtedly be modified to meet this fact. Hence the age of the patient seems to me a most important *indicium*.

76 But there are various *indicia* also within the youthful phase of life. Thus, in my estimation, it is a technical blunder to apply the Freudian viewpoint to a patient with the Adlerian type of psychology, that is, an unsuccessful person with an infantile need to assert himself. Conversely, it would be a gross misunderstanding to force the Adlerian viewpoint on a successful man with a pronounced pleasure-principle psychology. When in a quandary the resistances of the patient may be valuable signposts. I am inclined to take deep-seated resistances seriously at first, paradoxical as this may sound, for I am convinced that the doctor does not necessarily know better than the patient's own psychic constitution, of which the patient himself may be quite unconscious. This modesty on the part of the doctor is altogether becoming in view of the fact that there is not only no generally valid psychology today but rather an untold variety of temperaments and of more or less individual psyches that refuse to fit into any scheme.

77 You know that in this matter of temperament I postulate two different basic attitudes in accordance with the typical differences already suspected by many students of human nature – namely, the extraverted and the introverted attitudes.

306 Therapy and healing

These attitudes, too, I take to be important *indicia,* and likewise the predominance of one particular psychic function over the others.[4]

78 The extraordinary diversity of individual life necessitates constant modifications of theory which are often applied quite unconsciously by the doctor himself, although in principle they may not accord at all with his theoretical creed.

79 While we are on this question of temperament I should not omit to mention that there are some people whose attitude is essentially spiritual and others whose attitude is essentially materialistic. It must not be imagined that such an attitude is acquired accidentally or springs from mere misunderstanding. Very often they are ingrained passions which no criticism and no persuasion can stamp out; there are even cases where an apparently outspoken materialism has its source in a denial of religious temperament. Cases of the reverse type are more easily credited today, although they are not more frequent than the others. This too is an *indicium* which in my opinion ought not to be overlooked.

80 When we use the word *indicium* it might appear to mean, as is usual in medical parlance, that this or that treatment is indicated. Perhaps this should be the case, but psychotherapy has at present reached no such degree of certainty – for which reason our *indicia* are unfortunately not much more than warnings against one-sidedness.

81 The human psyche is a thing of enormous ambiguity. In every single case we have to ask ourselves whether an attitude or a so-called *habitus* is authentic, or whether it may not be just a compensation for its opposite. I must confess that I have so often been deceived in this matter that in any concrete case I am at pains to avoid all theoretical presuppositions about the structure of the neurosis and about what the patient can and ought to do. As far as possible I let pure experience decide the therapeutic aims. This may perhaps seem strange, because it is commonly supposed that the therapist has an aim. But in psychotherapy it seems to me positively advisable for the doctor not to have too fixed an aim. He can hardly know better than the nature and will to live of the patient. The great decisions in human life usually have far more to do with the instincts and other mysterious unconscious factors than with conscious will and well-meaning reasonableness. The shoe that fits one person pinches another; there is no universal recipe for living. Each of us carries his own life-form within him – an irrational form which no other can outbid.

82 All this naturally does not prevent us from doing our utmost to make the patient normal and reasonable. If the therapeutic results are satisfactory, we can probably let it go at that. If not, then for better or worse the therapist must be guided by the patient's own irrationalities. Here we must follow nature as a guide, and what the doctor then does is less a question of treatment than of developing the creative possibilities latent in the patient himself.

83 What I have to say begins where the treatment leaves off and this development sets in. Thus my contribution to psychotherapy confines itself to those cases where rational treatment does not yield satisfactory results. The clinical material at my disposal is of a peculiar composition: new cases are decidedly in the

minority. Most of them already have some form of psychotherapeutic treatment behind them, with partial or negative results. About a third of my cases are not suffering from any clinically definable neurosis, but from the senselessness and aimlessness of their lives. I should not object if this were called the general neurosis of our age. Fully two thirds of my patients are in the second half of life.

84   This peculiar material sets up a special resistance to rational methods of treatment, probably because most of my patients are socially well-adapted individuals, often of outstanding ability, to whom normalization means nothing. As for so-called normal people, there I really am in a fix, for I have no ready-made philosophy of life to hand out to them. In the majority of my cases the resources of the conscious mind are exhausted (or, in ordinary English, they are 'stuck'). It is chiefly this fact that forces me to look for hidden possibilities. For I do not know what to say to the patient when he asks me, 'What do you advise? What shall I do?' I don't know either. I only know one thing: when my conscious mind no longer sees any possible road ahead and consequently gets stuck, my unconscious psyche will react to the unbearable standstill.

85   This 'getting stuck' is a psychic occurrence so often repeated during the course of human history that it has become the theme of many myths and fairytales. We are told of the Open sesame! to the locked door, or of some helpful animal who finds the hidden way. In other words, getting stuck is a typical event which, in the course of time, has evoked typical reactions and compensations. We may therefore expect with some probability that something similar will appear in the reactions of the unconscious, as, for example, in dreams.

86   In such cases, then, my attention is directed more particularly to dreams. This is not because I am tied to the notion that dreams must always be called to the rescue, or because I possess a mysterious dream-theory which tells me how everything must shape itself; but quite simply from perplexity. I do not know where else to go for help, and so I try to find it in dreams. These at least present us with images pointing to something or other, and that is better than nothing. I have no theory about dreams, I do not know how dreams arise. And I am not at all sure that my way of handling dreams even deserves the name of a 'method.' I share all your prejudices against dream-interpretation as the quintessence of uncertainty and arbitrariness. On the other hand, I know that if we meditate on a dream sufficiently long and thoroughly, if we carry it around with us and turn it over and over, something almost always comes of it. This something is not of course a scientific result to be boasted about or rationalized; but it is an important practical hint which shows the patient what the unconscious is aiming at. Indeed, it ought not to matter to me whether the result of my musings on the dream is scientifically verifiable or tenable, otherwise I am pursuing an ulterior – and therefore autoerotic – aim. I must content myself wholly with the fact that the result means something to the patient and sets his life in motion again. I may allow myself only one criterion for the result of my labours: Does it work? As for my scientific hobby – my desire to know *why* it works – this I must reserve for my spare time.

87 Infinitely varied are the contents of the initial dreams, that is, the dreams that come at the outset of the treatment. In many cases they point directly to the past and recall things lost and forgotten. For very often the standstill and disorientation arise when life has become one-sided, and this may, in psychological terms, cause a sudden loss of libido. All our previous activities become uninteresting, even senseless, and our aims suddenly no longer worth striving for. What in one person is merely a passing mood may in another become a chronic condition. In these cases it often happens that other possibilities for developing the personality lie buried somewhere or other in the past, unknown to anybody, not even to the patient. But the dream may reveal the clue.

88 In other cases the dream points to present facts, for example marriage or social position, which the conscious mind has never accepted as sources of problems or conflicts.

89 Both possibilities come within the sphere of the rational, and I daresay I would have no difficulty in making such initial dreams seem plausible. The real difficulty begins when the dreams do not point to anything tangible, and this they do often enough, especially when they hold anticipations of the future. I do not mean that such dreams are necessarily prophetic, merely that they feel the way, they 'reconnoitre.' These dreams contain inklings of possibilities and for that reason can never be made plausible to an outsider. Sometimes they are not plausible even to me, and then I usually say to the patient, 'I don't believe it, but follow up the clue.' As I have said, the sole criterion is the stimulating effect, but it is by no means necessary for me to understand why such an effect takes place.

90 This is particularly true of dreams that contain something like an 'unconscious metaphysics,' by which I mean mythological analogies that are sometimes incredibly strange and baffling.

91 Now, you will certainly protest: How on earth can I know that the dreams contain anything like an unconscious metaphysics? And here I must confess that I do not really know. I know far too little about dreams for that. I see only the effect on the patient, of which I would like to give you a little example.

92 In a long initial dream of one of my 'normal' patients, the illness of his sister's child played an important part. She was a little girl of two.

93 Some time before, this sister had in fact lost a boy through illness, but otherwise none of her children was ill. The occurrence of the sick child in the dream at first proved baffling to the dreamer, probably because it failed to fit the facts. Since there was no direct and intimate connection between the dreamer and his sister, he could feel in this image little that was personal to him. Then he suddenly remembered that two years earlier he had taken up the study of occultism, in the course of which he also discovered psychology. So the child evidently represented his interest in the psyche – an idea I should never have arrived at of my own accord. Seen purely theoretically, this dream image can mean anything or nothing. For that matter, does a thing or a fact ever mean anything in itself? The only certainty is that it is always man who interprets, who assigns meaning. And that is the gist of the matter for psychology. It impressed the dreamer as a novel and interesting

idea that the study of occultism might have something sickly about it. Somehow the thought struck home. And this is the decisive point: the interpretation works, however we may elect to account for its working. For the dreamer the thought was an implied criticism, and through it a certain change of attitude was brought about. By such slight changes, which one could never think up rationally, things are set in motion and the dead point is overcome, at least in principle.

94 From this example I could say figuratively that the dream meant that there was something sickly about the dreamer's occult studies, and in this sense – since the dream brought him to such an idea – I can also speak of 'unconscious metaphysics.'

95 But I go still further: Not only do I give the patient an opportunity to find associations to his dreams, I give myself the same opportunity. Further, I present him with my ideas and opinions. If, in so doing, I open the door to 'suggestion,' I see no occasion for regret; for it is well known that we are susceptible only to those suggestions with which we are already secretly in accord. No harm is done if now and then one goes astray in this riddle-reading: sooner or later the psyche will reject the mistake, much as the organism rejects a foreign body. I do not need to prove that my interpretation of the dream is right (a pretty hopeless undertaking anyway), but must simply try to discover, with the patient, what *acts* for him – I am almost tempted to say, what is actual.

96 For this reason it is particularly important for me to know as much as possible about primitive psychology, mythology, archaeology, and comparative religion, because these fields offer me invaluable analogies with which I can enrich the associations of my patients. Together, we can then find meaning in apparent irrelevancies and thus vastly increase the effectiveness of the dream. For the layman who has done his utmost in the personal and rational sphere of life and yet has found no meaning and no satisfaction there, it is enormously important to be able to enter a sphere of irrational experience. In this way, too, the habitual and the commonplace come to wear an altered countenance, and can even acquire a new glamour. For it all depends on how we look at things, and not on how they are in themselves. The least of things with a meaning is always worth more in life than the greatest of things without it.

97 I do not think I underestimate the risk of this undertaking. It is as if one began to build a bridge out into space. Indeed, the ironist might even allege – and has often done so – that in following this procedure both doctor and patient are indulging in mere fantasy-spinning.

98 This objection is no counter-argument, but is very much to the point. I even make an effort to second the patient in his fantasies. Truth to tell, I have no small opinion of fantasy. To me, it is the maternally creative side of the masculine mind. When all is said and done, we can never rise above fantasy. It is true that there are unprofitable, futile, morbid, and unsatisfying fantasies whose sterile nature is immediately recognized by every person endowed with common sense; but the faulty performance proves nothing against the normal performance. All the works of man have their origin in creative imagination. What right, then, have we to

disparage fantasy? In the normal course of things, fantasy does not easily go astray; it is too deep for that, and too closely bound up with the tap-root of human and animal instinct. It has a surprising way of always coming out right in the end. The creative activity of imagination frees man from his bondage to the 'nothing but'[5] and raises him to the status of one who plays. As Schiller says, man is completely human only when he is at play.

99   My aim is to bring about a psychic state in which my patient begins to experiment with his own nature – a state of fluidity, change, and growth where nothing is eternally fixed and hopelessly petrified. I can here of course adumbrate only the principles of my technique. Those of you who happen to be acquainted with my works can easily imagine the necessary parallels. I would only like to emphasize that you should not think of my procedure as entirely without aim or limit. In handling a dream or fantasy I make it a rule never to go beyond the meaning which is effective for the patient; I merely try to make him as fully conscious of this meaning as possible, so that he shall also become aware of its supra-personal connections. For, when something happens to a man and he supposes it to be personal only to himself, whereas in reality it is a quite universal experience, then his attitude is obviously wrong, that is, too personal, and it tends to exclude him from human society. By the same token we need to have not only a personal, contemporary consciousness, but also a supra-personal consciousness with a sense of historical continuity. However abstract this may sound, practical experience shows that many neuroses are caused primarily by the fact that people blind themselves to their own religious promptings because of a childish passion for rational enlightenment. It is high time the psychologist of today recognized that we are no longer dealing with dogmas and creeds but with the religious attitude *per se,* whose importance as a psychic function can hardly be overrated. And it is precisely for the religious function that the sense of historical continuity is indispensable.

100   Coming back to the question of my technique, I ask myself how far I am indebted to Freud for its existence. At all events I learned it from Freud's method of free association, and I regard it as a direct extension of that.

101   So long as I help the patient to discover the effective elements in his dreams, and so long as I try to get him to see the general meaning of his symbols, he is still, psychologically speaking, in a state of childhood. For the time being he is dependent on his dreams and is always asking himself whether the next dream will give him new light or not. Moreover, he is dependent on my having ideas about his dreams and on my ability to increase his insight through my knowledge. Thus he is still in an undesirably passive condition where everything is rather uncertain and questionable; neither he nor I know the journey's end. Often it is not much more than a groping about in Egyptian darkness. In this condition we must not expect any very startling results – the uncertainty is too great for that. Besides which there is always the risk that what we have woven by day the night will unravel. The danger is that nothing permanent is achieved, that nothing remains fixed. It not infrequently happens in these situations that the patient has a

particularly vivid or curious dream, and says to me, 'Do you know, if only I were a painter I would make a picture of it.' Or the dreams are about photographs, paintings, drawings, or illuminated manuscripts, or even about the films.

102   I have turned these hints to practical account, urging my patients at such times to paint in reality what they have seen in dream or fantasy. As a rule I am met with the objection, 'But I am not a painter!' To this I usually reply that neither are modern painters, and that consequently modern painting is free for all, and that anyhow it is not a question of beauty but only of the trouble one takes with the picture. How true this is I saw recently in the case of a talented professional portraitist; she had to begin my way of painting all over again with pitiably childish efforts, literally as if she had never held a brush in her hand. To paint what we see before us is a different art from painting what we see within.

103   Many of my more advanced patients, then, begin to paint. I can well understand that everyone will be profoundly impressed with the utter futility of this sort of dilettantism. Do not forget, however, that we are speaking not of people who still have to prove their social usefulness, but of those who can no longer see any sense in being socially useful and who have come upon the deeper and more dangerous question of the meaning of their own individual lives. To be a particle in the mass has meaning and charm only for the man who has not yet reached that stage, but none for the man who is sick to death of being a particle. The importance of what life means to the individual may be denied by those who are socially below the general level of adaptation, and is invariably denied by the educator whose ambition it is to breed mass-men. But those who belong to neither category will sooner or later come up against this painful question.

104   Although my patients occasionally produce artistically beautiful things that might very well be shown in modern 'art' exhibitions, I nevertheless treat them as completely worthless when judged by the canons of real art. As a matter of fact, it is essential that they should be considered worthless, otherwise my patients might imagine themselves to be artists, and the whole point of the exercise would be missed. It is not a question of art at all – or rather, it should not be a question of art – but of something more and other than mere art, namely the living effect upon the patient himself. The meaning of individual life, whose importance from the social standpoint is negligible, stands here at its highest, and for its sake the patient struggles to give form, however crude and childish, to the inexpressible.

105   But why do I encourage patients, when they arrive at a certain stage in their development, to express themselves by means of brush, pencil, or pen at all?

106   Here again my prime purpose is to produce an effect. In the state of psychological childhood described above, the patient remains passive; but now he begins to play an active part. To start off with, he puts down on paper what he has passively seen, thereby turning it into a deliberate act. He not only talks about it, he is actually doing something about it. Psychologically speaking, it makes a vast difference whether a man has an interesting conversation with his doctor two or three times a week, the results of which are left hanging in mid air, or whether he has to struggle for hours with refractory brush and colours, only to produce in the

end something which, taken at its face value, is perfectly senseless. If it were really senseless to him, the effort to paint it would be so repugnant that he could scarcely be brought to perform this exercise a second time. But because his fantasy does not strike him as entirely senseless, his busying himself with it only increases its effect upon him. Moreover, the concrete shaping of the image enforces a continuous study of it in all its parts, so that it can develop its effects to the full. This invests the bare fantasy with an element of reality, which lends it greater weight and greater driving power. And these rough-and-ready pictures do indeed produce effects which, I must admit, are rather difficult to describe. For instance, a patient needs only to have seen once or twice how much he is freed from a wretched state of mind by working at a symbolical picture, and he will always turn to this means of release whenever things go badly with him. In this way something of inestimable importance is won – the beginning of independence, a step towards psychological maturity. The patient can make himself creatively independent through this method, if I may call it such. He is no longer dependent on his dreams or on his doctor's knowledge; instead, by painting himself he gives shape to himself. For what he paints are active fantasies – that which is active within him. And that which is active within is himself, but no longer in the guise of his previous error, when he mistook the personal ego for the self; it is himself in a new and hitherto alien sense, for his ego now appears as the object of that which works within him. In countless pictures he strives to catch this interior agent, only to discover in the end that it is eternally unknown and alien, the hidden foundation of psychic life.

107 It is impossible for me to describe the extent to which this discovery changes the patient's standpoint and values, and how it shifts the centre of gravity of his personality. It is as though the earth had suddenly discovered that the sun was the centre of the planetary orbits and of its own earthly orbit as well.

108 But have we not always known this to be so? I myself believe that we have always known it. But I may know something with my head which the other man in me is far from knowing, for indeed and in truth I live as though I did not know it. Most of my patients knew the deeper truth, but did not live it. And why did they not live it? Because of that bias which makes us all live from the ego, a bias which comes from overvaluation of the conscious mind.

109 It is of the greatest importance for the young person, who is still unadapted and has as yet achieved nothing, to shape his conscious ego as effectively as possible, that is, to educate his will. Unless he is a positive genius he cannot, indeed he should not, believe in anything active within him that is not identical with his will. He must feel himself a man of will, and may safely depreciate everything else in him and deem it subject to his will, for without this illusion he could not succeed in adapting himself socially.

110 It is otherwise with a person in the second half of life who no longer needs to educate his conscious will, but who, to understand the meaning of his individual life, needs to experience his own inner being. Social usefulness is no longer an aim for him, although he does not deny its desirability. Fully aware as he is of the

social unimportance of his creative activity, he feels it more as a way of working at himself to his own benefit. Increasingly, too, this activity frees him from morbid dependence, and he thus acquires an inner stability and a new trust in himself. These last achievements now redound to the good of the patient's social existence; for an inwardly stable and self-confident person will prove more adequate to his social tasks than one who is on a bad footing with his unconscious.

111 I have purposely avoided loading my lecture with theory, hence much must remain obscure and unexplained. But, in order to make the pictures produced by my patients intelligible, certain theoretical points must at least receive mention. A feature common to all these pictures is a primitive symbolism which is conspicuous both in the drawing and in the colouring. The colours are as a rule quite barbaric in their intensity. Often an unmistakable archaic quality is present. These peculiarities point to the nature of the underlying creative forces. They are irrational, symbolistic currents that run through the whole history of mankind, and are so archaic in character that it is not difficult to find their parallels in archaeology and comparative religion. We may therefore take it that our pictures spring chiefly from those regions of the psyche which I have termed the collective unconscious. By this I understand an unconscious psychic functioning common to all men, the source not only of our modern symbolical pictures but of all similar products in the past. Such pictures spring from, and satisfy, a natural need. It is as if a part of the psyche that reaches far back into the primitive past were expressing itself in these pictures and finding it possible to function in harmony with our alien conscious mind. This collaboration satisfies and thus mitigates the psyche's disturbing demands upon the latter. It must, however, be added that the mere execution of the pictures is not enough. Over and above that, an intellectual and emotional understanding is needed; they require to be not only rationally integrated with the conscious mind, but morally assimilated. They still have to be subjected to a work of synthetic interpretation. Although I have travelled this path with individual patients many times, I have never yet succeeded in making all the details of the process clear enough for publication.[6] So far this has been fragmentary only. The truth is, we are here moving in absolutely new territory, and a ripening of experience is the first requisite. For very important reasons I am anxious to avoid hasty conclusions. We are dealing with a process of psychic life outside consciousness, and our observation of it is indirect. As yet we do not know to what depths our vision will plumb. It would seem to be some kind of centring process, for a great many pictures which the patients themselves feel to be decisive point in this direction. During this centring process what we call the ego appears to take up a peripheral position. The change is apparently brought about by an emergence of the historical part of the psyche. Exactly what is the purpose of this process remains at first sight obscure. We can only remark its important effect on the conscious personality. From the fact that the change heightens the feeling for life and maintains the flow of life, we must conclude that it is animated by a peculiar purposefulness. We might perhaps call this a new illusion. But what is 'illusion'? By what criterion do we judge something to be an

illusion? Does anything exist for the psyche that we are entitled to call illusion? What we are pleased to call illusion may be for the psyche an extremely important life-factor, something as indispensable as oxygen for the body – a psychic actuality of overwhelming significance. Presumably the psyche does not trouble itself about our categories of reality; for it, everything that *works* is real. The investigator of the psyche must not confuse it with his consciousness, else he veils from his sight the object of his investigation. On the contrary, to recognize it at all, he must learn to see how different it is from consciousness. Nothing is more probable than that what we call illusion is very real for the psyche – for which reason we cannot take psychic reality to be commensurable with conscious reality. To the psychologist there is nothing more fatuous than the attitude of the missionary who pronounces the gods of the 'poor heathen' to be mere illusion. Unfortunately we still go blundering along in the same dogmatic way, as though *our* so-called reality were not equally full of illusion. In psychic life, as everywhere in our experience, all things that work are reality, regardless of the names man chooses to bestow on them. To take these realities for what they are – not foisting other names on them – that is our business. To the psyche, spirit is no less spirit for being named sexuality.

112 I must repeat that these designations and the changes rung upon them never even remotely touch the essence of the process we have described. It cannot be compassed by the rational concepts of the conscious mind, any more than life itself; and it is for this reason that my patients consistently turn to the representation and interpretation of symbols as the more adequate and effective course.

113 With this I have said pretty well everything I can say about my therapeutic aims and intentions within the broad framework of a lecture. It can be no more than an incentive to thought, and I shall be quite content if such it has been.

Notes

1 [*Delivered as a lecture, 'Ziele der Psychotherapie,' on April 12, 1929, at the 4th General Medical Congress for Psychotherapy, Bad Nauheim, and published in the *Bericht* of the Congress, 1929; republished in *Seelenprobleme der Gegenwart* (Zurich, 1931), pp. 87–114. Previously trans. by C. F. Baynes and W. S. Dell in *Modern Man in Search of a Soul* (London and New York, 1933).–EDITORS.]
2 [Published at Leipzig, 1904–13.–EDITORS.]
3 [*The attribution to Coleridge is incorrect, according to Coleridgean scholars who were consulted.–EDITORS.]
4 [Viz., thinking, feeling, sensation, and intuition.–EDITORS.]
5 [*The term 'nothing but' (*nichts als*) denotes the common habit of explaining something unknown by reducing it to something apparently known and thereby devaluing it. For instance, when a certain illness is said to be 'nothing but psychic,' it is explained as imaginary and is thus devalued. The expression is borrowed from James, *The Varieties of Religious Experience,* p. 12.–EDITORS.]
6 *This has since been remedied. Cf. 'A Study in the Process of Individuation.' [Also cf. *Psychology and Alchemy*, Part II.–EDITORS.]

Chapter 14

On synchronicity[1]

969 It might seem appropriate to begin my exposition by defining the concept with which it deals. But I would rather approach the subject the other way and first give you a brief description of the facts which the concept of synchronicity is intended to cover. As its etymology shows, this term has something to do with time or, to be more accurate, with a kind of simultaneity. Instead of simultaneity we could also use the concept of a *meaningful coincidence* of two or more events, where something other than the probability of chance is involved. A statistical – that is, a probable – concurrence of events, such as the 'duplication of cases' found in hospitals, falls within the category of chance. Groupings of this kind can consist of any number of terms and still remain within the framework of the probable and rationally possible. Thus, for instance, someone chances to notice the number on his street-car ticket. On arriving home he receives a telephone call during which the same number is mentioned. In the evening he buys a theatre ticket that again has the same number. The three events form a chance grouping that, although not likely to occur often, nevertheless lies well within the framework of probability owing to the frequency of each of its terms. I would like to recount from my own experience the following chance grouping, made up of no fewer than six terms:

970 On April 1, 1949, I made a note in the morning of an inscription containing a figure that was half man and half fish. There was fish for lunch. Somebody mentioned the custom of making an 'April fish' of someone. In the afternoon, a former patient of mine, whom I had not seen for months, showed me some impressive pictures of fish. In the evening, I was shown a piece of embroidery with sea monsters and fishes in it. The next morning, I saw a former patient, who was visiting me for the first time in ten years. She had dreamed of a large fish the night before. A few months later, when I was using this series for a larger work and had just finished writing it down, I walked over to a spot by the lake in front of the house, where I had already been several times that morning. This time a fish a foot long lay on the sea-wall. Since no one else was present, I have no idea how the fish could have got there.

971 When coincidences pile up in this way one cannot help being impressed by them – for the greater the number of terms in such a series, or the more unusual its character, the more improbable it becomes. For reasons that I have mentioned

elsewhere and will not discuss now, I assume that this was a chance grouping. It must be admitted, though, that it is more improbable than a mere duplication.

972 In the above-mentioned case of the street-car ticket, I said that the observer 'chanced' to notice the number and retain it in his memory, which ordinarily he would never have done. This formed the basis for the series of chance events, but I do not know what caused him to notice the number. It seems to me that in judging such a series a factor of uncertainty enters in at this point and requires attention. I have observed something similar in other cases, without, however, being able to draw any reliable conclusions. But it is sometimes difficult to avoid the impression that there is a sort of foreknowledge of the coming series of events. This feeling becomes irresistible when, as so frequently happens, one thinks one is about to meet an old friend in the street, only to find to one's disappointment that it is a stranger. On turning the next corner one then runs into him in person. Cases of this kind occur in every conceivable form and by no means infrequently, but after the first momentary astonishment they are as a rule quickly forgotten.

973 Now, the more the foreseen details of an event pile up, the more definite is the impression of an existing foreknowledge, and the more improbable does chance become. I remember the story of a student friend whose father had promised him a trip to Spain if he passed his final examinations satisfactorily. My friend thereupon dreamed that he was walking through a Spanish city. The street led to a square, where there was a Gothic cathedral. He then turned right, around a corner, into another street. There he was met by an elegant carriage drawn by two cream-coloured horses. Then he woke up. He told us about the dream as we were sitting round a table drinking beer. Shortly afterward, having successfully passed his examinations, he went to Spain, and there, in one of the streets, he recognized the city of his dream. He found the square and the cathedral, which exactly corresponded to the dream-image. He wanted to go straight to the cathedral, but then remembered that in the dream he had turned right, at the corner, into another street. He was curious to find out whether his dream would be corroborated further. Hardly had he turned the corner when he saw in reality the carriage with the two cream-coloured horses.

974 The *sentiment du déjà-vu* is based, as I have found in a number of cases, on a foreknowledge in dreams, but we saw that this foreknowledge can also occur in the waking state. In such cases mere chance becomes highly improbable because the coincidence is known in advance. It thus loses its chance character not only psychologically and subjectively, but objectively too, since the accumulation of details that coincide immeasurably increases the improbability of chance as a determining factor. (For correct precognitions of death, Dariex and Flammarion have computed probabilities ranging from 1 in 4,000,000 to 1 in 8,000,000.)[2] So in these cases it would be incongruous to speak of 'chance' happenings. It is rather a question of meaningful coincidences. Usually they are explained by precognition – in other words, foreknowledge. People also talk of clairvoyance, telepathy, etc., without, however, being able to explain what these faculties consist of or what means of transmission they use in order to render events distant in

On synchronicity 317

space and time accessible to our perception. All these ideas are mere names; they are not scientific concepts which could be taken as statements of principle, for no one has yet succeeded in constructing a causal bridge between the elements making up a meaningful coincidence.

975   Great credit is due to J. B. Rhine for having established a reliable basis for work in the vast field of these phenomena by his experiments in extrasensory perception, or ESP. He used a pack of 25 cards divided into 5 groups of 5, each with its special sign (star, square, circle, cross, two wavy lines). The experiment was carried out as follows. In each series of experiments the pack is laid out 800 times, in such a way that the subject cannot see the cards. He is then asked to guess the cards as they are turned up. The probability of a correct answer is 1 in 5. The result, computed from very high figures, showed an average of 6.5 hits. The probability of a chance deviation of 1.5 amounts to only 1 in 250,000. Some individuals scored more than twice the probable number of hits. On one occasion all 25 cards were guessed correctly, which gives a probability of 1 in 298,023,223,876,953,125. The spatial distance between experimenter and subject was increased from a few yards to about 4,000 miles, with no effect on the result.

976   A second type of experiment consisted in asking the subject to guess a series of cards that was still to be laid out in the near or more distant future. The time factor was increased from a few minutes to two weeks. The result of these experiments showed a probability of 1 in 400,000.

977   In a third type of experiment, the subject had to try to influence the fall of mechanically thrown dice by wishing for a certain number. The results of this so-called psychokinetic (PK) experiment were the more positive the more dice were used at a time.

978   The result of the spatial experiment proves with tolerable certainty that the psyche can, to some extent, eliminate the space factor. The time experiment proves that the time factor (at any rate, in the dimension of the future) can become psychically relative. The experiment with dice proves that moving bodies, too, can be influenced psychically – a result that could have been predicted from the psychic relativity of space and time.

979   The energy postulate shows itself to be inapplicable to the Rhine experiments, and thus rules out all ideas about the transmission of force. Equally, the law of causality does not hold – a fact that I pointed out thirty years ago. For we cannot conceive how a future event could bring about an event in the present. Since for the time being there is no possibility whatever of a causal explanation, we must assume provisionally that improbable accidents of an acausal nature – that is, meaningful coincidences – have entered the picture.

980   In considering these remarkable results we must take into account a fact discovered by Rhine, namely that in each series of experiments the first attempts yielded a better result than the later ones. The falling off in the number of hits scored was connected with the mood of the subject. An initial mood of faith and optimism makes for good results. Scepticism and resistance have the opposite effect, that is, they create an unfavourable disposition. As the energic, and hence also the causal,

approach to these experiments has shown itself to be inapplicable, it follows that the affective factor has the significance simply of a *condition* which makes it possible for the phenomenon to occur, though it need not. According to Rhine's results, we may nevertheless expect 6.5 hits instead of only 5. But it cannot be predicted in advance when the hit will come. Could we do so, we would be dealing with a law, and this would contradict the entire nature of the phenomenon. It has, as said, the improbable character of a 'lucky hit' or accident that occurs with a more than merely probable frequency and is as a rule dependent on a certain state of affectivity.

981 This observation has been thoroughly confirmed, and it suggests that the psychic factor which modifies or even eliminates the principles underlying the physicist's picture of the world is connected with the affective state of the subject. Although the phenomenology of the ESP and PK experiments could be considerably enriched by further experiments of the kind described above, deeper investigation of its bases will have to concern itself with the nature of the affectivity involved. I have therefore directed my attention to certain observations and experiences which, I can fairly say, have forced themselves upon me during the course of my long medical practice. They have to do with spontaneous, meaningful coincidences of so high a degree of improbability as to appear flatly unbelievable. I shall therefore describe to you only one case of this kind, simply to give an example characteristic of a whole category of phenomena. It makes no difference whether you refuse to believe this particular case or whether you dispose of it with an *ad hoc* explanation. I could tell you a great many such stories, which are in principle no more surprising or incredible than the irrefutable results arrived at by Rhine, and you would soon see that almost every case calls for its own explanation. But the causal explanation, the only possible one from the standpoint of natural science, breaks down owing to the psychic relativization of space and time, which together form the indispensable premises for the cause-and-effect relationship.

982 My example concerns a young woman patient who, in spite of efforts made on both sides, proved to be psychologically inaccessible. The difficulty lay in the fact that she always knew better about everything. Her excellent education had provided her with a weapon ideally suited to this purpose, namely a highly polished Cartesian rationalism with an impeccably 'geometrical'[3] idea of reality. After several fruitless attempts to sweeten her rationalism with a somewhat more human understanding, I had to confine myself to the hope that something unexpected and irrational would turn up, something that would burst the intellectual retort into which she had sealed herself. Well, I was sitting opposite her one day, with my back to the window, listening to her flow of rhetoric. She had had an impressive dream the night before, in which someone had given her a golden scarab – a costly piece of jewellery. While she was still telling me this dream, I heard something behind me gently tapping on the window. I turned round and saw that it was a fairly large flying insect that was knocking against the window-pane from outside in the obvious effort to get into the dark room. This seemed to me very strange. I opened the window immediately and caught the insect in the air as

it flew in. It was a scarabaeid beetle, or common rose-chafer (*Cetonia aurata*), whose gold-green colour most nearly resembles that of a golden scarab. I handed the beetle to my patient with the words, 'Here is your scarab.' This experience punctured the desired hole in her rationalism and broke the ice of her intellectual resistance. The treatment could now be continued with satisfactory results.

983 This story is meant only as a paradigm of the innumerable cases of meaningful coincidence that have been observed not only by me but by many others, and recorded in large collections. They include everything that goes by the name of clairvoyance, telepathy, etc., from Swedenborg's well-attested vision of the great fire in Stockholm to the recent report by Air Marshal Sir Victor Goddard about the dream of an unknown officer, which predicted the subsequent accident to Goddard's plane.[4]

984 All the phenomena I have mentioned can be grouped under three categories:

1   The coincidence of a psychic state in the observer with a simultaneous, objective, external event that corresponds to the psychic state or content (e.g., the scarab), where there is no evidence of a causal connection between the psychic state and the external event, and where, considering the psychic relativity of space and time, such a connection is not even conceivable.
2   The coincidence of a psychic state with a corresponding (more or less simultaneous) external event taking place outside the observer's field of perception, i.e., at a distance, and only verifiable afterward (e.g., the Stockholm fire).
3   The coincidence of a psychic state with a corresponding, not yet existent future event that is distant in time and can likewise only be verified afterward.

985 In groups 2 and 3 the coinciding events are not yet present in the observer's field of perception, but have been anticipated in time in so far as they can only be verified afterward. For this reason I call such events *synchronistic,* which is not to be confused with *synchronous*.

986 Our survey of this wide field of experience would be incomplete if we failed to take into account the so-called mantic methods. Manticism lays claim, if not actually to producing synchronistic events, then at least to making them serve its ends. An example of this is the oracle method of the *I Ching,* which Dr. Hellmut Wilhelm has described in detail.[5] The *I Ching* presupposes that there is a synchronistic correspondence between the psychic state of the questioner and the answering hexagram. The hexagram is formed either by the random division of the 49 yarrow stalks or by the equally random throw of three coins. The result of this method is, incontestably, very interesting, but so far as I can see it does not provide any tool for an objective determination of the facts, that is to say a statistical evaluation, since the psychic state in question is much too indefinite and indefinable. The same holds true of the geomantic experiment, which is based on similar principles.

987 We are in a somewhat more favourable situation when we turn to the astrological method, as it presupposes a meaningful coincidence of planetary aspects

and positions with the character or the existing psychic state of the questioner. In the light of the most recent astrophysical research, astrological correspondence is probably not a matter of synchronicity but, very largely, of a causal relationship. As Professor Max Knoll has demonstrated,[6] the solar proton radiation is influenced to such a degree by planetary conjunctions, oppositions, and quartile aspects that the appearance of magnetic storms can be predicted with a fair amount of probability. Relationships can be established between the curve of the earth's magnetic disturbances and the mortality rate that confirm the unfavourable influence of conjunctions, oppositions, and quartile aspects and the favourable influence of trine and sextile aspects. So it is probably a question here of a causal relationship, i.e., of a natural law that excludes synchronicity or restricts it. At the same time, the zodiacal qualification of the houses, which plays a large part in the horoscope, creates a complication in that the astrological zodiac, although agreeing with the calendar, does not coincide with the actual constellations themselves. These have shifted their positions by almost a whole platonic month as a result of the precession of the equinoxes since the time when the spring-point was in zero Aries, about the beginning of our era. Therefore, anyone born in Aries today (according to the calendar) is actually born in Pisces. It is simply that his birth took place at a time which, for approximately 2,000 years, has been called 'Aries.' Astrology presupposes that this time has a determining quality. It is possible that this quality, like the disturbances in the earth's magnetic field, is connected with the seasonal fluctuations to which solar proton radiation is subject. It is therefore not beyond the realm of possibility that the zodiacal positions may also represent a causal factor.

988 Although the psychological interpretation of horoscopes is still a very uncertain matter, there is nevertheless some prospect today of a causal explanation in conformity with natural law. Consequently, we are no longer justified in describing astrology as a mantic method. Astrology is in the process of becoming a science. But as there are still large areas of uncertainty, I decided some time ago to make a test and find out how far an accepted astrological tradition would stand up to statistical investigation. For this purpose it was necessary to select a definite and indisputable fact. My choice fell on marriage. Since antiquity, the traditional belief in regard to marriage has been that there is a conjunction of sun and moon in the horoscope of the marriage partners, that is, ☉ (sun) with an orbit of 8 degrees in the case of one partner; in ☌ (conjunction) with ☾ (moon) in the case of the other. A second, equally old, tradition takes ☾ ☌ ☾ as another marriage characteristic. Of like importance are the conjunctions of the ascendant (*Asc.*) with the large luminaries.

989 Together with my co-worker, Mrs. Liliane Frey-Rohn, I first proceeded to collect 180 marriages, that is to say, 360 horoscopes,[7] and compared the 50 most important aspects that might possibly be characteristic of marriage, namely the conjunctions and oppositions of ☉ ☾ ♂ (Mars) ♀ (Venus) *Asc.* and *Desc.* This resulted in a maximum of 10 per cent for ☉ ☌ ☾. As Professor Markus Fierz, of Basel, who kindly went to the trouble of computing the probability of my result,

informed me, my figure has a probability of 1: 10,000. The opinion of several mathematical physicists whom I consulted about the significance of this figure is divided: some find it considerable, others find it of questionable value. Our figure is inconclusive inasmuch as a total of 360 horoscopes is far too small from a statistical point of view.

990 While the aspects of these 180 marriages were being worked out statistically, our collection was enlarged, and when we had collected 220 more marriages, this batch was subjected to separate investigation. As on the first occasion, the material was evaluated just as it came in. It was not selected from any special point of view and was drawn from the most varied sources. Evaluation of this second batch yielded a maximum figure of 10.9 per cent for ☾ ☌ ☾. The probability of this figure is also about 1: 10,000.

991 Finally, 83 more marriages arrived, and these in turn were investigated separately. The result was a maximum figure of 9.6 per cent for ☾ ☌ *Asc*. The probability of this figure is approximately 1: 3,000.[8]

992 One is immediately struck by the fact that the conjunctions are all *moon conjunctions,* which is in accord with astrological expectations. But the strange thing is that what has turned up here are the three basic positions of the horoscope, ☉ ☾ and *Asc*. The probability of a concurrence ☉ ☌ ☾ and ☾ ☌ ☾ amounts to 1: 100,000,000. The concurrence of the three moon conjunctions with ☉ ☾ *Asc*. has a probability of 1: 3×10^{11}; in other words, the improbability of its being due to mere chance is so enormous that we are forced to take into account the existence of some factor responsible for it. The three batches were so small that little or no theoretical significance can be attached to the individual probabilities of 1: 10,000 and 1: 3,000. Their concurrence, however, is so improbable that one cannot help assuming the existence of an impelling factor that produced this result.

993 The possibility of there being a scientifically valid connection between astrological data and proton radiation cannot be held responsible for this, since the individual probabilities of 1: 10,000 and 1: 3,000 are too great for us to be able, with any degree of certainty, to view our result as other than mere chance. Besides, the maxima cancel each other out as soon as one divides up the marriages into a larger number of batches. It would require hundreds of thousands of marriage horoscopes to establish the statistical regularity of occurrences like the sun, moon, and ascendent conjunctions, and even then the result would be questionable. That anything so improbable as the turning up of the three classical moon conjunctions should occur at all, however, can only be explained either as the result of an intentional or unintentional fraud, or else as precisely such a meaningful coincidence, that is, as synchronicity.

994 Although I was obliged to express doubt, earlier, about the mantic character of astrology, I am now forced as a result of my astrological experiment to recognize it again. The chance arrangement of the marriage horoscopes, which were simply piled on top of one another as they came in from the most diverse sources, and the equally fortuitous way they were divided into three unequal batches, suited the sanguine expectations of the research workers and produced an over-all picture

that could scarcely have been improved upon from the standpoint of the astrological hypothesis. The success of the experiment is entirely in accord with Rhine's ESP results, which were also favorably affected by expectation, hope, and faith. However, there was no definite expectation of any one result. Our selection of 50 aspects is proof of this. After we got the result of the first batch, a slight expectation did exist that the ☉ ☌ ☽ would be confirmed. But we were disappointed. The second time, we made up a larger batch from the newly added horoscopes in order to increase the element of certainty. But the result was ☾ ☌ ☾. With the third batch, there was only a faint expectation that ☾ ☌ ☾ would be confirmed, but again this was not the case.

995 What happened in this case was admittedly a curiosity, apparently a unique instance of meaningful coincidence. If one is impressed by such things, one could call it a minor miracle. Today, however, we are obliged to view the miraculous in a somewhat different light. The Rhine experiments have demonstrated that space and time, and hence causality, are factors that can be eliminated, with the result that acausal phenomena, otherwise called miracles, appear possible. All natural phenomena of this kind are unique and exceedingly curious combinations of chance, held together by the common meaning of their parts to form an unmistakable whole. Although meaningful coincidences are infinitely varied in their phenomenology, as acausal events they nevertheless form an element that is part of the scientific picture of the world. Causality is the way we explain the link between two successive events. Synchronicity designates the parallelism of time and meaning between psychic and psychophysical events, which scientific knowledge so far has been unable to reduce to a common principle. The term explains nothing, it simply formulates the occurrence of meaningful coincidences which, in themselves, are chance happenings, but are so improbable that we must assume them to be based on some kind of principle, or on some property of the empirical world. No reciprocal causal connection can be shown to obtain between parallel events, which is just what gives them their chance character. The only recognizable and demonstrable link between them is a common meaning, or equivalence. The old theory of correspondence was based on the experience of such connections – a theory that reached its culminating point and also its provisional end in Leibniz' idea of pre-established harmony, and was then replaced by causality. Synchronicity is a modern differentiation of the obsolete concept of correspondence, sympathy, and harmony. It is based not on philosophical assumptions but on empirical experience and experimentation.

996 Synchronistic phenomena prove the simultaneous occurrence of meaningful equivalences in heterogeneous, causally unrelated processes; in other words, they prove that a content perceived by an observer can, at the same time, be represented by an outside event, without any causal connection. From this it follows either that the psyche cannot be localized in space, or that space is relative to the psyche. The same applies to the temporal determination of the psyche and the psychic relativity of time. I do not need to emphasize that the verification of these findings must have far-reaching consequences.

997 In the short space of a lecture I cannot, unfortunately, do more than give a very

cursory sketch of the vast problem of synchronicity. For those of you who would care to go into this question more deeply, I would mention that a more extensive work of mine is soon to appear under the title 'Synchronicity: An Acausal Connecting Principle.' It will be published together with a work by Professor W. Pauli in a book called *The Interpretation of Nature and the Psyche.*[9]

Notes

1 [Originally given as a lecture, 'Über Synchronizität,' at the 1951 Eranos conference, Ascona, Switzerland, and published in the *Eranos-Jahrbuch 1951* (Zurich, 1952). The present translation was published in *Man and Time* (Papers from the Eranos Yearbooks, 3; New York and London, 1957); it is republished with minor revisions. The essay was, in the main, drawn from the preceding monograph.–EDITORS.]
2 [For documentation, see supra, par. 830.–EDITORS.]
3 [Descartes demonstrated his propositions by the 'Geometrical Method'.–EDITORS.]
4 [This case was the subject of an English film, *The Night My Number Came Up.*–EDITORS.]
5 ['The Concept of Time in the Book of Changes,' originally a lecture at the 1951 Eranos conference.–EDITORS.]
6 ['Transformations of Science in Our Age,' ibid.]
7 This material stemmed from different sources. They were simply horoscopes of married people. There was no selection of any kind. We took at random all the marriage horoscopes we could lay hands on.
8 [These and the following figures were later revised by Professor Fierz and considerably reduced. See supra, pars. 901ff.–EDITORS.]
9 [See the foregoing.–EDITORS.]

Chapter 15

A psychological theory of types[1]

915 Character is the fixed individual form of a human being. Since this form is compounded of body and mind, a general characterology must teach the significance of both physical and psychic features. The enigmatic oneness of the living organism has as its corollary the fact that bodily traits are not merely physical, nor mental traits merely psychic. The continuity of nature knows nothing of those antithetical distinctions which the human intellect is forced to set up as aids to understanding.

916 The distinction between mind and body is an artificial dichotomy, an act of discrimination based far more on the peculiarity of intellectual cognition than on the nature of things. In fact, so intimate is the intermingling of bodily and psychic traits that not only can we draw far-reaching inferences as to the constitution of the psyche from the constitution of the body, but we can also infer from psychic peculiarities the corresponding bodily characteristics. It is true that the latter process is far more difficult, not because the body is less influenced by the psyche than the psyche by the body, but for quite another reason. In taking the psyche as our starting-point, we work from the relatively unknown to the known; while in the opposite case we have the advantage of starting from something known, that is, from the visible body. Despite all the psychology we think we possess today, the psyche is still infinitely more obscure to us than the visible surface of the body. The psyche is still a foreign, barely explored country of which we have only indirect knowledge, mediated by conscious functions that are open to almost endless possibilities of deception.

917 This being so, it seems safer to proceed from outside inwards, from the known to the unknown, from the body to the psyche. Thus all attempts at characterology have started from the outside world; astrology, in ancient times, even started from interstellar space in order to arrive at those lines of fate whose beginnings lie in the human heart. To the same class of interpretations from outward signs belong palmistry, Gall's phrenology, Lavater's physiognomy, and – more recently – graphology, Kretschmer's physiological types, and Rorschach's klexographic method. As we can see, there are any number of paths leading from outside inwards, from the physical to the psychic, and it is necessary that research should follow this direction until the elementary psychic facts are established with

sufficient certainty. But once having established these facts, we can reverse the procedure. We can then put the question: What are the bodily correlatives of a given psychic condition? Unfortunately we are not yet far enough advanced to give even an approximate answer. The first requirement is to establish the primary facts of psychic life, and this is far from having been accomplished. Indeed, we have only just begun the work of compiling an inventory of the psyche, not always with great success.

918   Merely to establish the fact that certain people have this or that physical appearance is of no significance if it does not allow us to infer a psychic correlative. We have learned something only when we have determined what psychic attributes go with a given bodily constitution. The body means as little to us without the psyche as the latter without the body. But when we try to infer a psychic correlative from a physical characteristic, we are proceeding – as already stated – from the known to the unknown.

919   I must, unfortunately, stress this point, since psychology is the youngest of the sciences and therefore the one that suffers most from preconceived opinions. The fact that we have only recently discovered psychology tells us plainly enough that it has taken us all this time to make a clear distinction between ourselves and the content of our minds. Until this could be done, it was impossible to study the psyche objectively. Psychology, as a science, is actually our most recent acquisition; up to now it has been just as fantastic and arbitrary as was natural science in the Middle Ages. It was believed that psychology could be created as it were by decree – a prejudice under which we are still labouring. Psychic life is, after all, what is most immediate to us, and apparently what we know most about. Indeed, it is more than familiar, we yawn over it. We are irritated by the banality of its everlasting commonplaces; they bore us to extinction and we do everything in our power to avoid thinking about them. The psyche being immediacy itself, and we ourselves being the psyche, we are almost forced to assume that we know it through and through in a way that cannot be doubted or questioned. That is why each of us has his own private opinion about psychology and is even convinced that he knows more about it than anyone else. Psychiatrists, because they must struggle with their patients' relatives and guardians whose 'understanding' is proverbial, are perhaps the first to become aware as a professional group of that blind prejudice which encourages every man to take himself as his own best authority in psychological matters. But this of course does not prevent the psychiatrist also from becoming a 'know-all.' One of them even went so far as to confess: 'There are only two normal people in this city – Professor B. is the other.'

920   Since this is how matters stand in psychology today, we must bring ourselves to admit that what is closest to us, the psyche, is the very thing we know least about, although it seems to be what we know best of all, and furthermore that everyone else probably understands it better than we do ourselves. At any rate that, for a start, would be a most useful heuristic principle. As I have said, it is just because the psyche is so close to us that psychology has been discovered so late. And because it is still in its initial stages as a science, we lack the concepts and

definitions with which to grasp the facts. If concepts are lacking, facts are not; on the contrary, we are surrounded – almost buried – by facts. This is in striking contrast to the state of affairs in other sciences, where the facts have first to be unearthed. Here the classification of primary data results in the formation of descriptive concepts covering certain natural orders, as, for example, the grouping of the elements in chemistry and of plant families in botany. But it is quite different in the case of the psyche. Here an empirical and descriptive method merely plunges us into the ceaseless stream of subjective psychic happenings, so that whenever any sort of generalizing concept emerges from this welter of impressions it is usually nothing more than a symptom. Because we ourselves are psyches, it is almost impossible to us to give free rein to psychic happenings without being dissolved in them and thus robbed of our ability to recognize distinctions and make comparisons.

921 This is one difficulty. The other is that the more we turn from spatial phenomena to the non-spatiality of the psyche, the more impossible it becomes to determine anything by exact measurement. It becomes difficult even to establish the facts. If, for example, I want to emphasize the unreality of something, I say that I merely 'thought' it. I say: 'I would never even have had this thought unless such and such had happened; and besides, I never think things like that.' Remarks of this kind are quite usual, and they show how nebulous psychic facts are, or rather, how vague they appear subjectively – for in reality they are just as objective and just as definite as any other events. The truth is that I actually did think such and such a thing, regardless of the conditions and provisos I attach to this process. Many people have to wrestle with themselves in order to make this perfectly obvious admission, and it often costs them a great moral effort. These, then, are the difficulties we encounter when we draw inferences about the state of affairs in the psyche from the known things we observe outside.

922 My more limited field of work is not the clinical study of external characteristics, but the investigation and classification of the psychic data which may be inferred from them. The first result of this work is a phenomenology of the psyche, which enables us to formulate a corresponding theory about its structure. From the empirical application of this structural theory there is finally developed a psychological typology.

923 Clinical studies are based on the description of symptoms, and the step from this to a phenomenology of the psyche is comparable to the step from a purely symptomatic pathology to the pathology of cellular and metabolic processes. That is to say, the phenomenology of the psyche brings into view those psychic processes in the background which underlie the clinical symptoms. As is generally known, this knowledge is obtained by the application of analytical methods. We have today a working knowledge of the psychic processes that produce psychogenic symptoms, and have thus laid the foundations for a theory of complexes. Whatever else may be taking place in the obscure recesses of the psyche – and there are notoriously many opinions about this – one thing is certain: it is the complexes (emotionally-toned contents having a certain amount of autonomy)

which play the most important part here. The term 'autonomous complex' has often met with opposition, unjustifiably, it seems to me, because the active contents of the unconscious do behave in a way I cannot describe better than by the word 'autonomous.' The term is meant to indicate the capacity of the complexes to resist conscious intentions, and to come and go as they please. Judging by all we know about them, they are psychic entities which are outside the control of the conscious mind. They have been split off from consciousness and lead a separate existence in the dark realm of the unconscious, being at all times ready to hinder or reinforce the conscious functioning.

924 A deeper study of the complexes leads logically to the problem of their origin, and as to this a number of different theories are current. Theories apart, experience shows that complexes always contain something like a conflict, or at least are either the cause or the effect of a conflict. At any rate the characteristics of conflict – shock, upheaval, mental agony, inner strife – are peculiar to the complexes. They are the 'sore spots,' the *bêtes noires*, the 'skeletons in the cupboard' which we do not like to remember and still less to be reminded of by others, but which frequently come back to mind unbidden and in the most unwelcome fashion. They always contain memories, wishes, fears, duties, needs, or insights which somehow we can never really grapple with, and for this reason they constantly interfere with our conscious life in a disturbing and usually a harmful way.

925 Complexes obviously represent a kind of inferiority in the broadest sense – a statement I must at once qualify by saying that to have complexes does not necessarily indicate inferiority. It only means that something discordant, unassimilated, and antagonistic exists, perhaps as an obstacle, but also as an incentive to greater effort, and so, perhaps, to new possibilities of achievement. In this sense, therefore, complexes are focal or nodal points of psychic life which we would not wish to do without; indeed, they should not be missing, for otherwise psychic activity would come to a fatal standstill. They point to the unresolved problems in the individual, the places where he has suffered a defeat, at least for the time being, and where there is something he cannot evade or overcome – his weak spots in every sense of the word.

926 These characteristics of the complex throw a significant light on its origin. It obviously arises from the clash between a demand of adaptation and the individual's constitutional inability to meet the challenge. Seen in this light, the complex is a valuable symptom which helps us to diagnose an individual disposition.

927 Experience shows us that complexes are infinitely varied, yet careful comparison reveals a relatively small number of typical primary forms, which are all built upon the first experiences of childhood. This must necessarily be so, because the individual disposition is already a factor in infancy; it is innate, and not acquired in the course of life. The parental complex is therefore nothing but the first manifestation of a clash between reality and the individual's constitutional inability to meet the demands it makes upon him. The primary form of the complex cannot be other than a parental complex, because the parents are the first reality with which the child comes into conflict.

328 Therapy and healing

928   The existence of a parental complex therefore tells us little or nothing about the peculiar constitution of the individual. Practical experience soon teaches us that the crux of the matter does not lie in the presence of a parental complex, but rather in the special way in which the complex works itself out in the individual's life. And here we observe the most striking variations, though only a very small number can be attributed to the special nature of the parental influence. There are often several children who are exposed to the same influence, and yet each of them reacts to it in a totally different way.

929   I therefore turned my attention to these differences, telling myself that it is through them that the peculiarities of the individual dispositions may be discerned. Why, in a neurotic family, does one child react with hysteria, another with a compulsion neurosis, the third with a psychosis, and the fourth apparently not at all? This problem of the 'choice of neurosis,' which Freud was also faced with, robs the parental complex as such of its aetiological significance, and shifts the inquiry to the reacting individual and his special disposition.

930   Although Freud's attempts to solve this problem leave me entirely dissatisfied, I am myself unable to answer the question. Indeed, I think it premature to raise the question of the choice of neurosis at all. Before we tackle this extremely difficult problem we need to know a great deal more about the way the individual reacts. The question is: How does a person react to an obstacle? For instance, we come to a brook over which there is no bridge. It is too broad to step across, so we must jump. For this purpose we have at our disposal a complicated functional system, namely, the psychomotor system. It is fully developed and needs only to be triggered off. But before this happens, something of a purely psychic nature takes place: a decision is made about what is to be done. This is followed by those crucial events which settle the matter in some way and vary with each individual. But, significantly enough, we rarely if ever recognize these events as characteristic, for as a rule we do not see ourselves at all or only as a last resort. That is to say, just as the psychomotor apparatus is habitually at our disposal for jumping, there is an exclusively psychic apparatus ready for use in making decisions, which functions by habit and therefore unconsciously.

931   Opinions differ widely as to what this apparatus is like. It is certain only that every individual has his accustomed way of making decisions and dealing with difficulties. One person will say he jumped the brook for fun; another, that there was no alternative; a third, that every obstacle he meets challenges him to overcome it. A fourth did not jump the brook because he dislikes useless effort, and a fifth refrained because he saw no urgent necessity to get to the other side.

932   I have purposely chosen this commonplace example in order to demonstrate how irrelevant such motivations seem. They appear so futile that we are inclined to brush them aside and to substitute our own explanation. And yet it is just these variations that give us valuable insights into the individual psychic systems of adaptation. If we observe, in other situations of life, the person who jumped the brook for fun, we shall probably find that for the most part everything he does or omits to do can be explained in terms of the pleasure it gives him. We shall

observe that the one who jumped because he saw no alternative goes through life cautiously and apprehensively, always deciding *faute de mieux*. And so on. In all these cases special psychic systems are in readiness to execute the decisions. We can easily imagine that the number of these attitudes is legion. The individual attitudes are certainly as inexhaustible as the variations of crystals, which may nevertheless be recognized as belonging to one or another system. But just as crystals show basic uniformities which are relatively simple, these attitudes show certain fundamental peculiarities which allow us to assign them to definite groups.

933 From earliest times attempts have been made to classify individuals according to types, and so to bring order into the chaos. The oldest attempts known to us were made by oriental astrologers who devised the so-called trigons of the four elements – air, water, earth, and fire. The air trigon in the horoscope consists of the three aerial signs of the zodiac, Aquarius, Gemini, Libra; the fire trigon is made up of Aries, Leo, Sagittarius. According to this age-old view, whoever is born in these trigons shares in their aerial or fiery nature and will have a corresponding temperament and fate. Closely connected with this ancient cosmological scheme is the physiological typology of antiquity, the division into four temperaments corresponding to the four humours. What was first represented by the signs of the zodiac was later expressed in the physiological language of Greek medicine, giving us the classification into the phlegmatic, sanguine, choleric, and melancholic. These are simply designations for the secretions of the body. As is well known, this typology lasted at least seventeen hundred years. As for the astrological type theory, to the astonishment of the enlightened it still remains intact today, and is even enjoying a new vogue.

934 This historical retrospect may serve to assure us that our modern attempts to formulate a theory of types are by no means new and unprecedented, even though our scientific conscience does not permit us to revert to these old, intuitive ways of thinking. We must find our own answer to this problem, an answer which satisfies the need of science. And here we meet the chief difficulty of the problem of types – that is, the question of standards or criteria. The astrological criterion was simple and objective: it was given by the constellations at birth. As to the way characterological qualities could be correlated with the zodiacal signs and the planets, this is a question which reaches back into the grey mists of prehistory and remains unanswerable. The Greek classification according to the four physiological temperaments took as its criteria the appearance and behaviour of the individual, exactly as we do today in the case of physiological typology. But where shall we seek our criterion for a psychological theory of types?

935 Let us return to the example of the four people who had to cross a brook. How and from what standpoints are we to classify their habitual motivations? One person does it for fun, another does it because not to do it is more troublesome, a third doesn't do it because he has second thoughts, and so on. The list of possibilities seems both endless and useless for purposes of classification.

936 I do not know how other people would set about this task. I can only tell you how I myself have tackled it, and I must bow to the charge that my way of solving

the problem is the outcome of my personal prejudice. This objection is so entirely true that I would not know how to defend myself. I can only point happily to old Columbus, who, following his subjective assumptions, a false hypothesis, and a route abandoned by modern navigation, nevertheless discovered America. Whatever we look at, and however we look at it, we see only through our own eyes. For this reason science is never made by one man, but many. The individual merely offers his own contribution, and it is only in this sense that I dare to speak of *my* way of seeing things.

937   My profession has always obliged me to take account of the peculiarities of individuals, and the special circumstance that in the course of I don't know how many years I have had to treat innumerable married couples and have been faced with the task of making husband and wife plausible to each other has emphasized the need to establish certain average truths. How many times, for instance, have I not had to say: 'Look here, your wife has a very active nature, and it cannot be expected that her whole life should centre on housekeeping.' That is a sort of statistical truth, and it holds the beginnings of a type theory: there are active natures and passive natures. But this time-worn truth did not satisfy me. My next attempt was to say that some persons are reflective and others are unreflective, because I had observed that many apparently passive natures are in reality not so much passive as given to forethought. They first consider a situation and then act, and because they do this habitually they miss opportunities where immediate action without reflection is called for, thus coming to be prejudged as passive. The persons who did not reflect always seemed to me to jump headfirst into a situation without any forethought, only to reflect afterwards that they had perhaps landed themselves in a swamp. Thus they could be considered 'unreflective,' and this seemed a more appropriate word than 'active.' Forethought is in certain cases a very important form of activity, a responsible course of action as compared with the unthinking, short-lived zeal of the mere busybody. But I soon discovered that the hesitation of the one was by no means always forethought, and that the quick action of the other was not necessarily want of reflection. The hesitation equally often arises from a habitual timidity, or at least from a customary shrinking back as if faced with too great a task; while immediate action is frequently made possible by a predominating self-confidence in relation to the object. This observation caused me to formulate these typical differences in the following way: there is a whole class of men who, at the moment of reaction to a given situation, at first draw back a little as if with an unvoiced 'No,' and only after that are able to react; and there is another class who, in the same situation, come out with an immediate reaction, apparently quite confident that their behaviour is self-evidently right. The former class would therefore be characterized by a negative relation to the object, and the latter by a positive one.

938   The former class corresponds to the *introverted* and the second to the *extraverted* attitude. But these two terms in themselves signify as little as the discovery of Molière's *bourgeois gentilhomme* that he ordinarily spoke in prose. They acquire meaning and value only when we know all the other characteristics that go with the type.

A psychological theory of types 331

939 One cannot be introverted or extraverted without being so in every respect. For example, to be 'introverted' means that everything in the psyche happens as it must happen according to the law of the introvert's nature. Were that not so, the statement that a certain individual is 'introverted' would be as irrelevant as the statement that he is six feet tall, or that he has brown hair, or is brachycephalic. These statements contain no more than the facts they express. The term 'introverted' is incomparably more exacting. It means that the consciousness as well as the unconscious of the introvert must have certain definite qualities, that his general behaviour, his relation to people, and even the course of his life show certain typical characteristics.

940 Introversion or extraversion, as a typical attitude, means an essential bias which conditions the whole psychic process, establishes the habitual mode of reaction, and thus determines not only the style of behaviour but also the quality of subjective experience. Not only that, it determines the kind of compensation the unconscious will produce.

941 Once we have established the habitual mode of reaction it is bound to hit the mark to a certain extent, because habit is, so to speak, the central switchboard from which outward behaviour is regulated and by which specific experiences are shaped. A certain kind of behaviour brings corresponding results, and the subjective understanding of these results gives rise to experiences which in turn influence our behaviour, in accordance with the saying 'Every man is the maker of his own fate.'

942 While there can be little doubt that the habitual mode of reaction brings us to the central point, the delicate question remains as to whether or not we have satisfactorily characterized it by the term 'introverted' or 'extraverted.' There can be a honest difference of opinion about this even among those with an intimate knowledge of this special field. In my book on types I have put together everything I could find in support of my views, though I expressly stated that I do not imagine mine to be the only true or possible typology.

943 The contrast between introversion and extraversion is simple enough, but simple formulations are unfortunately the most open to doubt. They all too easily cover up the actual complexities and so deceive us. I speak here from my own experience, for scarcely had I published the first formulation of my criteria[2] when I discovered to my dismay that somehow or other I had been taken in by them. Something was amiss. I had tried to explain too much in too simple a way, as often happens in the first joy of discovery.

944 What struck me now was the undeniable fact while people may be classed as introverts or extraverts, this does not account for the tremendous differences between individuals in either class. So great, indeed, are these differences that I was forced to doubt whether I had observed correctly in the first place. It took nearly ten years of observation and comparison to clear up this doubt.

945 The question as to where the tremendous differences among individuals of the same type came from entangled me in unforeseen difficulties which for a long time I was unable to master. To observe and recognize the differences gave me

comparatively little trouble, the root of my difficulties being now, as before, the problem of criteria. How was I to find suitable terms for the characteristic differences? Here I realized for the first time how young psychology really is. It is still little more than a chaos of arbitrary opinions and dogmas, produced for the most part in the study or consulting room by spontaneous generation from the isolated and Jove-like brains of learned professors, with complete lack of agreement. Without wishing to be irreverent, I cannot refrain from confronting the professor of psychology with, say, the psychology of women, of the Chinese, or of the Australian aborigines. Our psychology must get down to brass tacks, otherwise we simply remain stuck in the Middle Ages.

946   I realized that no sound criteria were to be found in the chaos of contemporary psychology, that they had first to be created, not out of thin air, but on the basis of the invaluable preparatory work done by many men whose names no history of psychology will pass over in silence.

947   Within the limits of a lecture I cannot possibly mention all the separate observations that led me to pick out certain *psychic functions* as criteria for the differences under discussion. I will only state very broadly what the essential differences are, so far as I have been able to ascertain them. An introvert, for example, does not simply draw back and hesitate before the object, but he does so in a quite definite way. Moreover he does not behave just like every other introvert, but again in a way peculiar to himself. Just as the lion strikes down his enemy or his prey with his fore-paw, in which his specific strength resides, and not with his tail like the crocodile, so our habitual mode of reaction is normally characterized by the use of our most reliable and efficient function, which is an expression of our particular strength. However, this does not prevent us from reacting occasionally in a way that reveals our specific weakness. According to which function predominates, we shall seek out certain situations while avoiding others, and shall thus have experiences specific to ourselves and different from those of other people. An intelligent man will adapt to the world through his intelligence, and not like a sixth-rate pugilist, even though now and then, in a fit of rage, he may make use of his fists. In the struggle for existence and adaptation everyone instinctively uses his most developed function, which thus becomes the criterion of his habitual mode of reaction.

948   How are we to sum up these functions under general concepts, so that they can be distinguished from the welter of merely individual events? A rough typization of this kind has long since existed in social life, in the figures of the peasant, the worker, the artist, the scholar, the fighter, and so forth, or in the various professions. But this sort of typization has little or nothing to do with psychology, for, as a well-known savant once maliciously remarked, there are certain scholars who are no more than 'intellectual porters.'

949   A type theory must be more subtle. It is not enough, for example, to speak of intelligence, for this is too general and too vague a concept. Almost any kind of behaviour can be called intelligent if it works smoothly, quickly, effectively and to a purpose. Intelligence, like stupidity, is not a function but a modality; the word

tells us no more than *how* a function is working, not *what* is functioning. The same holds true of moral and aesthetic criteria. We must be able to designate what it is that functions outstandingly in the individual's habitual way of reacting. We are thus forced to revert to something that at first glance looks alarmingly like the old faculty psychology of the eighteenth century. In reality, however, we are only returning to ideas current in daily speech, perfectly accessible and comprehensible to everyone. When, for instance, I speak of 'thinking,' it is only the philosopher who does not know what it means; no layman will find it incomprehensible. He uses the word every day, and always in the same general sense, though it is true he would be at a loss if suddenly called upon to give an unequivocal definition of thinking. The same is true of 'memory' or 'feeling.' However difficult it is to define these purely psychological concepts scientifically, they are easily intelligible in current speech. Language is a storehouse of concrete images; hence concepts which are too abstract and nebulous do not easily take root in it, or quickly die out again for lack of contact with reality. But thinking and feeling are such insistent realities that every language above the primitive level has absolutely unmistakable expressions for them. We can therefore be sure that these expressions coincide with quite definite psychic facts, no matter what the scientific definition of these complex facts may be. Everyone knows, for example, what consciousness means, and nobody can doubt that it coincides with a definite psychic condition, however far science may be from defining it satisfactorily.

950   And so it came about that I simply took the concepts expressed in current speech as designations for the corresponding psychic functions, and used them as my criteria in judging the differences between persons of the same attitude-type. For instance, I took thinking, as it is generally understood, because I was struck by the fact that many people habitually do more thinking than others, and accordingly give more weight to thought when making important decisions. They also use their thinking in order to understand the world and adapt to it, and whatever happens to them is subjected to consideration and reflection or at least subordinated to some principle sanctioned by thought. Other people conspicuously neglect thinking in favour of emotional factors, that is, of feeling. They invariably follow a policy dictated by feeling, and it takes an extraordinary situation to make them reflect. They form an unmistakable contrast to the other type, and the difference is most striking when the two are business partners or are married to each other. It should be noted that a person may give preference to thinking whether he be extraverted or introverted, but he will use it only in the way that is characteristic of his attitude-type, and the same is true of feeling.

951   The predominance of one or the other of these functions does not explain all the differences that occur. What I call the thinking and feeling types comprise two groups of persons who again have something in common which I cannot designate except by the word *rationality*. No one will dispute that thinking is essentially rational, but when we come to feeling, weighty objections may be raised which I would not like to brush aside. On the contrary, I freely admit that this problem of feeling has been one that has caused me much brain-racking.

However, as I do not want to overload my lecture with the various existing definitions of this concept, I shall confine myself briefly to my own view. The chief difficulty is that the word 'feeling' can be used in all sorts of different ways. This is especially true in German, but is noticeable to some extent in English and French as well. First of all, then, we must make a careful distinction between feeling and *sensation,* which is a sensory function. And in the second place we must recognize that a feeling of regret is something quite different from a 'feeling' that the weather will change or that the price of our aluminum shares will go up. I have therefore proposed using *feeling* as a proper term in the first example, and dropping it – so far as its psychological usage is concerned – in the second. Here we should speak of *sensation* when sense impressions are involved, and of *intuition* if we are dealing with a kind of perception which cannot be traced back directly to conscious sensory experience. Hence I define sensation as perception via conscious sensory functions, and intuition as perception via the unconscious.

952   Obviously we could argue until Doomsday about the fitness of these definitions, but ultimately it is only a question of terminology. It is as if we were debating whether to call a certain animal a leopard or a panther, when all we need to know is what name we are giving to what. Psychology is virgin territory, and its terminology has still to be fixed. As we know, temperature can be measured according to Réaumur, Celsius, or Fahrenheit, but we must indicate which system we are using.

953   It is evident, then, that I take feeling as a function *per se* and distinguish it from sensation and intuition. Whoever confuses these last two functions with feeling in the strict sense is obviously not in a position to acknowledge the rationality of feeling. But once they are distinguished from feeling, it becomes quite clear that feeling values and feeling judgments – indeed, feelings in general – are not only rational but can also be as logical, consistent and discriminating as thinking. This may seem strange to the thinking type, but it is easily explained when we realize that in a person with a differentiated thinking function the feeling function is always less developed, more primitive, and therefore contaminated with other functions, these being precisely the functions which are not rational, not logical, and not discriminating or evaluating, namely, sensation and intuition. These two are by their very nature opposed to the rational functions. When we think, it is in order to judge or to reach a conclusion, and when we feel it is in order to attach a proper value to something. Sensation and intuition, on the other hand, are perceptive functions – they make us aware of what is happening, but do not interpret or evaluate it. They do not proceed selectively, according to principles, but are simply receptive to what happens. But 'what happens' is essentially irrational. There is no inferential method by which it could ever be proved that there must be so and so many planets, or so and so many species of warm-blooded animals. Irrationality is a vice where thinking and feeling are called for, rationality is a vice where sensation and intuition should be trusted.

954   Now there are many people whose habitual reactions are irrational because they are based either on sensation or on intuition. They cannot be based on both at

once, because sensation is just as antagonistic to intuition as thinking is to feeling. When I try to assure myself with my eyes and ears of what is actually happening, I cannot at the same time give way to dreams and fantasies about what lies around the corner. As this is just what the intuitive type must do in order to give the necessary free play to his unconscious or to the object, it is easy to see that the sensation type is at the opposite pole to the intuitive. Unfortunately, time does not allow me to go into the interesting variations which the extraverted or introverted attitude produces in the irrational types.

955   Instead, I would like to add a word about the effects regularly produced on the other functions when preference is given to one function. We know that a man can never be everything at once, never quite complete. He always develops certain qualities at the expense of others, and wholeness is never attained. But what happens to those functions which are not consciously brought into daily use and are not developed by exercise? They remain in a more or less primitive and infantile state, often only half conscious, or even quite unconscious. These relatively undeveloped functions constitute a specific inferiority which is characteristic of each type and is an integral part of his total character. The one-sided emphasis on thinking is always accompanied by an inferiority of feeling, and differentiated sensation is injurious to intuition and vice versa.

956   Whether a function is differentiated or not can easily be recognized from its strength, stability, consistency, reliability, and adaptedness. But inferiority in a function is often not so easy to recognize or to describe. An essential criterion is its lack of self-sufficiency and consequent dependence on people and circumstances, its disposing us to moods and crotchetiness, its unreliable use, its suggestible and labile character. The inferior function always puts us at a disadvantage because we cannot direct it, but are rather its victims.

957   Since I must restrict myself here to a mere sketch of the ideas underlying a psychological theory of types, I must forgo a detailed description of each type. The total result of my work in this field up to the present is the establishing of two general attitude-types, extraversion and introversion, and four function-types, thinking, feeling, sensation, and intuition. Each of these function-types varies according to the general attitude and thus eight variants are produced.

958   I have often been asked, almost accusingly, why I speak of four functions and not of more or fewer. That there are exactly four was a result I arrived at on purely empirical grounds. But as the following consideration will show, these four together produce a kind of totality. Sensation establishes what is actually present, thinking enables us to recognize its meaning, feeling tells us its value, and intuition points to possibilities as to whence it came and whither it is going in a given situation. In this way we can orient ourselves with respect to the immediate world as completely as when we locate a place geographically by latitude and longitude. The four functions are somewhat like the four points of the compass; they are just as arbitrary and just as indispensable. Nothing prevents our shifting the cardinal points as many degrees as we like in one direction or the other, or giving them different names. It is merely a question of convention and intelligibility.

959   But one thing I must confess: I would not for anything dispense with this compass on my psychological voyages of discovery. This is not merely for the obvious, all-too-human reason that everyone is in love with his own ideas. I value the type theory for the objective reason that it provides a system of comparison and orientation which makes possible something that has long been lacking, a critical psychology.

Notes

1 [A lecture delivered at the Congress of Swiss Psychiatrists, Zurich, 1928, and published as 'Psychologische Typologie' in *Seelenprobleme der Gegenwart* (Zurich, 1931), pp. 101ff., reprinted in *Gesammelte Werke*, 6, Appendix, pp. 568ff. Translated into English by W. S. Dell and Cary F. Baynes as 'A Psychological Theory of Types,' in *Modern Man in Search of a Soul* (London and New York, 1933), pp. 85ff., which version is reproduced here with minor modifications.–EDITORS.]

2 Supra, pars. 858ff.

Chapter 16

The transcendent function[1]

Prefatory note

This essay was written in 1916. Recently it was discovered by students of the C. G. Jung Institute, Zurich, and was brought out in a private edition in its first, provisional form, in an English translation. In order to prepare it for publication, I have worked over the manuscript, while preserving the main trend of thought and the unavoidable limitedness of its horizon. After forty-two years, the problem has lost nothing of its topicality, though its presentation is still in need of extensive improvement, as anyone can see who knows the material. The essay may therefore stand, with all its imperfections, as an historical document. It may give the reader some idea of the efforts of understanding which were needed for the first attempts at a synthetic view of the psychic process in analytical treatment. As its basic argument is still valid today, it may stimulate the reader to a broader and deeper understanding of the problem. This problem is identical with the universal question: How does one come to terms in practice with the unconscious?

This is the question posed by the philosophy of India, and particularly by Buddhism and Zen. Indirectly, it is the fundamental question, in practice, of all religions and all philosophies. For the unconscious is not this thing or that; it is the Unknown as it immediately affects us.

The method of 'active imagination,' hereinafter described, is the most important auxiliary for the production of those contents of the unconscious which lie, as it were, immediately below the threshold of consciousness and, when intensified, are the most likely to irrupt spontaneously into the conscious mind. The method, therefore, is not without its dangers and should, if possible, not be employed except under expert supervision. One of the lesser dangers is that the procedure may not lead to any positive result, since it easily passes over into the so-called 'free association' of Freud, whereupon the patient gets caught in the sterile circle of his own complexes, from which he is in any case unable to escape. A further danger, in itself harmless, is that, though authentic contents may be produced, the patient evinces an exclusively aesthetic interest in them and consequently remains stuck in an all-enveloping phantasmagoria, so that once more nothing is gained. The meaning and value of these fantasies are revealed only through their integration into the personality as a whole – that is to say, at the moment when one is confronted not only with what they mean but also with their moral demands.

Finally, a third danger – and this may in certain circumstances be a very serious matter – is that the subliminal contents already possess such a high energy charge that, when afforded an outlet by active imagination, they may overpower the conscious mind and take possession of the personality. This gives rise to a condition which – temporarily, at least – cannot easily be distinguished from schizophrenia, and may even lead to a genuine 'psychotic interval.' The method of active imagination, therefore, is not a plaything for children. The prevailing undervaluation of the unconscious adds considerably to the dangers of this method. On the other hand, there can be no doubt that it is an invaluable auxiliary for the psychotherapist.

C. G. J.

Küsnacht, July 1958 / September 1959

131   There is nothing mysterious or metaphysical about the term 'transcendent function.' It means a psychological function comparable in its way to a mathematical function of the same name, which is a function of real and imaginary numbers. The psychological 'transcendent function' arises from the union of conscious and unconscious contents.

132   Experience in analytical psychology has amply shown that the conscious and the unconscious seldom agree as to their contents and their tendencies. This lack of parallelism is not just accidental or purposeless, but is due to the fact that the unconscious behaves in a compensatory or complementary manner towards the conscious. We can also put it the other way round and say that the conscious behaves in a complementary manner towards the unconscious. The reasons for this relationship are:

1. Consciousness possesses a threshold intensity which its contents must have attained, so that all elements that are too weak remain in the unconscious.
2. Consciousness, because of its directed functions, exercises an inhibition (which Freud calls censorship) on all incompatible material, with the result that it sinks into the unconscious.
3. Consciousness constitutes the momentary process of adaptation, whereas the unconscious contains not only all the forgotten material of the individual's own past, but all the inherited behaviour traces constituting the structure of the mind.
4. The unconscious contains all the fantasy combinations which have not yet attained the threshold intensity, but which in the course of time and under suitable conditions will enter the light of consciousness.

133   This readily explains the complementary attitude of the unconscious towards the conscious.

134   The definiteness and directedness of the conscious mind are qualities that have been acquired relatively late in the history of the human race, and are for instance

largely lacking among primitives today. These qualities are often impaired in the neurotic patient, who differs from the normal person in that his threshold of consciousness gets shifted more easily; in other words, the partition between conscious and unconscious is much more permeable. The psychotic, on the other hand, is under the direct influence of the unconscious.

135   The definiteness and directedness of the conscious mind are extremely important acquisitions which humanity has bought at a very heavy sacrifice, and which in turn have rendered humanity the highest service. Without them science, technology, and civilization would be impossible, for they all presuppose the reliable continuity and directedness of the conscious process. For the statesman, doctor, and engineer as well as for the simplest labourer, these qualities are absolutely indispensable. We may say in general that social worthlessness increases to the degree that these qualities are impaired by the unconscious. Great artists and others distinguished by creative gifts are, of course, exceptions to this rule. The very advantage that such individuals enjoy consists precisely in the permeability of the partition separating the conscious and the unconscious. But, for those professions and social activities which require just this continuity and reliability, these exceptional human beings are as a rule of little value.

136   It is therefore understandable, and even necessary, that in each individual the psychic process should be as stable and definite as possible, since the exigencies of life demand it. But this involves a certain disadvantage: the quality of directedness makes for the inhibition or exclusion of all those psychic elements which appear to be, or really are, incompatible with it, i.e., likely to bias the intended direction to suit their purpose and so lead to an undesired goal. But how do we know that the concurrent psychic material is 'incompatible'? We know it by an act of judgment which determines the direction of the path that is chosen and desired. This judgment is partial and prejudiced, since it chooses one particular possibility at the cost of all the others. The judgment in its turn is always based on experience, i.e., on what is already known. As a rule it is never based on what is new, what is still unknown, and what under certain conditions might considerably enrich the directed process. It is evident that it cannot be, for the very reason that the unconscious contents are excluded from consciousness.

137   Through such acts of judgment the directed process necessarily becomes one-sided, even though the rational judgment may appear many-sided and unprejudiced. The very rationality of the judgment may even be the worst prejudice, since we call reasonable what appears reasonable to us. What appears to us unreasonable is therefore doomed to be excluded because of its irrational character. It may really be irrational, but may equally well merely appear irrational without actually being so when seen from another standpoint.

138   One-sidedness is an unavoidable and necessary characteristic of the directed process, for direction implies one-sidedness. It is an advantage and a drawback at the same time. Even when no outwardly visible drawback seems to be present, there is always an equally pronounced counter-position in the unconscious, unless it happens to be the ideal case where all the psychic components are tending in

one and the same direction. This possibility cannot be disputed in theory, but in practice it very rarely happens. The counter-position in the unconscious is not dangerous so long as it does not possess any high energy-value. But if the tension increases as a result of too great one-sidedness, the counter-tendency breaks through into consciousness, usually just at the moment when it is most important to maintain the conscious direction. Thus the speaker makes a slip of the tongue just when he particularly wishes not to say anything stupid. This moment is critical because it possesses a high energy tension which, when the unconscious is already charged, may easily 'spark' and release the unconscious content.

139 Civilized life today demands concentrated, directed conscious functioning, and this entails the risk of a considerable dissociation from the unconscious. The further we are able to remove ourselves from the unconscious through directed functioning, the more readily a powerful counter-position can build up in the unconscious, and when this breaks out it may have disagreeable consequences.

140 Analysis has given us a profound insight into the importance of unconscious influences, and we have learnt so much from this for our practical life that we deem it unwise to expect an elimination or standstill of the unconscious after the so-called completion of the treatment. Many patients, obscurely recognizing this state of affairs, have great difficulty in deciding to give up the analysis, although both they and the analyst find the feeling of dependency irksome. Often they are afraid to risk standing on their own feet, because they know from experience that the unconscious can intervene again and again in their lives in a disturbing and apparently unpredictable manner.

141 It was formerly assumed that patients were ready to cope with normal life as soon as they had acquired enough practical self-knowledge to understand their own dreams. Experience has shown, however, that even professional analysts, who might be expected to have mastered the art of dream interpretation, often capitulate before their own dreams and have to call in the help of a colleague. If even one who purports to be an expert in the method proves unable to interpret his own dreams satisfactorily, how much less can this be expected of the patient. Freud's hope that the unconscious could be 'exhausted' has not been fulfilled. Dream-life and intrusions from the unconscious continue – *mutatis mutandis* – unimpeded.

142 There is a widespread prejudice that analysis is something like a 'cure,' to which one submits for a time and is then discharged healed. That is a layman's error left over from the early days of psychoanalysis. Analytical treatment could be described as a readjustment of psychological attitude achieved with the help of the doctor. Naturally this newly won attitude, which is better suited to the inner and outer conditions, can last a considerable time, but there are very few cases where a single 'cure' is permanently successful. It is true that medical optimism has never stinted itself of publicity and has always been able to report definitive cures. We must, however, not let ourselves be deceived by the all-too-human attitude of the practitioner, but should always remember that the life of the unconscious goes on and continually produces problematical situations. There is no

need for pessimism; we have seen too many excellent results achieved with good luck and honest work for that. But this need not prevent us from recognizing that analysis is no once-and-for-all 'cure'; it is no more, at first, than a more or less thorough readjustment. There is no change that is unconditionally valid over a long period of time. Life has always to be tackled anew. There are, of course, extremely durable collective attitudes which permit the solution of typical conflicts. A collective attitude enables the individual to fit into society without friction, since it acts upon him like any other condition of life. But the patient's difficulty consists precisely in the fact that his individual problem cannot be fitted without friction into a collective norm; it requires the solution of an individual conflict if the whole of his personality is to remain viable. No rational solution can do justice to this task, and there is absolutely no collective norm that could replace an individual solution without loss.

143   The new attitude gained in the course of analysis tends sooner or later to become inadequate in one way or another, and necessarily so, because the constant flow of life again and again demands fresh adaptation. Adaptation is never achieved once and for all. One might certainly demand of analysis that it should enable the patient to gain new orientations in later life, too, without undue difficulty. And experience shows that this is true up to a point. We often find that patients who have gone through a thorough analysis have considerably less difficulty with new adjustments later on. Nevertheless, these difficulties prove to be fairly frequent and may at times be really troublesome. That is why even patients who have had a thorough analysis often turn to their old analyst for help at some later period. In the light of medical practice in general there is nothing very unusual about this, but it does contradict a certain misplaced enthusiasm on the part of the therapist as well as the view that analysis constitutes a unique 'cure.' In the last resort it is highly improbable that there could ever be a therapy that got rid of all difficulties. Man needs difficulties; they are necessary for health. What concerns us here is only an excessive amount of them.

144   The basic question for the therapist is not how to get rid of the momentary difficulty, but how future difficulties may be successfully countered. The question is: what kind of mental and moral attitude is it necessary to have towards the disturbing influences of the unconscious, and how can it be conveyed to the patient?

145   The answer obviously consists in getting rid of the separation between conscious and unconscious. This cannot be done by condemning the contents of the unconscious in a one-sided way, but rather by recognizing their significance in compensating the one-sidedness of consciousness and by taking this significance into account. The tendencies of the conscious and the unconscious are the two factors that together make up the transcendent function. It is called 'transcendent' because it makes the transition from one attitude to another organically possible, without loss of the unconscious. The constructive or synthetic method of treatment presupposes insights which are at least potentially present in the patient and can therefore be made conscious. If the analyst knows nothing of these potentialities

he cannot help the patient to develop them either, unless analyst and patient together devote proper scientific study to this problem, which as a rule is out of the question.

146   In actual practice, therefore, the suitably trained analyst mediates the transcendent function for the patient, i.e., helps him to bring conscious and unconscious together and so arrive at a new attitude. In this function of the analyst lies one of the many important meanings of the *transference*. The patient clings by means of the transference to the person who seems to promise him a renewal of attitude; through it he seeks this change, which is vital to him, even though he may not be conscious of doing so. For the patient, therefore, the analyst has the character of an indispensable figure absolutely necessary for life. However infantile this dependence may appear to be, it expresses an extremely important demand which, if disappointed, often turns to bitter hatred of the analyst. It is therefore important to know what this demand concealed in the transference is really aiming at; there is a tendency to understand it in the reductive sense only, as an erotic infantile fantasy. But that would mean taking this fantasy, which is usually concerned with the parents, literally, as though the patient, or rather his unconscious, still had the expectations the child once had towards the parents. Outwardly it still is the same expectation of the child for the help and protection of the parents, but in the meantime the child has become an adult, and what was normal for a child is improper in an adult. It has become a metaphorical expression of the not consciously realized need for help in a crisis. Historically it is correct to explain the erotic character of the transference in terms of the infantile *eros*. But in that way the meaning and purpose of the transference are not understood, and its interpretation as an infantile sexual fantasy leads away from the real problem. The understanding of the transference is to be sought not in its historical antecedents but in its purpose. The one-sided, reductive explanation becomes in the end nonsensical, especially when absolutely nothing new comes out of it except the increased resistances of the patient. The sense of boredom which then appears in the analysis is simply an expression of the monotony and poverty of ideas – not of the unconscious, as is sometimes supposed, but of the analyst, who does not understand that these fantasies should not be taken merely in a concretistic-reductive sense, but rather in a constructive one. When this is realized, the standstill is often overcome at a single stroke.

147   Constructive treatment of the unconscious, that is, the question of meaning and purpose, paves the way for the patient's insight into that process which I call the transcendent function.

148   It may not be superfluous, at this point, to say a few words about the frequently heard objection that the constructive method is simply 'suggestion.' The method is based, rather, on evaluating the symbol (i.e., dream-image or fantasy) not *semiotically*, as a sign for elementary instinctual processes, but symbolically in the true sense, the word 'symbol' being taken to mean the best possible expression for a complex fact not yet clearly apprehended by consciousness. Through reductive analysis of this expression nothing is gained but a clearer view of the elements

originally composing it, and though I would not deny that increased insight into these elements may have its advantages, it nevertheless bypasses the question of purpose. Dissolution of the symbol at this stage of analysis is therefore a mistake. To begin with, however, the method for working out the complex meanings suggested by the symbol is the same as in reductive analysis. The associations of the patient are obtained, and as a rule they are plentiful enough to be used in the synthetic method. Here again they are evaluated not semiotically but symbolically. The question we must ask is: to what meaning do the individual associations A, B, C point, when taken in conjunction with the manifest dream-content?

149 An unmarried woman patient dreamt that *someone gave her a wonderful, richly ornamented, antique sword dug up out of a tumulus*. [For interpretation, see Table p. 344]

150 In this case there was no need of any supplementary analogies on the part of the analyst. The patient's associations provided all that was necessary. It might be objected that this treatment of the dream involves suggestion. But this ignores the fact that a suggestion is never accepted without an inner readiness for it, or if after great insistence it is accepted, it is immediately lost again. A suggestion that is accepted for any length of time always presupposes a marked psychological readiness which is merely brought into play by the so-called suggestion. This objection is therefore thoughtless and credits suggestion with a magical power it in no way possesses, otherwise suggestion therapy would have an enormous effect and would render analytical procedures quite superfluous. But this is far from being the case. Furthermore, the charge of suggestion does not take account of the fact that the patient's own associations point to the cultural significance of the sword.

151 After this digression, let us return to the question of the transcendent function. We have seen that during treatment the transcendent function is, in a sense, an 'artificial' product because it is largely supported by the analyst. But if the patient is to stand on his own feet he must not depend permanently on outside help. The interpretation of dreams would be an ideal method for synthesizing the conscious and unconscious data, but in practice the difficulties of analyzing one's own dreams are too great.

152 We must now make clear what is required to produce the transcendent function. First and foremost, we need the unconscious material. The most readily accessible expression of unconscious processes is undoubtedly dreams. The dream is, so to speak, a pure product of the unconscious. The alterations which the dream undergoes in the process of reaching consciousness, although undeniable, can be considered irrelevant, since they too derive from the unconscious and are not intentional distortions. Possible modifications of the original dream-image derive from a more superficial layer of the unconscious and therefore contain valuable material too. They are further fantasy-products following the general trend of the dream. The same applies to the subsequent images and ideas which frequently occur while dozing or rise up spontaneously on waking. Since the dream originates in sleep, it bears all the characteristics of an 'abaissement du niveau mental' (Janet), or of low energy-tension: logical discontinuity, fragmentary character,

Table Interpretation of dream (see par. 149)

Associations	Analytical interpretation	Constructive interpretation
Her father's dagger, which he once flashed in the sun in front of her. It made a great impression on her. Her father was in every respect an energetic, strong-willed man, with an impetuous temperament, and adventurous in love affairs. A Celtic bronze sword: Patient is proud of her Celtic ancestry. The Celts are full of temperament, impetuous, passionate. The ornamentation has a mysterious look about it, ancient tradition, runes, signs of ancient wisdom, ancient civilizations, heritage of mankind, brought to light again out of the grave.	Patient has a pronounced father complex and a rich tissue of sexual fantasies about her father, whom she lost early. She always put herself in her mother's place, although with strong resistances towards her father. She has never been able to accept a man like her father and has therefore chosen weakly, neurotic men against her will. Also in the analysis violent resistance towards the physician-father. The dream digs up her wish for her father's 'weapon.' The rest is clear. In theory, this would immediately point to a phallic fantasy.	It is as if the patient needed such a weapon. Her father had the weapon. He was energetic, lived accordingly, and also took upon himself the difficulties inherent in his temperament. Therefore, though living a passionate, exciting life he was not neurotic. This weapon is a very ancient heritage of mankind, which lay buried in the patient and was brought to light through excavation (analysis). The weapon has to do with insight, with wisdom. It is a means of attack and defence. Her father's weapon was a passionate, unbending will, with which he made his way through life. Up till now the patient has been the opposite in every respect. She is just on the point of realizing that a person can also will something and need not merely be driven, as she had always believed. The will based on a knowledge of life and on insight is an ancient heritage of the human race, which also is in her, but till now lay buried, for in this respect, too, she is her father's daughter. But she had not appreciated this till now, because her character had been that of a perpetually whining, pampered, spoilt child. She was extremely passive and completely given to sexual fantasies.

analogy formations, superficial associations of the verbal, clang, or visual type, condensations, irrational expressions, confusion, etc. With an increase of energy-tension, the dreams acquire a more ordered character; they become dramatically composed and reveal clear sense-connections, and the valency of the associations increases.

153   Since the energy-tension in sleep is usually very low, dreams, compared with conscious material, are inferior expressions of unconscious contents and are very difficult to understand from a constructive point of view, but are usually easier to understand reductively. In general, dreams are unsuitable or difficult to make use of in developing the transcendent function, because they make too great demands on the subject.

154   We must therefore look to other sources for the unconscious material. There are, for instance, the unconscious interferences in the waking state, ideas 'out of the blue,' slips, deceptions and lapses of memory, symptomatic actions, etc. This material is generally more useful for the reductive method than for the constructive one; it is too fragmentary and lacks continuity, which is indispensable for a meaningful synthesis.

155   Another source is spontaneous fantasies. They usually have a more composed and coherent character and often contain much that is obviously significant. Some patients are able to produce fantasies at any time, allowing them to rise up freely simply by eliminating critical attention. Such fantasies can be used, though this particular talent is none too common. The capacity to produce free fantasies can, however, be developed with practice. The training consists first of all in systematic exercises for eliminating critical attention, thus producing a vacuum in consciousness. This encourages the emergence of any fantasies that are lying in readiness. A prerequisite, of course, is that fantasies with a high libido-charge are actually lying ready. This is naturally not always the case. Where this is not so, special measures are required.

156   Before entering upon a discussion of these, I must yield to an uncomfortable feeling which tells me that the reader may be asking dubiously, what really is the point of all this? And why is it so absolutely necessary to bring up the unconscious contents? Is it not sufficient if from time to time they come up of their own accord and make themselves unpleasantly felt? Does one have to drag the unconscious to the surface by force? On the contrary, should it not be the job of analysis to empty the unconscious of fantasies and in this way render it ineffective?

157   It may be as well to consider these misgivings in somewhat more detail, since the methods for bringing the unconscious to consciousness may strike the reader as novel, unusual, and perhaps even rather weird. We must therefore first discuss these natural objections, so that they shall not hold us up when we begin demonstrating the methods in question.

158   As we have seen, we need the unconscious contents to supplement the conscious attitude. If the conscious attitude were only to a slight degree 'directed,' the unconscious could flow in quite of its own accord. This is what does in fact happen with all those people who have a low level of conscious tension, as for instance

primitives. Among primitives, no special measures are required to bring up the unconscious. Nowhere, really, are special measures required for this, because those people who are least aware of their unconscious side are the most influenced by it. But they are unconscious of what is happening. The secret participation of the unconscious is everywhere present without our having to search for it, but as it remains unconscious we never really know what is going on or what to expect. What we are searching for is a way to make conscious those contents which are about to influence our actions, so that the secret interference of the unconscious and its unpleasant consequences can be avoided.

159 The reader will no doubt ask: why cannot the unconscious be left to its own devices? Those who have not already had a few bad experiences in this respect will naturally see no reason to control the unconscious. But anyone with sufficiently bad experience will eagerly welcome the bare possibility of doing so. Directedness is absolutely necessary for the conscious process, but as we have seen it entails an unavoidable one-sidedness. Since the psyche is a self-regulating system, just as the body is, the regulating counteraction will always develop in the unconscious. Were it not for the directedness of the conscious function, the counteracting influences of the unconscious could set in unhindered. It is just this directedness that excludes them. This, of course, does not inhibit the counteraction, which goes on in spite of everything. Its regulating influence, however, is eliminated by critical attention and the directed will, because the counteraction as such seems incompatible with the conscious direction. To this extent the psyche of civilized man is no longer a self-regulating system but could rather be compared to a machine whose speed-regulation is so insensitive that it can continue to function to the point of self-injury, while on the other hand it is subject to the arbitrary manipulations of a one-sided will.

160 Now it is a peculiarity of psychic functioning that when the unconscious counteraction is suppressed it loses its regulating influence. It then begins to have an accelerating and intensifying effect on the conscious process. It is as though the counteraction had lost its regulating influence, and hence its energy, altogether, for a condition then arises in which not only no inhibiting counteraction takes place, but in which its energy seems to add itself to that of the conscious direction. To begin with, this naturally facilitates the execution of the conscious intentions, but because they are unchecked, they may easily assert themselves at the cost of the whole. For instance, when someone makes a rather bold assertion and suppresses the counteraction, namely a well-placed doubt, he will insist on it all the more, to his own detriment.

161 The ease with which the counteraction can be eliminated is proportional to the degree of dissociability of the psyche and leads to loss of instinct. This is characteristic of, as well as very necessary for, civilized man, since instincts in their original strength can render social adaptation almost impossible. It is not a real atrophy of instinct but, in most cases, only a relatively lasting product of education, and would never have struck such deep roots had it not served the interests of the individual.

162 Apart from the everyday cases met with in practice, a good example of the

suppression of the unconscious regulating influence can be found in Nietzsche's *Zarathustra*. The discovery of the 'higher' man, and also of the 'ugliest' man, expresses the regulating influence, for the 'higher' men want to drag Zarathustra down to the collective sphere of average humanity as it always has been, while the 'ugliest' man is actually the personification of the counteraction. But the roaring lion of Zarathustra's moral conviction forces all these influences, above all the feeling of pity, back again into the cave of the unconscious. Thus the regulating influence is suppressed, but not the secret counteraction of the unconscious, which from now on becomes clearly noticeable in Nietzsche's writings. First he seeks his adversary in Wagner, whom he cannot forgive for *Parsifal*, but soon his whole wrath turns against Christianity and in particular against St. Paul, who in some ways suffered a fate similar to Nietzsche's. As is well known, Nietzsche's psychosis first produced an identification with the 'Crucified Christ' and then with the dismembered Dionysus. With this catastrophe the counteraction at last broke through to the surface.

163   Another example is the classic case of megalomania preserved for us in the fourth chapter of the Book of Daniel. Nebuchadnezzar at the height of his power had a dream which foretold disaster if he did not humble himself. Daniel interpreted the dream quite expertly, but without getting a hearing. Subsequent events showed that his interpretation was correct, for Nebuchadnezzar, after suppressing the unconscious regulating influence, fell victim to a psychosis that contained the very counteraction he had sought to escape: he, the lord of the earth, was degraded to an animal.

164   An acquaintance of mine once told me a dream in which *he stepped out into space from the top of a mountain*. I explained to him something of the influence of the unconscious and warned him against dangerous mountaineering expeditions, for which he had a regular passion. But he laughed at such ideas. A few months later while climbing a mountain he actually did step off into space and was killed.

165   Anyone who has seen these things happen over and over again in every conceivable shade of dramatic intensity is bound to ponder. He becomes aware how easy it is to overlook the regulating influences, and that he should endeavour to pay attention to the unconscious regulation which is so necessary for our mental and physical health. Accordingly he will try to help himself by practising self-observation and self-criticism. But mere self-observation and intellectual self-analysis are entirely inadequate as a means to establishing contact with the unconscious. Although no human being can be spared bad experiences, everyone shrinks from risking them, especially if he sees any way by which they might be circumvented. Knowledge of the regulating influences of the unconscious offers just such a possibility and actually does render much bad experience unnecessary. We can avoid a great many detours that are distinguished by no particular attraction but only by tiresome conflicts. It is bad enough to make detours and painful mistakes in unknown and unexplored territory, but to get lost in inhabited country

on broad highways is merely exasperating. What, then, are the means at our disposal of obtaining knowledge of the regulating factors?

166 If there is no capacity to produce fantasies freely, we have to resort to artificial aid. The reason for invoking such aid is generally a depressed or disturbed state of mind for which no adequate cause can be found. Naturally the patient can give any number of rationalistic reasons – the bad weather alone suffices as a reason. But none of them is really satisfying as an explanation, for a causal explanation of these states is usually satisfying only to an outsider, and then only up to a point. The outsider is content if his causal requirements are more or less satisfied; it is sufficient for him to know where the thing comes from; he does not feel the challenge which, for the patient, lies in the depression. The patient would like to know what it is all for and how to gain relief. *In the intensity of the emotional disturbance itself lies the value, the energy which he should have at his disposal in order to remedy the state of reduced adaptation.* Nothing is achieved by repressing this state or devaluing it rationally.

167 In order, therefore, to gain possession of the energy that is in the wrong place, he must make the emotional state the basis or starting point of the procedure. He must make himself as conscious as possible of the mood he is in, sinking himself in it without reserve and noting down on paper all the fantasies and other associations that come up. Fantasy must be allowed the freest possible play, yet not in such a manner that it leaves the orbit of its object, namely the affect, by setting off a kind of 'chain-reaction' association process. This 'free association,' as Freud called it, leads away from the object to all sorts of complexes, and one can never be sure that they relate to the affect and are not displacements which have appeared in its stead. Out of this preoccupation with the object there comes a more or less complete expression of the mood, which reproduces the content of the depression in some way, either concretely or symbolically. Since the depression was not manufactured by the conscious mind but is an unwelcome intrusion from the unconscious, the elaboration of the mood is, as it were, a picture of the contents and tendencies of the unconscious that were massed together in the depression. The whole procedure is a kind of enrichment and clarification of the affect, whereby the affect and its contents are brought nearer to consciousness, becoming at the same time more impressive and more understandable. This work by itself can have a favourable and vitalizing influence. At all events, it creates a new situation, since the previously unrelated affect has become a more or less clear and articulate idea, thanks to the assistance and co-operation of the conscious mind. This is the beginning of the transcendent function, i.e., of the collaboration of conscious and unconscious data.

168 The emotional disturbance can also be dealt with in another way, not by clarifying it intellectually but by giving it visible shape. Patients who possess some talent for drawing or painting can give expression to their mood by means of a picture. It is not important for the picture to be technically or aesthetically satisfying, but merely for the fantasy to have free play and for the whole thing to be done as well as possible. In principle this procedure agrees with the one first described. Here too a product is created which is influenced by both conscious and

unconscious, embodying the striving of the unconscious for the light and the striving of the conscious for substance.

169 Often, however, we find cases where there is no tangible mood or depression at all, but just a general, dull discontent, a feeling of resistance to everything, a sort of boredom or vague disgust, an indefinable but excruciating emptiness. In these cases no definite starting point exists – it would first have to be created. Here a special introversion of libido is necessary, supported perhaps by favourable external conditions, such as complete rest, especially at night, when the libido has in any case a tendency to introversion. (''Tis night: now do all fountains speak louder. And my soul also is a bubbling fountain.'[2])

170 Critical attention must be eliminated. Visual types should concentrate on the expectation that an inner image will be produced. As a rule such a fantasy-picture will actually appear – perhaps hypnagogically – and should be carefully observed and noted down in writing. Audio-verbal types usually hear inner words, perhaps mere fragments of apparently meaningless sentences to begin with, which however should be carefully noted down too. Others at such times simply hear their 'other' voice. There are, indeed, not a few people who are well aware that they possess a sort of inner critic or judge who immediately comments on everything they say or do. Insane people hear this voice directly as auditory hallucinations. But normal people too, if their inner life is fairly well developed, are able to reproduce this inaudible voice without difficulty, though as it is notoriously irritating and refractory it is almost always repressed. Such persons have little difficulty in procuring the unconscious material and thus laying the foundation of the transcendent function.

171 There are others, again, who neither see nor hear anything inside themselves, but whose hands have the knack of giving expression to the contents of the unconscious. Such people can profitably work with plastic materials. Those who are able to express the unconscious by means of bodily movements are rather rare. The disadvantage that movements cannot easily be fixed in the mind must be met by making careful drawings of the movements afterwards, so that they shall not be lost to the memory. Still rarer, but equally valuable, is automatic writing, direct or with the planchette. This, too, yields useful results.

172 We now come to the next question: what is to be done with the material obtained in one of the manners described. To this question there is no *a priori* answer; it is only when the conscious mind confronts the products of the unconscious that a provisional reaction will ensue which determines the subsequent procedure. Practical experience alone can give us a clue. So far as my experience goes, there appear to be two main tendencies. One is the way of *creative formulation*, the other the way of *understanding*.

173 Where the principle of creative formulation predominates, the material is continually varied and increased until a kind of condensation of motifs into more or less stereotyped symbols takes place. These, stimulate the creative fantasy and serve chiefly as aesthetic motifs. This tendency leads to the aesthetic problem of artistic formulation.

174 Where, on the other hand, the principle of understanding predominates, the aesthetic aspect is of relatively little interest and may occasionally even be felt as a hindrance. Instead, there is an intensive struggle to understand the *meaning* of the unconscious product.

175 Whereas aesthetic formulation tends to concentrate on the formal aspect of the motif, an intuitive understanding often tries to catch the meaning from barely adequate hints in the material, without considering those elements which would come to light in a more careful formulation.

176 Neither of these tendencies can be brought about by an arbitrary effort of will; they are far more the result of the peculiar make-up of the individual personality. Both have their typical dangers and may lead one astray. The danger of the aesthetic tendency is overvaluation of the formal or 'artistic' worth of the fantasy-productions; the libido is diverted from the real goal of the transcendent function and sidetracked into purely aesthetic problems of artistic expression. The danger of wanting to understand the meaning is overvaluation of the content, which is subjected to intellectual analysis and interpretation, so that the essentially symbolic character of the product is lost. Up to a point these bypaths must be followed in order to satisfy aesthetic or intellectual requirements, whichever predominate in the individual case. But the danger of both these bypaths is worth stressing, for, after a certain point of psychic development has been reached, the products of the unconscious are greatly overvalued precisely because they were boundlessly undervalued before. This undervaluation is one of the greatest obstacles in formulating the unconscious material. It reveals the collective standards by which anything individual is judged: nothing is considered good or beautiful that does not fit into the collective schema, though it is true that contemporary art is beginning to make compensatory efforts in this respect. What is lacking is not the collective recognition of the individual product but its subjective appreciation, the understanding of its meaning and value for the *subject*. This feeling of inferiority for one's own product is of course not the rule everywhere. Sometimes we find the exact opposite: a naïve and uncritical overvaluation coupled with the demand for collective recognition once the initial feeling of inferiority has been overcome. Conversely, an initial overvaluation can easily turn into depreciatory scepticism. These erroneous judgments are due to the individual's unconsciousness and lack of self-reliance: either he is able to judge only by collective standards, or else, owing to ego-inflation, he loses his capacity for judgment altogether.

177 *One tendency seems to be the regulating principle of the other*; both are bound together in a compensatory relationship. Experience bears out this formula. So far as it is possible at this stage to draw more general conclusions, we could say that aesthetic formulation needs understanding of the meaning, and understanding needs aesthetic formulation. The two supplement each other to form the transcendent function.

178 The first steps along both paths follow the same principle: consciousness puts its media of expression at the disposal of the unconscious content. It must not do more than this at first, so as not to exert undue influence. In giving the content

form, the lead must be left as far as possible to the chance ideas and associations thrown up by the unconscious. This is naturally something of a setback for the conscious standpoint and is often felt as painful. It is not difficult to understand this when we remember how the contents of the unconscious usually present themselves: as things which are too weak by nature to cross the threshold, or as incompatible elements that were repressed for a variety of reasons. Mostly they are unwelcome, unexpected, irrational contents, disregard or repression of which seems altogether understandable. Only a small part of them has any unusual value, either from the collective or from the subjective standpoint. But contents that are collectively valueless may be exceedingly valuable when seen from the standpoint of the individual. This fact expresses itself in their affective tone, no matter whether the subject feels it as negative or positive. Society, too, is divided in its acceptance of new and unknown ideas which obtrude their emotionality. The purpose of the initial procedure is to discover the feeling-toned contents, for in these cases we are always dealing with situations where the one-sidedness of consciousness meets with the resistance of the instinctual sphere.

179   The two ways do not divide until the aesthetic problem becomes decisive for the one type of person and the intellectual-moral problem for the other. The ideal case would be if these two aspects could exist side by side or rhythmically succeed each other; that is, if there were an alternation of creation and understanding. It hardly seems possible for the one to exist without the other, though it sometimes does happen in practice: the creative urge seizes possession of the object at the cost of its meaning, or the urge to understand overrides the necessity of giving it form. The unconscious contents want first of all to be seen clearly, which can only be done by giving them shape, and to be judged only when everything they have to say is tangibly present. It was for this reason that Freud got the dream-contents, as it were, to express themselves in the form of 'free associations' before he began interpreting them.

180   It does not suffice in all cases to elucidate only the conceptual context of a dream-content. Often it is necessary to clarify a vague content by giving it a visible form. This can be done by drawing, painting, or modelling. Often the hands know how to solve a riddle with which the intellect has wrestled in vain. By shaping it, one goes on dreaming the dream in greater detail in the waking state, and the initially incomprehensible, isolated event is integrated into the sphere of the total personality, even though it remains at first unconscious to the subject. Aesthetic formulation leaves it at that and gives up any idea of discovering a meaning. This sometimes leads patients to fancy themselves artists – misunderstood ones, naturally. The desire to understand, if it dispenses with careful formulation, starts with the chance idea or association and therefore lacks an adequate basis. It has better prospects of success if it begins only with the formulated product. The less the initial material is shaped and developed, the greater is the danger that understanding will be governed not by the empirical facts but by theoretical and moral considerations. The kind of understanding with which we are concerned at this stage consists in a reconstruction of the meaning that seems to be immanent in the original 'chance' idea.

181 It is evident that such a procedure can legitimately take place only when there is a sufficient motive for it. Equally, the lead can be left to the unconscious only if it already contains the will to lead. This naturally happens only when the conscious mind finds itself in a critical situation. Once the unconscious content has been given form and the meaning of the formulation is understood, the question arises as to how the ego will relate to this position, and how the ego and the unconscious are to come to terms. This is the second and more important stage of the procedure, the bringing together of opposites for the production of a third: the transcendent function. At this stage it is no longer the unconscious that takes the lead, but the ego.

182 We shall not define the individual ego here, but shall leave it in its banal reality as that continuous centre of consciousness whose presence has made itself felt since the days of childhood. It is confronted with a psychic product that owes its existence mainly to an unconscious process and is therefore in some degree opposed to the ego and its tendencies.

183 This standpoint is essential in coming to terms with the unconscious. The position of the ego must be maintained as being of equal value to the counter-position of the unconscious, and vice versa. This amounts to a very necessary warning: for just as the conscious mind of civilized man has a restrictive effect on the unconscious, so the rediscovered unconscious often has a really dangerous effect on the ego. In the same way that the ego suppressed the unconscious before, a liberated unconscious can thrust the ego aside and overwhelm it. There is a danger of the ego losing its head, so to speak, that it will not be able to defend itself against the pressure of affective factors – a situation often encountered at the beginning of schizophrenia. This danger would not exist, or would not be so acute, if the process of having it out with the unconscious could somehow divest the affects of their dynamism. And this is what does in fact happen when the counter-position is aestheticized or intellectualized. But the confrontation with the unconscious must be a many-sided one, for the transcendent function is not a partial process running a conditioned course; it is a total and integral event in which all aspects are, or should be, included. The affect must therefore be deployed in its full strength. Aestheticization and intellectualization are excellent weapons against dangerous affects, but they should be used only when there is a vital threat, and not for the purpose of avoiding a necessary task.

184 Thanks to the fundamental insight of Freud, we know that emotional factors must be given full consideration in the treatment of the neuroses. The personality *as a whole* must be taken seriously into account, and this applies to both parties, the patient as well as the analyst. How far the latter may hide behind the shield of theory remains a delicate question, to be left to his discretion. At all events, the treatment of neurosis is not a kind of psychological water-cure, but a renewal of the personality, working in every direction and penetrating every sphere of life. Coming to terms with the counter-position is a serious matter on which sometimes a very great deal depends. Taking the other side seriously is an essential prerequisite of the process, for only in that way can the regulating factors exert an

influence on our actions. Taking it seriously does not mean taking it literally, but it does mean giving the unconscious credit, so that it has a chance to co-operate with consciousness instead of automatically disturbing it.

185   Thus, in coming to terms with the unconscious, not only is the standpoint of the ego justified, but the unconscious is granted the same authority. The ego takes the lead, but the unconscious must be allowed to have its say too – *audiatur et altera pars*.

186   The way this can be done is best shown by those cases in which the 'other' voice is more or less distinctly heard. For such people it is technically very simple to note down the 'other' voice in writing and to answer its statements from the standpoint of the ego. It is exactly as if a dialogue were taking place between two human beings with equal rights, each of whom gives the other credit for a valid argument and considers it worth while to modify the conflicting standpoints by means of thorough comparison and discussion or else to distinguish them clearly from one another. Since the way to agreement seldom stands open, in most cases a long conflict will have to be borne, demanding sacrifices from both sides. Such a rapprochement could just as well take place between patient and analyst, the role of devil's advocate easily falling to the latter.

187   The present day shows with appalling clarity how little able people are to let the other man's argument count, although this capacity is a fundamental and indispensable condition for any human community. Everyone who proposes to come to terms with himself must reckon with this basic problem. For, to the degree that he does not admit the validity of the other person, he denies the 'other' within himself the right to exist – and vice versa. The capacity for inner dialogue is a touchstone for outer objectivity.

188   Simple as the process of coming to terms may be in the case of the inner dialogue, it is undoubtedly more complicated in other cases where only visual products are available, speaking a language which is eloquent enough for one who understands it, but which seems like deaf-and-dumb language to one who does not. Faced with such products, the ego must seize the initiative and ask: 'How am I affected by this sign?'[3] This Faustian question can call forth an illuminating answer. The more direct and natural the answer is, the more valuable it will be, for directness and naturalness guarantee a more or less total reaction. It is not absolutely necessary for the process of confrontation itself to become conscious in every detail. Very often a total reaction does not have at its disposal those theoretical assumptions, views, and concepts which would make clear apprehension possible. In such cases one must be content with the wordless but suggestive feelings which appear in their stead and are more valuable than clever talk.

189   The shuttling to and fro of arguments and affects represents the transcendent function of opposites. The confrontation of the two positions generates a tension charged with energy and creates a living, third thing – not a logical stillbirth in accordance with the principle *tertium non datur* but a movement out of the suspension between opposites, a living birth that leads to a new level of being, a new situation. The transcendent function manifests itself as a quality of conjoined

opposites. So long as these are kept apart – naturally for the purpose of avoiding conflict – they do not function and remain inert.

190   In whatever form the opposites appear in the individual, at bottom it is always a matter of a consciousness lost and obstinately stuck in one-sidedness, confronted with the image of instinctive wholeness and freedom. This presents a picture of the anthropoid and archaic man with, on the one hand, his supposedly uninhibited world of instinct and, on the other, his often misunderstood world of spiritual ideas, who, compensating and correcting our one-sidedness, emerges from the darkness and shows us how and where we have deviated from the basic pattern and crippled ourselves psychically.

191   I must content myself here with a description of the outward forms and possibilities of the transcendent function. Another task of greater importance would be the description of its *contents*. There is already a mass of material on this subject, but not all the difficulties in the way of exposition have yet been overcome. A number of preparatory studies are still needed before the conceptual foundation is laid which would enable us to give a clear and intelligible account of the contents of the transcendent function. I have unfortunately had the experience that the scientific public are not everywhere in a position to follow a purely psychological argument, since they either take it too personally or are bedevilled by philosophical or intellectual prejudices. This renders any meaningful appreciation of the psychological factors quite impossible. If people take it personally their judgment is always subjective, and they declare everything to be impossible which seems not to apply in their case or which they prefer not to acknowledge. They are quite incapable of realizing that what is valid for them may not be valid at all for another person with a different psychology. We are still very far from possessing a general valid scheme of explanation in all cases.

192   One of the greatest obstacles to psychological understanding is the inquisitive desire to know whether the psychological factor adduced is 'true' or 'correct.' If the description of it is not erroneous or false, then the factor is valid in itself and proves its validity by its very existence. One might just as well ask if the duck-billed platypus is a 'true' or 'correct' invention of the Creator's will. Equally childish is the prejudice against the role which mythological assumptions play in the life of the psyche. Since they are not 'true,' it is argued, they have no place in a scientific explanation. But mythologems *exist*, even though their statements do not coincide with our incommensurable idea of 'truth.'

193   As the process of coming to terms with the counter-position has a total character, nothing is excluded. Everything takes part in the discussion, even if only fragments become conscious. Consciousness is continually widened through the confrontation with previously unconscious contents, or – to be more accurate – could be widened if it took the trouble to integrate them. That is naturally not always the case. Even if there is sufficient intelligence to understand the procedure, there may yet be a lack of courage and self-confidence, or one is too lazy, mentally and morally, or too cowardly, to make an effort. But where the necessary premises exist, the transcendent function not only forms a valuable addition to

psychotherapeutic treatment, but gives the patient the inestimable advantage of assisting the analyst on his own resources, and of breaking a dependence which is often felt as humiliating. It is a way of attaining liberation by one's own efforts and of finding the courage to be oneself.

Notes

1 [Written in 1916 under the title 'Die Transzendente Funktion,' the ms. lay in Professor Jung's files until 1953. First published in 1957 by the Students Association, C. G. Jung Institute, Zurich, in an English translation by A. R. Pope. The German original, considerably revised by the author, was published in *Geist und Werk . . . zum 75. Geburtstag von Dr. Daniel Brody* (Zurich, 1958), together with a prefatory note of more general import specially written for that volume. The author has partially rewritten the note for publication here. The present translation is based on the revised German version, and Mr. Pope's translation has been consulted.–EDITORS.]
2 [Nietzsche, *Thus Spake Zarathustra*, XXXI; Common trans., p. 156. – EDITORS.]
3 [Cf. *Faust: Part I*, Wayne trans., p. 46.]

Chapter 17

Healing the split[1]

578 When the medical psychologist takes an interest in symbols, he is primarily concerned with 'natural' symbols as distinct from 'cultural' symbols. The former are derived from the unconscious contents of the psyche, and they therefore represent an enormous number of variations on the basic archetypal motifs. In many cases, they can be traced back to their archaic roots, i.e., to ideas and images that we meet in the most ancient records and in primitive societies. In this respect, I should like to call the reader's attention to such books as Mircea Eliade's study of shamanism,[2] where a great many illuminating examples may be found.

579 'Cultural' symbols, on the other hand, are those that have expressed 'eternal truths' or are still in use in many religions. They have gone through many transformations and even a process of more or less conscious elaboration, and in this way have become the *représentations collectives* of civilized societies. Nevertheless, they have retained much of their original numinosity, and they function as positive or negative 'prejudices' with which the psychologist has to reckon very seriously.

580 Nobody can dismiss these numinous factors on merely rational grounds. They are important constituents of our mental make-up and vital forces in the building up of human society, and they cannot be eradicated without serious loss. When they are repressed or neglected, their specific energy disappears into the unconscious with unpredictable consequences. The energy that appears to have been lost revives and intensifies whatever is uppermost in the unconscious – tendencies, perhaps, that have hitherto had no chance to express themselves, or have not been allowed an uninhibited existence in our consciousness. They form an ever-present destructive 'shadow.' Even tendencies that might be able to exert a beneficial influence turn into veritable demons when they are repressed. This is why many well-meaning people are understandably afraid of the unconscious, and incidentally of psychology.

581 Our times have demonstrated what it means when the gates of the psychic underworld are thrown open. Things whose enormity nobody could have imagined in the idyllic innocence of the first decade of our century have happened and have turned the world upside down. Ever since, the world has remained in a state of schizophrenia. Not only has the great civilized Germany disgorged its primitivity, but Russia also is ruled by it, and Africa has been set on fire. No wonder the

Western world feels uneasy, for it does not know how much it plays into the hands of the uproarious underworld and what it has lost through the destruction of its numinosities. It has lost its moral and spiritual values to a very dangerous degree. Its moral and spiritual tradition has collapsed, and has left a worldwide disorientation and dissociation.

582   We could have seen long ago from primitive societies what the loss of numinosity means: they lose their *raison d'être,* the order of their social organizations, and then they dissolve and decay. We are now in the same condition. We have lost something we have never properly understood. Our spiritual leaders cannot be spared the blame for having been more interested in protecting their institutions than in understanding the mystery that symbols present. Faith does not exclude thought (which is man's strongest weapon), but unfortunately many believers are so afraid of science, and also of psychology, that they turn a blind eye to the numinous psychic powers that forever control man's fate. We have stripped all things of their mystery and numinosity; nothing is holy any longer.

583   The masses and their leaders do not realize that it makes no substantial difference whether you call the world principle male and a father (spirit), or female and a mother (matter). Essentially, we know as little of the one as of the other. Since the beginning of the human mind, both were numinous symbols, and their importance lay in their numinosity and not in their sex or other chance attributes. Since energy never vanishes, the emotional energy that manifests itself in all numinous phenomena does not cease to exist when it disappears from consciousness. As I have said, it reappears in unconscious manifestations, in symbolic happenings that compensate the disturbances of the conscious psyche. Our psyche is profoundly disturbed by the loss of moral and spiritual values that have hitherto kept our life in order. Our consciousness is no longer capable of integrating the natural afflux of concomitant, instinctive events that sustains our conscious psychic activity. This process can no longer take place in the same way as before, because our consciousness has deprived itself of the organs by which the auxiliary contributions of the instincts and the unconscious could be assimilated. These organs were the numinous symbols, held holy by common consent.

584   A concept like 'physical matter,' stripped of its numinous connotation of the 'Great Mother,' no longer expresses the vast emotional meaning of 'Mother Earth.' It is a mere intellectual term, dry as dust and entirely inhuman. In the same way, 'spirit' identified with 'intellect' ceases to be the Father of All. It degenerates into the limited mind of man, and the immense emotional energy expressed in the image 'our Father' vanishes in the sand of an intellectual desert.

585   Through scientific understanding, our world has become dehumanized. Man feels himself isolated in the cosmos. He is no longer involved in nature and has lost his emotional participation in natural events, which hitherto had a symbolic meaning for him. Thunder is no longer the voice of a god, nor is lightning his avenging missile. No river contains a spirit, no tree means a man's life, no snake is the embodiment of wisdom, and no mountain still harbours a great demon. Neither do things speak to him nor can he speak to things, like stones, springs,

plants, and animals. He no longer has a bush-soul identifying him with a wild animal. His immediate communication with nature is gone for ever, and the emotional energy it generated has sunk into the unconscious.

586 This enormous loss is compensated by the symbols in our dreams. They bring up our original nature, its instincts and its peculiar thinking. Unfortunately, one would say, they also express their contents in the language of nature, which is strange and incomprehensible to us. It sets us the task of translating its images into the rational words and concepts of modern speech, which has liberated itself from its primitive encumbrances – notably from its mystical participation with things. Nowadays, talking of ghosts and other numinous figures is no longer the same as conjuring them up. We have ceased to believe in magical formulas; not many taboos and similar restrictions are left; and our world seems to be disinfected of all such superstitious numina as 'witches, warlocks, and worricows,' to say nothing of werewolves, vampires, bush-souls, and all the other bizarre beings that populate the primeval forest.

587 At least the surface of our world seems to be purified of all superstitious and irrational admixtures. Whether, however, the real inner world of man – and not our wish-fulfilling fiction about it – is also freed from primitivity is another question. Is not the number 13 still taboo for many people? Are there not still many individuals possessed by funny prejudices, projections, and illusions? A realistic picture of the human mind reveals many primitive traits and survivals, which are still playing their roles just as if nothing had happened during the last five hundred years. The man of today is a curious mixture of characteristics acquired over the long ages of his mental development. This is the man and his symbols we have to deal with, and we must scrutinize his mental products very carefully indeed. Sceptical viewpoints and scientific convictions exist in him side by side with old-fashioned prejudices, outdated habits of thought and feeling, obstinate misinterpretations, and blind ignorance.

588 Such are the people who produce the symbols we are investigating in their dreams. In order to explain the symbols and their meaning, it is essential to learn whether these representations are still the same as they ever were, or whether they have been chosen by the dream for its particular purpose from a store of general conscious knowledge. If, for instance, one has to deal with a dream in which the number 13 occurs, the question is: Does the dreamer habitually believe in the unfavourable nature of the number, or does the dream merely allude to people who still indulge in such superstitions? The answer will make a great difference to the interpretation. In the former case, the dreamer is still under the spell of the unlucky 13, and will therefore feel most uncomfortable in room no. 13 or sitting at a table with thirteen people. In the latter case, 13 may not be more than a chiding or disparaging remark. In one case it is a still numinous representation; in the other it is stripped of its original emotionality and has assumed the innocuous character of a mere piece of indifferent information.

589 This illustrates the way in which archetypes appear in practical experience. In the first case they appear in their original form – they are images and at the same

time emotions. One can speak of an archetype only when these two aspects coincide. When there is only an image, it is merely a word-picture, like a corpuscle with no electric charge. It is then of little consequence, just a word and nothing more. But if the image is charged with numinosity, that is, with psychic energy, then it becomes dynamic and will produce consequences. It is a great mistake in practice to treat an archetype as if it were a mere name, word, or concept. It is far more than that: it is a piece of life, an image connected with the living individual by the bridge of emotion. The word alone is a mere abstraction, an exchangeable coin in intellectual commerce. But the archetype is living matter. It is not limitlessly exchangeable but always belongs to the economy of a living individual, from which it cannot be detached and used arbitrarily for different ends. It cannot be explained in just any way, but only in the one that is indicated by that particular individual. Thus the symbol of the cross, in the case of a good Christian, can be interpreted only in the Christian way unless the dream produces very strong reasons to the contrary, and even then the specifically Christian meaning should not be lost sight of.

590 The mere use of words is futile if you do not know what they stand for. This is particularly true in psychology, where we speak of archetypes like the anima and animus, the wise old man, the great mother, and so on. You can know about all the saints, sages, prophets, and other godly men, and all the great mothers of the world, but if they are mere images whose numinosity you have never experienced, it will be as if you were talking in a dream, for you do not know what you are talking about. The words you use are empty and valueless, and they gain life and meaning only when you try to learn about their numinosity, their relationship to the living individual. Then only do you begin to understand that the names mean very little, but that the way they are related to you is all-important.

591 The symbol-producing function of our dreams is an attempt to bring our original mind back to consciousness, where it has never been before, and where it has never undergone critical self-reflection. We *have been* that mind, but we have never *known* it. We got rid of it before understanding it. It rose from its cradle, shedding its primitive characteristics like cumbersome and valueless husks. It looks as if the unconscious represented the deposit of these remnants. Dreams and their symbols continually refer to them, as if they intended to bring back all the old primitive things from which the mind freed itself in the course of its evolution: illusions, childish fantasies, archaic thought-forms, primitive instincts. This is in reality the case, and it explains the resistance, even fear and horror, one experiences in approaching the unconscious. One is shocked less by the primitivity of its contents than by their emotionality. They are not merely neutral or indifferent, they are so charged with affect that they are often exceedingly uncomfortable. They can even cause real panic, and the more they are repressed the more they spread through the whole personality in the form of a neurosis.

592 It is just their emotionality, however, that gives them such a vital importance. It is as if a man who has lived through a period of life in an unconscious state should suddenly realize that there is a gap in his memory – that important events seem to

have taken place that he cannot remember. In so far as he assumes that the psyche is an exclusively personal affair (and this is the usual assumption), he will try to retrieve the apparently lost infantile memories. But the gaps in his childhood memories are merely the symptoms of a much greater loss, the loss of the primitive psyche – the psyche that lived and functioned before it was reflected by consciousness.

593   As the evolution of the embryonic body repeats its prehistory, so the mind grows up through the series of its prehistoric stages. Dreams seem to consider it their main task to bring back a sort of recollection of the prehistoric as well as the infantile world, right down to the level of the most primitive instincts, as if such memories were a priceless treasure. And these memories can indeed have a remarkably healing effect in certain cases, as Freud saw long ago. This observation confirms the view that an infantile memory-gap (a so-called amnesia) amounts to a definite loss and that its recovery brings an increase in vitality and well-being. Since we measure a child's psychic life by the paucity and simplicity of its conscious contents, we do not appreciate the far-reaching complexities of the infantile mind that stem from its original identity with the prehistoric psyche. That 'original mind' is just as much present and still functioning in the child as the evolutionary stages are in the embryo. If the reader remembers what I said earlier about the child who made a present of her dreams to her father, he will get a good idea of what I mean.

594   In infantile amnesia, one finds strange admixtures of mythological fragments that also often appear in later psychoses. Images of this kind are highly numinous and therefore very important. If such recollections reappear in adult life, they may in some cases cause profound psychological disturbances, while in other people they can produce astonishing cures or religious conversions. Often they bring back a piece of life, missing for a long time, that enriches the life of an individual.

595   The recollection of infantile memories and the reproduction of archetypal modes of psychic functioning create a wider horizon and a greater extension of consciousness, provided that one succeeds in assimilating and integrating the lost and regained contents. Since they are not neutral, their assimilation will modify the personality, even as they themselves will have to undergo certain alterations. In this part of the individuation process the interpretation of symbols plays an important practical role; for the symbols are natural attempts to reconcile and reunite often widely separated opposites, as is apparent from the contradictory nature of many symbols. It would be a particularly obnoxious error in this work of assimilation if the interpreter were to take only the conscious memories as 'true' or 'real,' while considering the archetypal contents as merely fantastic representations. Dreams and their ambiguous symbols owe their forms on the one hand to repressed contents and on the other to archetypes. They thus have two aspects and enable one to interpret in two ways: one lays the emphasis either on their personal or on their archetypal aspect. The former shows the morbid influence of repression and infantile wishes, while the latter points to the sound instinctive basis. However fantastic the archetypal contents may be, they

represent emotional powers or 'numinosities.' If one should try to brush them aside, they would only get repressed and would create the same neurotic condition as before. Their numinosity gives the contents an autonomous nature. This is a psychological fact that cannot be denied. If it is nevertheless denied, the regained contents are annihilated and any attempt at a synthesis is futile. But it appears to be a tempting way out and therefore it is often chosen.

596   Not only is the existence of archetypes denied, but even those people who do admit their existence usually treat them as if they were mere images and forget that they are living entities that make up a great part of the human psyche. As soon as the interpreter strips them of their numinosity, they lose their life and become mere words. It is then easy enough to link them together with other mythological representations, and so the process of limitless substitution begins; one glides from archetype to archetype, everything means everything, and one has reduced the whole process to absurdity. All the corpses in the world are chemically identical, but living individuals are not. It is true that the forms of archetypes are to a considerable extent interchangeable, but their numinosity is and remains a fact. It represents the *value* of an archetypal event. This emotional value must be kept in mind and allowed for throughout the whole intellectual process of interpretation. The risk of losing it is great, because thinking and feeling are so diametrically opposed that thinking abolishes feeling-values and vice versa. Psychology is the only science that has to take the factor of value (feeling) into account, since it forms the link between psychic events on the one hand, and meaning and life on the other.

597   Our intellect has created a new world that dominates nature, and has populated it with monstrous machines. The latter are so indubitably useful and so much needed that we cannot see even a possibility of getting rid of them or of our odious subservience to them. Man is bound to follow the exploits of his scientific and inventive mind and to admire himself for his splendid achievements. At the same time, he cannot help admitting that his genius shows an uncanny tendency to invent things that become more and more dangerous, because they represent better and better means for wholesale suicide. In view of the rapidly increasing avalanche of world population, we have already begun to seek ways and means of keeping the rising flood at bay. But nature may anticipate all our attempts by turning against man his own creative mind, and, by releasing the H-bomb or some equally catastrophic device, put an effective stop to overpopulation. In spite of our proud domination of nature we are still her victims as much as ever and have not even learnt to control our own nature, which slowly and inevitably courts disaster.

598   There are no longer any gods whom we can invoke to help us. The great religions of the world suffer from increasing anaemia, because the helpful numina have fled from the woods, rivers, mountains, and animals, and the God-men have disappeared underground into the unconscious. There we suppose they lead an ignominious existence among the relics of our past, while we remain dominated by the great *Déesse Raison,* who is our overwhelming illusion. With her aid we

are doing laudable things: we rid the world of malaria, we spread hygiene everywhere, with the result that under-developed populations increase at such a rate that food is becoming a problem. 'We have conquered nature' is a mere slogan. In reality we are confronted with anxious questions, the answers to which seem nowhere in sight. The so-called conquest of nature overwhelms us with the natural fact of over-population and makes our troubles more or less unmanageable because of our psychological incapacity to reach the necessary political agreements. It remains quite natural for men to quarrel and fight and struggle for superiority over one another. Where indeed have we 'conquered nature'?

599   As any change must begin somewhere, it is the single individual who will undergo it and carry it through. The change must begin with one individual; it might be any one of us. Nobody can afford to look around and to wait for somebody else to do what he is loath to do himself. As nobody knows what he could do, he might be bold enough to ask himself whether by any chance his unconscious might know something helpful, when there is no satisfactory conscious answer anywhere in sight. Man today is painfully aware of the fact that neither his great religions nor his various philosophies seem to provide him with those powerful ideas that would give him the certainty and security he needs in face of the present condition of the world.

600   I know that the Buddhists would say, as indeed they do: if only people would follow the noble eightfold path of the Dharma (doctrine, law) and had true insight into the Self; or the Christians: if only people had the right faith in the Lord; or the rationalists: if only people could be intelligent and reasonable – then all problems would be manageable and solvable. The trouble is that none of them manages to solve these problems himself. Christians often ask why God does not speak to them, as he is believed to have done in former days. When I hear such questions, it always makes me think of the Rabbi who was asked how it could be that God often showed himself to people in the olden days but that nowadays one no longer saw him. The Rabbi replied: 'Nor is there anyone nowadays who could stoop so low.'

601   This answer hits the nail on the head. We are so captivated by and entangled in our subjective consciousness that we have simply forgotten the age-old fact that God speaks chiefly through dreams and visions. The Buddhist discards the world of unconscious fantasies as 'distractions' and useless illusions; the Christian puts his Church and his Bible between himself and his unconscious; and the rationalist intellectual does not yet know that his consciousness is not his total psyche, in spite of the fact that for more than seventy years the unconscious has been a basic scientific concept that is indispensable to any serious student of psychology.

602   We can no longer afford to be so God-almighty as to set ourselves up as judges of the merits or demerits of natural phenomena. We do not base our botany on a division into useful and useless plants, or our zoology on a classification into harmless and dangerous animals. But we still go on blithely assuming that consciousness is sense and the unconscious is nonsense – as if you could make out

whether any natural phenomenon makes sense or not! Do microbes, for instance, make sense or nonsense? Such evaluations merely demonstrate the lamentable state of our mind, which conceals its ignorance and incompetence under the cloak of megalomania. Certainly microbes are very small and most despicable, but it would be folly to know nothing about them.

603 Whatever else the unconscious may be, it is a natural phenomenon that produces symbols, and these symbols prove to be meaningful. We cannot expect someone who has never looked through a microscope to be an authority on microbes; in the same way, no one who has not made a serious study of natural symbols can be considered a competent judge in this matter. But the general undervaluation of the human psyche is so great that neither the great religions nor the philosophies nor scientific rationalism have been willing to look at it twice. In spite of the fact that the Catholic Church admits the occurrence of dreams sent by God, most of its thinkers make no attempt to understand them. I also doubt whether there is a Protestant treatise on dogmatics that would 'stoop so low' as to consider the possibility that the *vox Dei* might be perceived in a dream. But if somebody really believes in God, by what authority does he suggest that God is unable to speak through dreams?

604 I have spent more than half a century investigating natural symbols, and I have come to the conclusion that dreams and their symbols are not stupid and meaningless. On the contrary, dreams provide you with the most interesting information if only you take the trouble to understand their symbols. The results, it is true, have little to do with such worldly concerns as buying and selling. But the meaning of life is not exhaustively explained by your business activities, nor is the deep desire of the human heart answered by your bank account, even if you have never heard of anything else.

605 At a time when all available energy is spent in the investigation of nature, very little attention is paid to the essence of man, which is his psyche, although many researches are made into its conscious functions. But the really unknown part, which produces symbols, is still virtually unexplored. We receive signals from it every night, yet deciphering these communications seems to be such an odious task that very few people in the whole civilized world can be bothered with it. Man's greatest instrument, his psyche, is little thought of, if not actually mistrusted and despised. 'It's only psychological' too often means: It is nothing.

606 Where, exactly, does this immense prejudice come from? We have obviously been so busy with the question of what *we* think that we entirely forget what the unconscious psyche thinks about us. Freud made a serious attempt to show why the unconscious deserves no better judgment, and his teachings have inadvertently increased and confirmed the existing contempt for the psyche. Before him it had been merely overlooked and neglected; now it has become a dump for moral refuse and a source of fear.

607 This modern standpoint is surely onesided and unjust. It does not even accord with the known facts. Our actual knowledge of the unconscious shows it to be a natural phenomenon, and that, like nature herself, it is at least *neutral*. It contains

all aspects of human nature – light and dark, beautiful and ugly, good and evil, profound and silly. The study of individual as well as collective symbolism is an enormous task, and one that has not yet been mastered. But at last a beginning has been made. The results so far gained are encouraging, and they seem to indicate an answer to many of the questions perplexing present-day mankind.

Note

1 [This text represents the seventh and final part of a long essay entitled by its editors, 'Symbols and the Interpretation of Dreams'. It was composed in English and completed shortly before Jung's death in June 1961, representing his last piece of scholarly writing. Without title, it was written to introduce a symposium, *Man and His Symbols* (© 1964 Aldus Books, London), consisting of essays by Jung and four colleagues, edited by Jung and after his death by Dr. Marie-Louise von Franz, with John Freeman as coordinating editor. The symposium was conceived as a popular presentation of Jung's ideas, and accordingly its contents were, with the author's agreement, extensively reworked and rearranged under the supervision of John Freeman and von Franz. It was given the title 'Approaching the Unconscious'. The present version is Jung's original text, revised by R. F. C. Hull. – Editor.]
2 *Shamanism: Archaic Techniques of Ecstasy.*

Index

Page references in **bold** indicate Jung's essays reproduced from his *Collected Works*.

abandonment, of the child 189–91
Abraham, Karl 6, 8
active imagination 298, 337–8
Acts of God 170
adaptation 39, 62–3, 71, 85, 111, 115, 169; adaptive function of consciousness 66; affects and weak adaptation 159; of the artist 269; of the Church 245, 247; and complexes 327; consciousness as the momentary process of 338; constant need for 341; disturbances in 77, 169; MBTI and social adaptation 296; through one's most developed function 332; projection, and disturbances in 77; psychic systems of 328; through thinking 333; through yoga 280; in young people 305, 312
Adler, Alfred 9, 68–9, 101–2, 289, 304–5; Adlerian theory of the transference 118
Adler, Gerhard 11
aesthetics (*see also* literature, and psychology): aesthetic problem of artistic formulation 349, 350, 351; art *see* art; creativity *see* creativity; dangers of aestheticism 290–1, 337
affects *see* emotions
African Christianity 227–8
after-life 90–1, 131–2
ageing/old age 88–9, 91
alchemy 146, 192
Alcoholics Anonymous 2
alienation 123, 207
altered states of consciousness 14; through the presence of the numinous 206
amnesia 360

analytical psychology *see* Jung, Carl Gustav: psychology/psychotherapy
androgyny (*see also* hermaphroditism) 194, 247
anger 14
anima (*see also* syzygy) 133, 143–6, 160–8, 172, 173, 247; autonomy of 166–7, 172; integration of 144, 166–7; and the integration of the shadow 168; and projection 144–5, 160–2, 165–6, 168, 196
Anima Mundi 273
animal instinct 54, 74
'animal magnetism' 70
animation 70, 292
animosity 163–4, 247
animus (*see also* syzygy) 143–6, 162–8, 172, 173–4, 196, 247; autonomy of 166–7, 172; integration of 144, 166–7; and the integration of the shadow 168; and power 163; and projection 144–5, 162–4, 165–6, 168, 196
Anquetil du Perron, Abraham 225
Anthroposophy 70, 204, 223–4, 226
anti-Semitism 8–11
Aphrodite 167
Apollo 35
apperception 280
archetypal images 138, 270–1
archetypes: anima *see* anima; animus *see* animus; archetypal contents 182–3, 212–13, 360–1; autonomy of 166–7, 172; as both images and emotions 358–9; child archetype *see* child archetype; critiques of Jung's theory 138–41; cultural/spiritual 'translation'

of 3; and dreams 360–1; Eastern thinking on cosmic forces/archetypes 206; and human autonomy/freedom 207; as the instinct's perceptions of itself 138; intelligence of archetypal forces 205–6; and intimate relationships 144; as links with the past 184–6; as living, psychic forces 182, 359, 360–1; *marriage quaternio* 168; moral neutrality of 270; mother *see* mother archetypes; of mother–son marriage 161; and myth 2–3, 148, 180–2; as primordial images *see* primordial images; viewed as psychic organs 91, 185; reactivated 100; regaining conscious contact with archetypal powers 3; and religion 2–3; in rituals and myths of indigenous peoples 148, 180–2; 'scientific' reduction of 148; Self *see* Self; shadow *see* shadow; in the spectrum of the psyche 138; spirit as an archetypal force 5 *see also* spirit; syzygy 143–6, 160–8, 174, 175, 176, 246–7; theory of 137–42, 151–4; as transpersonal factors 2–3; unknowability of 138, 149, 254; Wise Old Man 168, 270
Aristotle 151
art: as a collective therapy 212; and the dangers of aestheticism 290–1; expressive function of 291; literary *see* literature, and psychology; 'symbol' of 71; visionary 211–13
artists: creativity of *see* creativity; Freudian reading of 210; humanistic exaltation of 210; *participation mystique* of 271; personality/psychology of 210, 259, 268–71; vision of 129–30
astrology 115, 223, 224, 226, 228, 295, 319–22, 324, 329
Athanasius 250n12
Atman 146, 192, 204
attachment 41–2
attention 72
Attis 235
Augustine of Hippo 264
autochthonous myths 180, 181–2
Ayik 191

ba 132
Bachofen, Johann 257
Baldur 189

Barlach, Ernst, *Der tote Tag* 262
Barthé, Roland 211
Bascom, William 139
Bastian, Adolf 153, 179
Bataks 132
Baubo 161
Benoit, Pierre 260, 262
Besant, Annie 225
Bible 208, 242, 256, 283, 362
Binet, Alfred 61
Bion, Wilfred Ruprecht 14
bipolar disorder 43–4
bisexuality 193–6, 247
Blake, William 212, 262
Blavatsky, Helena 225
body: attitudes and health of the body 19; and the earth 68; machine paradigm of 19; and psyche 48–9, 50, 51–2, 54, 55, 324–5; split/distinguished from mind 18, 324
Bolshevism 227, 239
boredom 342
brain 50, 66, 236, 284
Buddha 46, 229–30, 235
Buddha-Mind 278
Buddhism 70, 277, 337, 362; gods of Tibetan Buddhism 276
Burckhardt, Jacob 267
Buss, David 141

Cambray, Joseph 16–17, 142, 292
Carroll, John 13–14
Carus, C. G. 179, 257, 269
Cassian 195
Catholic Church 234, 242, 245–7, 363; assessment of Jung as a false prophet 147; attitude to dreams 363; dogma 234; in a patient's dream 244–6, 247; sacraments 234
characterology 324–5; Jung's theory of types 294–6, 324–36
child archetype 147–9, 179–99; abandonment of the child 189–91; child as beginning and end 196–7; child god 183, 188–9; child hero 188–9, 192, 198; Christ child 183, 190; function of 186–7; futurity of 187–8; hermaphroditism of the child 193–6; and individuation 184, 187–8, 198; invincibility of the child 191–3; as a link with the past 184–6; phenomenology of 189–97; psychology of 184–9; as 'smaller than small yet bigger than big'

183, 189, 192; unity and plurality of child motif 188
childhood 82, 83, 91
Chinese metaphysics/philosophy 15–16, 35, 129, 130; and Chinese science 228; and civilizations 54
Chiron 270
Christian Science 70, 224
Christianity (*see also* religion): in Africa 227–8; and animals 74–5; Asiatic origin of 229; and the balance of opposites 35; and the Bible *see* Bible; Catholic Church *see* Catholic Church; Christ *see* Jesus Christ; Christian consciousness 177, 248; Christian symbols 73–5; Church as mediator with supernatural influences 241; *corpus mysticum* 188; creeds 234–5; dechristianization and the importation of strange gods 70; divine syzygy of Christ and the Church 167; a dream of a Christian woman 73–5; faith 74, 362; and the fall of man 37–8, 81; and the French Revolution 70; and the German psyche 35–6, 68, 69; Jung's metaphorical interpretation of mysteries of 208; and literalism 207–8, 253–6; moralism of 7; Nietzsche's attitude to 347; Protestant 234–5, 241–2, 246; sacraments 234; and the silence of God 301, 362; spiritualization and sublimation as principles of 245–6; and war 73–5, 218; and worldliness 248, 281–2; and the wounded healer 270
Christopher, St 183
cinema 230
civilization, psychosocial analysis of 33–4, 70–9
clairvoyance 296, 316–17, 319
Clement of Alexandria 168, 195
collective consciousness (*see also* collective psyche) 104, 105
collective images 115
collective psyche (*see also* collective consciousness; collective unconscious) 107, 108, 110–12; forces bursting from 115; fusion of the personal and 110; healing the splits 299–301, 356–64; identification with 44–5, 110, 121–2; and involuntary fantasies 115; negative attempts to free the individuality from 116–22; persona, and removal of the individual from 109; persona as a segment of 112–16; regressive dissolution in 109
collective unconscious 35, 40, 55, 66–8, 77; archetypes *see* archetypes; primordial images; and the augmentation of immorality and stupidity 110–11; autonomy expressed through anima and animus 166 *see also* anima; animus; and *buddhi* 280; and dreams 55, 127–9; images *see* archetypal images; and individuation 124–31; Jung on the personal and 61–8, 93–101, 112, 158; and Jung's theory of art 212; and mythological fantasies 65–6, 181–2; and mythology 77–8, 161; and the personal unconscious 40; projection of 77–8; and psychic inflation 43–4, 103–6, 112, 168–9; as suprapersonal 66; and visionary creations 266–7
Colonna, Francesco, *Hypnerotomachia* 262, 267
Communism 281
compensation 33, 46, 69, 72–5, 93, 103, 125–30, 162, 167, 186, 192, 212, 242, 266–7, 282, 284, 294, 296, 297, 331; collective 127–9; and the transcendent function 340, 341 *see also* transcendent function
complexes 326–8; and adaptation 327; as autonomous powers 238, 239, 327; and dreams 243; ego-complex stage of consciousness 82, 83; father complex 5, 40–1, 94–9, 114; Oedipus complex 7; parental complex 327–8 *see also* father complex; spirituality 'complex' 5
Conan Doyle, Sir Arthur 260
Confucius 235
coniunctio oppositorum 174; and hermaphroditism 193–6
consciousness: activation of the unconscious by one-sided conscious attitude 69, 76 *see also* compensation; adaptive function of 66 *see also* adaptation; altered states of 14, 206; analytical psychology and a change in 282; becoming conscious of the shadow 158; breaking through of the unconscious into 117; bridging the unconscious and the conscious 19–20, 72, 298, 341–55; Christian 177, 248; collective 104, 105; and the compensatory function of the

unconscious *see* compensation; dualistic stage of 83, 84; and Eastern thinking 279–80; effects of the unconscious on 40–3, 93–122; ego as centre of the field of 142, 155, 156, 157 *see also* ego; ego-complex stage of 82, 83; fear of becoming conscious 235, 238; and healing the splits of the collective psyche 299–301, 356–64; and instinct 37, 38, 80; 'knowing'/childish stage of 82, 83; as man's Promethean conquest 37, 80, 186; and the midlife crisis/ transition 39–40, 85–6, 88; modern Western consciousness and spiritual problem 203–5, 217–31; as the momentary process of adaptation 338 *see also* adaptation; moral 100; and nature 38–9; origins of 81–2; present-day 218; and problems 81, 82–5; and the psyche 50, 61 *see also* psyche/soul; and the Reformation 47; regaining conscious contact with archetypal powers 3; rootless 183; seat of 53; Self as centre of totality of the unconscious and 39, 142, 156–7 *see also* Self; and sense-perceptions 50; and the stages of life 37–40, 81–91; and the transcendent function *see* transcendent function; unconscious life as source of ego-consciousness 53, 55–6; widening of 16, 37, 46, 81, 126, 131, 354; without an ego 279; youth stage 82, 83–6

Corpus Hermeticum 151

creativity: and the collective unconscious 212; creative intuitions 124; creative personality 210, 259, 268–71; the creative process 131, 212; and fantasies 66; literary *see* literature, and psychology; psychological mode of 211, 260–1, 262; and reductionism 210; and the shadow 36; transcendent function and creative formulations 349, 350, 351; and the unconscious 36, 66, 72, 131; 'visionary' mode of 211–13, 261, 262–7

creeds 234–5

cryptomnesia 100

culture: cultural symbols 356; cultural 'translation' of archetypes 3; and the difference between Eastern and Western thinking 213–15, 273–85; Jewish 3, 68–9; Jung's psychology as a therapy of 3, 33, 71–9; modern Western man's spiritual problem 203–5, 217–31; religious *see* religion; and the second half of life 89; Western culture as Jung's 'patient' 33

Cybele 235

Dacqué, Edgar 48, 60n2
Dadaism 78
daemons/daimons 42, 69, 99, 171, 234, 237, 263
Daniel 347
Dante Alighieri 261, 262, 267; *The Divine Comedy* 211–12, 264, 266
darkness 189, 191, 192, 224–5
Daudet, Léon, *L'Hérédo* 124
death: and the after life 90–1, 131–2; of the father 86; fear of 87; as a goal/ transition 90; preparation for 88; and rebirth 66
deflation 43–4
Demeter 161
demons 3, 77, 127, 164, 238, 250, 265, 356; fear of 73; of sickness 67
depression 43–4, 298; and mid-life 85
Deussen, Paul 228
Devil 35
Dionysus (*see also* Wotan) 35, 246, 347
discipleship 122
dissociation 3, 34, 185–6, 188, 198, 298, 299, 340, 357
dogma 234
Doyle, Sir Arthur Conan 260
dragons 121, 161, 183, 184, 189, 266
Drake, Carlos 140
dreams/dreaming 41–2, 245, 248–9, 249–51n12; aim of dream work 291, 307–13; in ancient cultures 54; archetypal contents 360–1; archetypal images in 270–1; and the Catholic Church 363; child motif/archetype in 147–8, 180, 184; childhood dreams 182, 187; collective dreams 126–7; and the collective unconscious 55, 127–9; and complexes 243; and cryptomnesia 100; difficulties of working with dreams 297–8, 307–9, 343; god-image of dreams 96–100; God speaking through dreams 363; and healing/therapy 42, 290, 291, 307–13; incest motif 7; man's lack of control over 53; and mythology 176, 180, 266; and the numinous 360–1; painting what is seen in dreams 311–13, 351; of a patient with imaginary cancer 240, 242–9; psychology of 180; religion

and the revealing function of dreams 242–9; and repression 94; and the revelation of the unknown 241, 243; snake-dreams 189; symbol-producing function 300, 358, 359; and the transcendent function 343–5, 351; and the unconscious 73–5, 96–100, 290, 297, 307–12, 347; as the voice of the unknown 241, 243; as warnings 347
Dreisch, Hans 291
dualism 38; dualistic model of knowledge 18; dualistic stage of consciousness 83, 84; ecopsychology as a way out of 18
Dundes, Alan 139–40

earth 68; mother earth and the feminine 38; and spirit 18, 38
Eastern thinking (*see also* Buddhism): Chinese *see* Chinese metaphysics/philosophy; on cosmic forces/archetypes 206; and the devaluation of the world 227; introversion of 192, 214, 215, 277, 279, 285; Taoist 15–16, 35, 129; understanding of mind 276, 278, 279; vs Western thinking 15–16, 213–15, 273–85; Western turn to the East 147, 204–5, 223–4, 225–6, 228–30
Eckermann, Johann Peter 272n19
Eckhart, Meister 14, 183
ecology of the soul 18–20
ecopsychology 18
Eddy, Mary Baker 224
Eden myth 37–8, 81
ego (*see also* individuality; persona; personality) 142–3, 155–8; and the assimilation of the unconscious 43–4, 99–100, 101–12, 168–74; as centre of field of consciousness 142, 155, 156, 157; clinging to power 40; complex 82; deflation 43–4; dominance in first half of life 39; and Eastern thinking 279–80; effect of anima and animus on 164; exclusive pursuit of 300; hubristic 43, 146, 147; inflation *see* inflation; personalistic view of 291; and personality 156–7; relations with the unconscious 7, 40–6, 93–133, 158, 298, 352–3; as seat of identity in Freud's thinking 205; as seat of unconsciousness 206; 'second ego' *see* Self; and the Self 142, 155, 156–7, 168–70; somatic basis of 155–6; and therapy 291

egotism 20, 84, 85, 89, 123, 147, 240, 269
Eigen, Michael, *The Psychoanalytic Mystic* 14
Einstein, Albert 17, 291
Elgonyi 126
Eliade, Mircea 356
Ellis, Havelock 226, 303
emotions: affective value 171–2; affects and weak adaptation 159; archetypes as both images and 358–9; dealing with emotional disturbance 348–9; emotionality of contents of the unconscious 359–60; man's lack of control over 53, 159; and the shadow 158–9
empiricism 151–2, 232; empirical reality of the soul 31, 47, 48–9, 51–6
enantiodromia 222
endosomatic stimuli/perceptions 155–6
energy, psychic 41, 42, 64–5, 70, 82, 83, 94, 116, 119, 224, 254, 269–70, 297, 338; and active imagination 338; falling into the unconscious 116; forces bursting from collective psyche 115; and God 56; high energy-tension 340; libido *see* libido; low energy-tension 343; in the transference 97; uprush of collective forces 239
entelechy 187–8
Eros 64, 145, 160, 161, 162–3, 164, 167, 171
eternity (*see also* timelessness) 143
Eustachius, Brother (Eustachius Kugler) 183
Evans-Wentz, W. Y. 273
evil 33, 34–6, 78, 222–3, 224–5; Catholic assessment of Jung as an evil-doer 147; and collective compensations 128–9; good and 58, 102, 108–9; pacts with 129; war *see* war
extraversion: and the theory of types 294–5, 305–6, 331; of the West 146, 215, 277, 280, 281–2, 284, 285

fairytales 77, 180, 182, 307
faith 209, 274–5, 317, 322, 357; Christian 74, 362; and knowledge 224, 274; mysteries of 250; and superstition 72, 139, 152, 194–5
fall of man 37–8, 81
fanaticism 40, 86
fantasies: and active imagination 298; and creativity 66; dream fantasies *see*

dreams/dreaming; involuntary 115; man's lack of control over 53; mythological 65–6, 181–2; painting what is seen in 311–13; as real things 193; release of repressed personal fantasies 115; and repression 94; and therapy 290, 309–10; and the transcendent function 345, 348; and the unconscious 297

father complex (*see also* parental complex) 5, 40–1, 94–9, 114

fear: of becoming conscious 235, 238; of being alone 103; of the dark 191; of death 87; of demons 73; of ghosts 58, 265; 'irrational' 191; of magical influences 181; pneumaphobia 11–14, 206; of the unconscious 175, 279, 356, 359

feeling: affect *see* emotions; and the theory of types 296, 333–4

femininity 87–8, 144, 145; feminine side of men *see* anima; mother archetypes 151; mother earth and the feminine 38

feminist scholarship 16

Ferenczi, Sándor 9

fetishism 70

Fierz-David, Linda 267

Fierz, Markus 320–1

Forel, August 303

Fox, Robin 141

France/the French: French psychologists 61–2; French psychopathology 70; French Revolution 70, 225; French school of hypnotism 70

free association 298, 337, 351

freedom 206–7; self-liberating power of the introverted mind 215, 279; self-liberation 215, 277, 279, 284; tearing loose from maternal womb of 217–18

Freud, Sigmund 5, 6–9, 11–13, 33, 55, 63–4, 93, 95, 205, 209, 224–5, 226, 228, 245, 268, 277, 292, 293, 351, 363; aims of therapy 289; *Civilization and its Discontents* s; 'History of the Psycho-Analytic Movement' 9; *Interpretation of Dreams* 226; and Jung 5, 6–9, 11–13, 293; *Moses and Monotheism* 33; and older patients 289, 305; 'Psychoanalysis and Telepathy' 12; reductionism 6–8, 13, 64–5, 68–9, 210; sexual theory of neurosis 6, 7, 118, 303, 304–5; *Totem and Taboo* 12, 13; 'The Uncanny' 12; view of the unconscious 97

Frey-Rohm, Liliane 320

Frye, Northrop 141

Futurism 78

Gallant, Christine 12–13, 15

Gardner, Russell 141

gender identity (*see also* anima; animus) 145

German Medical Society of Psychotherapy 9–11

Germany 356; German psyche 35–6, 68, 69; German psychology and the development of psychoanalysis 62; National Socialism/Nazism 9–11, 36, 277, 281; pagan tendencies of 246

ghost-stories 184

ghosts 218, 237, 240–1, 280, 358; fear of 58, 265

Gilbert, Paul 141

Gilgamesh 239–40

Gnosticism 195, 223–4

God: Acts of 170; and 'all-powerful' matter 49; as archetypal light 151; belief in the goodness of 74; death of 147; divine need for humanity 143; God-images 13, 42, 96–100, 168, 174, 255; the God Within 146; image of God fashioned by the unconscious 42, 96–100; known through faith 274; proximity of the divine 146–7; and the psyche 277–8; as the quintessence of reality 56; rebirth of 147; religious statements about 254; silence of 301, 362; speaking through dreams 363; as spirit 99; and the theology of incarnation 143; as the Wholly Other 278; will of 170, 171

Goddard, Sir Victor 319

godlikeness 101–2, 110

gods: of ancient Greece 35; archaic god-image 42, 96–100; as archetypal forces 3; bisexual 193–4; child god 183, 188–9; and creeds 235; dechristianization and the importation of strange gods 70; personification of 292; as producers of psychological changes 237; and psychic experience 58; Roman 70; of Tibetan Buddhism 276; union with 42

Goethe, Johann Wolfgang von 70, 84, 258; *Faust* 119, 120, 184, 196, 211–12, 258, 260, 261, 264, 266–7, 270

Goetz, Bruno 184, 262

good and evil 58, 102, 108–9
Göring, Matthias Heinrich 10
Gothic Age 32, 47, 49
Great Mother 151
Greek gods 35
Grof, Stanislov 14
Grotstein, James S. 14
guilt 143, 160–1

habitus 171
Haggard, Rider 260, 262
hallucinations 349
Harms, Ernest 11
Haule, John 140
healing (*see also* medicine): through active imagination 298, 337–8; aims and tasks of psychotherapy 289–91, 303–14; and the dialectic between the ego and the unconscious 298; and dreams 42, 290, 291, 307–13; and fantasies 290; forces of the unconscious 72; and memories 360; Self as seat of 147; and solidarity with the world 107; and spirituality 290; of the splits in the collective psyche 299–301, 356–64; and synchronicity 291–3, 315–23; therapy and the patient's inferior function 295–6; and the transcendent function 297–9, 337–55; and transference 41, 95–6, 299, 342 *see also* transference; and the transpersonal 291
Hecate 167
Hegel, Georg Wilhelm 297
Helen (Selene) 167
Heracles 189
Heraclitus 222
hermaphroditism: of the child 193–6; of the creator 247
Hermes 167, 196, 235
hermeticism 146, 195
hero, child 188–9, 192, 198
hieros gamos 161, 195, 196
Hillman, James 2, 18, 137
Hobson, R. F. 139
Hoffman, E. T. A., *The Golden Bowl* 262
Hölderlin, J. C. Friedrich 70, 172–3, 231
holistic practice 18–20, 59
Holy Spirit (*see also* spirit) 204
homunculi 184
Hosea 195, 241
hostility 14
Hubert, Henri 153
hubris 43, 103, 146, 147

humanism 210
humility 103, 147
Hurwitz, Sigmund 11
hypnotism 70

I Ching 319
ideas: collective 172–3; innate possibilities of 66; Platonic 137, 138–9, 151–2
identification: with business or titles 104; with the collective psyche 44–5, 110, 121–2
Ignatius Loyola, *Exercitia* 281
illness *see* mental health/illness; sickness
images: archetypal 138, 270–1; archetypes as both emotions and 358–9; and artists' vision 129–30; collective 115; fear of a ghost as a psychic image 58; of God, fashioned by the unconscious 42, 96–100; imagos 132, 160–1 *see also* archetypes; knowledge and psychic images 57, 236, 275, 277; numinous 359, 360; 'primordial images' *see* primordial images; sacred 207; symbolic 41 *see also* symbols/symbolism; transformation of material objects into psychic images 280
incarnation, theology of 143
incest 7
Indian civilizations 54
indigenous/'primitive' mentality 67, 148, 180–1, 182, 191, 192, 241, 283, 346; synchronicity and 'primitive' philosophy 292–3
individualism (*see also* egotism) 45, 123
individuality (*see also* ego; persona; personality) 45, 110, 111, 112; analysis of the personal unconscious and the emergence of 113–15; and identification with the collective psyche 44–5, 121–2; negative attempts to free from collective psyche 116–22; and regressive restoration of the persona 116–21
individuation 45–6, 112; as aim of therapy 289; and the child motif 184, 187–8, 198; and the function of the unconscious 123–33; neurosis and the road of self-realization 99; and the transcendent function *see* transcendent function; urge towards self-realization 131, 192
infantile amnesia 360
inferiority, sense of 83, 99, 103, 108, 159, 164, 198, 235, 304, 350

inflation (*see also* megalomania): with annexation of the collective unconscious 43–4, 103–6, 112, 168–9; identification with the collective psyche 44–5, 121–2; with proximity of the divine 146–7
instinct 50, 64, 76; abandonment of 37, 38, 80–1; animal 54, 74; archetypes *see* archetypes; collective instincts 111 *see also* collective unconscious; and consciousness 37, 38, 80; and healing the splits of the collective psyche 299–301, 356–64; power of 50, 74; sexuality as a fundamental instinct 63–4 *see also* sexuality; in the spectrum of the psyche 138; and the unconscious 36, 72
interdisciplinary studies 18
internationalism 230
intolerance 40, 86
introversion 278, 280, 283–4; of Eastern thinking 192, 214, 215, 277, 279, 285; of the libido 349; self-liberating power of the introverted mind 215, 279; and the theory of types 294–5, 305–6, 331
intuition 3, 16, 32, 36, 54, 65, 72, 124, 197, 246–7, 264, 265; and the theory of types 295, 296, 334–5

Jacobi, Jolande 11
Jacobs, Gregg 141–2
Jaffé, Aniela 11
James, William 124, 234
Janet, Pierre 61, 63
Jaques, Elliott 39
Jesus Christ 46, 146, 176, 218, 235, 274; androgyny of the Christ 194; Christ child 183, 190; divine syzygy of Christ and the Church 167; identification with the 'Crucified Christ' 347; imitation of Christ 203–4, 274, 278; literalism, myths and 207–8, 253; as universal symbol of the spirit 208; as the wounded healer 270
Jews: anti-Semitist allegations against Jung 8–11; and the earth 68; Jewish cultures 3, 68–9; Jewish doctors 10; Jewish psychology 11; and mysticism 6
Joachim of the Flowers 204
John of the Cross 14
Jones, Ernest 7–8, 9
Joyce, James, *Ulysses* 212
Jung, Carl Gustav: **the man**: assessment by Western religions 147; chronology of life and work 25–8; clash with authorities 5; and the emergence of holistic science 15–18; explorations in and beyond science and religion 3–5 *see also* religion; and his father 5; father complex 5; and Freud 5, 6–9, 11–13; and the German Medical Society of Psychotherapy 9–11; as a hermeneut 32; and his mother 5; and mysticism 6, 14; national typology 11; and Nazism 9–11 *see also* National Socialism/Nazism; pneumaphobic opposition to 11–14; racist allegations against 8–11; reputation in its historical context 1–14; resilience 32; and romantic transferences 41; swimming against the tide 32; writings of *see* Jung, Carl Gustav: writings
Jung, Carl Gustav: **psychology/ psychotherapy**: aims and tasks of psychotherapy 289–91, 303–14; archetypal theory *see* archetypes; based on an autonomous, spiritual principle 51–6; compensation theory *see* compensation; consciousness *see* consciousness; dealing with patients' religious problems 75–6; dreams *see* dreams/dreaming; and the ecology of the soul 18–20; ego *see* ego; and the emergence of individuality 113–15; and the future 14–20; healing *see* healing; as holistic clinical practice 18–20, 59; incest theory 7; individuation *see* individuation; libido *see* libido; and literature *see* literature, and psychology; moral philosophy at heart of 35, 78–9; and myth *see* mythology; names for 2; overviews and 'basic postulates' 1–20, 31–3, 47–60; projection *see* projection; psyche, collective *see* collective psyche; psyche, individual *see* psyche/soul; as psychology of *homo religiousus* 206; and religion *see* religion; repression *see* repression; Self *see* Self; sexism in 145–6; and sexuality 6–7, 63–4 *see also* sexuality; shadow *see* shadow; soul *see* psyche/soul; spirit *see* spirit; and the stages of life *see* life stages; synchronicity *see* synchronicity; syzygy 143–6, 160–8, 174, 175, 176 *see also* anima; animus; and theory of art 212–13 *see also* literature, and psychology; theory of types 294–6, 324–36; as a therapy of culture 3, 33, 71–9;

transcendent function *see* transcendent function; transference *see* transference; the unconscious *see* [the] unconscious; the unconscious, collective *see* collective unconscious

Jung, Carl Gustav: **writings**: 'The aims of psychotherapy' (1931) 289–91, **303–14**; 'Basic postulates of analytical psychology' (1931) 31–3, **47–60**; chronology 25–8; 'The difference between Eastern and Western thinking' (1939/1954) 213–15, **273–85**; 'Healing the split' (1961) 299–301, **356–64**; 'On the concept of the archetype' (1938/1954) 137–42, **151–4**; 'On synchronicity' (1951) 291–3, **315–23**; 'Phenomenology of the Self: The ego; The shadow; The syzygy: Anima and animus; The Self' (1951) 142–7, **155–77**; Preface to *Answer to Job*: Lectori benevolo (1952) 207–9, **253–6**; 'A psychological theory of types' (1931) 294–6, **324–36**; 'Psychology and literature' (1930/1950) 17, 209–13, **257–71**; 'Psychology and religion: The autonomy of the unconscious' (1938/1940) 205–7, **232–49**; 'The psychology of the child archetype' (1940) 147–9, **179–99**; *The Red Book* 4, 290; 'The relations between the ego and the unconscious' (1928) 40–6, **93–133**; 'The role of the unconscious' (1918) 33–7, **61–79**; social dimension of 32; 'The spiritual problem of modern man' (1928/1931) 203–5, **217–31**; 'The stages of life' (1930/1931) 37–40, **80–91**; 'The state of psychotherapy today' (1934) 9, 20; *Symbols of Transformation* 7, 139; *Synchronicity: An acausal connecting Principle* (with Pauli) 292; 'The transcendent function' (1916/1957) 297–9, **337–55**; *Transformations and Symbols of the Libido* 139

Jung, Emilie Preiswerk (mother of Carl) 5
Jung, Paul (father of Carl) 5

ka 132
Kant, Immanuel 134n26, 138, 152, 179, 297; categories 137, 152
Keats, John 149
Kerényi, Karl 17, 179, 193
Keyserling, Hermann 230
Kierkegaard, Søren 278

Kirsch, Hilda 11
Kirsch, James 11
Kluger, Rivkah 11
Knoll, Max 320
knowledge: academic compartmentalization of 17; Cartesian basis of 293; and consciousness 82; dualistic model of 18; and faith 224, 274; fragmentary knowledge and ecology 18; and godlikeness 102; of good and evil 102; higher/divine 54; inflation through 104 *see also* inflation; and interdisciplinary studies 18; and psychic images 57, 236, 275, 277; and the subject of cognition 192; technical 220; tree of 82, 134; the unconscious as a source of 54–5; Western and Eastern systems of 15–16
Knox, Jean 142
Kretschmer, Ernst 9
Krishnamurti, Jiddu 226
Kubin, Alfred, *Die andere Seite* 262
Kugler, Eustachius, Brother 183
Kundalini-yoga 224

La Barre, Weston 139
Lamarckism 140
League of Nations 230
Leibniz, Gottfried 179
Lévi-Strauss, Claude 140
Lévy-Bruhl, Lucien 172
libido 6, 15, 41, 42, 64, 349; sudden loss of 308
life stages 37–40, 80–91; adult stage 86–9; childhood 82, 83, 91; and the ego 39; life after death 90–1, 131–2; midlife crisis/transition 39–40, 85–6, 88; puberty 82; and the Self 39; youth 82, 83–6
light 151, 189, 191, 192
literature, and psychology 209–13, 257–71; the artist 210, 259, 268–71; and myth 265–7; 'psychological' creation 211, 260–1, 262; the 'psychological novel' 211, 259–60; a psychologist's approach to a work of art 259–67; 'visionary' creation 211–13, 261, 262–7
Logos 145, 162–3, 167
love 163

magic 53, 58, 67, 131, 234, 241, 274; fear of magical influences 181; magical

prestige 109; magical *représentations collectives* 105; witchcraft 67, 237
Maitland, Edward 247
mandalas 174, 204
Mani 235
manic depression 43–4
manticism 319
marriage quaternio 168
Martin, Stephen 9
Marx, Karl 207, 209
masculinity 87–8, 144, 145; masculine side of women *see* animus
masks (*see also* persona) 109
materialism (*see also* scientism/scientific materialism) 16, 31–2, 47–50, 236, 265, 274–5, 306
matter 17, 32, 48, 49–50, 274, 357; metaphysics of 32, 48; and mind 47, 48, 49; observation of 16; and spirit 15–16, 58
maturity (*see also* life stages) 40
Maui 189
Mauss, Marcel 153
Maya 58, 160–1
Mayer, Robert 70
MBTI (Myers-Briggs Type Indicator) 296
Mechtild of Magdeburg 98, 195
Medical Society of Psychotherapy 9–11
medicine 19, 59, 236; complimentary treatments 19
medicine-men 108, 241
megalomania (*see also* inflation) 104, 108, 121, 198, 227, 267, 347, 363
Meissner, William, *Psychoanalysis and Religious Experience* 14
Melville, Herman, *Moby Dick* 260
memory: artificial acquisition of 55; a child's islands of 82; and the forgotten 65; gaps in 359–60; and healing 360; recollection of infantile memories 360; tricks of 53
mental health/illness (*see also* healing): illness as a response to lack of symbolic/ spiritual life 40, 59–60; and medication 19; mental health industry 19; neurosis *see* neurosis; paranoia 117, 175; psychic disequilibrium/disturbance 45, 60, 62–3, 70, 83, 86, 111, 116, 122, 236–7, 266, 268, 303, 348–9, 357, 360; psychic equilibrium 33, 50, 83, 99, 116, 198, 212, 266, 284; psychosis *see* psychosis; schizophrenia 106, 117, 175, 188, 282, 283, 352

Mercurius 183
Merton, Thomas 14
Mesmer, Franz 70
metaphysics: Chinese *see* Chinese metaphysics/philosophy; of matter 32, 48; of mind 32, 48; unconscious 308–9
Meyrink, Gustav, *Das grüne Gesicht* 262
midlife crisis/transition 39–40, 85–6, 88
midrash 3
mind: Buddha-Mind 278 *see also* universal mind; collective psyche *see* collective psyche; and the difference between Eastern and Western thinking 213–15, 273–85; Eastern mind in the Western unconscious 214 *see also* Eastern thinking; Eastern understanding of 276, 278, 279; enlightened 280; healing the split 299–301, 356–64; and matter 47, 48, 49; as part of a continuum 214; psyche *see* psyche/soul; self-liberating power of the introverted mind 215, 279; split/distinguished from body 18, 324; thinking *see* thinking; unconscious *see* [the] unconscious; unconscious, collective *see* collective unconscious; universal/One Mind 214, 273, 276, 278, 283, 284, 285
miracles 209, 253–4, 322
Mithraism 74, 229
Mithras 235
Mohammed 46, 146, 235
mood 53
moral attitude 59
moral conflict 102, 191, 248
moral consciousness 100
moral control, resistance to 143, 159
moral inferiority, sense of 99, 108
moral philosophy 35, 78–9; conflicts of duty and moral problems 170; and moral freedom 170–1; society and the augmentation of immorality and stupidity 110–11
Moses 46, 146
mother archetypes 151; Chtonic Mother 168; mother-imago 160–1
mother-goddess 151
mother–son marriage 161
mother–son secret conspiracy 160–1
Müller, Max 228
Myers-Briggs Type Indicator (MBTI) 296
mysterium iniquitatis 195
mysticism 6, 14; and identification with

the collective psyche 121–2; *participation mystique* 105, 217, 271
mythology (*see also* fairytales): and archetypes 2–3, 180; autochthonous myths 107, 180, 181–2; child motif/archetype in 147–8, 179, 183–4, 191; of death and rebirth 66; and dreams 176, 180, 266; Eden myth 37–8, 81; experience of myths 181; and indigenous/'primitive' mentality 148, 180–1, 182; literalism, myths and religion 207–9, 253–6; and literature 265–7; living and lived myth 198; mythical world 181; mythological fantasies 65–6; mythological projection 190; and night 191; and projections of the collective unconscious 77–8, 161; recapitulation of 38; 'scientific' reduction of 148; and the syzygy 161

National Socialism/Nazism 9–11, 36, 277, 281
national typology 11
nature 38–9, 361–2; and the child 190; loss of communication with 357–8; neurosis and separation from 20; and spirit 38–9, 56, 57–8
Nazism *see* National Socialism/Nazism
Nebuchadnezzar 347
Negro tribes 53
Neumann, Erich 11
neurosis: and archetypal problems 3; and attitude to life 59; causes of 76, 290, 297; 'choice of neurosis' 328; and the collective unconscious 40–2, 94–101; and demoralization 235; and the disturbance of spiritual processes in the psyche 60; Freud's sexual theory of 6, 7, 118, 303, 304–5; healing of *see* healing; and lack of consciousness of problems 83–4; and megalomania *see* megalomania; and mid-life transition 85–7; and moral sense of inferiority 99, 108; and the nature of the psyche 236–9; neurotic power psychology 102; and one-sidedness 290, 339–40; of a patient with imaginary cancer 237–8, 239–40, 242–9; religious interpretation of 40–1, 239–49; and the road of self-realization 99; and separation from nature 20; solidarity with the world and the healing of 107; as the suffering of a soul which has not discovered its meaning 19; in a woman with a father complex 40–1, 94–9, 114
Nietzsche, Friedrich 14, 50, 69, 147, 225, 246, 257, 266, 267; *Thus Spake Zarathustra* 211–12, 347
numinosity/the numinous (*see also* spirit) 13, 206, 233–4; and dreams 360–1; fear of 206; loss of 357–8, 361; numinous character of the child 190 *see also* child archetype; numinous images 359, 360; numinous symbols 357, 360–1

objectivity 16, 131, 284–5; *of représentations collectives* 172
occultism 5, 12, 61
Oedipus complex 7
old age 88–9, 91
Oldenberg, Hermann 228
O'Murchu, Diarmuid 15, 16
Opicinus de Canistris 195
opposites: Christianity and the balance of 35; *coniunctio oppositorum* 174, 193–6; dissolution of personality into its paired opposites 108; *hieros gamos* 161, 195, 196; intellectual freedom from 57; and the transcendent function 353–4 *see also* transcendent function
Otto, Rudolph 233

Paglia, Camille 206
pain 57
paradigm theory 16
Paradise 37–8, 81, 82
paranoia 117, 175
parapsychology (*see also* clairvoyance; telepathy) 12, 223, 316–18, 322
parental complex 327–8; father complex 5, 40–1, 94–9, 114
participation mystique 105, 217, 271
Paul, apostle 84, 133–4n17, 347
Pauli, Wolfgang 17, 292
Pererius, Benedictus, S.J. 249–51n12
Persephone 161, 167
persona 44, 109; disintegration of 115–16; regressive restoration of 116–21; as a segment of the collective psyche 112–16
personality 39–40, 112; development of the person 108–9, 110–11; dissolution of 108; and the dynamics of the unconscious 33, 34, 64–70; ego *see* ego; individuality *see* individuality; integration of 43; persona *see* persona; and psychology of the artist 210, 259,

268–71; and regressive restoration of the persona 116–21; retarded maturation of 131; therapy and the transformation of 290, 299; as a total phenomenon *see* Self; transformations of 106
Peucer, Kaspar 250–1n12
philosophy: Chinese 15–16, 35, 54, 129, 130; Indian 54; Jung's use of philosophical arguments 32; moral *see* moral philosophy; National Socialist 277, 281; 'primitive' 292 *see also* indigenous/'primitive' mentality; psychology linked with 50–1, 257; of science 16; Taoist 15–16, 35, 129; and ultimate meaning 16
Plato 153, 277; Diotema 171; Ideas 137, 138–9, 151–2; Platonic spirit 152
pneumaphobia 11–14, 206
post-structuralism 210–11
postmodernism 16, 210–11
power: and the animus 163; breaking the power principle 78; of child hero 192; of a collective image 106; a complex as an autonomous power 238, 239, 327; of conviction 117, 260; of the *daimon* 171; demonic 238, 250; deposition of the conscious mind from 115–16; drives 69, 118, 192; ego's clinging to 40; of instincts 50, 74; magical 274, 343 *see also* magic; neurotic power psychology 102; of the *numinosum* 206; of primordial images 124; psychic energy *see* energy, psychic; renunciation of 109; self-liberating power of the introverted mind 215, 279; of the spirit of the age 49; of spirituality 215; suggestive 124, 293; transference as an infantile power-aim 118; unconscious powers 167; of the Wholly Other 278; will to 44, 101, 107, 109; women and 163
predisposition 100, 153
prestige 109
primitive man 58, 60, 66–7, 132, 186, 191, 192, 197, 240; development of the person 108–9, 110; and dreams 54; and the loss of numinosity 357; philosophy of 292; and projections of the collective unconscious 77–8; psyche 67, 68, 185, 360; views of the soul 51–2, 53, 54
'primitive' mentality *see* indigenous/'primitive' mentality
primitive tribes (*see also* indigenous/'primitive' mentality) 89, 181
primordial images (*see also* archetypes) 77, 91, 100, 122, 123, 124, 139–40, 153–4, 180, 195–6, 270
problems: arising with consciousness 82–5; collective 126; conflicts of duty and moral problems 170; spiritual problem of modern man 203–5, 217–31
progress 94, 110, 186, 187, 194–5, 222, 299
projection 6, 12, 13, 34, 77–8; and the anima 144–5, 160–2, 165–6, 168, 196; and the animus 144–5, 162–4, 165–6, 168, 196; dissolution of 165–6; and inflation 168–9; mythological 190; as obstacle to the integration of the shadow 143, 159–60; projected images 132; and synchronicity 292; thoughts as projected sensuous projections 67; upon the opposite sex 144
prophets/prophecy 44–5, 122; Catholic assessment of Jung as a false prophet 147; Hebrew prophets 195, 241; manticism 319
Protestantism 234–5, 241–2, 246
psyche/soul: abnormal psychic phenomena/processes 61 *see also* clairvoyance; parapsychology; telepathy; after death 90–1, 131–2; and apperception 280; archaic souls 132; archetypes *see* archetypes; awakening the symbolic life of the soul 2; and the body 48–9, 50, 51–2, 54, 55, 324–5; and the brain 236; civilizations where the psyche is outside 220; collective *see* collective psyche; collective unconscious *see* collective unconscious; complexity/ambiguity of the psyche 289, 306; and consciousness 50, 61 *see also* consciousness; and the divine 54; dreams as products of the psyche 96 *see also* dreams/dreaming; ecology of the soul 18–20; ego *see* ego; empirical reality of the soul 31, 47, 48–9, 51–6; etymologies of words for 'soul' 52; existence of autonomous individual souls 51; fusion of the personal and collective psyche 110; German psyche 35–6, 68, 69; and God 277–8; immortality of the soul 53; individuation *see* individuation; infantile preconscious psyche 153; instinct in the spectrum of

138 see also instinct; man's lack of control over psychic happenings 52–3; materialistic conceptions of 47–50; mind see mind; and modern Western man's spiritual problem 203–5, 217–31; nature of 236–9; neuroses and the disturbance of spiritual processes in the 60; neurosis and the nature of the psyche 236–9; 'perils of the soul' 182, 238, 240; personality see personality; phenomenology of 326 see also Self: phenomenology of; primitive psyche 67, 68, 185, 360 see also primitive man; primitive views of the soul 51–2; psyche as a religious phenomenon 206; psychic birth 82; psychic disequilibrium/ disturbance 45, 60, 62–3, 70, 83, 86, 111, 116, 122, 236–7, 266, 268, 303, 348–9, 357, 360; psychic energy see energy, psychic; psychic equilibrium 33, 50, 83, 99, 116, 198, 212, 266, 284; psychic experiences 58, 189, 191, 197, 254; psychic images see images; psychic objectivity 131; psychic reality 57–8, 148, 205, 215, 264, 276–7, 314; psychogenic disturbance 62–3; psychoneurosis as a suffering of a soul 19; religions as alien to the soul 203–4; search for the soul 2; Self see Self; soul as life-breath 51–2; soul-force 70; and the stages of life 37–40, 80–91; transcendent function and the tendency to wholeness see transcendent function; the unconscious see [the] unconscious; the unconscious, collective see collective unconscious; World Soul 276
psychic time (see also synchronicity) 292
psychoanalysis: and Eastern practices 228; German psychology and the development of 62; Jungian see Jung, Carl Gustav: psychology/psychotherapy; post-Freudian 14; trauma theory 132
psychogenic disturbance 62–3
psychokinesis 317
psychological adaptation see adaptation
psychology: analytical see Jung, Carl Gustav: psychology/psychotherapy; based on an autonomous, spiritual principle 51–6 see also Jung, Carl Gustav: psychology/psychotherapy; of the child archetype 147–9, 179–99; collective 112 see also collective psyche; and the difference between Eastern and Western thinking 213–15, 273–85; of dreams 180; ecopsychology 18; French 61–2; Freudian 227, 228, 262 see also Freud, Sigmund; German psychology and the development of psychoanalysis 62; indigenous/'primitive' see indigenous/'primitive' mentality; Jewish 11; Jung on the goal and reach of 17; medical 180, 193, 356 see also Jung, Carl Gustav: psychology/psychotherapy; multiplicity of modern psychologies 50, 257; and myth 198 see also mythology; personality/psychology of artists 210, 259, 268–71; philosophy linked with 50–1, 257; primitive 67–8, 283, 309 see also primitive man; and religion 205–7, 232–49; and spirit 17; 'without the soul' 32, 47, 51; as the youngest of the sciences 325
psychoneurosis see neurosis
psychosis 116, 117, 124–5, 175, 183, 339, 347; psychotic art products 262; 'psychotic interval' 338
psychotechnics 257
psychotherapy, Jungian see Jung, Carl Gustav: psychology/psychotherapy
puberty 82
Pueblo Indians 53, 227

Quispel, Gilles 292

racism 8–11
Rank, Otto 9, 268
rationalism 6, 54, 78, 119, 170, 193, 248, 259, 293, 318–19, 361–2
rationality 14, 339; and the theory of types 333–4
rebirth 7, 66, 69, 183; of God 147; rituals 84; of spirit 152
reductionism: Adler 68–9; charges against Jung 4; Freudian 6–8, 13, 64–5, 68–9, 210; materialistic see materialism; 'scientific' reduction of archetype and myth 148
Reformation 47
regression 109; regressive restoration of the persona 116–21
Reich, Wilhelm 9
religion: and the after life 90, 131–2; as alien to the soul 203–4; and archetypes 2–3; assessment of Jung by Western religions 147; Buddhism see Buddhism;

as a call to personal transformation 209; Christian *see* Christianity; conflict with science as a misunderstanding 274; creeds 234–5; dealing with patients' religious problems 75–6; dogma 234; faith *see* faith; former function as schools for later life 88; healing and the religious attitude 290; intolerance and fanaticism in 86; Jung's explorations in and beyond 3–5; linking back of *religio* 185, 206; literalism in Western religions 207–9, 253–6; Mithraism 74; mystery religions 70; mystical *see* mysticism; 'new age' 147; new religious expressions 203–5; the numinous as Jung's interest in 'religion' 206, 233–4 *see also* numinosity/the numinous; and psychology 205–7, 232–49; reductionist charges against Jung 4; religious education 84; religious interpretation of neurosis 40–1, 239–49; religious sentimentality 248; religious tendencies of the unconscious 206–7; and the revealing function of dreams 242–9; science and the dismissal of 2, 4; shamanistic 70; and spirit 5; and the spiritual problem of modern man 203–5, 217–31; spirituality *see* spirituality; Taoism *see* Taoist philosophy; Western turn to the East 147, 204–5, 223–4, 225–6, 228–30
renunciation 109
représentations collectives 105, 172, 356
repression 34, 62, 63, 69, 75, 93–4, 100, 110, 187, 238, 359; and the cinema 230
resentment 14
resistance 84, 130, 213, 265, 279, 305, 307, 317, 342, 349, 351, 359; intellectual 293, 319; to moral control 143, 159; and projection 159; and the shadow 143, 158
responsibility 19, 34–5, 88, 101, 122, 143, 157, 237
Rhine, J. B. 317–18
Roazen, Paul 14
Roman Empire 228–9
Rumi 14

sacraments 234
Samuels, Andrew 11, 15, 289
Satan 35
scarab beetle 318–19

scepticism 187, 219, 222, 229–30, 317, 350, 358
Schelling, Friedrich 179
Schiller, Friedrich 71, 194, 310
schizophrenia 106, 117, 175, 188, 282, 283, 352
Schmitz, Oscar 228
Schopenhauer, Arthur 70, 97, 104, 225, 257, 277; prototypes 137
science: Chinese 228; conflict with religion as a misunderstanding 274; and the destruction of the medieval world-view 222; and the dismissal of religion 2, 4; Jung and the emergence of holistic science 15–18; Jung's explorations in and beyond 3–5; philosophy of 16; psychology as the youngest of the sciences 325; 'scientific' reduction of archetype and myth 148; and the unconscious 205
scientism/scientific materialism (*see also* materialism) 4, 16, 31–2, 47, 274–5
secrecy 63, 109, 172; intuitions of secret things 264; primitive secret teachings 265; ritual secrets 108; secret conspiracy between mother and son 160–1; secret needs/fears 103, 238; secret participation of the unconscious 346, 347
Seelig, Carl 291
Self 39, 126, 146–7, 168–77; as centre of totality of consciousness and the unconscious 39, 142, 156–7; and ego 142, 155, 156–7, 168–70; as a God-image 168; and historical/messianic persons 46, 146; and individuation 45–6, 123–33, 187 *see also* individuation; phenomenology of 142–7, 155–77; psychic 'otherness' of 192; as seat of spirituality and healing 147; as 'second ego'/'also I' 39, 83, 84; as 'smaller than small yet bigger than big' 192; symbols of 193, 204 *see also* mandalas; transcendent function as operational arm of *see* transcendent function
self-alienation 123, 207
self-liberation 215, 277, 279, 284
self-realization *see* individuation
Semon, Richard 100
sensation, theory of types 295, 334–5
serpents 184, 189
sexism 145–6

sexuality (*see also* libido) 6–7, 63–4; bisexuality/hermaphroditism 193–6, 247; Freud's sexual theory of neurosis 6, 7, 118; *hieros gamos* 161, 195, 196; and psychic birth 82; and spirit 13, 42–3
shadow 35–6, 103, 143, 158–60, 172; becoming conscious of 158; integration of 143, 168; projection as obstacle to the integration of 143, 159–60
shamanism 70
Shamdasani, Sonu 4
Sheldrake, Rupert 142
Shepherd of Hermas 261, 264, 267
sickness (*see also* mental health/illness): and medicine 59; as a response to lack of symbolic/spiritual life 40, 59–60
Siegfried 189
slips of the tongue 340
Smith, Noel 140
society: and immorality/stupidity 110–11; and new ideas and emotionality 351; social catastrophe 33–4, 58–9, 74 *see also* war; the unconscious, and a psychosocial analysis of civilization 33–4, 70–9
Socrates 218
soul *see* psyche/soul
Spielrein, Sabina 9
spirit: of the age 47, 48–9, 212, 230; *antimimon pneuma* 177; as an archetypal force 5; autonomous 51; and a doctor's responsibility 19; and earth 18, 38; God as 99 *see also* God; Great Spirit 87; and healing the splits of the collective psyche 299–301, 356–64; Holy Spirit 204; individual spirits 5, 49, 58, 67, 77–8, 131–2, 234, 292 *see also* daemons/daimons; gods; influence on primitive man 67; Jesus as universal symbol of 208; as masculine 38; and matter 15–16, 58; and nature 38–9, 56, 57–8; personification of spirits 292; Platonic 152; pneumaphobia and dread of the spirit 11–14, 206; post-Christian 177; psychology based on an autonomous, spiritual principle 51–6 *see also* Jung, Carl Gustav: psychology/psychotherapy; rebirth of 152; and religion 5; religion based on indwelling 204; and the sciences 16; search for 2; and sexuality 13, 42–3; spiritual source of neuroses 19; and spiritual truth 207–8

spirit-world 49, 51, 56, 131
spiritualism 70, 132, 223, 226
spirituality: 'complex' 5; and Freud 5; and healing/therapy 290; illness as a response to lack of symbolic/spiritual life 40, 59–60; and maturity 40; mystical *see* mysticism; neuroses and the disturbance of spiritual processes in the psyche 60; and pneumaphobia 11–14, 206; Self as seat of 147; spiritual problem of modern man 203–5, 217–31; spiritual 'translation' of archetypes 3; and the spiritual world 49, 51, 56, 131; and Western integration of the metaphorical East 147; and worldliness 248
spiritualization 245–6
Spitteler, Carl 162, 262, 263, 267
splitting (*see also* dissociation; projection) 18, 68, 106, 187, 194; body–mind split/distinction 18, 324; healing the splits of the collective psyche 299–301, 356–64; split-off autonomous complexes 238, 239, 327 *see also* complexes
spontaneity/the spontaneous 36, 96, 131, 154, 162, 174, 180–1, 183–4, 190, 233, 237, 242, 255–6, 282, 318, 337, 343, 345
stages of life *see* life stages
Steiner, Rudolf 224
Stekel, Wilhelm 268
Stevens, Anthony 138, 140, 141
subjectivity 82, 280–1
sublimation 64, 195, 245–6, 280
subliminal perceptions 65
sun-wheels 265
Superman 147
superstition 12, 58, 66–7, 72, 152, 194–5, 358
suppression 34, 62, 69, 78, 93
Swedenborg, Emanuel 225, 319
Swiss Federal Institute of Technology 17
symbols/symbolism: and archetypes 356; awakening the symbolic life of the soul 2; bearers of 191; Christian 73–5; cultural 356; dissolution of the symbol 343; of dreams 360–1; illness as a response to lack of symbolic/spiritual life 40; killing of symbols 73; mandalas 174, 204; meaningfulness of 363; natural 356; numinous 357, 360–1; quaternity 174; *représentations collectives* 105, 172, 356; of the Self

193, 204 *see also* mandalas; 'symbol' of art 71; symbol-producing function of dreams 300, 358, 359; symbolic images 41 *see also* images; the symbolic life and the healing of the split 300; and the unconscious 72–5; and the union of rational and irrational truth 71–2; of unity and totality 174; as the voice of the world 193

Symington, Neville, *Emotion and Spirit* 14

synchronicity 3, 17, 291–3, 315–23; and 'primitive' philosophy 292–3; and projection 292

syzygy (*see also* anima; animus) 143–6, 160–8, 174, 175, 176, 246–7

table-turning 70
taboo 5, 11, 12–13, 63, 81, 165, 240, 358; infringements 109, 134
Talmud 245
Tao 16, 146, 204
Taoist philosophy 15–16, 35, 129
Teilhard de Chardin, Pierre 14, 15
telepathy 12, 316–17, 319
Teresa of Avila 14
Tertullian 254–5, 277
Theosophy 70, 204, 223–4, 227, 228, 229
therapy, Jungian *see* Jung, Carl Gustav: psychology/psychotherapy
thinking (*see also* mind) 91; adaptation through 333; collective 109; and cryptomnesia 100; Eastern *see* Eastern thinking; ideas *see* ideas; indigenous/'primitive' mentality 67, 148, 180–1, 182, 191, 192, 241, 283; Logos function 145, 162–3; man's lack of control over obsessive thoughts 53; and the theory of types 296, 333, 334; thoughts as projected sensuous projections 67; 'unconscious thinking' 154; Western turn to the East 147, 204–5, 223–4, 225–6, 228–30; Western vs Eastern 15–16, 213–15, 273–85
time 143, 283; psychic 292 *see also* synchronicity
timelessness (*see also* eternity) 51, 283
the transcendent 6, 168, 192
transcendent function (*see also* individuation) 282–3, 284, 297–9, 337–55
transference 41, 95–6, 97–8, 114, 299; energy 97; as an infantile power-aim 118; and regressive restoration of the persona 118; and the transcendent function 342

the transpersonal 41–2, 98, 105; archetypes as transpersonal factors 2–3 *see also* archetypes; and healing 291; the numinous *see* numinosity/the numinous; spirit *see* spirit

trauma theory 132

tree of knowledge 82, 134

types, theory of 294–6, 324–36

the unconscious: activated by one-sided conscious attitude 69, 76 *see also* compensation; and analytical technique that produces new level of consciousness 282; assimilation of 43–4, 99–100, 168–74; and attention 72; autonomy of 205–7, 232–49; beginnings of talk of 69–70; breaking through into consciousness 117; bridging the conscious and 19–20, 72, 298, 341–55; collective *see* collective unconscious; compensation function/theory of 33, 46, 69, 72–5, 93, 103, 125–30, 162, 167, 186, 192, 212, 242, 266–7, 282, 284, 294, 296, 297, 331, 340; complexes *see* complexes; contents of the personal unconscious 65, 93–4; and creativity 36, 66, 72, 131; and dreams *see* dreams/ dreaming; Eastern mind in the Western unconscious 214 *see also* Eastern thinking; effects upon consciousness 40–3, 93–122; ego as seat of unconsciousness 206; emotionality of contents of 359–60; fantasies as primary data of 290, 297; fear of 175, 279, 356, 359; as a field of experience 131; and the forgotten 65; Freud's view 97; healing forces of 72; image of God fashioned by 42, 96–100; individuation and the function of 123–33; innocent/ childlike unconsciousness 37–8, 81; instinct *see* instinct; intelligence of 205; intuition arising from *see* intuition; Jung on the personal and collective unconscious 61–8, 93–101, 112, 158; Jung's 'The role of the unconscious' 33–7, 61–79; language of 71; as a multiple consciousness 205; neutrality of 363; and our lack of control over psychic happenings 52–3; personality and the dynamics of 33, 34, 64–70; phenomena resulting from assimilation of 43–4, 101–12, 168–74; primordial images of *see* primordial images; projection of *see* projection; and a psychosocial analysis of civilization 33–4, 70–9; relations between the ego and 7, 40–6, 53, 55–6, 93–133, 158, 298, 352–3; religious tendencies of 206–7; and repression *see* repression; secret participation of 346, 347; Self as centre of totality of consciousness and 39, 142, 156–7 *see also* Self; shadow *see* shadow; as a source of knowledge 54–5; and spontaneity *see* spontaneity/the spontaneous; as the starting point of Jung's psychology 31; and subliminal perceptions 65; symbol-creating function of 72–5; taking responsibility for the darkness within 34–5, 78; tearing loose from maternal womb of 217–18; and the transcendent function *see* transcendent function; unconscious life as source of ego-consciousness 53, 55–6; unconscious metaphysics 308–9; unconscious predisposition 100, 153; 'unconscious thinking' 154; as the world of the past 69

Underhill, Evelyn 14

understanding, and the transcendent function 349, 350, 351

universal mind 214, 273, 276, 283, 284, 285; Buddha-Mind 278

the unknown 107, 138, 155, 183, 190, 324, 325; revealed through dreams 241, 243

unus mundus 17

Upanishads 225, 277

Usener, Hermann 154

visionary experiences 42, 54, 87, 98, 104–6, 126, 183–4, 185; artist's vision 130

von Hartmann, Eduard 61, 257

Wagner, Richard 261–2, 266, 347; *The Ring of the Nibelungen* 211–12, 259, 261

war 33–4, 58, 221; and Christian nations 73–5, 218

Watson, Grant 4

Wells, H. G., *Christina Alberta's Father* 124, 128

Wenegrat, Brant 141

White, Victor 17

Wilhelm, Hellmut 319

Wilhelm, Richard 17, 228

will: of God 170, 171; to power 44, 101, 107, 109; progress enforced by 187

Wise Old Man 168, 270

witchcraft 67, 237

witches 77, 126, 127, 132, 237, 280

wizards 237, 270

World Soul 276

worldliness (*see also* materialism) 248, 281–2

Wotan 42, 99, 246

wounded healer 270

yoga 60, 228, 234, 281, 284; hatha 279–80; kundalini 224

youth 82, 83–6

Zarathustra 235

Zen 337

Zentralblatt für Psychotherapie 10

Zimmer, Heinrich 17